6th Edition

Social Psychology
in the '90s

Kay Deaux
*Graduate Center of
City University of New York*

Francis C. Dane
Mercer University

Lawrence S. Wrightsman
University of Kansas

In association with
Carol K. Sigelman

Brooks/Cole Publishing Company
Pacific Grove, California

I(T)P® The ITP logo is a registered trademark under license.

Brooks/Cole Publishing Company
A division of International Thomson Publishing Inc.

Printed in the United States of America

10 9 8 7 6

Library of Congress Cataloging-in-Publication Data

Deaux, Kay.
    Social psychology in the '90s / Kay Deaux, Francis C. Dane, Lawrence S. Wrightsman, in association with Carol K. Sigelman. —6th ed.
        p.   cm.
    Rev. ed. of: Social psychology.   5th ed.   1988.
    Includes bibliographical references and index.
    ISBN 0-534-10398-7
    1. Social psychology.   I. Wrightsman, Lawrence S.   II. Dane, Francis C.   III. Deaux, Kay.   Social psychology.   IV. Title.
HM251.D358   1993
302—dc20   92-16505
                                                    CIP

Sponsoring Editor: *Marianne Taflinger*
Editorial Associate: *Heather L. Graeve*
Editorial Assistant: *Virge Pirelli-Minetti*
Production Editor: *Penelope Sky*
Manuscript Editor: *Laurie Vaughn*
Permissions Editor: *Mary Kay Hancharick*
Interior and Cover Design: *Roy R. Neuhaus*
Cover Photo: *Robert Llewellyn*
Art Coordinator: *Lisa Torri*
Interior Illustration: *Precision Graphics*
Photo Editor: *Larry Molmud*
Photo Researcher: *Sue C. Howard*
Proofreaders: *Micky Lawler and Linda Ruth Dane*
Indexer: *Do Mi Stauber*
Typesetting: *GTS Graphics*
Cover Printing: *Lehigh Press Lithographers/Autoscreen*
Printing and Binding: *R. R. Donnelley & Sons Company, Crawfordsville*

For
Sam, Linda, and Bea

Preface

Social psychologists have been attempting for nearly a century to understand how and why people influence each other. Some of the earliest explanations of social behavior remain viable, others have changed considerably, and still others have been set aside entirely. In every edition of this textbook, we stress the notion that change is one of the constants of social psychology.

The foundation of social psychology is the "fact" that the thoughts, feelings, and behaviors of each person affect and are affected by the thoughts, feelings, and behaviors of others. In the 1990s, attempting to understand the *how* and *why* of this deceptively simple observation restores the importance of cognition; affirms the integrity of individual, social, and physical components of the self-concept; and demonstrates the unarguable connection among a wide variety of research methods and settings.

The sixth edition of *Social Psychology* reflects the expansion of the field upon its modern foundation. The various ways in which social knowledge is represented are introduced in Chapter 4 and incorporated into other chapters whenever appropriate. Similarly, the interaction between the self and others is introduced in Chapter 3, but not confined to a single chapter. The coverage of such methodological developments as grounded research is greatly expanded, but traditional experimental methods are presented as the mainstay of testing hypotheses. The centrality of research is emphasized throughout the text, beginning in Chapter 1 with the professional activities of social psychologists. Finally, exemplary research in the fields of health, law, and business illustrates how social psychology works in everyday life.

Every chapter in this edition has been revised, in most cases substantially. The nearly 2,000 references represent recent research and theory, their historical bases, and their limitations. The major structural change is the integration of related subjects into fewer chapters. For example, material on leadership, formerly a separate chapter, has been incorporated into Chapter 12, "Behavior in Groups." As in previous editions, each chapter is an independent unit, and instructors are free to develop sequences that serve their own purposes. To encourage this flexibility, we have included some glossary terms in more than one chapter and have cross-referenced numerous discussions.

As in previous editions, we attempt to make the learning process effective and engaging. Each chapter opens with a chapter outline and closes with a summary. Important terms are boldfaced in the text and defined in the Glossary. A study guide and an instructor's manual accompany the text. The instructor's manual, prepared by Mary Kite and Georgia Green, provides multiple-choice and discussion questions for each chapter, as well as extensive suggestions for further reading, classroom discussion, demonstrations, and individual-involvement exercises. The study guide, prepared by Glenn Littlepage, lets students evaluate their understanding of the material in the text. For each text chapter the study guide includes a chapter preview; a list of basic terms, concepts, and theories; a set of completion items; and sample multiple-choice and short-answer questions.

Just as the social-psychological investigators of the past one-hundred years developed the material on which this book is based, so have instructors and students helped establish the book's identity. We know that you will benefit from these contributions. We hope that this text will convey some of the challenge and excitement that initiated and maintained our involvement in social psychology. Perhaps some of you will embark on a path that will lead to your making contributions of your own to the second one-hundred years of social psychology.

▶ Acknowledgments

As *Social Psychology* continues to evolve, the list of contributors lengthens. During the past twenty years, hundreds—perhaps thousands—of people have helped shape the book. Students filled out questionnaires included in the text, professors offered written comments and personal conversations, and many editors and production people at Brooks/Cole worked with real dedication. Without doubt, the book is better as a result of these varied contributions.

When we began this revision, we asked a number of colleagues to make recommendations. Their suggestions, whether adopted or not, influenced our decisions about how best to present an accurate and engaging portrait of social psychology today. For their helpful reviews, we thank the following people: Karin Ahim, DePauw University; Galen Bodenhausen, Michigan State University; Paul D. Cherulink, Southeast Missouri State University; Aaron Cohen, California State University, Long Beach; Michael Conn, City University of New York; Robert Croyle, University of Utah; Rachel Ann Foster, Central Michigan University; Mary Kite, Ball State University; Christopher Leone, University of North Florida; Glenn Littlepage, Middle Tennessee State University; Jacqueline Pope-Tarrence, Western Kentucky University; Christopher Grace, Biola University; Nancy Rhodes, Texas A&M University; Phillip R. Shaver, S.U.N.Y. at Buffalo; and Russ Veitch, Bowling Green State University.

Almost all of this book was written while Charles Boorman, Melissa Burgamy, Marcus Durham, and Lisa Fulford were matriculating at Mercer University. Their viewpoints as undergraduates and their devotion as research assistants keenly interested in social psychology cannot be described adequately in a few words. The expertise and cooperation of Virginia Cairns is also greatly appreciated. As reference librarian at Mercer University, her skill at tracking down references may be without equal.

The enthusiasm and dedication of the Brooks/Cole staff continues to be a source of invigoration and pleasure. Many people in the Brooks/Cole family are a part of this book even if they were not directly involved in the current edition. This time we must give particular recognition and thanks to a number of people. The sequential contributions of Claire Verduin and Marianne Taflinger as sponsoring editors produced a one–two punch of continuity and innovation. Gay Bond and Heather Graeve accomplished the remarkable feat of smoothly coordinating communication among editors, authors, and reviewers. The speed with which the manuscript became a book reflects the remarkable talents of the production editor, Penelope Sky.

To all of these people, and to others whose contributions are not listed here, a heartfelt thanks.

Kay Deaux
Francis C. Dane
Lawrence S. Wrightsman

Brief Contents

Contents

3 **The
Self
51**

4 **Understanding
Others
81**

5

Interpersonal Communication 115

10 Aggression and Violence 253

13 Behavior between Groups   347

6th Edition

Social Psychology in the '90s

The purpose of psychology is to give us a completely different idea of the things we know best.

Paul Valéry

Seek simplicity and distrust it.

Alfred North Whitehead

1

History and Systems of Social Behavior

It's Saturday morning. You are in bed, momentarily relishing the fact that you do not have to get up. The sun is shining and birds are singing. Yet something seems strange; it is too quiet. Looking out the window, you see no one, even though others should be up and about. The world looks the same, except for one thing—there are no people in sight, absolutely none. What's going on?

You turn on the television and quickly scan the channels with the remote control. There is only snow and static. Even the ever-present MTV channel is gone. Nothing on the stereo receiver, either; it lights up but produces no intelligible sound. You pick up the phone, are relieved to get a dial tone, and call a friend. You hear ring after ring, but no answer. You make phone calls to other people and hear only endless ringing or answering machines.

Increasingly panicked, you get dressed and go downtown, but you see no one. Stores look open—lights on, doors unlocked—but no one is inside. There is food, electricity, telephones—all the usual physical aspects of your world—but there are no people.

How would you react? Consider what life without people would be like. No television, no radio, no newspapers or magazines; they all require human effort to produce. Perhaps you could continue some activities, but only those that did not involve people. Even electricity would eventually become unavailable, because no one is there to maintain the equipment. The university would continue to exist as a physical plant, at least until it fell into disrepair, but no teaching or learning could occur. There could be no traffic jams, no football, no high school reunions, no Thanksgiving dinners. No spouses or lovers, no friends or enemies, no parents or children.

And no social psychology. As a discipline, social psychology focuses on human interaction, exploring all the ways in which our behaviors affect and are affected by others. Gordon Allport suggested social psychologists *"attempt to understand and explain how the thought, feeling, and behavior of individuals are influenced by the actual, imagined, or implied presence of others"* (1985, p. 3). This well-accepted definition is quite comprehensive—little human behavior escapes it. "Implied presence," for example, means our behavior is often shaped by awareness that we belong to particular cultural, oc-cupational, or social groups. Even when we are alone, our behavior may be influenced by our perceptions of how others might react if they knew what we were doing.

What if those others are gone; if cultural, occupational, and social groups no longer exist? Imagining the total absence of people, as in our opening scenario, may give you some sense of how pervasive others' influence can be. With no other people, there could be no group effort—you would do everything on your own. Aggression would be impossible, but so would love and friendship. No one would give you orders, but no one would give you social support or comfort, either. Easy decisions might become difficult because there would be no one to give you needed information. And it would be difficult to judge your own condition, because we often compare how we are doing with how others are doing in the same situation. Human beings are indeed social animals, and an asocial life would be severely restricted.

Of course, not all activities carried out by humans are social behaviors. For example, if you pick an apricot off a tree, eat it, get sick, and thereafter avoid eating apricots (at least those straight off the tree), your reactions occur whether other people are present or not and probably do not reflect an awareness of others. Reflex actions, such as removing your hand from a hot stove, are nonsocial; the immediate physical response is the same regardless of the presence or the awareness of others. However, your oral response to touching a hot stove may well be affected by the presence of others. Certain internal responses—glandular, digestive, excretory—are generally considered to be beyond the realm of social psychology. Yet nausea, constipation, and other physical responses may result from feelings associated with the actions or presence of other people. The research of David Phillips (1970, 1972) indicates even the time of dying may be a response to social considerations. In Jewish populations in both New York City and Budapest, for example, Phillips found a "death dip"—a significant decrease in death rates—during the months leading up to Yom Kippur, the holiest of Jewish holidays.

Clearly, much of any person's behavior, perhaps more than you first realized, is social. Although social behavior is something about which we all have a great deal of information, studying social psychology enables us to look differently at and increase our understanding of what we know and to discover what we do not know.

▸ A History of Social Psychology

To understand modern-day social psychology, we should look at its historical roots. As suggested in Table 1.1, one origin of social psychology can be pinpointed at the year in which two very different publications appeared. In one publication, the French philosopher Gabriel de Tarde (1898) wrote at length about imitation, the basis of social learning theory, and much of the conformity research discussed in Chapter 8 (Allport, 1985; Pepitone, 1981). In the other, Norman Triplett (1898) described an experiment concerning

Table 1.1   Milestones in Social Psychology

1898: Gabriel de Tarde publishes *Etudes de Psychologie Sociale* (Studies of Social Psychology), and in the *American Journal of Psychology,* Norman Triplett publishes an experiment demonstrating that physical activity can be affected by the mere presence of other people.

1908: Edward Ross and William McDougall each publish a textbook titled *Social Psychology.*

1918–1920: W. I. Thomas and F. Znaniecki's five-volume study, *The Polish Peasant in Europe and America,* makes attitude a central concept for social psychology.

1921: The *Journal of Abnormal Psychology* becomes the *Journal of Abnormal and Social Psychology.*

1924: Floyd Allport publishes the influential *Social Psychology.*

1934: George Herbert Mead's book *Mind, Self, and Society* is published, in which he stresses the interaction between self and others.

1935: The first *Handbook of Social Psychology,* edited by Carl Murchison, is published.

1936: Muzafer Sherif explains the process of conformity in *The Psychology of Social Norms.*

1939: Kurt Lewin, with his students Ronald Lippitt and Ralph White, reports an experimental study of leadership styles, showing that social issues can be studied in the laboratory. In the same year, John Dollard and his associates introduce the frustration-aggression theory.

1941: In *Social Learning and Imitation,* Neal Miller and John Dollard present a theory that extends behavioristic principles to the realm of social behavior.

1945: Kurt Lewin founds the Research Center for Group Dynamics.

1954: The first modern edition of the *Handbook of Social Psychology,* edited by Gardner Lindzey, is published.

1957: Leon Festinger publishes *A Theory of Cognitive Dissonance,* presenting a model that stresses the need for consistency between thought and behavior.

1958: Fritz Heider lays the groundwork for attribution theory with the publication of *The Psychology of Interpersonal Behavior.*

1959: John Thibaut and Harold Kelley publish *The Social Psychology of Groups,* a foundation for social exchange theory.

1965: The *Journal of Abnormal and Social Psychology* splits into two separate publications, the *Journal of Abnormal Psychology* and the *Journal of Personality and Social Psychology.*

1985: The third edition of *Handbook of Social Psychology,* edited by Gardner Lindzey and Elliot Aronson, is published.

social facilitation,[1] the influence of the presence of other people, which will be discussed in Chapter 12. Of course, interest in social-psychological topics existed before 1898. For example, both Plato and Aristotle discussed persuasion and other social behaviors extensively.

In 1908 two textbooks, both titled *Social Psychology,* were published in the United States, thus calling attention to a newly defined field. That the authors—Edward Ross and William McDougall—had anything at all to say suggests that people were thinking, conducting studies, and proposing theories about issues that would eventually fit under the rubric of social psychology. Early on, however, exactly what was and what was not social psychology was still uncertain.

This lack of clarity is illustrated by the difference in the pictures of social psychology presented by Ross and by McDougall. The distinctions reflected the differences in their intellectual traditions. Ross was a sociologist, and he endorsed the concept of a group mind (Pepitone, 1981; Post, 1980). His textbook dealt with such topics as the mob mind, public opinion, and social conflicts. McDougall, in contrast, came from a psychological tradition that focused on instincts; he emphasized individual motivations and sentiments.

The direct influence of both of these approaches was short-lived. Their global concepts—group mind and instinct—were too general to be useful, particularly for the increasingly popular experimental methods of psychology. During the early years of the 20th century, social psychologists began to define their domain. Attitudes, for example, became a central concept, and the phrase "social psychology" was first used in the title of a professional journal (see Table 1.1). Psychoanalytic theory and behaviorism also had an impact on social psychology at this time.

Sigmund Freud's (1905) **psychoanalytic theory,** a theory of personality development derived from his experiences as a therapist, emphasized internal processes brought about by conflict between the individual and society. Freud's theory included an emphasis on **socialization,** the process of acquiring behaviors soci-

ety considers appropriate. How, for example, does a child learn to be a responsible, moral person? According to Freud, the **superego,** or conscience, develops as a result of the teachings and admonitions of parents, teachers, other authorities, and peers. Although psychoanalytic concepts rarely contribute directly to modern social-psychological theory, the concepts of internal processes and social conflict still affect our thinking about human behavior.

Almost the opposite of psychoanalytic theory, John B. Watson's (1913) **behaviorism** stressed the importance of experimental methods and the influence of environmental factors on behavior. It was Watson, for example, who claimed he could take any infant and raise the child to be anything: doctor, artist, or thief. The characteristics of the infant were not important to Watson; only the environment in which the infant behaved was important. Watson argued that internal processes, such as Freud's superego development, should be avoided; only observable, verifiable behaviors constituted the scientific part of psychology for Watson. Although his emphasis on observable phenomena remains in modern social psychology, it has been tempered considerably. An emphasis on environment also remains, but only as part of an overall pattern of influence.

While proponents of Freud and Watson were engaging in heated debates, the shape of modern social psychology became much clearer in the 1920s with the publication of Floyd Allport's social psychology text (Post, 1980). Unlike the earlier works of Ross and McDougall, this new book offered experimental work as well as theoretical development. A new rigor was evident in this presentation, and Allport's discussions of such topics as social influence were early signs of an increasingly vital social psychology discipline. George Herbert Mead (1934), for example, emphasized the importance of the influence of other people in the development of an individual's concept of self. Some uncertainty about the content of social psychology remained, however, as was illustrated by discussions of insect populations and domesticated animals in Carl Murchison's (1935) first *Handbook of Social Psychology.* But it was the theoretical and empirical rigor of the 1930s that eventually characterized the remainder of the history of social psychology. The value of the experimental

---

[1]Terms printed in **boldface** type are listed in the "Key Terms" section at the end of each chapter and are defined in the glossary, which follows Chapter 14.

method for analyzing social issues, for example, was demonstrated when Kurt Lewin and his colleagues compared the consequences of authoritarian, democratic, and laissez-faire leadership styles in a laboratory setting. Lewin further capped the developments of the 1930s by introducing field theory, a model of social behavior that incorporates both the person and the environment.

The fundamental contribution of **field theory** is the proposition that human behavior is a function of both the person and the environment (Lewin, 1951). This proposition is expressed symbolically in the equation $B = f(P, E)$, in which behavior, B, results from the combination of the person, P (that is, aspects such as heredity, abilities, and personality), and the environment, E (aspects such as the presence of others and physical and social impediments to goals). Personal and environmental variables function, f, together to influence any given behavior. Your behavior in the classroom, for example, is probably very different from your behavior at a party; you are the same person, but you act differently in different environments. Although Lewin's proposition may seem obvious now, its statement in the early development of social psychology marked a clear shift from the individual emphasis of psychoanalytic theory on one hand and the external emphasis of behaviorism on the other. The interdependence of the person and the environment remains an important concept in modern social psychology. Another major emphasis of field theory that has survived is the *here and now:* the relative importance of the present. Events that happened to us ten years ago may be less explanatory of our current behavior than what we remember about those events—our current reactions—and the reactions of others upon discovering our past.

Lewin also emphasized the practical value of social-psychological research, which was tested and demonstrated most thoroughly during World War II. The U.S. Army, for example, called on psychologists to assess the effectiveness of its morale and propaganda films. Other government agencies wanted to persuade consumers to eat unusual foods, such as sweetbreads, in order to reserve beef for the fighting forces. In these and other efforts, persuasion and social influence became major areas of research. After the war, theory and research in attitude change continued, led by Carl Hov-

Kurt Lewin (1890–1947)
AP/Wide World Photos

land and others who had participated in the war effort (Jones, 1985; Pepitone, 1981).

Since the end of World War II, research and theorizing in social psychology have accelerated. Work on such problems as conformity, aggression, and the interaction of society and self has continued, building upon the efforts of pioneering investigators and revealing more complex patterns of behavior. Many new questions about human behavior have also been raised— the nature of love and close relationships, the processes of communication, and the ways in which we perceive other people and process information about our social environment. Concern for social problems has generated new research as well, on such issues as the impact of media violence, the consequences of crowding and stress, and the willingness of people to help others in emergencies. The need for a modern edition of *Handbook of Social Psychology* (the first modernized edition was published in 1954), the growth of *Journal of Personality and Social Psychology* into the largest journal published by the American Psychological Association, and the subsequent need for a third edition of *Handbook of Social Psychology* are some results of the expansion of social-psychological research. With the proliferation of research has come growth in theoretical work—efforts to give us a way of viewing and interpreting the wealth of data now available.

Theories in Social Psychology

Anyone who offers an explanation about why a social relationship exists or how it functions is proposing a social theory. In this sense, we are all theorists, for we all form explanations for the events that occur around us. Our personal theories, however, may be vague, idiosyncratic, and untestable. Despite these shortcomings, our personal theories help us make sense of things that happen in our world and are therefore essential.

Within science, theories are also essential, again because they help us understand how and why things happen. The term *theory,* however, is used more specifically among scientists—a **theory** is a description of relationships among symbols that represent reality (Hall & Lindzey, 1978). Attitude, for example, is an abstract symbol used to represent the reality that individuals have preferences concerning specific objects. You can't see or touch an attitude—it's not real—but we use the concept of attitude to represent things that are real, such as a preference for clay courts over grass courts when playing tennis. The term **construct** is applied when an abstract symbol in a theory is defined in terms of observable events. The construct *prejudice,* discussed in Chapter 13, is often defined in terms of responses to a questionnaire. Because they are abstract, all theories contain aspects that cannot be proven true in any absolute sense. Yet all theories serve common purposes.

One of these purposes is to organize and clarify diverse bits of knowledge about social phenomena (Hendrick & Jones, 1972). We each have a tremendous accumulation of knowledge about human behavior. Some of this knowledge is based on personal experience; some is based on recent public events; and some is based on what we glean from books, movies, or the accounts of friends. Similarly, the scientists of human social behavior have an extensive set of observations and empirical data, and theories provide a convenient way of organizing them (Shaw & Costanzo, 1982). In short, a theory integrates known empirical findings within a logically consistent and reasonably simple framework (Hall & Lindzey, 1978).

Another purpose of any theory in social psychology is to indicate gaps in knowledge so that further research can lead to a more comprehensive understanding of social phenomena. That is, theories are used not only to integrate existing information, but also to define more clearly what we don't know. Suppose, for example, as you peruse an album of family photographs, you notice there are no baby pictures of your older sister. Such a gap might lead you to ponder several explanations. Are the photographs in a different album? Have they been misplaced? Is your sister adopted? In much the same way, gaps in research concerning a particular theory guide future research; they provide a source of **hypotheses**—anticipated relationships about the concrete variables in the world—which are then tested through research. Similarly, theories may also be used to anticipate the outcomes of events that we can expect to occur, even if the particular conditions have not yet been encountered (Shaw & Costanzo, 1982). For example, knowing about the relationship between attitudes and behavior, and knowing that Sally likes you and likes jazz, you might expect Sally to agree to accompany you to a "jazz in the park" concert.

And if Sally says "no"? Data generated through research do not always support the original theoretical framework—the research may, in fact, show that the theory has to be revised or even rejected. It may be difficult to think in terms of revising or rejecting a theory on the basis of research, but history is replete with examples of rejected theories: "The earth is flat"; "The sun revolves around the earth"; and "There is air on the moon." Therefore, any theory is best understood as a model, and even as a model any theory has a limited life span. Without the use of some theory, however, the task of understanding the variety of social behavior would be tremendously difficult.

Judging the ultimate validity or "goodness" of a theory is difficult and often requires the accumulation of considerable data. Shaw and Costanzo (1982) have suggested three necessary characteristics of a good theory: (1) the propositions of a theory must be logically consistent among themselves, (2) the theory must agree with known facts, and (3) the theory must be testable. Shaw and Costanzo also noted other desirable characteristics of a theory, including simplicity, ease of relating to real-world observations, and usefulness in generating further research.

By these criteria, some theories are better than others. Yet several different theories may simultaneously meet these criteria. No one theory adequately accounts for all social phenomena, and each of several theories may do a good job of explaining a single phenomenon. The theoretical approach an investigator adopts will lead that investigator to ask certain questions about the behavior he or she is researching and to ignore others. Some theories focus on the individual, and others focus on the situation or the social structure. Some theories emphasize a person's present circumstances, whereas other theories contain propositions about early learning or biological causes. In other words, there is no perfect theory. Social scientists use a variety of perspectives to generate hypotheses and to interpret events (Georgoudi & Rosnow, 1985; Gergen, 1985). As William McGuire has said in explaining his use of the term *perspectivism,* "any one theoretical viewpoint depicts the known just from one perspective and . . . a creative scientist should view it from multiple theoretical perspectives" (1984, p. 29).

Following McGuire's advice, we shall describe three broad theories, or perspectives, of social psychology: role, learning, and cognitive. Each perspective has its own orientation, assumptions, and constructs. Each also has served as a base from which social psychologists have developed theories to explain a relatively narrow range of human behavior. Many of these theories will be discussed in subsequent chapters. As we discuss each theoretical orientation, we will first consider its basic concepts and assumptions. Then we will give examples of research that has been guided by each theoretical perspective. And finally, we will provide comparisons of the three perspectives.

▶ Role Theories

The role perspective originates in the theatrical notion of roles as parts that actors play in a dramatic presentation (Shaw & Costanzo, 1982). The concept of role, which can be traced back to classical times, has more recently been found useful by sociologists. George Herbert Mead, as we noted earlier, talked about the development of self in relation to the social structure. Other uses of the concept of role can be found in anthropology, sociology, philosophy, and psychology.

Basic Assumptions and Concepts

As is illustrated in Figure 1.1, a **role** can be defined as the functional aspects associated with a specific position in a social context (Shaw & Costanzo, 1982). The concept of role is shared by a variety of theoretical perspectives (Stryker & Statham, 1985). We are using role theory as if it were a single perspective, however, because these different perspectives do have several things in common. Generally, role theories do not include such individual determinants of behavior as personality, attitudes, and motivation. Instead, explanations for behavior mainly involve roles, the social context, and expectations people have about the roles in a particular social interaction. Further, in contrast to the more psychological theories we will discuss later, role theories include a particular emphasis on large social networks and organizations. To gain additional understanding of roles, let's look at a student named Gloria McWilliams.

As a student, Gloria performs certain behaviors—she attends classes, prepares assignments, applies for graduation, and so on. When interacting with Gloria in her role as a student, other people assume she will act in certain ways. Their assumptions about her behavior are called **role expectations.** Professors, for example,

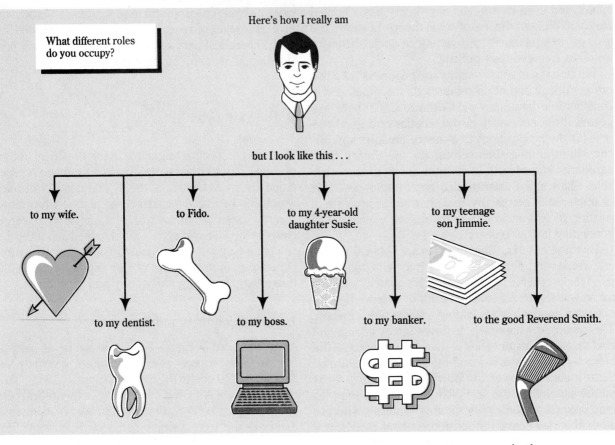

Figure 1.1 *Different roles involve serving different functions, even when the same person occupies them.*

expect Gloria (and other students) to attend class with some regularity, to show some concern about grades, and to be interested in learning. Some instructors may expect a certain amount of deference from Gloria; others may not. Similarly, Gloria may have role expectations in regard to her professors, expecting them to be on time for class, to be dynamic lecturers, to be experts on the topic, and to be understanding when she misses an exam.

When role expectations are shared by a group of individuals, they are considered **norms,** more generalized expectations about behavior that are learned in the course of interactions with other members of a society (Biddle & Thomas, 1966). Depending upon what we have learned from specific role relationships, we may

hold general norms about the appropriate interactions between women and men, between authority figures and subordinates, or between other roles. Suppose, for example, most of the authority figures Gloria has encountered have been distant and formal. Generalizing from such experiences, Gloria may adopt a norm consistent with the notion that all her professors—authority figures in the student-faculty relationship—prefer to remain distant and formal. She may even expect professors to be generally unfriendly, and perhaps she will avoid discussion in class unless called upon.

But there is more to Gloria than being a student. Like all of us, she performs a variety of roles every day. Sometimes conflict results when a person holds several roles that make incompatible demands. While studying for a final exam, for example, Gloria may receive a call from a friend who needs a 90-mile ride to the airport for an emergency trip home. Before Gloria can decide what to do, her boss may call and ask her to come in to work. Gloria's roles of student, friend, and employee cannot all be satisfied at the same time, which produces interrole conflict. At other times, a single role may involve incompatible expectations or activities. Gloria would experience intrarole conflict if she had to choose between studying for a history exam and typing a psychology term paper that was due the same day. In this case, her role as student requires her simultaneously to conduct two incompatible activities.

To say that people *perform* a series of roles does not mean that people are pretending; nor does it mean that they are being deceitful or deceptive. To a significant extent, we behave in ways that are in agreement with our settings and the positions we hold. It is difficult, for example, to adopt the role of an airline pilot in a psychology classroom. Even if one's occupation is that of airline pilot, the functions of that role—flying, navigating, and so on—generally have little utility while taking notes during a lecture on the history of social psychology. Then again, the range of behaviors considered acceptable in a particular setting is fairly broad; an airline pilot may use global navigation as a metaphor during a class discussion. But the role also defines the limits of what is appropriate in the setting. Navigation as a metaphor might be useful from time to time, but interrupting the class to map the route from Los Angeles to Hong Kong would not be acceptable.

Contributions to Social Psychology

The concept of role has been used often in social psychology: such terms as *role model, role playing,* and *role taking* appear frequently in the literature. The concept of role helps us to understand, for example, why people's behavior may change when their position in a social system is altered; changes in social position also mean changes in roles.

A vivid demonstration of the effect of roles is illustrated in Seymour Lieberman's (1956) study of the attitudes of factory workers. In initial testing, Lieberman assessed attitudes toward union and management policies held by virtually every worker in a midwestern

People perform a series of roles every day.
Dion Ogust/The Image Works

home-appliance factory. About a year later he went back to the same factory and again assessed workers' attitudes—this time selecting two specific groups of workers. In the intervening year, some workers had been promoted to foreperson, a position that should ally them more closely with management. Other workers had been elected as union stewards, a role that generally involves confrontations with management. For both types of workers, attitudes changed as a function of their new roles in the organization. Compared with a group of workers who had retained their previous positions, those who became forepersons expressed more positive attitudes toward management officers and management policies, such as an incentive system that paid workers according to how much they produced. In contrast, workers who had been elected union stewards became more positive in their attitudes toward union officers and union policies, such as a seniority system under which pay was connected to time

Employees' attitudes change as a function of their roles in an organization.
Alan Carey/The Image Works

on the job. In each case, attitudes shifted according to the new role the worker occupied.

Eighteen months later, Lieberman returned to the factory. At that point, some of the forepersons had been returned to nonsupervisory jobs, and some of the stewards had also returned to their original positions. Again, shifts in the workers' attitudes mirrored changes in roles. The former forepersons once again were less positive toward management, and the former stewards were now less strongly in favor of union officers. Back and forth, attitudes shifted with the roles, a striking demonstration of the extent to which roles influence attitudes and beliefs.

Social psychologists interested in self-concept also have relied heavily on role theories. Charles Cooley (1902/1964) and George Herbert Mead (1934), for example, both discussed self-concept in terms of interactions with others. As illustrated earlier in Figure 1.1, part of our self-concept is based on how we think others see us, and their perceptions are partially based on the roles we occupy. More recent developments in the concept of self, discussed in Chapter 3, also have relied heavily on role theories. Mark Snyder (1987), for example, used role theories and the earlier work of Cooley and Mead in his empirical and theoretical development of the concept of **self-monitoring,** the extent to which people pay attention to the way they are perceived by others and alter their behavior in response to the social context. Role theories also have been used as

a basis for understanding the communication process (Chapter 5) and the positions of leaders and subordinates in organizations (Chapter 12).

Alice Eagly (1987) has argued that gender differences can be explained in terms of **gender-role norms,** expectations that individuals have about appropriate behavior for men and women. Women, for example, are expected to show concern for others, to express their emotions, and generally to direct their behavior toward interpersonal relations. In contrast, men are expected to be independent and assertive and generally to direct their behavior toward accomplishment. Eagly's social-role theory, illustrated in Figure 1.2, includes the proposition that differences observed in the social behavior of men and women partially result from the differences in men's and women's roles in society. For example, traditionally restricted occupations, such as secretary and military pilot, lead people to develop gender-role expectations as well as sex-typed skills and beliefs. Secretaries generally have a supportive function, whereas pilots' skills are directed toward accomplishing a particular task independently. Gender-role expectations and gender-typed skills, in turn, result in differences in social behavior. Social-role theory will be discussed in more detail in Chapter 13.

Think back to our opening scenario. Clearly, role theory could be used to predict some serious distortions in a person's life if other people were to disappear. If, for example, the self is a product of interactions with

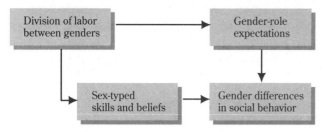

Figure 1.2 *A social-role theory of gender differences in social behavior.*

Source: From "Explaining Sex Differences in Social Behavior: A Meta-Analytic Perspective" by A. H. Eagly and W. Wood, 1982, *Personality and Social Psychology Bulletin, 17,* pp. 306–315.

others, how would you evaluate your own behavior in the absence of other people? Think, for example, how often you compare your test results with those of your classmates. For that matter, who would construct the test that enables you to determine how much you know? And if you play roles in larger social structures, what would you do in a world that was suddenly without groups, communities, and organizations? Only your memories of those relationships would be influential, and in time their influence would wane, leaving you with few guides for behavior. Even conventions about "male" and "female" clothing would become irrelevant.

Role theory helps us understand and predict some, but not all, social behavior. Therefore, we turn to our second theoretical perspective.

▶ Learning Theories

As we noted earlier, experimental psychologists were strongly influenced by the behaviorist principles of John Watson. Later psychologists such as Clark Hull, Kenneth Spence, and B. F. Skinner elaborated the process by which learning takes place.

Basic Assumptions and Concepts

The central focus of learning theory is an analysis of the relation between stimulus and response. A **stimulus** is any event (external or internal) that changes an organism's behavior (Kimble, 1961). This change is called a **response.** If reading this book (the stimulus) changes

the way you (the organism) relate to other people (the response), then learning has occurred. Obvious? Yes, but then you live in a society that has benefited from almost a hundred years of developments in learning theory. Obvious, too, may be the concept of **reinforcement,** any favorable outcome that results from a response. Reinforcement increases the probability that a response will be repeated. Responses that are not rewarded, in contrast, tend to be discarded, and actions that are punished may be actively avoided.

Early learning theorists, including Ivan Pavlov, extended learning theory's power of explanation by developing the concepts of generalization and discrimination. **Stimulus generalization** is a process through which the same response can be invoked by more than one stimulus (Shaw & Costanzo, 1982). If, for example, you have been reinforced for studying social psychology, perhaps by good grades or better social interactions, then stimulus generalization might leave you inclined to put forth the same amount of effort to study geometry, even if you had not been reinforced for studying geometry in the past. This principle allows learning theorists to explain a wider range of behaviors than they could if each single behavior had to be reinforced separately.

The flip side of generalization is **stimulus discrimination,** a process of learning to respond differently to different stimuli. Thus, through experience you may learn that understanding social psychology makes it easier to talk to strangers, whereas other experiences convince you that understanding geometry leads to more favorable outcomes when you play pool. After you have learned to discriminate between social psychology and geometry, the area of knowledge you apply, social psychology or geometry, will depend on the stimulus—strangers or a game of pool. Our ability to make such distinctions allows us to develop more complex ways of responding to our social environment.

Basic learning theorists (sometimes called S-R theorists, for stimulus-response) traditionally have little interest in what occurs between the stimulus and the response—the cognitive and subjective aspects of behavior. Theirs is a "language of observables" (Lott & Lott, 1985, p. 110) that deals with specific antecedent and consequent events. What thoughts go through our mind, for example, when we are deciding whether to talk to a stranger about the weather or challenge the stranger to a game of eight ball matters little to S-R theorists. Instead, they are more interested in how a particular behavior was learned and how it is maintained.

Contributions to Social Psychology

The basic ideas of learning theory remain influential, but social psychologists generally have moved beyond the simple S-R model. One major development has been increased reliance on what occurs during the learning process. The functioning person is recognized as an intermediary between the stimulus and the response, and the model is sometimes called an S-O-R model (Stimulus-Organism-Response). As we discuss the contributions of learning theory, we will examine two S-O-R learning theories that are prominent in social psychology: social learning theory and social exchange theory.

Neal Miller and John Dollard (1941) laid the foundation for modern social learning theory when they proposed that imitation could be explained by basic principles of stimulus, reward, and reinforcement. Much of the socialization process, according to Miller and Dollard, is a result of children being reinforced, intentionally or not, for imitating others. Consider, for example, the extent to which parents respond positively when an infant successfully imitates the sounds *mama* or *dada*. From that foundation, Albert Bandura (1973, 1977) developed **social learning theory,** whose basic proposition is that learning can occur by observing, though not necessarily performing, the behavior of another person. The behavior of the other person (a *model*) serves as a source of information, which the observer then uses to perform the same behavior later.

Social learning theory's major departure from traditional learning theory is the proposition that reinforcement may have little influence in determining whether or not a behavior is learned—reinforcement affects only the performance of a behavior. That is, paying attention to a model and mentally rehearsing the model's actions are sufficient for learning. Parents, for example, are often models for their children's behavior, either in-

Parents, intentionally or unintentionally, serve as models for their children.
Leonard Freed/Magnum Photos, Inc.

tentionally or unintentionally. A mother completing her makeup may be unaware that she is serving as a model for her child. Wanting to look like "Mommy," her daughter watches closely and learns how to apply makeup. Although the child's performance may be sloppy the first few times—as anyone who has been around young children will recognize—the elements of the behavior have been established, and practice will refine the skills. Such learning can have embarrassing outcomes; as Kaufmann (1973) notes, a 5-year-old boy may hear certain obscenities but give no evidence of having learned them until he shouts them in front of his kindergarten class.

Whether or not someone pays attention to a model, thereby starting the social learning process, depends upon characteristics of both the model and the observer. Such characteristics of a model as novelty and attractiveness (discussed in Chapter 4) increase the likelihood that someone will pay attention to the model. Similarly, an observer's belief that the model's behavior is functional will enhance the extent to which he or she attends to the model. Mental rehearsal—imagining oneself performing the behavior—completes the learning process. The actual performance of the behavior, however, partly depends on the person's ability. Someone can carefully observe Eric Clapton play guitar, for example, and mentally rehearse how he produces a specific blues progression, but the observer may be incapable of duplicating Clapton's behavior because of shorter fingers or a slower reaction time. Thus, the person knows *how* to play the progression, but can't *perform* the way Clapton does. Another influence on motor production is the presence of reinforcements, either from others or from oneself. Clapton is reinforced for playing guitar, whereas an observer may be reinforced for studying social psychology.

Social learning theory allows for much more complicated forms of learning than the earlier reinforcement models did. Yet like its predecessors, social learning theory's central concepts are the stimuli that elicit social behaviors and the reinforcements that the individual anticipates. And like basic learning theory, social learning theory is primarily a model of individual behavior.

The second theory that relies on principles of reinforcement is focused more strongly on the interactions between people. According to **social exchange theory,** social interactions depend on the rewards and costs involved. As the name suggests, the theory characterizes social behavior as an exchange, a give-and-take relationship. What gets exchanged are rewards and investments, and they can be either material or nonmaterial goods—money and jewelry are material, whereas approval and prestige are nonmaterial.

George Homans (1958, 1974), who proposed one of the first models of social exchange, relied heavily upon the concept of **distributive justice,** the belief that rewards should be proportional to investments. That is, what one gets out of a relationship should be proportional to what one puts into it. According to social exchange theory, a relationship may be terminated if rewards and investments are not proportional. If you purchase a stereo that doesn't work properly, for example, you probably would return it for one that does work (a "just" exchange) or demand a refund (terminate the relationship).

John Thibaut and Harold Kelley have developed a more complex version of social exchange theory. They call it a theory of interdependence (Kelley & Thibaut, 1978; Thibaut & Kelley, 1959). Their theory emphasizes the dynamic aspects of dyadic (two-person) interaction—one person acting with and reacting to another person. Unlike Homans, Thibaut and Kelley argue that the costs and rewards of one person cannot be considered in isolation. According to the theory of interdependence, the interaction process depends on maximizing the satisfaction of both participants.

Another element that distinguishes Thibaut and Kelley's model from Homans's simpler framework is the proposition that people make comparisons between their present outcomes and other possible alternatives (Jones, 1985). In other words, you not only evaluate the costs and rewards involved in an ongoing relationship, you also consider the costs and rewards that might be attached to a potential, alternative relationship. If you think the alternative relationship is a "better deal," you may be tempted to leave the present relationship, even if the present relationship is not a bad one. Suppose, for example, that two different sections of your social psychology class are both taught by the same instructor and are otherwise academically equivalent. The section you are attending is rewarding, but your friend is enrolled in the other section. Because your friend's presence makes the other section a "better deal," you may be tempted to change sections, even though there is nothing wrong with the section in which you are enrolled.

To analyze the interaction process, Thibaut and Kelley introduced the outcome matrix. Basically, this matrix illustrates each person's costs and rewards regarding a set of alternative interactions. Consider the matrix in Figure 1.3 in which roommates Ann and Lisa are trying to decide how to spend a Saturday. Ann observes that their apartment is a mess and suggests that they clean it together. Lisa has planned to go cycling for the day and suggests that Ann join her. (To keep the ex-

ample simple, we assume cleaning and cycling are the only two options available and that these options are mutually exclusive.) For Lisa, cycling is more rewarding; for Ann, cleaning is more rewarding. If these two women were not interacting, there would be no question about which choice would be made—Lisa would grab her bike, and Ann would grab her broom. Yet, because the outcomes of these choices are related, we have to consider each in relation to the other.

If they both go cycling (upper left quadrant), they both live with a dirty apartment, but that involves a greater cost and lesser reward for Ann than for Lisa. If they both clean (lower right quadrant), Lisa has the greater cost and lesser reward, although Ann's cost—tension with Lisa—is not insignificant. If Lisa goes cycling and Ann cleans the apartment (upper right quadrant), they both incur costs as well. For Lisa, the cost is guilt; she would realize that Ann was doing more than her fair share of domestic work. For Ann, the cost is resentment aroused by Lisa's pleasure-seeking. To maintain their relationship, Ann and Lisa must calculate the rewards and costs in order to determine which outcome will maximize mutual benefit. Perhaps the only outcome we can be sure will not occur is that in which Ann cycles and Lisa cleans (lower left quadrant); it is a theoretically possible outcome, but it involves costs without rewards for Lisa. We will again encounter social exchange theory in Chapter 9 when we discuss interpersonal attraction.

Social psychologists have applied the principles of learning theories to a wide variety of areas. Perhaps the best example is seen in the contributions of simple reinforcement and observational learning to our understanding of aggressive behavior, discussed more thoroughly in Chapter 10. Similarly, both direct reinforcement and observational learning can help us understand how people learn to be helpful and the conditions under which they are most likely to do so (see Chapter 11). Learning models have also been used to show why the presence of an audience sometimes facilitates performance and at other times impairs it (Chapter 12). Many of our basic attitudes may be acquired through a process of learning and reinforcement, a process that will be described further in Chapters 6 and 7.

What would learning theories lead us to predict about the sole survivor in our opening scenario? Tradi-

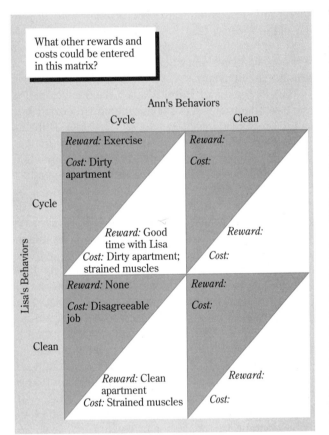

Figure 1.3   *A social exchange outcome matrix. In each quadrant, words above the diagonal describe Lisa's costs and rewards; words below the diagonal describe Ann's costs and rewards.*

tional behaviorists would probably be more able than role theorists to make specific predictions because they could look to behaviors acquired in the past as key predictors of current behavior. Even so, behaviorists agree that people can act as stimuli for behaviors and would predict that many behaviors would be less likely to occur in the absence of other people. Social learning theorists, with their emphasis on other people as models for behavior, would predict a number of restrictions for the survivor's behavior. The absence of models, for example, would preclude the survivor's learning many new behaviors. Social exchange theorists, with their emphasis on interactions between people, would have little basis for predicting behavior of any kind. Our lone survivor would have no social relationships and no interdependency; therefore, social exchange theory would not be applicable.

▶ Cognitive Theories

Since Watson first proposed the behaviorist orientation, many psychologists have reacted strongly against it. Rather than shunning mentalistic concepts, these psychologists have considered such concepts necessary for understanding human behavior. Gestalt psychologists, led by Kurt Koffka and Wolfgang Köhler in the 1930s, were one such group. Taking their name from the German word for "shape" or "form" (*Gestalt*), these psychologists stressed perception and thought. By making the basic assumption that "the whole is greater than the sum of its parts," they moved beyond the simple S-R associations proposed by the behaviorists. Pieces of wood and wrapped steel wires, for example, become something more than parts when formed into an acoustic guitar. Similarly, studies on problem solving led Gestalt psychologists to argue that people learn not only by repetitive, trial-and-error processes, but often by experiencing sudden insights that involve broad reorganization of thoughts. Whereas Watson suggested the unobservable was unimportant, Gestalt psychologists suggested unobservable cognitive processes were all-important.

The **phenomenological approach** represents another reaction against behaviorist principles. According to this view, we can understand a person's behavior only if we know how that person perceives the world.

Stimuli and responses are influential, but only as they are represented in a person's consciousness. Whatever *you* may think about staying up all night in a dingy bar listening to someone play blues guitar is irrelevant if you are trying to understand someone else's behavior; what counts is what *the other person* thinks about it. Lewin's field theory, discussed in the history section of this chapter, is strongly related to the phenomenological approach.

Basic Assumptions and Concepts

Gestalt psychology, the phenomenological approach, and Lewin's field theory provide a background for current cognitive models of social psychology. The word *cognition* comes from a Latin word (*cognoscere*) meaning "to become acquainted with or to know." Accordingly, psychologists use *cognition* to refer to thinking or knowing and consider cognition separate from feeling (emotion) and behaving (Landman & Manis, 1983). Whereas behaviorists adopted the S-R model, cognitive theorists focus almost exclusively on the *O* (organism) of the S-O-R model of behavior.

Cognitive psychologists are interested in two basic issues: mental representation and mental processing. A representation is something that stands for something else; your diploma will eventually represent your college education, but it obviously is not the same thing as a college education. When we talk about mental representation, we mean how an event or an experience is represented in the mind (Markus & Zajonc, 1985). Landman and Manis (1983) consider mental representations to be like building blocks. Instead of forming physical structures, however, the building blocks of mental representation form a **cognitive structure,** the set of principles that organizes our cognitive experience (Shaw & Costanzo, 1982). Mental processing, in contrast, refers to the workings of the mind—how we perceive, how we remember, and how cognition leads to action. In other words, cognitive processes deal with how the building blocks are put together, how they are stored, and how they affect what we do.

Social cognition is a special form of cognitive psychology that deals specifically with the ways in which we think about people and the social aspects of our environment. The world of people differs in many respects from the world of objects (Fiske & Taylor, 1984).

Our schemas regarding people with disabilities might lead us to believe they are unable to pursue creative endeavors.
Alan Carey/The Image Works

For example, social cognition is a mutual process—the target of your perception (another person) can look back at you; a rock cannot. People are also flexible, changing from situation to situation and from year to year in a way that most objects do not. The bicycle you bring out of storage after a year is the same bicycle you put into storage. Friends to whom you return after a year's absence, however, probably are not the same people you left behind. So the process of social cognition differs from and in many ways is more complex than the more basic process of cognition.

One structural concept used by most social cognition theorists is **schema,** an organized body of knowledge about past experiences that is used to interpret present experiences. Suppose, for example, a friend suggests you go to a poetry recital. You may have some direct experience with previous recitals, or you may have heard about them from other people. Whether di-

rect or indirect, those organized experiences constitute your schema about poetry recitals. When your friend asks you to attend the recital, that "old" information is activated—called back from storage—and you use it in your decision about whether to accept the invitation. Based on the information in the schema, you form expectations about the recital to which you have been invited. That is, a schema both organizes what we have already experienced and influences our perception of new events, including events that have not yet happened.

Figure 1.4 shows how this process is represented. Unless you happen to be thinking about poetry recitals at the time you receive the invitation, you first search your memory for a "poetry recital" schema. Once the schema is activated, the information about previous recitals enables you to anticipate how enjoyable tonight's recital might be. Based on those inferences, you either decline or accept the invitation. Your decision then is incorporated into the schema as new information. The schema is then stored in memory until you need to use it again; for example, when you go to the recital if you decide to accept the invitation.

If, however, you have no schema about poetry recitals, you may ask your friend to provide additional information. What happens at a poetry recital? Is there something more to it than someone reciting poetry? What kind of poetry will be recited? As is illustrated in Figure 1.4, the answers to these and other questions you ask become part of a new schema for poetry recitals and serve as the basis for your response to the invitation. Again, the schema is stored in memory, ready for reactivation should poetry recitals come up in the future.

Notice that Figure 1.4 includes the notion that the schema may be altered every time it is used. Every time a schema is activated, the information and inferences produced by the process are incorporated into the schema before it is stored. As we shall see in Chapter 3, Abraham Tesser (1988) used this notion in his theory concerning the ways in which we evaluate ourselves. According to Tesser, resistance to changing the beliefs we have about ourselves results in several different processes that serve to maintain schemas concerning our self-image. Each time a self-schema is activated, these processes strengthen the schema before it is again stored in memory.

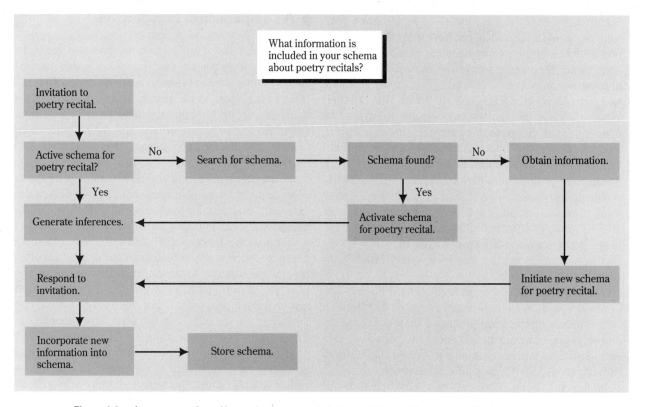

Figure 1.4 *A representation of how schemas operate in the social cognition process. Much cognitive activity occurs between the invitation and the response.*

The cognitive perspective has been a part of social psychology for a long time (Zajonc, 1980). Newer models of social cognition, for example, follow social psychology's well-established tradition of using cognitive concepts, such as attitudes and stereotypes, to explain social behavior. A *stereotype* about college professors, for example, could easily be considered a *schema* about college professors. Newer models of social cognition differ from older ones, however, in their emphasis on process as well as on structure. In addition to attempts to understand what schemas are—what information goes into them, how they relate to each other—social cognition theorists are interested in developing models about the way schemas are used. For example, several theorists have proposed a variety of processes through which schemas and other cognitive concepts affect our thoughts and behaviors without our being aware of the ongoing process (Uleman & Bargh, 1989).

Susan Fiske and Steven Neuberg (1990), for exam-

ple, have developed a model of the ways in which we form impressions about other people that relies heavily on the social cognition perspective. They outline processes concerning when schemas about others are activated, how such schemas are stored and recalled, and how and when the schemas we have about people we have known or heard about in the past affect the impressions we form about new people we encounter. Details about Fiske and Neuberg's model are presented in Chapter 4.

Contributions to Social Psychology

It is easy to find examples of cognitive theories throughout the history of social psychology, from the early interest in attitudes through Fiske and Neuberg's (1990) model of impression formation. In addition to those previously noted, cognitive concepts will appear in many of our later chapters. In Chapters 6 and 7, for example, we explore the concept of attitude and consider some of the theories that have been developed to predict when and how our attitudes change. Cognitive consistency theories, for example, include the assumption that we want our various attitudes, or our attitudes and our behaviors, to be consistent with one another. When they are not consistent, we are motivated to make changes. Suppose, for example, that you admire football heroes and oppose the use of drugs. How do you reconcile your attitudes when you read about drug use among professional football players? This contradiction might cause some shift in your attitudes, either away from football players ("They're not so great after all") or toward drug use ("Maybe the dangers have been exaggerated"). These changes may not be directly observable, but they can be inferred if we rely on cognitive theory.

The ways in which our thoughts can influence our behaviors will be demonstrated in other chapters as well. The communication process (Chapter 5), for example, is fueled by our beliefs about the person we talk with, and discriminatory behavior can be understood, in part, as a consequence of our stereotyped beliefs (Chapter 13). Even more centrally, our beliefs about ourselves reflect the functioning of cognitive variables (Chapter 3). We will see the analysis of cognitive processes most directly in Chapter 4, when we discuss in more detail the assumptions of cognitive theories.

Because cognitive theories emphasize what goes on inside people's heads, they may seem to provide little help with predicting disruptions for the individual who has suddenly lost his or her society. To some extent that is true. Cognitive theorists say far less than role and learning theorists about the actual interchange of human life. Yet social cognition theories would lead us to predict that past schemas would soon prove ineffective in our opening scenario and that the sole survivor would have to create new schemas to deal with the new experiences. Beliefs about the self might shift to incorporate increasing evidence of self-reliance; schemas about the environment would focus more on animals and physical features and less on people. How the individual would act would then depend on the characteristics of the new schemas adopted to deal with this unprecedented situation.

A Comparison of Perspectives

Each of the three major perspectives we have discussed involves certain assumptions about human behavior; some concepts are considered important and others incidental. As a result, a specific perspective leads researchers in certain directions, to ask some questions and to ignore others. Having considered the central features of each perspective separately, let's now compare them directly. Table 1.2 summarizes these comparisons across five dimensions: central concept, historical emphasis, locus of influence (internal or external), individuality versus social influence, and assumptions about human nature.

Each of the three perspectives we have examined has one concept as its centerpiece. For role theories, the central concept is role expectations, formed as people interact with one another in a social system consisting of defined positions. Learning theory's central concept is more specific: it is the stimulus-response unit that results from associating specific behaviors with specific stimuli. Although some learning theories, such as social exchange and social learning, can involve rather complex units, the focus remains on discrete behaviors. For cognitive theories, the central concept is cognition or, more specifically, a variety of cognitive structures and processes.

In contrast to their disparate central concepts, the three perspectives diverge only slightly in the extent to which they emphasize historical versus contemporary causes of behavior. Role theories place the greatest weight on the present by emphasizing expectations concerning the current role being played. Both learning and cognitive theories give more attention to historical antecedents, which results in a combination of historical and contemporary causes. Learning and cognitive theories assume that behavior can and does change with new experience, but it's rarely the case that new experience completely replaces either reinforcement history or cognitive structures stored in memory.

The third dimension on which these perspectives differ is the emphasis placed on internal and external events. Role theories tend to stress socially defined positions and situations. As we shall see in Chapter 3,

Table 1.2 A comparison of three theoretical perspectives in social psychology

| | Perspective | | |
	Role	Learning	Cognitive
Central concept	Role expectations	Stimulus-response units	Cognitive structures
Historical emphasis	Present; expectations are based on present position and context	Past and present; reinforcement history and present contingencies are equally important	Past and present; structures stored in memory and current events are equally important
Locus of influence	External; socially defined roles in the situation	External; stimuli and contingencies present in the environment	Internal; cognitive processes occur within the individual
Individual versus social influence	Social; role expectations result from socialization	Individual; learning experiences are more important	Individual; cognitions are more important
Assumptions about human nature	People respond to expectations about the roles they play	People respond to patterns of reinforcement	People form cognitive structures to create meaning for experiences

however, the more recent emphasis on beliefs about the self allows some weight to be given to internal events. Traditional learning theories, in contrast, are concerned only with external events; they are uninterested in and even antagonistic to the notion of "mentalistic" concepts. More contemporary theories, such as social learning and social exchange, include some internal processes but still involve an essentially external locus of influence. Cognitive theories are extremely focused on the internal and stress internal cognitive structures almost exclusively. They do not preclude external influence, but they generally presume external events to be filtered through internal cognitive structures.

Although the learning and cognitive perspectives differ in the importance they attach to external events, they are alike in the extent to which they focus on the individual. Learning theories give more attention to individual learning histories and, in the case of social learning and social exchange theories, to individual differences in interaction goals. Cognitive theories focus on individual differences among cognitive structures such as schemas, perhaps reflecting psychologists' continuing interest in analyzing individuals rather than groups. Role theories, in contrast, almost ignore indi-

vidual differences. Instead, their focus is on the common features of roles, role conflicts, and role expectations as determinants of behavior.

Both the learning and the role perspectives assume that human nature lacks an essence; rather, people act in response to stimuli or in response to the expectations of the roles they are fulfilling. Within both perspectives, however, recent modifications have inserted the person more directly into theories, acknowledging an organism (an *O* between the stimulus and response) in the case of learning theories and giving greater attention to the self-concept in the case of role theories. Cognitive theories, in contrast, assume that people think, interpret, and find meaning in events. At the same time, cognitive theorists have been accused of giving too little attention to other aspects of human behavior, such as emotion and action, and of allowing the analogy of the computer to direct attention away from these other basic features of human nature.

Clearly, theories within the role, learning, and cognitive perspectives differ considerably in what is considered important and how our understanding of social behavior develops from their propositions. As we suggested earlier, no perspective can be used by itself to explain the broad range of behavior that social psychology incorporates. Each perspective offers valuable insights; at the same time, there are facets of behavior with which none of the theories within a single perspective really comes to grips.

Thus, we return to the purpose of having theories in the first place—to help us organize and interpret information obtained through research. We should not expect any single theory to be all-encompassing or to be "the truth." Runkel and McGrath's (1972) description of theories as "guide[s] to tell you where to look for what you want to observe" (p. 23) reminds us that theories can limit our understanding if used incorrectly. Depending on the theoretical perspective we adopt, we can observe diverse aspects of human behavior. The most significant lesson to be learned is, perhaps, the importance of being aware of our assumptions and of their consequences. At that point we can begin to recognize the full complexity of human social behavior and follow Whitehead's advice quoted at the beginning of this chapter. Theories enable us to simplify what we have learned about social behavior. At the same time, we must avoid falling into the trap of believing that our simplistic views of social behavior are correct in any absolute sense.

▶ What Social Psychologists Do

Having learned about the major perspectives that guide social psychologists, it is time to turn our attention to what specifically is guided by these perspectives. Just what do social psychologists do as they attempt to understand social behavior? They teach, build theories, solve problems, and conduct research.

Although many social psychologists work in other settings, most are employed in academic settings and spend much of their time teaching (Stapp & Fulcher, 1981). According to Marianne LaFrance (1990), teaching attracts students to the discipline and "can re-activate in teachers the fascination that drew them into the field in the first place" (p. 34). Robert Cialdini (1990), for example, credits one of his undergraduate students as the source of an idea that formed the basis of 15 years of research on what became known as the "door-in-the-face" technique of persuasion (Chapter 7).

But there is much more to social psychology than teaching others about it. Role, learning, and cognitive perspectives provide the foundations on which social psychologists build their understanding of social behavior. You will encounter many theories in this book, primarily because "social psychologists are intense theory builders" (Aron & Aron, 1989, p. 109). Some of these theories seem to contradict one another, but that is usually because we simply don't yet know enough about the social behavior in question. Because there is so much to understand about complex and pervasive social behavior, social psychologists rely heavily on the variety of theories that characterize their discipline. According to John Touhey:

[Social psychology] hasn't crystallized or hardened or limited itself to any narrow approaches. What I find wonderful about doing social psychology is that I'm free to bring in ideas from all of the allied social sciences and from the humanities as well. That's the charm, that to me is the cream—the fascination, the addiction if you will—of modern social psychology. [Aron & Aron, 1989, p. 127]

What do social psychologists do with these theories? Usually, they use the theories in attempts to solve social problems. Social action—research and theory designed to solve social problems—is part of the legacy of Kurt Lewin. As you will discover in the coming chapters, the problems to which social-psychological theories have been applied range from arranging furniture in the classroom to preventing and reducing international conflict (Capshew, 1986; McGrath, 1980). Obviously, not every theory is designed to solve a social problem, but social psychologists generally seem to adopt a problem-oriented approach to the discipline. Indeed, many social psychologists work in businesses, government agencies, law firms, hospitals, and a variety of other settings in which problem solving is a full-time occupation. Stanley Schachter, whose work is so pervasive it could be cited in almost every chapter of this book, put it this way:

It's hard to talk about some of these things without sounding pompous. But if I were forced to give advice, I'd say, get problem-oriented, follow your nose and go where problems lead you. Then if something opens up that's in-

"I'm a social scientist, Michael. That means I can't explain electricity or anything like that, but if you ever want to know about people I'm your man."

Drawing by Handelsman; © 1986 The New Yorker Magazine, Inc.

teresting and that requires techniques and knowledge with which you are unfamiliar, learn them. [Evans, 1976, p. 168]

Where our noses lead us—how we obtain the information we teach others, the information we use to build (and tear down) theories, and the information we apply to social problems—brings us to research.

Conducting research may be the most important activity social psychologists perform. Consider the "funny thing" that happened to John Arrowood on his way to law school:

I had an undergraduate research scholarship for a summer and got to meet a number of . . . social psychologists who all seemed to be having the time of their lives doing things that you probably couldn't have stopped them from doing anyway. They were professionally nosy; they were curious. They were finding out new things—and they were getting *paid* for doing it!

This came as a great revelation to me . . . And so I was hooked at that point on research. There was simply no thought thereafter of going into law school. [Aron & Aron, 1989, p. 90]

▶ Summary

Social psychology is the field of study concerned with interpersonal behavior. Its concerns include not only actual interpersonal behavior but any behavior in which the presence of others is imagined or anticipated. Imagining what the world would be like without other human beings gives you some sense of how broad the concerns of social psychology are.

Although the writings of early philosophers and the experiments of 19th-century psychologists indicate an interest in social behavior, the beginning of social psychology as a recognized discipline is often set at 1908, when two textbooks titled *Social Psychology* were published. During the next 30 years, many important developments set the tone for modern social psychology as a research-based discipline, and both research and theory have continued to accelerate.

Theories are formulated to explain phenomena. The three theoretical perspectives that dominate current social psychology are the role, learning, and cognitive perspectives.

Role theories are used to explain social behavior by an analysis of the expectations that accompany roles, socially defined patterns of behavior that accompany a particular position within a social context. In recent years, concepts derived within the role perspective have been used to explain a variety of phenomena related to the self and the self-concept.

Learning theories were once limited to stimuli, responses, and reinforcements, and learning theorists concentrated only on events external to the person. More recent theories within the learning perspective include social learning theory and social exchange theory, both of which include numerous cognitive concepts. Thibaut and Kelley, with their theory of interdependence, shifted the focus from the individual to the interacting dyad, considering the rewards and costs for both partners in an interaction.

The cognitive perspective has roots in early work by both Gestalt and phenomenological theorists. More recently, cognitive theorists have developed much more elaborate concepts of cognitive structure, often by borrowing models from the field of computer technology. *Social cognition* refers specifically to the ways in which we think about people and the social aspects of our environment.

Theories can be compared on several dimensions, including central concepts, emphasis on historical or contemporary situations, focus on internal or external events, emphasis on individuals or social structures, and basic assumptions about human nature.

Each theoretical perspective offers a unique view of social behavior, and no single theory within any perspective explains everything. Our understanding is often increased when we take several different perspectives into account.

The profession of social psychology involves teaching, building theories, solving problems, and conducting research. These activities are interconnected, but if one activity must be chosen to be of primary importance, research would be that one.

▶ *Key Terms*

behaviorism
cognitive structure
construct
distributive justice
field theory
gender-role norm
hypothesis
norm
phenomenological approach
psychoanalytic theory
reinforcement
response
role
role expectations
schema

self-monitoring
social exchange theory
social facilitation
social learning theory
socialization

stimulus
stimulus discrimination
stimulus generalization
superego
theory

Research is the invasion of the

unknown.

DeWitt Stetton, Jr.

The whole of science is nothing more

than a refinement of everyday thinking.

Albert Einstein

2

Methods of Studying Social Behavior

In this chapter, we discuss social-psychological research. "Its continuing mission—to explore strange new worlds, to seek out new life and new civilizations, and boldly go where no one has gone before." Yes, it does sound a little pretentious, perhaps a bit silly, and possibly sacrilegious to *Star Trek* (first and *Next Generation*) fans. But you need not spend much time talking to a social psychologist to discover the description is applicable. Instead of a starship, social psychologists use research as their vehicle of exploration; instead of star charts, social psychologists use theories to navigate.

As we saw in Chapter 1, theories enable us to look at the world in certain ways. We use theories to provide a general framework for our understanding. We also use them to decide what specific events to look for and to form tentative explanations for the events we observe. A social learning theorist, for example, may look for influential people in the environment and consider modeling as a possible explanation for someone's behavior. On the other hand, a social cognition researcher may investigate what information was available to that same person and consider the extent to which a schema may explain the person's behavior. Beveridge said, "we are prone to see what lies behind our eyes rather than what appears before them" (1964, p. 99); what we expect or want to see is probably what we will see.

"Behind our eyes" encompasses considerable territory, and it is from this territory that social psychologists develop the ideas they examine through research. Like any other scientists, social psychologists begin their pursuit of knowledge with an idea, which itself is based on existing knowledge. The idea is then tested to determine its worth. In other words, new knowledge results from a mixture of old knowledge, an idea, and an empirical test of the idea. All the research discussed in this book began with an idea—sometimes a formally derived hypothesis, sometimes an intuitive leap, and sometimes just a lucky happenstance. How ideas develop will be the first topic of this chapter. How we translate ideas into scientific studies will be our focus in the rest of the chapter.

▶ **Research Hypotheses**

Where do ideas come from? Curiosity and observation are the starting points in the research process (Silver-

man, 1977). Social psychologists focus their curiosity on human behavior and their observations on people and social interactions. Research ideas may develop from a general interest in some topic: persuasion, group processes, love, and so forth. In other instances, a specific event may be perplexing, and, like Sherlock Holmes, the social psychologist will try to unravel the mystery. This approach resembles Schachter's problem-solving approach, discussed in Chapter 1. In still other cases, an investigator may be involved in one project and, like the fabled princes of Serendip, accidentally discover other, even more interesting information about human behavior. The new information may have little to do with the original research focus. In each case, curiosity and observation are at the root of the investigation.

William McGuire (1973) has suggested some specific ways in which testable hypotheses about human behavior may be derived. (See Table 2.1.) Some of these approaches are based on a considerable body of past research; the investigator builds on past theory and data and develops increasingly complex hypotheses from those sources. Other approaches begin with direct observation of people's behavior, from which the investigator tries to define the basic psychological processes that may underlie the observed events. The latter approach is seen in attempts to analyze the practitioner's rule of thumb.

Consider the rule of thumb that Joule, Gouilloux, and Weber (1989) call the "lure." Walking past a store window, you notice a pair of shoes on sale for, say, 50% of its original cost. Intrigued, you attempt to buy a pair but are told your size is not available. As you are about to leave, the salesperson offers to show you a similar pair of shoes that happen not to be discounted. According to the "lure" hypothesis, the commitment you made to buy the discounted, but unavailable, shoes will probably result in your buying the substitute, regular-priced shoes. Joule, Gouilloux, and Weber found support for this hypothesis in their research, which is discussed at greater length in Chapter 8. For the present, the "lure" hypothesis serves to illustrate how mundane the sources of some research ideas can be.

Each approach McGuire suggested can be used to develop a hypothesis. Once you have a hypothesis, how do you decide whether the idea is a good one? Bibb Latané (quoted in Hunt, 1985) suggests four criteria: (1) the idea should be theoretically interesting; (2) the idea should suggest an advance in methodology; (3) a well-designed experiment should follow from the idea; and (4) the idea should have social relevance. Not all research hypotheses can satisfy each of these criteria, but some do. For example, Bibb Latané and John Dar-ley developed a productive research program that investigated the conditions under which people are willing to help others in emergencies. This research was prompted by a newspaper story about an incident in which many people witnessed a long-drawn-out mur-

Table 2.1 Some approaches to hypothesis formation

1. *Case study and introspection*
   Example: Upon wondering why he testified that burglars had broken a window to enter his house when in fact they had forced open a door, Hugo Münsterberg (1913) generated a number of studies concerning the accuracy of eyewitnesses.

2. *Accounting for a paradoxical incident*
   Example: A cult of Illinois citizens in the mid-1950s fervently predicted the end of the world. When the designated day arrived and the world did not end, the believers' enthusiasm for their cause did not wane (Festinger, Riecken, & Schachter, 1956). This incident led to a hypothesis about the effects of commitment on subsequent behavior.

3. *Use of analogy*
   Example: Borrowing from the medical principles of immunization, William McGuire (1964) developed research showing how information about a topic could "inoculate" individuals against persuasive messages.

4. *Hypothetico-deductive method*
   Example: In this more formal method, the investigator combines several principles derived from theory and previous research and, through logical deduction, arrives at a set of predictions. The work of Hui, Triandis, and Yee (1991), discussed later in this chapter, exemplifies this approach.

5. *Functional or adaptive approach*
   Example: The investigator considers a particular pattern of events, then generates the principles that must be operating for the event to occur. James Pennebaker (1989) did this when, after working with people whose spouses died unexpectedly, he developed several hypotheses about thinking patterns during stress.

6. *Analyzing the practitioner's rule of thumb*
   Example: Based on tactics employed by salespeople in clothing and shoe stores, Joule, Gouilloux, and Weber (1989) developed and tested a hypothesis concerning one way in which individuals attempt to convince people to do something they don't want to do.

7. *Trying to account for conflicting results*
   Example: While reviewing the accumulation of research on a specific topic, a researcher may notice conflicting results. Mullen, Salas, and Miller (1991) have described a variety of instances in which conflicting results have led to new hypotheses directed toward explaining the conflicts.

8. *Accounting for exceptions to general findings*
   Example: Most research shows that a performance by a woman will be rated less favorably than an equivalent performance by a man. Yet on some occasions, such devaluation will not occur (Taynor & Deaux, 1973). These exceptions to the rule provide an intriguing source of hypotheses.

9. *Reducing observed complex relationships to simpler component relationships*
   Example: Patricia Devine (1989) used this approach when she separated the process of making prejudicial inferences into spontaneous and actively controlled components. Devine's research led to several hypotheses about tactics for reducing prejudice.

THE PRIVATE DOUBTS OF CHRISTOPHER COLUMBUS.

IT SURE **LOOKS** FLAT.

Drawing by M. Stevens; © 1991 The New Yorker Magazine, Inc.

der, but none called for help. Latané and Darley designed a set of research studies to answer the question "Why don't people help?" (Latané & Darley, 1970). They hypothesized, among other things, that the presence of other people can reduce an individual's sense of responsibility. Thus, a victim is less likely to receive help from someone in a crowd. (This area of research will be described in more detail in Chapter 11.) Latané and Darley's work addressed questions that have both theoretical and practical importance. It also made methodological contributions to research, and the experiments were unquestionably sound in their design.

Testing Hypotheses

Simply formulating a hypothesis is not enough; one also must devise a means to test the hypothesis. An untested hypothesis is like an old trunk found in a deserted barn; it might contain valuable articles, or it might contain rotted clothing. Thus, hypothesis generation provides the initial direction, but the latter stages of the research process are critical. They are also not simple or automatic, though research reports in professional journals often make the process seem easy. It seems as though the investigators came up with a good

hypothesis, tested it, obtained interesting results, and then quickly published their findings. In truth, the course of research is not so smooth, but it usually is enjoyable.

Consider the study by Anthony Doob and Alan Gross (1968), who wanted to examine the link between frustration and aggression. Specifically, they wanted to know whether the status of the frustration agent might affect the amount of aggression resulting from frustration. What kind of frustration? What kind of aggression? What kind of status? Answering these questions will illustrate the process of testing research hypotheses.

Testing any hypothesis requires translating theoretical concepts into concrete variables that represent the concepts in reliable and valid ways. **Reliability** refers to the consistency with which a concrete variable represents a theoretical concept. Just as a reliable person is someone from whom you can expect a certain amount of consistency, such as in fulfilling promises, a reliable variable is one from which you can expect to obtain consistent representation of an abstract concept. When you use a calculator, for example, you expect to obtain *4* every time you add *2* and *2.* If instead it sometimes produced *6, 3, 14,* or *75,* it would be unreliable, and you would not want to use it. If a research variable sometimes represented a theoretical concept and sometimes did not, it would be unreliable and should not be used. In contrast, **validity** refers to the extent to which a variable represents what it is supposed to represent. If a calculator produced 6 every time you used it to add 2 and 2, it would not be a valid calculator. It would be reliable because it consistently produced 6 every time you added 2 and 2, but it would not represent what it should represent—the concept of addition. Thus, both reliability and validity are important considerations in the process of hypothesis testing.

Before they could test their hypothesis, Doob and Gross needed reliable and valid ways to measure frustration, aggression, and status. They decided to use a stalled car at a traffic light to represent frustration. Being stuck behind a stalled car certainly is valid; it represents the concept of **frustration**—the experience of having something or someone interfere with one's goal. A stalled car is also a reliable way to produce frustration; one's goal at a traffic light rarely involves anything other than moving forward when the light turns green, and a stalled car consistently interferes with that goal.

Doob and Gross measured aggression by observing whether the driver behind the stalled car honked the horn. Is that valid? It is if the definition of **aggression** includes any behavior accomplished for the purpose of hurting a living being that does not want to be hurt (Baron, 1977). It may not be the same as a punch in the nose, but honking one's horn is a way to annoy someone. Is it reliable? Although people do honk their horns for other reasons, honking at someone in a stalled car blocking a traffic lane is more likely to be aggression than to be, say, a friendly greeting. Therefore, observing whether the driver behind the stalled car honks the horn is a valid and reliable way to measure aggression.

Because the behavior in which Doob and Gross were interested was horn-honking, it became their **dependent variable**—a measure of the participants' responses in the research situation. The term derives from the fact that subjects' responses *depend on* or are a reaction to what occurs in the study. It is called a *variable* because responses may differ; for example, some drivers may honk their horns, and others may not.

The valid, reliable measure of status Doob and Gross chose was the make of the stalled car; the quality and cost of one's car consistently represent socioeconomic status. Doob and Gross used the status of the stalled car as an **independent variable**—a set of different conditions presumed to have some effect upon the research participants' responses. Doob and Gross were testing the hypothesis that the status of the stalled car (the independent variable) would affect the horn-honking responses of drivers in cars immediately behind the stalled car (the dependent variable). For graduate students, finding a low-status car—old, well-used, and inexpensive—was no problem. A high-status car was harder to come by, so they went out and rented a Chrysler.

The choice of independent and dependent variables is linked closely to the procedures and setting one plans to employ in a study. It would not make much sense, for example, for Doob and Gross to use horn-honking as a dependent variable if they were planning to run their study in a college classroom. Certain procedures, in turn, may reduce the validity of the variables by introducing **demand characteristics**—any cues that indicate what behavior is expected—into the research situation (Orne, 1969). For example, if someone in a study were asked first to complete a questionnaire about nuclear disarmament, then to listen to a speech advocating nuclear disarmament, and finally to complete a questionnaire similar to the previous one, the subject might suspect that the researcher was studying attitude change. Someone who wanted to please the researcher or "do the right thing" might well report a change of attitude that had not really occurred. Such a response would reflect the influence of the demand characteristics of the situation rather than the influence of the independent variable. Similarly, if the participants in Doob and Gross's study knew what hypothesis was being tested, horn-honking might no longer be a valid measure of aggression. Instead, horn-honking might represent the concepts of cooperation, helpfulness, or sympathy for poor graduate students who stand on street corners conducting research.

Even being aware that one is participating in a research study might reduce the validity of the dependent variable. **Evaluation apprehension,** concerns about being observed and judged by others,[1] might

[1]This problem is related to the more general issue of impression management, which is discussed in Chapter 3.

lead some of Doob and Gross's subjects to alter their normal behavior. Some participants may not want to seem too aggressive, and others might want the researchers to think that they have no tolerance for stalled cars although they are usually more patient. Evaluation apprehension reduces the validity of the dependent measure; it represents what the participants want the researcher to think about them, which is not necessarily the concept it is supposed to represent (Sigall, Aronson, & Van Hoose, 1970). To control for such problems as demand characteristics and evaluation apprehension, Doob and Gross chose not to inform their participants that they were participating in a research study. (Informing research participants about research procedures is discussed with other ethical issues in the section titled "Ethics of Research.")

Knowledge about research hypotheses can also affect the behavior of the researchers themselves. Robert Rosenthal (1966) has argued that **experimenter expectancies,** beliefs about what results should be obtained from a research study, can influence the results of the study even when the research subjects are not human. When human interaction is involved, a researcher's expectations are even more likely to influence the research results; vocal inflection or subtle facial movements are two of many ways to convey information (see Chapter 5). After reviewing research on gender differences, for example, Eagly and Carli (1981) noted several effects that depended on the researcher's gender, perhaps because male and female researchers convey different expectancies to male and female subjects. Thus, experimenter expectancies can reduce the validity of the dependent variable by making it, in part, a measure of what the experimenter thinks will happen. Reducing the influence of experimenter expectancies often involves minimizing the interaction—which can include using recorded or printed instructions—between researcher and participants. Sometimes the researchers who developed the research hypotheses will have someone who is unaware of the hypotheses complete the research procedures.

After considering the reliability and validity of their research variables and controlling for demand characteristics, evaluation apprehension, and experimenter expectancies, Doob and Gross (1968) were ready to test their hypothesis. They used an apparently stalled car—sometimes the low-status car, sometimes the high-status car—to block the way at traffic lights and counted the number of times drivers behind the stalled car honked their horns. When the data were collected and analyzed, Doob and Gross found support for the initial hypothesis. People were less likely to honk at the driver of the high-status car. So far, so good. But when Doob and Gross wrote the report and submitted it to a journal, the editor of that journal found the study uninteresting. The editor of a second journal had a similar opinion. Fortunately, a third editor responded positively, and Doob and Gross's study of horn-honking now occupies a place in the social psychology literature.

▶ **Major Methods of Social-Psychological Research**

There is no one right way to test a hypothesis, nor is there necessarily a single, best way. Therefore, social psychologists have developed a warehouse of methods, many of which may be appropriate for any single question. Every method has strengths and weaknesses, and understanding the relative utility of different research methods is important. Without such understanding it is relatively easy to misinterpret research results; this can sometimes have far-reaching consequences. In 1970, for example, the U.S. Supreme Court considered the question of whether using juries of fewer than twelve people violated the constitutional requirement of due process (*Williams v. Florida*). The Court decided juries containing as few as six individuals would satisfy due process and cited several "experiments" in its written opinion. Unfortunately, many of the "experiments" cited were "uncontrolled, haphazard observation by court clerks and attorneys interviewed . . . after the fact" (Saks & Hastie, 1978, p. 77). Some of the "experiments" did involve valid, reliable research procedures, but the Court's conclusion about the results of many of these studies was directly opposite that of the researchers who conducted the studies (Saks, 1977; Wrightsman, 1991).

In this section, we will discuss six of the research methods social psychologists employ most often: experiments, quasi-experimental research, field studies,

Socioeconomic status often affects our judgments about people's capabilities.
Left: Mark Antman/The Image Works. Right: Alan Carey/The Image Works

archival research, simulation and role playing, and surveys and interviews. In each case, we will consider both the advantages and disadvantages of the method.

Experimental Research

The study conducted by Doob and Gross (1968) was an **experiment,** a study in which the independent variable is manipulated in order to test a causal hypothesis. The status of the stalled car (that is, the independent variable) was under the experimenters' control. Doob and Gross tested the hypothesis that the status of the car would *cause* different amounts of aggression, which was measured by horn-honking.

The following study by John Darley and Paget Gross (1983) is another example of experimental research. Princeton University students volunteered for a study that allegedly was designed to assess the rating forms elementary school teachers used to place individual pupils in academic programs. The students observed a videotape of a 9-year-old girl named Hannah and used the rating forms to make judgments about her capabilities. Approximately half the students saw a scene of Hannah in a home environment that was decidedly upper middle class—a suburban neighborhood with large five- and six-bedroom homes, a modern school, and tree-lined parks. Darley and Gross told these subjects that Hannah's parents were both college graduates and were currently employed as professionals, her father as an attorney and her mother as a freelance writer. The other students saw a different videotape of Hannah's environment, one that showed a run-down urban neighborhood, with a schoolyard made of asphalt and enclosed by a chain-link fence. These students were told that Hannah's parents had little education and worked as a meat packer and a seamstress.

In Darley and Gross's experiment, the status of the neighborhood depicted in the videotape of Hannah's environment was an independent variable—the researchers decided which videotape would be seen by which students. Darley and Gross expected the videotapes and the information about Hannah's parents to produce expectations among their subjects, expectations that would influence the judgments they would make about Hannah's academic potential. This experiment included a second independent variable as well. Before making their judgments, half the students assigned to view each of the two videotapes of Hannah's environment received information about her ability level in the form of a 12-minute videotape of Hannah performing a series of achievement tests. The others (again, half of those who saw the videotape of Hannah in the middle-class environment and half who saw her in the working-class environment) made their judgments without the benefit of this performance information. The dependent variables in this experiment included several questionnaire ratings of Hannah's ability, motivation, and academic potential, including estimates of the grade level at which she could function.

What did Darley and Gross learn from their experiment? As you can see in Figure 2.1, when the students did not have any actual information about Hannah's performance on the achievement tests, the manipulation of Hannah's environment did not cause very different ratings concerning the grade in which Hannah should be placed. Perhaps the students were unwilling to make such judgments on obviously inadequate evidence. But when the students did have information about Hannah's performance on the achievement tests, the manipulation of Hannah's environment caused the students to place her in very different grades. These students filtered the performance information through their expectancies. Both groups saw the same videotape of Hannah's performance on the achievement tests, but students who believed Hannah was from a working-class environment placed her in a much lower grade than students who believed Hannah was from a middle-class environment. More information about how our expectations about others affect the ways in which we evaluate them will be provided in Chapter 4.

The most important characteristic of an experiment is the researcher's ability to control the independent variables. This ability is important because it enables the researcher, and everyone else, to draw conclusions about the cause-and-effect relationship between the independent and dependent variables. In the Darley and Gross experiment, for example, the same child portrayed Hannah in all the videotapes so that the child's appearance was the same for all the experimental conditions. Also, Hannah's videotaped performance on the achievement tests was identical in the working-class and middle-class conditions. This allowed the experimenters to conclude that any difference between the groups meant that subjects were reading into the film what they expected to see rather than simply responding to what was there. Darley and Gross exercised similar control of the dependent variables, asking the subjects precise questions about their judgments concerning Hannah.

One other characteristic of experimental research should be mentioned—the **manipulation check,** a dependent measure used specifically to assess the extent to which the different conditions associated with the independent variable really are different. Although experimenters control the independent variable, it is still important for them to be sure that the subjects perceive the manipulation as it is intended. Darley and Gross, for example, asked their subjects to identify Hannah's socioeconomic class in order to ensure that the subjects had perceived the difference between the two environments depicted in the videotapes.

Sometimes, however, there is little doubt that manipulation of the independent variable effectively created different conditions. Clive Seligman and his colleagues

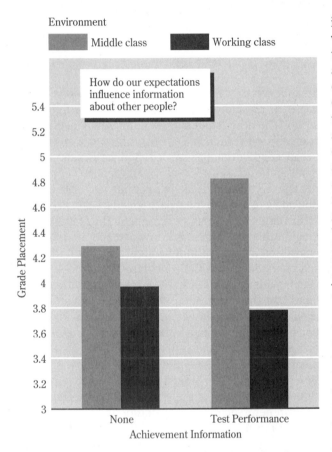

Figure 2.1 *Both expectations and specific information about academic achievement affect judgments concerning academic potential.*

Source: "A Hypothesis-Confirming Bias in Labeling Effects" by J. M. Darley and P. H. Gross, 1983, *Journal of Personality and Social Psychology, 44,* pp. 20–33.

(Seligman, Finegan, Hazlewood, & Wilkinson, 1985), for example, conducted an experiment to test the causal relationship between being blamed for a negative outcome (or receiving credit for a positive outcome) and the reactions of those who experience the outcome. Specifically, they wanted to determine if mitigating circumstances would modify someone's reaction to either a negative or a positive outcome. To test their hypothesis, Seligman et al. telephoned sixty customers who had ordered pizzas from a local pizza parlor and manipulated the outcome of the delivery. They told half the customers that the delivery of their pizzas would be delayed (negative outcome) and told the others that their pizzas would be delivered earlier than the estimated time (positive outcome). The researchers also manipulated the reason for the change in delivery time. Sometimes the customer was told the driver caused the change in delivery time, and sometimes the customer was told that such circumstances as traffic conditions caused the change in delivery time. Seligman and his colleagues used the size of the tip the customer gave the driver as their dependent variable.

What kinds of tips did the driver receive in each of the experimental conditions? Figure 2.2 shows the results. The different outcomes did not produce any difference in tips when situational reasons were given for the change in delivery time. But the driver who was held responsible for the outcome either benefited or suffered, depending on whether the change in delivery time was positive or negative.

The experiment by Seligman and his colleagues illustrates another important characteristic of experimental research. **Randomization,** the process of ensuring that each subject has an equal chance of experiencing any one of the different conditions in an experiment, enables researchers to be certain that the independent variables are the cause of whatever changes occur in the dependent variable. Looking at the results in Figure 2.2, for example, one might argue that they merely indicate that some people give bigger tips than some other people. One might also argue that more "big tippers" happened to be in the group that was told the driver was responsible for the early pizza delivery. Such an argument, if correct, would make the study an invalid test of the hypothesis. But by randomly assigning customers to the different conditions in their experiment, Seligman and his colleagues were able to

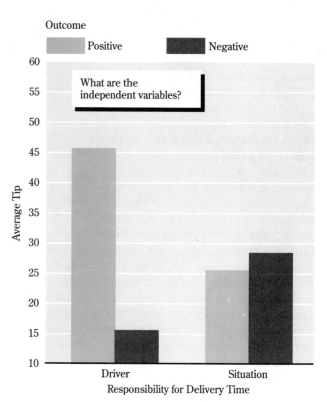

Figure 2.2 *Delivery outcome influenced the tip only when the driver was responsible for the outcome.*
Source: Adapted from "Manipulating Attributions for Profit: A Field Test of the Effects of Attributions on Behavior" by C. Seligman, J. E. Finegan, J. D. Hazlewood, and M. Wilkinson, 1985, *Social Cognition, 3*, pp. 313–321.

ensure that both "big tippers" and "little tippers" were equally likely to experience either early or late delivery and were equally likely to be told that either the driver or the traffic was the reason for the change in delivery time. Thus, any differences in the size of the tips among the experimental conditions were caused by the independent variables.

Advantages The major advantage of experimental research procedures is that they enable researchers to test hypotheses about cause-effect relationships. The experimenter's ability to manipulate the independent variables and to assign subjects randomly to the different conditions provides the basis for drawing conclusions about cause and effect. Also, experiments allow the investigator to "sort out" variables—to simplify more complex events of the natural world by breaking them down into components. Seligman and his fellow researchers, for example, were able to separate the outcome from the entity responsible for the outcome.

Other advantages of experiments are somewhat more mundane and depend on the type of experiment being conducted. Experiments conducted in laboratories, such as the one conducted by Darley and Gross (1983), are relatively convenient. Most psychological laboratories are located on university campuses, where there is an abundant supply of students to serve as subjects, and the experimenter has easy access to facilities. Procedures at many universities make a pool of subjects readily available, usually from introductory psychology classes, and the investigator avoids the difficulty of recruiting subjects individually. Experiments conducted in the field, such as those by Doob and Gross (1968) and Seligman and his colleagues (1985), are less convenient but enable researchers to focus on behavior in a natural setting. Thus, the reduction of evaluation apprehension and demand characteristics in field experiments is often offset by the increased difficulty in recruiting subjects and manipulating independent variables.

Disadvantages In addition to the relative inconvenience of field experiments, experimental research in general has some substantial disadvantages. To the extent that subjects are aware that they are participating in research, experiments—particularly those conducted in laboratories—are prone to the problems of demand characteristics and evaluation apprehension discussed earlier. These problems affect the **internal validity** of the experiment (Campbell & Stanley, 1966), the extent to which the results are due to the independent variables that were manipulated in the experiment. Solving these problems often raises ethical questions, which we address later in this chapter.

Another disadvantage of experimental research is its lack of relevance to everyday behavior. Many situations created in laboratory experiments bear little direct relation to the situations a person encounters in everyday life. Field experiments, too, can produce anomalous situations: how often does someone at a pizza parlor call to tell you that your pizza will be delivered *early*? For this reason, Aronson, Brewer, and Carlsmith (1985)

have distinguished between experimental realism and mundane realism. **Experimental realism,** which is often measured by manipulation checks, refers to the amount of impact inherent in the research situation; that is, the extent to which the subject is involved in the experiment and paying attention to it. **Mundane realism** refers to the similarity of the situation to everyday life. How often, for example, does one evaluate academic potential the same way that the subjects in the Darley and Gross (1983) experiment evaluated Hannah?

External validity refers to the extent to which research situations represent situations that occur in everyday life (Campbell & Stanley, 1966). The college students' evaluations of Hannah's performance, for example, *might* parallel the judgments of a supervisor rating male and female employees in an organization or a college professor grading essays written by middle- and working-class students, but we cannot be certain. Experiments conducted outside the laboratory generally have greater external validity than experiments conducted in laboratory settings.

Critics have also argued that reliance on college students as subjects in academic laboratories can introduce distortions into our understanding of human behavior (Sears, 1986). Compared with the general population, college students may be more cognitive, more concerned with material self-interests, less crystallized in their attitudes, and more responsive to some situational pressures that are not likely to affect other people. Very different people in very different settings need to be studied, Sears suggests, if we are to understand the full range of human experience.

In summary, experimental research offers the best way to test cause-effect hypotheses through control of the research setting and the greatest ability to isolate those variables believed to be important. However, control and isolation of variables can create another set of problems that reduces the correspondence between the results of experiments and everyday behavior. Therefore, we generally make a distinction between what *can* and what *will* happen in a social setting. Darley and Gross (1983) showed people *can* interpret the same performance in different ways if they have different expectations. Their results do not necessarily mean that people *will* make different interpretations in every social situation.

Quasi-Experimental Research

There are many potential independent variables for which manipulation is simply impossible, excessively difficult, or ethically inappropriate. In such instances, quasi-experimental research is one alternative to an experiment. The label *quasi* means the researcher does not have full control over the independent variables but does have a choice about how, when, and for whom the dependent variable is measured. Consider, for example, the success of medical procedures such as kidney transplants. Patients whose kidneys fail to function normally face several treatment options, one of which is a kidney transplant. For some patients this treatment succeeds; for others it does not. Interested in how someone's experience affects judgments of other events, Clark McCauley and his colleagues (McCauley, Durham, Copley, & Johnson, 1985) asked kidney patients to estimate the general survival rates of people who have had kidney transplant operations. They focused on two groups of patients: Patients in one group had received donor kidneys successfully, whereas the other group had to return to kidney dialysis because the transplant failed. Both groups were asked: "What percentage of kidney transplants from an unrelated person (cadaver) are functioning successfully one year after the transplant operation?" The two groups of patients differed markedly in their answers. On average, patients whose transplant had succeeded estimated that 53% of all transplants were successful, while patients whose transplant had failed guessed a more pessimistic 29%. Thus, one's experience does affect judgments about what happens to "everyone else."

McCauley and his colleagues could not have manipulated their independent variable—whether or not someone received a *successful* kidney transplant. Many independent variables used in quasi-experimental research include natural changes in ongoing behavior, such as policy decisions, a natural disaster, and changes in health or financial status. In other cases, quasi-experimental independent variables are preexisting conditions, such as research concerning gender differences, personality variables, intelligence, and so on. Cross-cultural research falls into the latter category of quasi-experiments.

Consider, for example, a quasi-experimental study conducted by Harry Hui, Harry Triandis, and Candice Yee (1991). They noted that a number of previous researchers had reported results consistent with the notion that Chinese were more generous than Americans in situations involving dividing rewards among people who worked together to complete a task. One possible explanation for this difference is that Chinese culture tends more toward collectivism—affiliation, nurturance, sharing, and so on—whereas American culture tends more toward individualism—autonomy, deference, and so on. To test their hypothesis, Hui and his colleagues asked students from Chinese (Hong Kong) and American (Indiana) cultures, culture being an independent variable they could not manipulate, to divide rewards between themselves and a fictitious co-worker. For half the students in each culture, the subject's contribution to the completion of the task was high; the subject had completed about 80% of the work. For the other half of the students in each culture, the contribution was low, only about 20% of the work.

The results, as illustrated in Figure 2.3, demonstrated that the Chinese students were more generous with the rewards. Whether their contribution was high or low, Chinese students kept less of the reward for themselves than did American students. Hui, Triandis, and Yee also had the students complete a measure of collectivism. When Hui and his colleagues statistically controlled for the collectivism scores of their subjects, the difference in generosity between the Chinese and American students was about the same. Thus, they concluded that the difference between the two cultures is probably not related to the collectivism-individualism difference between Chinese and Americans. What does explain the difference in generosity? The answer to that question will have to wait for additional research.

Advantages One unique advantage of quasi-experimental research is that it allows us to study strong variables that cannot be manipulated or controlled, such as the outcome of a kidney transplant or the results of a lifetime of experience within a specific culture. Often, too, quasi-experimental research deals with policy decisions that have consequences for very large numbers of people. This gives the research findings a measure of external validity rarely matched in more limited experimental research.

Disadvantages Because the investigator cannot control the independent variable in quasi-experimental re-

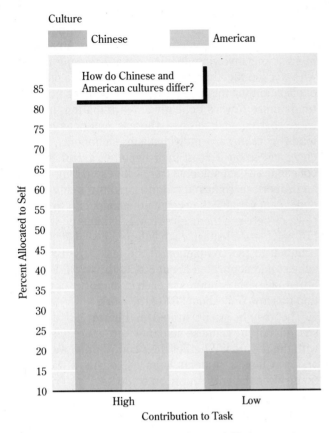

Figure 2.3 *Culture as an independent variable in a quasi-experimental study.*

Source: "Cultural Differences in Reward Allocation: Is Collectivism the Explanation?" by C. H. Hui, H. C. Triandis, and C. Yee, 1991, *British Journal of Social Psychology, 30,* pp. 145–157.

1966; Cook & Campbell, 1979), the lack of random assignment precludes the level of certainty that can be attained in an experiment. Even the most sophisticated statistical analyses cannot replace random assignment (Tanaka, Panter, Winborne, & Huba, 1990).

When a natural disaster or similar event is the independent variable, the investigator faces the additional problem of preparation. Natural disasters usually arrive with little or no warning, thus giving the investigator little time to design a study and to prepare appropriate measuring instruments. Often such research must be done on the run. Also, the arbitrariness of events in the quasi-experimental world does not allow the researcher to choose variables according to any theoretical model. It is difficult to predict how people will respond to stress, for example, before one knows the magnitude of the stressful event. Because it is clearly impossible for researchers to control such a variable, they must accept the level of stress inherent in the situation they find: sometimes a tornado warning, sometimes a devastating twister.

In summary, quasi-experimental research offers some clear advantages to investigators in the impact and complexity of situations that can be studied. In addition, it allows investigators to study some situations that cannot be studied in any other way. However, researchers have less control in quasi-experimental research than in true experiments, so they must interpret results more cautiously.

Field Research

Contrary to experiments and quasi-experiments, field studies are characterized by in-depth observation of a limited number of people in a natural location. Instead of manipulating some aspect of the environment and observing the changes that occur, the field investigator observes and records as much information as possible about the situation as it unfolds and does not intentionally alter the situation in any substantial way. Depending on the research, people in the environment may or may not be aware of the investigator's presence and the general purpose of the investigation. At other times, researchers may become **participant observers,** researchers who actively engage in ongoing activities as they maintain records of the behaviors of those around them.

search, it is always possible that other uncontrolled variables are affecting the dependent variable. In the study of kidney patients, for example, certain differences among patients may have influenced both their judgments of events and their responsiveness to their operations. Pessimistic people, for example, also are less likely to have a successful kidney transplant. Random assignment of subjects to conditions is impossible; no one can ethically assign some patients to experience an unsuccessful transplant, nor could a researcher randomly assign some people to experience socialization within a particular culture. Although several statistical procedures can increase confidence in the proposed cause-effect relationship (see Campbell & Stanley,

Natural disasters usually arrive with little or no warning.
Bob Daemmrich/The Image Works

Whether one is a participant observer or not, observation is the key element of the field study. Because people-watching is a common activity for most of us, it is often hard to appreciate how difficult systematic scientific observation can be. First, a researcher must become thoroughly familiar with the environment and aware of the kinds of behaviors that are most likely to occur. Next, the researcher must decide which types and what level of behavior should be observed. For example, should gross behavioral movement be observed, or is it necessary to observe finer levels, such as facial expressions or vocal pitch? The choices, of course, depend on the questions the researcher wants to answer. Field researchers may not purposely manipulate conditions, but they do formulate specific questions and hypotheses. Without specific hypotheses, field observation becomes mired in a hopeless array of competing events; the researcher may feel like a child viewing a three-ring circus for the first time.

Once categories of behavior are selected for observation, the investigator must devise specific methods of recording the desired information. Here, too, social psychologists have an opportunity to engage in the creativity often associated with developing manipulations of independent variables in an experiment. Creativity alone is not sufficient, however; preliminary data collection is often required to assess the reliability of one's observation techniques. In a field study, reliability often involves ensuring that different observers will code the behavior in the same way. Without such reliability, a coding system merely reflects one observer's biases and cannot become the basis of a scientific statement.

Consider the field study conducted by Judith Hall and Ellen Veccia (1990), who tested hypotheses concerning age and gender differences in interpersonal touching. They sent a team of five observers to twenty different locations such as malls, subway stations, downtown shopping areas, and parks. Armed with microcassette recorders, the observers noted who touched whom among 4,500 dyads, what part of the body was touched, and the gender of each dyad member. The observers also estimated the ages of the dyad members. Training sessions for the observers included observing a variety of different kinds of touches recorded on a videotape, as well as "live" practice sessions in which the recorded observations of pairs of observers were compared.

As can be seen in Figure 2.4, Hall and Veccia found both gender and age differences with respect to interpersonal touching in mixed-gender dyads. Males were much more likely to initiate touch among teenagers, but females were the primary initiators of touch among dyads over 40. As is the case in quasi-experimental research, that the independent variables were not manipulated and random assignment to conditions was not employed prevents any definite conclusions about the cause of the age difference illustrated in Figure 2.4. As Hall and Veccia noted, the age difference may reflect either a generational difference or differences in marital status that are associated with age.

As we noted earlier, some field researchers participate in the activities they are observing. Barker and Schoggen (1973), for example, focused their field research on the residents of a small midwestern town,

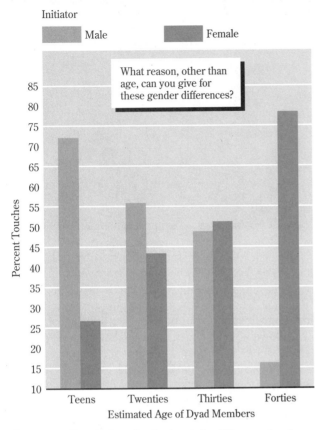

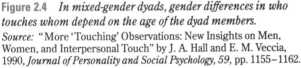

Figure 2.4 *In mixed-gender dyads, gender differences in who touches whom depend on the age of the dyad members.*
Source: "More 'Touching' Observations: New Insights on Men, Women, and Interpersonal Touch" by J. A. Hall and E. M. Veccia, 1990, *Journal of Personality and Social Psychology, 59,* pp. 1155–1162.

population 830. They compared behaviors there with those seen in an English village of similar size. A major goal of this research was to make a complete classification of each town's behavior settings. As we discuss in greater detail in Chapter 14, certain settings, such as a church or classroom, are associated with typical patterns of behavior that are not produced in other settings, such as a bar or baseball stadium.

The settings for field studies are not limited to the everyday locations observed by Hall and Veccia (1990) and Barker and Schoggen (1973). Other researchers have conducted field research in considerably more exotic settings, such as 200 feet below the surface of the Pacific Ocean (Radloff & Helmreich, 1968), in a space station orbiting above the earth (Stewart, 1988), and in Antarctica (Harrison, Clearwater, & McKay, 1990).

Advantages   The major advantage of the field study is its realism. The focus of the study is on events as they normally occur in a natural setting. Because most field studies take place over an extended period, they provide information that cannot be gained in the brief period of observation typical of experimental and quasi-experimental research. Additionally, the duration of the field study generally allows collection of several types of dependent measures. Barker and Schoggen (1973), for example, observed behavior at a variety of levels in a variety of situations as they studied the quality of small-town life. A variety of measures directed at the assessment of a few concepts gives us greater confidence in the conclusions than we could derive from any one measure taken alone.

Disadvantages   Although well-conducted field studies furnish a wealth of data, the lack of control in such settings can be a problem. As we noted earlier, the absence of a manipulated independent variable and of randomization precludes firm conclusions about cause and effect. As with quasi-experimental research, some statistical techniques can be used to narrow the possibilities, but firm conclusions require a controlled experimental design.

A second potential problem in some field research is the subjects' awareness of the investigator's observations. When subjects know they are being observed, their behavior may be affected by evaluation apprehension. Just as in other types of research, the potential influence exerted by the researcher can be a problem, particularly when the researcher is a participant observer.

In summary, the field study allows the investigator to study intensively a series of events in a natural setting. Field studies are not always the best means of testing particular hypotheses, but they may serve as a source of information that can provide the basis for more stringent experimental tests.

Archival Research

Archival research is the general term applied to any study in which the information or records being analyzed were not produced for the purpose of the study itself. Usually the records were collected for something other than a social-psychological study. This is the case when archival researchers analyze government documents, newspaper reports, books and magazines, folk stories, personal letters, and speeches by public figures.

For example, Philip Tetlock and his colleagues (Tetlock, Bernzweig, & Gallant, 1985) used written opinions by the U.S. Supreme Court to test their hypothesis that the justices' political stances—liberal, moderate, or conservative—were related to the complexity of their judicial decisions. Specifically, Tetlock and his colleagues were interested in integrative complexity—the degree to which multiple dimensions of issues and a variety of evidence are considered in arriving at judgments. To test their hypothesis, they selected two kinds of cases—civil liberties and economic issues—from among those heard by the Court between 1946 and 1978. They used an accepted coding procedure to assess the integrative complexity demonstrated in each justice's written opinions for the two kinds of cases. Then they compared the complexity scores of justices falling into each of the three political groupings. As Figure 2.5 shows, the opinions of liberal and moderate justices exhibited greater complexity than those of conservative justices—but only when economic issues were at stake. In the area of civil liberties and rights, the written opinions of all justices were equivalently complex.

Virtually any kind of record is "fair game" for archival research, including research reports themselves. As we noted earlier, a theoretical concept can be translated into several different research variables, which means a given theory can be used to derive many research hypotheses. Thus, researchers periodically publish literature reviews, articles in which individual research reports are integrated in order to arrive at general conclusions that are beyond the scope of any one research study. A narrative review of research on sex differences in children's behavior by Eleanor Maccoby and Carol Jacklin (1974), for example, has often been cited in support of the conclusion that there are very few behavioral differences between men and women.

More recently, researchers have employed a technique called **meta-analysis,** the practice of analyzing the statistical results of individual studies. Although one technique for combining the results of individual studies appeared in the first modern *Handbook of Social Psychology* (Mosteller & Bush, 1954), meta-analysis was not widely used by social psychologists until the late 1970s (Cooper & Lemke, 1991). That meta-analysis has

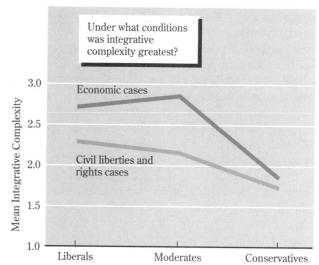

Figure 2.5 *Mean integrative complexity of U.S. Supreme Court justices for two types of cases.*
Source: "Supreme Court Decision Making: Cognitive Style as a Predictor of Ideological Consistency of Voting" by P. E. Tetlock, J. Bernzweig, and J. L. Gallant, 1985, *Journal of Personality and Social Psychology, 48,* pp. 1227–1239.

found its place as an important tool in the social-psychological research arsenal is illustrated by the fact that it was the focus both of a chapter in a recent volume on social-psychological research methods (Cooper, 1990) and of a special issue of *Personality and Social Psychology Bulletin* (Miller & Cooper, 1991).

Meta-analysis enables researchers to identify trends across empirical studies more clearly and with greater confidence than is usually possible with nonstatistical literature reviews. Harris Cooper's (1979) meta-analysis of some of the same studies reviewed by Maccoby and Jacklin (1974), for example, identified a tendency for women to conform more than men in studies concerning group pressure. Later, Eagly and Wood (1991) argued that a number of meta-analyses have produced strong support for social-role theory as an explanation of behavior differences between men and women (Chapter 13).

Advantages   Archival research has several advantages. First, it allows the investigator to test hypotheses over a wider range of time and societies than would otherwise be possible. Many records date back for centuries, a period beyond the scope of the other methods we have discussed. A hypothesis about general human behavior that receives support across several cultures and historical periods can be accepted with much greater confidence than one tested only in a single society at one time period.

A second advantage of the archival method is that it usually involves **unobtrusive measures**—assessments of behavior obtained without the knowledge of the person being studied (Webb, Campbell, Schwartz, & Sechrest, 1966). That is, because the information used in archival research is often collected for another purpose, there is little chance that demand characteristics will be a problem for the present investigator. Evaluation apprehension, too, is reduced, though one can never be certain that those who created the record were completely unconcerned about their intended audience.

Disadvantages Although archival researchers do not collect the data personally and may have fewer problems with demand characteristics and evaluation apprehension, they may have difficulty locating the kind of data they need. Unable to design the dependent measures, archival researchers are at the mercy of the people who collected the data. Sometimes, of course, creativity and ingenuity help investigators to locate the kinds of data they need; in other cases, missing or inaccurate records prevent an adequate analysis of the data. Even if the material is available, it is sometimes difficult to categorize in a way that will yield an answer to the research question. Careful methods of content analysis must be developed for material that is primarily linguistic (such as Supreme Court opinions), much as categories are developed for observational research. Such procedures are simultaneously time-consuming and challenging, although the development of computer programs has provided a welcome assist.

In summary, archival research offers the investigator tremendous opportunities to examine data from a wide range of times and places. Reliance on data collected for another purpose may cause problems for the investigator, but the appeal of archival research is strong. This is particularly true when it is used with other research methods.

Simulation Research

Many of the behaviors and situations in which social psychologists are interested cannot be studied directly. Limitations concerning legal access, for example, pre-vent direct observation of jury deliberations, and ethical limitations prevent experimental research concerning extremely stressful environments. Other phenomena, such as the resolution of a long-standing conflict between two groups, do not occur with sufficient regularity to enable one to study the process systematically. In such cases, social psychologists turn to **simulations,** attempts to imitate some crucial aspects of a real-world situation, in which research participants are asked to role-play or act *as if* the simulation were real.

For example, Geoffrey Kramer, Norbert Kerr, and John Carroll (1990) used a jury-trial simulation to examine the effects of two different kinds of pretrial publicity: factual and emotional. They recruited more than 600 people eligible for jury duty, plus 174 college students, to view a videotape of an armed-robbery trial and deliberate as if they were serving on a real jury. Some of the subjects were exposed to pretrial publicity concerning facts in the case; they learned that the defendant had an extensive criminal record and learned of incriminating evidence that had been ruled inadmissible and therefore not included in the trial. Other subjects were exposed to highly emotional publicity that was unrelated to the charge of armed robbery; they learned that the defendant was also a suspect in a hit-and-run accident in which a little girl had been killed. Still other subjects were exposed to innocuous pretrial publicity in which the robbery was briefly described and the defendant was identified as the person who had been arrested. For each type of publicity, some of the jurors were exposed to the information just before viewing the trial videotape, whereas others were exposed to the publicity about two weeks before they viewed the trial videotape. Finally, some jurors were randomly assigned to receive special instructions from the trial judge to disregard any information that was not presented as evidence during the trial; television and newspaper reports were specifically mentioned in the instructions.

Kramer and his colleagues found that, compared with juries exposed to the innocuous pretrial publicity, those exposed to the emotional pretrial publicity were much more likely to convict the defendant. Neither the delay nor the judge's instructions had any effect upon the conviction-prone bias caused by the emotional publicity. The judge's instructions also did not eliminate the conviction-prone bias caused by the factual publicity. However, the delay between the publicity and the trial reduced the impact of the factual publicity; among juries exposed to the factual publicity, only those who received the publicity immediately before the trial were more likely to convict. When Kramer and his colleagues analyzed recordings of the jury deliberations, they discovered that juries exposed to the emotional pretrial publicity also made more conviction-prone statements. Interestingly, the amount of time the jurors spent talking about the pretrial publicity was not related to the jury verdicts, even though the publicity affected the verdicts. Presumably, the publicity caused jurors who wanted to convict the defendant to be more persuasive during the deliberations.

Aside from enabling social psychologists to study behaviors to which they normally do not have access, simulations also provide information about the impact of adopting a particular role. One of the most dramatic studies in social psychology, for example, is the simulation conducted by Philip Zimbardo and his colleagues (Haney, Banks, & Zimbardo, 1973) at Stanford University. The simulation began with wailing police sirens as nine young men were picked up at their homes. Police officers frisked and handcuffed the men, drove them to the police station, booked them, blindfolded them, and finally drove them to a specially constructed "prison" in the basement of the Stanford psychology building. There, three other young men dressed as guards supervised the prisoners' activities. A small area of the building was outfitted with typical prison cells, a small prison yard, and even a solitary confinement cell.

The subjects in this research project were selected from a group of college students who had answered a newspaper ad for volunteers to take part in a psychological study of prison life. All applicants were screened, and those selected were judged the most stable, most mature, and least antisocial of the volunteers. The subjects agreed to be randomly assigned to play the role of prisoner or guard, which also qualifies this study as an experiment. As you will see, however, the degree to which the researchers were able to control the procedures was not as extensive as is usually the case in most experiments.

Conditions at the "prison" were as realistic as possible. Prisoners were identified only by number, their meals were bland, and their toilet visits were supervised. They were assigned to work shifts and were lined up three times a day for a count. The guards were allowed to devise most of the rules for running the prison, although neither punishment nor physical aggression was permitted. The experimenters maintained constant observation of the situation by audio- and videotape equipment, and they administered a series of questionnaire measures. Although the project was scheduled to run for two weeks, Haney et al. terminated the simulation study abruptly after six days.

Why did the researchers stop the simulation after only six days? Within that period, the behavior of the college men had degenerated. Guards increasingly enjoyed their power; they arbitrarily commanded the prisoners to do pushups, for example, and refused requests to go to the toilet. Prisoners lapsed into depression and helplessness and began to develop symptoms of both physical and emotional distress. It was clear to the experimenters that the reality of a prison had been created, and the situation was too dangerous to continue. After terminating the experiment, the researchers held several sessions with the participants to deal with their emotional reactions to the experience. They also maintained contact with each student for a year after the study to ensure that the negative effects of the prison simulation did not persist.

Not all simulation studies are so dramatic, but the Stanford prison simulation illustrates how adopting a role may alter an individual's behavior. The influence of adopting a role, for example, also makes it possible to use simulation research to study international decision making by having subjects make political and economic decisions for imaginary countries (Streufert, Castore, & Kliger, 1967). In still another form of simulation, computer programs model some aspect of behavior, and hundreds or thousands of hypothetical subjects (or computer runs) can be used to test a hypothesis (Stasser, 1990). Although simulation studies take many forms, all imitate some aspect of a real-world situation to increase our understanding of psychological processes.

Advantages The success of a simulation or role-play study depends greatly on the degree of involvement the research setting can engender (Geller, 1978; Greenwood, 1983). If the subjects become deeply involved in the setting, then the simulation may well approximate the real-life conditions it intends to match. Because participants know the purpose of the study in advance, they take on the role of co-investigator. That role is both ethically and humanistically more satisfying in many respects than the more typical experimental subject role, in which the subject is often unaware of the experimenter's intentions (Kelman, 1968). Another advantage of simulation is that it may allow the investigator to study phenomena and situations that are difficult to study in the real world. It is difficult for social scientists to examine prisons or negotiations between warring countries, for example, but they can simulate them in the laboratory or on the computer. The simulation also can include experimental control of variables and random assignment of subjects.

Disadvantages In spite of their advantages, simulation and role playing are among the most controversial methods in the social-psychological repertoire (Cooper, 1976; Forward, Canter, & Kirsch, 1976; Hendrick, 1977; Miller, 1972). Critics claim the subjects will do only what they think they *might* do, not necessarily what they *would* do in the real situation (Carlsmith, Ellsworth, & Aronson, 1976). We can wonder, for example, whether the individuals in a jury-trial simulation would behave the same way if they were asked to decide whether a real defendant was guilty or not guilty (Bray & Kerr, 1982). Similarly, simulations accomplished via computer depend entirely on the theoretical principles and assumptions that are programmed into the computer.

In addition, the problems of experimental demands and evaluation apprehension are even more serious when the subject is fully informed of the purposes of the study. Proponents of role playing argue that the participant in an experiment is always playing a role, whether it is the general role of subject or a more specific role defined by the investigator. Computer simulations avoid these particular criticisms, but questions can be raised about these simulations' correspondence to actual behavior.

This controversy is difficult to resolve and probably will continue for several years. Some issues in the controversy can be resolved empirically by experiments focused on the methodological practices themselves. Other aspects of the argument may be more philosophical and, like the theories in Chapter 1, may reflect overriding views of human nature. Despite the controversy, simulation and role playing retain their shelf in the methodological warehouse of social psychology. The studies produced by these methods continue to add to our knowledge about the social world.

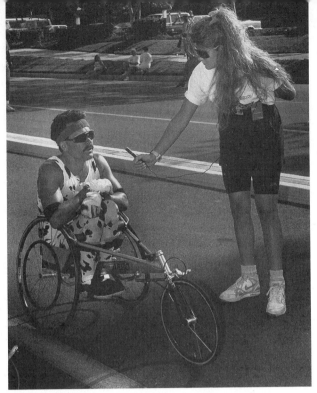

Personal interviews are the source of much research information.
Spencer Grant/Monkmeyer Press

Survey Research

Social psychologists often ask questions of research participants, but survey research involves relying *solely* on data obtained from questionnaires or interviews. In an **interview** survey, the researcher asks a predetermined set of questions and records the respondent's answers. The set of questions used in an interview is usually called a schedule. In a **questionnaire** survey, the respondent reads the questions from and writes answers on a printed form. If the questionnaire is distributed through the mail, the respondent might never even see the researcher. In both cases, the researcher develops one or more hypotheses and then designs a set of questions that will elicit beliefs, attitudes, and self-reported experiences related to the research topic.

Designing a good interview schedule or questionnaire, like preparing to make observations in field research, is not as easy as it may seem. A researcher cannot, for example, put "any old thing" on a questionnaire or interview schedule. Considerations include the wording of questions, the provision of sufficient response alternatives, and the format of the instrument itself. The wording of an item, for example, systematically may bias the answers. Politicians often use this tactic to their advantage. An item that begins "I agree that Candidate X...," for example, is more likely to receive a positive response than one that begins "Does Candidate X...?" Considerable pretesting is necessary to ensure that the items are objective, unbiased, understandable to the average respondent, and specific enough to elicit the desired information. (Schuman and Kalton [1985] offer much more detail on this topic.) Like other research methods, using a survey to obtain information requires knowing something about the information to be obtained.

One example of survey research through an interview is the large-scale study conducted by Campbell, Converse, and Rogers (1976) to assess the quality of life in the United States. After carefully selecting a sample of 2,164 persons aged 18 years or older, which represented all segments of the population and all regions of the country, Campbell, Converse, and Rogers conducted lengthy interviews to determine how satisfied people were with their lives. The researchers assessed both general satisfaction and particular aspects such as job, marriage, and health.

The initial findings of the study showed most people were happy with their lives. A closer look at the results, however, showed that subjective feelings of satisfaction are related to some of the characteristics of one's life situation. Degree of marital satisfaction, for example, is related to educational level, as Figure 2.6 illustrates. A greater percentage of less-educated people report being completely satisfied with their marriage than those with more education. It is also worth noting that the differences between men and women in reported marital satisfaction are greatest at the two extremes of educational level.

To obtain straightforward, honest responses to questions concerning such topics as marital satisfaction, an interviewer must develop rapport with the respondents. At the same time, however, interviewers must standardize the way they conduct the interview to prevent bias caused by being intentionally or unintentionally encouraging or discouraging, or seeming to be uninterested in a particular kind of response. The difficulty of establishing rapport in a standardized manner is one of the reasons survey research is often accom-

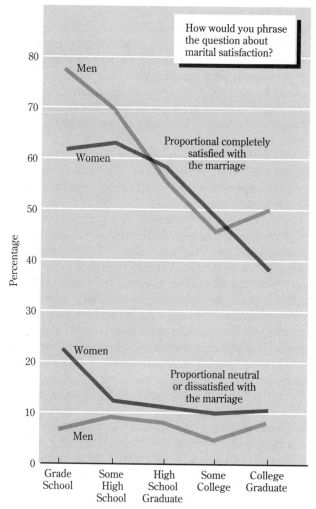

Figure 2.6 *Education is associated with a decline in the proportion of people who report being completely satisfied with their marriage.*

Source: *The Quality of American Life: Perceptions, Evaluations, and Satisfactions* by A. Campbell, P. E. Converse, and W. L. Rogers, 1976.

plished through questionnaires. Another reason for using questionnaires is that they eliminate the need for a large number of interviewers that might be required for an interview survey of, say, hundreds of people. Ikhlas Abdalla (1991), for example, used questionnaires to examine several hypotheses about social support and job stress among 511 employees in Kuwait.

One hypothesis in which Abdalla was specifically interested was the extent to which men and women in an Arab culture might differ in their use of support from co-workers to maintain job satisfaction in the face of role conflict at work. In Arab culture, female employees "are severely limited in their circle of friends, especially at work where their relations are mostly confined to other women with similarly limited work experience" (Abdalla, 1991, p. 277). Despite the different levels of co-worker support available to men and women, Abdalla found high levels of such support enabled males and females equally to maintain higher levels of job satisfaction than employees with low levels of co-worker support. Perhaps, as Abdalla speculated, Arab women's greater experience with using social support in their home environment enabled them to "do more with less" in the work environment.

Both questionnaires and interviews require paying attention to *sampling procedures*. If the researcher wants to generalize to a larger population—for example, the entire population of the United States and Canada—it is not necessary to contact every member of that population. A sample or a subset of perhaps 2,000 people can, if selected properly, accurately represent the total population. Although the variety of sampling techniques that can be employed to obtain a representative sample is beyond the scope of this chapter (for further information, see Dane, 1990), we should note that improper sampling is almost certain to produce inaccurate results. Many televised news programs, for example, feature a "roving reporter" who asks passing pedestrians their opinion on some topical issue. Such procedures are not systematic and probably tell us very little about the attitudes of the general population.

Advantages   A major advantage of survey research is that it can be very straightforward and specific. Rather than devising a situation to elicit desired behavior or finding a natural setting in which to observe that behavior, survey researchers directly question people about the topic under investigation. Sometimes this is the only practical approach to obtaining desired information. If, for example, you want to know about events of a person's childhood, directly asking the person may be the only way to find out.

Questionnaires and interviews also have particular advantages and disadvantages, which tend to balance out. For instance, questionnaires are easier and more economical to use than interviews. In addition, questionnaires provide greater anonymity for the respon-

dent, which is important when sensitive or personal issues are being examined. Face-to-face interviews, however, allow the interviewer to gather additional information from observation. The interviewer also can clarify questions that may be confusing to the respondent and can be sure which person in the household is answering the questions.

Disadvantages   Perhaps the major difficulty with survey research is the accuracy of self-report data. When asked about childhood events, for example, a respondent may or may not correctly recall what happened. Even when more recent events are discussed, either unintentional or deliberate bias may intrude. Surveys of sexual behavior are frequently contested on these grounds: critics suggest that people may be less than honest in describing their sexual practices. Other topics may precipitate evaluation apprehension, leading to embellishment as the respondent attempts to create a favorable impression.

Questionnaires and interviews also have opposite sets of weaknesses. A questionnaire gives the investigator less control over the situation. One cannot guarantee the conditions under which the questionnaire is being administered, who is answering it, and whether the respondent fully understands the questions. On the other hand, the interview is more costly, more time-consuming, and more susceptible to experimenter expectancy effects.

In summary, survey research allows the investigator to ask directly about the issues of concern. Questionnaires in particular permit very large-scale studies and thus may produce conclusions applicable to a wide range of individuals. Survey research, however, relies on the accuracy and honesty of the respondent and depends on self-reports of behavior rather than on observations of the behavior itself.

Selecting a Research Method

Each method has its own set of advantages and disadvantages, and in the abstract, there is no best method. At the concrete level of specific hypotheses, however, one method is likely to include more advantages than other methods.

In the initial stages of research, questions may be only vaguely defined. An investigator may be interested in something concrete, such as communes, the jury system, or a particular religious group. Such topics probably would guide the investigator to a particular setting—that is, to field research—or to the use of a survey method. Hall and Veccia's (1990) interest in interpersonal touching, for example, led to malls, parks, and other locations where they could observe people touching people. Lieberman's (1956) interest in attitudes and behavior produced his surveys of factory workers, discussed in Chapter 1. In other cases, the investigator's questions may involve something more abstract—for example, why people like each other, what causes aggression, or how we share what we have with others. Here the possibilities for study are greater. Hui, Triandis, and Yee's (1991) comparison of Chinese and American students' reward allocation strategies, for example, is only one of perhaps hundreds of studies that have dealt with that topic.

Phoebe Ellsworth (1977), in discussing the selection of a research method, notes some basic concerns that the investigator always has. First among these is finding a situation or instance that could lead to disconfirming one's hypothesis. Although scientists, including social psychologists, enjoy finding out that they are right, it is crucial that their studies be more than a simple demonstration of what was known all along. Instead, research must be a true questioning process. As the eminent biologist Albert Szent-Györgyi once stated,

> Research means going out into the unknown with the hope of finding something new to bring home. If you know in advance what you are going to do or even find there, it is not research at all: then it is only a kind of honorable occupation. [1971, p. 1]

At a party, knowing how everyone is going to get along—exactly what will be done and said—may make a "nice" party, but it does not make an interesting party.

Sometimes an investigator will begin in the laboratory, testing a theory under highly controlled conditions, and then move out to the field to see whether the same principles hold. At other times, a reverse strategy is used, as when relationships observed in a field study are then taken back to the laboratory to test cause-effect relationships. You should recall from Chapter 1 that such a back-and-forth strategy was prescribed by Kurt Lewin, often considered one of the founders of modern social psychology.

The advantages of that strategy should be evident after our discussion of the various research methods. Because each method has its own particular set of weaknesses, it is impossible to rely on any single one for a full understanding of a phenomenon. Thus, the question is not which method is best, but which *set* of methods will be best. As Eugene Webb and his colleagues note, "if a proposition can survive the onslaught of a series of imperfect measures, with all their irrelevant error, confidence should be placed in it" (Webb et al., 1966, p. 3). This notion of focusing on a single concept from a variety of vantage points represents a key strategy in social-psychological research.

▶ Simple Statistics

An investigator's decisions do not end with defining a question and choosing a research method. The next decisions to be made concern the types of data to be collected and the procedures to be used in analyzing those data. Depending on the way a hypothesis is framed, an investigator may be interested in the *frequency,* the *rate,* or the *level* of a particular behavior. For example, we might ask how often married couples engage in physical aggression or what percentage of people are willing to help a person who has fallen in a subway; these are questions about frequency of occurrence. On other occasions, the concern may be with the rate of a behavior, as measured in units per person or per segment of time. For example, we might want to know how many contacts a kindergarten teacher has with pupils each day. Still other questions might focus on the specific level of a behavior, as when one measures the degree of attraction between two persons or the level of shock a subject administers in an aggression experiment.

A second, related issue is the way the data we collect are to be analyzed. Although this is not the place for an elaborate discussion of statistics, a few basic concepts will help you understand the research discussed in later chapters. Social psychologists usually are interested in four characteristics of data: central tendency, variability, correlation, and measures of difference.

Central tendency refers to the average or a general response. It is used to represent a group of scores with a single number. Your own grade point average is one example; it is a single number that represents all the grades you have earned. One central-tendency statistic is called a *mean;* it is the sum of all the scores divided by the number of scores. That is, "mean" is just another word for what is usually called an "average."

Variability refers to the dispersion, or "spreadedness," of responses. Rather than knowing the average opinion of Canadians about independence for Quebec, for example, it might be more helpful to know the degree to which those opinions vary. Are most Canadians generally favorable toward the separatist movement, or do the opinions vary widely from strong opposition to strong support?

Suppose, for example, we asked 1,000 people to rate their agreement with the statement "The province of Quebec should be entirely independent from Canada" on a scale from 1 (strongly disagree) to 5 (strongly agree). The fictitious results in Figure 2.7 illustrate how the same central tendency—in this case, a mean of 3 (neutral)—can lead to very different interpretations, depending on the variability of the responses. The data at the top of the figure reflect the notion that opinions are extreme and equally divided. The data at the bottom of the figure reflect the notion that most people are neutral, and only a few have strong opinions.

The third type of result that interests researchers involves **correlation,** the extent to which a change in one variable is related to a change in another variable. The amount of time students spend studying, for example, is usually correlated with examination scores; more studying is related to higher grades. Sometimes two variables can be related in an inverse fashion, such as the temperature and the amount of clothing people wear; most people wear *fewer* clothes as the temperature climbs *higher.* As another example, in the study of Supreme Court decisions (Tetlock et al., 1985) the analysis dealt with the relationship between two variables—complexity of ideas and political ideology. Similarly, Figure 2.6, from the satisfaction survey by Campbell, Converse, and Rogers (1976), illustrates the association between marital satisfaction and education. As education levels rose, fewer respondents reported complete satisfaction with their marriage; this indicated a negative, or inverse, correlation.

Although the existence of a correlation indicates two variables are related, it does not necessarily mean that one of the variables causes the other. That is, one cannot draw a conclusion about cause and effect from a

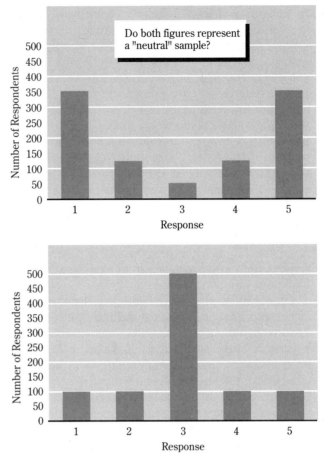

Figure 2.7 *Although both data sets have the same mean, differences in variability lead to two different interpretations.*

correlation. It would be incorrect, and reasonably ludicrous, to conclude, for example, that going to college causes people to become less than completely satisfied with their marriages. Similarly, we cannot conclude that becoming less than satisfied with one's marriage causes one to attend college. A correlation only indicates two variables have something in common, but does not mean that the commonality is causal.

Finally, an investigator may be concerned with the *differences* among two or more groups. "Are men more satisfied with marriage than women?" is a question of this type. Another researcher might test a hypothesis concerning the difference between high-status and low-status speakers' effectiveness at persuading an audience. Typically, the central tendencies of the groups are compared, as when one looks for differences between the grade point averages of male and female students. In experimental research, a difference in the central tendencies of the groups experiencing different levels of an independent variable indicates that the independent variable has had an effect.

As we have seen in several of the studies described in this chapter, social psychologists are often interested in the simultaneous effects of two or more independent variables. Earlier we described the Darley and Gross (1983) experiment, in which subjects were asked to evaluate a young girl after they had been led to believe she lived in a working-class or middle-class environment and either had or had not observed the child's performance on achievement tests. This experiment included two independent variables: one was environment; the other, performance information.

Experiments involving more than one independent variable give us more information than we would have if we studied only one variable at a time. Their results frequently take the form of an interaction, as shown in Figure 2.8. **Interaction** is a statistical term referring to the situation in which the effect of one independent variable depends on the level or state of the other independent variable. Thus, in Figure 2.8, the effect caused by knowing about Hannah's environment depends on the level of performance information made available to the subjects. Only when subjects had information about Hannah's performance on achievement tests did knowing about her environment cause the subjects to make very different recommendations concerning her grade placement. When two independent variables interact, information about the **main effect**—the effect produced by one independent variable, without considering the impact of any other independent variable—is much less informative. To say that subjects in the Darley and Gross experiment suggested generally higher grade placements when Hannah's background was middle class, for example, oversimplifies the results of the experiment.

Ethics of Research

Beyond the technical issues already discussed, an investigator must consider another set of concerns before he or she conducts any research project—the project's ethical aspects. Research ethics are of great

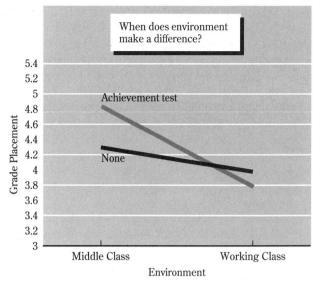

Figure 2.8 *An interaction between environment and information about performance.*

Source: "A Hypothesis-Confirming Bias in Labeling Effects" by J. M. Darley and P. H. Gross, 1983, *Journal of Personality and Social Psychology, 44,* pp. 20–33.

concern to social psychologists, and there are many sources to which we can turn for information about ethical conduct of research. The U.S. Department of Health and Human Services, for example, has issued a set of guidelines that all recipients of grants and contracts must follow. In addition, numerous books and articles (for example, Carlsmith et al., 1976; Cook, 1976; Dane, 1990; Kelman, 1968; Schlenker & Forsyth, 1977) on the subject have been published, and the American Psychological Association (1973, 1990) has developed a set of guidelines on ethics. Social psychologists tend to subject research practices to far more stringent ethical evaluation than do other academicians, law professors, and the students who frequently participate in such research (Rugg, 1975; Schwartz & Gottlieb, 1981).

The ethical issues involved in research are many and complex, and they cannot be fully resolved here. A few important points, however, should be considered briefly.

One concern is the level of pain or stress a subject experiences. This question is more prominent in the medical and biological sciences because experimentation with new drugs or surgical procedures can produce irreversible damage. Social psychologists are generally more concerned with psychological than with physical harm. An investigator interested in the effects of negative feedback on someone's subsequent behavior, for example, may purposely expose a subject to uncomplimentary information such as a report of a low score on an intelligence test. Such information can cause considerable stress. In other situations the subject may be instructed to administer increasingly intense electrical shocks to another person. Even if no shock is actually delivered, subjects may become very upset as they try to comply with the researcher's instructions.

A researcher should always try to minimize the amount of stress a subject experiences. At the same time, it is difficult to argue that stressful events should never be studied (West & Gunn, 1978). Although it is certainly more pleasant to focus one's research attention on positive forms of human behavior, humans display undesirable behavior as well. The social psychologist who seeks to understand the full range of human behavior is obligated to consider both positive and negative aspects of human interaction.

One solution is to rely on informed consent. As much as possible, the researcher should inform subjects in advance about the requirements of a study and obtain their consent to participate. Thus, if a subject is to be exposed to electrical shock, it is the researcher's obligation to inform the subject of that fact in advance. Informed consent is important in any area of study, particularly when the potential for stress or pain is great.

Informed consent procedures are easy to institute in the laboratory experiment, in which the investigator has control over the total situation. But what of research conducted outside the laboratory? As we noted earlier, field studies and field experiments are often conducted without the knowledge of the participants. For that reason, the investigator must plan field research carefully. Invasion of privacy is an important consideration. If a subject has been fully informed of procedures and has given consent, the researcher probably will not be intruding unfairly. In a field research situation, however, where revealing the information necessary to obtain informed consent would defeat the purposes of the study, the investigator must be particularly concerned about unreasonable intrusion.

Although it is difficult to formulate specific criteria for an acceptable field study or experiment, similarity

to a normal situation is a working rule of thumb. When the researcher does not tamper with the environment, for example, some ethical concerns are resolved. Even in this setting, however, investigators must consider carefully the potential for invading the privacy of individuals.

Another ethical concern of researchers relates to the practice of deceiving subjects either by withholding certain information or by misleading them intentionally. Such procedures are common in social-psychological research (Gross & Fleming, 1982), partly because so many social-psychological studies include inherent risk of evaluation apprehension. If a researcher is studying helping behavior, for example, telling the subjects about the purpose of the study could undermine the researcher's ability to learn anything about how helpful people are. Instead, the researcher might learn only how helpful the subjects want the researcher to believe they are. In such cases, the researcher is likely to provide a false description of the purpose of the study. Thus, some justification exists for withholding information and, sometimes, for deception. It is also true, unfortunately, that deception has been abused.

Subjects are less likely to be deceived when informed consent is required. If deception is a necessary part of the procedure, it is critical that the researcher undertake a thorough debriefing as soon as the project is completed. **Debriefing,** a term borrowed from the military, refers to the process whereby a researcher reveals the complete procedure to the subject. If the subjects have been given a false purpose for the study, for example, the researcher should fully explain the real purpose at the end of the study. Part of the debriefing process also should include an explanation as to why deception was necessary. Another part of the debriefing should include ensuring that subjects leave the study feeling no worse than they did when they arrived. Haney, Banks, and Zimbardo (1973), for example, conducted multiple debriefing sessions after the Stanford prison study.

A final ethical concern of the social psychologist involves the confidentiality of data and the anonymity of participants. Investigators should protect subjects' confidentiality routinely, and the subjects should be assured that confidentiality will be preserved.

Few questions of ethics are easily resolved, and the investigator must carefully weigh the question of scientific value against the subject's rights. Ultimately, investigators must decide for themselves whether to conduct a particular project, although numerous checks exist in the form of sanctions by colleagues and review committees. For example, federal guidelines require all institutions receiving federal funds to review research procedures before any study is conducted. Each time a study is begun, the investigator must consider all the available options and decide the best way to answer the research question. That decision requires keeping a multitude of complex issues in balance.

Venturing into any unknown territory is a complex but exciting process. The investigator must make many judgment calls along the way, and each judgment will contribute to the ultimate success or failure of the project. Just as social psychologists have a variety of research methods at their disposal, they have innumerable questions that they can ask. Far from being an orderly process, research is often accidental and always somewhat opportunistic. Some authors have even suggested that a garbage can may be the most accurate way to represent the accidental conjunctions of methods, theories, resources, and solutions that take place (McGrath, Martin, & Kulka, 1982). But treasures rarely come out of garbage cans. We prefer to think of the research process as a series of parties. The mixture of guests is often stimulating and thoroughly enjoyable, but it sometimes leaves one unsatisfied and thinking about how to make changes that will improve the next one.

▶ Summary

Research is an exacting, exciting endeavor. The process of research is lengthy, beginning with an idea and moving through decisions concerning the method of testing the hypothesis, completion of the actual research, and, finally, analysis and interpretation of the data. Each stage is important to the final product, which is the answer to some question about human behavior.

Sources of experimental hypotheses are numerous, ranging from casual observation to complex hypothetico-deductive systems. Once a hypothesis is formulated, it can be tested in many ways; any question can be answered by several methods.

At least six specific methods are available to the social psychology researcher: experiments, quasi-experiments, field studies, archival research, simulations, and surveys. Each of these methods has certain advantages and disadvantages.

The selection of any one research method depends in part on the question being asked. Eventually, it is important for the investigator to test each question with a variety of methods, thus mitigating the disadvantages of each single method and increasing confidence in the validity of the research results. Further, different techniques of statistical analysis are required to test different hypotheses.

Finally, investigators must give careful thought to ethical issues. Social-psychological research involves people, and the rights of these participants in the research process always must be recognized and protected.

▶ Key Terms

aggression
archival research
central tendency
correlation
debriefing
demand characteristics
dependent variable
evaluation apprehension
experiment
experimental realism
experimenter expectancies
external validity
frustration
independent variable
interaction
internal validity
interview
main effect
manipulation check
meta-analysis
mundane realism
participant observer
questionnaire
randomization
reliability
simulation
unobtrusive measure
validity
variability

Show me the sensible person who likes himself or herself! I know myself too well to like what I see. I know but too well that I'm not what I'd like to be.

Golda Meir

The image of myself which I try to create in my own mind that I may love myself is very different from the image which I try to create in the minds of others in order that they may love me.

W. H. Auden

3

The Self

As the King of Hearts tells the White Rabbit in *Alice in Wonderland,* "Begin at the beginning." So we begin our understanding of social behavior with the self. The concept of the self is one of the oldest and most enduring in psychology, but it is not limited to psychology. Early philosophers advised us to "know thyself," and Shakespeare told us, "To thine own self be true." Authors have written hundreds of books about systems of self-knowledge. Further reflecting the importance of the concept of self, the *Oxford English Dictionary* contains six pages devoted to the word *self* and lists more than one hundred words that focus on the self, from *self-abasement* to *self-wisdom.*

What about you? How often do you think about yourself? When you decided to go to college, did you wonder whether you had the ability or the drive to succeed? When you go out with someone, do you worry about whether your date will find you charming, interesting, and fun? When you're alone, do you sometimes weigh your good and bad points?

The self is clearly important—but should it be a topic for social psychology? The answer is yes; the self is a *social* construct—we know ourselves through our interaction with others. Not only is the self defined by social interactions, but it can affect a wide range of social behaviors, such as how we judge others, how we communicate with them, whether we choose to lead or follow, or when we are willing to help a person in need. Without an understanding of the self, we cannot understand much about social behavior.

In later chapters we discuss some consequences of self-reference. In this chapter we will consider how the notion of self develops and what influences our self-definitions. Then, recognizing that people are not always introspective, we will describe some situations that tend to make people aware of themselves. We will then consider how people deal with various aspects of themselves—how they regard themselves, how they experience emotions, and how they evaluate their abilities and the situations in which they find themselves. Finally, we will consider the self in social interaction, describing the ways in which people choose to present themselves to others.

▶ The Nature of the Self

How do you think about yourself? What images do you have of yourself? What talents do you think you have?

What do you consider your weak points? All such thoughts constitute your **self-concept,** which can be defined more precisely as all the thoughts and feelings that have reference to the self as an object (Rosenberg, 1979). Where do these thoughts come from? How do we arrive at certain beliefs about ourselves and certain ways of dealing with the world? We must answer these questions as we try to understand the self.

Theories of the Development of Self

The philosopher and psychologist William James, one of the most articulate theorists of the self, defined the self in the broadest possible terms (James, 1890). Any experience that involves any reference to one's self, he believed, affects one's sense of well-being and self-worth. Nearly 100 years later, most contemporary psychologists agree that the self includes many elements and that almost any experience can affect our self-concept. For example, Harold Proshansky and his colleagues (Proshansky, 1978; Proshansky, Fabian, & Kaminoff, 1983) have proposed that part of one's sense of self includes physical environments that have meaning for each of us—home, neighborhood, and workplace—a point we discuss further in Chapter 14.

James also believed that the self-concept is very much a social experience. That is, our personal identities are critically dependent on our relationships with other people. It was James (1890) who first sensitized us to the identity-threatening consequences we would suffer if, in the flip side of the opening scenario in Chapter 1, our relationships with other people were eliminated:

> If no one turned around when we entered, answered when we spoke, or minded what we did, [and] if every person we met "cut us dead," and acted as if we were nonexisting things, a kind of rage and impotent despair would ere long well up in us, from which the cruelest bodily tortures would be a relief; for these would make us feel that, however bad might be our plight, we had not sunk to such a depth as to be unworthy of attention at all. [pp. 293–294]

Among social theorists, James was not alone in recognizing that the self is a product of social interaction. Charles Cooley (1902/1964) used the term "looking-glass self" to convey the idea that self-concepts reflect the evaluations of other people in the environment. This idea, elaborated by George Herbert Mead (1934) and Harry Stack Sullivan (1953), is known as the prin-

We tend to see ourselves as others see us.
Gale Zucker

ciple of *reflected appraisals.* According to this principle, we see ourselves as others see us. *Which* others is a critical question because different people may have contradictory views of us. Some people may be more important at one point in our life than at others. For example, our parents' views are usually paramount when we are young, and our spouse's views are likely to be most important when we are older. Similarly, different people rely on different others for self-reference. In a study of high school students, for example, Jon Hoelter (1984) found that females relied more on the evaluations of peers, and males looked to parental appraisals.

Other people are important to the development of self-concept, but others do not define the self exclusively. We take actions ourselves, and the outcomes of those actions help define the self (Gekas, 1982; Gekas & Schwalbe, 1983). When we learn to play the piano, for example, we discover something about our musical ability, our finger dexterity, and our willingness to com-

mit time to practice. All this information can become part of our self-concept.

Our own actions and the views of others contribute to our self-concept, and later we will consider some ways in which those contributions take place. Before doing so, we must consider what exactly we mean when we refer to self-concept.

The Structure of the Self-Concept

From a social cognition perspective, the self-concept is one of many types of cognitive structure (Greenwald & Pratkanis, 1984; Kihlstrom & Cantor, 1984). In Chapter 1 we introduced the concept of a **schema**—an organized pattern of knowledge that we use to interpret our experience. When the knowledge organized in a schema concerns one's self, it is called a self-schema. As Hazel Markus defines them, **self-schemas** are "cognitive generalizations about the self, derived from experience, that organize and guide the processing of self-related information contained in the individual's social experiences" (1977, p. 64).

Because self-schemas are derived from experience, the contents of self-schemas vary from individual to individual. Some people, for example, may think of themselves as very independent; others may think of themselves as dependent. For still other people, the independence/dependence dimension may be irrelevant. To understand how different self-schemas can affect our organization and use of information, Markus (1977) included three groups of people in a quasi-experimental study; one group consisted of people who rated themselves as extremely independent, another group rated themselves as extremely dependent, and the third group was neutral with respect to independence. Weeks later, in a different study, Markus asked members of each of these groups to participate in a series of tasks that included making judgments about the self and providing descriptions of behavioral events that related to independence or dependence. One of these tasks was to respond to a series of adjectives by pressing one of two buttons, labeled "me" and "not me."

Markus's results clearly indicated that one's self-schema can affect how one processes information. Consider, for example, the speed with which subjects made "me" judgments, as illustrated in Figure 3.1. Independent people responded "me" more quickly to adjectives consistent with independence (such as *independent, individualistic, assertive*) than they responded to adjectives concerning dependence (such as *cooperative, tactful, tolerant*). People who had described themselves as dependent showed the opposite pattern, responding "me" more quickly when dealing with adjectives associated with dependence but taking more time with those associated with independence. The aschematics—people who did not define themselves clearly as either independent or dependent—showed no differences in the speed with which they judged the different adjectives to be self-descriptive. Also, both independent and dependent subjects recalled more specific incidents of behavior consistent with their self-schema and fewer occasions in which behavior was inconsistent with their self-schema. Equally important, the three groups showed no differences when responding to adjectives unrelated to independence—for example, *honest, intelligent, friendly*. From this we can infer that Markus's

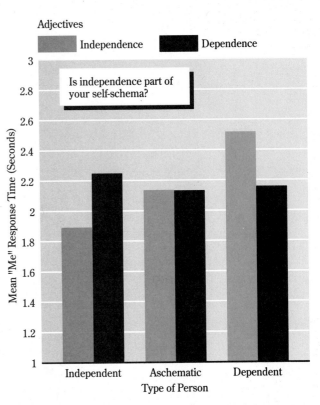

Figure 3.1 *People make judgments about self-descriptive information more quickly when the information is consistent with their self-schema.*

Source: Adapted from "Self-Schemata and Processing Information about the Self" by H. Markus, 1977, *Journal of Personality and Social Psychology, 35,* pp. 63–78.

results did not occur simply because the three groups differed in general ability to respond faster or to generate more self-descriptive items.

Independence is just one dimension used to illustrate the operation of the self-schema. Almost any personality trait is probably central to the schemas of some people and irrelevant to others. Honesty may be the organizing principle for some people, whereas consistency may be a central concept for other people. Nor are self-schemas limited to verbal material. Part of our self-concept also involves visual images—for example, what we look like and how we would like to look. People remember photographs of themselves that most closely resemble their physical self-image better than they remember pictures that differ from that self-image, even when all the photos were taken at the same time (Yarmey & Johnson, 1982). Think of how many times you have looked at a photograph of yourself and thought, "That doesn't look like me." Chances are, your expression—serious, smiling, silly, and so on—did not match your self-schema.

Our beliefs about ourselves affect us in a variety of ways: what we think about, what we talk about, and even what we prefer to look at. Also, the self-concept is multifaceted. From a role perspective, we can talk about the different roles we play to express different aspects of the self-concept. For example, you probably think of yourself as a student, as a son or daughter, as a citizen, and perhaps as a member of a particular religious or ethnic group. The characteristics associated with each role are incorporated into the self-concept. With the identity of athlete, for example, one may think of oneself as strong, limber, and adventurous. As a son or daughter, the same person may be most aware of obedience and respectfulness. Different roles, however, can share certain characteristics, representing continuity in one's personality. As a parent, as a friend, and as a physician, for example, someone can be equally caring and warm.

The roles that constitute the self-concept can be considered in terms of a hierarchy, with the most important ones at the top and less important roles falling lower on the scale (Rosenberg & Gara, 1985; Stryker, 1982). That is, some aspects of the self-concept frequently guide thoughts and behavior, while others come to mind only on specific occasions. The more important an aspect of the self-concept is—the higher it stands in the hierarchy—the more likely it is to influence our choices and our behavior. For example, Mark Leary and his colleagues (Leary, Wheeler, & Jenkins, 1986) compared the sports interests of people whose self-concepts were defined primarily in personal terms with the interests of people whose self-concepts were defined primarily in social terms. The "personal" people were much more likely to engage in individual sports than in team activities. They ran and they swam, but they were less likely to play volleyball. The reverse was true of individuals who defined themselves in social terms. People's reasons for engaging in the sports of their choice differed as well. Individuals who scored high in personal identity said they felt better physically and got a feeling of self-satisfaction from participation in sports. In contrast, people who scored high in social

identity were more likely to say that they liked others to know they were physically active or that they enjoyed competing and exercising with other people. In summary, although the self-concept may be stable, certain aspects of it will be prominent in one role—intellectual as a student—but not in another role—physical as a weekend athlete (Tesser & Campbell, 1983).

If all these aspects are part of a single self-concept, why don't all of them influence behavior all the time? One answer to this question relates to the fact that schemas differ in their accessibility; that is, in how readily they come to the forefront of our thinking (Higgins & King, 1981; Wyer & Srull, 1981). For any schema, including the various aspects of the self-concept, the immediate situation affects accessibility through a process called priming. **Priming** is the process through which a cue in the situation activates a pathway in memory (Logan, 1989). When we see someone walking a dog, for example, priming may cause us to recall fond memories of our own dog. Similarly, a shopping list primes memories of the decisions we made when we made the list. Thus, the cues associated with the role we are playing make some aspects of our self-concept more accessible than others.

The term **working self-concept** has been used to denote the specific aspects of one's identity that are activated by the role one is playing at any particular moment (Markus & Nurius, 1986). As an illustration of this blend of role and cognitive perspectives, consider an experiment by Hazel Markus and Ziva Kunda (1986). They examined the working self-concept by randomly assigning subjects to one of two conditions. One group of undergraduate women was led to believe their opinions on a variety of issues were nearly identical to the opinions of three strangers (who were actually confederates of the experimenter). The other group was led to believe their opinions were very different from the opinions espoused by the same three confederates. How would you react to this situation? Depending upon which group you were in, you would probably think, "Am I really so similar?" or "Am I really so different?" Thus, Markus and Kunda hypothesized that the experience would prime the self-schema concerning similarity; that is, it would make similarity part of the working self-concept. To test this hypothesis, the subjects were shown a series of slides containing adjectives related either to similarity (*normal, follower*), to uniqueness (*original, independent*), or to something entirely different (*introverted, extroverted*). While viewing each slide, the subject pressed one of two buttons—"me" or "not me"—to indicate whether the adjective on the slide was an accurate description. If the manipulation had, in fact, made similarity part of the working self-concept, then its heightened accessibility should increase the speed with which the subjects were able to react to the adjectives. Subjects concerned with appearing "too similar" to the confederates should be quick to avoid similarity-related adjectives, whereas subjects who appeared to be unique should be quick to claim similarity-related adjectives as descriptive. Such responses reflect a **confirmatory bias,** a tendency to obtain information that is consistent with our beliefs.

When Markus and Kunda measured the speed with which the subjects responded to the adjectives, they obtained support for their hypothesis. As illustrated in Figure 3.2, subjects led to believe they were unique took fewer milliseconds to decide the similarity-related adjectives were "me" words. In contrast, subjects led to believe they were "too similar" were much faster at denying that the similarity-related adjectives described them. Reactions to the uniqueness-related adjectives also supported the hypothesis. Finally, there were no group differences in the speed with which the subjects responded to the unrelated adjectives, indicating that only that part of the self-concept concerning similarity had been primed. Thus, the working self-concept changes as we change roles. In other words, to some extent we become different people as we move from situation to situation.

You might think this diversity of selves and aspects of the self-concept would be problematic, perhaps causing an "identity crisis." In fact, just the opposite is true: diversity and complexity of the self-concept are associated with lower levels of stress. As Patricia Linville (1985, 1987) has suggested, greater self-complexity provides a buffer against stressful events. If an individual has only one or two major identities, any single event is going to have an impact on most aspects of the self-concept. The woman who sees herself primarily as a wife, for example, is likely to be devastated if the marriage ends. When the role of "wife" is no longer available, a large part of her self-concept, her identity, also ends. In contrast, the individual who has a more complex representation of self may be more protected from negative events that primarily involve only one or two

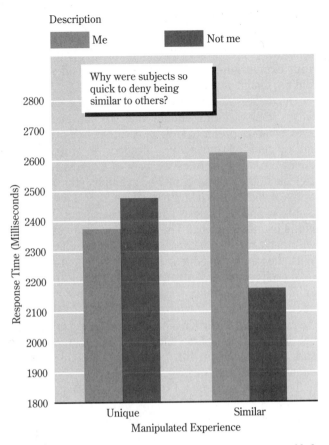

Figure 3.2 *The accessibility of the working self-concept enabled subjects to more quickly correct the false impression they believed the experimenter had formed of them.*
Source: "Stability and Malleability of the Self-Concept" by H. Markus and Z. Kunda, 1986, *Journal of Personality and Social Psychology, 51,* pp. 858–866.

of several roles. The woman who sees herself not only as a wife, but also as a mother, lawyer, friend, and tennis player, will have other roles to fall back on if the role of spouse is no longer available. Linville's research has shown that people with more complex self-concepts are less prone to depression and illness; they also experience less severe mood swings following success or failure in one area of performance.

Influences on Self-Definition

The concepts of self-schema, working self-concept, and multiple identities in general all deal with the structure of self-concept. The content of a specific self-concept, in contrast, depends very much on one's culture as well as individual experiences. Roy Baumeister (1987) noted that societies historically have stressed different aspects of the self, even to the point of whether self-conceptions and self-knowledge were considered important at all. Literature suggests that in the late medieval period, for example, people did not engage in much introspection. More recently, Freudian psychoanalytic theory proposed that it is impossible to know the self totally because unconscious forces set barriers to self-inquiry. Today self-knowledge is believed to be not only within reach but of critical importance. There is even a magazine called *Self*, which provides information for those who a short time ago were called the "me" generation.

As concern with self-knowledge varied across historical periods, so did the dimensions considered most important for self-definition. The themes of self-reliance and individualism characteristic of the Victorian period (mid- to late nineteenth century) were replaced by concerns for socioeconomic status in the early twentieth century. Which themes are central now? External guidelines are less apparent today, Baumeister suggests, and more responsibility lies with the individual to develop criteria for self-evaluation.

In general, any visible characteristic is likely to be incorporated into one's self-concept (Herman, Zanna, & Higgins, 1986; Jones et al., 1984; Kanter, 1977). Height, weight, physical appearance—each of these characteristics probably will become part of our self-concept because people may shape their behavior toward us according to their beliefs about certain characteristics (an instance of stereotyping, which we will discuss in Chapter 4). Some characteristics, gender and race for example, are almost inevitably part of one's self-concept, perhaps because they are the most visible characteristics. Through interactions with others we learn, implicitly or explicitly, what cultural beliefs and values may be associated with our gender (Bem, 1987; Spence, 1985) and our race (Cross, 1978; Parham, 1989). As these beliefs become part of our self-concept, they affect our preferences for interaction with others. In childhood, for example, one's **gender identity** as a girl or a boy may influence one's choice of playmates and preferences among toys; in later life, one's beliefs about gender can affect occupational choices and marital roles (Katz, 1986). Like gender, one's sense of **racial identity** develops early. When black children are asked

Different dimensions are considered important for self-definition at different time periods.
Culver Pictures

whether a white or a black doll looks most like them, for example, most will select the black doll by the age of about 5 (Clark & Clark, 1947; Fine & Bowers, 1984).

Physical characteristics are particularly likely to be part of the self-concept if they are distinctive (McGuire & McGuire, 1981). William McGuire and his colleagues (McGuire, McGuire, & Winton, 1979), for example, found that fourth-graders were much more likely to mention their gender spontaneously when they came from households in which their gender was in the minority (see Figure 3.3). Being female, for example, was a particularly important feature of the self-concepts of girls whose families included more males than females. If a girl came from a family that had a large proportion of females, in contrast, she was much less likely to mention her gender when asked for a self-description. College students also are sensitive to the gender of their companions. Even in groups of only three people, students describing themselves are more likely to mention their gender if they are the sole representative of their gender in that group than if the other two members are of the same gender as the stu-

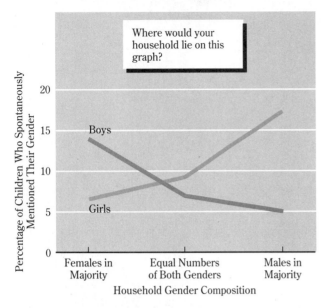

Where would your household lie on this graph?

Figure 3.3 *Gender is more likely to be included in the working self-concept when one's gender is in the minority.*
Source: Adapted from "Effects of Household Sex Composition on the Salience of One's Gender in the Spontaneous Self-Concept" by W. J. McGuire, C. V. McGuire, and W. Winton, 1979, *Journal of Experimental Social Psychology, 15,* pp. 77–90.

dent (Cota & Dion, 1986). Similarly, McGuire and Padawer-Singer (1976) reported that children who are taller or shorter than average are more likely to mention their height than are children of average height; further, children who are older or younger than most of their classmates are more likely to mention age.

Particular experiences and environments also affect our thoughts about ourselves. Research shows, for example, that our self-evaluations are influenced by the self-appraisals of our friends (Felson & Reed, 1986). If we associate with people who stress athletics and card games, those dimensions are likely to find their way into our self-concept. Of course, the causal direction goes both ways. A person for whom athletics is a prominent aspect of the self-concept is likely to seek out friends who share an interest in active sports. The broader cultural context also may influence the contents of the self-concept. When Michael Bond and Tak-Sing Cheung (1983) compared Japanese students with students from Hong Kong and the United States, they found many differences in the kinds of descriptors used

in self-description. Japanese students were more likely to describe personal aspirations and choices (possible selves) and less likely to mention psychological attributes.

Clearly, many things influence the self-concept, and it is easy to see why a concept of multiple selves or multiple self-schemas is more useful than the notion of a single self-concept. When and how these various selves come to the forefront is the next issue to consider.

▶ Becoming Aware of the Self

Although our self-concept is always with us, our awareness of it varies from time to time. If you are in the habit of waking up, walking immediately to the television set, switching on the national news, and then walking into the kitchen for coffee, you probably do not engage in much self-reflection when you follow this routine for the fiftieth day in a row. Ellen Langer (1978a, 1989a, 1989b) has called such behaviors "mindless," suggesting that self-awareness is not part of the process of performing overlearned behaviors. In other situations, a sense of anonymity may minimize attention to the self. In contrast, if you walk into a party filled with people you have never met, all of whom turn to stare at you as you enter, you probably will engage in considerable self-reflection, wondering how you look and what your next move should be. In this second case, we again see how important the environment can be to our awareness of our selves.

A Theory of Self-Perception

Daryl Bem (1967, 1972) has proposed a **self-perception theory** that suggests we often become aware of ourselves simply by watching what we do. As Bem has described this process, "individuals come to 'know' their own attitudes, emotions, and other internal states partially by inferring them from observations of their own overt behavior and/or the circumstances in which this behavior occurs" (1972, p. 5). In other words, Bem suggests that people don't have much inside information about who they are or why they do things. Instead, like an outside observer, people look at what they are doing and infer a reason for that behavior.

Some people choose to make their self-evaluations public.
Robert V. Eckert, Jr./EKM-Nepenthe

Bem's theory brings us to the learning theory perspective on self-concept. Suppose, for example, you spend an hour every day exercising. Why are you spending so much time on this activity, and what does it say about you? Perhaps, when you stop to think about it, you realize you have been working out ever since you found out your favorite date liked only thin, well-conditioned people. In that case, you may conclude that the reinforcement from your favorite date is the main cause of your behavior. What if your date doesn't care about your physical condition? Without this external motivator, you, and a neutral observer as well, may conclude that exercise reflects an internal value or attitude—perhaps a belief in the importance of fitness—that functions as reinforcement for the activity. Thus, observing your behavior leads to inferences about the self. Bem does not claim that all aspects of the self depend on this after-the-fact observation process, but he claims that the process operates whenever internal cues are weak or ambiguous. If, for example, you got

on a scale, noticed an excessively high number, decided to do something about it, and *then* decided to exercise every day, self-perception theory would not apply.

Can we also learn about ourselves from being aware of what we don't do? If you jog every afternoon, you may conclude that jogging reflects something about your self-definition. What if you don't jog—does that say something as well? Research on the psychology of problem solving indicates people use negative instances of an event very poorly when they try to find a solution (Rips, 1990). The same tendency seems to operate in the self-perception process. People tend to infer characteristics about themselves more from what they have done than from what they have not done (Fazio, Sherman, & Herr, 1982). Thus, if you are a regular jogger, you may see yourself as energetic and athletic. If you do not jog or engage in other sports, you probably will not label yourself unathletic or lazy (even if you are both). Such reasoning, of course, makes perfect sense from the learning perspective of self-perception theory—inferences about the self are based on behaviors we *perform*. If there is no behavior, there is nothing about which to make an inference.

Behavior is only one source of information about our selves; thoughts and feelings provide insight as well. As Susan Andersen and her colleagues have shown, people are sometimes more influenced by cognitive and affective elements than by behavioral factors (Andersen, Lazowski, & Donisi, 1986). In one study, for example, students responded to statements that concerned either religious behaviors ("I prayed") or thoughts and feelings about religion ("I have felt like praying"). The statements presented to some students were worded in a positive way, such as "I have devoted time to religious or spiritual activities." Other students read a negative form of the same statement: "I fail to devote time to religious or spiritual activities." After responding to these statements, the students rated their general degree of religiosity. The results showed that students were more likely to be influenced by the phrasing of cognitive and affective statements than by behavioral statements. Thus, Andersen and her colleagues reasoned, self-perception may sometimes be affected less by thinking about our behavior than by thinking about what we feel and believe about behaviors.

States of Self-Awareness

How often do people think about themselves during the day? Do people think about themselves more often than they think about, say, their families, their jobs, or their favorite TV shows? To answer such questions, Csikszentmihalyi and Figurski (1982) asked 107 persons, ranging in age from 19 to 63 and in occupation from clerical worker to manager, to record their thoughts at selected times each day for one week. Subjects did not know when they would be asked to record their thoughts; they responded whenever they heard a beep from an electronic paging device that they carried with them. Approximately 45 times during the week, each person recorded his or her thoughts and feelings, for a total of more than 4,700 observations.

As Figure 3.4 shows, the self was not at the top of the list. People reported thinking more often about their work or about chores and home, or they reported

having no thoughts at all. Yet thoughts about the self were more common than thoughts about food, about television and radio, or about the research project itself. The investigators also asked their subjects to describe how happy, active, and alert they felt and whether they would rather be doing something else. Responses to these questions when subjects were thinking about themselves suggest that self-reflection is uncomfortable. When subjects were thinking about themselves, they reported being less happy and less active than when they were thinking about other topics. Also, subjects more often wished they were doing something other than thinking about themselves.

Why might thinking about oneself be uncomfortable? Robert Wicklund and his associates proposed a theory of objective self-awareness to explain when people will focus attention on themselves and what happens when they do (Duval & Wicklund, 1972; Wicklund, 1975; Wicklund & Frey, 1980). Wicklund defines **self-awareness** as "focused attention directed toward just one facet of the self" (Wicklund & Frey, 1980, p. 36). Self-awareness can be aroused in many ways. The classic technique used in laboratory experiments involves placing a mirror in front of the subject. However, self-awareness can be induced by any stimulus that focuses attention upon the self, including such things as hearing your recorded voice, looking at pictures of yourself, stubbing a toe, or unexpectedly failing at something.

What happens when your attention is focused on the self? According to Frederick Gibbons's (1990) expanded model of self-awareness processes, the first thing that occurs is activation of the self-schema. Of course, not "everything" about your self will come into awareness every time you confront a mirror or similar stimulus. Instead, the components of your self-concept that are likely to be activated are those related to whatever cues draw your attention. Your new haircut may activate aspects of your self concerning appearance, for example, or the clock behind you may activate aspects concerning your ability to meet deadlines and manage your work load. If salient cues are absent, aspects of the self related to whatever you were thinking about or doing when attention was directed to the self will be activated. Your reflection in a window while taking a test, for example, may call to mind anxiety about doing

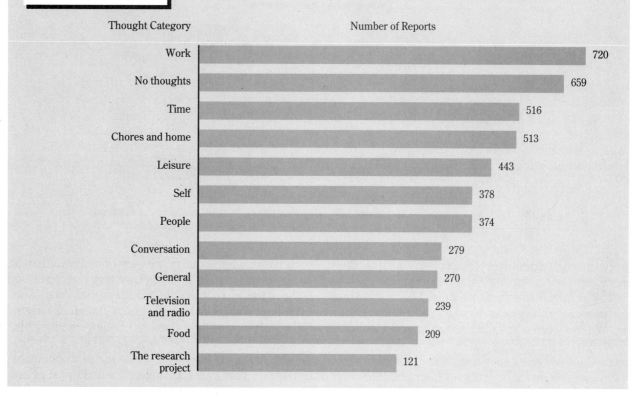

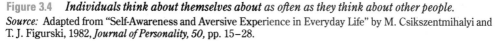

What emotions do you experience when thinking about each of these topics?

Thought Category	Number of Reports
Work	720
No thoughts	659
Time	516
Chores and home	513
Leisure	443
Self	378
People	374
Conversation	279
General	270
Television and radio	239
Food	209
The research project	121

Figure 3.4 *Individuals think about themselves about as often as they think about other people.*
Source: Adapted from "Self-Awareness and Aversive Experience in Everyday Life" by M. Csikszentmihalyi and T. J. Figurski, 1982, *Journal of Personality, 50,* pp. 15–28.

well or the instructor's admonition to avoid looking at others' answers.

As is illustrated in Figure 3.5, after "the self-schema is accessed, self-assessment is inevitable" (Gibbons, 1990, p. 286). The process that begins with self-focus leads to self-examination, a comparison between the accessed self-schema and some standard. As a result of the comparison, your subsequent behavior is likely to become more consistent with the standard.

Arthur Beaman, Bonnel Klentz, Edward Diener, and Soren Svanum (1979), for example, demonstrated the effects of self-focus on subsequent behavior in two field studies involving children who were trick-or-treating at Halloween. In different homes, a bowl filled with bite-sized candy bars was placed on a table in a room near the front door. Beaman and his colleagues manipulated self-awareness by placing a large mirror in such a way that the children would see themselves as they took candy from the bowl. Sometimes the female experimenter who answered the door told the children to help themselves to the candy, and sometimes she told them to take only one candy, but she was always out of sight while the children were taking the candy. Finally, some of the children, all of whom were in costume,

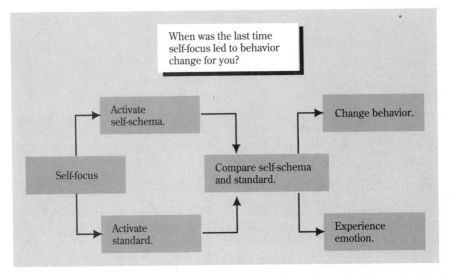

When was the last time self-focus led to behavior change for you?

Activate self-schema.

Self-focus

Activate standard.

Compare self-schema and standard.

Change behavior.

Experience emotion.

Figure 3.5   *Focusing attention on the self can lead both to negative affect and to changes in behavior.*

were asked to identify themselves by stating their name, and others remained anonymous.

The results, illustrated in Figure 3.6, clearly show the influence of self-awareness on subsequent behavior. When told to take only one candy, fewer children disobeyed in the presence of the mirror than in its absence, but only when they had recently thought about themselves by giving their names to the experimenter. Even when told to help themselves, fewer children took more than one candy in the presence of a mirror than in its absence. Presumably, norms against greedy behavior were the standards to which they compared their own behavior. The presence or absence of the mirror had no effect in the anonymous conditions, perhaps because the children's costumes were the most salient cues in these conditions. Instead of obedience, the mirror in the anonymous conditions may have activated aspects of the self-concept concerning appearance.

The relatively low percentage of trick-or-treaters who took more than one candy when admonished to take only one indicates they were capable of changing their behavior to match the standard. Often, however, doing the "right thing" is not so easy. Therefore, part of the self-awareness process usually involves assessing one's ability to perform behaviors that are consistent with standards. For example, college students are better at resisting conformity pressure to abandon their

personal standards under self-focus conditions than at other times, but only if they believe they are capable of doing what is required to maintain their standards (Froming, Walker, & Lopyan, 1982; Gibbons & Wright, 1983). When someone does not believe meeting the standards is possible, the discrepancy between behavior and standards is likely to make the person uncomfortable. In such cases, particularly when the standard is an unattainable ideal, the person will avoid self-awareness, usually by leaving the situation (Duval & Wicklund, 1972; Greenberg & Musham, 1981).

Finally, we should note that self-awareness does not always involve contemplating behaviors or ideals. If a particular mood or pain instigates self-focus, the self-schema will involve aspects of what Gibbons calls the physical/emotional self, and subsequent behavior is likely to be consistent with the physical or emotional experience. In one experiment, for example, people with a snake phobia were asked to approach and hold a snake; some people were asked to do so in the presence of a mirror, others without a mirror. Consistent with Gibbons's model, people were much more likely to refuse to hold the snake or leave the room when they were in the presence of the mirror (Scheier, Carver, & Gibbons, 1981). Presumably, the self-aware subjects said to themselves, "I'm afraid—my heart is racing, my palms are sweaty—and I'm going to behave consistent

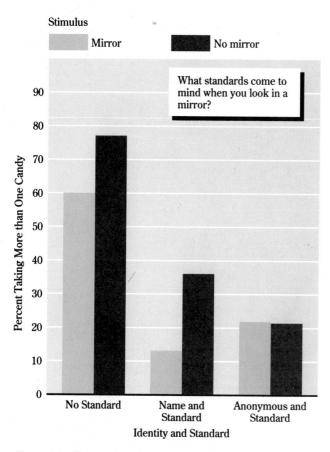

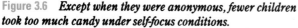

Figure 3.6 *Except when they were anonymous, fewer children took too much candy under self-focus conditions.*
Source: Adapted from "Self-Awareness and Transgression in Children: Two Field Studies" by A. L. Beaman, B. Klentz, E. Diener, and S. Svanum, 1979, *Journal of Personality and Social Psychology, 37,* pp. 1835–1846.

with my fear and stay far away from that snake." Thus, self-awareness may heighten emotional experiences as well as facilitate attempts to maintain standards.

Individual Differences in Self-Awareness

Some people spend more time in a self-aware state than others. To measure this tendency, Alan Fenigstein, Michael Scheier, and Allan Buss (1975) developed the "Self-Consciousness Scale," which measures **self-consciousness,** the disposition to focus attention on the self in terms of public and private aspects. (The public aspects of self-consciousness will be discussed later,

with other topics concerning public presentations of one's self.) **Private self-consciousness** involves a focus on personal aspects of the self, such as bodily sensations, beliefs, moods, and feelings. People who obtain high scores on the private self-consciousness scale agree with items such as "I'm always trying to figure myself out," "I reflect about myself a lot," and "I'm generally attentive to my inner feelings" (Fenigstein, Scheier, & Buss, 1975).

Consistent with Gibbons's (1990) model of self-awareness, people who score high on measures of private self-consciousness are more aware of their internal feelings and more readily describe themselves (Carver, 1979; Mueller, 1982). Thus, it is perhaps not surprising that they and their close friends tend to agree about what they are really like (Franzoi, 1983). People high in private self-consciousness also tend to be more aware of changes in their internal bodily states (Scheier, Carver, & Gibbons, 1979). It has even been suggested that such people may tend to be healthier than others because they can recognize stresses to their bodies and take action before the stress is physically damaging (Mullen & Suls, 1982). If, for example, you are able to identify subtle changes in your body as early signs of stress, then you may be in a better position to alter or avoid stressful stimuli before they take too great a physical toll.

▶ Dealing with the Self

The self-concept is active, is evaluative, is a source of emotions, is an influence on behavior, and may be described as more than occasionally nonrational as self-awareness shifts from one point of focus to another. As we discuss how individuals deal with their self-concepts, we will consider specifically the concept of self-esteem, how and why emotions are experienced, and how individuals evaluate their abilities and explain their behavior.

Self-Esteem

The singer Pearl Bailey once said, "There's a period of life when we swallow a knowledge of ourselves and it becomes either good or sour inside." She described what social psychologists less graphically call **self-es-**

"Call it vanity, call it narcissism, call it egomania. I love you."
Drawing by Koren; © 1986 The New Yorker Magazine, Inc.

teem—the evaluation of oneself in either a positive or a negative way. Several measures are available to assess self-esteem; they generally involve asking people to respond to such statements as "On the whole, I am satisfied with myself" (Rosenberg, 1979). Although momentary changes in self-esteem occur, during episodes of self-focus for example, most measures include the assumption that a person's self-esteem is somewhat stable. In other words, some people tend to feel good about themselves most of the time, whereas others rate themselves more negatively a good part of the time.

Evaluations of the self are based on a variety of experiences. Successful outcomes, for example, tend to result in positive self-esteem, whereas negative self-esteem follows from repeated unsuccessful outcomes (Gekas & Schwalbe, 1983). Satisfaction with one's current activities, friendships, and romantic involvements contributes to positive self-esteem, but deficits in such areas lower one's self-esteem (Bohrnstedt & Fisher, 1986). Physical characteristics and facial appearance also affect a person's self-esteem. The self-evaluations

of males have been found to be related to muscular strength, for example (Tucker, 1983).

Some aspects of the self-concept are more important to self-esteem than others. Among sixth-grade children, for example, the roles of athlete, son or daughter, and student seemed to have the greatest impact on self-esteem; friendship and club membership were less influential (Hoelter, 1986). People also vary in the values they attach to specific facets of their self-concept. Whereas one person's self-esteem may be linked primarily to facial attractiveness, another person may rely primarily on academic achievement as a yardstick of self-worth. Interestingly, the link between self-esteem and the importance of a self-concept facet may be an all-or-none phenomenon (Hoge & McCarthy, 1984; Marsh, 1986). That is, if a specific facet has some importance, the fact that it might be more or less important than some other facet does *not* mean that its impact on the self-esteem will differ from that of the other facet.

Overestimating positive aspects of our self-concepts

also may be the way in which we define self-esteem for ourselves. Most people, for example, consider themselves to be more physically attractive than others rate them (Pittenger & Baskett, 1984). In a study designed to measure the relative importance of positive and negative aspects of the self-concept, David Roth, C. R. Snyder, and Lynn Pace (1986) asked students whether each of 60 items was a true description of themselves. Half the items were positive but were too good to be true of most people (for example, "I am always courteous, even to disagreeable people"). The other half were negative, but worded such that they should be true of most people ("I feel sad sometimes"). Thus, responding "true" to the positive items or "false" to the negative items suggested an unrealistic self-concept. On average, both males and females scored about 28 (out of 60), indicating a tendency to overestimate positive aspects and to underestimate negative aspects. More important, a second study showed that accepting the too-good items was related to scores on a self-esteem scale, but denying the negative items was not. The more unrealistic, positive aspects subjects included in their self-concept, the higher their score on the self-esteem scale.

Despite its unrealistic base, positive self-esteem is generally considered good, the mark of a psychologically healthy person. Indeed, there is evidence that self-esteem is associated with a variety of positive outcomes (Ellis & Taylor, 1983; Shamir, 1986). Low self-esteem, in contrast, is generally considered bad, the mark of an unhealthy person. Higgins (1989), for example, noted that the connection between low self-esteem and distress is "so fundamental that many recent perspectives on the psychological nature of severe distress are based upon it" (p. 93). It should not be surprising, then, that many of our emotional experiences are tied to self-esteem.

Experiencing Emotions

High self-esteem, unrealistic or not, is pleasurable and satisfying, and it is not surprising that many theorists have considered it a dominant human goal (Rosenberg, 1979). Most people prefer to be in a positive state and to experience positive emotions. In fact, people report that they experience more positive than negative emotions. Shula Sommers (1984) asked college students to describe their experiences on a typical day, using a list of adjectives representing positive and negative emotions. By a large margin, students believed that mildly positive emotions best characterized a typical day. When they used the same set of adjectives to describe an atypical day, they most frequently chose adjectives that applied to mildly negative emotions.

Often the unpleasant emotions we experience are a consequence of negative self-evaluation. The self-awareness process makes it more difficult to maintain unrealistic positive aspects of our self-concepts (Gibbons, 1990). Possible selves—identities we believe we might take on—can also be a cause of substantial negative emotion (Markus & Nurius, 1986). Concern about becoming unemployed or homeless, for example, can create feelings of distress, which may be one reason that policy makers, researchers, and the general public all seem unwilling to confront such problems (Shinn & Weitzman, 1990).

Two types of potential selves that occupy a place in our self-concept are what Tory Higgins (1987) calls the ideal self and the ought self. The **ideal self** is defined as the self-concept that we desire to attain: hopes, wishes, and aspirations concerning different facets of our self. The **ought self,** in contrast, refers to facets of the self-concept that should exist: duties, obligations, responsibilities, and so on. The ideal and ought selves are part of everyone's self-concept.

According to self-discrepancy theory (Higgins, 1987, 1989), it is not the negative facets of our self-concept that produce negative emotions. Instead, the key to such emotions is the amount of discrepancy between the actual self and either the ideal self or the ought self. As is illustrated in Figure 3.7, the kind of emotion we experience depends upon the type of discrepancy. Discrepancies between facets of one's actual self and the ought self, for example, produce social anxiety and other agitated emotions. For the sake of argument, assume that you believe you are obligated to be honest on all occasions. As you talk with your professor the day before an essay exam, you see a copy of the exam on the desk. The phone rings, and the professor is distracted for a few minutes. You unobtrusively make notes on the questions you see on the exam so you can prepare answers for use the next day. How do you feel about the discrepancy between what you think you ought to be (honest) and what you have done (a dis-

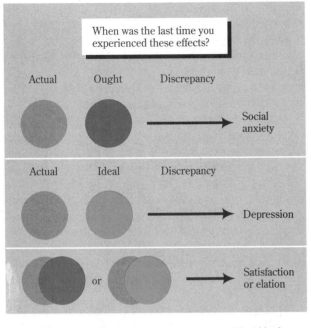

Figure 3.7 *Discrepancies between actual and either ideal or ought selves produce negative emotions.*

Thus, self-evaluation is an important process in the generation of both positive and negative emotions.

How people interpret their emotional experiences varies. Emotional experience depends on both a state of physiological arousal and an appropriate cognitive label for that arousal (Schachter & Singer, 1962; Zillman, 1978). In other words, how a person interprets an event influences what emotions he or she will experience. "Butterflies in the stomach" as your professor returns your exam can be interpreted as either excitement or fear. If the professor says "Very good!" while returning it, the arousal will be interpreted as excitement. If the professor winces while returning the exam, the same arousal will be interpreted as fear. If the professor seems to take too long to return the exam, the arousal may be interpreted as anxiety. The physiological experience—butterflies—is the same in all cases, but the cognitive interpretations differ. These variations in interpretation, like the evaluations discussed in the next section, demonstrate how flexible beliefs about oneself can be.

Exploring the Self

Exploring objective facets of the self-concept is relatively easy; generally, discovering characteristics such as weight, height, and eye color requires little effort. For other facets, though, one cannot make judgments with so much certainty because there are no objective standards on which a person can rely.

That we do wish to explore facets of the self is evidenced by people's preferences for tasks that test abilities about which they are uncertain (Trope & Ben-Yair, 1982). That is, one way to find out more about subjective facets is to gain some experience. For instance, if Charles is uncertain about his ability at video games, he may play frequently to discover just how well he can perform. With more experience, he will be in a better position to evaluate his ability. After some time, however, Charles may decide he has no talent or liking for video games, and his attempts at exploration on that particular dimension may cease. People who believe they have little ability at a task tend to avoid situations that provide additional feedback (Meyer & Starke, 1982). On the other hand, people who have considerable ability may sometimes continue to seek opportunities for evaluation, perhaps still seeking to learn just how good they are.

honest act)? You would be likely to feel guilty and uneasy in future interactions with the professor and, perhaps, in other situations in which honesty plays a role.

In contrast, one is most likely to feel dejection and depression—emotions concerning motivational deficits—if the discrepancy is between an actual self and an ideal self. Again for the sake of argument, assume that you would like to be an effective leader of an organization; one facet of your ideal self is to be a great leader. If an episode of self-awareness leads you to admit that your leadership qualities are not terribly strong, and other members of your group are regularly sought for leadership roles instead of you, how will you feel? In all likelihood you will feel downcast, sad, and dejected because you are failing to attain the ideal you set for yourself. The accompanying lower levels of motivation may generalize to other situations that involve leadership.

Reductions in actual-ideal or actual-ought discrepancies may, to turn the issue around, be a source of positive emotions. If you as a would-be leader begin to develop more effective leadership skills and are selected increasingly often to lead your group, you probably will experience a sense of elation or satisfaction.

Unlike the scores one receives at the end of a video game, many facets of the self can be evaluated only through comparisons with other people. Leon Festinger (1954) developed **social comparison theory** to explain this process. According to the theory, in the absence of a physical or objective standard of correctness, we will seek other people as a means of evaluating ourselves. The first time we encounter a full table setting and are uncertain about which fork to use first, for example, we wait for others to use their forks. Similarly, others' opinions may be particularly influential for physical appearance, where the objective criteria are not altogether clear (Felson, 1985). Whether the issue is table forks, our physical attractiveness, opinions about the latest rock group, or our emotions, we are often motivated to explore our beliefs and abilities by comparing them with social reality (Goethals, 1986; Latané, 1966; Suls & Miller, 1977).

Joanne Wood (1989) has identified three reasons people use social comparison—evaluation, improvement, and enhancement. Because the goals differ, each of these motivations involves a slightly different way of comparing.

When one's goal is self-evaluation, people use social comparison to obtain an accurate impression of the self. Therefore, social comparison is more fruitful when we choose to compare ourselves with people whose abilities are similar to our own (Castore & DeNinno, 1977; Goethals & Darley, 1977; Wheeler, Koestner, & Driver, 1982). If you are trying to evaluate your tennis-playing ability, for example, you probably would not compare yourself with last year's winner at Wimbledon, nor would you compare yourself with a 6-year-old who has never held a racket. Instead, you probably would compare yourself with someone who plays slightly better than you, reflecting what Festinger (1954) termed a "unidirectional drive upward." When choosing a "comparison other" for self-evaluation, people generally select someone whose performance represents a standard they may be able to match in the future. Later, if one's performance improves, the standard of comparison probably will rise as well.

Sometimes, however, exploration involves unfamiliar facets or dimensions of the self, such as a personality trait about which you just learned or a new game that bears no resemblance to those you already know how to play. In such circumstances, Wood (1989) suggests an individual will seek information about people

"*Of course you're going to be depressed if you keep comparing yourself with successful people.*"
Drawing by Wm. Hamilton; © 1991 The New Yorker Magazine, Inc.

who represent the extremes of the dimension: "For example, a young girl seeking to understand what extroversion is may look to an extremely outgoing friend and to an extremely timid friend" (p. 235). Why? Because knowing your own level on a dimension is not very informative unless you also know whether that level is high, low, or in the middle of the range of possible levels of the dimension. As we learn more about our level on a particular dimension, we tend to choose comparison others who are similar to us (Wheeler et al., 1969).

Gender, for example, is an important characteristic of the comparison other. When subjects in an experiment chose one person whose performance they would like to compare with their own, both males and females generally showed a strong preference for someone of the same gender (Suls, Gaes, & Gastorf, 1979; Zanna, Goethals, & Hill, 1975). The choice of someone of the same gender for comparison purposes is particularly likely if the individual believes the task is somehow related to gender and if the individual has a strong tendency to refer to gender in processing information (Miller, 1984). Thus, people seek relevant others with whom to compare their performances, and similarity often serves as a cue for potential relevance.

Festinger's unidirectional drive upward is most apparent when self-improvement is the goal of social comparison. According to Wood (1989), people who are especially achievement oriented or competitive are likely to compare themselves with others who are better on the relevant dimension—intelligence, tennis ability, and so on—but otherwise are similar. Comparing ourselves to people who are better on the relevant dimension enables us to improve ourselves. At the same time, the fact that the "better person" is similar to us in other ways is a source of inspiration. If someone "like me" can become a success, for example, then perhaps I, too, can become a success.

Finally, Wood notes that self-enhancement, attempts to convince ourselves that we are better off than we are, usually leads to downward comparisons. That is, when we need to enhance our self-esteem, we compare ourselves with those who are worse off than we are (Taylor & Lobel, 1989; Wills, 1981, 1983). If we do not have direct information about others who are "worse off" than we are, Wood suggests we may either fabricate comparison with others—"imagine how much worse things are for *really* poor people"—or generalize from secondhand information—"I heard that University X has a limit on how many A's professors can give in each class."

Social comparison is an active process. We are motivated by different goals that, in turn, affect the others with whom we choose to compare ourselves. Exploring the self, however, often goes beyond deciding how well we did compared with other people. Often we want to discover *why* we acted in a particular way or why a certain outcome occurred. This process of explaining or inferring the causes of events has been termed **causal attribution.** (As we shall see in Chapter 4, causal attributions are made about the behavior of other people as well.)

Fritz Heider, whose work (1944, 1958) is the mainspring for most of the work on attribution processes, suggested that we all act as "naive psychologists," trying to discover cause-and-effect relations in the events that occur around us. These attempts to make sense of our world are the central focus of attribution theory.

Any event can have several possible causes. To create some order in this abundance, Heider (1958) suggested that the causes to which we attribute events may be either of two basic types: dispositional (something about the person; in this case, oneself) and situational (something in the environment in which the event took place). In the "Hi and Lois" cartoon, for example, Lois has come up with several situational causes for her first gray hair. Each of these claimed causes is external to her—they involve some person or event in the environment. Alternatively, Lois could assign to the event a dispositional cause—her growing older, for example.

"Growing old" is an attribution that would require a change in Lois's self-concept—a change many people find aversive. People often avoid making such attributions, preferring to accentuate the positive and eliminate the negative, at least when it comes to themselves. This tendency to accept greater personal responsibility for positive outcomes than for negative outcomes has been termed the **self-serving attribution bias.** It is a pervasive form of self-enhancement. Miron Zuckerman (1979) analyzed several dozen studies on people's explanations of their performance and found that people systematically tend to claim that their success on a task is due to their ability or the amount of effort they exerted. We attribute positive outcomes to qualities associated with ourselves. However, we are much more likely to seek situational causes when we fail; we prefer to look outside ourselves for an explanation for failure. The self-serving bias is also evident when people estimate their effect on other people's outcomes. Professors, for example, are more likely to claim responsibility when their students do well than when they do poorly.

Not everyone is given to attributing positive outcomes to oneself, and the situation exerts some influence on the process (Arkin, Cooper, & Kolditz, 1980). For example, people who suffer from depression (as a pervasive condition, not as an isolated reaction to an unfortunate turn of events) are likely to explain events using a reverse form of self-serving bias (Sweeney, Anderson, & Bailey, 1986). After negative outcomes, the depressive person is likely to offer explanations that stress dispositional and stable causes—"It's all my fault." The depressive's explanations for positive outcomes are also the reverse of those predicted by the self-serving model. Good things may happen, but ac-

Attributions of causality

cording to the depressive person's attributions, they are not really under one's own control.

Claude Steele (1988) has proposed a theory of self-affirmation that accounts for a variety of differences in attributions about the self. He argues that it is not necessarily negative attributions about oneself—"I am getting old"—that attributional biases enable us to avoid. Instead, self-attributional biases are motivated by avoiding *any* change in the self-concept. We know, for example, that self-focus leads to behavior that is more consistent with the self-concept, even if the behavior reflects negatively on the person. We also enjoy being around those who affirm our self (Swann, 1984). Thus, the self-serving bias, according to Steele's theory, will operate only when a potential explanation of a negative outcome threatens our self-concept. If poor performance on an examination is not consistent with our self-concept, then self-serving bias leads us to consider the difficulty of the test or the devious nature of the professor as causes for our performance. On the other hand, if poor test performance is consistent with our self-concept, then the self-serving bias will not operate; we will be more likely to view ourselves as the cause, even if the test really was extremely difficult.

These patterns of attributions are interesting, but are they important? That is, does how a person interprets events really make any difference? Attribution theorists have always assumed that a connection exists between the explanations people offer and their subsequent behavior (Jones et al., 1972). Several studies support this assumption. A particularly relevant case is the work of Timothy Wilson and Patricia Linville (1985),

who investigated the explanations offered by first-year college students who did poorly in their initial studies. Wilson and Linville wanted to help students whose grades were below the class median (below a 3.0 or "B" average, in this case) and who reported being worried about their academic performance. The researchers' strategy was to give students information that might alter their attributions. Students in the treatment condition listened to third- and fourth-year students talk about their academic experiences. The advanced students revealed that they too had poor grades during their first year, but steady improvement had followed. This information was designed to show the faltering first-year students that their performance was typical and was subject to change. A control group of first-year students received no such information. Did the information affect the students' subsequent performance?

Wilson and Linville sought to answer this question in two ways: for short-term and for long-term performance. Short-term effects were assessed using the students' performance on questions from the Graduate Record Examination, administered immediately after the interview sessions. The researchers found the intervention was effective for male students, but not for female students. More important, perhaps, were the effects on long-term performance, reflected in the grades the students earned in the semester following the study. As illustrated in Figure 3.8, the program was again effective for male students, whose performance improved dramatically in comparison with that of the control group. Women in both the treatment and control groups improved; improvement was greater for

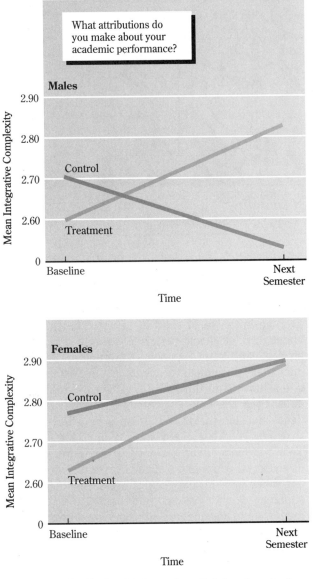

Figure 3.8 *Attributional information affects long-term performance of males, but not of females.*
Source: "Improving the Performance of College Freshmen with Attributional Techniques" by T. D. Wilson and P. W. Linville, 1985, *Journal of Personality and Social Psychology, 49,* pp. 287–293.

cussion of their problems and more comparison with others. Women in the control group, therefore, may have gained on their own much of the same information the investigators were providing for the treatment group.

Attributional effects go beyond the classroom. When Antonia Abbey and her colleagues interviewed law school students who were seeking jobs, they found that students who believed their ability to find a job was contingent on dispositional factors reported being much happier than students who made situational attributions (Abbey, Dunkel-Schetter, & Brickman, 1983). In a year-long study of life insurance sales agents, Seligman and Schulman (1986) found that agents who attributed negative outcomes to situational causes were much more likely to keep their jobs and sold considerably more insurance than agents who attributed negative events to themselves. In both studies, then, people who used self-serving biases to explain outcomes fared better than people who did not employ such biases.

We cannot say that the way one explains events is always going to have major consequences. But attributions do influence what we think about ourselves. Attributions also affect the way we deal with the people and events in our world.

▶ Relating to Others

Knowing oneself is no easy task. As individuals, we attempt to evaluate our worth, understand our emotions, and explain our outcomes. As we have seen, this process can sometimes be aversive. But individuals are more than self-contained units. Each of us is part of an ongoing social process, an interaction between the self and others. In those interactions, we make many choices about how we wish to represent ourselves to others.

Presenting the Self

Given the multiplicity of selves or identities contained in the self-concept, how does the individual decide which self to present? The general process by which people behave in particular ways to create a desired social image has been called **impression management,** defined as "the conscious or unconscious attempt to control images that are projected in real or imagined

women in the treatment condition, who inexplicably had lower initial grades than those in the comparison group. To account for the differences between males and females in their study, Wilson and Linville suggested that women may typically engage in more dissocial interactions" (Schlenker, 1980, p. 6). In other words, we are often concerned about the image we present to others, and that concern leads to attempts to control what others think about us. Different situations may arouse different identity concerns; people's goals may vary from one situation to the next. These and other factors affect the presentation of the self.

The sociologist Erving Goffman (1959, 1967) used analogies to the world of theater to formulate his theory of the *presentation of self in everyday life.* Goffman described social interaction as a theatrical performance in which each individual uses a set of carefully chosen verbal and nonverbal acts that express one's self. That is, Goffman suggested any given image we present to others is like a role played by an actor. Like an actor, each of us puts a great deal of effort into presenting a particular image; we try to stay "in character" to obtain the benefits associated with a particular image—status, advancement, money, and so on.

According to Goffman, normal social interaction is not possible unless each person not only stays in character, but helps others in the interaction to maintain their images. Otherwise, like a real actor waiting for someone else to say the correct line, we may be left standing on stage wondering what to do next. We not only avoid insulting others, we may go out of our way to overlook or help others apologize for the social blunders they commit. That is, social interaction requires each participant to regulate his or her self-presentation so that others will perceive and evaluate it appropriately.

Some people think of impression management as a deliberate strategy of manipulation, as opposed to an expression of one's true inner feelings and beliefs. That notion is usually mistaken (Tetlock & Manstead, 1985). In choosing which aspect of the self to present in a particular situation, an individual may be choosing among equally true selves. A common goal pursued in social interaction is self-verification—presenting the self as one believes it to be (Swann, 1986). You *are* a student, for example, so you engage in self-presentation to make sure your professor thinks of you as a student.

The Goals of Self-Presentation

How an individual goes about presenting the self depends on the individual's goals. Some goals may suggest that certain attributes of the self are most important to display, whereas other goals may call for a different presentation of self. Edward Jones and Thane Pittman (1982) have identified five major strategies of self-presentation, each designed to help the individual attain a particular goal. These five strategies are ingratiation, intimidation, self-promotion, exemplification, and supplication.

1. Ingratiation Perhaps the most common presentation strategy, ingratiation consists of behaviors "designed to influence a particular other person concerning the attractiveness of one's personal qualities" (Jones & Wortman, 1973, p. 2). In other words, the main goal of the ingratiator is to be seen as likable.

One can approach this task in a variety of ways, including complimenting the other person and conforming to the other person's opinions and behaviors. As one character says in Molière's play *The Miser,* "I find the best way to win people's favor is to pretend to agree with them, to fall in with their precepts, encourage their foibles, and applaud whatever they do." This view assumes, correctly, that we tend to like people whose beliefs, attitudes, and behaviors are similar to our own (see Chapter 8). This strategy will not work, however, if the target suspects that one is deliberately being ingratiating (Kauffman & Steiner, 1968). The ingratiating person is often a *reactor,* one who responds to the comments and actions of the other person (Godfrey, Jones, & Lord, 1986) rather than initiating comments and actions. The ingratiator can be friendly, a good listener, and willing to look for common ground in a conversation.

2. Intimidation In contrast to the goal of affection sought by the person who relies on ingratiation, the goal of the person who uses intimidation is to arouse fear. By creating the image of a dangerous person, the intimidator tries to control an interaction by the exercise of power. Jones and Pittman (1982) offer the example of a sidewalk robber, who attempts to create fear in the victim and thereby gain money or jewelry. One also can think of cases in which parents attempt to intimidate a child or in which a professor intimidates a student. Threats are obviously unpleasant, and they may cause the other person to try to escape the situation. For this reason, Jones and Pittman suggest that intimidation may be used most often in relationships that are in some respects involuntary, from which escape is not easy.

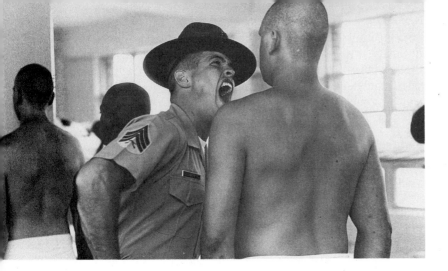

The intimidator's goal is to arouse fear.
David Wells/The Image Works

3. Self-promotion If a person's goal is to be considered competent, by virtue either of some general quality (such as intelligence) or of some specific skill (such as playing the banjo), self-promotion is the strategy most often used. In contrast to the reactive ingratiator, the self-promoter tends to be proactive (Godfrey, Jones, & Lord, 1986). Self-promoters take the lead in conversations, describing their strengths and attempting to impress others with their accomplishments. Sometimes self-promoters acknowledge minor flaws in order to appear more credible when they claim specific skills (Jones, Gergen, & Jones, 1963). Similarly, the self-promoter may acknowledge weaknesses if they are already known to the target person, and then go on to emphasize positive traits that the other person was not aware of (Baumeister & Jones, 1978). A danger in self-promotion is the possible mismatch between claims of competence and actual competence. Someone who claims to be a great racquetball player, for example, either should be good or should avoid getting on the court with the person on whom the self-promotion strategy was used. Another danger in self-promotion is that self-promotional remarks inserted inappropriately into a conversation will result in the self-promoter being perceived as egotistical and less well liked (Holtgraves & Srull, 1989).

4. Exemplification "You go on home. I'll stay here this weekend and work at the library to finish our paper, even though I may have to miss my parents' anniversary party." This is an example of exemplification, a strategy designed to elicit perceptions of one's integrity and moral worthiness—and often to arouse guilt in the target person. The exemplifier may be a martyr, the leader of a revolutionary cause, or simply a person who likes to appear as a sufferer. In each case, the goal is to influence the impressions that others form and their behaviors regarding either the exemplifier or the cause.

5. Supplication In this self-presentation strategy, a person advertises weakness and dependence on another person. Unlike the exemplifier, who seeks respect, the supplicant seeks sympathy. Jones and Pittman suggest that supplication is often the person's last hope, tried when other goals appear unattainable. Although it may not be the preferred strategy, we can think of many occasions when people resort to it. The person who claims to be "all thumbs," for example, may persuade someone else to connect the stereo components; the student who claims ignorance of word processing may prompt a generous roommate to offer to type a term paper. In each case, the supplicant is presenting an image of helplessness in the hope of arousing a sense of obligation in the target.

Many other goals are possible when people decide how they want to present themselves to others. Often it is important to present oneself as a member of a particular group, such as when students wear clothing and jewelry to display their fraternity or sorority affiliation. At other times, self-presentation may be used to affirm some central aspect of one's personality. Jennifer Crocker and Brenda Major (1989) reviewed research showing that stigmatized people—those toward whom others react negatively because of a specific characteristic, such as facial disfigurement—may sometimes emphasize their stigma for self-esteem affirmation. Gender role is another such case. In some situations, a person may feel it is very important to be seen as particularly masculine or feminine; in other circumstances, this self-presentational goal may not exist (Deaux & Major, 1987).

Consider an experiment in which female job applicants were scheduled to be interviewed by male interviewers who were described either as valuing the traditional female stereotype of emotionality and deference or as favoring more independent, career-oriented women (von Baeyer, Sherk, & Zanna, 1981). When the women arrived for their interviews, the experimenters carefully observed what the women wore and recorded their answers to the interviewer's questions. The values the women expected the interviewer to hold clearly affected the self-presentation strategies they chose. Women who expected a traditional interviewer looked more "feminine," not only in their general appearance and demeanor, but also in their use of makeup and choice of accessories. These women also gave more traditional responses to questions about marriage and children. In contrast, those women who expected the interviewer to favor career-oriented women tended less to fulfill the traditional female stereotype in their behavior and appearance.

Such tailoring of one's gender-role image is not limited to women. Similar studies have found that men also alter their presentation to fit the presumed values of another person (for example, Jellison, Jackson-White, Bruder, & Martyna, 1975). Other basic characteristics also can be subject to self-presentational concerns. A black person, for example, may choose to speak and dress differently with a predominantly black group than with a predominantly white group. Similarly, a white may follow the same kind of strategy in an attempt to create a positive impression on one or the other group. In these and many other cases, concerns with self-presentation may cause marked shifts in behavior as a person moves from one audience to another.

Self-Handicapping and BIRGing

Self-presentation is not limited to the five major strategies described by Jones and Pittman (1982). Another widely used strategy, particularly when perceived competence is the goal, is the self-handicapping strategy. As Stephen Berglas and Edward Jones (1978) define it, a **self-handicapping strategy** is "any action or choice of performance setting that enhances the opportunity to externalize (or excuse) failure and to internalize (accept credit for) success" (p. 406). Consider a student who approaches an exam with the following story: "I didn't get any sleep last night. The phone kept ringing, two cats were fighting in the alley, and the people upstairs had the stereo blasting for hours. How could I study or sleep? I'll never do well on this exam." Such a student is carefully setting up excuses in preparation for possible failure on the exam. If the student does succeed, the credit he or she can take for overcoming such difficulty is greater than the credit he or she can take for doing well on an exam for which the student could study.

In an empirical demonstration of self-handicapping strategies in action, Berglas and Jones (1978) asked two groups of college students to work on a problem-solving task. One group received problems that could be solved, but the other group unknowingly worked on problems that had no solutions. Before proceeding to a second problem-solving session, subjects were given a choice of two drugs that were ostensibly of interest to the experimenter. One of these drugs was supposed to enhance performance; the other was described as impairing performance. Subjects who had previously worked on solvable problems generally chose the drug that would improve their performance. The other group of subjects, whose experience probably led them to believe they might not do well on the next task either, showed a strong preference for the interfering drug. By handicapping themselves with a drug, they provided themselves with a convenient excuse in case they did poorly on the second task. In the language of attribution theory, they had prepared a situational explanation for their possible failure and thus could avoid negative dispositional explanations.

Self-handicapping is not limited to academic performance; athletes also deliberately handicap themselves in an attempt to protect their self-esteem in case they lose. Frederick Rhodewalt and his students observed the performance of 27 members of the Princeton men's swimming team to learn more about self-handicapping strategies (Rhodewalt, Saltzman, & Wittmer, 1984). Using a scale developed to assess people's general tendencies to handicap themselves, the investigators divided the swimmers into two groups—high self-handi-cappers and low self-handicappers. Records of attendance at practice were kept during each week leading up to a meet. In addition, the swimming coaches evaluated the practice performance of each swimmer during each week.

One would expect swimmers who have strong tendencies toward self-handicapping to practice less before a meet than those low in such tendencies. By cutting back on practice, high self-handicappers give themselves an excuse for poor performance. Such differences should be particularly strong when the upcoming meet is an important one because more self-esteem is at stake.

The results of the study are shown in Figure 3.9. Although high and low self-handicappers differed little regarding practice before unimportant meets, differences increased—both in actual attendance and in the coach's ratings—before important meets. Presumably collegiate swimmers are not alone in these tendencies. Rhodewalt and his colleagues have found similar tendencies among professional golfers, and we suspect that the self-handicapping net spreads to other sports as well.

A person who has taken no self-handicapping actions before a failure may try to find some excuse for the failure afterward, particularly if the failure is not consistent with the self-concept. One may make such attributions not only to affirm the self-concept, but to influence an audience as well. A good excuse dissuades an audience from linking a person with an undesirable outcome (Snyder, Higgins, & Stucky, 1983). Excuses take many forms. A person who has failed may try to convince an audience that his or her performance is highly inconsistent, thus suggesting that no single failure should be taken too seriously. Or a person may claim that this particular situation was unique, thus preventing generalization of the outcome to general competence (Mehlman & Snyder, 1985).

Even the distant past may be appealed to when excuses are needed. People may claim they are not responsible for their outcomes because of early traumatic experiences. As the psychoanalyst Alfred Adler once said, "the neurotic does not suffer from ... reminiscences, he (or she) makes them ... raises them to rank and dignity" (quoted in DeGree & Snyder, 1985, p. 1512). Nor is it only the neurotic who makes such excuses. College students who faced probable failure on

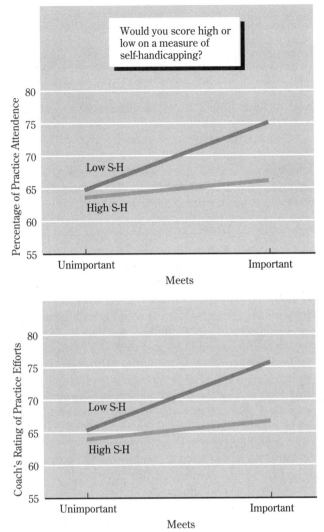

Figure 3.9 *Athletes who obtained high scores on a measure of self-handicapping practiced less, and with less effort, than athletes with low self-handicapping scores, but only before important meets.*

Source: "Self-Handicapping among Competitive Athletes: The Role of Practice in Self-Esteem Protection" by F. Rhodewalt, A. T. Saltzman, and J. Wittmer, 1984, *Basic and Applied Social Psychology, 5,* pp. 197–209.

a task reported more adversity in their backgrounds when such a tactic seemed to provide a suitable excuse for failure (DeGree & Snyder, 1985).

Promises candidates make when they campaign for election often seem to be forgotten when the candidates take office. One possible explanation for these apparent shifts in position is that new information leads to a real change in opinion. According to this *cognitive adjustment* interpretation, the officeholder may be exposed to arguments that did not surface during the campaign and may be forced to alter his or her view of the proper course. Remember George Bush's promise: "Read my lips. No new taxes"? Once president, Bush suggested that new information about the federal deficit required him to reconsider that promise. A second, more cynical explanation is that politicians never intend to fulfill their campaign promises. Instead, the claims candidates present on the campaign trail may simply represent a self-presentation strategy designed to make a favorable impression on their audiences and thus to win votes.

To test these competing hypotheses, Philip Tetlock (1981) compared preelection and postelection statements made by twentieth-century U.S. presidents. Preelection statements were those made during the five months before the election; postelection statements were gathered at three points—one month after the president took office, during the second year of office, and during the third year. Tetlock reasoned that if cognitive adjustment were the major reason for policy shifts, then changes should be gradual as the president acquired increasing amounts of information. In contrast, using the self-presentation hypothesis, one would predict more rapid changes in policy statements, changes that should be evident during the first month in office. To assess these possible changes, Tetlock evaluated the complexity of statements the presidents made, ranging from simple, unidimensional statements at one end of the scale to more complex, multidimensional statements at the other end.

Tetlock's findings give strong support to the self-presentation interpretation. Presidents' policy statements became significantly more complex immediately after they took office and did not change much over their first three years. The suddenness of this shift and the level pattern after election are not consistent with a gradual accumulation of information leading to cognitive adjustment. The trends were very similar for all the presidents during the twentieth century with one exception: statements made by Herbert Hoover became simpler after he took office.

Sometimes the desire for favorable self-presentation leads people to associate themselves with the success of others. Have you ever told people that you come from the same town as a well-known television personality, that you went to school with a prominent politician, or that you are distantly related to a famous historical figure? Such attempts to *bask in reflected glory* (BIRGing) occur on many college campuses the Monday morning after a big football game (Cialdini, Borden, Thorne, Walker, & Freeman, 1976). Students are more likely to wear clothing and buttons that associate them with their school after a victory than after a defeat. Students say "we won" after a winning game, but "they lost" after the other team won. "Cutting off reflected failure" coexists with basking in glory as a self-presentation strategy (Snyder, Lassegard, & Ford, 1986).

It may seem contradictory that we (1) sometimes go out of our way to hurt our own chances of performance, (2) sometimes undermine another's performance, (3) sometimes compare ourselves with those less fortunate than ourselves, and (4) sometimes associate ourselves with those who are much more successful than we are, all for the sake of maintaining our self-concept. According to Abraham Tesser's (1988) Self-Evaluation Maintenance Model, the key to unraveling the apparent contradiction is the concept of relevance. If someone else's performance is relevant to our self-concept, social comparison processes become important, and we are likely to compare ourselves if the other's performance is worse than ours or to maintain our self-concept if the other's performance is better. Tesser's review of research indicates that maintaining our self-concept in the face of a superior performance can include many different reactions: finding excuses for our (inferior) performance, finding fault with the other's (superior) performance, projecting unfavorable characteristics onto a successful other, handicapping our future performances, and even actively undermining the future performance of the other. In contrast, when relevance is low, the importance of social comparison is also low, and we are free to engage in BIRGing if the other's performance is good or dissociate ourselves if the other's performance is bad.

We use self-presentation strategies to present a particular image to an audience on a specific occasion. Do these strategies have any lasting effect? Does the image we present on one occasion have any impact on our private self-conceptions? Rhodewalt and his colleagues have shown that self-presentation strategies can have carryover effects (Jones, Rhodewalt, Berglas, & Skelton, 1981; Rhodewalt, 1986; Rhodewalt & Agustsdottir, 1986). They suggest that self-presentations can influence the self-concept through what Markus (1977) called the working self-concept. As we discussed earlier, the working self-concept contains those particular aspects of the self that are accessed—on our mind—at a given time. Carryover effects refer to the tendency for often-used working self-concepts to become even more accessible and more likely to be used in the future. Also, the content of self-concepts can be changed by self-presentation. When an individual chooses to engage in a behavior that conflicts somewhat with the sense of self, that behavior can cause an alteration in the working self-concept. When the changed working self-concept is "put away" in memory, the changes are stored as well. That an individual's sense of self can be changed by the very means chosen to express the self testifies to both the stability and the flexibility of the self-concept.

Individual Differences in Self-Presentation

Everyone engages in self-presentation behaviors; yet important differences exist in the extent to which people can and do control their presentations. Some people engage in impression management more often and with greater skill than others. Professional actors, for example, are trained to manipulate the images they project to the audience. As we noted earlier, successful politicians, too, have long practiced the art of presenting the right image for the right constituency.

Earlier we discussed individual differences concerning private self-consciousness, the tendency to engage in self-focus. We now turn to **public self-consciousness,** concern about how one is projecting the self to the social world and awareness of how one is seen as a social object by others (Scheier & Carver, 1981). The Self-Consciousness Scale developed by Fenigstein, Scheier, and Buss (1975) includes the following items to assess public self-consciousness: "I'm concerned about what other people think of me," "I'm self-conscious about the way I look," and "I'm concerned about my style of doing things." Notice that these items tend to focus on the self, but they do so from the point of view of others. People high in public self-consciousness tend to be more concerned about others' evaluations

and are more sensitive to social rejection (Fenigstein, 1979), whereas people low in public self-consciousness show less concern for this kind of evaluation (Franzoi & Brewer, 1984).

In one experimental attempt to validate the public self-consciousness scale, R. Glen Hass (1984) asked people to draw an *E* on their foreheads (see Figure 3.10). People who were low in public self-consciousness were more likely to draw an *E* from an internal perspective (right side of Figure 3.10). Their *E* could be read if they faced a mirror. People who were high in public self-consciousness drew an *E* that an observer could read (left side of Figure 3.10). Hass obtained the same results when he had people draw an *E* in the presence of a video camera, a symbol of the attention of others (viewers). The importance of the social component of public self-consciousness is illustrated by the fact that the direction in which people drew the *E* was not related to their scores on a measure of private self-consciousness.

Although it may seem trivial, drawing an *E* for an experimenter demonstrates individual differences in the extent to which we depend on the feedback of others to maintain our self-concepts. Mark Snyder's (1979, 1987) concept of **self-monitoring** also indicates people vary in the extent to which they can and do exercise control over their verbal and nonverbal self-presentation. High self-monitoring persons are particularly sensitive to the expressions and self-presentations of others in social situations, and they use these cues in monitoring their self-presentation for purposes of impression management. High self-monitoring persons are identified by their high scores on the Self-Monitoring Scale (Snyder & Gangestad, 1986). The high self-monitoring person endorses such statements as these:

1. In different situations and with different people, I often act like very different persons.

2. I'm not always the person I appear to be.

3. I may deceive people by being friendly when I really dislike them.

High self-monitoring persons are good at learning what is socially appropriate in new situations, have good control of their emotional expressions, and can effectively use these abilities to create impressions that reflect whatever aspects of themselves they want others to see. In fact, they are such polished self-presenters that they can effectively adopt the mannerisms of a reserved, withdrawn, and introverted person and then do an abrupt about-face and portray themselves, equally convincingly, as friendly, outgoing, and extroverted (Lippa, 1976, 1978). In self-presentation situations, high self-monitoring persons are likely to seek out and consult social comparison information about appropriate patterns of self-presentation. They invest considerable effort in attempting to "read" and understand others (Berscheid, Graziano, Monson, & Dermer, 1976; Jones & Baumeister, 1976).

In contrast, low self-monitoring people tend not to observe, regulate, or control the impressions that they convey to others. They may observe them but not regulate them; they may be able to control these impressions but do not do so for one reason or another. Instead, they are much more likely to exhibit consistent images across a variety of situations. Low self-monitors agree with statements such as:

1. I have trouble changing my behavior to suit different people and different situations.

2. I can only argue for ideas which I already believe.

3. I would not change my opinion (or the way I do things) in order to please people or to win their favor.

Before you go too far in building your personal schema about self-monitoring, a note of caution is in order. Although it may seem that high self-monitors are superficial fakes and low self-monitors are deeply sincere, this is not necessarily the case. The Self-Monitoring Scale measures how much people work at self-presentation and how well they succeed, but it does not measure the purposes for which people use self-presentations. High self-monitors may tell people what they want to hear to cheat them out of their life savings, or they may alter their behavior to make a client feel more comfortable in therapy. Similarly, low self-monitors may come across as sincere individuals who withstand conformity pressures, or they may appear to be boring clods who cannot adapt to changes in social situations.

You also may detect similarities between the concept of self-monitoring and that of public self-consciousness. The two concepts are related, though only moderately so (Scheier & Carver, 1980). The person high

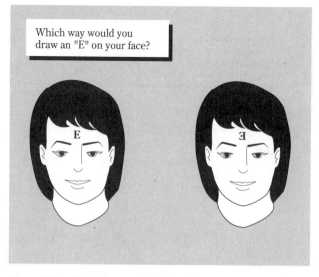

Figure 3.10 *A simple test of public self-consciousness: high score on the left, low score on the right.*

in public self-consciousness may be aware of the impression he or she is making but does not necessarily act on that information. High self-monitors, in contrast, use this information to guide their self-presentations in an interaction. In other words, a high degree of public self-consciousness may be necessary for self-monitoring behavior, but it is not sufficient for impression management.

An experiment by Mark Snyder and Thomas Monson (1975) illustrates one way in which self-monitoring alters social behavior. In this study, discussions indicated that the subject's group favored either autonomy or conformity. High self-monitoring persons were keenly attentive to these differences, as Figure 3.11 shows. They were conforming when conformity was the most appropriate interpersonal orientation, and nonconforming when reference-group norms favored autonomy in the face of social pressure. Low self-monitoring persons were unaffected by the differences in social setting. In a similar study, high self-monitoring subjects were more likely to be cooperative when they expected future interaction with a partner than when they did not, whereas low self-monitors did not vary their behavior in response to such prospects (Danheiser & Graziano, 1982).

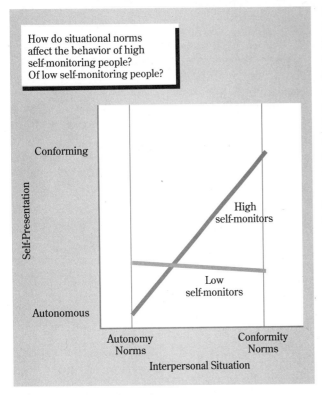

How do situational norms affect the behavior of high self-monitoring people? Of low self-monitoring people?

Figure 3.11 *High self-monitoring people are more likely to match their behavior to group norms.*
Source: "Persons, Situations, and the Control of Social Behavior" by M. Snyder and T. C. Monson, 1975, *Journal of Personality and Social Psychology, 32,* pp. 637–644.

Self-monitoring may be a useful skill in the work world. Some positions in organizations are called "boundary-spanning" positions because people in these positions must interact regularly with various organizational subgroups. An area manager who must coordinate sales, repair, and production staff is one example; the academic department chair who deals with students, faculty, and administration is another. People who hold such positions are responsible for filtering and transmitting information across organizational boundaries, and they must adapt to a variety of pressures and competing opinions. David Caldwell and Charles O'Reilly (1982) reasoned that persons who score high in self-monitoring should be more successful in such positions because they can perceive cues

and modify their behavior accordingly. Caldwell and O'Reilly measured the self-monitoring tendencies of 93 field representatives whose jobs required boundary spanning and assessed their job performance. High self-monitors did better in these jobs, and the differences were particularly important during the early stages of employment. These findings are important, for they suggest that self-monitoring, far from being a skill to be cultivated only by people who wish to deceive, can be helpful to anyone in an environment that contains a complex mix of people and policies.

Clearly impression management can be either good or bad. Goffman (1955) pointed out both the potentials and the pitfalls:

> Too little perceptiveness, too little *savoir faire* [that is, too little impression management], too little pride and considerateness, and the person ceases to be someone who can be trusted to take a hint . . . or give a hint that will save others embarrassment. Such a person comes to be a real threat to society; there is nothing much that can be done . . . Too much *savoir faire* or too much considerateness, and [the person] becomes someone who is too socialized, who leaves the others with the feeling that they do not know how they really stand . . . , nor what they should do to make an effective long term adjustment. [p. 227]

The same tactic of self-presentation can foster an honest image or a deceptive one and can influence others for altruistic purposes or for exploitive ones. We may or may not approve of a particular goal served by self-presentation, but presentation of self is an integral part of everyday social interaction.

Thus, the self-concept both results from and affects social interactions. Our interactions with others enable us to define and explore more fully the different images that constitute who we are. As we present those images to others, we reinforce (and sometimes change) the images, and we rely on feedback from others to determine the extent to which the image we present is the one we want to present.

▶ Summary

Social knowledge and social behavior begin with the self-concept, the totality of an individual's thoughts about the self. As such early social scientists as George

Herbert Mead and Harry Stack Sullivan pointed out, we learn about ourselves from the reflected appraisals of others. We also learn about ourselves through the outcomes of actions we take.

Self-schemas are cognitive generalizations about the self that influence the way we organize and remember events and experiences. The self-concept consists of multiple schemas. We may usefully think of the self as consisting of multiple identities arranged in a hierarchy of importance. The self-concept also includes ideas about what we would like to be or think it possible to become, as well as specific physical characteristics.

Self-perception theory contains the proposition that we become aware of ourselves by watching what we do, much as outside observers form judgments of us based on what they see. Certain conditions can create a state of objective self-awareness or concentrated self-focus; at such times we focus attention on some aspect of the self. The particular aspect of self that predominates at any given time depends in part on the accessibility of that aspect, which can be affected by priming through situational cues. People who are high in private self-consciousness are more likely to engage in self-focus than people who are low in private self-consciousness.

Because the concept of self is an active one, it is important to consider the processes involved. Self-esteem refers to the evaluation of oneself, an assessment of how good or bad one is. Negative emotions are generally aroused when a discrepancy exists between the perceived or working self and some standard of comparison (an ideal self, an ought self, or a possible self).

To evaluate their abilities, people often engage in social comparison, looking to others as a way of gauging their performance. People also make causal attributions to explain their outcomes. Frequently such comparisons and attributions are self-serving; that is, they are designed to permit us to maintain a consistent self-concept in the face of changes in our behavior or in the situation. Attributions are important because they can affect subsequent choices and actions.

The attempt to control the images of the self that one presents to others is called impression management. Self-presentation can serve many goals, and people can use several different strategies. People who anticipate failure, for instance, may resort to self-handicapping strategies. Although all people engage in some impression management, people who score high in self-monitoring are more attuned to impression management than people who score low in self-monitoring.

▶ Key Terms

causal attribution
confirmatory bias
gender identity
ideal self
impression management
ought self
priming
private self-consciousness
public self-consciousness
racial identity
schema
self-awareness
self-concept
self-consciousness
self-esteem
self-handicapping strategy
self-monitoring
self-perception theory
self-schema
self-serving attribution bias
social comparison theory
working self-concept

To know one's self is wisdom, but to

know one's neighbor is genius.

Minna Antrim

Rather than humbly regarding our

impressions of the world as

interpretation of it, we see them as

understandings or correct

apprehensions of it.

Edward Jones & Richard Nisbett

4

Understanding Others

I magine you are sitting in a chair reading, and you happen to glance out the window toward the house next door. Suddenly you see a person run out through the front door, jump into a car in the driveway, and speed away. What would you notice first? You probably would notice first whether the person was a man or a woman. Having established that it was a woman, you might next note her approximate height and weight, and perhaps her ethnicity. If she was someone you had seen before, these features might help you to identify her; it's Susan, your neighbor's sister. But why did she seem in such a hurry to leave? Why didn't her sister come out with her to say good-bye? Answers to questions like these are the basis of understanding others.

Now let's change this scenario slightly. Suppose you did not recognize the person, but you're sure it was a middle-aged white man. A little later you find out that a burglary has been committed next door, and, having volunteered what you saw, you are called to the police station. Will you recognize the man in a police lineup? In this case, the concern is not with interpreting events but with recognizing an individual you have seen before. And later, as you think about these events, what do you recall? In succeeding months, can you recreate the scene you witnessed? Does your account of the event change with the passage of time?

More generally, we can ask about the process of thinking about people. How is information about other people represented in our memories? Are our impressions of other people usually accurate? Does our knowledge affect our judgments of and interactions with others? These questions, too, fall within the domain of understanding others.

As you read in Chapter 3, knowing ourselves provides us with some understanding of social behavior. Knowing about other people adds to that understanding. It may be that, as Minna Antrim suggests at the beginning of this chapter, truly knowing another person requires genius. If that is true, then most of us aspire to genius status.

The major reasons for trying to understand and interpret the behavior of the people around us are obvious. Other people are part of our lives, and they affect our lives in many ways. For example, if we can predict whether an approaching stranger is a harmless pedestrian or a dangerous mugger, then we may be able to avoid theft or injury. Knowing something about people we may seek out at a party can mean the difference between good conversation and bad or between love and rejection. The actions of other people, strangers and friends alike, have such important consequences for us that the ability to interpret their behavior is crucial to our well-being.

▶ Forming Impressions of People

We are often told that first impressions are important. And although we are also advised not to judge a book by its cover, there is considerable evidence that people do just that—judge people on the basis of appearance alone. Such judgments involve a set of inferences as to what the person we see is like "underneath." How accurate are such inferences? To answer this and other questions about how impressions are formed, we must look first at the raw material that goes into the impressions on which we base our initial judgments.

Physical Appearance

When we meet someone for the first time, appearance provides the first and most obvious information we have about the person. Some characteristics, such as gender and race, are almost always noted and remembered (Grady, 1977; Kessler & McKenna, 1978; McArthur, 1982). Indeed, we may not need a good look at people to decide their gender. The way people walk (Cutting & Proffitt, 1981), or simply the way they move their faces and heads while talking (Berry, 1990a), enable us to decide whether they are male or female.

We are also likely to notice other physical features, such as height, weight, and facial expressions, particularly if the person varies strikingly from the average (DeJong & Kleck, 1986; Roberts & Herman, 1986). We are unlikely, for example, to overlook exceptionally tall or short persons, or a single angry face among a crowd of happy people (Hansen & Hansen, 1988). John Bargh (1989) has argued that we engage in such processes without any specific goal, intent, or awareness of the stimulus that produces them. That is, we do not see a single angry face in a crowd and then decide to pay attention to that person. Instead, the mere fact that the face is unusual automatically draws our attention to it, and only then do we notice that the expression indicates anger. The same perceptual process has been demonstrated in nonsocial situations (for example, see Friedman, 1979). When the situation is not entirely what we expect it to be, our attention is drawn immediately to the unusual aspects.

Similarly, noting a stranger's appearance usually results in an initial judgment about the person's physical attractiveness. It is reported that Queen Victoria once said, "An ugly baby is a very nasty object" (quoted in Langlois, 1986), making clear both her awareness of appearance and her feelings about it. Although most of us are less outspoken, our first impressions of people, adults as well as babies, are strongly influenced by the degree of the person's physical attractiveness (Dion, 1986; R. Freedman, 1986; Patzer, 1985).

Why are physical features so central a part of first impressions? People's physical features are immediately apparent, so we generally know whether people are tall or short before we know whether they are honest or conniving or know anything else about their "inner" qualities. Also, many people believe that physical features provide information about a person's underlying characteristics and, therefore, about his or her probable behavior (R. M. Baron, 1990; McArthur & Baron, 1983). If, like Shakespeare's Julius Caesar, you believe it's best to be cautious of people who look "lean and hungry," then paying attention to these physical signs provides an apparent advantage.

Consider, for example, the work of Leslie McArthur and her colleagues, who have investigated people's perceptions of infants' faces (Berry & McArthur, 1985, 1986; McArthur & Apatow, 1983/1984). Certain characteristics of the infant face are distinctive. Infants' heads are larger in relation to their bodies than adults' are, for example, and infants' eyes are larger in relation to their faces. A baby's features are lower on the face, giving the impression of a large forehead and a tiny chin. (Figure 4.1 illustrates the relative placement of features across the life span.) Such features serve as cues to inform people that this person is an infant. People may infer from certain physical characteristics a set of behavioral tendencies, in this case helplessness and dependency. These inferences are not necessarily accurate or reliable, but they affect our judgments (Alley, 1990).

Adults with infantile features—large eyes placed low on the face, for example, as in the face on the left in Figure 4.1—are often judged to have childish traits (Berry & McArthur, 1985; McArthur & Apatow, 1983/

What features vary among these faces?

Figure 4.1 *These faces vary in apparent age. The one on the left is the youngest; the one on the right, the oldest.*

Source: "Impressions of Baby-Faced Adults" by L. Z. McArthur and K. Apatow, 1983/1984, *Social Cognition, 2,* pp. 315–342.

1984). They are assumed to be weaker, less dominant, and less intellectually astute than the average adult. At the same time, such adults are also judged to be exceptionally honest, kind, and warm—a judgment that reflects the widespread belief in the naiveté of childhood. As a potential roommate, the person with childlike features is seen as likely to respond to friendly conversation but unlikely to be able to move heavy boxes of books. Beliefs about infantile features are so pervasive that individuals sometimes employ such inferences when making judgments about themselves (Berry & Brownlow, 1989). All in all, a large set of inferences may be drawn from a small set of physical signs.

Other features also tend to be associated with a variety of psychological traits. For that matter, almost every physical feature has accumulated a history of associations, from the nose—a long one has been seen as a sign of energy—to wrinkles, which presumably testify to depth of character (Berry & McArthur, 1986). At one time or another, tall people have been assumed to be delicate, introverted, stupid, and intelligent, while short people have been said to be passionate, petty, and given to negativity (Roberts & Herman, 1986). Overweight individuals are judged more harshly than muscular or thin people on a variety of characteristics ranging from intelligence to cleanliness (Ryckman, Robbins, Kaczor, & Gold, 1989).

Perhaps most studied by psychologists are the inferences we make about physically attractive people. Considerable research has shown that most people believe "what is beautiful is good." In fact, it is difficult to overestimate the effect of another person's physical appearance on our initial impressions. Studies have shown that the highly attractive person is more likely to be recommended for hiring after a job interview (Dipboye, Arvey, & Terpstra, 1977; Dipboye, Fromkin, & Wiback, 1975), to have his or her written work evaluated favorably (Landy & Sigall, 1974), and to be considered an effective psychological counselor (Cash, Begley, McCown, & Weise, 1975), and less likely to be judged maladjusted or disturbed (Cash, Kehr, Polyson, & Freeman, 1977). On the other hand, those whose physical features are perceived as less attractive are often judged to be less admirable, and the outcomes of their encounters with others tend to be less satisfying than those of people who are considered more attractive (Jones, Howard, & Haley, 1984).

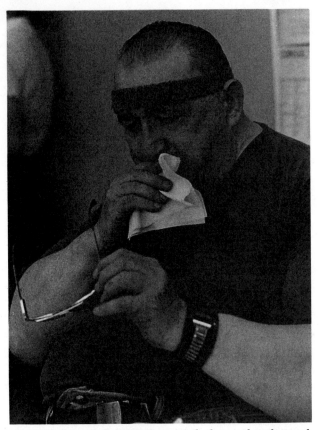

We tend to make inferences about people that are based on such physical characteristics as weight.
Robert Kalman/The Image Works

In summary, physical features are an important ingredient of first impressions. As the aspects of people we notice first, physical features often are a source of information in themselves. For people who associate certain characteristics with specific features, which we discuss later in this chapter, physical features also serve as clues to the characters of others.

Character Traits

The inferences people draw from physical features are often inferences about personality. We decide whether someone is honest or sneaky, generous or stingy, assertive or shy. That is, we make decisions about **traits,** which Stephen Briggs (1985) defined as terms that refer to "the regularities and peculiarities that we observe in the actions and expressions of others" (p. 37). In addition to making our own judgments based on traits, we hear from others about traits they have decided to apply to someone. Because trait descriptions are so common in everyday language, social psychologists have taken great interest in the role of traits in impression formation and in how positive or negative certain traits might be.

What is the best thing you can say about someone's personality? What is the worst? Answers to these questions come from Norman Anderson (1968), who obtained likableness ratings of 555 words that describe personality traits. Subjects rated each word on a 7-point scale ranging from "least favorable or desirable" to "most favorable or desirable." For research purposes, each word was assigned a value that was determined by the average of the ratings it received from 100 college students. Table 4.1 contains the relative rankings of selected words from the list.

The list is tremendously useful in research on impression formation because it gives us an empirical indication of the values associated with various traits. Of course, these ratings are colored by the particular group of raters; some other group might rate the word *polite* more or less favorably than did this group (which made it 53rd in the list of 555 terms). Anderson's list is also interesting for what it reveals about our preferences. The term in the exact middle of the list (278th in rank), for example, is *ordinary.* Perhaps because being able to understand and predict the behavior of others is so important to us, *sincere* is rated most favorably of all 555 terms, and *liar* and *phony* receive the lowest ratings.

How do we combine all this information to form an impression? Are some traits more important than others? Solomon Asch (1946), who conducted some of the first research on the impression formation process, proposed the concept of central traits. According to Asch, **central traits** are characteristics that exert such a strong influence on impressions that they can change completely the impression people form. For example, when the adjective *cold* was included in a list of seven stimulus words that purportedly described a person, only about 10% of the subjects believed that the person in question was also likely to be generous or humorous. When the adjective *warm* was used, however, about 90% of the subjects described the person as generous or humorous.

Table 4.1 Favorability ratings of some words used to describe personality traits

Rank	Term	Rank	Term
1	sincere	278	ordinary
2	honest	305	critical
3	understanding	355	unhappy
4	loyal	405	unintelligent
5	truthful	465	disobedient
6	trustworthy	500	prejudiced
7	intelligent	520	ill-mannered
8	dependable	531	loud-mouthed
9	open-minded	540	greedy
10	thoughtful	546	deceitful
20	kind-hearted	547	dishonorable
30	trustful	548	malicious
40	clever	549	obnoxious
53	polite	550	untruthful
80	ethical	551	dishonest
100	tolerant	552	cruel
150	modest	553	mean
200	soft-spoken	554	phony
251	quiet	555	liar

Source: Adapted from "Likableness Ratings of 555 Personality-Trait Words" by N. H. Anderson, 1968, *Journal of Personality and Social Psychology, 9,* pp. 272–279.

erous, and more than 75% described the person as humorous. In contrast, comparisons between the words *polite* and *blunt* produced almost no differences in the resulting impressions. Therefore, Asch concluded that warmth/coldness was a central trait, but politeness/bluntness was not.

Even when people have an opportunity to interact with an individual, impressions formed before the interaction can have pronounced effects. In an extension of Asch's work, Harold Kelley (1950) introduced a guest lecturer to several university classes after leading some students to believe that the lecturer was a warm person and others to believe that he was cold. The lecturer then gave the identical talk to all groups. The impressions class members reported after the lecture varied considerably and were consistent with the initial description of him as warm or cold. Furthermore, class members who had been led to expect a warm person interacted more with the lecturer in discussion.

Later research showed that the role of central traits is not quite so simple as Asch thought. The importance of any particular trait depends both on what other information is presented about a person and on the judgments that the subject is asked to make (Wishner, 1960). Other research has shown that individuals' uses of various traits produce two dimensions for judgment: a social/interpersonal dimension and an intellectual/ competence dimension (Rosenberg, Nelson, & Vivekananthan, 1968). The specific effect of *warm* or *cold,* extreme examples on the social/interpersonal dimension, may be weak if one already has other information about sociability. Thus, the information that someone is warm adds little to your impression if you already think the person is good-natured, happy, and helpful. Asch obtained large differences between *warm* and *cold* in his research because most of the other information he provided concerned intellectual abilities. Similarly, Kelley's introduction of the guest lecturer contained primarily intellectual information, so his results concerning *warm* and *cold* may also have been due to the paucity of other information about the lecturer's interpersonal warmth. Thus, there probably are no central traits; instead, there may be only collections of traits that constitute central dimensions. Intellectual competence and interpersonal warmth are two of the most important dimensions concerning judgments about people (Rosenberg et al., 1968).

Although some information about others comes to us as trait descriptions, we infer many traits from behaviors, and we must decide whether we have enough information to make a trait inference. Therefore, another important feature of trait descriptions is the ease with which they can be inferred or confirmed (Rothbart & Park, 1986). Confirmation of a trait from behaviors depends on several factors. First, the behaviors associated with some traits are more commonly displayed than others, and it is easier to confirm a trait when the behaviors associated with it are more frequently displayed. For example, one generally has more opportunities to observe cheerful behaviors than clever behaviors. Second, some traits require less behavioral evidence than others. At one end of the confirmation spectrum are traits that allow what Reuben M. Baron (1990) calls a *critical events test,* a single behavior that seems to make a trait judgment "obvious." A single instance of cheating, for example, may suffice to convince us that someone is dishonest (Birnbaum, 1972, 1973, 1974). On the other hand, the sight of someone's disordered apartment probably will not convince us that its occupant is basically messy. Third, some traits are simply more concrete than others; that is, the behaviors associated with the traits are easy to identify. It is quite clear, for example, whether or not a person is talkative; it is more difficult to say whether someone is imaginative.

Winning a spelling bee is one behavior from which we might make inferences about intellectual ability.
Dennis Cook/AP/Wide World Photos

Finally, part of the impression formation process involves disconfirming a trait, removing it from our impression of a specific person. Traits vary in the ease with which they can be disconfirmed. In general, favorable traits are disconfirmed rather easily, whereas we require a considerable amount of contrary evidence before we remove an unfavorable trait from an impression (Rothbart & Park, 1986; Skowronski & Carlston, 1989). Once we have inferred that someone is honest, for example, one lie might be enough to void that decision. On the other hand, once we have inferred that someone is cruel, perhaps after observing the individual kick a dog, repeated evidence of kindness may not wipe out the impression of cruelty.

The Question of Accuracy

There is little doubt that we form impressions about people and that we use physical appearance and inferences about character traits to do so. But are these impressions accurate? That question is not so easy to answer as it may appear at first glance.

For many years, the study of social perception focused mainly on the issue of impression accuracy. Despite much research, the overall result was frustration, resulting in part from methodological dead ends. What, for example, does it mean when George is labeled "honest"? Has he told the truth on several occasions? Probably. Does he always tell the whole truth? Probably not. How many people have to agree with that impression of George before we conclude that it is accurate? Traits, like theories, are abstract conclusions drawn from concrete information. As we discussed in Chapter 1, theories cannot be proven true in any absolute sense. Therefore, recent investigators have concentrated on assessing the accuracy with which people can interpret and predict behaviors, which are objective events.

For example, Diane Berry (1990a) has argued that sometimes "we can literally see and hear dominance, and attraction, and depression and warmth" (p. 146). That is, our lifetime of experience with social behavior enables us to identify particular patterns of consistent behaviors in others. In one demonstration of this effect, Berry (1990b) affixed circular patches of reflective material to individuals' faces, then videotaped each individual reciting the alphabet and conversing with a research assistant. The lighting was such that anyone who viewed the videotape would be able to see only the light reflected by the patches. The three individuals whose videotapes were shown to students included a child about 5 years old and two adults aged 35 and 70. The research assistant with whom they conversed was in her early twenties. Berry asked her subjects to view

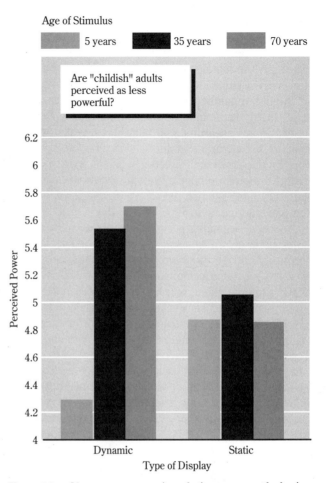

Figure 4.2 *Observers can perceive relative power on the basis of facial movement.*
Source: "What Can a Moving Face Tell Us?" by D. S. Berry, 1990, *Journal of Personality and Social Psychology, 58,* pp. 1004–1014.

a videotape and rate the power of the stimulus face in terms of physical strength, dominance, vulnerability, and so on. Berry hypothesized that subjects would perceive the older faces as more powerful, particularly when interacting with the young research assistant.

The results, illustrated in Figure 4.2, support Berry's hypothesis. When the stimulus persons were interacting with the research assistant, subjects were able to accurately perceive the relatively low power displayed in the child's face. However, when the stimulus persons' faces were static—posing for the camera—the subjects perceived no differences in power. The subjects, unaware of the actual ages of the stimulus persons, assumed all three faces belonged to adults. Thus, it was only when the child was interacting with the research assistant that perceivers were able to determine accurately the relative powerlessness of a 5-year-old interacting with an adult research assistant.

The difference between the power ratings assigned under the dynamic and the static conditions in Berry's study also indicates the importance of context when we consider the accuracy of impressions. People don't always act the same in all situations. As you read in Chapter 3, for example, people high in self-monitoring are likely to engage in self-presentation, and their behaviors may change considerably from one social context to the next. Thus, it is possible to form an impression of someone on the basis of his or her behavior in the dormitory and be quite wrong in predicting how that person will behave at a job interview. As William Swann (1984) has suggested, we need to distinguish between circumscribed accuracy and global accuracy.

Circumscribed accuracy refers to the correctness of impressions that are based on specific traits a person displays in specific situations. Your impression of another student in your social psychology course, inferred from that student's behavior in class, might enable you to predict, for example, how talkative he or she will be in a philosophy class. This kind of accuracy is relatively easy to attain, primarily because you have some direct behavioral evidence and the contexts are similar. **Global accuracy,** in contrast, refers to one's ability to form impressions that are valid in many situations and on many occasions. How well could you predict, for example, whether that same student will be talkative with family members, on a date, and at a job interview? Accuracy of this kind, as the early investigators discovered, is more difficult to achieve. One reason global accuracy is difficult to achieve is that, as we noted earlier, we often form first impressions on the basis of very little information. That is, we begin making predictions long before we have enough information to attain global accuracy. Another reason involves the manner in which we organize social knowledge.

▶ Organizing Impressions

In coming to know other people, we do not respond passively to their external characteristics or their behaviors. Instead, we hold certain assumptions about

people, assumptions through which we filter information we receive. At a general level, we may have overriding **philosophies of human nature**—expectations that people will possess certain qualities and will behave in certain ways. An analysis of writings by philosophers, theologians, and social scientists, for example, suggests that our beliefs about human nature have six basic dimensions: trustworthiness, rationality, altruism, independence, variability, and complexity (Wrightsman, 1964, 1974). The first four dimensions can be combined into a generally positive or negative view of the world; the fifth and sixth dimensions concern beliefs about the extent of individual differences in human nature.

These dimensions define a basic framework, or template, by which we judge the actions and characteristics of others. For example, if you believe that people are basically trustworthy, you are likely to require more behavioral evidence before inferring someone is dishonest than would be required by someone who believes people are basically untrustworthy. Similarly, if you believe that people are extremely complex, you may refrain from making inferences about global traits, preferring instead to limit yourself only to attaining a certain level of circumscribed accuracy. Beliefs about human nature can vary widely from one individual or group of people to another, but the existence of such beliefs does indicate that people organize information about others at a global level.

Psychologists also have been trying to understand how social knowledge is organized at more specific levels. Several of these more specific concepts or categories have been identified, including implicit theories, schemas and scripts, and stereotypes.

Implicit Personality and Social Theories

Through socialization and independent experiences, each of us arrives at his or her own **implicit personality theory,** a set of unstated assumptions about what personality traits are associated with one another. These theories often include beliefs about what behaviors are associated with specific traits (Reeder & Brewer, 1979; Skowronski & Carlston, 1989). Such theories are considered implicit because they are rarely stated in formal terms and are often not part of conscious awareness; nonetheless, they dominate our judgments of other people (Schneider, 1973; Wegner & Vallacher, 1977).

For example, when asked to describe the people they know, college students use the terms *intelligent, friendly, self-centered, ambitious,* and *lazy* with the greatest frequency (Rosenberg & Sedlak, 1972), but they don't apply all these terms to the same person. People described as intelligent are also likely to be described as friendly but are rarely described as self-centered. Thus, many people apparently have an implicit personality theory in which intelligence and friendliness go together, whereas intelligence and self-centeredness do not. Like that of any theory, the validity of implicit personality theories can be tested by measuring objectively the actual occurrence of the traits included in them. In fact, however, one of the things that distinguishes implicit personality theories from more formal psychological theories is the lesser likelihood of their being tested. Without testing, implicit personality theories are rarely found to be incorrect. Because we may not even be aware that we make an association between specific traits—for example, intelligence and friendliness—we may be unlikely to notice those times at which our implicit theories are wrong.

Each of us probably has his or her own implicit personality theory that could be assessed by reference to conversations and letters or to free descriptions elicited by experimenters. In an interesting application of the archival method, Rosenberg and Jones (1972) showed that it is possible to assess the implicit personality theories of historical figures, in this case the writer Theodore Dreiser. Analyzing *A Gallery of Women* (1929), a collection of sketches about 15 women, these investigators tabulated all the traits that Dreiser ascribed to the women in his sketches; Table 4.2 summarizes the 99 descriptors Dreiser used most frequently. By statistical analysis, Rosenberg and Jones reduced these traits to three basic dimensions: hard/soft, male/female, and conforms/does not conform. Hardness was closely related to maleness in Dreiser's implicit theory but was not identical with it; by contrast, the characteristics of gender and conformity seemed to be independent of each other. It is interesting to consider this pattern of Dreiser's in conjunction with current stereotypes of men and women. Dreiser was clearly concerned with women's outward physical characteristics as evidenced by the relative frequencies of the descriptions listed in Table 4.2. Although his descriptions

Table 4.2 The ninety-nine most frequently occurring trait categories in Theodore Dreiser's *A Gallery of Women*

Trait category	Frequency
Young	100
Beautiful	67
Attractive	44
Charming, dreamer	41
Poetic	39
Interesting, worker	32
Artistic	29
Gay	26
Practical, romantic, writer	25
Conventional, girl	24
Free, strong	23
Woman	22
Unhappy	20
Intellectual, radical, sensitive, sensual	19
Kind, cold	18
Vigorous	17
Able, drinker, generous, troubled	16
Colorful, graceful, intelligent, poor, reads, religious, studies, tall	15
Fool, good-looking, literary, pagan	14
Aspirant, determined, good, had means, sad, society person, not strong, tasteful	13
Ambitious, careful, defiant, different, erratic, genial, happy, lonely, man, varietistic	12
Clever, genius, indifferent, Irish, manager, nice, old, pale, quiet, restless, serious, shrewd, sincere, successful, suffering, sympathetic, thin, understanding	11
American, communist, crazy, critical, emotional, enthusiastic, fearful, fighter, forceful, great, handsome, hard, lovely, had money, painter, physically alluring, playful, repressed, reserved, skilled, sophisticated	10

Source: "A Method for Investigating and Representing a Person's Implicit Theory of Personality: Theodore Dreiser's View of People" by S. Rosenberg and R. A. Jones, 1972, *Journal of Personality and Social Psychology, 22,* pp. 372–386.

might suggest a rather superficial view of women, in his work Dreiser deviated from at least one aspect of the commonly-held stereotype: he did not associate independence predominantly with males.

Just as people have implicit personality theories about the extent to which traits are related, so they have implicit social theories about how events are related. More specifically, we can define a **social theory** as a belief "about how and in what way variables in the social environment are related" (Anderson & Sechler, 1986, p. 24). That is, social theories typically deal with a cause-and-effect relationship: the reasons that things happen. Thus, a person can have beliefs about the relationship between capital punishment and murder rates, between child-rearing practices and moral development, or between diet and mental health. Social psychologists, of course, develop theories concerning the very same things, but their theories differ from implicit social theories in at least two ways. First, implicit social theories are often unstated, so they are not subjected to the public scrutiny that formal social theories are. Second, formal social theories are based on logic and tested through research; implicit social theories usually are based on casual observation.

Another approach to understanding people's implicit theories is represented in the work of the psychologist George Kelly. In developing a cognitive theory of human behavior, Kelly was concerned about the links between perceptions and behavior. A crucial mediating link in this chain is our interpretation of the events and stimuli in our world. As Kelly (1955) asserts:

> [People] look at [their] world through transparent patterns or templates which [they] create and then attempt to fit over the realities of which the world is composed . . . Let us give the name constructs to these patterns that are tried on for size. They are ways of construing the world. [Vol. 1, pp. 8–9]

"Construct" is a key term for Kelly. A **construct** is a way of interpreting the world and a guide to behavior. Implicit personality theory itself is a construct that social psychologists devised to help interpret the manner in which people assume certain traits are related. Kelly's fundamental assumption is that we are all scientists who try to understand and predict events, and each of us tries in the same way to choose constructs that will make the world understandable and predictable. According to Kelly's theory, people's main motivation is not to strive for reinforcement in general or to avoid anxiety. Instead, they try to *validate their own construct systems;* that is, to obtain information that supports their view of the world. Further, Kelly has discarded the notion of an objective, absolute truth in favor of the phenomenological approach described in Chapter 1—conditions have meaning only as they are construed by the individual.

Such implicit theories and construct systems reflect our need to simplify and integrate information so as to deal effectively with the complexities of human interaction. Given a limited amount of information, we fill in details in order to make people and events more comprehensible. For example, when people are confronted with two essentially random events and are asked to imagine a link between them, they are more likely than not to believe that the events are indeed related (Anderson & Sechler, 1986). Implicit personality and social theories persist, even in the face of contradictory evidence, because people develop a rationale for the theories that they form (Anderson, Lepper, & Ross, 1980).

Schemas, Prototypes, and Scripts

Implicit theories and construct systems emphasize the various elements that enter into our judgments of other people. Among these elements are schemas, prototypes, and scripts, all of which are cognitive structures we use to interpret the world around us. The concepts of schema, prototype, and script are similar, but each represents a slightly different way in which information about people and places is organized.

The concept of a **schema** was defined in Chapter 1 as an organized configuration of knowledge, derived from past experience, that we use to interpret our current experience. One particular set of schemas, those related to the self, was discussed in Chapter 3. Just as we have schemas in regard to the self, we also have schemas in regard to other people. In fact, the two sorts of schema may be quite similar. The content of a self-schema also can be applied to other people (Fong & Markus, 1982; Markus, Smith, & Moreland, 1985). Although a great deal of recent attention has been devoted to schemas, the concept is not a new idea. The psychologist Sir Frederick Bartlett (1932), for example, introduced the term *schema* to refer to a way of representing the memory process, and even he was not the first to use the term.

You probably have a script on "eating in a restaurant" stored in your memory.
Alan Carey/The Image Works

Despite a certain vagueness that often makes it difficult to pin down, the concept of schema is useful for explaining how we form impressions and react to other people's behavior (Fiske & Taylor, 1984; Hastie, 1981). Part of the concept's vagueness is due to the existence of many forms of schemas. As we noted, some schemas concern the self. One may also have schemas concerning visual material; evaluating houses according to memories of one's childhood home is an example. Two other kinds of schemas—prototypes and scripts—are discussed in more detail in the following paragraphs.

A **prototype** is a collection of abstract features associated, to varying degrees, with a category (Cantor, 1981); that is, a prototype is a schema concerning a group of things or people. For any category you can think of—"rock star," for example—a set of characteristics may come to mind. You may consider some characteristics as likely for a rock star to have—a penchant for wild clothes and jewelry, for example. You may associate other characteristics with rock stars occasionally, but not so often—outrageous public behavior, for example. Like most social constructs, specific prototypes can change as one's experience with those representing the prototype change.

Prototypes can be associated with situations as well as with people (Cantor, Mischel, & Schwartz, 1982; Schutte, Kenrick, & Sadalla, 1985). Thus, you may associate a particular set of characteristics with a baseball field, a concert hall, or a dormitory room.

Prototypes can also operate at different levels of categorization. For example, under the general idea of ex-troversion, you may think of a comic or a public relations type. At an even more specific level, you may think of different types of comics—a circus clown, a stand-up comedian, or the practical joker in a local fraternity. Typically, people will use the level that provides the greatest differentiation between concepts while providing the most meaningful, or "richest," definition within concepts (Andersen & Klatzky, 1987).

Another specific kind of schema used to categorize our experiences is the **script** (sometimes called an event schema), defined as a "conceptual representation of a stereotyped event sequence" (Abelson, 1981, p. 715). To use a common example, consider a restaurant script. When you first enter a restaurant, your previous experience with restaurants, stored as a script, leads you to expect certain things to happen in a certain sequence: You will receive a menu from the waiter, decide what to order, place your order, and then wait for your food. At the beginning of a familiar event sequence, the script for that sequence is activated spontaneously, just as seeing your reflection in a mirror activates the self-schema.

Most people have dozens of scripts in their memory, perhaps hundreds. Of course, not all people share the same scripts. Some may have a "taking the car to a repair shop" script, for example, whereas others do not. Even when people have scripts for the same situation, the scripts are likely to differ in detail, depending on each person's experience in that situation. John Pryor and Thomas Merluzzi (1985) looked at one particular script for an experience that varies widely in detail

Table 4.3 The dating script according to Notre Dame students

1. Male arrives (55%).
2. Female greets male at the door (33%).
3. Conversation with date after arrival (43%).
4. Introduce date to parents or roommates and leave the house (36%).
5. Discuss where you will go (16%).
6. Talk about common interests: "small talk" (33%).
7. Go to a movie (43%).
8. Male buys refreshments at movie (16%).
9. Go to get something to eat and drink while talking (23%).
10. Male takes female home (65%).
11. Male walks female to door (20%).
12. Complimentary summary of evening (27%).
13. If interested ask to call/hope he asks to call again (53%).
14. Kiss (71%).
15. Say "good night" and thank date for the evening (34%).
16. Male returns home (25%).

Source: "The Role of Expertise in Processing Social Interaction Scripts" by J. B. Pryor and T. V. Merluzzi, 1985, *Journal of Experimental Social Psychology, 21,* pp. 362–379.

among individuals: the first-date script. Table 4.3 contains some elements of that script that were identified by students at Notre Dame. The figure in parentheses after each statement represents the percentage of students who mentioned that action. As you can see, the more general actions—male arrives, male takes female home, kiss—were noted by a majority of the subjects, whereas lower percentages for the more specific actions—discuss where to go, male buys refreshments—reflect individual differences concerning event sequences that make up the script.

Individuals also differ in their familiarity with a particular script. Those who have dated many people could be considered to have more expertise with the dating script than those who have had few dates. How would this difference in expertise be shown? Pryor and Merluzzi asked two groups of students, one consisting of men who had dated six or more women in the past year ("experts") and the other of men who had dated three

or fewer women ("novices"), to arrange in order a randomly listed set of statements from the dating script. Experts did the job faster, a finding that supports the idea that available schemas affect information processing.

Each of these concepts—schema, prototype, and script—is a way of representing our organization of social knowledge. All are considered important, not just because they are ways of organizing knowledge that we already have but because they affect future action as well. As we will see when we discuss social cognition processes, these categories influence us in a number of ways (Higgins & Bargh, 1987; Markus & Zajonc, 1985). Existing schemas, prototypes, and scripts affect how we interpret new information. They also affect our ability to remember events, the judgments we make about others, and our behavior concerning attempts to obtain additional information about others. Before discussing the process in more detail, we consider yet another way in which we organize information about others.

Stereotypes

A **stereotype** can be thought of as a schema about members of an identifiable group (Hamilton, 1979, 1981). Thus, when you see a person with red hair, your "red-haired person" schema (assuming you have one) is activated, and you may react to that person on the basis of your more general beliefs about and experiences with people with red hair instead of reacting to the person as an individual. Activation of a stereotype, as for most schemas, is automatic (Devine, 1989). That is, upon seeing someone with red hair, your beliefs about such people will come to mind. You may be able to ignore them, but the only way to prevent them from coming to mind is not to have a stereotype in the first place. However, avoiding stereotypes completely may not be possible, as we shall see later.

It was the journalist Walter Lippmann (1922) who first introduced the term *stereotype* to the social science literature, describing stereotypes as "pictures in our heads." In many respects, this idea of a picture or template is similar to the concept of schema. Yet, whereas the word *schema* is not pejorative, Lippmann viewed stereotypes in negative terms, seeing them as a means by which people protect their relative standing in society. In a society in which white people are dominant, for example, whites may use negative stereotypes of blacks to justify their social position. Psychoanalytic theorizing reinforced this idea of the stereotype as a defense mechanism, emphasizing stereotypes as products of unconscious needs and defensive drives. Work by Theodore Adorno and his colleagues (1950) on the authoritarian personality firmly placed stereotypes in the category of "bad things to have."

Stereotypes often contain negative elements. Many white people in the United States, for example, describe blacks in more negative terms than they do whites. In cognitive terms, we can say that, for such people, the schematic representation of blacks contains more negative elements than the schematic representation of whites does. How would one demonstrate this difference? One method that cognitive psychologists have developed relies on reaction time—the length of time it takes a person to respond to some kind of information. The assumption is that people will respond more quickly to information that fits a category already available in memory. In a study based on this assumption, John Dovidio and his colleagues asked people to decide whether a series of positive and negative adjectives did or did not apply to a black and a white person (Dovidio, Evans, & Tyler, 1986). Their results showed the predicted differences in reaction times. Subjects in the study (all white) responded more quickly to descriptors of positive traits in reference to a white person and to descriptors of negative traits in reference to a black person.

It would be a mistake, however, to assume that stereotypes are always negative. Some information they contain is positive, and some is neutral. A stereotype, like other cognitive categories, embraces the range of our information about a particular group and our associations with it (Andersen & Klatzky, 1987; Jussim, Coleman, & Lerch, 1987). Consider the stereotypes many people hold regarding women and men, for example. As Figure 4.3 shows, people are more likely to think that men are independent and competitive and that women are warm and emotional. None of these traits is necessarily bad, however. When you think about stereotypes, you should keep in mind the notion of probabilities, suggested by the concept of prototypes. For as Figure 4.3 also shows, people in general do not think it impossible that women are independent or that men are warm; rather, each trait is simply seen

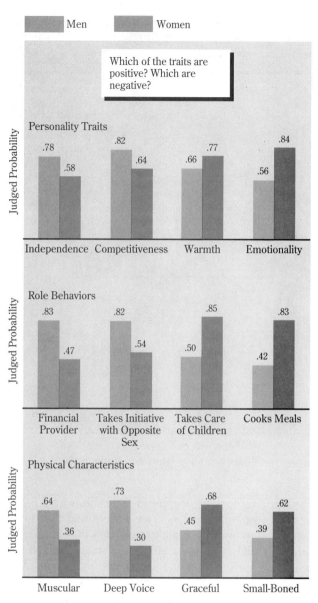

Figure 4.3 *Stereotypes of women and men.*
Source: "Components of Gender Stereotypes" by K. Deaux and L. L. Lewis, 1983, *Psychological Documents, 13,* p. 25. (Ms. No. 2583)

as more likely to occur in one gender than in the other (Deaux & Lewis, 1983).

In discussing person prototypes, we suggested that there are various levels of categorization—for example, an extroverted person, a comic, and a stand-up co-

Most people hold stereotypes of the elderly.
Left: Alan Carey/The Image Works. Right: Alan Zak

median. Stereotypes operate in the same way. In the case of gender stereotypes, we have found that four types of women come readily to people's minds: housewives, athletic women, businesswomen, and sexy women. Types of men that people frequently consider are businessmen, macho men, blue-collar working-men, and athletic men (Deaux, Winton, Crowley, & Lewis, 1985). Even more specific types of men and women may emerge on a college campus, such as fraternity and sorority members. Other groups are also differentiated; among the elderly, for example, we find the grandmother, the senior citizen, and the elder statesman (Brewer, Dull, & Lui, 1981).

Stereotypes, particularly those based on physical features, are easily developed and can have pervasive effects. In one series of studies, for example, researchers were able to create stereotypes about tall and short

people, and stereotypes about men and women, in less than a half hour. In their third experiment, Thomas Hill and his associates (Hill, Lewicki, Czyzewska, & Boss, 1989) showed their subjects six videotaped episodes, each less than two minutes long. For the relevant episodes, a voice-over indicated that the person was thinking about a self-related problem about which no one knew. To create the gender stereotype, half the subjects were shown episodes in which it was always a man who had the problem, and the other subjects saw episodes in which a woman had the problem. Before seeing the episodes, and again two weeks after viewing them, subjects rated the "sadness" (among other traits) of such people as their dating partner, a female and a male student they thought were particularly busy, and so on. Hill and his colleagues reasoned that subjects would incorporate the manipulated gender differences into a stereotype and that this stereotype would influence later judgments about men and women the subjects knew.

The results, illustrated in Figure 4.4, indicate that before the subjects saw the episodes, they believed men and women did not differ in sadness. That is, the subjects did not have any existing gender-specific stereotypes about sadness. After viewing the episodes, however, subjects who saw videotapes in which men were purported to be sad rated males they knew as sadder (higher scores reflect greater sadness) and women they knew as less sad. The opposite pattern of ratings was obtained from those who saw the episodes in which women were depicted as sad. Despite the fact that interviews indicated the subjects did not even notice whether men or women had more problems in the videotaped episodes, simply viewing the manipulated gender differences between *strangers* caused the subjects to alter their judgments about *people they knew.*

Sometimes, as we have just seen, stereotypic categories may form to account for social behaviors we have observed. At other times, however, stereotypic beliefs result from false inferences about what we have seen. Such is the case of the **illusory correlation,** defined as an overestimation of the strength of a relationship between two variables (Chapman, 1967). The variables in an illusory correlation may not be related at all, or the relationship may be much weaker than it is believed to be. One explanation for this kind of bias relates to the frequency or the distinctiveness of the events that we try to explain (Hamilton, 1981). If two types of information both occur infrequently, we will tend to make an association between them even if no real association exists.

In a demonstration of this bias, subjects were given a set of descriptive statements about a variety of people (Hamilton & Gifford, 1976). Two-thirds of these people were identified as members of group *A,* and the remaining third were identified as members of group *B.* In addition to their group identification, each person was described by a single behavior, either a desirable behavior (for example, "John visited a sick friend in the hospital") or an undesirable behavior (for example, "John always talks about himself and his problems"). Approximately two-thirds of the members of both group *A* and group *B* were described by positive behaviors, and about one-third by negative behaviors. Thus,

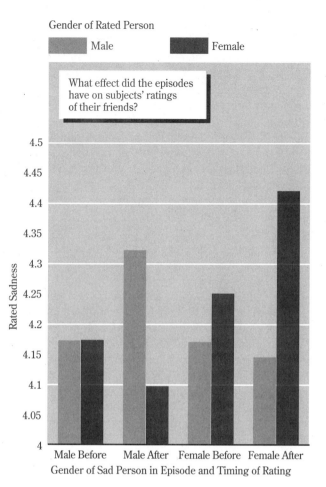

Gender of Rated Person

What effect did the episodes have on subjects' ratings of their friends?

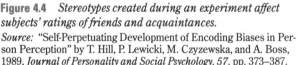

Figure 4.4 *Stereotypes created during an experiment affect subjects' ratings of friends and acquaintances.*
Source: "Self-Perpetuating Development of Encoding Biases in Person Perception" by T. Hill, P. Lewicki, M. Czyzewska, and A. Boss, 1989, *Journal of Personality and Social Psychology, 57,* pp. 373–387.

although the proportion of "nice" people was the same in both groups, group *B* contained fewer "nice" people because group *B* had fewer people in total. The subjects had two kinds of information—group membership and type of behavior—but no real association existed between these two variables. When asked to make judgments about the typical member of each group, subjects showed evidence of the illusory correlation. They liked group *B* less than they liked members of group *A,* evidence of a perceived link between frequencies. There were *fewer* people in group *B,* and there were *fewer* undesirable behaviors. Even though the proportions of undesirable behaviors were identical for the two groups, the less frequent group was linked with the less frequent behavior, and the subjects liked members of group *B* less.

The key component in forming illusory correlations is the distinctive character of the behaviors (Hamilton, Dugan, & Trolier, 1985). We pay more attention to events that we see infrequently simply because they are unusual. Put two such events together, and the distinctiveness is particularly great. If, for instance, the minority position on a political issue is voiced by a citizen of a small town, that association is more likely to be remembered than, say, the majority position voiced by a citizen of either a large or a small town, or a minority protest made by a citizen of the large town (Spears, van der Pligt, & Eiser, 1985).

As we suggested earlier, stereotypes affect our judgments and actions. Imagine, for example, you have been watching a debate between a black and a white candidate for political office. The black candidate appears to lose the debate, and the person sitting next to you takes that opportunity to make an ethnic slur on blacks in general. Would that slur affect your evaluation of the black candidate? That is, how different would your evaluation be from that made in a situation in which (a) the black candidate won or (b) you heard no ethnic slur? Jeff Greenberg and Tom Pyszczynski (1985) predicted that an ethnic slur uttered in such a situation would activate whatever negative stereotype of blacks was present and that one's evaluation of the black candidate would be lower with the slur than if the black candidate won the debate or no slur had been made. That is exactly what happened. It is important to note, however, that neither the ethnic slur alone nor the losing performance alone was sufficient to cause the black candidate to be judged more negatively than the white candidate. Once the stereotype was activated, however, the negative evaluation resulted.

Stereotypes are not based solely on individual experience. Stereotypes are also the product of social learning and, as Greenberg and Pyszczynski's (1985) experiment demonstrated, are supported through social learning. As children mature, they acquire information about categories of people that tend to be shared by members of their culture. In other words, an individual's categories may share many features with those categories other members of the society use.

The structure and content of our beliefs about members of recognizable groups come into play on numerous occasions. Later on, in discussing the ways in which groups of people interact (Chapter 13), we will again have occasion to consider stereotypes and their consequences. First, however, we must consider how information is actually processed.

▶ The Process of Social Cognition

Schemas, stereotypes, and similar concepts represent ways of thinking about the structure of social knowledge—an issue of *content* of social knowledge. The other questions that must be considered involve the process of acquiring and using social knowledge—how do we think about other people, how do the categories work, and how do we process information? We will consider the answers to these questions as we discuss a model of impression formation proposed by Susan Fiske and Steven Neuberg (1990). As we work our way through the model, illustrated in Figure 4.5, we will consider how existing information is used, how new information is stored, and some errors and biases that enter into the process along the way.

Initial Categorization

According to the model, the first part of the process involves spontaneously categorizing the target person, who could be someone we meet or someone we hear about from another source. That is, we immediately "pigeonhole" the person as belonging to one of the types of people that exist among our prototypes and stereotypes, and we do so without necessarily being aware of the process (Devine, 1989).

Why spontaneously categorize everyone? Some theorists have stated that we do so because we are "cognitive misers." That is, it is more efficient to think in terms of categories than to try to process all the information with which we are bombarded from moment to moment (Fiske & Taylor, 1984). Although efficiency may be part of the reason, Penelope Oakes and John Turner (1990) have argued that categorization is the way in which we are able to attach meaning to social stimuli. Merely categorizing someone as "a human being," for example, enables us to make inferences

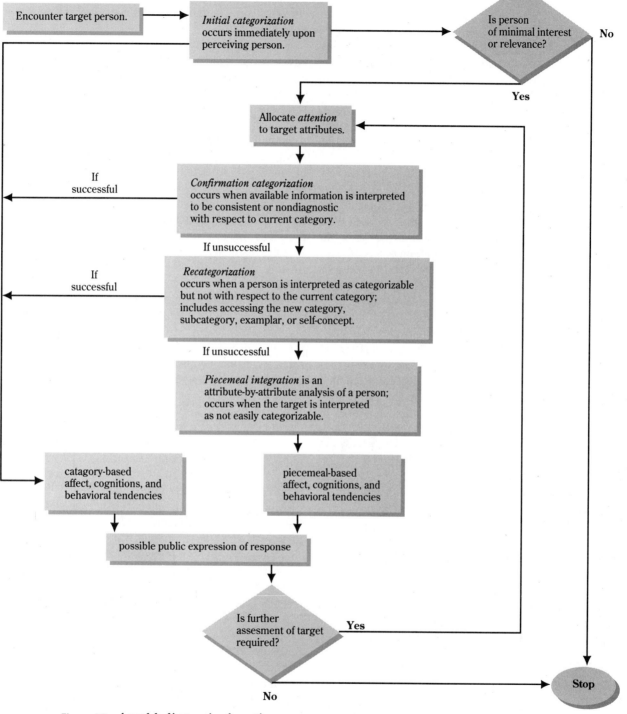

Figure 4.5 *A model of impression formation.*

Source: "A Continuum of Impression Formation, from Category-Based to Individuating Processes: Influences of Information and Motivation on Attention and Interpretation" by S. T. Fiske and S. L. Neuberg, 1990, *Advances in Experimental Social Psychology, 23,* pp. 1–74.

about the individual on the basis of our philosophies of human nature. Further categorization of the target person—in terms of gender, race, student or faculty status, and so on—activates stereotypes and schemas that provide additional information about the person. According to Oakes and Turner, categorization enables us to begin to interact with others on an expanded basis. Through categorization, "things we see" become transformed into "people" and other, more specific categories.

The level at which we categorize the target person, ranging from "human being" to "my friend Akimi," depends on characteristics to which our attention is drawn. Several factors can affect our attention and thus the schemas that are activated. One of these factors is the vividness or prominence of a person or event. **Vividness** refers to the intensity or emotional interest inherent in a stimulus (Fiske & Taylor, 1984). A movie filmed in color, for example, is more vivid than a black-and-white film. During categorization, our attention is drawn to more vivid stimuli. Emotional interest, in turn, suggests that the current state of the person forming the impression will also affect the categorization process. Elizabeth Loftus (1979), for example, has applied the term "weapon focus" to the tendency among eyewitnesses at a crime scene to focus their attention on the more vivid and more threatening weapon. Such focus reduces the subsequent accuracy with which victims and bystanders can identify the perpetrator (Loftus, Loftus, & Messo, 1987; Tooley, Brigham, Maass, & Bothwell, 1987). As a result, the person later identified, perhaps incorrectly, as the perpetrator may be someone who fits the witness's prototype of, say, a knife-wielding assailant instead of someone whose facial features match those of the individual holding the knife at the time the crime took place.

Less intense emotional and motivational factors can also affect the categorization process. Alice Isen and her colleagues have found, for example, that people create and use more general categories when they are in a positive mood than when their mood is more serious (Isen & Daubman, 1984). People asked to sort color chips into as many or as few categories as they wished created fewer categories when they had just viewed a funny film; subjects were more likely to say that such things as camels, feet, and elevators were good examples of the category "vehicle" after they had

viewed a comedy than after they had viewed a sobering documentary.

The distinctiveness of a stimulus or event also influences categorization. *Distinctiveness* refers to the degree to which a stimulus stands out in relation to its context. A 6'8" basketball player stands out in a roomful of people of average height and would be distinctive in that context, but not on a professional basketball court. A woman would be distinctive at an otherwise all-male meeting of a corporate board of directors but would not be readily distinguished at a professional-women's luncheon. Distinctive stimuli attract our attention by virtue of being different from their surroundings. Distinctive events are unexpected, generally not predictable on the basis of our prior knowledge. If a person or event is distinctive, we evaluate it more extremely and recall it more readily (Fiske & Taylor, 1984).

Categorization also can be affected by **priming.** As we saw in Chapter 3, priming refers to the effects of prior context on the retrieval of information. Thus, one is more likely to use a category if it has been activated recently; it is more accessible, more readily called to mind, than some other schemas that have not been primed by recent use (Higgins, Rholes, & Jones, 1977; Wyer & Srull, 1981). E. Tory Higgins and Gillian King (1981) distinguish between chronic and momentary accessibility. Momentary accessibility depends on the situation or the context. At school, Tom is much more likely to categorize people according to their majors than he is at work, where he is likely to categorize them according to their roles in the organization. Chronic accessibility, in contrast, involves the individual's own stable set of categories and beliefs. If Lisa is an active campaigner against smoking, she will be more likely than Pam, a heavy smoker, to remember and be able to retrieve information about the hazards of cigarettes. Lisa will have referred to that particular category so frequently that it will be readily accessible in her memory.

Although a variety of factors affect the category first employed in the impression formation process, Fiske and Neuberg's point is that categorization *will* occur; it cannot be avoided. If the target is of little interest or relevance, the impression formation process ends. We might, for example, do little more than say to ourselves, "Hmmm, another engineering major," and shift our attention to someone or something else. On the other hand, if the person merits further consideration, we begin to pay attention to attributes other than those that prompted the initial categorization. How deeply into the impression formation process we delve before producing some sort of response to the target person depends on the fit between these attributes and the initial category; this brings us to the second phase in the model.

Confirmatory Biases

If the person's additional attributes are consistent with the category into which we have placed the target, no further formation of our impression is necessary. For example, a 6'8" man wearing a basketball uniform and signing basketballs for children probably would not require much additional attention. We might stop the impression *formation* process and respond to him as we would to any basketball player. But what would happen if the person's other attributes did not fit so neatly into the category, or if we were motivated to find out more about the person?

When we have already categorized someone, how we encode additional information about the person will be influenced by categorical expectancies (Higgins & Bargh, 1987). We tend to encode events that fit into an existent category as additional evidence of the validity of that representation. We may even seek out behavioral evidence that supports our categorization. Such confirmatory biases were discussed in Chapter 3 with respect to maintaining one's self-concept, but they apply equally well to confirming one's impressions about others. Consider, for example, the Darley and Gross (1983) experiment discussed in Chapter 2, in which subjects' ratings of the academic potential of a girl named Hannah were affected by what they believed to be Hannah's socioeconomic status. The scenes of Hannah's impoverished or suburban environment presumably called to mind an initial categorization of "poor person" or "rich person," respectively, and the inferences associated with such category labels. When the subjects later received information about Hannah's performance on achievement tests, the subjects confirmed their initial categorization. Those who categorized Hannah as "poor" predicted much lower levels of academic achievement than those who categorized her as "rich," despite having seen exactly the same achievement test performance. Presumably, subjects sought, and found,

information in the videotape of Hannah's performance that confirmed their initial categorization.

Other goals in a situation also influence the way we attempt to confirm our initial categorization. Imagine that you are given a written description of a person named Wanda. First you read the description to yourself; then you are asked to describe Wanda to a Mr. Jones. Now add one other detail. You are told either that Mr. Jones likes Wanda or that he dislikes her. Would this information affect not only what you said about Wanda but the impression you actually coded in memory about her? Yes, if your behavior is anything like that of the subjects studied by Higgins and Douglas McCann (1984). Either immediately or several days later, subjects remembered the individual more positively when they had tailored their description to suit someone who liked her. Categorizing Wanda as "someone Mr. Jones likes" influenced the subjects' judgments about Wanda's other attributes.

Recategorization

In some circumstances, confirmatory biases cannot resolve the apparent lack of fit between one's initial categorization and the target person's specific attributes. When such a mismatch occurs, we attempt to develop more specific beliefs about certain types of individuals within that general category; that is, we create subcategories. If you met a husband who did all the family's cooking, for example, you might develop a stereotypic category for "gourmet chefs" or "men who are married to professional women who can't cook." The more deviant the observed individual is from the general stereotype of his or her category, the more likely subtypes are to form (Deaux & Lewis, 1984; Weber & Crocker, 1983).

Recategorization can also be prompted when the additional attributes are irrelevant to the initial category (Locksley, Hepburn, & Ortiz, 1982). This usually occurs when the initial category is not very strong, such as a recently formed stereotype or one based on social rather than physical attributes. The process, sometimes called *dilution* of a stereotype, is not well understood and does not occur with just any irrelevant attributes (Fiske & Neuberg, 1990). However, there is some research support (for example, Hilton & Fein, 1989) for the notion that attributes useful in a variety of judgmen-

tal situations (intelligence, for example) can prompt recategorization.

Information Integration

Despite the pervasiveness of categorization, instances occur in which we encounter someone whose attributes simply do not fit neatly into any of our existing categories, stereotypes, or schemas. In other instances, such as interviewing job applicants or evaluating dating partners, we may be motivated to make our specific predictions about behavior as accurate as possible and be unwilling to rely solely on categories. In either case, Fiske and Neuberg propose that we integrate single attributes and react to that person as an individual (sometimes called an *individuated* response). That is, we consider each attribute or behavior separately and build an impression of the person "piece by piece."

Although other models have been developed to explain how individual pieces of social information are combined, most of the research evidence supports Norman Anderson's (1965, 1974) *weighted averaging model.* Essentially, the model proposes that we attach some positive or negative value to a particular attribute, assign a weight to the attribute, and combine all the weighted attributes to arrive at an average score for the person. Although it sounds complicated, a weighted average model is what is used to determine your grade point average. First, a value is assigned to each of your grades (A = 4, B = 3, C = 2, D = 1, F = 0). Each value is then weighted according to the number of credit hours assigned to the course; an "A" in a 3-credit course earns $4 \times 3 = 12$ grade points, and a "C" in a 5-

credit course earns $2 \times 5 = 10$ grade points. The grade points for all the courses you have taken are summed, and then, finally, the grade point average is obtained by dividing that sum by the number of credit hours you have taken.

The notion of a weighted average reflects the fact that some traits have more influence on our impressions in some situations than in others. The qualities that interest you in a potential roommate, for example, may have no relevance to your assessment of someone you hire to mow your lawn. Where do the weights come from? John Skowronski and Donal Carlston (1989) have proposed that behaviors with the greatest diagnostic value for inferring a particular trait will be given the greatest weight in the weighted averaging process. Imagine, for example, you are trying to decide whether Mavis is honest or dishonest—traits that rank very high and very low, respectively, in Table 4.1. Suppose Mavis tells you your new haircut looks good. She could be either telling the truth or lying. Even if she is lying, she may just be trying to spare your feelings. Such behavior does not have much diagnostic value because it is not very useful for categorizing Mavis as honest or dishonest, so you would not assign a large weight to that particular behavior. On the other hand, suppose Mavis tells an instructor she cannot take a test because there was a death in her family when you know she merely wanted to leave a day early for spring break. Such behavior has more diagnostic value—honest people do not lie for selfish purposes—and should carry greater weight. Irrelevant behaviors, such as Mavis arriving on time for class every day, do not carry much weight because they have no diagnostic value; honest people are not necessarily any more or less prompt than dishonest people.

Whether we begin to weigh each attribute or behavior separately—that is, we reach the level of piecemeal integration in Fiske and Neuberg's (1990) model—will determine whether we react to someone as "the waiter" or as "Tom." If we are in a hurry or there is nothing particularly striking about Tom, categorizing him as a waiter and following the restaurant script is likely to serve our purpose very well. As we notice things about Tom during the meal, we will interpret those attributes so that they are consistent with our stereotype about waiters and their role. If one of Tom's attributes is inconsistent with our waiter prototype—for example, he tells us not to leave a tip—we might develop a subcategory of waiters but still respond to Tom as "a waiter." We are not likely to respond to Tom as "Tom" unless he defies categorization—perhaps he has a Ph.D. in computer science and is second violinist in the symphony—or we are motivated to predict his behavior outside the role of waiter—perhaps he mentions that he also works at the day-care center our children attend.

Errors and Biases

Fiske and Neuberg's model of the impression formation process may seem to suggest that the process proceeds orderly and logically, but such is not the case. In fact, a host of biases, shortcuts, and misplaced assumptions influence our interpretation of social life. In Chapter 3, for example, we introduced one type of bias, **confirmatory bias**—the tendency to seek information that is consistent with one's beliefs. Confirmatory bias applies as well to confirming beliefs about the self as it does to confirming beliefs about others. In this section we discuss two other types of bias: heuristics and false consensus bias.

Heuristics   We have already noted that impressions and judgments about people are often formed on the basis of very little information. One way this occurs is through the use of **heuristics**, defined as shortcuts or rules of thumb we use to make judgments for which we have insufficient or uncertain information (Tversky & Kahneman, 1974, 1980). Like initial categorization, heuristics are cognitive processes that enable us to

glean more information (often incorrectly) from a situation. They are part of the routine business of social perception and judgment.

In particular, consider two heuristics that Amos Tversky and Daniel Kahneman (1974) have identified: the representativeness heuristic and the availability heuristic. The **representativeness heuristic** refers to our tendency to consider some events more representative of the total population than they are. Suppose, for example, you are told two tests for intelligence exist; one test requires an hour to administer, and the other requires only ten minutes. In which test would you have greater confidence? If you are like most people, you chose the longer test (Tversky & Kahneman, 1980). As we explained in Chapter 2, however, a longer measurement instrument is not necessarily a more valid one. But, using the representativeness heuristic, you might have reasoned that most valid intelligence tests are long and thereby placed your faith in the longer test. The correct solution is to place equal confidence in the two tests until you receive additional information about each test's reliability and validity. Consider another example: You are given information about Henry, who belongs to a club whose membership consists of twenty-five engineers and five artists. Henry is described as flamboyant, creative, bearded, and rarely seen in a suit. Is Henry an engineer or an artist? Although the odds (5 to 1) suggest that Henry is probably an engineer, most people peg Henry as an artist. Again, information about base rate or overall distribution tends to be ignored in favor of one's own beliefs about people and the perceived similarities of their behavior.

The **availability heuristic** refers to our tendency to be biased by events that are readily accessible in our memory; it might better be called the "accessibility heuristic." If you were asked whether the average musician is rich or poor, for example, what would you say? If you have seen a lot of rock concerts or read about the lavish lifestyle of popular musicians, you might be inclined to answer "rich." If, however, you had more experience hanging around the musicians' union hall and listening to stories of unemployment, your answer might be "poor." However, the "average" musician probably has an "average" income, so the best answer to the question is neither "rich" nor "poor." In a very different illustration of the availability heuristic, consider the widespread publicity in the United States that initially linked acquired immune deficiency syndrome (AIDS) with gay men. The accessibility of that publicity led many people to assume anyone infected with the human immunodeficiency virus (HIV) must be gay. Thus, Christian Crandall (1991a) found that people who contract HIV through heterosexual relations report feeling *more* stigmatized than do people infected through homosexual relations. That is, heterosexuals with HIV may feel odd and embarrassed by the threat to their self-concept that stems from their own beliefs about the link between HIV and homosexuality. In contrast, heterosexuals who are not infected with HIV do not report negative reactions toward infected heterosexuals, although they have strong negative reactions toward infected homosexuals (Crandall, 1991b). Thus, the bias introduced by the early, memorable publicity concerning AIDS influences people's reactions to present events through the availability heuristic.

Of course, people can avoid using heuristics, particularly when they are aware of the advantages of avoiding them (Nisbett, Krantz, Jepson, & Kunda, 1983). When people are asked to estimate the distribution of other people's beliefs and attitudes, for example, they often can judge the general range of such attitudes quite accurately (Nisbett & Kunda, 1985).

False consensus bias Although people generally can judge the range of others' opinions on an issue, they also tend to think that other people are more similar to themselves than is actually the case. This tendency to believe that many others share our attitudes and behaviors is called the **false consensus bias.** We tend to consider our own behaviors and judgments as quite common and appropriate and to view alternative responses as uncommon, inappropriate examples of extreme ends of a range (Ross, Greene, & House, 1977). This bias is evident even in regard to simple, minor issues. College students who preferred brown bread, for instance, estimated that 52% of students also prefer brown bread; students who preferred white bread estimated that only 37% of others prefer brown bread. Although some people have suggested that this egocentric bias may be a self-presentation strategy—an attempt to demonstrate that one is like others—the evidence suggests that it is basically a cognitive and perceptual error (Mullen et al., 1985).

We often seek answers for why *people behave as they do.*
Ajit Kumar/AP/Wide World Photos

▶ Explaining Behavior: Attributions of Causality

Thus far, we have described social cognition in terms of the content of impressions and the process by which those impressions come about—the *what* and *how* of impression formation. But social knowledge involves more than assigning trait descriptions to people; it includes attempting to understand *why* people behave the way they do (Weiner, 1985b). Why did Amy move to the country? Why did Tony quit the football team? As we have seen, understanding the answers people might give for such questions requires knowing something about the content and the process of social knowledge. It also requires knowing something about the way in which people engage in **causal attribution**—the process of explaining or inferring the causes of events.

In Chapter 3 we considered the process of causal attribution as it operates in our attempts to explain our own behavior and outcomes. The same general principles apply when we consider how we explain the behavior of other individuals. In their simplest form, causal attributions consist of distinguishing between *dispositional* (or personal) causes and *situational* (or environmental) causes, as Fritz Heider (1958) first suggested. Yet this distinction, although quite useful, is too simple to describe the sometimes elaborate explanations that people devise. More recent theorists have offered several detailed models that attempt to map the causal attribution process.

Before discussing those theories, however, we must caution you that we and other social psychologists have taken some liberties in the language we use. You will read in the following discussion and elsewhere about making dispositional attributions and situational attributions. At first glance, the language seems to convey that people make *either/or* decisions. That notion is due more to ease of communication than to direct implication. As John Medcof (1990) has so strongly argued, attributions are best understood as statements of probability: The *most probable* reason Amy moved to the country is her love of fresh air (high dispositional probability); the *most probable* reason Tony quit the football team is his father's losing his job (high situational probability). But such language is awkward, so we use the simpler terminology for the sake of convenience.

Covariation and Causal Schemas

Harold Kelley (1967, 1972, 1973; Kelley & Michela, 1980) has proposed that we try to explain events in much the same way a scientist would; armed with a series of observations of people's behavior, we try to figure out what might be responsible for a particular action. One difference, of course, is that scientists are likely to test their explanations through controlled research. In everyday causal attribution, we rarely test our explanations. Instead, we rely on the principle of *covariation,* in which "an effect is attributed to the one of its possible causes with which, over time, it varies" (Kelley, 1967, p. 108). Recall that apparent covariation between traits and group members is also one basis for developing stereotypes—descriptions of behavior—through illusory correlations. Kelley proposed the same process applies to how we explain behavior in everyday circumstances—we look for a systematic pattern of relationships and infer cause and effect from

that pattern. This model obviously assumes that we have more than one opportunity to observe a particular person and that we have observed other people in similar situations as well.

Building on Heider's general distinction between dispositional and situational causes, Kelley has pointed to three general types of explanations that people may offer when they try to interpret someone's behavior: an attribution to the *actor,* or the person who is engaging in the behavior in question; an attribution to the *entity,* or the target of the actor's behavior; and an attribution to the *circumstances,* or the particular setting in which the behavior occurs (Kelley, 1967). Thus, if Susan runs away from Joe at a restaurant, we might attribute the event to something about Susan ("She is basically a hysterical person"), to something about Joe ("He is an insulting boor"), or to the particular circumstances ("The food was terrible and made Susan sick").

Each of these explanations is reasonable, but people are generally motivated to decide on one as *the* explanation. Kelley suggests that to reach this decision we use three basic kinds of information: consensus, consistency, and distinctiveness. **Consensus** information consists of our knowledge about the behavior of other actors in the same situation. If everyone in the restaurant jumped up and ran out, we would say the behavior had high consensus; if Susan ran out alone, her behavior would have low consensus. The second source of information, **consistency,** is our knowledge about the actor's behavior on other occasions. Does Susan habitually run out of restaurants and out of movies and concerts as well, or is this the only time that she has done so? Finally, one can use distinctiveness as a source of information. **Distinctiveness** is concerned with the variation in the actor's behavior with respect to different entities, or targets. Does Susan run away only from Joe, or has she also run away from Rita, Peter, and Lila on other occasions?

Kelley suggests that if we have information about each of these three factors, our causal explanations will be quite predictable. These predictable explanations, which have been confirmed by subsequent research (Major, 1980; McArthur, 1972; Orvis, Cunningham, & Kelley, 1975), are outlined in Table 4.4. Depending on the particular combination of information we have about the people involved, we will explain the event by attributing it to the actor, to the entity, or to the circum-

Table 4.4 Kelley's model of attribution: Why did Professor Martinez (actor) criticize Paul (entity)?

- Attributions are made to the actor when:

  Consensus is low.
  Consistency is high.
  Distinctiveness is low.

  Example: No other professors criticize Paul (low consensus); Professor Martinez criticized Paul last year, last month, and twice last week (high consistency); and Professor Martinez criticized every other student in the class as well (low distinctiveness). Conclusion: The behavior is attributed to Professor Martinez—for example, "Professor Martinez is a mean professor."

- Attributions are made to the entity when:

  Consensus is high.
  Consistency is high.
  Distinctiveness is high.

  Example: Every other professor criticizes Paul (high consensus); Professor Martinez criticized Paul last year, last month, and twice last week (high consistency); and Professor Martinez was friendly to all the other members of the class (high distinctiveness). Conclusion: The behavior is attributed to Paul—for example, "Paul is stupid and lazy."

- Attributions are made to the circumstances when:

  Consistency is low.

  Example: Professor Martinez has never criticized Paul before (low consistency). Conclusion: The behavior is attributed to a particular set of circumstances rather than to Paul or to Professor Martinez—for example, "Paul said something today that Professor Martinez misinterpreted."

stances. When the pattern of information is less clear than that outlined in the table, we may base our explanations on some combination of these three factors.

Consensus, consistency, and distinctiveness are the main ingredients of Kelley's model of the attribution process, but they are not the only ingredients. The covariation model also includes what has become known as the **augmentation principle:** "When there are known to be constraints, costs, sacrifices or risks involved in taking an action, the action once taken is attributed more to the actor than it would be otherwise" (Kelley, 1973, p. 114). That is, when a behavior is diffi-

cult to perform, we assume the actor is responsible for the behavior. For example, the risk inherent in Boris Yeltsin's resistance to the unsuccessful coup d'état by "hardliners" during August 1991 in the USSR led many people to credit him with foiling the coup. Hundreds of thousands of Soviet citizens also resisted the coup, but Yeltsin's prominence placed him at greater risk; therefore, many people attributed Yeltsin's behavior to his disposition rather than to pressure from his aides or some other situational cause.

Although the covariation model has a kind of precise elegance, it is clearly an idealized model. Often the information the model requires is not available: We may not have observed a person on previous occasions, or we may not know how other people have behaved in the same situation. What do we do in such cases? Kelley suggests that we rely on causal schemas. According to Kelley, a **causal schema** is "a conception of the manner in which two or more causal factors interact in relation to a particular kind of effect" (1972, p. 152). (A causal schema is one particular kind of social theory.) Our observations of people lead us to develop certain beliefs about causes and effects. We then explain a particular person's behavior on the basis of those beliefs. In other words, Kelley is suggesting that in the absence of all possible information about one person in one situation, we rely on general beliefs when we attempt to explain a particular behavior.

As one example of a causal schema, consider the *multiple sufficient-cause* schema. According to this schema, when we decide that any number of factors may be responsible for a particular event, the factor we select will depend on the information we have available. Again using Susan's hasty exit from the restaurant as an example, if Susan looked angry, we might decide Joe is the cause of the event. If Susan looked disgusted, but Joe did not, we might decide it was something she ate (or didn't want to eat). Either attribution would be sufficient to explain the event. The existence of more than one sufficient cause, however, often results in **discounting,** a reduction in the importance of any one cause by the presence of other plausible causes. Thus, because Susan's behavior reasonably could be attributed to Susan, Joe, or the food, we are less likely to place blame for the incident on one particular cause.

In other cases, we apply a *multiple necessary-cause* schema. In this schema, at least two causes are neces-

In a multiple necessary-cause schema, more than one cause explains an event. Why are these people smiling?

sary to explain the event. Often we apply the multiple necessary-cause schema to explain fairly extreme events. For example, if both Susan and Joe looked angry, we might conclude *they* had an argument. It takes two to start an argument, as the saying goes, so both Joe and Susan caused her departure. In this case two causes are needed to explain an effect.

In summary, causal schemas are a kind of shorthand. If we have unlimited information, the covariation model may represent our inference processes accurately. But in many situations we try to explain events without having all the information, and in such cases we will rely on a causal schema to make sense of the behavior we observe.

Correspondent Inference

In our attempts to explain the events that occur around us, we do, as the covariation and causal schema models suggest, make a general distinction between dispositional and situational causes. Beyond this general process, however, we also make very specific attributions

about the personal characteristics of the actor. At the very least, according to our earlier discussion of the impression formation process, we categorize the participants (Fiske & Neuberg, 1990). Edward Jones and his colleagues (Jones & Davis, 1965; Jones & McGillis, 1976) have proposed correspondent inference theory to explain the way we infer the intentions and characteristics of the actor once we have decided that the actor is the cause of the behavior. That is, the theory deals with the decisions we make about which intentions correspond to someone's behavior.

According to correspondent inference theory, the potential consequences of a behavior are important considerations in our decisions about the intentions of an actor. For example, if you see John (a sales manager) give Maria (the vice-president) a bouquet of flowers at the office, your decision about which potential consequence John intended will affect your attributions about John. You may decide, for instance, that John's intention was simply to make Maria happy. Then again, you may decide that John is trying to curry favor to get a promotion, a raise, or some other benefit Maria controls. A third possibility is that John may be trying to enhance his reputation as a "nice person."

How do we decide which consequence was the intended consequence? One way is to focus on the **noncommon effect,** defined as a consequence that could only be achieved by the specific manner in which the behavior was performed (Newtson, 1974). If John wanted to make Maria happy or curry favor, for example, he could have produced the same effect by bringing the flowers to Maria's home. The noncommon effect, in this case, is enhancing his reputation among the other employees; only by giving Maria flowers at the office could John be sure that the other employees would know about his "niceness." In general, the consequence chosen as the intended consequence is the one with the fewest noncommon effects.

A second way in which we attribute dispositional characteristics to the behavior of others is through our initial expectations. Unexpected actions or out-of-role behaviors, for example, are likely to be attributed to some characteristics of the actor (Jones, Davis, & Gergen, 1961). Also, any unexpected event is likely to be examined in some detail and to prompt a search for explanations (Hastie, 1984). Thus, if someone does something quite divergent from what we expect, we are much more likely to wonder why the event happened and to seek an explanation in the personality of the actor. If we are familiar with the setting in which this unexpected event occurs, person attributions are apt to be particularly strong (Lalljee, Watson, & White, 1982). For example, the action of someone who comes into your room and recites Hamlet's soliloquy is much more likely to invoke a dispositional attribution than the same behavior at a party in an unfamiliar locale (unless you are an actor, accustomed to dramatic monologues recited in your room).

We form two basic kinds of expectancies. The first, *category-based expectancies,* are assumptions we make based on the individual's membership in a particular group or category. Stereotypes, discussed earlier, are one form of such category-based expectancies. If we assume that most men are not gentle, then we would probably take particular note of a man who was playing gently with children, and we would tend to attribute his behavior to something special about his personality. *Target-based expectancies* are based on information we

have about a particular individual. For example, having seen Lionel behave gently with many children on many occasions, we would probably expect Lionel to be gentle, no matter what our expectations of men in general might be.

A third influence on our attributions is the extent to which the behavior of others affects us. Jones and Davis (1965) have noted stronger tendencies to make dispositional attributions when the behavior of others is rewarding or costly to the person making the attribution. To the extent that Anna's behavior has a direct effect on you, you are more likely to attribute causality to Anna than you would be if her actions did not affect you. Similarly, if you even suspect someone intended to influence you with his or her behavior, your attributions will be more strongly dispositional. When others' behaviors affect us, we are more strongly motivated to determine what dispositional characteristics caused the behavior.

You may notice some overlap between Kelley's covariance model and Jones's correspondent inference model. Category-based and target-based expectancies, for example, are very similar to Kelley's respective concepts of consensus and consistency. Both category-based expectancies and consensus involve information we have about a group of people, from which we may infer the causes of a particular person's behavior. Similarly, target-based expectancies and consistency both rely on our information about the particular actor. Jones's correspondent inference theory, however, takes us one step further in the process of explaining behavior, from pointing generally to something about the person to labeling the specific traits that we believe to be responsible.

Overestimating dispositional causes   If it seems as though correspondence inference theory has a decidedly dispositional bent, you are correct. That emphasis results from the fact that the theory was developed to explain how people make attributions about others: among people from Western cultures, the way attributions about others are made does, in fact, have a decidedly dispositional bent. Jones and Harris (1967), for example, demonstrated that students who knew that an essay author had been *assigned* to take a particular political position nevertheless made inferences about the author's attitudes from the essay content. In recognition of its pervasiveness, the tendency to emphasize dispositional causes for the behavior of others has been called the **fundamental attribution bias** (Fiske & Taylor, 1984; Ross & Fletcher, 1985).

As an example of this bias, imagine yourself watching a quiz show in which a woman is asked to make up questions and a man is asked to answer them. The questioner, drawing on her own area of expertise, poses a difficult set of questions, and the respondent is only moderately successful in providing answers. If you were asked to judge the general intellectual ability of each contestant, whom would you rate more favorably? If you are like the subjects in an experiment conducted by Ross, Amabile, and Steinmetz (1977), you would probably rate the questioner as more intelligent than the respondent. Yet in making this judgment you would be neglecting an important situational factor—the control and choice assigned to the questioner. The questioner was able to select particular areas and avoid others; it's easier to ask questions than it is to answer them. Had the roles in the situation been reversed so that the woman became the respondent and the man became the questioner, the man might well have displayed similar finesse, and your judgments of intelligence would have been reversed. Ross and his colleagues point out the pervasiveness of this particular bias in judgments of the powerful and the powerless: we tend to overestimate the capability of those in power, forgetting to consider the role requirements that give the powerful an advantage over the powerless.

How pervasive is the fundamental attribution bias? According to Daniel Gilbert (1989), it is as automatic as initial categorization in the impression formation process: We cannot avoid making a dispositional attribution; we can only attempt to amend it after we have made it. Gilbert and his colleagues (Gilbert & Krull, 1988; Gilbert, Krull, & Pelham, 1988; Gilbert, Pelham, & Krull, 1988) demonstrated in a series of experiments that distractions and other tasks designed to occupy thinking produced more extreme fundamental attribution biases than those in undistracted conditions. Gilbert argues that the *very first* attribution we make is dispositional—we automatically blame (or credit) the actor. After the automatic attribution, we may consider information such as Kelley's consensus or Jones's non-

common effects and alter our initial attribution. Thus, situational attributions come about only as "second" thoughts.

The primacy of dispositional attributions for the behaviors of others is very strong. Daniel Gilbert and Edward Jones (1986), for example, had subjects press a button to prompt a male "target" to read either a conservative or a liberal statement concerning a variety of different issues. The procedure was such that some subjects told the target to make predominantly liberal statements, and others told the target to make predominantly conservative statements. Later, the subjects were asked to judge the political opinions of the target. Despite the fact that the subjects were telling the target which statement to read, those who heard the target read conservative statements thought he was more conservative than did subjects who heard the target read liberal statements. As is illustrated in Figure 4.6, this effect was obtained for ratings both of the target's general political views (general rating) and of the target's views about the issues specifically mentioned (all items). On four occasions, the statement the target read was exactly the same, regardless of whether the subject told the target to read a conservative or a liberal statement. Even on these issues (constant items), the subjects thought the conservative target was more conservative. That is, we tend to make a dispositional attribution about the behavior of another person even when we are the primary influence on that person. Apparently, the fundamental attribution bias can be overcome only when additional, objective information convinces us that the other person could not possibly be the cause of the behavior (Miller & Lawson, 1989).

What accounts for the fundamental attribution bias? One explanation, suggest Jellison and Green (1981), is that people in Western society tend to have a strong belief in personal responsibility. We believe people should be held accountable for their own outcomes. Internally caused outcomes are therefore valued, whereas externally caused ones are disparaged. It may be that such strong values lead us to automatically hold people accountable—that is, to make dispositional attributions—and then to consider alternative explanations.

Although there appears to be consistency across a wide variety of cultures in terms of the content and

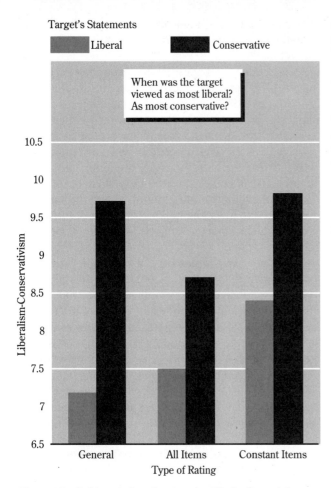

Target's Statements

■ Liberal   ■ Conservative

When was the target viewed as most liberal? As most conservative?

Figure 4.6 *Subjects inferred a target's attitudes from statements they told him to make.*

Source: "Perceiver-Induced Constraint: Interpretations of Self-Generated Reality" by D. T. Gilbert and E. E. Jones, 1986, *Journal of Personality and Social Psychology, 50,* pp. 269–280.

structure of values (Schwartz & Bilsky, 1990), evidence also exists that cultures vary in the extent to which they place importance on certain values. For example, in a cross-cultural study comparing Americans and Indians, Joan Miller (1984) found that as American children grew older (and perhaps internalized the value of accountability), they increasingly referred to internal dispositions in their explanations of outcomes. Hindu children of India, in contrast, tended to base their

explanations on situational context. Thus, the fundamental attribution bias may be fundamental only in Western culture.

The Actor-Observer Effect   Edward Jones and Richard Nisbett (1972) proposed that differences in the attentional focus of actors and observers should produce different attributions about the causes of the actor's behavior. As observers, we pay more attention to the actor's behavior than to the surrounding context (Heider, 1958). An actor, however, is more likely to pay attention to the surrounding context. Because people rely on what they have observed more closely when they make judgments, Jones and Nisbett suggested there should be an **actor-observer effect:** actors should weigh the situation more heavily when explaining their behavior, and observers should weigh the actor's dispositions more heavily when explaining the same behavior. The "observer" portion of this effect is, of course, the result of the fundamental attribution bias.

Do actors' attributions differ from observers' attributions as a result of differential attention focus? Through an ingenious experiment, Michael Storms (1973) provided a resounding yes. He asked pairs of subjects (the actors) to carry on a conversation that was shown to another pair of subjects (the observers) via closed-circuit television. When the subjects rated the conversations, the actors weighed the situation as more influential, but observers considered the conversation to be influenced more heavily by the actors' dispositions; the actor-observer effect occurred. Then Storms shifted the actors' attentional focus by showing them a videotape of their conversation. When these actors-turned-observers rated the conversation from this vantage point, their ratings indicated stronger dispositional attributions. The shift in attention created a change in the actors' attributions concerning their own behavior.

Why do actors-turned-observers change their attributions? One reason involves the process of self-focus, discussed in Chapter 3. Generally, we focus attention more often on the situation than on ourselves. Watching oneself on a videotape, however, prompts the self-focus process (Gibbons, 1990). During this process, we interpret our behavior so as to confirm our self-concept

(Steele, 1988; Tesser, 1988). Thus, an actor-turned-observer is not just any observer; he or she is a self-aware actor. If self-aware actors' behaviors are consistent with their self-concept, their attributions will be about as dispositional as any other observer's attributions. On the other hand, when self-aware actors' behaviors are not consistent with their self-concept, their attributions will be situational; they will interpret their behavior in a way that enables them to affirm their self-concept. We can speculate that if the subjects in Storms's study were videotaped doing something out of the ordinary—some behavior that did not fit their self-concept—then their ratings probably would not have become more dispositional. Thus, the actor-observer effect enables us to understand why two people in the same situation can arrive at different explanations for what happened.

Causes of Success and Failure

Bernard Weiner has developed a model of attribution that concerns a much more specific area of behavior than the models of Kelley and Jones. Weiner's model deals with the explanations we arrive at for people's success and failure at particular tasks (Weiner, 1974, 1979, 1985a; Weiner et al., 1972). Why was Linda promoted so quickly? Why did David flunk the calculus exam? How we answer such questions is what Weiner attempts to explain in his model.

Like Kelley's and Jones's models, Weiner's basic model rests on a foundation established by Heider. Weiner bases his model on three independent dimensions: locus of causality, stability, and controllability. **Locus of causality** refers to the extent to which an individual's behavior results from dispositional (internal) or situational (external) influences. **Stability,** in contrast, concerns the extent to which the cause of a behavior can change. One's mood, for example, is unstable in that it is usually temporary, whereas intelligence is generally considered as stable. **Controllability** refers to the extent to which an individual has the power to change a cause of behavior. The amount of training or preparation one has for a specific task, for example, is generally viewed as something an individual can control by increasing it, whereas the difficulty of the task is typically considered to be outside the control of the individual

Ability is a stable cause of success, but so are preparation and training.
David Jones/Topham/The Image Works

performing it. Weiner suggests that these three dimensions are independent of one another and that we use them to understand our own successes and failures (as discussed in Chapter 3) and those of others. As abstract dimensions, locus, stability, and controllability each can be represented by a variety of possible explanations. Ability is a stable cause, but so are preparation, training, task difficulty, and so forth. Yet, when these different concrete explanations have been subjected to statistical analyses designed to assess the extent to which they "go together," Weiner's three dimensions receive considerable research support (Russell, 1982; Vallerand & Richer, 1988).

The dimensions also have different consequences for future behavior. The stability dimension is most important in the formation of expectancies, or predictions of how someone will do in the future under similar circumstances (Valle & Frieze, 1976). For example, if we believe that Linda's excellent job performance was due to something stable, such as her ability or the ease of the assignment, we would expect her to do well again if she were given the same assignment. If we decide that the reason for her success was something temporary, such as a fleeting good mood or pure chance, we would be less confident of her future success. The same principles hold when we try to explain failure. Failure attributed to stable factors is likely to yield predictions of future failure, whereas failure attributed to more temporary factors allows the possibility of future improvement.

The locus of causality dimension in Weiner's model—internal versus external explanation—relates primarily to the rewards or punishments that follow a performance. We are more likely to reward people if we believe their success was of their own making—due to their ability, for example, or to their hard work—than if we think chance or some other external factor was responsible. Punishment is also more likely when failure is attributed to an internal rather than an external cause. If David failed his exam because he didn't try hard enough, we are likely to be much more critical of him than we would be if we thought his failure was the consequence of an unreasonably hard test.

The controllability dimension involves attributions concerning the potential for intended change. If we think someone's failure was due to an uncontrollable cause, such as low aptitude, we may be skeptical of his or her chances for improvement even if the person is motivated to improve. Similarly, success attributed to uncontrollable causes is likely to be viewed as luck and may not produce expectations for similar success in the future.

Our choice among these possible causes can be affected by a variety of factors. Initial expectancies may be important, for example, in decisions between a stable cause and a more temporary cause. If we expect someone to do well, then we will probably attribute that person's success to ability or skill. If we expect the person to fail, in contrast, then we will be more apt to attribute the person's success to some more temporary cause. Category-based expectancies regarding members of a particular group may affect attributions as well. For example, people are more likely to attribute a woman's success to temporary factors but to attribute a man's similar success to his ability (Deaux, 1976b; Deaux & Emswiller, 1974). Similarly, whites are more likely to see ability as responsible for the success of a white than of a black (Yarkin, Town, & Wallston, 1982); both blacks and whites are more likely to attribute failure to a lack of ability in the other group than in their own group (Whitehead, Smith, & Eichhorn, 1982).

Such biases in evaluation are important in their own right. They become even more important when we realize that attributions are not the end of the line, that the explanations we form may influence other kinds of behavior. Madeline Heilman and Richard Guzzo (1978) have provided a vivid demonstration of some of these consequences. In a simulated organizational setting, business students were asked to assume the role of an employer and to decide on the raises and promotions to be given to a set of hypothetical employees. The information provided about the employees included one of four explanations for their recent successful job performance: superior ability, considerable effort, a relatively easy assignment, or pure chance. The behavior of the role-playing supervisors strongly supported the validity of Weiner's dimensions. Employers recommended raises only to those employees whose performance had been explained by either ability or effort; in other words, rewards were given for internally caused success but were not given when external factors were believed to be responsible. Promotion was reserved for those employees who were said to be superior in ability. Presumably subjects believed that future performance could be ensured only if the employee had superior ability (an internal, stable, *and* uncontrollable characteristic), but not necessarily if the employee had shown exceptional effort (a less stable but more controllable characteristic).

Weiner's model of attribution is more limited than the others we have considered, focusing strictly on explanations for successful and unsuccessful performances in an achievement context. Nevertheless, Weiner's model is important because it points more clearly than the others to some of the behavioral consequences that attribution patterns may have.

Belief in a Just World

Explanations of the outcomes of individual events may reflect a more general view of the way the world works. The social psychologist Melvin Lerner has suggested that many people have a **belief in a just world**—a belief that "there is an appropriate fit between what people do and what happens to them" (Lerner, 1966, p. 3). For Lerner, the belief in a just world is not only a cognitive principle; it develops out of a motivational context as well. Lerner suggests that we develop a sense of our own deservingness and that to maintain that comforting belief, we need to believe that others also get what they deserve in the world.

But what happens if situations appear unjust? Lerner suggests that such events threaten our belief in a just world and that accordingly we will try to correct the situation in some way (Lerner, 1975, 1977; Lerner, Miller, & Holmes, 1976). On some occasions we may rectify the situation by compensating the victim of injustice—by giving aid to refugees, for example. At other times we may try to punish the source of harm (if we can find one). And if we cannot reestablish justice, we may convince ourselves that no injustice has occurred.

Blaming the victim is one way we can maintain our belief that people get what they deserve (Ryan, 1971). Martin Symonds (1975), a psychiatrist who has interviewed hundreds of victims of rape, assault, and kidnapping, found that many of these victims receive censure instead of sympathy. When a person has been mugged, for example, friends, family, and the police frequently interrogate the person relentlessly about why he or she was in such an unfortunate situation. "Why were you walking in that neighborhood alone?" "Why didn't you scream?" "Why were you carrying so much money?" Such reactions reflect our pervasive need to find rational explanations for apparently senseless events. Observers are particularly likely to place the responsibility for rape on the victim. This tendency is most pronounced when other explanations for the attack are not apparent. For example, a victim who is unacquainted with her assailant is seen as more responsible for a rape than one who is acquainted with him (Smith, Keating, Hester, & Mitchell, 1976). In general, men are more likely to attribute responsibility to the female victim than women are (Feild, 1978; Selby, Calhoun, & Brock, 1977). Such beliefs affect jurors' verdicts in trials concerning rape and other crimes (Dane & Wrightsman, 1982).

Some people have used the same type of rationale to account for the assassination of public figures. For example, in April 1968, right after Dr. Martin Luther King, Jr., was murdered, a representative sample of 1,337 American adults were asked: "When you heard the news [of the assassination], which of these things was your strongest reaction: (1) anger, (2) sadness, (3) shame, (4) fear, (5) he brought it on himself?" About one-third (426) of the respondents chose the response "he brought it on himself" (Rokeach, 1970). For these respondents, Lerner's "just world" hypothesis applies. Presumably, they believed that because he had been killed, he must have deserved to die.

We do not always blame the victim, however. Indeed, we are particularly unlikely to do so when the victim's suffering results from events that we also may experience. Observers who are told to expect a fate similar to that of the victim are less likely to malign the victim (Sorrentino & Boutilier, 1974). Subjects in Sorrentino and Boutilier's experiment observed a female undergraduate receive a series of electrical shocks as a "learner" in a teaching-effectiveness project. Some of the subjects were told that they would also serve as learners later; others were told that they would not. Anticipation of a similar fate led to a significant reduction in the assignment of negative characteristics to the learner. Such a pattern is, of course, consistent with the gender differences in attribution of responsibility for rape, a case where we can assume that women are more likely than men to anticipate a similar fate.

At a more general level, Lerner (1977) has suggested that the individual's first concerns are his or her own deservingness and the ability to believe in a world where justice prevails. Often this belief leads a person simply to ignore evidence of injustice. Thus, we may skip articles in the newspaper that deal with suffering in other countries and avoid neighborhoods in our own town where evidence of poverty is prominent. Yet many of those same occasions may lead us to offer direct assistance—perhaps because they represent only a minimal threat to our sense that justice prevails in our own lives. Not being personally threatened, we may feel free to offer assistance to correct the injustices suffered by others. When we see a threat to our own state of deservingness, though, we are much more likely to choose other strategies, such as blaming the victims and seeing them as directly responsible for their own misfortunes, thereby sparing ourselves the fear that a similar fate may befall us.

▶ Summary

Understanding other people is a useful skill that makes the world more predictable. Our initial impressions of other people are often based on surface characteristics, such as physical appearance, which are immediately visible. We typically categorize someone immediately and infer character and personality traits from characteristics we believe are associated with the category. As we learn more about the person, we try to confirm our initial categorization, or we may construct subcategories. Sometimes we may integrate information about someone in a piecemeal, trait-by-trait fashion.

Some traits are more important than others in the process of impression formation. Traits concerning personality dimensions about which we have little information, for example, carry a great deal of diagnostic value. We also believe they enable us to predict behavior. Traits vary in the degree to which they can be confirmed or disconfirmed by observation. In combining a series of trait descriptors, people tend to weight the value of each trait and average the weighted values to arrive at an overall judgment. Accuracy of impressions is an elusive issue, as eyewitness testimony in the courtroom has demonstrated.

The mental categories that represent social knowledge can be conceptualized in several ways. Most people have a set of implicit personality theories and social theories that represent their understanding of human behavior. More specific events are represented by schemas, prototypes, and scripts. A stereotype is a schema that summarizes beliefs about members of a particular group. In some instances, particularly in the case of a negative belief, a stereotype may reflect an illusory correlation between two actually unrelated factors.

Both the vividness and the distinctiveness of an event will affect our interpretation of it. Moods, goals, and emotional states are also influential. Priming can affect the accessibility of a particular social category.

Because social information is so extensive, people have developed a set of heuristics, or shortcuts, to make their task simpler. The social inference process is also subject to a number of biases, including the false consensus bias.

The specific form of social inference that concerns explanations for the outcomes of events is called causal attribution. In general, actions may be attributed to either a dispositional factor or a situational factor. Several models have been developed to explain various aspects of the attribution process. Biases are evident in our attributions as well. We tend, for example, to overestimate the influence of dispositional factors (the fundamental attribution bias). At a more general level, explanations of events often reflect a belief in a just world.

▶ *Key Terms*

actor-observer effect
augmentation principle
availability heuristic
belief in a just world
causal attribution
causal schema
central trait
circumscribed accuracy
confirmatory bias
consensus
consistency
construct
controllability

discounting
distinctiveness
false consensus bias
fundamental attribution bias
global accuracy
heuristics
illusory correlation
implicit personality theory
locus of causality
noncommon effect
philosophies of human nature

priming
prototype
representativeness heuristic
schema
script
social theory
stability
stereotype
traits
vividness

Language exists only when it is listened to as well as spoken. The hearer is an indispensable partner.

John Dewey

Those of us who keep our eyes open can read volumes into what we see going on around us.

E. T. Hall

5

Interpersonal Communication

I magine what it would be like if no one returned your greeting as you walked around campus, if no one met your eyes, if no one acknowledged your presence, if everyone seemed to look through you as if you weren't there. That is, imagine what life would be like without communication. In fact, shunning—the complete absence of talking with, looking at, or gesturing toward someone—is used in some cultures as the ultimate punishment (Miller, 1988). Even shunning, however, communicates a message: "You are no longer welcome in our society."

Very simply, communication is the basis for all social interaction. Communication makes possible the self-presentation strategies discussed in Chapter 3 and the majority of impression formation and attribution processes discussed in Chapter 4. While communicating, individuals both present themselves to and interpret the other person. How this occurs is the concern of this chapter. What does it mean to communicate? How are messages sent and received? Through what channels of communication do messages flow?

When we understand the elements of the communication process, we can then examine specific communication situations, from those in which people try to be completely honest with one another to those in which they aim to deceive. Finally, the issues of self, social knowledge, and communication will be linked together in a general model of social interaction.

▶ The Meaning of Communication

It has often been said that one can't *not* communicate. Even though in some situations so much tension and stress exists that verbal communication actually ceases, the communication process continues. Signs and messages continue to be transmitted between people even if the goals of the interaction may have changed.

The widely used term *communication* has been applied to situations ranging from information processing within the individual to large-scale sociocultural systems, such as mass media and computer networks. We will focus primarily on a phenomenon somewhere between those extremes: interpersonal communication—the interactions that take place between two people.

Communication theorists have developed many models in an attempt to represent the communication process. For example, an early, influential model proposed by Shannon and Weaver (1949) included four necessary components—source, transmitter, receiver, and destination—and one usual but unnecessary component—noise or interference (see Figure 5.1). Later this model was revised to include the concept of feedback, which attempted to explain why the receiver may not always receive the same message the transmitter has sent.

Shannon and Weaver's model had a tremendous in-

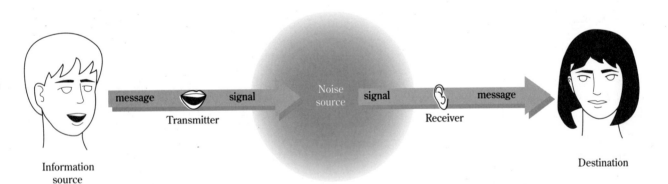

Figure 5.1 *A simple model of communication.*
Source: The Mathematical Theory of Communication by C. Shannon and W. Weaver, 1949, Urbana, IL: University of Illinois Press.

fluence on the early analysis of communication, particularly in the then-developing field of computer science. But their model was too simple. First, they assumed communication was unidirectional. Communication, however, involves at least two people, both of whom are simultaneously sending and receiving messages. Second, Shannon and Weaver did not include the context in which communication occurs. An adequate model of communication must also include the ways in which particular people, topics, and situations may shape the process (Clark, 1985).

More recent work on interpersonal communication includes a number of assumptions, such as those illustrated in Figure 5.2. First, it is assumed that communication represents an interaction between two parties, both of whom have sending and receiving parts to play. From this viewpoint, communication is seen as a shared social system rather than as a one-way street (Scott, 1977). Second, both parties bring to the interaction their expectations and understandings. Represented by the "self" and the "context" in Figure 5.2, these expectations and understandings shape the nature of the communication by what have been called the rules of the communication game (Higgins, 1981; Krauss & Glucksberg, 1977). If you were asked how today's history lecture was, for example, would you respond to a friend the same way you would to the university president or to the instructor who gave the lecture? The question is the same, but the form of your answer could differ substantially. And third, speakers must share what Herbert Clark (1985) has termed a common ground for communication to flow most effectively. In other words, the participants must share certain beliefs and suppositions that will enable them to coordinate their communicative efforts.

Although not specifically illustrated in Figure 5.2, a fourth assumption that most current communication experts share is that verbal and nonverbal channels are part of the same system. It is sometimes useful to focus on one or the other channel, but one must remember that communication takes place through many channels simultaneously. For example, a speaker may display some facial expression, stand a particular way, and use a particular set of gestures. Sometimes the communications sent through these channels may parallel each other, conveying the same message. Sometimes,

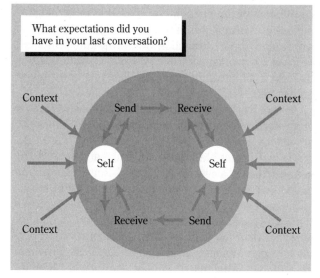

Figure 5.2 *A model of the interpersonal communication process.*

however, the messages from different channels may be contradictory, so interpretation becomes more difficult.

Channels of Communication

When the word *communication* is mentioned, many people think automatically of language. *Webster's New World Thesaurus* (C. Laird, 1974), for example, provides *talk, utterance,* and *announcing* as the first three synonyms for communication, and virtually all the means of communication noted involve speech or writing. Yet messages can be exchanged through many other channels of communication: facial expressions, eye contact, physical touch, body gestures, even the distance we put between ourselves and others. Because speech is the most obvious of the communication channels, however, we shall begin there.

Language and Paralanguage

"When I use a word, it means just what I choose it to mean, neither more nor less," said Humpty-Dumpty in Lewis Carroll's classic, *Through the Looking Glass.* Such confidence in the encoding of one's message is admirable, but perhaps unrealistic. Although the choice of words and the combination of words into sentences represent our most controlled form of communication, the levels of meaning involved in such choices are numerous.

A word has both a **denotation**—its explicit meaning or definition—and a **connotation**—implicit associations with the word. The word *drink,* for example, denotes any ingestible liquid, but it usually carries the connotation of "alcoholic beverage." Roger Brown and his colleagues also have noted that some words, particularly verbs, may predispose people to make certain kinds of causal attributions (discussed in Chapter 4). Most active verbs, such as *hit* and *help,* predispose people to assign causality to the actor (Au, 1986; Brown & Fish, 1983). That is, when someone says, "Jennifer helped Jared" we are more likely to perceive Jennifer as helpful than we are to consider the possibilities either that Jennifer's helping was an accident or that Jared was in a state such that anyone would have helped him. In contrast, verbs that Brown has labeled "experience" verbs, such as *astonish* and *admire,* predispose one to assign causality to the stimulus. When Jennifer admires Jared, we are more likely to assume the admiration stems from characteristics of Jared (the stimulus) than to assume that some characteristic of Jennifer leads her to admire others (Brown & Van Kleeck, 1989; Van Kleeck, Hillger, & Brown, 1988).

The philosopher John L. Austin (1962) pointed out that similar distinctions apply to sentences and phrases. A **locution** consists of words arranged in some sequence—a sentence or phrase that conveys a particular message. For example, the literal meaning of the sentence "It's cold in this room" is clear. The term **illocution** refers to the intended meaning of the sentence. When someone says, "It's cold," he or she may mean (1) "Shut the door behind you"; (2) "I know you just turned down the heat, but would you please turn it up again?"; (3) "This is a crummy, drafty room"; (4) "I want to talk and this is the best I can do for a conversational opening"; or any of a host of other possibilities.

What other meanings do people intend to convey by their language? According to the linguist John Searle (1979), there are five general possibilities: (1) to describe something, (2) to influence someone, (3) to express feelings and attitudes, (4) to make a commit-

ment, and (5) to accomplish something directly. The speaker's task is to phrase the message so that the intent is clear, and the listener's task is to decide which intention motivated the speaker. To accomplish these tasks, people rely on a variety of implicit rules and agreements that are shared in the society—the common ground we referred to earlier.

Not all verbal communication is expressed in words and sentences. Vocal sounds and modifications, called **paralanguage,** convey meaning even though they are not considered language. The study of paralanguage deals with *how* something is said, not *what* is said (Knapp, 1978). Examples of paralanguage include speech modifiers such as pitch, rhythm, intensity, and pauses, as well as vocalizations such as laughing, crying, yawning, groaning, sneezing, and snoring (Trager, 1958). Someone who laughs while saying, "Get out of here," for example, probably does not intend to convey the literal meaning of the phrase; less obviously, perhaps, the person who speeds up his or her speech may be conveying either anxiety or excitement.

Some claims have been made that spoken lies can be detected via paralanguage cues, such as analysis of the speaker's voice patterns. Proponents of the spectrographic analysis of vocal stress patterns have argued for this method as a reliable lie detector. Although such claims appear to be exaggerated (Brenner, Branscomb, & Schwartz, 1979; O'Hair & Cody, 1987; O'Hair, Cody, & Behnke, 1985), we can transmit a considerable amount of information through paralinguistic cues. Low voice pitch, for example, tends to convey pleasantness, boredom, or sadness, whereas high pitch conveys anger, fear, surprise, or general activity. Moderate variations in pitch may communicate anger, boredom, or disgust, whereas more extreme voice variations indicate pleasantness, happiness, and surprise (Knapp, 1978; LaFrance & Mayo, 1978).

Roger Brown (1986) has used the term **social register** to refer to a way of expressing a message addressed to a particular type of listener. A classic example of such stylized ways of talking, which combine linguistic and paralinguistic cues, is baby talk. Listen carefully to someone talking to a very young child. Typically the pitch will be higher than normal, the sentences very simple, and the intonation exaggerated. These characteristic features of the baby talk register have been noted in countries throughout the world and can easily be detected by someone who cannot actually see the speaker's target. This particular social register is not limited to situations in which people talk to babies, as Lynn Caporael (1981) found when she studied the speech of caregivers in nursing homes. The speech of staff members to elderly patients bore a striking resemblance to the speech of adults to children, suggesting similarities in the assumed dependency of these two groups.

Even though words sometimes fail us, it may seem that the tremendous variety of linguistic and paralinguistic forms of communication should be sufficient to communicate virtually any thought or feeling. Yet beyond these verbal forms of communication lies a wealth of nonverbal communication modes that sometimes support, sometimes contradict, and sometimes go beyond the verbal message.

Gaze

"Drink to Me Only with Thine Eyes," "the eyes of a woman in love," "seeing eye to eye"—all these expressions testify to the importance of eyes as communicators. So does the fact that when people merely look in our general direction, we tend to assume they are gazing at us (Teske, 1988). The pervasiveness of optic symbols in myth and religion also testifies to the importance we assign to this mode of communication. In some cultures, for example, people wear veils to protect themselves from the "evil eye" (Kleinke, 1986). Indeed, we perhaps depend more on the eye behavior of other people than on any other form of nonverbal communication, although this dependence sometimes causes problems.

Gazing,[1] like all nonverbal behaviors, serves several purposes. Miles Patterson (1982, 1983) has identified five specific functions of such behaviors: (1) providing information, (2) regulating interaction, (3) expressing intimacy, (4) exercising social control, and (5) facilitating the accomplishment of a task. Note the similarity between these specific functions and the general mean-

[1]The term *eye contact* is often used interchangeably with *gaze* (a fixed look directed at the face of another person) and *mutual gaze* (the fixed looks of two persons directed at each other). Most investigators prefer the latter terms, however, because actual eye contact is difficult to measure; a look in the general direction of someone's face cannot be distinguished from actual eye-to-eye contact.

ings conveyed by language, as we described earlier. Functionally, gazing is as much a part of communication as language.

Providing information People convey information by the amount and pattern of their gazing behavior. A gaze (but not a sustained stare) communicates liking, attentiveness, competence, and credibility (Kleinke, 1986). Our dependence on the eyes as a source of information is manifested in the discomfort we feel when we converse with people who are wearing opaque sunglasses. "I can't tell what they're thinking" is a frequent complaint in such a situation.

People tend to look more frequently at people they like than at people they dislike. Even the belief that another person has gazed frequently at us can engender liking. In a demonstration of this effect, Chris Kleinke and his colleagues (Kleinke, Bustos, Meeker, & Staneski, 1973) asked male and female subjects to engage in a ten-minute conversation. At the end of the period, the subjects were told that their partner had gazed at them far more or far less often than the average number of times, regardless of the actual frequency of gazes. Subjects who were told that the gaze frequency was lower than normal rated their partners as less attentive. Interestingly, being told about above-average rates of gazing produced different effects on men than on women. When women thought their male partner had looked at them more than might be expected, their attraction to him did not increase. The same belief had the opposite effect on men: they were more attracted to women who they believed had gazed at them more than the average number of times.

Gaze is also an important indicator of perceived status differences in a relationship. Ralph Exline and his colleagues have explored the gaze patterns of high- and low-status people interacting with each other (Exline, 1971; Exline, Ellyson, & Long, 1975). In some of their studies, the experimenter manipulated status differences; in others, the investigators looked at real-life status relationships, such as that between an ROTC officer and a cadet. In all cases, the low-status person gazed at a partner more than the high-status person did.

Nancy Henley (1977) has suggested that perceived status differences may be related to the pervasive gender differences in eye behavior. In general, women engage in more frequent eye contact than men do (Duncan, 1969), consistent with a finding that a lower-status person looks directly at others more often than does a higher-status person. Women are also less likely to engage in staring and are more apt to avoid the gaze of the other (Henley, 1977). According to Henley, these differences reflect the extent to which both women and men are socialized to believe that women have less status than men, a point we also address in Chapter 13.

Regulating interaction   Gaze serves an important role in initiating communication and in maintaining a conversation once it has begun. For example, if your professor is looking around the classroom for someone to supply a correct answer, you are likely to avoid eye contact if you failed to read the material the night before; however, you will probably return the professor's gaze if you know the correct answer and can discuss it. In this case, mutual gaze, or the lack of it, is used in an attempt to control the relationship by signaling willingness to engage in an exchange. Similarly, you will probably ignore a gaze from a stranger at a bar if you don't want to be bothered, but you might return the look if you were interested in establishing a new relationship. Observing unacquainted college students meeting in a laboratory setting, Mark Cary (1978) found that mutual gaze predicted the beginning of conversations. If students looked at each other at their first encounter, they were likely to engage in conversation. If they looked a second time, conversation was even more likely.

Although mutual gaze may initiate conversation, its role is often diminished once a conversation begins. Consider these figures from a study of typical two-person conversations (Argyle & Ingham, 1972). One or both participants gaze at the other about 61% of the time, but mutual gaze accounts for only 31% of the total interaction time. The average length of an individual gaze is about three seconds, about three times longer than the average duration of mutual gaze. Lengthy mutual gazing, as we shall see later, is usually reserved for messages that are more intense than those employed in a typical conversation.

We noted earlier that socialization produces gender differences in gaze; it also produces ethnic differences. For example, white adult speakers tend to gaze at the other person more often when they are listening (75% of the time) than when they are speaking (41%). This pattern is reversed among blacks, although the overall amount of gaze remains the same (see Figure 5.3). Ethnic differences in typical patterns of gaze can create substantial problems in communication. Marianne LaFrance and Clara Mayo (1976) observed, for example, that when blacks and whites converse, they often misinterpret the signals for taking turns in the conversation.

> When the white listener . . . encountered a pause with sustained gaze from a black speaker, the white was cued to speak, and both found themselves talking at once. In the obverse situation, by directing his gaze at the black listener, the white speaker often did not succeed in yielding

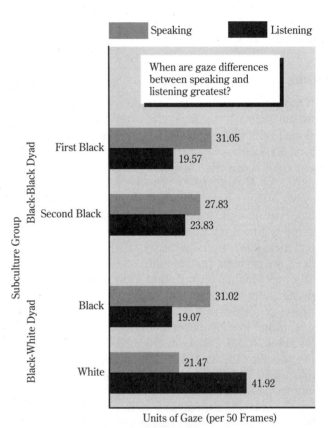

Figure 5.3   *Blacks gaze more often while talking than while listening; whites show the opposite pattern.*

Source: "Racial Differences in Gaze Behavior during Conversations: Two Systematic Observational Studies" by M. LaFrance and C. Mayo, 1976, *Journal of Personality and Social Psychology, 33,* pp. 547–552.

the floor and had to resort to direct verbal questioning. [p. 551]

Such differences can certainly create discomfort in a conversation and may cause errors in judgment about the other person's intentions and motives as well.

Expressing intimacy A third function of gaze is to express intimacy or involvement in a relationship. As noted earlier, people look more often, but do not stare, at others whom they like than at those they dislike (Exline & Winters, 1965). This gaze pattern has been observed in the laboratory in people who have interacted only briefly, as well as in dating couples whose interactions are more extensive.

While frequent gaze may convey positive feelings, extended gaze may indicate the intensity of a relationship. For example, couples who score high on a measure of romantic love spend more time looking at each other than those who report being less involved in a relationship (Rubin, 1970). Kimble and Forte (1978) asked women to communicate either a positive or a negative message to a male assistant. When the women were asked to act as if they were strongly involved in the message, they looked at the assistant more than when they were instructed to appear less certain about the message. This effect of intensity was found whether messages were positive or negative. In fact, it was slightly stronger when the messages were negative, lending credence to most people's concerns about the intentions of someone who is staring at them.

Exercising control Gaze often accompanies attempts to exert control. People gaze more when they are attempting to be persuasive; they also gaze more when they are attempting to ingratiate themselves with the other person (Kleinke, 1986). Phoebe Ellsworth and her colleagues have shown that a stare can also cause flight. When drivers are stopped at an intersection, for example, a stare from a person standing on the corner causes them to depart much more rapidly than they do when no one is staring at them (Ellsworth, Carlsmith, & Henson, 1972).

Although higher-status people tend to gaze at a partner less often than people of lower status, a specific pattern of gaze behavior is seen in high-status people when they wish to exert control. The **visual domi-**

nance behavior of people in high-status positions involves a tendency to look at the other person more fixedly when they speak than when they listen. The effectiveness of this visual dominance pattern was demonstrated convincingly by Ralph Exline in a field study of ROTC officers at their training camp (Exline, Ellyson, & Long, 1975). Those leaders who showed a visual dominance pattern were given the highest leadership ratings, whereas those who engaged in a lower speaking-to-listening ratio of direct gaze were rated less favorably on leadership abilities. This study gives no indication, of course, whether individuals who engage in visual dominance behavior are more likely to be selected as leaders or whether the holding of a leadership position encourages the development of visual dominance behavior. Nevertheless, the effectiveness of such behavior in communicating power and status is clear.

Facilitating task accomplishment Gaze can facilitate communication between people who are working together on the same project (Patterson, 1983). If you and a friend are sailing a boat, for example, some decisions or agreements may be made primarily by an exchange of gazes. In service relationships, such as that between a physician and a patient, a person's gaze may transmit information that is not easily expressed in words. A patient's eyes may indicate fear, acceptance or a variety of other responses to a physician's explanation of the problem. When speech is impossible, as when a patient is in a dentist's chair, gaze may be a major medium of communication.

Overall, it is evident that eye contact or gaze provides substantial amounts of information in the communication process. The eyes are not the only channel, however; other nonverbal channels also convey information effectively.

Facial Expressions

The scientific study of facial expressions has a long history, dating from the classic work of Charles Darwin, *The Expression of the Emotions in Man and Animals* (1872). Darwin proposed, for example, that facial expressions communicate specific messages and that evolutionary connections should make it possible for humans and other animals to interpret these messages across species. Investigators since Darwin have contin-

Our emotions can be conveyed quite clearly by facial expressions.
Daemmrich/The Image Works

ued to be interested in the ways in which facial expressions convey emotions, primarily surprise, fear, anger, disgust, happiness, and sadness.

An extensive research program conducted by Paul Ekman and his colleagues has provided an exact description of the facial expressions that accompany each of these emotional states (Ekman, 1972, 1982; Ekman & Friesen, 1975). A person caught by surprise, for example, will typically raise the eyebrows and drop the jaw; horizontal wrinkles will appear across the forehead; the upper eyelid will be raised while the lower lid is drawn down, and the white of the eye will show above the iris and often below as well. Subtle muscular activity, detectable with a technique called *facial electromyography,* also differentiates the various emotions (Rinn, 1984; Schwartz, 1982). Ekman uses the term **facial affect program** to designate the pattern of facial-muscle activity that accompanies a particular emotional experience.

In support of the universality of emotional expression Darwin postulated, Ekman and others have also shown that members of very different cultural groups demonstrate consistency in associating facial expressions with emotions. Samples of people in Eastern and Western Europe, the Middle East, Asia, South America, and preliterate societies of New Guinea all were able to identify correctly the six primary emotions displayed in photographs of faces of North Americans (Ekman, 1972; Ekman & Friesen, 1971; Ekman et al., 1987; Izard, 1969). Similarly, Robert Krauss and his colleagues compared the reactions of Japanese and American soap-opera viewers (Krauss, Curran, & Ferleger,

1983). Even though the Americans did not understand the Japanese spoken by the soap-opera characters, the two groups gave very similar interpretations of both American and Japanese shows. That is, the Americans were able to follow the soap opera merely by identifying the emotions portrayed in the Japanese actors' faces and voice qualities.

Christine and Ranald Hansen (1988) further reasoned that if detecting a threat presumably had more survival value than detecting pleasure, then people should be able to detect an angry face more quickly than a happy face. To test this hypothesis, they showed pictures of "crowds" consisting of nine faces and asked people to decide whether the crowd contained a face that did not fit with the others. The amount of time subjects took to report whether or not there was a discrepancy was recorded. As is illustrated in Figure 5.4, the fastest decision times (fewest seconds) were obtained when an angry face was embedded in either a neutral or happy crowd. Interestingly, subjects detected a neutral face in a happy crowd as quickly as they detected angry faces, perhaps because a neutral face surrounded by happy faces is considered a threat. Notice, too, that in the angry crowd it took about the same amount of time to decide there was no discrepant face as it did to detect the discrepant neutral or happy face. It may be that angry faces command our attention, and therefore the discrepant neutral or happy faces were the last to be scanned in the angry crowd condition.

That facial displays of emotion can be recognized by respondents of different cultures and that some facial displays are recognized more quickly than others pro-

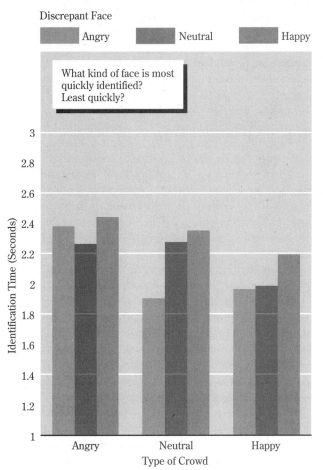

Discrepant Face

Angry Neutral Happy

What kind of face is most
quickly identified?
Least quickly?

Identification Time (Seconds)

Type of Crowd: Angry, Neutral, Happy

Figure 5.4 *People identify a discrepant angry face more quickly than they identify discrepant neutral or happy faces.* *Source:* "Finding the Face in the Crowd: An Anger Superiority Effect" by C. H. Hansen and R. D. Hansen, 1988, *Journal of Personality and Social Psychology, 54,* pp. 917–924.

vides information about their relative importance as sources of information about people. However, such findings do not mean that the same emotion will always be displayed in similar circumstances. In some societies, for example, it is not considered appropriate to display emotional reactions publicly. In North America, certain situations may call for restraining emotional reactions. Consider what your reaction would be to the sight and smell of an overflowing, malodorous garbage can in a neighbor's kitchen. Although you might experience disgust, it is quite likely that you would attempt to mask your emotional expression as you talked with your neighbor. Such controls or restraints are called **display rules,** personal, situational, or cultural norms concerning the expression of emotions.

The recognition of display rules brings us closer to the central issue of communication. Although the abstract expression of emotions is of interest in its own right, it is the ways in which we transmit those emotions to another person that affect the communication process. This distinction between the expression and the communication of emotion is an important one. Consider a series of studies conducted by Kraut and Johnston (1979) on smiling behavior. Exploring a wide range of natural settings, including bowling alleys, hockey arenas, and public walkways, these investigators observed the frequency of smiling and attempted to relate those occasions to simultaneously occurring events. Their findings indicated that people were most likely to smile when they were talking with other people; they were far less likely to smile when an event caused them to experience positive emotions while they were alone. Susan Jones and her colleagues (Jones, Collins, & Hong, 1991; Jones & Raag, 1989) have demonstrated the same effects in 18-month-old and 10-month-old infants; infants playing with toys smile more often in the presence of an attentive mother than an inattentive mother. Thus, one major function of a smile is to *communicate* happiness to other persons.

Alan Fridlund (1991) has also demonstrated that even when we are alone, smiling may be a form of communication. Subjects in his experiment watched a videotape constructed to elicit smiles. The videotape included images of cute babies, a dog playing, sea otters in an aquarium, and a Steve Martin comedy routine. Most of the subjects arrived for the experiment with a friend, and some watched the videotape with their friend. Other subjects who brought a friend were led to believe their friend was viewing the same videotape in a separate room; still others were led to believe their friend was filling out a questionnaire in another room. Finally, some subjects arrived alone for the experiment and watched the videotape alone.

Using facial electromyography to measure movement of the cheek muscles, Fridlund showed that smiling increased with the sociality of the setting (see Figure 5.5). When subjects brought no friend or the friend was completing a questionnaire, subjects smiled considerably less than when their friends were with them or were watching the same videotape in a different room. In contrast, self-report ratings of happiness did

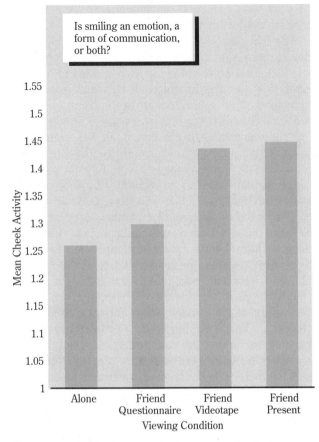

Is smiling an emotion, a form of communication, or both?

Figure 5.5 *Smiling is greater in the actual or implied presence of a friend.*

Source: "Sociality of Solitary Smiling: Potentiation by an Implicit Audience" by A. J. Fridlund, 1991, *Journal of Personality and Social Psychology, 60,* pp. 229–240.

erate emotions in the person displaying them. Beginning with Darwin (1872), a number of theorists have proposed what is known as the **facial feedback hypothesis:** facial displays consistent with an emotional expression produce physiological effects that an individual interprets as an emotion (Buck, 1980; Ekman, Levenson, & Friesen, 1983; Izard, 1977; J. Laird, 1974; Tomkins, 1962; Zajonc, Murphy, & Inglehart, 1989). Although it is controversial (Adelmann & Zajonc, 1989), one aspect of the facial feedback hypothesis that has received support is the notion that forming the facial display associated with an emotion—a smile, for example—may prompt the experience of the emotion—may cause someone to *feel* happier—even if the initial reason for display had nothing to do with the emotional experience.

In an experimental test of the facial feedback hypothesis, Fritz Strack, Leonard Martin, and Sabine Stepper (1988) asked subjects to make both cognitive (objective funniness) and affective (feeling amused) judgments about cartoons under two different conditions. In one condition, subjects held a pen in their mouth using only their teeth, which forced their facial muscles to form a smile. In the other condition, subjects held the pen in place using only their lips, thus preventing the formation of a smile. As is clear from Figure 5.6, the subjects' affective judgments differed between the two conditions—the cartoon was rated more amusing when subjects held the pen between their teeth—but the cognitive judgments did not differ.

On the other hand, not all facial displays typically associated with a particular emotional experience necessarily represent that emotion. For example, blushing is a display that has long been associated with shame and embarrassment (Darwin, 1872). Blushing, however, also occurs in situations involving positive emotions, such as being paid a compliment. Mark Leary and Sarah Meadows (1991) further argue that blushing is a form of communication used to reduce the possibility of appearing to deviate from group norms, of standing out by being too much better or worse than others in the situation. Using self-reports, Leary and Meadows identified two general classes of situations that elicit blushing. One primarily included emotional situations: being embarrassed, being judged stupid or incompetent, being paid a compliment, and having others sing "Happy Birthday." The other class involved merely *an-*

not differ across viewing conditions. Thus, Fridlund concludes that smiling may not be the result of an experienced emotion, but rather a means by which to communicate an emotion, even to an implicit other. In other words, facial expressions such as a smile may be less an automatic response to a particular stimulus than a conscious choice to relate to another person. This idea, of course, allows for the possibility that a smile may be used to mask some other emotion that is being experienced, and, as we shall see later, such masking attempts are common.

Facial expressions, however, may do more than communicate emotions to others. They also may gen-

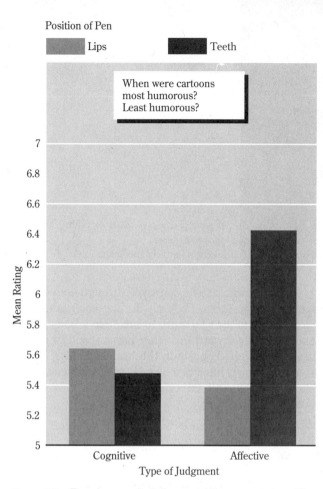

Position of Pen

Lips | Teeth

When were cartoons most humorous? Least humorous?

Mean Rating

7
6.8
6.6
6.4
6.2
6
5.8
5.6
5.4
5.2
5

Cognitive   Affective

Type of Judgment

Figure 5.6 *Forming a smile before watching an amusing videotape enhances the emotional experience.*
Source: "Inhibiting and Facilitating Conditions of the Human Smile: A Nonobtrusive Test of the Facial Feedback Hypothesis" by F. Strack, L. L. Martin, and S. Stepper, 1988, *Journal of Personality and Social Psychology, 54*, pp. 768–777.

ticipating a social situation in which one might be anxious. For example, self-reports of blushing were obtained in situations such as being called upon in class, being introduced to a stranger, talking to a teacher or employer, and talking to someone of the opposite sex. Although not emotional per se, such situations often involve the possibility of violating social norms and being perceived as someone who does not fit in. Blushing in such situations, therefore, may communicate an individual's awareness of having threatened one's accep-

tance—a way of saying "oops" (Castelfranchi & Poggi, 1990).

Body Movements and Gestures

Other parts of the body are involved in the communication process as well. Movements of the head, hands, legs, feet, and torso can all communicate messages to another person. To impose some order on the multitude of possible body movements, Ray Birdwhistell (1978) proposed a model called **kinesics**—a scheme for classifying body motions in terms of structure and meaning—as an analogy to *linguistics,* the term that designates the study of human language. On the basis of extensive observations, Birdwhistell proposed that there are approximately fifty to sixty basic classes of body movements that form the core of nonverbal body language. The basic units occur simultaneously to produce meaning, much like basic spoken sounds combine to form meaningful syllables. Despite Birdwhistell's important contribution, one major point of argument is whether kinesics describes a separate language or whether the meaning of body movements depends primarily on the verbal context.

Nonverbal behaviors that are directly linked with spoken language have been termed **illustrators** (Ekman & Friesen, 1972). If you are asked to direct someone to the library, for example, you will probably gesture as well as use words. You may, for example, make a turning motion with your hand as you say, "Turn left at the corner." Illustrators are an integral part of language (Graham & Heywood, 1975).

Not all body gestures accompany verbal language, however. Sometimes a gesture substitutes for a spoken phrase. Such gestures, termed **emblems,** are nonverbal acts that are clearly understood by the majority of the members of a culture (Johnson, Ekman, & Friesen, 1975). A wave of the hand in greeting, for example, is widely recognized in most North American cultures. Less friendly hand gestures may be equally well recognized. Other emblems may be shared by smaller groups, such as the two-fingered "hook 'em, Horns" sign of Texas football fans. As you might suspect, the meaning an emblem conveys can vary dramatically across cultures. A single gesture may convey two very different meanings. In North America, for example, a circle formed by the thumb and index finger, with other

A gesture can emphasize or substitute for a spoken phrase.
George Gardner/The Image Works

fingers upraised, is an emblem for "I'm all right" or "Everything is fine," but in and around France it also means "zero" or "worthless." In Mediterranean countries and in the Middle East, it is an obscene gesture (Morris, Collett, Marsh, & O'Shaughnessy, 1979). Similarly, two very different gestures can convey the same meaning; an arm wave can be either a greeting or a warning. Because emblems replace rather than accompany other forms of communication, these disparities in meaning can cause confusion in relationships between members of different cultures.

Body movements and gestures do more than support and replace spoken language; they can also indicate the nature of the relationship between two persons. A perceived status difference in a relationship is one example of this function of nonverbal communication. The higher-status person in a relationship will generally look more relaxed: arms and legs in asymmetrical positions and a backward lean to the body. The lower-status person is more likely to maintain a fairly rigid position, with body upright, feet together and flat on the floor, and arms close to the body (Mehrabian, 1972). Once again, perceived status differences in nonverbal behavior frequently parallel observed gender differences in body language that result from the different socialization of men and women (Henley, 1977). Men are far more apt to adopt an open stance, whereas women more frequently adopt the closed positions typical of a lower-status person.

Attraction can also be conveyed through body movements and gestures. People who like each other are more likely to lean forward, to maintain a body orientation directly toward the other person, and to take a more relaxed body position (Mehrabian, 1972). These signs are clearly interpreted and may arouse feelings of liking or disliking in the other person (Clore, Wiggins, & Itkin, 1975).

Touch

Touch is, perhaps, one of the most basic means of communication. Long before we develop language skills or learn body illustrators and emblems, we communicate through tactile contact. Parent and child depend on touch for much of their early communication.

Touch takes different forms in different kinds of relationships. At a professional or functional level, we may be touched by a hairstylist, a dentist, or a tennis instructor without giving the contact much thought. Social-polite touch is more personal but not intimate, exemplified by routine handshakes when people first meet. Other forms of touch may involve more intimate interactions, as in friendship, love, or sexual involvement. In general, men and women initiate touching at about equal frequencies, but there are situationally specific differences. Judith Hall and Ellen Veccia (1990), for example, reported male-initiated touching occurs

Touch is a major channel of communication between this father and his young child.
Arlene Collins/Monkmeyer Press

more frequently than female-initiated touching among couples under 30 years old, but female-initiated touching occurs more frequently among couples over 30. Hall and Veccia also found males were more likely to initiate a touch to the hand, but females were more likely to initiate a touch to the arm.

Even seemingly accidental touches can affect behavior. In a restaurant, for example, both male and female customers who were briefly touched on the hand or the shoulder when the server returned the change left larger tips than those who were not touched (Crusco & Wetzel, 1984).

Men and women do not always respond in the same way to touch, however. In a study conducted at the Purdue University library, for example, students who checked out books were briefly touched or not touched on the hand by the library clerk (Fisher, Rytting, & Heslin, 1976). The female students who were touched briefly responded positively; they liked the clerk and the library more than those who had not been touched. Men, however, did not respond to touch with similar increases in liking. Sheryl Whitcher and Jeffrey Fisher (1979) provided an even more striking demonstration of gender differences in reaction to touch. Male and female patients in an eastern U.S. university hospital were either touched or not touched during a preoperative teaching interaction with the nurse. The touches themselves were part of the professional role—a light touch on the patient's hand and an approximately one-minute contact on the patient's arm. The dependent measures in this study included both questionnaire responses and physiological measures taken immediately after surgery. The findings constituted striking evidence of the positive effects of touch on women. Female patients who had been touched reported less fear and anxiety on the questionnaire measures, and their blood pressure readings after surgery were lower. The nurse's brief touch produced negative effects in the male patients; they indicated less positive reactions than a no-touch control group and had higher blood pressure readings.

In general, women react more positively than men to touch (Major, 1981; Stier & Hall, 1984). Brenda Major (1981) has suggested that the existence of such a gender difference is dependent upon differences in status. When the status of two persons is approximately equal or when their status is ambiguous, Major argues, the reactions of men and women differ in the way we have just described—women's reactions are positive, and men's are negative. When the toucher is clearly higher in status than the recipient, however, both men and women react positively to touch.

Touch also conveys information about status to onlookers. As observers, we are more apt to attribute dominance and high status to the person who initiates a touch, while attributing submissiveness and low status to the person who receives the touch (Major & Heslin, 1982). Thus, like many nonverbal communication channels, touching may convey information to unintended as well as intended targets.

*These individuals are maintaining a social distance zone,
which indicates that they are not well acquainted.*
James Carroll

Interpersonal Distance

The forms of communication discussed so far have all
involved some part of the body as a means of transmitting messages. At this point we turn to something more
abstract—the distance between bodies as a mode of
communication. The anthropologist Edward Hall
(1959, 1966) is probably the individual most responsible for pointing out how distance between two or more
persons can communicate a variety of messages. On
the basis of extensive observations, primarily within
the United States, Hall has proposed a categorization of
distance zones to describe the patterns typically found
in different types of relationships. The four major zones
are termed intimate, personal, social, and public.

Intimate zones range in distance from actual physical
contact to about 18 inches (approximately 0.5 meter).
This zone generally indicates a high level of intimacy
between the participants, although there are exceptions, as when strangers are crowded together in an elevator. In such forced closeness, the distance is uncomfortable because it conflicts with the feelings that may
be aroused in the occupants by close physical contact
with total strangers. The *personal distance zone* extends
from 1½ to 4 feet (about 0.5 to 1.25 meters) and typifies

the distance usually maintained between friends (at the
closer end) and between acquaintances (at the farther
end) in everyday conversations. Greater distances,
ranging from 4 to 12 feet (1.25 to 3.5 meters), represent
the *social distance zone* and are typically found in business interactions or very casual social interactions.
Your interactions with a clerk at a store probably fall
into this category, as do typical professor/student interactions. Finally, Hall describes a *public distance zone,* in
which interpersonal distance ranges from 12 to 25 feet
(about 3.5 to 7.5 meters). Interactions at these distances are typically quite formal, as at a public address
or in an interaction with a judge or similar official.

As Hall's categorization indicates, greater liking is
usually communicated by smaller interpersonal distance. The optimal distance between friends, for example, tends to be less than the distance between two
strangers who interact (Hayduk, 1983). Because intimacy and interpersonal distance are so closely related,
we often use distance to send messages to other people
and to establish, or attempt to alter, limits of a relationship. If you want to communicate liking for another person, for example, you will probably decrease the interpersonal distance. If you're not fond of a person, you
will probably choose instead to "keep your distance."
In a demonstration of this behavior, Howard Rosenfeld
(1965) asked female students to talk with another student (actually a confederate of the experimenter) with
the goal either of appearing friendly or of avoiding the
appearance of friendliness. Approval-seeking women
placed their chairs an average of 4.75 feet from the confederate; students seeking to avoid affiliation placed
their chairs an average of 7.34 feet away.

Interpersonal distance can convey status messages
as well as affiliative messages. In general, peers stand
closer together than do people of unequal status
(Mehrabian, 1969b). When Lott and Sommer (1967)
observed seating patterns of students of different academic rank, they found that seniors sat closer to other
seniors than to either first-year students or professors.
In a field study, Dean, Willis, and Hewitt (1975) observed conversations between military personnel. Navy
men maintained a greater distance when they initiated
a conversation with a superior than when they initiated
a conversation with a peer, and this difference grew
larger as the difference in rank increased. Such differ-

ences were not observed when a superior initiated the conversation, thus indicating the freedom of the higher-status person to define the boundaries of the conversation.

Combining the Channels

Communication is a multichanneled process. In only the most unusual cases do we rely on just one form of communication. Most often, particularly in an ongoing relationship, messages are transmitted back and forth through a variety of verbal and nonverbal modes. Thus far we have assumed, to paraphrase Gertrude Stein, that a channel is a channel is a channel. In other words, we have acted as if all nonverbal channels of communication were equally important. They are not, of course, but which channel is most effective depends on several factors, including the truthfulness of the speaker, the topic of conversation, and the kind of judgment being made (O'Sullivan, Ekman, Friesen, & Scherer, 1985).

Evidence shows, however, that people tend to rely more on facial cues than on vocal cues or on the verbal message itself (Mehrabian & Weiner, 1967; O'Sullivan et al., 1985). In one series of experiments, Bella DePaulo and her colleagues paired various combinations of auditory and visual messages and examined their effects in the communication of dominance and liking (DePaulo, Rosenthal, Eisenstat, Rogers, & Finkelstein, 1978). Visual cues proved more influential than vocal cues. The subjects' preference for visual information was most noticeable when facial expressions were paired with auditory cues; body gestures did not exert as strong an effect as facial cues. These investigators also found that visual cues are more significant when people are interpreting messages of liking than when the messages concern status or dominance. Finally, women revealed a greater reliance on visual messages than men did.

In some instances, however, the visual message may be discarded in favor of the spoken message. Consider a series of studies by Daphne Bugental and her colleagues (Bugental, Kaswan, & Love, 1970; Bugental, Love, & Gianetto, 1971). These investigators asked children to interpret situations in which either a woman or a man was conveying one message with the face while expressing a contradictory verbal message. In

judging women, the children tended to believe a negative verbal message and ignore an accompanying smile. With men, in contrast, the children relied more on the facial expression than on the verbal message.

Why would the children react differently to men than to women? To explore this question, Bugental and her colleagues observed the behavior of fathers and mothers with their children. They found that mothers tended to be less consistent in combining channels of communication—they were just as likely to smile when saying negative things as when saying positive things. Fathers were more consistent, smiling when they said positive things and not smiling when they said negative things. As a result, children may learn to disregard the facial channel of their mothers' communication because it is a less reliable indicator of meaning, and to pay more attention to their fathers' facial messages.

▶ Patterns of Communication

The verbal and nonverbal channels we have described are the tools of communication that people learn to use in social situations to convey meaning and to relate to other people. It is now time to look more closely at the patterns of communication—the ways in which one person relates to another.

Basic Dimensions of Communication

The ways we communicate with other people may seem to be a series of unique combinations of specific partners in specific situations. However, investigators of different channels of communication have concluded that there are only three major dimensions of communicative behavior. Osgood, Suci, and Tannenbaum (1957), who concentrated mainly on verbal material, defined these three dimensions as *evaluation, control,* and *activity.* Using different channels, investigators of facial movements and the expression of emotion used different labels for the same three dimensions: pleasantness/unpleasantness, attention/rejection, and sleep/ tension (Schlosberg, 1954). Upon analyzing a variety of nonverbal behaviors, Albert Mehrabian (1969a) described these same basic dimensions as immediacy, relaxation, and activity. Despite considerable variety in the *who, what, where,* and *when* of communication, the *why* of communication is limited to three dimensions: expressing general likes or dislikes, exerting control, and indicating responsiveness to or acceptance of others.

Equilibrium and Arousal Models

We have described the communication process as a two-way street on which at least two persons send and receive messages. We turn now to two models of the dynamics of communication, the equilibrium model and the arousal model, both of which focus on the ebb and flow of interactions. According to Michael Argyle and Janet Dean (1965), who proposed the equilibrium model, every interpersonal encounter includes pressures toward both approach and avoidance; a person may seek friendship or security while at the same time fearing rejection. Depending on the situation, an appropriate balance, or state of equilibrium, will be established by regulation of the nonverbal channels of communication. Argyle and Dean suggest that if this equilibrium is disturbed, as when one person presses for more intimacy than the other wants, the latter person will compensate—will alter the messages conveyed through some of the nonverbal channels to restore the equilibrium. During a casual conversation, for instance, an acquaintance may sit much closer to you than seems appropriate. Such an imbalance would probably lead you to alter your own nonverbal communication—either by increasing the distance between the two of you or perhaps by avoiding eye contact, orienting your body away from the person, or making facial signs that indicate discomfort. Thus, the model's basic assumption is that a loss of equilibrium created by a message conveyed through one channel can be compensated for by alterations in the messages sent through the same or other channels.

To test this model, investigators generally have manipulated one communication channel and looked at the effects of the manipulation on another channel. For example, as people interact at closer distances, the amount of eye contact tends to decrease (Argyle & Dean, 1965; Russo, 1975), and body orientation becomes less direct (Patterson, Mullens, & Romano, 1971). Still other research has shown that as an interviewer's questions become increasingly personal, the interviewee will initiate less eye contact with the interviewer (Carr & Dabbs, 1974; Schulz & Barefoot, 1974).

Not all research supports the equilibrium model, however. For example, men and women often react differently to disturbances of equilibrium in a relationship (Aiello, 1977a, 1977b). Men generally increase their gaze behavior as the distance between them and another person increases, but a different pattern is seen in women's behavior. When the distance between participants is greater than 6 to 8 feet, women no longer increase their gaze behavior. Cultural differences also affect the way in which equilibrium is established (Grujic & Libby, 1978). French Canadians exhibit more intimacy through nonverbal channels when speaking French than when speaking English. The preferred channel also changed with the language they spoke; intimacy was established by gaze when speaking English, by smiling when speaking French. A further problem with the equilibrium model is that compensation is not the only response to a change in equilibrium. Sometimes an increase in the level of intimacy initiated by one person is reciprocated rather than avoided. When you are with someone you like in a romantic setting, aren't you more apt to respond positively to increases in intimacy than to try to reduce the intimacy level?

Miles Patterson (1976) has proposed an *arousal model* (see Figure 5.7) that accounts for both reciprocal and compensatory reactions to a loss of equilibrium. Patterson suggests that small changes in the intimacy level of an interaction will probably not be noticed, and hence no behavior changes will occur. At some threshold point, however, a sufficient change in the intimacy level of the interaction will be noticed, and some behavioral adjustment will be made.

The precise adjustment that will be made, however, depends on the label one attaches to the state of arousal; a given state of arousal can be labeled either positive or negative, depending on the circumstances. In the romantic setting suggested earlier, physical contact or intensified gazes initiated by your lover would probably be a positive experience and would lead you to reciprocate the behavior. The same behavior displayed by a stranger on a park bench would most likely be labeled negatively and would lead to compensatory adjustments on your part—turning your body away, avoiding the gaze, or getting up and leaving. As an expansion of the equilibrium principles proposed by Argyle and Dean (1965), the arousal model leads us to predict that a change in the behavior of one person may lead to any of a variety of reactions in the other person, depending on situational factors (Dane & Storms, 1977).

Patterson's arousal model can also be applied to other dimensions of communication than immediacy. Consider, for example, an experiment by Linda Carli (1990) concerning the reactions of male and female subjects to a female communicator's use of status cues during a persuasive message. For half the subjects, the communicator's behavior reflected a lower status. She spoke tentatively; the message included tag questions, such as "That's true, isn't it?" and qualifiers, such as "sort of" and "maybe." Other subjects heard the same message without the tag questions and qualifiers; Carli labeled this the "assertive" message. As is clearly illustrated in Figure 5.8, the reactions of male and female listeners differed markedly, despite the fact that the topic was one with which most of them agreed and for which pretesting had indicated no gender differences. When the woman spoke as an equal (assertively) to men, their reaction was to "distance" themselves through disagreement. Men evidenced agreement with the female speaker only when she exhibited a speech pattern consistent with a lower status. The opposite reactions were obtained from women, who accepted (agreed with) the female speaker when she spoke as an equal but evidenced less agreement when the speaker acted as though she were lower in status. The listeners' ratings of the speaker's trustworthiness and likableness followed the same pattern.

Conversational Patterns

Nonverbal channels combine to provide some structure to communication. Verbal patterns also exist in the form of conversational rules and conventions. In its simplest form, a conversation between two people can be divided into three parts: the opening section, the

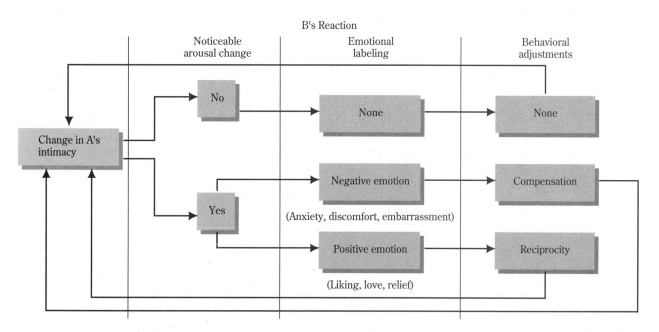

Figure 5.7 *Patterson's arousal model of interpersonal communication.*
Source: "An Arousal Model of Interpersonal Intimacy" by M. L. Patterson, 1976, *Psychological Review, 83,* pp. 235–245.

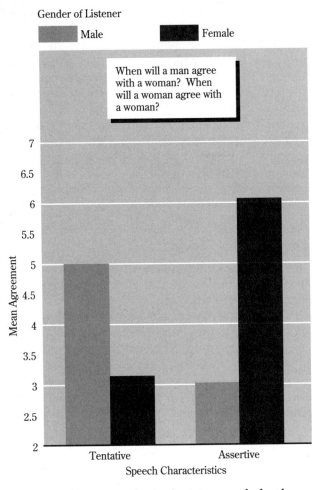

Gender of Listener

Male   Female

When will a man agree with a woman? When will a woman agree with a woman?

Figure 5.8 *Listener reactions to the status cues of a female speaker.*
Source: "Gender, Language, and Influence" by L. L. Carli, 1990, *Journal of Personality and Social Psychology, 59,* pp. 941–951.

Emanuel Schegloff, and Gail Jefferson (1974) have identified the following:

1. Length of conversation is not specified in advance.
2. Occurrences of more than one speaker at a time are common, but very brief.
3. Turn order and size are not fixed, but vary.
4. Turn allocation techniques are used.

Turn taking, for example, can occur in several ways. Direct questions may shift the focus from one partner to another, as may a pause at the end of a sentence. For example, Gerald Stasser (1988, 1990; Stasser & Taylor, 1991) has demonstrated that linguistic cues for turn-taking behavior are sufficiently regular to enable the development of a computer simulation. In group discussions, turn taking is also strongly related to the eventual decision of the group.

Paralinguistic cues also play an important role in the management of conversation (Duncan & Fiske, 1977; Wiemann & Knapp, 1975). If you want to keep talking even though you sense that the other person wants to take a turn, for example, you are not likely to say, "I know you want to talk, but I'm not finished with what I have to say." Instead, you may increase the volume and rate of your speech and decrease the frequency and duration of pauses (Knapp, 1978). At the same time, the other person may persist in an attempt to gain entrance by using vocal "buffers" ("Ah ..." or "Er ...") or by increasing the rapidity of responses, as if to say, "Hurry up so I can talk."

As we noted earlier, communication requires that participants share some common ground (Clark, 1985). Because people who already know each other have a common store of shared experiences, conversation can develop quickly between them. People who are not acquainted, however, need to engage in certain preliminaries to determine just where the common ground may lie (Maynard & Zimmerman, 1984). For example, upon first meeting, two students may try to find out about each other's living quarters, majors, or hometowns in order to establish areas of common experience.

Participants in a conversation also make certain assumptions about the nature of their interaction. They adhere to what H. P. Grice (1975) has called the **coop-**

body of the conversation, and the closing section (Clark, 1985).

To open a conversation, people must first recognize each other as potential conversants and either make some kind of contact or gaze at each other (Schiffrin, 1977). Initial greetings begin a simple interchange: "Hello," "How are you doing?," "What's up?" Once conversation is initiated, it proceeds according to a set of more or less strict rules. Among the numerous characteristics of the typical conversation, Harvey Sacks, erative principle—each participant assumes the other person is informative, truthful, relevant, and concise. Thus, if you ask your roommate what he or she thinks of Professor Wong, you expect to receive an answer consistent with the cooperative principle. "Professor Wong is a good lecturer, but he makes the exams too hard" would fulfill your expectations. But what if your roommate answered, "He wears elegant ties"? Such a response would probably lead you to seek an alternative explanation for the response (which Grice has termed a **conversational implicature**). That is, you would attempt to determine the indirect meaning conveyed by the response; perhaps your roommate wants to avoid a truthful answer, is being sarcastic, or simply misunderstood the question. In other words, people take from conversation not only what the other person is literally saying but what is implied as well (Krosnick, Li, & Lehman, 1990).

In several different studies, Thomas Holtgraves and his colleagues (Holtgraves, 1991; Holtgraves, Srull, & Socall, 1989; Holtgraves & Yang, 1990) have found that the relative status of communicators influences interpretations of the direct and indirect meanings of statements and requests. Statements by people of higher status, for example, are more likely to be perceived as assertive than are statements by equal-status persons. Communications from high-status people are also more memorable, and people expect communications from high-status people to be more direct, or less polite, than communications from lower-status or equal-status others. On the other hand, communications that threaten a conversant's relative status are more likely to be phrased in terms of indirect meaning; instead of asking Juan directly about the size of his raise, for example, the speaker is more likely to elicit the information indirectly by asking Juan whether he thinks his raise was fair. How we interpret others' remarks, as well as how we decide to phrase our own remarks, results from our beliefs about ourselves, the other person, and experience with people's behavior in general.

The ending of a conversation also follows some predictable patterns. The topic of conversation is exhausted, the participants prepare to leave, and the contact ends (Clark, 1985). A preclosing statement, such as "Well, I gotta go now," may signal that one person wishes to end the conversation. People may also make statements that point to future interaction, assuring the partner that the break is only temporary. Nearly every language has a set of ritualized phrases that signal a temporary end: *au revoir, hasta la vista, auf Wiedersehen, so long*.

Conversation in Close Relationships

Conversations between people who know each other well tend to follow a slightly different pattern from conversations between acquaintances. In general conversation, for example, good friends tend to raise more topics and are generally more responsive to each other, asking more questions in reaction to the other person's statements (Hornstein, 1985). Close friends are also more likely to engage in **self-disclosure,** or the process of revealing information about the self.

Not all information about oneself is equally likely to be revealed in the process of self-disclosure, even among friends. Sidney Jourard (1971) found that people reveal more information about their attitudes and opinions than about their personalities and their bodies. Gender differences are also apparent in self-disclosure: women report, and actually engage in, more self-disclosure than men, and the things they talk about tend to differ from the topics introduced by men (Cline, 1989).

In studying communication between pairs of best friends, Davidson and Duberman (1982) found that although women and men were equally likely to talk about topical issues, such as politics, current events, work, and movies, they differed in their discussion of relational and personal topics. Women were more likely to talk specifically about their relationship with their friend and about personal aspects of their lives. These women also reported much more reliance on nonverbal cues in communicating with their best friends. Snell (1989) found these differences are exaggerated by social anxiety. The self-disclosures of socially anxious males to male and female friends, for example, tended to be limited to information consistent with gender-role stereotypes about masculine behavior, such as defending their opinions and being assertive. Similarly, the self-disclosures of socially anxious females to friends of either gender were limited to stereotypically feminine topics, such as friendship and being understanding.

Although men's and women's communications may differ in content, they are alike in their evidence of reciprocity in self-disclosure. In other words, if one person increases the intimacy of the disclosures, the other person is likely to respond with a similar increase in intimacy (Cozby, 1973). In longer-term relationships, however, strict reciprocity does not appear to be the rule (Altman, 1973; Morton, 1978). The overall intimacy level of exchanges in long-term relationships tends to be higher than in new relationships, but there does not seem to be a one-for-one exchange of intimate information in any single interaction. Over the course of many interactions, however, the self-disclosures of one partner tend to balance those of the other. Thus, the specific rules of communication may change considerably as we move from the initial encounter to more stable relationships.

In addition to self-disclosure, conversations in relationships also communicate speakers' desires concerning control of a situation. Relational analysts, for example, have proposed that individual messages can be described by one of three control dimensions (Rogers & Farace, 1975). A "one-up" message represents an attempt to gain control in an exchange; a "one-down" message indicates that one is yielding control by either seeking or accepting the control of the other person; and a "one-across" message represents a movement toward neutralizing the control in the interaction. Questions, unless they are rhetorical, generally involve transfer of control; they give the "floor" to the other person. Arguments are often characterized by mutual "one-up" messages; both people simultaneously attempt to control the situation.

Patricia Noller (1984) has investigated some of the ways in which married couples communicate, examining both the encoding and decoding abilities of the partners. To study encoding abilities, she presented one partner with a description of a situation and a hypothetical reaction to that situation. For example, the wife might be told to imagine she was sitting alone with her husband on a winter evening and felt cold. She would be asked also to assume that she wondered whether her husband was cold as well and to say, "I'm cold, aren't you?"

It was then the other partner's task to decode the message. Noller provided the second partner with three possible interpretations of the message and asked him to select one on the basis of his understanding of his wife's statement. Possible interpretations might be the message actually intended (she wondered whether he, too, was cold), a request for physical affection, or an accusation that the partner showed a lack of consideration in keeping the house too cold.

Noller found couples who scored high on a measure of marital adjustment communicated significantly better than couples who scored low on this measure, a finding that testifies to the association between effective communication and marital happiness. As for the encoding of the messages they wished to send, women were generally better than men at this task. This superiority was especially evident in the sending of positive messages, which men encoded surprisingly poorly.

Why were the men, particularly men in less satisfactory marriages, not as effective in this communication task? Perhaps they simply lacked communication skills in general. Another explanation focuses on the marital relationship itself, suggesting that these men tended to show communication deficits only in interaction with their wives. To answer this question, Noller asked the same subjects to decode messages sent by strangers. In this case, the men evidenced few decoding problems. Thus, the ability to decode messages is not just a general trait but can be sharply influenced by particular features of a relationship. Husbands and wives may indeed experience failures of communication, but such failures are often as likely to be a consequence of the problem as they are to be a cause of the problem.

▶ Deceptive Communication

Not all communication is intended to convey accurate information from one person to another. Political scandals, criminal proceedings, and extramarital affairs are often occasions for determined attempts to tell another person something other than the truth. Even though most people consider lying to be "bad" most of the time, deception is a ubiquitous form of communication (Saxe, 1991).

It is often believed that deceptive communications are easily detected. In 1905, for example, Freud suggested that "he that has eyes to see and ears to hear may convince himself that no mortal can keep a secret. If his lips are silent, he chatters with his fingertips; betrayal oozes out of him at every pore" (Freud, 1905/1959). More recently, the trial lawyer Louis Nizer (1973) has pointed to cues that are associated with witnesses' attempts to deceive jurors. Among such cues are a tendency to look at the ceiling, a self-conscious covering of the mouth before answering questions, and crossing of the legs.

Are these beliefs in the detectability of deception justified? Do liars regularly expose themselves through the various communication channels? To answer these questions we must determine whether people who lie "give themselves away" reliably through the verbal and nonverbal messages they send; then we must find out whether an observer can reliably interpret those cues.

Those Lying Ways

Several cues accompany deception. Although a liar may control the verbal content of a message, other communication channels may leak information.

The speech content of people who are being deceptive tends to vary from the norm. They make fewer factual statements than usual; they are prone to vague, sweeping statements; and they frequently leave gaps in their conversation, apparently in an attempt to avoid saying something that would give them away (Knapp, Hart, & Dennis, 1974). The voice alters as well; liars tend to speak at a higher pitch than truth tellers (Ekman, Friesen, & Scherer, 1976). An increase in manipulative gestures also accompanies lying in many instances: the deceiver is more apt to touch the face with the hand, for example (Ekman & Friesen, 1974)—a finding that echoes the observations of Louis Nizer (1973)—or to play with glasses or some other external object (Knapp et al., 1974).

Facial expression is somewhat less reliable as an indicator of deception. This finding may be explained in part by the fact that people are more aware of their facial expressions than they are of some of the other nonverbal channels, and thus they can attempt to control the face they present to others. People also vary considerably in the face they present; some people smile while they are lying, for example, whereas others maintain a placid expression. Some other facial signs may indicate emotion but do not reliably point to the specific emotion that calls them forth. For example, the blinking rate or the extent of pupil dilation may increase when a person is lying, but the same signs may accompany general nervousness as well. The face gives more microscopic cues that are less easily controlled (Ekman, 1985), but such cues are not so readily interpreted by the average observer.

Some people are better at lying than others. Recalling the discussion of self-monitoring in Chapter 3, you might expect that people high in self-monitoring would be more successful in controlling at least some of the cues of deception. Aron Siegman and Mark Reynolds (1983) found that to be the case when they examined the ability to control the temporal pacing of speech: people high in some aspects of self-monitoring can speak at the same pace when they lie as when they tell the truth. People who are highly motivated to lie—because they believe, for example, that the ability to lie is related to career success—tend to be good at controlling the verbal aspects of their presentation. The same people are apparently less successful in controlling the other nonverbal channels, however, a failing that often permits their deception to be detected (DePaulo, Lanier, & Davis, 1983).

Detecting Deception

Paul Ekman (1985), who has studied deceptive communication for years, has identified a number of conditions under which lying is relatively easy to detect. Some of them include the following:

1. The liar does not anticipate exactly when he or she has to lie.
2. The lie involves emotions felt at the moment.
3. Amnesty is available to the liar who confesses.
4. The punishment that will follow discovery is severe.
5. The liar and the target are personally acquainted.
6. The lie is not authorized by some official body.
7. The liar is not practiced in lying.
8. The liar does not have a good memory.
9. The liar has not successfully deceived the target before.

Although these conditions are helpful, and liars provide a large variety of nonverbal cues to their deceit, observers do not use all this information. Even those whose occupation relies on the ability to detect deception are not necessarily very good at the task. U.S. Customs officers, for example, should be particularly skillful in distinguishing travelers who are likely to be carrying contraband, yet a study that compared a sample of these workers with a random group of college students indicated no superiority in the customs agents (Kraut & Poe, 1980).

Why is our ability to detect deception so poor? For one thing, observers tend to rely too much on the vocal aspects of a message. People who have access to both vocal and facial cues, for example, are no better at detecting deception than people who only hear the deceptive message (Zuckerman, DePaulo, & Rosenthal, 1981). Reliance on verbal cues may make people inattentive to channels through which more reliable information is being conveyed. Of course, when only the verbal message is available, detection of deceit is particularly difficult. Reading the transcript of a trial, for example, is probably not a very good way to tell if a witness was lying. People may also rely on their own theories as to which cues are relevant, and those theories may be wrong. If nervous blinking is not a valid indicator of lying, for example, then it will not do much good to pay attention to that sign.

Another reason for our poor ability to detect lies is that we often do not receive feedback that would permit us to know whether our assumptions were right or wrong. As Leonard Saxe (1991) has noted: "There is an ambiguity to most lies that makes their detection, as well as their understanding, difficult. Uncomfortable as it may be, there is often no objective way to identify the truth" (p. 413). In the absence of such feedback, faulty theories can persist.

A further reason why detecting deception is difficult is that many cues used to detect deception are also cues for other communication processes. Consider, for example, the observation that people are more likely to exhibit speech disfluencies—interruptions of the normal flow of speech, such as "uh," "er," and "um"—when they are lying than when they are telling the truth (DePaulo, Lanier, & Davis, 1983). Stanley Schachter and his colleagues (Schachter, Christenfeld, Ravina, & Bilous, 1991) have demonstrated that such disfluencies generally are more likely to occur when content is relatively unstructured or when the speaker has a larger number of synonyms for a particular word. Thus, "hemming and hawing" may indicate that the speaker

is actively constructing a deceptive communication, but it may also indicate only that the speaker is choosing from several equally truthful but different ways to express a point.

Even the use of specialized equipment, such as the polygraph or "lie detector," does not provide an infallible means by which to detect deception. A polygraph enables one to detect changes in physiological arousal by measuring heart rate, respiration, and skin conductivity. Saxe (1985), however, has argued that the arousal measured under typical testing conditions is fear of detection, as opposed to arousal associated with deception per se. For example, in one study (Saxe, Schmitz, & Zaichkowsky, described in Saxe, 1991) subjects were given a chance to take money from a desk drawer and told they would be able to keep the money if they could pass a polygraph test. In one condition, subjects were informed that the polygraph was not particularly reliable. Under such circumstances, all the subjects who had taken the money passed the polygraph test. Presumably, the guilty subjects were not afraid of being caught by the faulty machine. On the other hand, about half the subjects who had not taken the money failed the test; perhaps they were (correctly) afraid the polygraph results would not substantiate their innocence. Thus, the validity of measures of arousal as a means of detecting deception depends on the extent to which those being tested believe the measure to be reliable.

Despite our generally poor ability to detect deception, we can more readily detect deceit in some people than in others. For example, lies told by women seem to be more readily detected than lies told by men. Further, lies told by a person of the other gender are more easily spotted than lies told by someone of our own gender (DePaulo, Stone, & Lassiter, 1985). Exactly why these disparities are found is not clear, but they suggest that our experience may be more beneficial in some areas than in others.

What makes some lies more believable than others? According to Ralph Rosnow's (1991) recent review of research on rumors, there are four conditions under which deceptive communications will be believed, even to the point that we are willing to pass them along to others as "true." The first condition occurs when listeners are generally uncertain; rumors and other lies are believable when listeners can use them to relieve cognitive ambiguity and create perceptions of predictability. The second condition occurs when listeners are experiencing personal anxiety, are concerned about the outcome of a situation addressed in the rumor. Third, deceptive communications that are elaborations built upon a "kernel of truth" are more believable than are complete fabrications. Finally, all other conditions being equal, rumors are more likely to be believed when listeners' levels of outcome-relevant involvement are low. That is, the less directly involved in the outcome listeners are, the more likely they are to believe a deceptive communication and relay it to others.

▶ Communication and Social Interaction

As we noted at the beginning of this chapter, communication links one person with another. Looking inward, each of us is concerned with our own identities, goals, and motivations. Looking outward, each of us has a set of beliefs and theories about other people,

both as individuals and as groups. It is through communication that these identities and beliefs take shape.

As we discussed in Chapter 4, individuals often approach other people with some prior expectations that are not necessarily valid. Yet the process of communication may confirm one's initial expectations. This general phenomenon is known as the **self-fulfilling prophecy**—the fact that a perceiver's beliefs about another person may elicit from that person behavior that confirms the initial expectation. As one example of the self-fulfilling prophecy, consider the philosophy, "Be nice to others, and they will be nice to you."

Researchers have closely examined the process by which we elicit reactions that conform to the expectations we have conveyed (Jones, 1986; Miller & Turnbull, 1986; Snyder, 1984). John Darley and Russell Fazio (1980) have termed this process the **expectancy confirmation sequence.** As Figure 5.9 indicates, the expectancy confirmation sequence involves five steps. For the sake of clarity, the figure considers the process from the viewpoint of one person, *A*. In fact, of course,

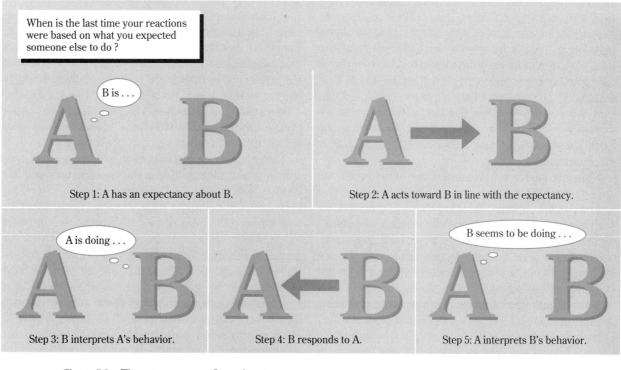

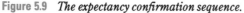

Figure 5.9   *The expectancy confirmation sequence.*

both people in an interaction are simultaneously perceivers and targets.

In the first two steps of the sequence, the perceiver has a set of beliefs about the target and behaves toward the target on the basis of those beliefs. Again, as we saw in Chapter 4, a perceiver's beliefs can originate from any number of sources. They may be based on past interaction with the target. The wife of twenty years may know from experience, for example, that her husband will react angrily when she tells him he needs a haircut; therefore she may speak more tentatively or stand at a greater distance than usual when telling him. Alternatively, beliefs about an individual may derive from stereotypes about a group to which the individual belongs. Whatever the beliefs, it is quite likely that the perceiver will communicate them in some way to the target.

This communication sequence has been confirmed by numerous studies. Mark Snyder and William Swann (1978), for example, told subjects that their partner in a competitive game was either hostile or nonhostile. Perceivers who believed their partner was hostile acted more competitively toward the partner than did subjects who had no such belief. In another study demonstrating the influence of stereotypes, male students engaged in a ten-minute telephone conversation with a female student who they believed to be either physically attractive or unattractive (Snyder, Tanke, & Berscheid, 1977). Analysis of conversations revealed that men who believed their partner was an attractive woman were friendlier, more outgoing, and generally more sociable than those who believed their partner was less attractive.

How do perceivers communicate such beliefs to their targets? As we might expect, they use both verbal and nonverbal channels. Monica Harris and Robert Rosenthal (1985) identify the following behaviors as those that convey a positive expectancy: maintaining closer physical distances, having longer interactions, interacting more often, encouraging more, engaging in more eye contact, smiling more, and praising more.

The target who receives such a communication must then interpret exactly what the perceiver is doing (step 3 in Figure 5.9). For example, if Linda believes Kirby is hostile and therefore stands farther away from him than is normal for their interaction, Kirby may compensate and attempt to move closer. If she, believing his move is hostile, moves away again, Kirby may conclude Linda does not like him. Whether or not the interpretation is correct, the target's response is based on what he or she believes the perceiver has communicated. The target's response, whether in words or in action, in turn sends a message back to the perceiver. Sometimes the response confirms the perceiver's initial belief, an instance of the self-fulfilling prophecy. In Snyder and Swann's study of competitive behavior, for example, targets whose partners thought they were hostile, and who accordingly acted hostile, tended to respond in a hostile manner. Similarly, the women in the telephone conversation study whose partners believed they were attractive responded with more sociability, poise, and humor than did women who were believed to be unattractive—even though the women in the two conditions did not actually differ in degree of physical attractiveness and were unaware that their partner knew anything about their looks. In yet another demonstration of the expectancy confirmation effect, people in a study of conversational interchange were told that their partners either liked them very much or didn't particularly like them. People who believed they were liked responded in kind: they disclosed more information about themselves, they had a more pleasant tone of voice and general attitude, and they were less likely to disagree or express feelings of dissimilarity in later conversations (Curtis & Miller, 1986). After the conversation, their partners really did like them better than partners who had been described as less approving.

The expectancy confirmation sequence has been shown to affect interaction in the classroom as well. Rosenthal and Jacobson (1968) found that teachers' beliefs about the abilities of their students could affect the performance of those students. When teachers were led to believe that a (randomly selected) group of students were brighter than average, the students scored higher on an intelligence test at the end of the school year than another group of randomly selected students who had not been described as above average. In such situations, as subsequent research confirms, the expectancy confirmation sequence is played out: first, the teachers develop expectations; second, their beliefs affect their behavior toward the students; and third, the students tend to react to the differential treatment in ways that confirm the initial beliefs (Jussim, 1986). Such is the power of beliefs.

It would be a mistake, however, to assume that a perceiver can always shape the behavior of a target. Targets are, after all, individuals with their own self-identities and goals, and they may just as easily choose to disconfirm a perceiver's expectancies (Miller & Turnbull, 1986). Predicting just when a target will and will not confirm a communicated expectancy is one of the challenges of this particular approach (Deaux & Major, 1987). Investigators have identified some conditions that favor nonconfirmation. When a perceiver's expectation is highly discrepant from the target's firmly held self-conception, for example, the target is not likely to engage in the expected response (Swann & Ely, 1984). Also, if the perceiver's beliefs are made explicit, the target is better able to ignore them (Hilton & Darley, 1985). Nonconfirmation is particularly likely when the perceiver has conveyed a negative expectation, which most of us would be unlikely to endorse.

The final step in the expectancy confirmation sequence is the perceiver's interpretation of the target's behavior. This perception may accurately reflect the target's response, particularly when behavioral confirmation is provided by the target's response. Sometimes, however, perceivers elect to maintain their initial beliefs, even in the face of nonconfirming evidence, through a process of cognitive confirmation. In other words, a perceiver may choose to see what he or she believes, ignoring information that tends to be inconsistent with that belief (Darley & Gross, 1983).

The sequence of expectancy confirmation does not necessarily stop when a particular conversation ends (Jones, 1986). If people treat you as competent, for example, and you act competently in response, you may begin to see yourself as a competent person. This self-conception of competence may cause you to act more confidently in the future, continuing the sequence a step further. Consider, for example, males' responses to the tentative female speakers in Linda Carli's (1990) study, discussed earlier and illustrated in Figure 5.8. Based on stereotypic beliefs, the men expected the women to behave in a manner consistent with lower status and so rewarded them by agreeing with them when they spoke tentatively. In subsequent attempts to

Teachers' beliefs about the abilities of their students can affect the performance of those students.
Nita Winter/The Image Works

persuade men, the women are likely to speak tentatively because that particular style worked well. The resulting self-fulfilling prophecy provides further support for men's expectations about the relative status of women, strengthens the stereotype, and increases the likelihood of continued gender differences in communication.

Of course, there are limits to the expectancy confirmation sequence. In one experiment, for example, Thomas Holtgraves, Thomas Srull, and Daniel Socall (1989) asked subjects to observe a staged conversation between two men. Half the subjects believed one conversant was the other's boss, and the other half believed the conversants were co-workers. In addition, sometimes one conversant was instructed to act as the other's boss, and at other times both conversants were instructed to act as co-workers. The results indicated that a speaker's verbal and nonverbal cues are as important as the expectations of people attending to the speaker. That is, subjects perceived one of the conversants as "the boss" only when the subjects were told he was the boss *and* the conversant was told he was the boss.

Thus, communication both results from and contributes to the outcomes of social interactions. It constantly shapes our views of ourselves and of others, defines present realities, and lays the groundwork for future interaction. We will again return to communication, the core of all social interaction, as we discuss liking, hating, helping, harming, and other topics in later chapters.

▶ Summary

Communication is fundamental to most social behavior. Although the forms of communication are varied, it has been truthfully said that we can't *not* communicate. Current models stress that communication is a shared social system, with both partners bringing a set of expectations and understandings to the interaction. Both verbal and nonverbal communications are part of this shared system.

We communicate through many channels, including language, paralanguage, gaze, facial expressions, body movements, gestures, touch, and interpersonal distance. The study of our use of language, the most obvious form of communication, reveals how important intention and interpretation can be. The nonverbal behaviors, including gaze, serve a variety of purposes. Five specific functions are (1) to provide information, (2) to regulate interaction, (3) to express intimacy, (4) to exercise social control, and (5) to facilitate the accomplishment of tasks.

Facial expressions convey a variety of emotions, and these basic emotional expressions can be identified by people in very different cultures. Cultures may differ, however, in the display rules that govern the circumstances in which an emotion will be expressed. Interpersonal distance is a more abstract form of communication, but it too is an important means of conveying information. Four major zones (intimate, personal, social, and public) define the distances between people that accompany different types of interchange.

All these verbal and nonverbal channels combine in the communication process to convey meaning. Three major dimensions of communication have been identified (liking, status, and responsiveness); each dimension is associated with a distinctive set of nonverbal cues. Two models have been proposed to explain how nonverbal cues are combined to convey liking. The equilibrium model proposes that participants in an interaction seek to achieve a balance between pressures toward approach and avoidance, and that participants compensate for an excess of pressure in one direction by sending nonverbal messages designed to restore the balance. The arousal model suggests that the way a change in arousal level is interpreted depends on the way the situation is defined. Sometimes compensation will be the rule, and at other times reciprocity is more likely.

Conversations have a regular structure, and the elements of that structure—an opening, a body, and a close—are typically regulated by a set of rules or conventions. Conversations between partners in a close relationship tend to follow somewhat distinctive rules. Self-disclosure, for example, is both more common in such conversations and less subject to rules of strict reciprocity.

Deceptive communication is accompanied by specific patterns of verbal and nonverbal behaviors. However, although deceit may be leaked, observers are often unable to distinguish the truth teller from the liar.

Self and social knowledge combine in the communication process. Often a person's beliefs about another can influence that other person's behavior, creating a self-fulfilling prophecy. Five steps constitute the expectancy confirmation sequence, in which the perceiver's beliefs are conveyed to a target, who interprets the message and then acts in accordance with that interpretation. The target's response may thus tend to confirm the perceiver's beliefs. In other circumstances the target will disconfirm expectations in order to communicate some other message to the perceiver.

▶ *Key Terms*

connotation
conversational implicature
cooperative principle
denotation
display rules
emblems
expectancy confirmation sequence
facial affect program
facial feedback hypothesis
illocution
illustrators
kinesics
locution
paralanguage
self-disclosure
self-fulfilling prophecy
social register
visual dominance behavior

People are disturbed not by things but by the views that they take of them.

Epictetus

We have too many high sounding words, and too few actions that correspond with them.

Abigail Adams

6

The Nature of Attitudes

In 1940 few people were aware of the existence of atomic bombs. Nor did many people understand the potential of nuclear power. That situation changed with the bombings of Hiroshima and Nagasaki. People who a short time before had never heard of atomic fission formed strong opinions on both sides of the issue. Most Americans supported President Truman's decision to use atomic weapons. In a 1945 public opinion poll, 93% of a random sample of the U.S. population said they would have used the bomb (Fiske, Fischhoff, & Milburn, 1983). By 1982, attitudes had shifted somewhat, although a majority of U.S. citizens still supported Truman's decision. Asked whether it was necessary and proper to have dropped the atomic bombs on Japan during World War II, 63% said it was, and 26% said they thought it was wrong. The remaining 11% were not sure. Different distributions of attitudes could undoubtedly be found outside the United States, reflecting different experiences with nuclear power.

Nuclear power is only one of many issues on which people take a stand. What do you think about gun control, abortion, space exploration, social science research, and the killing of whales? Attitudes are equally pervasive in less controversial realms. What kind of ice cream do you prefer, which is the best television show, who is your favorite performer, and what brand of toothpaste do you like? Each of these questions is a question about your attitudes.

Attitudes serve as an index of individuals' thoughts and feelings about the people, the objects, and the issues in their environment. More important, they provide clues to future behavior, enabling us to predict how people will act when they encounter the objects of their beliefs. For example, as we stated in Chapter 4, we are much more likely to arrive at a dispositional explanation if someone's behavior is consistent with what we believe their attitudes to be. In this chapter we consider what attitudes are, how they develop, and how they relate to other beliefs and to behavior. In Chapter 7 we will examine persuasion and its influence on attitudes.

▶ The History of Attitudes

More than fifty years ago the distinguished Harvard psychologist Gordon Allport described attitudes as "the keystone in the edifice of American social psychol-

ogy" (1935, p. 798). But just what *is* this concept that not only is central to social psychologists but is part of the common language as well?

Definitions of Attitudes

In one of the earliest uses of the word, *attitude* meant a physical posture or body position; it still holds this meaning for kinesiologists (Williams & Lissner, 1962). In early experiments on reaction time, experimenters referred to a subject's "attitude" when they meant a readiness to respond to the onset of a stimulus (Himmelfarb & Eagly, 1974). In more recent times the term has generally been limited to mental states. Thus, attitudes are not directly observable events. Rather, they are abstract constructs that can represent internal structures and processes (like the schemas discussed in Chapters 3 and 4).

The term *attitude* is widely used by psychologists and the public alike—for example, "Jeremy has an attitude problem" and "try to adopt a positive attitude." Many different definitions have been offered, often reflecting particular theoretical positions that are accepted by some investigators but rejected by others. To allow room for a variety of such positions, we will use a flexible definition: an **attitude** is an evaluation of some object about which an individual has some knowledge (Pratkanis & Greenwald, 1989). By evaluation we mean any judgment on a dimension, such as good-bad or positive-negative. The object of an attitude can be anything. Someone may think his or her parents are wonderful, volleyball is a good sport, cats are so-so pets, and anchovies taste awful. Each of these thoughts represents an attitude, an evaluation of the object on a particular dimension. It is not necessary to know a great deal about a particular object in order to have an attitude about it, but one must have enough knowledge to be able to represent the object in memory, to think about it.

Two other terms—*value* and *opinion*—should be mentioned before we go further. *Values* are broad, abstract goals that lack a specific object or reference point. Bravery, beauty, and freedom are values. They serve as dimensions of judgment or as abstract standards for decision making, through which the individual may develop specific attitudes and beliefs (Rokeach, 1973). Thus, if beauty is one of your primary values, many of your beliefs may be based on judgments as to whether a particular object is beautiful. The value of practicality may be more important to other people, and so their attitudes and beliefs regarding the same object may differ sharply from yours. For example, Pamela Homer and Lynn Kahle (1988) found internal values such as self-fulfillment, sense of belonging, and security to be strongly related to attitudes about nutrition, which in turn were related to food-shopping behavior. However, the values were not directly related to behavior. Thus, attitudes play a mediating role in translating our values into actions.

Opinion is less easily defined. Closely associated with public opinion polling, which focuses on the shared attitudes and beliefs of large groups of people, *opinion* is often used to refer to expressed attitudes. The term has also been used interchangeably with *attitude*. Following McGuire (1985), we will simply note that there is little point in attempting to distinguish between attitudes and opinions. If a more specific term (such as *expressed attitude*) is required, it makes sense to use that term instead of *opinion*.

Values such as freedom provide abstract standards for decision making.
Laurent Rabours/AP/Wide World Photos

Components of Attitudes

Early attitude theorists proposed that attitudes have three basic components: the cognitive, the affective or emotional, and the behavioral or conative (Katz & Stotland, 1959). As McGuire (1985) has noted, the proposition that people take three existential stances regarding the human condition—knowledge, feeling, and acting—has been advanced by philosophers throughout history. As far back as Plato, terms designating cognition, affect, and behavior were used to refer to the three components of what we call attitude (Oskamp, 1977).

However, recent theorists have questioned the utility of the three-component view of attitudes (Fazio, 1990; Pratkanis & Greenwald, 1989; Tesser & Shaffer, 1990; Zanna & Rempel, 1988). These theorists consider behavior to be separate from attitude and include the proposition that behavior itself may be an attitudinal object. One may, for example, either like or dislike one's tennis playing; that is, one can have an attitude about a behavior. Affect, too, has been considered separately, primarily because the role it plays in attitudes depends on the situational context (Millar & Tesser, 1986) and on the particular object of the attitude (Breckler & Wiggins, 1989; Burke & Edell, 1989). Most people's attitudes toward anchovies, for example, probably do not involve a great deal of emotion. On the other hand, attitudes toward parents usually include some emotional aspect.

Consistent with our earlier definition, only *knowledge* (information associated with the object) and *evaluation* (judgments based on knowledge) remain as essential parts of an attitude. It is necessary to distinguish between knowledge and evaluation because the components of one person's attitude do not always match those of another person's about the same object. Two people may share the knowledge that jogging is an aerobic exercise, for example, but may differ sharply in their judgments about jogging. As a further example, two people can evaluate recycling positively, but one may consider it a "rebate" on newspaper subscriptions, whereas the other's relevant knowledge may concern ecological survival. Different evaluations lead to different behaviors, but so does different knowledge about the object. We need to know something about both components of an attitude if we are to predict behavior.

Measurement of Attitudes

Measuring attitudes is easier said than done. You can't see, smell, or touch an attitude; it is an underlying construct that must be inferred. To make such inferences, psychologists have developed many methods of measurement, all designed to tap people's underlying attitudes toward various objects and issues in their environment (Dawes & Smith, 1985).

In its simplest form, an attitude measure might consist of open-ended questions—for example, "What do you think about space exploration?" Such questions have the advantage of eliciting a broad range of views and, sometimes, more detail than some of the other forms. However, open-ended questions also have the disadvantage of low reliability (a person may answer differently on different occasions even though his or her attitude has not changed), and it is difficult to compare the answers of different respondents because their answers can vary so widely. Although open-ended questions can be quite useful in the initial stage of an investigation—when one is not sure of all the issues that may be involved—later stages of attitude research generally call for more closed-ended questions that allow more precision.

Many types of questionnaires and rating scales have been developed to measure attitudes more precisely. To give you an idea of what these scales look like, we will discuss two types of scales in some detail—the Likert method and the semantic differential technique.

The Likert method of summated ratings In 1932 Rensis Likert proposed a procedure for measuring attitudes that has been widely used ever since. A **Likert scale** consists of a set of declarative statements with which subjects are asked to indicate the degree of their agreement or disagreement. A sample item from such a scale is shown in Figure 6.1. The number of response categories may vary, but five or seven is the most common number.

A Likert scale will contain a series of such items, and a person's final attitude score will be the sum of the responses to all items. For example, if there are twenty items on the scale, each with five categories, a person's score can range from 20 to 100. In refining a Likert scale, an investigator will generally conduct analyses to determine which questions are the best measures of

Nuclear power plants are a safe means of energy production.

Strongly disagree	Disagree	Undecided	Agree	Strongly agree
1	2	3	4	5

Figure 6.1 *A sample item from a Likert scale of attitude measurement.*

the attitude being studied. The investigator will elect to keep only those items that are related to the same attitude.

The semantic differential technique The Likert method requires the investigator to create a series of items specific to the issue at hand and then to determine whether the items are worthwhile measures of attitudes toward the issue. The **semantic differential technique,** in contrast, relies on ratings of bipolar adjectives that are general enough to be applied to any topic (Osgood et al., 1957).

This method, which was originally developed to measure the meaning of an object (hence the term *semantic*), requires a person to rate a given concept on a series of seven-point bipolar rating scales, as shown in Figure 6.2. Any concept—a person, a political issue, a work of art, a group, or anything else—can be rated. In

Nuclear Energy

Fair	— — — — — — —	Unfair
Large	— — — — — — —	Small
Clean	— — — — — — —	Dirty
Bad	— — — — — — —	Good
Valuable	— — — — — — —	Worthless
Weak	— — — — — — —	Strong
Active	— — — — — — —	Passive
Cold	— — — — — — —	Hot
Fast	— — — — — — —	Slow

Figure 6.2 *A sample item from a semantic differential scale of attitude measurement.*

the usual format, the respondent places an *X* at one of the seven points on the scale to indicate his or her rating of the item on each bipolar dimension.

The adjective scales used in this format have been found to represent the same three dimensions identified for communication in general (see Chapter 5): evaluation (as represented by such pairs as good-bad and clean-dirty), potency (for example, weak-strong), and activity (such as active-passive or fast-slow). Investigators interested in attitudes usually concentrate on the evaluative dimension, but at times the other dimensions may be of interest as well.

Both the Likert and semantic differential scales are relatively direct techniques for measuring attitudes. However, attempts to measure attitudes directly can produce **evaluation apprehension**—defined in Chapter 2 as an individual's concern about the impression he or she is making—and make it difficult to obtain an accurate response. Subjects may, for example, feel a need to express a position they think the interviewer favors rather than to state their true opinion. Also, the order in which items appear on even the most well-developed scale can affect responses to the items. Roger Tourangeau and his colleagues (Tourangeau & Rasinski, 1988; Tourangeau, Rasinski, Bradburn, & D'Andrade, 1989) have shown that, through **priming,** questions concerning one attitude can alter responses to questions about a different attitude. Earlier questions will make certain information more accessible in memory, thus affecting subjects' responses to later questions. For example, if an item about aborting a fetus with serious birth defects appeared early in a questionnaire about abortion, subjects would be less likely to agree with later pro-choice items than they would if the birth-defect item were not included (Schuman & Presser, 1981).

Because self-report responses should always be treated with caution, researchers have developed several indirect techniques for measuring attitudes. One such measure is the *lost-letter procedure,* conceived by Stanley Milgram and his colleagues (Milgram, Mann, & Harter, 1965). Stamped letters or postcards addressed to organizations associated with the issue that interests the researcher are dropped in parking lots and on street corners, and the experimenter waits to see how many are picked up and mailed to their destinations. If you wanted to know how residents of a community felt about gun control, for instance, you could address one hundred letters to the National Rifle Association (NRA) and another one hundred letters to the National Committee to Ban Handguns (NCBH). The address on both sets of envelopes would be a post office box that you rented so you could keep track of the outcome. If more letters were mailed to the NCBH than to the NRA, you might conclude that community opinion tended to favor gun control. Of course, this method has its problems. Letters may not be returned for many reasons, including loss or destruction by the weather; conversely, many people would probably mail the letter no matter how they felt about the organization to which it was addressed. Thus, although it avoids the problems of self-report, the lost-letter technique is at best a rather crude measure of attitudes.

Other indirect measures of attitudes rely on responses over which people have little control, such as pupil dilation or skin conductance (Blascovich & Kelsey, 1990; Dawes & Smith, 1985). John Cacioppo and his colleagues, for example, have demonstrated that slight muscle movements around the mouth can be used as an indicator of mental processes associated with attitudes (Cacioppo, Petty, & Marshall-Goodell, 1984; Cacioppo, Petty, & Tassinary, 1989). The mere fact that a measure does not require self-report, however, does not necessarily mean it is better than one that does. Ultimately, the technique must measure attitude-related behaviors—the only reason to measure attitudes at all.

▶ The Formation of Attitudes

People have attitudes about many things. But where do these attitudes come from? As you might suspect, there is no single answer to this question. Some attitudes are based on direct experience with the attitude object, whereas others are acquired less directly. For example, a person may develop an attitude toward pizza as a result of eating pizza, but the same person could develop an attitude toward squid without ever actually tasting it. Attitudes can be learned through direct reinforcement or acquired through imitation and social learning. In short, there are a great many routes to attitude formation.

Direct Experience with the Attitude Object

Perhaps the most obvious way to develop an attitude toward some object or issue is through a personal experience that results in an evaluation of the object. You taste your first piece of pizza, you like the taste, and you develop a positive attitude toward pizza. Conversely, your first taste of pizza may be so unpleasant that a negative attitude is formed. Both of these cases illustrate simple processes by which an attitude can be acquired. Sometimes the single event is more dramatic (McGuire, 1985). A religious experience, a childhood trauma, a wartime bombing—such incidents can create strong attitudes toward relevant issues and objects.

Sometimes one acquires an attitude by virtue of an object's association with other objects about which attitudes have already been formed. Such are the principles of classical conditioning. Building on earlier work by Leonard Doob (1947), Arthur Staats (1967) used a classical conditioning model to explain one way of acquiring attitudes. In the now-familiar experiments associated with Ivan Pavlov and his dogs, an unconditioned stimulus (UCS) is paired with a new stimulus, called the conditioned stimulus (CS). Through the process of association, Pavlov's dogs learned to respond to a bell that was paired with meat powder. The same type of learning can occur for attitudes (see Figure 6.3). The new response is called a conditioned response (CR), and Staats defines an attitude as such a response—a conditioned evaluative response to some object in the environment.

To apply these principles to the acquisition of attitudes, consider your associations with the word *stupid*. Most people would react negatively to this description. Now assume that a particular politician is always described as stupid. Presumably you would learn to evaluate that politician negatively as well, even if you know nothing else about him or her.

A simple encounter with an object does not necessarily lead a person to develop an attitude toward that object. Every day the average person encounters innumerable objects, issues, and groups, many of which may call forth no attitude at all. For example, you may walk into a large department store and encounter hundreds of different products. Do you have an attitude toward each of them? Probably not. If an employee of the department store approaches you and *asks* what you

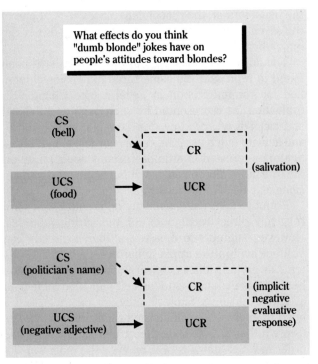

What effects do you think "dumb blonde" jokes have on people's attitudes toward blondes?

Figure 6.3 *Classical conditioning model. The original Pavlovian situation is represented in the top half of the diagram; the parallel process for social attitudes is shown in the lower half.*

think of portable vacuum cleaners, however, you may form an attitude on the spot. In other words, direct questioning may cause attitudes to form. Even the expectation that one will be asked about a particular object or issue in the future seems to be enough to cause attitudes to develop (Fazio, Lenn, & Effrein, 1983/1984). Presumably such anticipation is functional, allowing an individual to be prepared to understand and react to situations that would otherwise be unfamiliar.

Parents and Peer Groups

Many attitudes are acquired from other people. Parents are the earliest and most obvious sources of acquired attitudes. The political attitudes of children, for example, are remarkably similar to those of their parents on the average (McGuire, 1985). Peers are also a major influence on attitude acquisition, as the cycles of teenage fads testify. Attitudes toward music, clothing styles,

Attitudes about clothing styles and hairstyles develop in the context of peer interaction.
Martin Benjamin/The Image Works

hairstyles, and many other things develop in the context of interaction with peers. Children's ideas about smoking are related to the opinions of both parents and peers. A study of British 15-year-olds, for example, indicated that boys who smoked were more likely to have fathers and friends who smoked. Further, according to the boys' reports, their parents were more tolerant of smoking than those of boys who did not smoke (Eiser & van der Pligt, 1984).

Various principles of learning can help to explain how such attitudes and the correspondent behaviors are acquired. Principles of operant reinforcement apply to the situation in which a reward immediately follows the expression of an attitude. Imagine that you express an opinion about nuclear disarmament, and a listener excitedly says, "You're right!" Would you be more likely to endorse that opinion in the future?

A classic study of the role of reinforcement in attitude acquisition was conducted at the University of Hawaii (Insko, 1965). Students were phoned by an interviewer who sought their opinions about "Aloha Week" (festivities held every fall in Honolulu). To half the students, the investigator responded with "good" when the student said something favorable about Aloha Week; the other half received a "good" response following unfavorable statements about Aloha Week. By this means, verbal reinforcement was accomplished—positive evaluations were reinforced in some of the students, negative evaluations in others.

About one week after the telephone calls, the same students completed an apparently unrelated "Local Is-

sues Questionnaire" in their regular class meeting, and one of the items on this questionnaire asked for their attitudes toward Aloha Week. Students in the group whose positive evaluations had been verbally reinforced by the telephone interviewer expressed more favorable views than subjects in the group that had been verbally reinforced for negative evaluations. The effect of verbal reinforcement thus appeared in another setting one full week later.

Why does a verbal response such as "good" have an effect on expressed attitudes? One possibility is that the response leads the person to believe that adopting the other's apparent attitude will result in future reinforcements. Some people have questioned whether the reinforcement itself is really the cause of changes in attitudes, suggesting that **demand characteristics** may be a more reasonable explanation. It is possible that students who participated in Insko's study expressed either more favorable or more unfavorable attitudes toward Aloha Week on the Local Issues Questionnaire because they felt they were supposed to rather than because any true shift in attitude had occurred (Page, 1974).

Although demand characteristics may account for some experimental findings, there is little doubt that attitudes can be conditioned. A child who knows that her parents approve when she says school is good and disapprove when she says school is bad is aware of what her parents want to hear (their demands); yet it is still possible that the child's positive attitude toward school may be due in part to the reinforcement she re-

Advertisers attempt to foster favorable attitudes toward their products.
Dion Ogust/The Image Works

ceives. In a similar manner, praise and approval from friends and relatives can effectively mold attitudes.

The principles of **social learning theory** also help to explain how some attitudes are formed. As we saw in Chapter 1, people can learn simply by observing the behaviors of others. Those others (called models) can express particular attitudes, which then may be adopted by the individual who witnesses their expression. In the case of parents and children, observational learning is at least as important as direct reinforcement and is probably more common. Similarly, people probably acquire many of their attitudes through imitation of their peers without having any direct experience with the targets of the attitudes. Someone may imitate statements made by friends—"drugs are dangerous," for example—and as a result may form a negative attitude toward drugs without any direct experience with them. Imitating the behavior of peers also leads to direct experiences that produce attitudes toward behaviors.

Attitudes also form (and change) as a result of the roles we occupy. In a classic study described in Chapter 1, Seymour Lieberman (1956) demonstrated that attitudes of workers promoted to managers became more pro-management and more anti-union than those of workers who were not promoted. Similarly, workers elected to the position of union steward changed in di-

rections consistent with their new roles. In a laboratory simulation of Lieberman's study, Randy McCombe and Lloyd Stires (1990) replicated the original results. In the latter study, the college students being "promoted" or "elected" presumably formed their attitudes as they played out their roles in the experiment.

Media Influence

Parents, peers, and the roles we perform are not the only models that affect the formation of attitudes. The media, and in particular television, are another powerful source of attitudes (Oskamp, 1988; Roberts & Maccoby, 1985). Research has shown that the media can both create attitudes and reinforce those that already exist. For example, children's requests for specific foods are correlated with the frequency with which those foods are advertised on television (Taras et al., 1989). Advertisers attempt to foster a favorable evaluation of the product through the information conveyed in the advertisement, as well as indirectly through creating a favorable attitude toward the advertisement itself. The latter is often accomplished by manipulating viewers' emotional response (Burke & Edell, 1989).

Nor is attitude formation limited to advertising. In one study, Eskimo children were exposed to television for the first time when they saw a series about other cultures and values. Children who watched this series underwent significant changes in their beliefs about other cultural groups (Caron, 1979). In the case of gender-role stereotypes, differences in the amount of television viewing have been shown to affect the sexism scores of adolescent girls. Heavy television viewing increased sexism scores, particularly among girls of middle-class families. Interestingly, this effect was not found among boys. Although boys who initially were more sexist in their views did watch more television, their attitudes were not altered by their viewing experience (Morgan, 1982).

Political campaigns, particularly U.S. presidential campaigns, increasingly depend on television to create positive attitudes toward the candidates. The attempts to create favorable attitudes are not always successful, of course. On occasion an advertising campaign has backfired, fostering negative rather than positive attitudes. Even those who report the actions of political candidates, such as news broadcasters, can affect the formation of attitudes toward the candidates (Mullen et al., 1986).

Attitude formation can also be influenced by existing attitudes via priming. Shanto Iyengar and his colleagues designed an experiment that considered the effects of news programs on viewers' attitudes (Iyengar, Kinder, Peters, & Krosnick, 1984). Students at Yale University watched televised evening newscasts that covered a variety of issues, including civil rights, United States–Soviet relations, and energy problems. The students were divided into three groups that differed only in their level of exposure to stories about energy (none, intermediate, or high). The investigators predicted that students who were exposed more frequently to energy stories would be more likely to evaluate the performance of the president, Jimmy Carter, on this dimension because it would be more accessible to them. The investigators' findings supported their hypothesis. The students who had high exposure to the energy issue based their overall evaluation of President Carter primarily on their beliefs about his performance on energy issues. If they thought he was strong in this area, they rated his overall performance favorably; if they thought he was weak in this area, his overall performance was devalued. Other issues were less important for these students. In contrast, students who had less exposure to energy stories did not base their overall evaluation on this issue. Thus, television broadcasters, by making some issues more salient than others, can influence the dimensions on which potential voters base their attitudes. This influence of the media is a fairly subtle one, affecting the dimensions of judgment rather than affecting the evaluation of the candidate directly.

In summary, individual attitudes can be formed in many ways. Some attitudes may be developed through the operation of basic learning and reinforcement principles; others are formed as a person acquires information about new topics. Because we have attitudes about people as well as about objects and issues, the process of attitude formation may mirror the process of impression formation (Fiske & Neuberg, 1990) described in Chapter 4. That is, as we directly or indirectly encounter an attitudinal object, we may first categorize the object and determine whether additional attention is required. If more attention is required, new information may lead us to confirm the initial categori-

zation, recategorize the object, or develop an entirely new category. Once formed, attitudes are then in a position to affect other attitudes and behavior as well.

▶ The Structure and Functions of Attitudes

Attitudes are pervasive, encompassing a broad spectrum of topics and issues. Although it would be fairly easy to study attitudes if each attitude were self-contained, the situation is in fact complex. Sets of attitudes tend to be interrelated, and, as we will discuss in the next chapter, anyone attempting to change an attitude must recognize these interrelationships. Also, attitudes affect the processing of related information and serve some of the same functions—priming, organization, and so on—as schemas (Chapters 3 and 4). In this section we shall consider some additional structural issues and functions specific to attitudes.

Complexity and Values

One way to think about the structure of attitudes is in terms of their complexity and flexibility. Two people can have the same general attitude on a particular issue, yet they can differ greatly in the way they express that attitude. One person may be rigid in defense of the attitude and never question it; the other may have developed the same general attitude after frequent questioning and consideration of alternative views. The differences among members of political elites in regard to complexity of thought have been a major question for the psychologist Philip Tetlock. In Chapter 2, when we discussed archival research, we examined Tetlock's study of Supreme Court justices' decisions. Tetlock has investigated other decision makers as well, including members of the British House of Commons (Tetlock, 1984). Once again his interest was in what he calls integrative complexity—the degree to which people have multidimensional views of an issue and integrate a variety of information in arriving at their position. Consider the following statements, representing the two extremes of this dimension, made by two parliamentarians who were interviewed about their views on the economy.

Person A: The key problem is that we have been living way beyond our means for far too long. We have to tighten our belts. Nobody likes to face this unpleasant truth, but that's the way it is.

Person B: We always have to deal with competing priorities in making up the budget. Most basically, we face the tension between the need to fund social welfare programs to which we are committed and the need to stimulate private sector expansion. But there is no simple rule to resolve that tension. [Tetlock, 1984, p. 369]

Person *A* represents a simplified position in this case, whereas person *B* reveals consideration of more than one dimension of the problem. (It is, of course, a matter of debate as to which style of thought is better or more effective.)

The politicians investigated in the course of this study were classified into four groups on the basis of their political stance: extreme socialists, moderate socialists, moderate conservatives, and extreme conservatives. As Figure 6.4 shows, the level of attitudinal complexity varied with the parliamentarians' political stance. Those who took extreme positions to either the right or the left were more unidimensional in their attitudes than the more moderate politicians.

Why should moderates differ in complexity from those who take more extreme attitudinal positions? Tetlock suggests that one needs to examine the values that underlie attitudes. In the case of political attitudes, at least two values are paramount in a democracy—equality and freedom. Tetlock suggests that people who take extreme positions clearly favor one of these values over the other. Freedom is more important to the conservative; equality is more important to the socialist. Given such clear priorities, attitudes regarding a particular position should also be quite clear. Moderates of both persuasions, in contrast, attach more nearly equal importance to both values. Consequently, many issues arouse in such people a conflict between fundamental values, thereby complicating the process of arriving at a final position. Tetlock calls this model *value pluralism*. The more equal weight people give to potentially conflicting values, the more complex their attitudinal positions tend to be.

Value pluralism is not an issue for political elites alone. As Tetlock (1986) has shown, one can understand the complexity of many attitudes in terms of value conflict. College students who highly value both the beauty of nature and personal prosperity, for example, are more likely to have complex attitudes toward opening public lands to mining and drilling oper-

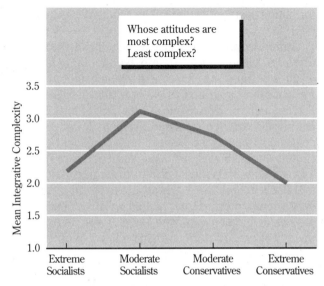

Figure 6.4 *Attitudinal complexity and political beliefs of British parliamentarians*

Source: "Cognitive Style and Political Belief Systems in the British House of Commons" by P. E. Tetlock, 1984, *Journal of Personality and Social Psychology, 46,* pp. 365–375.

ations. As we noted earlier, such conflicts may be a major factor in the moderation of the attitudes of the people who experience them (Chaiken & Stangor, 1987; Homer & Kahle, 1988).

Complexity also applies to the knowledge structure of an attitude (Pratkanis & Greenwald, 1989). Some attitudes are *bipolar,* so named because the knowledge component of such attitudes contains information that is both favorable to (supports) and unfavorable to (refutes) the evaluation of the object. That is, regardless of an individual's evaluation of an object, his or her knowledge about the object includes both positive and negative information. Attitudes concerning controversial issues, such as majority rule in South Africa, capital punishment (Judd & Kulik, 1980), and abortion (Hymes, 1986), are likely to be bipolar. Other attitudes are labeled *unipolar* because the knowledge component contains only information that supports the evaluation of the object. For example, if your knowledge about anchovies is limited primarily to how they taste and to the fact that they are small fish, your attitude toward anchovies is probably unipolar.

Why are some attitudes bipolar? One function of attitudes involves presentation of the self (Pratkanis &

Greenwald, 1989; see also Chapter 3). We are more likely to encounter disagreement from others concerning our attitudes on controversial issues. Perhaps we make the extra effort to remember information on both sides of the issue because we wish to avoid appearing uninformed, because we want to be able to hold our own in such disagreements, or simply because we are exposed repeatedly to information on both sides.

How Attitudes Interrelate

Attitudes toward seemingly different topics are not always independent of one another. Basic values that underlie a set of attitudes provide a kind of glue that holds those attitudes together. Thus, the person who values equality may see women's rights, homosexual rights, and aliens' rights as interrelated issues. Attitudes may also be held together by their connection to a general world view. David Buss and Kenneth Craik (1983) have identified two contemporary world views that tie together beliefs on such diverse issues as economic growth, societal goals, and world responsibility. Items characteristic of each of these views are shown in Table 6.1.

World view *A* endorses high growth and high technology. Proponents of this view tend to take a pro-business stance and favor rational, quantified decision-making processes. World view *B,* in contrast, suggests that material and technological growth should level off. Proponents of this view are concerned with redistribution of wealth from richer to poorer nations, the social and environmental impacts of growth, and decentralization of control and decision making.

People who endorse these two different world views differ in many other ways. Proponents of world view *B,* for example, are more likely to anticipate catastrophic outcomes from modern technologies (such as X rays and pesticides). The urban setting appeals to people who hold world view *A;* the *B*'s prefer open spaces and natural environments. These general patterns are important, Buss and Craik suggest, because they can guide the formation of new attitudes. People do not necessarily form individual attitudes toward each new form of technology that arises. Confronted by a particular technology, however, the individual may rely on his or her general world view to come to terms with it.

Attitudes relate not only to other attitudes but also

Table 6.1   Contemporary world views: Sample items from two orientations

WORLD VIEW *A*

1. A high-growth, high-technology society provides the best hope for raising the poor to a high state of material and social well-being.

2. Some of the decentralization talk heard nowadays is romantic nonsense; we can never go back to the family farm.

3. On the whole, centralization promotes efficiency and effective management.

WORLD VIEW *B*

1. The social and environmental costs of continued technological growth and rising per capita energy consumption are intolerably high.

2. Decision making in our society should be made as participative as possible and guided more by humane criteria.

3. The rich nations of the world consume far more than their fair share of the earth's limited resources and contribute far more than their share of environmental damage.

Source: "Contemporary Worldviews: Personal and Policy Implications" by D. M. Buss and K. H. Craik, 1983, *Journal of Applied Social Psychology, 13,* pp. 259–280.

to general moods and feelings. Beliefs about the use of nuclear power and the possibility of nuclear war, for example, not only relate to each other but form a general cluster that has been termed *nuclear anxiety* (Newcomb, 1986; Zur, 1990). People who are characterized by this cluster of attitudes tend to feel a greater sense of powerlessness and depression and to be less satisfied with their lives generally. Further, such people—particularly men—have a greater tendency to use drugs on a regular basis. Thus, ways of coping with life may be related to particular attitudinal positions.

Attitudes and Information

The influence attitudes have on the way related information is perceived is the *schematic* function of attitudes (Pratkanis & Greenwald, 1989). Having established an attitudinal position on a particular issue, for example, people often interpret new information in ways that will be consistent with their beliefs. They also are more likely to remember information that is consistent with their particular beliefs (Roberts, 1985). Though selective, the schematic function is not limited to information that supports attitudes. Bipolar attitudes also contain information that opposes the evaluation of the object, and people sometimes pay especially close attention to information that contradicts their beliefs (Chaiken & Stangor, 1987).

Enjoyment of support for one's attitudes leads to other behaviors as well, including **selective exposure,** a combination of seeking consistent information and avoiding inconsistent information. For example, people sometimes actively look for information that will support their beliefs. At the same time, they will take steps to avoid encountering information that contradicts those beliefs.

People often hold political attitudes with a great deal of fervor, and it is not surprising that selective exposure operates here. Consider the case of the U.S. voter who, in the 1972 election, voted either for George McGovern or for the successful candidate, Richard Nixon. Six months later the U.S. Senate opened its hearings on the Watergate break-in, investigating President Nixon's involvement in or knowledge of the illegal activities of the Republican reelection committee. Were McGovern and Nixon supporters equally likely to watch the televised hearings? The selective exposure hypothesis predicts not, a prediction supported in a series of interviews conducted by Paul Sweeney and Kathy Gruber (1984). McGovern supporters reported paying more attention to the hearings and being more interested in politics than they had been previously. Nixon supporters, in contrast, reported a significantly lower level of interest in the Watergate coverage. Supporting a selective exposure interpretation, the findings of this study also revealed that McGovern supporters could recall the names of more people involved in the scandal than could Nixon supporters, as well as the names of members of the investigating committee and of witnesses who testified before the committee. Thus, the supporters of both McGovern and Nixon showed evidence of selective exposure: McGovern supporters by seeking information that damaged the opposition candidate, and Nixon supporters by avoiding information that threatened their beliefs. Such activities help to maintain the attitudes people already have.

▶ **Attitudes and Behavior**

Do attitudes predict behavior? People who study attitudes have traditionally assumed that the answer is yes. Find out a person's attitude, and you should be able to predict what that person will do. For example, if you assess a person's attitude toward environmental protection and find that it is positive, then you might expect the person to save bottles and newspapers for recycling. But would your prediction be accurate? Not necessarily.

What Attitude and What Behavior?

Early in the history of attitude research, investigators learned that attitudes and behaviors were not always directly related. Early evidence that called such linkage into question was provided by Richard LaPiere (1934). In the early 1930s strong feelings existed against Asians in the United States, particularly along the West Coast. LaPiere, a highly mobile sociologist, took a Chinese couple on a three-month automobile trip, twice across the United States and up and down the West Coast. The trio stopped at 250 hotels and restaurants during their trip, and only once were they refused service. Later LaPiere wrote to each of these establishments, asking whether it would accept Chinese patrons. Only about half the proprietors bothered to answer, but of those who did, 90% said they would not serve Chinese! In a similar study, Kutner, Wilkins, and Yarrow (1952) arranged for a black woman to join two white women seated in a restaurant, repeating this procedure in eleven restaurants. In no case was the black woman refused service. However, later telephone calls requesting reservations for an interracial party produced six refusals and five grudging acceptances of the reservation.

These studies suggest some discrepancy between behavior and attitude, but some problems can be seen in each of the studies. For example, in neither case was attitude actually assessed. Instead, an indication of intended behavior was compared with an actual behavior. Further, there is no way of knowing whether the person who refused the reservation by letter or by phone was the same person who had admitted the Chinese or black persons when they visited the establishment. If they were not the same people, then it makes no sense

Individuals' attitudes about the environment may result in the specific behavior of volunteering to pick up debris along a highway.

Dan Chidester/The Image Works

to talk about inconsistency. An additional question raised by these studies concerns the existence of other attitudes that might be relevant to the behavior. The hotel and restaurant personnel might also have had attitudes regarding embarrassing people, causing a scene, filling empty hotel rooms and restaurant tables, or any number of other beliefs that took precedence at the time (Dawes & Smith, 1985).

In the face of failures (some more sophisticated than the preceding studies) to find expected relations between measured attitudes and observed behavior, many social psychologists (for example, Wicker, 1969) began to believe that the concept of attitude was not useful in their attempts to understand human behavior. But other investigators, rather than throwing out the baby with the bath water, have pointed to several reasons that the expected relationship may not always be strong and, at the same time, have charted new directions for the investigation of attitudes. Let us consider some of these reasons for the weakness of the relationship found.

First, consider the *level of specificity* at which attitudes and behaviors are defined. Investigators have often used a very general measure of attitudes (for example, attitudes toward psychology) and then looked at a very specific measure of behavior (such as willingness to enroll in a social psychology course taught at Classic University by Professor Knowlittle). It is not surprising that such a general measure of attitude has little power to predict such a specific behavior.

Experiments in which the measure of attitude is more specific have been much more successful in predicting specific behavior. For example, Weigel, Vernon, and Tognacci (1974) measured people's attitudes toward general issues, such as the environment, and toward more specific objects, such as the Sierra Club. Later the investigators gave subjects the opportunity to volunteer for Sierra Club activities. Although no relation between general environmental attitudes and Sierra Club activities was found, the researchers discovered a strong relation between the more specific attitudinal measures and the actual behavior. Similarly, Wilson, Kraft, and Dunn (1989) found a high correlation between attitudes toward a political candidate and the number of campaign posters the subjects took for distribution, but only for those subjects who were knowledgeable about the candidate.

A related issue concerning the attitude-behavior relation is the question of single acts versus multiple acts. Investigators have generally selected a single behavior to test their predictions. Yet if we are interested in a general issue, such as attitudes toward the environment, then it probably makes more sense to examine a series of possible behaviors. In other words, although a person's general attitude toward the environment may not be an accurate predictor of his or her response to any single activity, such as joining the Sierra Club or recycling bottles, that attitude may be a much more accurate predictor when a whole series of behaviors related to the environment is taken into account. Many factors can influence a decision to engage in any single act. Over a wide range of behaviors, however, the general attitude is likely to exert a more powerful influence.

One of the reasons for seeking a broader range of behavioral indexes is that behavior is complex and multidetermined. Our attitude toward an object will affect some of our behavior, but other factors can influence our behavior as well. Suppose an older man tells his friend, "The less contact I have with teenagers, the better; they're loud and disrespectful," and then boards a bus. Noting that all the seats but one are occupied, the man takes the available one—next to a teenager. We cannot conclude that his verbal statement is false just because his choice of seats has repudiated it. Even the apparently simple action of taking a seat may be multidetermined. Although the man might prefer not to sit next to a teenager, perhaps his feet hurt so much that sitting anywhere is preferable to standing. Observation of future behavior, however, might prove more enlightening. Perhaps the man would refuse to take that bus again or would change his schedule to avoid traveling when the bus was crowded. Other situations involving the man's interactions with teenagers might show a consistency between expressed attitude and actual behavior. In short, one-time measures of behavior don't give us much information about the strength of the attitude-behavior relation.

When situational pressures are strong, people of widely differing attitudes may act in a similar way. If a child were about to be hit by a car, for example, most people, no matter what their attitude toward the child's racial or ethnic group, would probably try to save the child. Yet in other situations that did not involve a threat to life, attitudes toward various groups might influence one's reaction to a child. In general, we can say that the stronger the situational pressures toward some behavior, the less likely individual differences in attitudes are to affect the behavior. (We shall return to this general point in Chapter 13.)

Another issue regarding the attitude–behavior relation is that a given behavior may be linked to more than one attitude. In the case of a child about to be struck by a car, a person might have one set of attitudes toward the child's ethnic group and another set of attitudes toward children. Which attitude would best predict behavior? Thus, the relation between behavior and a single attitude may appear inconsistent because other attitudes have greater influence.

A Theory of Planned Behavior

Our ability to predict when and how attitudes influence behavior has been increased tremendously by the work of Izek Ajzen (1985, 1987), who developed the *theory of planned behavior*. This theory is an extension of an earlier theory of reasoned action, which Ajzen developed with Martin Fishbein (Fishbein & Ajzen, 1975; Ajzen & Fishbein, 1980). Both theories include the assumption that behaviors are performed for a reason— that people think about the consequences of their actions and make deliberate decisions to achieve some outcomes and avoid others.

The elements of the theory of planned behavior are illustrated in Figure 6.5, which shows that intention is the key antecedent to behavior. It is the behavioral intention, rather than the attitude itself, that predicts the behavior. As is also illustrated, however, three major components—attitude toward the behavior, subjective norms, and perceived control—combine to produce a behavioral intention. It is important to note that Ajzen has defined his task very precisely: he is concerned with the prediction of very specific behaviors on the basis of attitudes. Therefore, Ajzen assesses each of the model's components in terms of the specific behavior with which they are concerned. Nearly any behavior and its correspondent behavioral intention could be studied within this framework, from a decision to use birth control to the choice of a particular toothpaste.

According to the theory, an individual's attitude toward the behavior in question is the product of two factors: (1) beliefs about the consequences of that specific behavior and (2) an evaluation of those possible outcomes. Each of these factors varies among individuals, as do behaviors. Consider a student's decision to spend an additional ten hours a week studying. Two people may agree on the likely outcomes of this behavior— better grades and less time to spend with friends, for example—but differ in their evaluation of those outcomes. Julie may value a high grade point average much more than time spent with friends. Consequently, her attitude toward additional study will be more positive than that of Hal, who views friendships as very important and grades as only moderately so.

The second component of the model, subjective norms, introduces a social element: the person's beliefs about what other people think he or she should do, and the strength of the person's motivation to comply with those expectations. Julie and Hal, for example, may consider the expectations of their parents, their friends, and perhaps their favorite professor when they decide whether to spend more time studying. Julie may be sure her parents favor study and be motivated to comply with their expectations, whereas Hal may have the same perception of his own parents but not care about complying with their wishes. Similarly, the expectations of friends and peers influence some people more than others.

The third component, perceived behavioral control, involves the notion that some behaviors are under greater control than others. More important, according to Ajzen, are the individual's beliefs about control. Thus, even though Julie may place a high value on good grades and be motivated to comply with her parents' expectations, she is less likely to study if she believes she has little control over the grade she receives (Ajzen & Madden, 1986). Similarly, Stephan may have a positive attitude toward donating money to charity and believe that others also endorse such action. Yet if he believes he has no money to spare, our ability to predict his behavior from his attitude will be weakened.

These three factors combine to determine a person's intention to perform the behavior in question. As you might expect, the relative importance of attitudes, norms, and perceived control will vary from issue to issue. The relative importance of these components may also be affected by aspects of one's self-concept. Lynn Miller and Joseph Grush (1986) reasoned that attitudes should be most influential for people who tend to be very aware of their own attitudes and who are relatively unconcerned about the behaviors and opinions of others. To test their hypothesis, Miller and Grush measured subjects' attitudes, perceived norms, private self-consciousness, and self-monitoring (see Chapter 3). Miller and Grush found that among people who scored high in private self-consciousness and low in self-monitoring, the attitude component was strongly related to behavior. But among people who scored in the opposite direction on both measures, the researchers found greater correspondence between subjective norms and behavior and much weaker relationships between attitudes and behavior.

The theory of planned action can be used even more effectively to predict behavior when one also takes into account attitudes toward *not* performing the behavior. For example, Jaccard, Helbig, Wan, Gutman, and Kritz-Silverstein (1989) found the *difference* between attitudes toward diaphragm use and attitudes toward becoming pregnant was strongly related to consistent diaphragm use. Neither attitude predicted behavior very well separately, but when the difference between them was large enough, 90% of the women consistently used

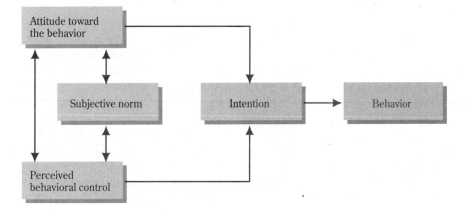

Figure 6.5 *A theory of planned behavior.*
Source: "Attitudes, Traits, and Actions: Dispositional Prediction of Behavior in Personality and Social Psychology" by I. Ajzen, 1987, *Advances in Experimental Social Psychology, 20,* pp. 1–63.

diaphragms. That is, women who used diaphragms consistently had both a very positive attitude toward diaphragm use *and* a very negative attitude toward becoming pregnant.

In summary, the theory of planned behavior has been very useful in efforts to predict behavior in relation to a wide range of issues and objects. It does not predict all behavior, but it does predict quite well, particularly with well-planned behavior. However, although in most instances it would seem that one would need to look no further than behavioral intention to predict actual behavior, such is not the case. Other factors also affect behavior. For example, past behavior is often the best single predictor of future behavior, independent of expressed attitudes and normative concerns. Further, not all behaviors are planned (Mittal, 1988; Tesser & Shaffer, 1990). What the theory of planned behavior does not do is tell us *how* and *why* attitudes do or do not influence behavior. To answer those questions, as well as to predict unplanned behavior, we need to consider the processes involved.

How Do Attitudes Influence Behavior?

Confident that attitudes indeed predict behavior, investigators have begun to consider the hows and the whys of the attitude-behavior relationship. That is, investigators are studying the process by which an attitude in the mind is translated into a behavior that can be observed objectively.

A major component of the process of converting an attitude into a behavior, according to Russell Fazio (1986), is whether a particular attitude is active in working memory. As we saw in Chapter 4, some schemas or knowledge structures in an individual's memory may not be immediately accessible. If an attitude is made accessible, however, then it is much more likely to guide behavior. In that case, the behavior is consistent with the attitude.

What kinds of events are likely to make attitudes accessible? Various cues in the environment can make a person think about a particular topic. The sight of your class notebook, for example, might make you think about studying, just as signs announcing a nuclear disarmament rally might activate your attitudes toward nuclear energy. A direct request that you think about your attitudes toward some issue will, not surprisingly, make that attitude more accessible. So, too, will performing a

Various cues in the environment can make us think about a particular topic.
Mimi Forsyth/Monkmeyer Press

behavior that has implications for an attitudinal position. **Self-perception theory** suggests that we sometimes infer our attitudes from observations of our own behavior (see Chapter 3). Thus, helping a friend stuff envelopes for a student government campaign will make a person think about his or her attitudes toward the candidate. As Fazio and his colleagues have shown, the presence of the attitude object spontaneously accesses the attitude. This process not only makes attitudes accessible at the moment but also increases the accessibility of that attitude in the future (Fazio, Herr, & Olney, 1984).

The accessibility of an attitude is also determined by its overall strength. The stronger the attitude, the more likely it is to become available. Several factors contribute to the strength of an attitude and hence to its general accessibility (measured in laboratory experiments by the speed of reaction time). Attitudes that have been expressed often, for example, are more likely to be accessible than attitudes that are rarely expressed. Attitudes that are formed on the basis of direct experience are also more readily accessed than attitudes that are formed more indirectly (Fazio & Williams, 1986).

In one study in which actual (as opposed to self-reported) behavior was examined, Fazio, Powell, and Williams (1989) measured the accessibility of attitudes toward a variety of candy bars and other snacks. Accessibility was measured in terms of the speed with which subjects pressed a "like" or "dislike" button upon seeing the name of each product. Subjects also rated their attitude toward each product on a seven-point scale. At the end of the study, all the products were laid out on a table, and the subjects chose five of the ten as payment for participating. The attitude-behavior correlation was directly related to the accessibility of the attitude; the higher the accessibility, the stronger the attitude-behavior correlation.

Although thinking about one's attitude will often increase its correspondence with behavior, there are exceptions. Asking people to analyze the reasons for their attitudes, for example, may sometimes weaken the attitude-behavior link. In a study conducted in a university dining hall, female students were asked about their attitudes toward a variety of beverages, such as milk, diet colas, and iced tea (Wilson & Dunn, 1986). In one condition, the students were first asked to analyze the reasons they liked or disliked various beverages. In a second condition, the students were asked simply to think about how much they liked each beverage. A third set of students, in a control condition, received neither set of instructions. All students then were asked about their attitudes toward the beverages, and later their actual choice of beverage during dinner was assessed. As Figure 6.6 indicates, the relationship between attitude and behavior was lowest among students who first analyzed the reasons for their attitudes.

Thinking about the reasons one holds an attitude does not always reduce attitude-behavior consistency. Wilson, Kraft, and Dunn (1989), for example, demonstrated that the effects of thinking about reasons seem to be limited to attitudes that have a poorly developed knowledge component. Subjects who knew much about a political candidate's stands on various issues, for example, evidenced a strong attitude-behavior cor-

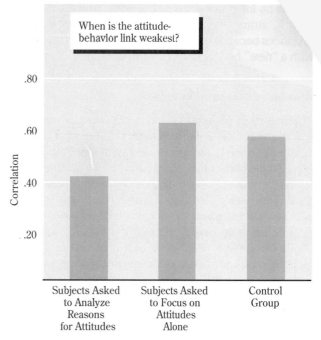

Figure 6.6 *Correlations between attitudes toward beverages and actual consumption of beverages.*
Source: "Effects of Introspection on Attitude-Behavior Consistency: Analyzing Reasons versus Focusing on Feelings" by T. D. Wilson and D. S. Dunn, 1986, *Journal of Experimental Social Psychology, 22,* pp. 249–263.

relation, with or without thinking about why they supported the candidate. It was only those subjects who did not know very much about their candidate whose attitude-behavior correlations were lower after thinking about the reasons they held the attitude.

Why should a request that one analyze one's reasons for holding an attitude have this effect? According to Wilson, Kraft, and Dunn, focusing on why one holds an attitude should, for knowledgeable people, confirm the evaluative component of the attitude. That is, if you *know* why you hold a particular attitude, thinking about those reasons should not produce any change in the attitude. On the other hand, when asked to provide reasons for their attitudes, those with a poor knowledge base may generate reasons that do not fit their evaluative component or may decide that their reasons are not very good ones. Either outcome could change the attitude. Thus, when people don't know much about an attitude object, the attitude that is measured *before* they think about reasons may be changed; the original attinger operative at the time of the behavior. ...de-behavior consistency is lower in such ...ause the "old" attitude is being compared ...ehavior.

Reason versus Spontaneity

The theory of planned behavior involves the assumption that the attitude-behavior link is based on a careful deliberation of attitudes, subjective norms, and perceived control over the intended behavior. On the other hand, the process of spontaneous attitude accessibility described earlier does not involve reasoning except, perhaps, after the fact. Which is correct? Russell Fazio (1990) has proposed a model in which he answers "both are correct" and provides a mechanism for explaining which processing mode is likely to operate.

Fazio proposes that, most of the time, spontaneous processing is likely to occur. An attitude is activated that, together with norms, creates selective perception of the situation, and appropriate behavior follows. Past behavior, the strength of the attitude, and the presence of the attitude object all increase the accessibility of the attitude, which increases the likelihood that the attitude will be activated. Habits, such as seat belt use, form because a strong attitude about the behavior is automatically activated in the presence of the attitude object. A more deliberative process, such as the theory of planned behavior, will occur only when people have both the motivation and the opportunity to engage in such reflection. Fazio calls his model the MODE model—"referring both to its emphasis on different processing modes for linking attitudes to behavior and its depiction of **m**otivation and **o**pportunity as **de**terminants of which processing mode is likely to operate in any given situation" (1990, p. 92).

To explain the motivations that might precipitate planned behavior, Fazio has borrowed from Arie Kruglanski's (1980, 1989) theory of how people acquire knowledge. Kruglanski proposes that *fear of invalidity,* a propensity to acquire information so as to avoid mistaken or invalid conclusions, is the basis for motivation to acquire information. (You may recall that similar concerns underlie the social comparison process discussed in Chapter 3.) According to Fazio, we interrupt the spontaneous processes of the attitude-behavior link whenever the potential cost of a mistaken judgment is high. When there is no fear of invalidity, we simply allow the spontaneous processing of attitudes to guide our perceptions of the situation and our subsequent behavior. But motivation is not enough; we must also have the opportunity. If the situation requires an immediate response, for example, we may not have time to reflect carefully about our attitudes.

In a test of the MODE model, Sanbonmatsu and Fazio (cited in Fazio, 1990) manipulated both general and specific evaluations of two department stores, Smith's and Brown's. Two-thirds of the information about various departments in Smith's store was positive, whereas two-thirds of the information about various departments in Brown's store was negative. In general, then, Smith's was the better department store. The information about the camera department in each store, however, was opposite to that of the general information. Smith's, the better store, had the poorer camera department; Brown's, the poorer store, had the better camera department. Later, subjects in the experiment were asked to imagine they needed to buy a camera and were given an opportunity to choose the store at which they would prefer to make their purchase. If the subjects were following a planned process to arrive at their intentions, they should choose Brown's better camera department. But if subjects were following a spontaneous process, they should choose Smith's, the better store.

Sanbonmatsu and Fazio manipulated opportunity by telling half the subjects to take their time in arriving at their decision and telling the other half they must decide within fifteen seconds. Motivation, specifically fear of invalidity, was manipulated by telling half the subjects in each opportunity condition that their decisions would be compared with those of other subjects and that they would have to explain their decisions to those other subjects and the experimenter. The other half of the subjects, those in the low motivation conditions, were not told anything about what would be done with their decisions. According to the MODE model, only those subjects who were allowed to take their time *and* were told their decisions would be compared to others' decisions should engage in planned action. This is exactly what happened. These subjects were more likely to prefer Brown's (the poorer store with the better camera department) than the subjects in any of the other three conditions. Planned intentions resulted, but only when there was sufficient motive *and* sufficient opportunity to interrupt the spontaneous attitude-behavior link.

Given some of these complexities, it is not surprising that early investigators sometimes despaired of finding a relationship between attitudes and behavior. Yet our understanding of just how and why attitudes influence behavior has improved considerably, thanks in large part to advances in our understanding of cognitive processes. Attitudes will continue to be a central issue for social psychologists because their consequences for social behavior are so extensive. And as we discuss in the next chapter, the attempts made by various people, institutions, and media to change our attitudes make our understanding of the attitude formation process all the more important.

▶ Summary

The many definitions of attitude that have been offered through the years have referred to both physical and mental states. As a working definition, we can consider attitudes to be evaluations of objects of thought on some particular dimension of judgment. The attitudes of a large group of people are referred to collectively as public opinion.

Most attitudes have two components: a cognitive or knowledge aspect and an evaluation aspect. Historically, a third component—behavior—has been included, but recent theorists have considered behavior separately. Different questions and measures may emphasize different aspects of an attitude. Two major measurement techniques are the Likert method and the semantic differential technique. Among the numerous other measures that have been developed, some are rather indirect indexes of attitudes.

Attitudes are formed in a variety of ways. Direct experience with the attitude object itself is a common means of developing an attitude, and learning theory principles can help to explain the acquisition process. Attitudes are also influenced by the opinions and behaviors of parents and peers and by the media, whose influence can be explained partially by social learning theory.

Attitude structure refers to the makeup of attitudes. Attitudes vary, for example, in their complexity. Value pluralism suggests that attitudinal complexity results from the amount of conflict between competing values that are relevant to a particular issue. Attitudes are related not only to basic values but to other attitudes as well. They also affect the ways in which other information is selected and retained in memory, so that this information often supports existent attitudes.

A major issue regarding attitudes is the relationship between assessed attitudes and observed behaviors. Some early investigators found little relationship between the two, but more recent work has substantially advanced our understanding of when and how such relationships will be found. In the theory of planned behavior, predictions of behavioral intentions, and in turn of behavior, are based on three factors: one's attitude toward the behavior, subjective norms in regard to that behavior, and perceived control over the behavior. More recent theory and research, however, indicates planned behavior occurs only when people have sufficient motivation and opportunity. At other times, the attitude-behavior link is spontaneous.

An understanding of the relationships between attitude and behavior entails an understanding of the processes involved. Advances in social cognition have helped to develop such understanding. The accessibility of an attitude is a major determinant of its ability to predict behavior, and conditions that make attitudes accessible continue to be researched.

▶ *Key Terms*

attitude
demand characteristics
evaluation apprehension
Likert scale
priming
selective exposure
self-perception theory
semantic differential technique
social learning theory

TRIUMPH OVER TYRANNY!

BUY WAR BONDS

Some praise at morning what

they blame at night,

But always think the last opinion right.

Alexander Pope

We are incredibly heedless in the

formation of our beliefs, but find

ourselves filled with an illicit passion

for them when anyone proposes to rob

us of their companionship.

James Harvey Robinson

7

Persuasion and Attitude Change

onsider a few moments in the life of a young woman named Joan. On a dreary Monday morning, Joan gets out of bed and turns on the television. She hopes the early-morning program will provide some positive information about the economy. Instead, an advertisement praises a new hair rinse that promises to transform her into the essence of charm, popularity, and sexuality. That's the last thing I need, Joan thinks—to heighten my sexuality. The phone rings. It's Ernie, still trying to persuade her to go away with him for the weekend. But Joan is resistant; she's not sure their relationship has progressed that far. She finally terminates the conversation by agreeing to meet for lunch and discuss it further then. She sighs, wondering when she will be able to finish the work she was going to do during lunch; quickly swallows her sugar-coated cornflakes; and scans the front page of the newspaper. The headlines are about the latest budget compromise winding its way through Congress. Joan wonders how effective the letter she wrote to her own congressional representative has been. As she leaves for work, the mail arrives, but it contains nothing but some throwaway ads.

If Joan had nothing else to do all day, she might be able to keep track of all the attempts to change her attitudes or behavior. On this particular morning, she has already been inundated by advertisements emanating from several media, including the cereal box. It seems that every story in the newspaper is about changing attitudes or behavior: pressures on a world leader, a local campaign to increase recycling, a story extolling the thrills of attending the state fair. And then there's always Ernie and his constant persuasion campaign.

Of course, persuasion operates in both directions. Not only do other people attempt to persuade us, but we also try to persuade others. To understand more about the occurrence of persuasion, Brendan Rule and her colleagues asked students at the University of Alberta two questions: "Who tries to persuade you in the course of your everyday life?" and "Whom do you try to persuade in the course of your everyday life?" (Rule, Bisanz, & Kohn, 1985). The students' answers, shown in Table 7.1, indicate that family and friends are the major sources of persuasion; over half the reported attempts to persuade came from these sources. Compared with other people, family and close friends are even more likely to be targets of our attempts at persuasion. Yet people on the average reported more attempts to persuade them (mean = 5.8) than they reported attempts at persuasion (mean = 4.6). Perhaps we perceive others as attempting to persuade us when they do not do so, or perhaps we are less likely to consider our own attempts to persuade others as persuasion.

As we saw in Chapter 6, the formation of attitudes

Table 7.1   The targets of persuasion: Percentage of responses in nine categories

	"Who tries to persuade you?"	"Whom do you try to persuade?"
Immediate family	27%	35%
Extended family	7%	5%
Close friends	18%	24%
Circumstantial friends	7%	12%
Instructors	13%	7%
Sales people	11%	2%
Other professionals	10%	3%
Trait-defined people (for example, religious people)	5%	9%
Goal-defined people (for example, people who are trying to impress me)	2%	3%
Average number of attempts within each category	5.8%	4.6%

Source: "Anatomy of a Persuasion Schema: Targets, Goals, and Strategies" by B. G. Rule, G. L. Bisanz, and M. Kohn, 1985, *Journal of Personality and Social Psychology, 48,* pp. 1127–1140.

has been a prominent topic of social-psychological research. So, too, is attitude change. Numerous theories have been developed to predict and explain the process of attitude change, and we will discuss several of them in this chapter. The theories differ in the mechanisms considered important in the attitude change process. Some theories emphasize perceptual processes, others emphasize cognitive consistency, and still others look to the motivations and functions that beliefs serve. In each case, the principles can be applied to persuasion that occurs not only in the psychological laboratory but also in such areas as advertising, health care, and politics. Later, we consider some general features of the attitude change process, including circumstances under which persuasion may be resisted.

▶ Theories of Attitude Change

Psychologists have developed many theories to explain how and when attitude change occurs. Some theories focus on the way individuals analyze incoming information and judge it against their own beliefs. Others pay more attention to learned habits or perceptual judgments. Although their emphases differ, all these theories identify some important factors in the broad process of attitude change.

Social Judgment Theory

At the core of **social judgment theory** is the assumption that people know what their attitudes are and are able to determine what attitudinal changes they are willing to accept and what changes they would reject. The theory proposes that an individual considers this knowledge when evaluating any persuasive communication. By way of analogy, think of shopping for a car and assume that you have an ideal price in mind, as well as an upper limit on what you can afford. If the price of a car is between your ideal price and your limit, you are likely to consider buying the car; but if a car's price is clearly beyond your limit, you will reject the car. In much the same way, social judgment theory proposes that each persuasive message is compared to the individual's current attitude: if the message is close to the existing attitude, change may occur; but if the message

is too far from the current position, the individual will reject the message, and attitude change will not occur.

The major developer of the social judgment approach to attitude change has been Muzafer Sherif (Sherif & Hovland, 1961; Sherif, Sherif, & Nebergall, 1965). In developing his theory, Sherif borrowed some perceptual concepts from psychophysics. One such concept is that of an **anchor,** a reference point used in making judgments. In social judgment theory, an anchor refers to one's current attitude, the reference point with which one compares persuasive messages. Two other principles Sherif used in his social judgment theory are assimilation effects and contrast effects. **Assimilation effects** refer to perceptual shifts *toward* an anchor point. Basing his ideas on this concept, Sherif proposed that we will perceive persuasive communications that are similar to our current attitude as more similar than they really are. **Contrast effects** refer to shifts in judgments *away from* an anchor point. According to this principle, we will perceive messages that differ from our own attitude as more discrepant than they actually are.

To explain how these judgments of assimilation and contrast are related to actual attitude change, Sherif introduced three new concepts: latitude of acceptance, latitude of rejection, and latitude of noncommitment (Sherif & Hovland, 1961; Sherif et al., 1965). As illustrated in Figure 7.1, each latitude refers to a range of specific attitudinal positions, reflecting Sherif's belief that a person's attitude is somewhat fluid and is best represented as a range of positions. For example, if you were presented with a set of statements on a particular issue, social judgment theory would predict that you would judge some to be consistent with your attitude and some to be inconsistent with it. The statements you judged to be consistent with your attitude would constitute your **latitude of acceptance.** The statements you perceived as inconsistent with your attitude would define the **latitude of rejection.** Finally, the **latitude of noncommitment** refers to the range "in between," neither particularly consistent nor particularly inconsistent.

According to social judgment theory, when a person encounters a persuasive communication, his or her first reaction is to consider whether the message falls inside or outside the latitude of acceptance. Once the person makes this judgment, attitude change may or

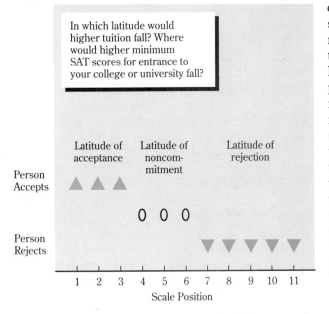

Figure 7.1 *Latitudes of acceptance, rejection, and noncommitment. Each number represents a particular attitudinal position.*
Source: "Width of the Latitude of Acceptance as a Determinant of Attitude Change" by A. H. Eagly and K. Telaak, 1972, *Journal of Personality and Social Psychology, 23*, pp. 388–397.

committed to either a Republican or a Democratic position, for example, did not differ from uncommitted or neutral people in the *size* of their latitudes of acceptance; of course, the content of statements within the latitude differed between committed and neutral people. Instead, the differences between committed and neutral people were in the width of latitudes of noncommitment and rejection. People at either extreme of the scale had larger latitudes of rejection and smaller latitudes of noncommitment than did people whose attitudes fell at the midpoint. In other words, the person who is a fanatic about some issue, such as gun control, will not necessarily find any fewer positions acceptable than will a less ego-involved advocate. Instead, the fanatic will reject more positions at the opposite end of the spectrum and be neutral about very few positions. Not all research is consistent with Sherif's findings, however, and the exact relation between ego involvement and size of latitudes is still uncertain (Eagly & Telaak, 1972; N. Miller, 1965).

The size of the latitude of rejection is important in Sherif's theory because it is the basis for predictions of attitude change. A person with a wide latitude of rejection would not be expected to change his or her position easily because a greater proportion of persuasive messages would fall in the latitude of rejection. For example, attitude change for a fanatic must occur in very small increments. Two fanatics at opposite ends of a continuum, therefore, could presumably spend all night trying to persuade each other to no avail.

Effects of discrepancy between communication and recipient's position On the basis of the principle of the latitudes, social judgment theory predicts a curvilinear or inverted-U relationship between discrepancy and attitude change. If you consider the implications of the various latitudes, the reasons for this prediction become clear. Messages that fall very close to the person's own position will probably be assimilated, and no real change will be necessary. That is, an attempt to persuade someone to change "just a little bit" should not work because the target will not perceive the message as different from his or her current attitude. On the other hand, messages that are highly discrepant with one's own position will probably fall within the latitude of rejection and will not be acceptable or effect any change. Between these two extremes, when

may not occur. Social judgment theory states that attitude change will occur only when a communication is judged to be within either the latitude of acceptance (Atkins, Deaux, & Bieri, 1967) or the latitude of noncommitment (Peterson & Koulack, 1969). Most research within the framework of social judgment theory has concentrated on two issues: (1) What are the effects of ego involvement in an issue on attitude change? and (2) How much is attitude change influenced by the discrepancy between the communication and the recipient's position?

Ego involvement and the latitudes If you are extremely committed to an issue, will you have a smaller acceptable range of positions than someone who is less intensely concerned with the issue? Surprisingly, Sherif and his colleagues say no; they found no difference in the size of the latitude of acceptance as a function of involvement in an issue. People who were strongly messages fall somewhere in the latitude of noncommitment, their persuasive impact should be the greatest. Research findings generally support this prediction (Hovland, Harvey, & Sherif, 1957; Peterson & Koulack, 1969).

Because the measurement procedures are somewhat cumbersome, some researchers have examined "crossing the midpoint" of a measurement scale as an alternative to explicitly measuring the latitude of rejection. Their reasoning is straightforward: a message that falls on the "other side" of someone's attitude is more likely to be perceived as within one's latitude of rejection (Nemeth & Endicott, 1976). That is, trying to persuade someone to change an evaluation from positive to negative, or vice versa, involves persuading someone to cross the neutral midpoint of the relevant dimension. Martin Fishbein and Rense Lange (1990) used such straightforward reasoning to examine the extent to which messages from the other side of the midpoint are persuasive. The answer they obtained was, essentially, "it depends." When the fact that the persuasive message fell on the other side of the midpoint was made explicit to their subjects, Fishbein and Lange's results indicated the subjects were less likely to change their attitudes. But when the scale position of the persuasive message was *not* explicit, the subjects were as likely to change their attitudes as were subjects who received a persuasive message from the same side of the midpoint. These results support the importance of a latitude of rejection but call into question the social judgment theory's assumption that people usually know where their own attitude position, and that of a persuasive message, falls on a scale.

Thus, the two main attractions of social judgment theory are (1) the notion that attitudes are best understood as ranges rather than pinpoint-specific positions and (2) the recognition of an optimum distance between the subject's attitude position and the position of the persuasive communication. Although some applications of social judgment theory have been made, it has not been used so extensively in the practical arena as some other models. The theory is somewhat limited, dealing only with the variables of message discrepancy and a person's ego involvement in the issue. Also, social judgment theory is not particularly useful for understanding situations that involve more than one attitude.

Balance Theory

Balance theory relies on the principle of cognitive consistency to explain attitude change. Like social judgment theory, consistency theories assume that we are aware of our attitudes and behaviors. And like the self-concept theories described in Chapter 3, consistency theories assume that we are motivated to keep our attitudes and behaviors consistent. Holding inconsistent attitudes, like holding inconsistent self-schemas, is assumed to be an uncomfortable experience that leads to attitude change. (Cognitive dissonance theory, discussed in the next section, also emphasizes this principle.) Thus, consistency theories deal primarily with self-persuasion, situations in which we change our attitudes, as opposed to situations in which someone else tries to change our attitudes.

Although consistency theories assume that we are thoughtful, they do not necessarily posit that we are rational. Robert Abelson and Milton Rosenberg (1958) coined the term *psycho-logic* to refer to the process whereby we may alter our beliefs so that they are psychologically consistent without necessarily following the strict rules of formal logic. For example, if you know cigarettes can cause cancer and yet continue to smoke, the belief and the behavior are inconsistent. To resolve this uncomfortable state of inconsistency, you may deny that cigarettes have anything to do with disease or presume you are immune to the link between smoking and cancer. Such choices are not totally rational, but denial allows your continued smoking behavior to be consistent with your beliefs.

Fritz Heider (1946, 1958) was the first to develop a consistency theory to explain how people view their relationships with other people and with their environment. For simplicity, Heider limited his analysis to two persons (P and O) and to one other entity (X). The person P is the focus of analysis, and O represents some other person; X can be an idea, another person, a thing, or any attitude object. Heider's goal was to discover how the relationships among P, O, and X are organized in P's cognitive structure. Heider proposed that two possible relationships could exist among these three elements—a *unit relationship* (belonging together, as in ownership or membership in a group) and a *liking relationship*. Both relationships may come into play in any given situation. For example, members of a group (unit relationship) often assume that other members of the same group share their opinions (liking relationship) on a variety of issues (Spears & Manstead, 1990).

In formulating **balance theory,** Heider proposed that the relations among P, O, and X can be either balanced or unbalanced, depending on the pattern of relationships among elements. Consider the following example. Paul (P), who has spent all summer as a volunteer worker for the Republican presidential candidate, begins his first year at the state university intending to major in political science. His faculty adviser is Professor O'Hara (O). At their first meeting, Paul notices that Professor O'Hara is wearing a campaign button for the Democratic candidate. Will Paul like Professor O'Hara? Will Paul think much of the professor's recommendations about which courses to take or career plans? Probably not, because Paul should feel a little uncomfortable in an unbalanced relationship. If X in this example stands for the Democratic candidate, an unbalanced state exists if Paul likes Professor O'Hara, because they disagree about the Democratic candidate. As long as Paul dislikes Democrats and the professor likes them, the only way a balanced state can exist within Paul's cognitive structure is for Paul to dislike Professor O'Hara. Paul can say, in effect, "Professor O'Hara doesn't know what she's talking about, which figures because she supports the Democratic candidate."

Heider proposed that balanced states exist either when all three relations are positive (as in liking) or when two relations are negative (disliking) and one is positive (see Figure 7.2). The preceding example fits the latter possibility. Of course, if Paul had found that his adviser was a Republican and had come to like her, then balance theory would describe the relationship as "P likes O, P likes X, and O likes X." As Figure 7.2 indicates, unbalanced states do occur; people do like other people who differ in their attitudes toward important issues or objects. The reverse situation is also possible: you may discover that someone you hate intensely likes the same science fiction author that you do. In general, unbalanced states exist wherever there is an odd number of negative relationships. What do you do about unbalanced states? Heider proposed that such states produce tension and generate forces to achieve or restore balance. If you dislike both ballet (−) and Henry (−), and you discover that Henry also dislikes ballet (−), you may be motivated to reconsider

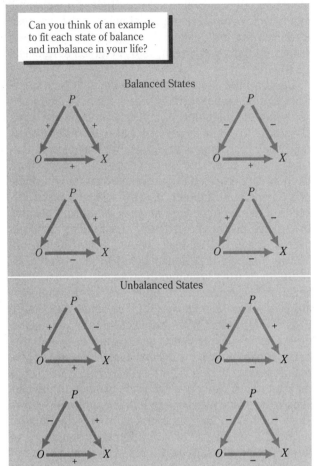

Figure 7.2 *Heider's balance theory: Examples of balanced and unbalanced states according to Heider's definition of balance.*
Source: "The Concepts of Balance, Congruity, and Dissonance" by R. B. Zajonc, 1960, *Public Opinion Quarterly, 24,* pp. 280–296.

your evaluation either of ballet—there must be something good about it if that no-good Henry hates it—or of Henry—anyone who hates ballet can't be all bad.

In the realm of political opinion, balance theory can often explain how voters view candidates and their positions. Donald Kinder (1978), for example, studied voters' perceptions of the 1968 U.S. presidential candidates: Richard Nixon, Hubert Humphrey, and George Wallace. At the same time, Kinder asked the voters about their own stands on several issues, such as the problem of urban unrest. In line with balance theory, voters who thought using more force was the solution to urban unrest tended to see their preferred candidate as having similar views on the issue. Voters who were opposed to the use of force saw *the same candidate* as sharing their views. Because they liked their candidate, voters assumed their candidate shared their likes and dislikes about a variety of issues. In balance theory terms, voters attempted to achieve a balanced relationship among the triad consisting of (1) their attitude toward an issue, (2) their attitude toward a candidate, and (3) the candidate's attitude toward that issue.

In addition to predicting situations in which people are motivated to change their attitudes, balance theory provides one explanation for the false consensus bias discussed in Chapter 4; people tend to assume others' attitudes are similar to their own. When Donald Granberg and Edward Brent (1983) studied U.S. election survey data collected between 1952 and 1980, they found that voters systematically biased their estimates of which candidate would win. By a ratio of about 4 to 1, voters thought their own candidate would win. In the 1932 election, for example, 93% of the voters who preferred Franklin D. Roosevelt predicted he would win. In contrast, only 27% of Herbert Hoover's supporters thought Roosevelt would win. Using the framework of balance theory, we can consider P to represent the individual voter, O to represent the general electorate, and X to represent the issue of who should be president. Balance occurs if all views are consistent: P likes a particular candidate (X), and P belongs to the general electorate (O); therefore, P believes that voters also like the candidate and will vote for X.

As described here, balance theory is a fairly simple approach to the understanding of attitude change. Research support for balance theory, as for many other simple theories, has not been overwhelmingly consistent despite the development of more complicated versions of the theory that incorporate more elements and different types of relationships among the elements (Insko, 1981, 1984). However, the basic principle of balance theory—the importance of consistency among various attitudes—has remained an extremely influential part of research and theory concerning attitude change.

Cognitive Dissonance Theory

Another type of consistency theory, first proposed by Leon Festinger (1957), is **cognitive dissonance theory,** illustrated in Figure 7.3. Cognitive dissonance exists when two related cognitions—thoughts, attitudes,

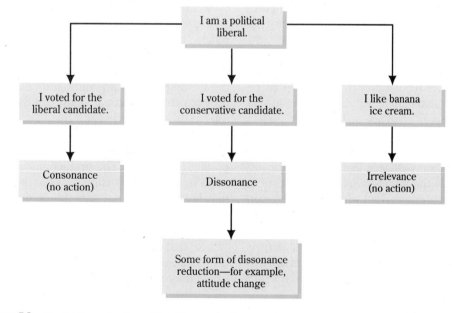

Figure 7.3 *Basic elements of cognitive dissonance theory.*

or beliefs—are inconsistent. Like other consistency theories, this theory proposes that dissonance is an uncomfortable state that motivates us to reduce dissonance; changing one of the cognitions is one way to reduce the discomfort.

According to Festinger, cognitions must be relevant before dissonance theory is applicable. For example, "I'm a thoughtful person" and "It's a nice day today" would probably be considered irrelevant—that is, one cognition does not imply anything about the other. Therefore, dissonance theory would not be applicable. In contrast, "I'm a thoughtful person" is relevant to "I forgot my father's birthday" because the first relates to the second in a psychological sense; therefore, dissonance theory is applicable. Again according to Festinger, two relevant cognitions can exist either in a state of *consonance* or in a state of *dissonance*. The conjunction of "thoughtful person" and "called father on his birthday" is consonant; the cognitions fit together. When cognitions do not fit together—"thoughtful person" and "forgetting father's birthday"—they create dissonance. If the dissonance is sufficiently uncomfortable, one of the cognitions will be changed to restore consistency and reduce the discomfort.

In its original form, cognitive dissonance theory was quite simple; the discomfort of dissonant cognitions motivates a change in one of the relevant cognitions. As researchers directed their attention to it, however, they identified numerous shortcomings, and the theory has undergone considerable change since Festinger proposed it more than thirty-five years ago.

One of the most intriguing features of cognitive dissonance theory is its recognition that a change in behavior can lead to a change in attitude. If a person behaves in a way that is contrary to his or her beliefs, cognitive dissonance theory predicts the person will change those attitudes to make them consistent with the already-performed behavior. A classic demonstration of this effect is the *forced-compliance* experiment. Dissonance theory proposes that when people are convinced to take a public position contrary to their attitude, the conflict will lead to a change in the private attitude. The theory also makes the somewhat surprising prediction that the *smaller* the inducement to advocate a public position that violates a private attitude, the *more* likely a shift in the privately held attitude.

In the first test of this prediction, Festinger and Merrill Carlsmith (1959) paid male students either $1 or $20 to lie to other students. After participating for an hour in a series of dull, meaningless tasks (for example, putting twelve spools in a tray, emptying the tray, and then refilling it, time and time again), the subject was paid to tell another student waiting for the experiment that it was interesting, educational, and highly worthwhile. Later, on a questionnaire that presumably was not part of the experiment, each subject who had lied indicated his private attitudes toward the experiment. Festinger and Carlsmith found that subjects who had been paid only $1 rated the experimental task as more enjoyable than did subjects who were paid $20. Presumably, the students who were paid $20 for the lie could easily justify their behavior—in this instance, money talked. The students who were paid only $1 had to find some other reason for their behavior. The only reason they would tell someone else the experiment was enjoyable, unless they were willing to consider themselves the kind of people who would lie for a mere dollar, was that the experiment must have been enjoyable.

This study was a dramatic demonstration of what can happen when cognitions are inconsistent. It was particularly striking because it appeared to contradict basic principles of reinforcement, which suggest that the greater the reward, the greater the attitude change. As you might expect, such contradiction did not go unchallenged. Daryl Bem (1967, 1972), for example, proposed self-perception theory as an alternative to dissonance theory. As described in Chapter 3, **self-perception theory** proposes we determine our attitudes from our behavior. According to Bem, subjects in the Festinger and Carlsmith study did not experience dissonance; they simply examined their behavior and inferred their attitude from that. To support his argument, Bem (1967) described the Festinger and Carlsmith study to a group of subjects and asked them to predict the results. The predictions of these objective observers were very similar to the original results, indicating one need not experience dissonance to conclude that the experiment was interesting. That is, $1 is not enough money to induce someone to lie, so subjects in that condition looked back at their behavior and decided they must have enjoyed the experiment because they had said they enjoyed it; no inconsistency, no discomfort, no dissonance.

The "war" between dissonance theory and self-perception theory raged for several years. Proponents of each theory mustered considerable empirical support for their preferred theoretical interpretation. Like many battles over the correctness of two opposing theoretical perspectives, this one ended when Russell Fazio, Mark Zanna, and Joel Cooper (1977) declared both sides were correct. Their extensive review of the research indicated that Bem's self-perception theory provided the better account of ordinary situations in which behaviors differed slightly from attitudes, but dissonance theory provided the better account of situations in which people's behaviors differed substantially from their attitudes.

Later, another review of research on dissonance theory led Cooper and Fazio (1984) to further qualify the original formulation of dissonance theory. Cooper and Fazio found that the arousal of dissonance depends on two critical conditions. First, the consequences of the behavior must in some way be aversive; the behavior must lead to "an event that blocks one's self-interest or an event that one would rather not have occur" (p. 232). In Festinger and Carlsmith's experiment, for example, lying to someone would be aversive to most people, especially in combination with the knowledge that they were leading that student on to a very boring experience. In contrast to this situation, imagine that you are alone in your room, reciting a speech with which you disagree. Would merely saying the attitude-discrepant words cause you to experience dissonance? Probably not, because the event would be less aversive; there are no witnesses to your behavior. Equally important, you could easily change what you say without any aversive consequences.

In another example of the importance of discomfort in cognitive dissonance, Claude Steele and his colleagues conducted a series of laboratory experiments in which they examined the effects of alcohol (Steele, Southwick, & Critchlow, 1981). They recruited college students who were at least 21 years old and who had experience with alcohol for a study presumably concerned with beer tasting. The experimenters initially created dissonance by asking these students to write a counterattitudinal essay—an essay in favor of increased tuition, which most students in fact opposed. Having created this inconsistency between behavior and belief, the experimenters then gave subjects the opportunity to sample a variety of beers. Although dissonance did not affect the amount of beer that students drank, the beer did affect their subsequent attitudes.

Students who drank beer after writing the counterattitudinal essay were less likely to change their attitudes than subjects who indicated their attitudes immediately after completing the essay and before drinking any beer. In a further demonstration of the specific effect of alcohol, these investigators found that neither water nor coffee had any noticeable effect on attitudes. Thus, alcohol may serve many people as a means of reducing uncomfortable tension and avoiding recognition of the contradictions between their behaviors and their beliefs.

According to Cooper and Fazio, a second condition necessary for the arousal of dissonance is the assumption of personal responsibility. To experience dissonance, a person must attribute the event to some personal, internal factor (Croyle & Cooper, 1983). You may recall from our discussion of attribution in Chapter 3 that such personal attributions are most likely when people believe that they had a choice in making the event happen and that they were able to foresee the consequences. When these conditions are not met, dissonance is unlikely to be aroused.

In experimental studies of cognitive dissonance, investigators are careful to give subjects the appearance of choice in order to create the conditions necessary for the arousal of dissonance. These two conditions, aversive consequences and responsibility, are sufficient to produce dissonance arousal, provided the individual's self-concept does not include being the kind of person who causes aversive consequences. Thus, even if the behavior that produced the aversive consequences is consistent with other, relevant attitudes, the fact that the consequences are different from one's self-concept will produce dissonance (Scher & Cooper, 1989).

The integral role of the self-concept in dissonance phenomena led Steele (1988) to add yet another refinement to dissonance theory. According to Steele, virtually all instances in which attitude change results from dissonance reduction involve behavior that is inconsistent with a positive self-concept: lying to another, arguing against one's self-interest, acting foolishly, and so on. Within the confines of laboratory experiments, Steele argues, subjects who engaged in such behaviors could either change their self-concept—an unlikely event, as we discussed in Chapter 3—or change their attitudes to make them more consistent with their self-concept. Thus, attitude change occurs as a result of **self-affirmation,** responding to a threat to self-esteem by enhancing some facet of the self-concept. For example, in several experiments in which Steele and his colleagues provided alternative means for self-affirmation, such as completing a questionnaire about values, subjects who engaged in behaviors inconsistent with their attitudes did not change those attitudes. Instead, the self-affirming activities the experimenter provided were sufficient to reduce the dissonance arousal.

Where does all this leave cognitive dissonance theory? As illustrated in Figure 7.4, the modern version of dissonance theory does include several necessary conditions that must occur before people will change an attitude that is inconsistent with their behavior, but the theory still provides a means by which to explain why self-persuasion occurs under certain circumstances.

More than most other theories of attitude change, dissonance theory has served to explain the effects of making a decision on subsequent attitudes and behavior. According to the theory, having to choose between two attractive options is one circumstance under which dissonance is likely to be aroused. The more difficult or important the decision—the more relevant it is to one's self-concept—the more likely a person is to find reasons that support his or her choice and to minimize the attractive qualities of the forgone choice. In such instances, the aversive consequences involve denying oneself the unchosen alternative. For example, if you are undecided about which of two majors to declare, dissonance theory predicts that once you have made your choice, you will find many ways of "spreading apart" the alternatives. After you make the decision, your chosen major will seem even more attractive: better employment opportunities, more interesting courses, perhaps even better faculty. This same strategy has been evidenced in a variety of settings, including election polling areas and racetracks.

Robert Knox and James Inkster (1968), for example, were not content to test cognitive dissonance theory only under controlled laboratory conditions. These researchers went to a racetrack in Vancouver and interviewed bettors at the $2 window about the chances of their horse's winning. Subjects who were interviewed as they stood in line waiting to place their bets thought their horse had a little better than fair chance to win. Subjects interviewed immediately after they had placed their bets were significantly more confident, rating

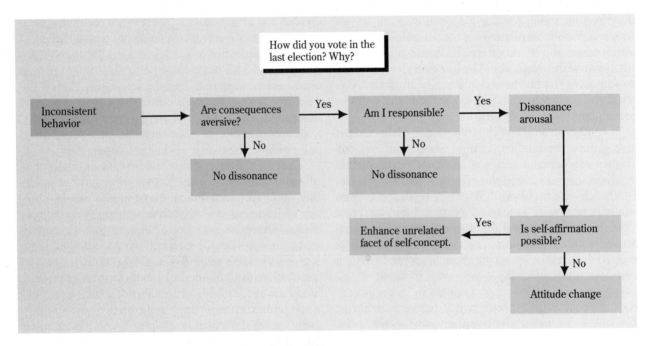

Figure 7.4 *Cognitive dissonance theory in the 1990s.*

Bettors are less confident about their selections while waiting in line than they are after they have placed their bets.
Alan Carey/The Image Works

their chances as good. These findings suggest that the act of committing oneself by placing a bet creates dissonance and leads to a dissonance-reducing boost in confidence in one's choice. The aversive consequences are, of course, foolishly wasting one's money on a bad bet. Frenkel and Doob (1976) observed a similar process at polling areas during a Toronto election. Voters polled after they had cast their ballot were more likely to believe that their candidate was best and that he or she would win than voters polled before they entered the polling area. In this case, the aversive consequences involved wasting one's vote.

Behavior following a decision takes other forms as well. **Selective exposure,** a concept introduced in Chapter 6, was a phenomenon predicted by cognitive dissonance theorists. Specifically, they predicted that people would prefer supportive information and would avoid information that contradicted existent cognitions. Such selective information seeking does not always occur (Frey, 1986). If people know they can effectively refute some discrepant information, for example, they may seek it out for the sheer pleasure of refuting it. Similarly, most people are fairly rational about their needs, and if they realize that future decisions will require familiarity with the dissonant information, they will pay attention to it. Thus, there appear to be limits

to the selective exposure effect, but within those limits, biased information search often occurs.

In general, cognitive dissonance theory can be applied to any situation in which individuals commit themselves to a position relevant to their self-concept. For example, in an early experiment within the cognitive dissonance tradition, Elliot Aronson and Judson Mills (1959) found that people who had to exert great effort to join a group liked that group more than potential members who had to exert less effort. Applying those results, Danny Axsom and Joel Cooper (1985) hypothesized that patients in a weight therapy program who were required to exert a great deal of effort on a task, even a task that had no apparent relation to the therapy program, would justify their effort by becoming more committed to the goal of the program and consequently would lose more weight. The results of this experiment were striking, even when they were assessed six and twelve months after the effortful procedures had taken place. Six months later, for example, patients who had completed the more effortful series of tasks over a four-day period had lost an average of 8.5 pounds, but patients whose tasks had been relatively easy lost virtually no weight. In this case, behavior affected behavior through the mediation of attitudinal processes.

The act of voting increases our feelings that our chosen candidate is best and is going to win the election.
Alan Carey/The Image Works

In another practical demonstration of the consequences of cognitive dissonance, consumers of electric power in Australia were given one of several kinds of information about their use of energy (Kantola, Syme, & Campbell, 1984). All the subjects were heavy users of electricity, and their behavior in this regard was inconsistent with their belief that energy should be conserved. How might people resolve such inconsistency? Faced with a contradiction between an important value and the evidence that they were consuming large amounts of energy, consumers might try to alter their future behavior in an attempt to bring their behavior in line with values they expressed. To explore this possibility, the Australian investigators aroused dissonance in some consumers by pointing out the contradiction, but they did not mention the contradiction to another group. Even though both groups were given feedback on their energy use as well as tips on reducing it, only the dissonance arousal group showed a significant decrease in energy consumption. As we might expect, the attitudes of people in this experiment did not change because self-affirmation was accomplished by reducing their energy consumption.

In a very different context, Theodore Blumoff (1990) noted evidence of dissonance in the written opinions of U.S. Supreme Court justices. In his examination of *Bowsher v. Synar,* the decision in which the Court ruled that certain portions of the Gramm-Rudman budget reduction act were unconstitutional, Blumoff noted several instances of selective exposure; in the majority opinion, for example, the Court completely ignored a precedent it had set only twelve months before. Blumoff also pointed out several ways in which the Court reinterpreted both historical records and its own precedents.

Functional Theories

The theories discussed thus far emphasize flexibility or consistency. Some theorists, however, have focused their attention on the reasons we have attitudes. **Functional theories** assume that attitudes exist and change to fulfill an individual's needs (Katz, 1960; Pratkanis, Breckler, & Greenwald, 1989; Smith, Bruner, & White, 1956).

The basic proposition of a functional theory of attitude change is simple: the attitudes people have are those that fit their needs, and attitude change occurs when someone's need state changes. Change someone's need or the extent to which an attitude fulfills that need, and the attitude will change. Functional theories are phenomenological; proponents of these theories maintain that a stimulus for attitude change, such as a television commercial, can be understood only within the context of the perceiver's needs and personality. Different people may have quite different needs, and consequently a message that might promote attitude change in some people may not be effective for others.

What functions do attitudes serve? Although early theorists proposed a variety of different attitude functions (Katz, 1960; Smith, 1947; Smith, Bruner, & White, 1956), the five functions listed in Table 7.2 exemplify the emphases of most of the modern functional theories of attitude change (Tesser & Shaffer, 1990). For example, the knowledge function reflects the cognitive view of an attitude as an evaluation of an object, suggesting that attitudes serve some of the same purposes as the various schemas described in Chapters 3 and 4. The instrumental function, consistent with the learning theory perspective, reflects the extent to which people use their attitudes to obtain rewards. The ego defense function, rooted in psychoanalytic theory, serves to help an individual cope with some internal anxieties. Derogatory attitudes concerning a group of people, for example, may enhance someone's self-esteem in order to resolve concerns about insecurity. Attitudes toward individuals are most likely to serve a social-adjustment function, and attitudes associated most closely with the self are sometimes used for value-expressive or self-presentation purposes.

To some extent, the various functions of attitudes may overlap (Herek, 1986), such as when someone's preference for a particular model of car might enhance self-esteem (ego defense) or might enable the individual to present a specific image to others (value expression). Thus, functional theories require the investigator to determine just what function a particular attitude serves for a particular individual before deciding how to change the attitude. One approach to this problem has been to classify individuals on the basis of personality dimensions. For example, in an early test of functional theory, Charles McClintock (1958) measured subjects' need for conformity and ego defensiveness before presenting one of several messages designed to change prejudicial attitudes. One message was tailored specifically to appeal to people concerned about conformity; it stressed information about societal values. Another was designed to appeal to people who were ego defensive; it stressed interpretations of the internal dynamics that can lead to prejudice. Among subjects who read the informational message, more high-conformity subjects than low-conformity subjects changed their attitudes. The interpretational message, in contrast, had more effect on subjects who scored in the middle range of the ego defensiveness scale. More recently, Mark Snyder and Kenneth DeBono (1987, 1989) have obtained evidence that, among people high in self-monitoring (see Chapter 3), attitudes serve needs for social adjustment and approval, whereas people low in self-monitoring use attitudes primarily to express individual values.

Another approach to identifying the different functions of different attitudes involves directing attention to the objects of attitudes (Abelson & Prentice, 1989; Prentice, 1987). For example, according to the research of Gregory Herek (1986), attitudes that are related to one's social class or occupational group are more likely to be based on value-expressive functions, whereas attitudes related to sexuality may be more closely tied to defensive needs. In contrast, Pratkanis and Greenwald (1989) have focused on the content of attitudes to differentiate functions. The content of social adjustment attitudes, for example, includes information about the value that other people place on the attitude object.

That different attitude functions exist for different objects and for different personality dimensions complicates functional strategies for changing attitudes. One needs to know, for example, whether an attitude is based on the function of the object or based on a function of the individual's personality. Consequently, any particular attempt to change the attitudes of a large group of people, such as product advertisements or an election campaign, will probably be effective for only

Table 7.2 Some functions of attitudes

Type of attitude	Function served
Knowledge	Evaluating objects and organizing information
Instrumentality	Maximizing rewards and minimizing punishments
Ego defense	Coping with conflict related to the self-concept, enhancing self-esteem
Social adjustment	Defining or enhancing interpersonal relationships
Value expression	Expressing aspects of the self-concept

some of the people, and then perhaps only some of the time. And that is, of course, exactly what occurs with mass media attempts at persuasion.

In summary, the different concerns of attitude theorists are reflected in existing theories of attitude change. For example, concerns about how to phrase a message so as to persuade people to change a specific attitude led to the development of social judgment theory. Attempting to understand why self-persuasion occurs produced cognitive dissonance theory, whereas interest in the relationships between attitudes and the self-concept and different personality types produced the functional theories. That each of these theories has received empirical support illustrates the importance of attitudes for social behavior, as well as the complicated nature of attitude change. Therefore, we must turn our attention to the process by which attitude change takes place.

▶ The Process of Attitude Change

During the late 1940s and 1950s, a highly energetic and productive group of social psychologists gathered at Yale University under the direction of Carl Hovland. This group was known as the Communication Research Program, and its theoretical perspective was based on the reinforcement principles of learning theory. Members of the group believed, for example, that the same principles that applied to the acquisition of verbal and motor skills could be applied to attitude formation and change (Hovland, Janis, & Kelley, 1953). Together these investigators conducted a massive amount of research on the process of attitude change. Though nearly "ancient" by social psychological time standards, the results of their research remain pertinent.

Sequence Models

Using the stimulus-response terminology of learning theory, Hovland and his colleagues proposed the model of attitude change shown in Figure 7.5. The model is called a sequence model because it posits a series of required stages between the persuasive attempt and any resulting attitude change. Any disruption of the series foils the attitude change process.

The first stage, *attention,* recognizes the fact that we do not always notice or pay attention to all message stimuli. If the television is not turned on, for example, television advertisements will not affect us. Similarly, we may notice only a fraction of the persuasive messages as we drive down a highway lined with billboards. Without attention, the attempted persuasion will very likely not be successful. But even when an appeal is noticed, it may not be effective.

The second stage posited by Hovland and his colleagues, *comprehension,* recognizes that some messages may be too complex or too ambiguous for the intended audience to understand. When you don't understand what your instructor is saying, you don't learn very much from the lecture. Similarly, a complex treatise on the balance-of-payments deficit may be totally ineffective in persuading a senator who has little background in economics to vote for or against a particular bill.

Finally, in the third step, a person must decide to accept the communication before any real attitude

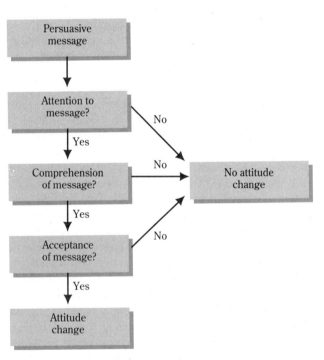

Figure 7.5 *A sequential model of attitude change.*

change takes place. From the perspective of the reinforcement theorist, the degree of *acceptance* depends largely on the incentives (or threats) offered. A message may provide arguments or reasons for accepting the advocated point of view, engender expectations of rewards or other pleasant experiences, or provide instructions for avoiding unpleasant experiences. For example, the billboard on the highway may inform you that a filling station at the next exit is your "last chance for gas" in the next 50 miles.

Later investigators have retained the idea of a sequence of stages but have elaborated on just what those stages are. William McGuire (1968a), for example, proposed a five-stage sequence consisting of (1) attention, (2) comprehension, (3) yielding, (4) retention, and (5) action. In this formulation, the acceptance stage of the early Hovland model has been divided into two separate stages: first, the yielding or changing of one's attitude, and second, the retention of that changed belief. Further, in adding an action stage, McGuire has pointed to the importance of considering behavior as well as internalized beliefs. Even more detailed analyses of this sequence are possible, as McGuire has shown in his more recent writings (1985). Drawing on some of the more recent work in cognition, he has proposed a twelve-stage model that considers how beliefs are stored in and retrieved from memory during the course of attitude change.

One important assumption inherent in most of these sequence models is that the stages are dependent on one another. In other words, each preceding stage is necessary before the next one can take place. Comprehension cannot occur unless a person has paid attention to the message, yielding is dependent on prior comprehension, and so forth.

Parallel Models

Other researchers have proposed models in which the attitude change process is not sequential. Instead, such parallel models involve two processes for attitude change and specify the conditions that determine which potential process will operate (Chaiken, Liberman, & Eagly, 1989; Chaiken & Stangor, 1987; Eagly & Chaiken, 1984; Petty & Cacioppo, 1986). Parallel models generally involve the assumption that people are motivated to hold correct or valid attitudes, an assumption that also dates back to the late 1940s (for example, Festinger, 1950). A companion assumption common to the parallel models is that people are not always able or sufficiently motivated to engage in full-scale, sequential processing.

Consider the parallel processing model in Figure 7.6, the elaboration likelihood model proposed by Richard Petty and John Cacioppo (1986). One must be both motivated and able to employ the *central processing*, or sequential, mode of thinking about the persuasive message. People who engage in central processing think about the issues, pay attention to the arguments presented in the persuasive message, and evaluate the implications of those arguments. But even after some central processing, individuals may resort to peripheral processing if the information contained in the message does not produce a strong evaluation—decidedly favorable or unfavorable thoughts—or if the cognitions produced do not involve any new information.

Many factors can increase the likelihood that someone will engage in central processing (Tesser & Shaffer, 1990). Personal relevance of the topic, a neutral mood, and direct experience with the attitude object, for example, increase an individual's motivation to employ central processing. Written messages, multiple messages, multiple communicators, and extensive topical knowledge, on the other hand, tend to increase an individual's ability to engage in central processing. In general, central processing is more likely when fewer demands are made on one's cognitive capacity and when one is able and motivated to take the time to pay attention to the message content.

Some people seem particularly motivated to engage in central processing even when the preceding characteristics are not present. Such people, considered high in need for cognition, tend to treat most persuasive communication as an intellectual challenge. John Cacioppo and Richard Petty (1982; Cacioppo, Petty, & Kao, 1984) have developed a scale to measure need for cognition. On this scale, people with a high need for cognition tend to endorse statements such as "I usually end up deliberating about issues even when they do not affect me personally" and "I prefer my life to be filled with puzzles that I must solve." People with a low need for cognition, in contrast, tend to endorse statements such as "Ignorance is bliss" and "Thinking is not my idea of fun."

Peripheral processing is a general term applied to any type of processing in which little thought is given to the message itself. Instead of thinking about the message, individuals rely on external characteristics such as the attractiveness of a source or the rewards associated with a particular attitudinal position. As you might expect, peripheral processing is more likely when the characteristics associated with central processing are absent. Even the simple frequency with which one encounters an object may cause attitude change under peripheral processing (Grush, McKeough, & Ahlering, 1978).

Models of attitude change that stress simple conditioning of attitudes, such as those described in Chapter 5, involve peripheral processing. Perhaps anticipating peripheral processing among television viewers, advertisers often attempt to associate positive emotions with products that have little or no relationship to the emotional event. In some advertisements, for example, the joy of a son or daughter coming home from the Army

or the excitement of a family reunion are associated with a particular brand of coffee or laundry detergent. As we noted in Chapter 5, such associations affect the formation and change of attitudes (Burke & Edell, 1989).

One specific type of peripheral processing, suggested by Shelly Chaiken, is heuristic processing. You may recall from Chapter 4 that **heuristics** are relatively simple schemas or "rules of thumb" for making decisions. With regard to persuasion, such rules may include "experts usually have valid arguments," or "people like me are usually correct." Whatever rules may be applied during heuristic processing, the net result is that the message context is given priority over the message content (Chaiken et al., 1989). For example, if you do not have enough time to consider carefully the pros and cons of all available cars, you may base your purchase decision on the salesperson who "seems nice." Sometimes people apply heuristics without conscious recognition, but on other occasions people are aware

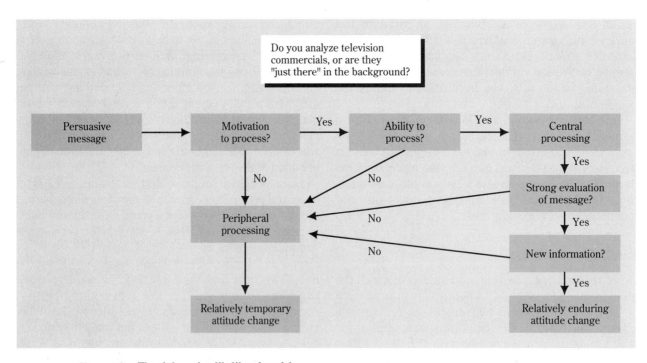

Figure 7.6   *The elaboration likelihood model.*
Source: "The Elaboration Likelihood Model of Persuasion" by R. E. Petty and J. T. Cacioppo, 1986, *Advances in Experimental Social Psychology, 19*, pp. 123–205.

they are using heuristics. A newcomer to the stock market, for instance, may find it necessary to rely on a broker's advice because the amount of potentially relevant information seems overwhelming.

As suggested by the elaboration likelihood model, it is also possible for individuals to employ both central and peripheral processing, hence the description of the model as *parallel*. Wendy Wood and Carl Kallgren (1988) demonstrated this in an experiment in which they manipulated the expertise and likability of the source of a persuasive communication. Subjects read the transcript of an interview in which a student argued against land preservation. Half the subjects were led to believe the communicator was an expert; he was completing a graduate degree in geology and had experience in reclaiming land that had been used for strip mining. The other half believed the communicator was not an expert; he was working toward a graduate degree in French, and no mention was made of any experience with land preservation. Within each of the expertise conditions, either the communicator was likable—he said the subjects' school was better than the one from which he had recently transferred—or he was not very likable—he said his former school was better than the subjects' school.

Building upon earlier research that demonstrated that people with more knowledge about a topic are more likely to engage in central processing (Wood, 1982), Wood and Kallgren also divided their subjects into three groups. Based on how much information they could recall about land preservation, the subjects were classified as high, medium, or low with respect to the likelihood they would engage in central processing. Wood and Kallgren hypothesized that subjects who were least likely to engage in central processing would be most influenced by the communicator's expertise or likability. That is, subjects using heuristic processing— "agree with experts" or "agree with nice people"— should be more affected by the communicator's expertise or likability than subjects using central processing.

As expected, the results demonstrated that the communicator was generally more persuasive when he was perceived as an expert and when he was likable. The specific test of Wood and Kallgren's hypothesis is illustrated in Figure 7.7, which shows the extent to which subjects in the study disagreed with the source. Only those subjects who knew little about land preservation

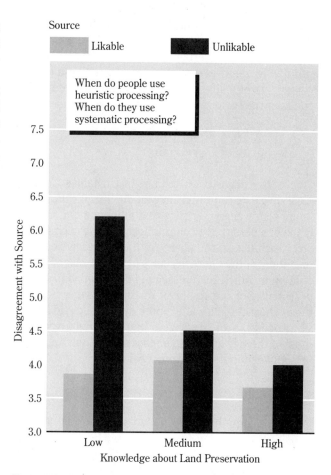

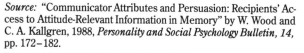

Figure 7.7 *Evidence of both heuristic and systematic processing.*
Source: "Communicator Attributes and Persuasion: Recipients' Access to Attitude-Relevant Information in Memory" by W. Wood and C. A. Kallgren, 1988, *Personality and Social Psychology Bulletin, 14,* pp. 172–182.

were affected by the communicator's likability; they seemed to be using a "disagree if the communicator is not nice" heuristic. (The expertise of the communicator, on the other hand, affected all subjects equally.) Although the subjects with relatively high knowledge about land preservation could recall more of the message and were therefore engaging in more central processing, they were just as likely to use an "agree with the expert" heuristic as were subjects who could not recall the graduate student's message.

Wood and Kallgren's research demonstrates that attitude change is not an either-or process. We use both systematic and heuristic processes, although circumstances may make one or the other type of processing more probable at certain times. Therefore, to understand why one message may produce attitude change when a slightly different message may not, we need to consider the various elements of persuasion.

▶ Elements of Persuasion

One of the major contributions of Hovland's Communication Research Program was the specification of an initial set of characteristics that influence one's acceptance of a persuasive communication. These characteristics include: (1) the source of the persuasive communication, (2) the characteristics of the message, (3) the context in which the message is delivered, and (4) the personality of the recipient of the message. Some of these characteristics affect both systematic and heuristic processors of messages, but the effectiveness of most of them is limited to instances in which recipients are engaged in heuristic processing.

Source

Who says something may be just as important as what is said. Hovland and his colleagues (1953) suggested that the credibility of a source would affect the incentives for changing one's attitude. Therefore, the more believable the source, the more likely a change in attitude. In the early research that tested this hypothesis, the manipulations of credibility were quite strong. For example, several decades ago Hovland and Weiss (1951) contrasted the effectiveness of the American physicist Robert Oppenheimer with that of the Soviet newspaper *Pravda*. Not surprisingly, U.S. subjects were more persuaded by the message from Oppenheimer in those "Cold War" days.

Recent research has considered more specific components of a communicator's credibility, including expertise, trustworthiness, attractiveness, and similarity to the recipient (Petty & Cacioppo, 1981). Each of these factors has been shown to affect attitude change. For example, a message advocating a certain number of hours of sleep was more effective when the source was a Nobel Prize–winning physiologist than when the source was a YMCA director. As we saw in Wood and

Kallgren's (1988) study, communicator expertise affects those engaged in systematic as well as heuristic processing of the message. That is, even when people are paying close attention to the content of a message (systematic processing), they also consider communicator expertise to be important. And when portions of a message defy systematic processing, perhaps because the message is too complex, an expert's arguments are perceived as more valid.

Similarly, a communicator may also be more effective when arguing *against* his or her best interest (Walster, Aronson, & Abrahams, 1966). Alice Eagly and her colleagues have discussed this process in terms of attribution theory (Eagly, Chaiken, & Wood, 1981). Messages that seem unlikely to reflect the communicator's self-interest, such as a millionaire supporting higher taxes for the rich or a politician supporting a limit on campaign expenses, lead to correspondent inferences (Jones & Davis, 1965). As we saw in Chapter 4, novelty attracts our attention, leads to a more detailed analysis of the situation (Hastie, 1984), and produces particularly strong dispositional attributions (Lalljee et al., 1982). That is, when people argue against their best interests, we are more likely to pay attention to what they are saying and assume they believe what they are saying. All this cognitive effort is, of course, consistent with systematic processing.

Both the physical appearance of communicators and their similarity to us can affect attitude change. After the 1960 U.S. presidential election, many commentators attributed John F. Kennedy's victory to the fact that he appeared more attractive on the televised debates than did his opponent, Richard Nixon (McGinniss, 1970). Closer to home, Shelly Chaiken (1979) asked students to persuade other undergraduates to sign a petition. Physically attractive sources were more effective than less attractive sources. In trying to explain this effect, Chaiken found that the more attractive student sources had a number of other characteristics as well, such as better communication skills and higher SAT scores, all of which may have contributed to their greater effectiveness.

Wood and Kallgren's (1988) study demonstrated that the likability of a communicator affects only those engaged in heuristic processing. The fact that the effects of communicator attractiveness and likability depend on the medium of communication also supports this conclusion. If a persuasive message is presented through either a visual or an auditory medium, a communicator's likability affects the amount of attitude change that occurs. Persuasive messages transmitted in written form, which are more likely to be processed systematically, seem to be less affected by the likability and attractiveness of the source (Chaiken & Eagly, 1983).

People are also more easily persuaded if the source is similar to them in ways that are relevant to the issue (Berscheid, 1966). The importance of this similarity factor was demonstrated by Dembroski, Lasater, and Ramirez (1978). Studying ways to increase toothbrushing behavior, these investigators found that when the target group was black, a black communicator was much more effective than a white communicator. Most people assume similar others also hold similar attitudes (Marks & Miller, 1988), which may underlie the "agree with people like me" heuristic.

Advertisers make extensive use of these various source characteristics in planning their advertising campaigns. It is quite common for a famous person from the world of sports or entertainment to be shown endorsing a product. The credibility, trustworthiness, or attractiveness of the source makes the message more convincing. Other ads attempt to create a feeling of similarity between the viewer and the source. Someone who acts just like your neighbor or your parents should be more persuasive than someone who seems to have nothing in common with you.

Message

A persuasive message can vary in content, organization, and the medium used. Each of these aspects can affect the effectiveness of a message, either by making systematic or heuristic processing more likely, or directly through systematic processing of the message itself.

A major issue in regard to the content of persuasive messages has been the effectiveness of fear-arousing appeals. Is trying to frighten people about the consequences of maintaining their present attitudes an effective way to change those attitudes? Or is it better to minimize the negative consequences of their current attitudes?

In an early experiment, Irving Janis and Seymour

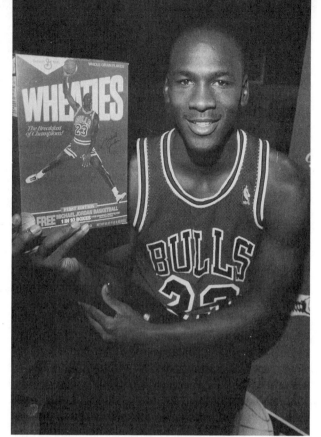

People are more easily persuaded if the source is familiar to them.
Mark Elias/AP/Wide World Photos

Feshbach (1953) used different levels of fear in a message designed to encourage proper dental care. The level of fear ranged from low (some small cavities might occur) to high (pictures of advanced gum disease were shown). They found the greatest reported change among those subjects who had been exposed to material designed to arouse low levels of fear. Later evidence contradicted this conclusion, however; investigators often found greater attitude change following high-fear appeals (Higbee, 1969; Leventhal, 1970).

These contradictions suggested the need to look more carefully at the content of fear-arousing messages. After doing just that, Ronald Rogers (1975, 1983; Maddux & Rogers, 1983) proposed four factors that are important in any fear appeal: (1) the magnitude of unpleasantness of the event described, (2) the probability that the negative consequences will occur if the recommended action is not taken, (3) the perceived effectiveness of the recommended action for avoiding the negative consequences, and (4) the perceived ability to complete the recommended action. For example, most people probably see the chances of developing severe gum disease as slim, even though they may forget to brush their teeth for days (low probability of consequences). Other people may know that quitting smoking is an effective way to reduce the probability of lung cancer, but they believe the recommended action is too difficult. In general, then, fear appeals will be most persuasive if the described event is relatively unpleasant, if the person believes the event really will occur, if the recommended action sounds effective, and if the person believes he or she can accomplish the recommended action.

Even when only a little fear is aroused, fear-based messages may be more effective than incentive-based messages. For example, Beth Meyerowitz and Shelly Chaiken (1987) randomly assigned female students to read one of three different pamphlets concerning monthly breast self-examination. All the pamphlets included information about the prevalence of breast cancer, as well as instructions about how to conduct a breast self-examination. For one group of women, the loss condition, the pamphlet also contained a message about the consequences of failing to engage in self-examination, such as being *unable* to detect tumors early. For another group, the gain condition, the pamphlet included positive consequences for engaging in self-examination, such as being *better able* to detect tumors early. A third group, the neutral condition, received pamphlets without any information about consequences. Finally, a fourth group, the no-pamphlet control, did not receive the pamphlet.

About four months later, the same women were interviewed about (1) their attitudes toward monthly breast self-examination, (2) the number of times they intended to conduct a self-examination during the coming year, and (3) the number of times they had actually

Fear-based messages may be more effective than incentive-based messages at changing attitudes.
Skjold/The Image Works

conducted a self-examination in the previous four months. The results, illustrated in Figure 7.8, clearly indicated that only the loss-oriented message inserted into the pamphlet produced changes in either attitudes, intentions, or behaviors. Thus, while high fear-arousing messages are more effective than low fear-arousing messages under the conditions outlined by Rogers, even low fear-arousing messages may be more effective than messages offering incentives.

Another issue regarding the content of persuasive messages is whether messages containing only one point of view (one-sided) or messages containing pros and cons (two-sided) are more effective. For example, if you are arguing in favor of reduced television time for children, should you present only arguments that are favorable to your position, or should you acknowledge and attempt to refute an opposing viewpoint? In answering this question, we again see that few answers are "all or none"; instead, specific conditions must be considered in each case. As Karlins and Abelson put it:

> When the audience is generally friendly, or when your position is the only one that will be presented, or when you want immediate, though temporary, opinion change, present one side of the argument. [But when] the audience initially disagrees with you, or when it is probable that the audience will hear the other side from someone else, present both sides of the argument. [1970, p. 22]

That is, one-sided communications are better if you can assume the audience will be engaging in primarily heuristic processing, particularly if the audience is receptive to your point of view. In contrast, if the audience will be engaging primarily in systematic processing of your message, perhaps because they are already aware of the issues, then a two-sided communication may be more effective.

If sometimes it is more effective to present both sides of an argument, which side should be presented first for maximum impact? In general, the answer to this question depends on the time between the two messages and on the time between the messages and the measurement of attitude (Petty & Cacioppo, 1981). Figure 7.9 shows how these factors interact. As can be seen, the first message will be more effective (primacy effect) when the two messages are presented at about the same time, but the attitude is measured much later. When the second message is delayed but presented

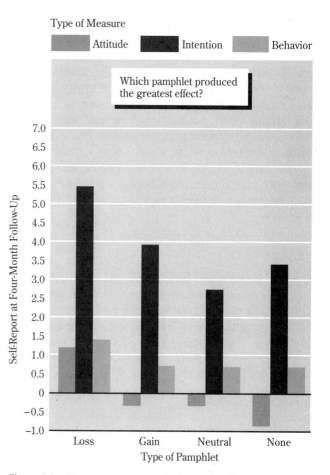

Figure 7.8 *Reactions to persuasive messages about monthly breast self-examination.*

Source: "The Effect of Message Framing on Breast Self-Examination Attitudes, Intentions, and Behavior" by B. E. Meyerowitz and S. Chaiken, 1987, *Journal of Personality and Social Psychology, 52,* pp. 500–510.

just before the attitude is measured, the second message has the greater impact (recency effect). When the message and measurement are contemporaneous, and when all three are about equally spaced in time, neither message necessarily has an advantage.

In addition to the content and organization of the persuasive message, the medium by which the message is delivered can affect its persuasiveness. As with previous message characteristics, the effect of medium depends partly on whether one is interested in having people understand the message (systematic processing) or in creating only attitude change, with or without understanding (Chaiken & Eagly, 1976). A written message may be more effective in conveying information and initiating systematic processing, particularly information that is complex and difficult to grasp. More direct communications, such as videotaped or live presentations, tend to initiate heuristic processing. Therefore, if you want to present a complex proposal to your supervisor at work, written communication may be preferable in the initial presentation stage. Later, however, when the options have been reduced to yes and no, a face-to-face presentation should be more effective.

Context

Up to this point, we have discussed persuasive communications as though they were the only event occurring in a situation. Some laboratory experiments have structured situations in just that way, but in a real-life persuasion context, many events occur simultaneously.

For instance, a television advertisement suggesting that you buy a particular brand of aspirin may have to compete with a family argument, the stereo in the next room, and a knock at the door. What effect do distractions have on the effectiveness of a persuasive message?

You might think that any distraction would reduce the effectiveness of a persuasive message, but that is not necessarily true. Distraction, of course, makes it more difficult to think about the persuasive message (Petty, Wells, & Brock, 1976). For example, if a message is one with which we might normally disagree, distraction prevents us from thinking about arguments against the message; that is, from rehearsing a refutation. Thus, distractions increase the probability of heuristic processing, thereby decreasing the influence of the message itself. So, if the communicator is likable and we are distracted, we may be more likely to change our attitude in favor of the message than if we were not distracted. A "busy" television advertisement that is pleasing to the eye and conjures up many positive emo-

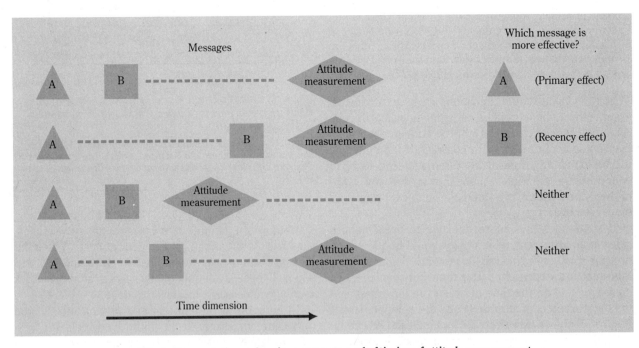

Figure 7.9 *Effects of presentation order of two messages and of timing of attitude measurement.*
Source: "The Need for Cognition" by J. T. Cacioppo and R. E. Petty, 1982, *Journal of Personality and Social Psychology, 42,* pp. 116–131.

tions, for example, may accomplish the desired attitude change even if the advertisement contains no real information about the product.

When investigators want to distract subjects in the laboratory, they generally ask them to do two tasks simultaneously. A more natural version of distraction can be seen in the political heckler, who makes comments from the audience while a speaker tries to present an argument. Studies of heckling have found that this form of distraction, in contrast to that used in a laboratory situation, generally reduces the persuasiveness of a message among listeners who are initially neutral, although it may serve to moderate positions that were originally extreme (Silverthorne & Mazmanian, 1975; Sloan, Love, & Ostrom, 1974). Why do these findings differ from those of laboratory-based studies of distraction? One reason may be that a heckler not only serves as a distractor (as a competing laboratory task does), but also provides information and an opposing viewpoint. When uninvolved members of an audience are presented with another side of an argument, the speaker's position may seem much less convincing than it otherwise would. Consistent with the research on two-sided communications, however, a speaker who responds to a heckler calmly and refutes the heckler's claims apparently can overcome their negative effects (Petty & Brock, 1976).

Recipient

We have already discussed the notion that some people, those high in need for cognition, are more likely to engage in systematic processing than others. We can also ask whether some people, by nature of their personalities, are more responsive than others to an attempt to change their attitudes, regardless of the source, the content, or the context of a message. Conversely, are some people able to resist efforts—even the best-designed and most appropriate ones—to change their attitudes? The answer is yes, to a slight degree (McGuire, 1968a, 1968b). In most cases, however, the recipient's personality interacts with other factors to determine whether a change in attitude will take place.

Early attempts to relate personality to persuadability focused on single variables, such as intelligence, self-esteem, the need for social approval, and gender. Generally, these simple approaches met with little success. For example, despite the frequently held belief that women are more easily persuaded than men, systematic reviews indicate men and women have nearly equal tendencies to change their attitudes (Eagly & Carli, 1981). Although early research suggested that people low in self-esteem would be more prone to change their attitudes (Janis & Field, 1959), this assumption proved inaccurate when it was subjected to a wider range of tests (Bauer, 1970).

One alternative to this simple but unsuccessful approach has been proposed by William McGuire (1968b). As we noted earlier, the learning model considers three distinct stages in the attitude change process: attention, comprehension, and acceptance. If we examine these stages separately, we may find that a personality variable has different effects at different stages. For example, people of high intelligence may be able to comprehend a complex message more easily than persons of lesser intellectual endowment, or more intelligent people may be less prone to yield to persuasion because they have greater confidence in their own critical abilities. In testing this hypothesis, Eagly and Warren (1976) found that intelligence is related to attitude change as a function of message complexity. Highly intelligent people changed their attitudes more than less intelligent people when the message was complex. But when a message was weak and unsupported by arguments, people of lower intelligence were more likely to change their attitudes.

As we noted in our discussion of functional theories, personality differences, such as *self-monitoring,* also affect the type of message that people prefer. For example, two general approaches to advertising are often identified within the trade, emotional and rational. The major emphasis of the emotional approach is on the visual image—the form, color, and appearance of the ad—and emotional reactions to the ad. In emotional ads, relatively little is said of the product itself. The depicted individuals, typically very attractive and likable, get most of the attention. A rational approach, in contrast, emphasizes the characteristics of the product—its quality, its value, its utility. For example, a soft-drink producer, may emphasize the taste of the beverage, or a manufacturer of automobile tires may stress the tires' safety features and durability.

Mark Snyder and Kenneth DeBono (1985) suspected that individuals who differ in their tendencies toward self-monitoring may prefer different advertising approaches. According to their analysis, high self-monitoring individuals, who are more sensitive to the demands of situations, should be more sensitive to the emotional approach, with its stress on images. In contrast, the low self-monitoring person, who relies more on internal attitudes and dispositions as guides, may be more influenced by ads that stress the characteristics of the product itself. Their hunch was correct. Not only did high self-monitoring individuals evaluate image-oriented advertisements more favorably, but they were more willing to try products that were marketed with an appeal based on image and to pay higher prices for such products. Low self-monitors, as predicted, were more influenced by claims of quality than by projected images.

The relative effectiveness of emotional versus rational messages also depends on the reasons people hold their current attitudes about the product. Murray and Karen Millar (1990) demonstrated this in a series of two experiments. First they determined whether students liked or disliked a particular brand of soft drink. Then they assessed whether the reasons for liking or disliking the drink were emotional (feelings about the product) or rational (attributes such as taste). About eight weeks later, the Millars presented magazine ads promoting the soft drink to the same students. For those who liked the drink, the ads were proattitudinal; for those who disliked the drink, the ads were counterattitudinal. Some ads presented emotional reasons for drinking the brand name, and other ads presented rational reasons. After randomly assigning students to view the different ads, the Millars asked the students to rate how much they agreed with the particular ad they saw.

The results, presented in Figure 7.10, clearly show that the relative effectiveness of emotional and rational ads depends on why people like (or dislike) the product. When people's initial attitude toward the product was positive, the rational ad produced more agreement with the ad regardless of why people liked the product. But when the initial attitude toward the product was negative, the ad that was pitched toward a different type of reason than that which produced the initial atti-

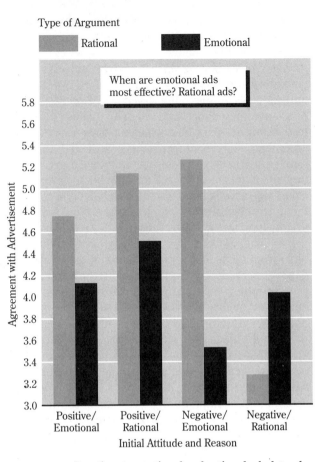

Figure 7.10 *Reactions to emotional and rational ads depend on the initial attitude and the reasons for the initial attitude.* *Source:* "Attitude Change as a Function of Attitude Type and Argument Type" by M. G. Millar and K. U. Millar, 1990, *Journal of Personality and Social Psychology, 59,* pp. 217–228.

tude was more effective. Interestingly, the greatest agreement was produced by the rational ads directed at people who initially had a negative, emotional reaction to the product.

Perhaps not surprisingly, the mood of recipients also affects the extent to which a persuasive message will produce attitude change. What may be surprising is that recipients' moods interact with the strength of the message. People in a bad mood (such as sad or angry) are much more likely to engage in systematic processing, so strong messages produce more attitude change in them than do weak messages. People in a good mood, however, tend to process messages heuristically and are equally affected by strong and weak arguments (Bless, Bohner, Schwartz, & Strack, 1990). Thus, if you have strong arguments, you need not worry about the mood of the audience or how much the audience likes you. But if you ⬚⬚⬚⬚⬚⬚ ⬚⬚⬚⬚ are better off if the audience ⬚⬚⬚⬚⬚⬚⬚⬚⬚⬚⬚⬚ likes you.

Once again, ⬚⬚⬚⬚⬚⬚⬚⬚⬚⬚⬚⬚ simple process. The proce⬚⬚⬚⬚⬚⬚⬚⬚⬚⬚ be either systematic or heuristi⬚⬚⬚⬚⬚⬚⬚⬚ nts of persuasion have different effec⬚⬚, ⬚⬚⬚⬚ as a function of the type of processing employed and sometimes as a function of the initial attitudes and the reasons for those attitudes. But not every persuasive communication is successful, so we now turn our attention to research and theory concerning resistance to persuasion.

▶ Resistance to Persuasion

Discussions of attitude change often convey the impression that all people change their attitudes almost all the time. That is simply not the case. Shifts in attitude are often temporary, and people sometimes resist strongly any attempt to change their attitudes.

Anticipatory Attitude Change

If people expect to receive a persuasive message, they sometimes appear to change their attitude even before receiving the message. In the initial demonstration of *anticipatory attitude change*, William McGuire and his colleagues observed that people who expected a persuasive message shifted their attitudes in the direction of the forthcoming message before it was even presented (McGuire & Millman, 1965; McGuire & Papageorgis, 1962). Do such shifts involve "real" attitude change? For two reasons, the answer is no.

First, we know from social judgment theory that there is "elasticity" in a person's attitudes (Cialdini, Levy, Herman, & Evenbeck, 1973; Cialdini, Levy, Herman, Kozlowski, & Petty, 1976). In response to various pressures, such as an expected persuasive message, people moderate their position within a limited range. However, when the outside pressures disappear (that is, when the persuasive attempt is finished), their attitudes snap back to their original positions. Robert Cialdini and his colleagues raise the possibility that most attitude change observed in the laboratory may reflect this elasticity rather than any real change.

Second, what appear to be anticipatory attitude changes are likely to be a form of impression management (Deaux, 1968; Hass, 1975; Hass & Mann, 1976; McGuire & Millman, 1965). That is, when people anticipate a persuasive message, they may temporarily moderate their position in an attempt to appear broad-minded or to avoid conflict. Such strategies are no doubt common in real life as well as in the laboratory. Consider how you would state your opinion concerning a baseball team toward which you have little allegiance if you were discussing the team with a friend who was a devoted fan. Even if you don't think the team is very good, you might temporarily present your attitude as more positive than it really is, if only to demonstrate that you are not inflexible.

Reactance

Concerns with appearing moderate and reasonable may occur only when people have no personal investment in an issue. Indeed, Cialdini and his colleagues (Cialdini, Levy, et al., 1976) found that when an issue is of great importance to a subject, anticipating a persuasive message may make someone's attitude stronger instead of more moderate. Further, the subjects who had initially strengthened their attitudes maintained their more extreme position even when the threat of persuasion was removed, a finding that suggests resistance to persuasion.

Why should people resist persuasion? According to Jack Brehm's (1966; Brehm & Brehm, 1981) theory of psychological **reactance**, any attempt to reduce someone's perceived control will motivate that person to reassert control. Attitudes concerning important issues, for example, are likely to be incorporated into an individual's self-concept (Schlenker, 1980). Thus, any attempt to change such attitudes may be perceived as a threat to one's ability to engage in impression management. To reassert control in such instances, an individual may change his or her position to a more extreme attitude. By doing so, the individual who is threatened by a persuasive attempt not only reaffirms his or her control, but reduces the likelihood that future persuasive attempts will be made by the same person. As Richard Petty and John Cacioppo (1977) have stated in this context, "forewarned is forearmed." (Reactance theory is discussed in more detail when we consider general social influence processes in Chapter 8.)

Inoculation

In an experiment conducted during the months preceding President Truman's announcement that the Soviet Union had produced an atomic bomb, Arthur Lumsdaine and Irving Janis (1953) compared one-sided and two-sided messages to determine their relative effectiveness for encouraging resistance to subsequent persuasive attempts. Their findings indicated that two-sided messages were more effective, and Lumsdaine and Irving suggested that including both sides of an issue "inoculated" subjects against later attempts to persuade them.

William McGuire (1964) pursued this explanation in a more elaborately designed set of studies. Before hearing a persuasive message designed to change their initial attitude, subjects were presented with one of three types of "defenses." Some subjects received arguments that supported their initial beliefs. Others received arguments that refuted the persuasive arguments that would be used in the subsequent message. A third group received arguments that refuted persuasive arguments that would not be used in the later communication. As is illustrated in Figure 7.11, subjects who had heard only the arguments that supported their initial position showed the least resistance to subsequent persuasion. In fact, they changed their attitudes almost as much as the control group, which received no defenses at all. In contrast, subjects who had already been exposed to a weakened form of the counterarguments resisted the actual message when it was presented; their attitudes were about the same as those of subjects who were never exposed to the persuasive communication.

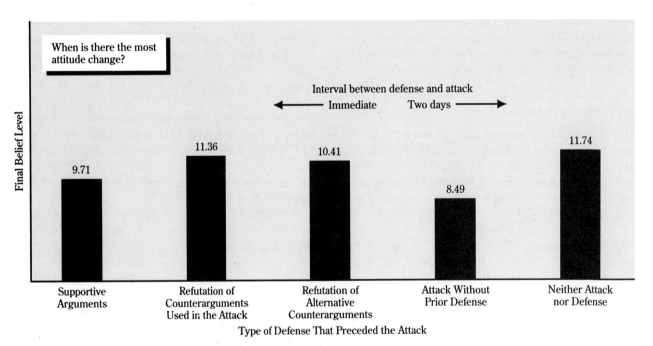

Figure 7.11 *Resistance to persuasion produced by three types of defenses.*
Source: "Inducing Resistance to Persuasion" by W. J. McGuire, 1964, *Advances in Experimental Social Psychology, 1,* pp. 191–229.

Applying this rationale to a marketing context, Szybillo and Heslin (1973) studied the effectiveness of various defenses when people were exposed to arguments favoring the installation of inflatable air bags in cars. (In 1973, negative attitudes about inflatable air bags were relatively unchallenged.) Szybillo and Heslin, too, found that prior arguments could increase resistance to persuasion and that refutational arguments were more effective than supportive arguments in building resistance.

In an interesting twist on the resistance-to-persuasion technique, John Lydon, Mark Zanna, and Michael Ross (1988) tested subjects' resistance to "backsliding" from a recent attitude change. Subjects who were generally in favor of exercise were exposed to a persuasive message that argued against vigorous exercise. Immediately after the persuasion, some subjects were asked to list the various exercises they had done in the last five months. Others were asked to list the times they had used seat belts. In this first session, both groups showed considerable attitude change as compared with a control group who had not received the persuasive message.

Two weeks later, all subjects were again questioned about their attitudes toward vigorous exercise in the context of a different experiment. Again, compared with the control group, the subjects who had thought about exercise thought a no-vigorous-exercise statement was more plausible than did the subjects who had thought about using seat belts. The subjects who thought about exercise also remembered more about the initial persuasive message. Further, Lydon and his colleagues had given all subjects a pamphlet that *encouraged* exercise when they left the first session. The results of a multiple-choice test on the pamphlet indicated that the subjects who had thought about exercise paid less attention to that pamphlet than did subjects who thought about using seat belts. Inoculation tactics, it would appear, also can be used to reinforce a recent attitude change.

Even when counterarguments are not supplied, inoculation can enable people to build resistance to later attacks. Petty and Cacioppo (1977) have found, for example, that when people are warned of a forthcoming message and are given time to think about the issue involved, they consider their own positions and alternative positions. They also generate cognitive defenses against the impending assault. Therefore, one of the most effective ways of encouraging resistance to persuasion is to warn a person that an attempt to persuade him or her is about to be made and to identify the specific content of a message so that refutation can be rehearsed. A somewhat similar strategy for increasing resistance to persuasion is to encourage people to think about behaviors that are relevant to the attitude, as in the study by Lydon, Zanna, and Ross (1988). When people were asked to think about how often they had brushed their teeth in the past two weeks, for example, they were more resistant to a persuasive message that questioned the effectiveness of tooth brushing (Ross, McFarland, Conway, & Zanna, 1983). Given these findings, it isn't surprising that commercials are often introduced with little warning or that government leaders often call surprise press conferences to announce new policy initiatives. What is surprising, however, is the position of those who don't want their children (or others) exposed to new ideas because they don't want to risk attitude change. Such avoidance tactics, as we have just seen, are likely to make children more, not less, susceptible to persuasive messages.

▶ Summary

Attempts to change our attitudes are ubiquitous, as are our own attempts to change others' attitudes. Many theories have been developed to predict when attitudes will and will not change. Among them are social judgment theory, balance theory, cognitive dissonance theory, and functional theories.

Social judgment theory emphasizes the individual's perception and thoughts about a persuasive message as prerequisites to attitude change. Attitudes are described by a range of positions along a scale called the "latitude of acceptance." Other opinion points on the scale may fall either in the latitude of rejection or in the latitude of noncommitment.

Research within the social judgment framework has focused on two major variables: (1) the effects of a person's ego involvement in an issue and (2) the amount of discrepancy between a persuasive communication and the person's own position. Persuasive messages, for example, are most effective when they fall within an individual's latitude of noncommitment. High levels of ego involvement are associated with wider latitudes of rejection and narrower latitudes of noncommitment. Thus, fanatics' attitudes may be no more extreme than others' attitudes; instead, the range of attitudes they refuse to consider may be wider.

The cognitive consistency theories of attitude change include Heider's balance theory and Festinger's cognitive dissonance theory. Common to these theories is an assumption that people change their attitudes in order to reduce or eliminate inconsistency between conflicting attitudes and behaviors. Although these theories assume that we are thoughtful, they do not require that we be rational either in our perception of inconsistency or in its resolution.

Balance theory deals with the relationships among a person (P), another person (O), and some object (X). If an imbalance exists among these elements—for example, if two people like each other but disagree in their attitudes toward their home—then attitude change is expected to occur. Although empirical support for balance theory has not been overwhelming, its basic principle of attitudinal consistency has had a great impact on research and theory concerning attitude change.

Cognitive dissonance theory is also based on the principle of consistency, but it deals with behaviors as well as attitudes. In its initial statement, the theory proposed that dissonance is aroused when a person's behavior is inconsistent with his or her attitude. Such dissonance is believed to be uncomfortable, and the resultant discomfort motivates the person to eliminate the dissonance by changing either the behavior or the attitude.

However, inconsistency itself is not sufficient, or even necessary, to arouse dissonance. The behavior must be relatively unusual and have aversive consequences, the individual must accept personal responsibility for the outcome, and there must be little or no opportunity for self-affirmation. Under those conditions, dissonance will be aroused, and a person will be motivated to reduce it.

Dissonance theory is particularly applicable to attitude change following a decision. Selective exposure and other techniques reduce dissonance by justifying one's decision.

Functional theories of attitude change assume that people hold attitudes that fit their needs and that to change those attitudes we must determine what those needs are. Some attitudes are evaluative, based on the rewards and punishments associated with the attitude object itself; others are expressive, directed toward objects that are means to a desired end. Still others enable individuals to maintain their level of self-esteem.

Considerable research has demonstrated that there is more than one process of attitude change. The central, or systematic, process can be considered a sequence of steps. In its simplest form, this sequence consists of attention to, comprehension of, and acceptance of a persuasive message. Because people are not always motivated to or able to engage in systematic processing, another process, called peripheral or heuristic processing, has also received empirical support. Heuristic processing requires very little attention to the content of a persuasive message.

Central processes tend to result in relatively enduring attitude change. People with a high need for cognition are likely to engage in central processing more often than are people with a low need for cognition. Peripheral processing results in relatively temporary attitude change and often includes simple rules or heuristics, such as "agree with attractive people" or "follow the advice of experts."

The major elements in persuasion are the source, the message, the context, and the recipient. Many studies have been conducted to show how variations in each of these elements can affect the amount of attitude change that occurs.

People who argue against their best interests, for example, are often more persuasive than people whose arguments are consistent with their self-interests. Communicators who are similar to the recipients are also more effective than dissimilar communicators.

Messages that focus on fear about the consequences of not changing an attitude can be effective, but only under very specific conditions. The level of fear must not be too great, and listeners must believe that the consequences are likely to occur if they do not change, that the recommended action will enable them to avoid the consequences, and that they are able to complete the recommended action.

Distraction in the context of a persuasive message tends to promote peripheral processing. However, if the distraction is itself a persuasive message, such as a heckler's comments during a speech, the communicator may have the advantage if he or she can calmly refute arguments conveyed in the distractive message.

More intelligent people are better able to comprehend a persuasive message, but they are also better able to refute the arguments contained in a simplistic message. People high in self-monitoring are more likely to engage in peripheral processing, whereas people low in self-monitoring are more likely to pay attention to the content of a persuasive communication.

Although emphasis has been placed on the factors that bring about change, we should consider also the factors that increase resistance to change. Studies of anticipatory attitude change suggest that some changes may simply reflect "elasticity," that people consciously present their opinions as moderate in order to appear flexible. When a person is forewarned of a persuasive communication, he or she may experience reactance to the apparent attempt to reduce personal control. In such cases, the person's attitude may become more extreme, making the persuasion attempt less effective. People who have information about the content of persuasive messages may be inoculated against subsequent change as a result of the opportunity to think about ways to refute the persuasive arguments.

▶ *Key Terms*

anchor
assimilation effects
balance theory
cognitive dissonance theory
contrast effects
functional theory
heuristics
latitude of acceptance
latitude of noncommitment
latitude of rejection
reactance
selective exposure
self-affirmation
self-perception theory
social judgment theory

As for conforming outwardly, and

living your own life inwardly, I do not

think much of that.

Henry David Thoreau

Don't compromise yourself. You are

all you've got.

Janis Joplin

8

Social Influence and Personal Control

Imagine you have volunteered to participate in a research project on visual perception. Along with six other subjects, you are shown a vertical line—the "target" line—and then are asked which of three other vertical lines match it in length (see Figure 8.1). One of the three lines is identical in length to the first line. The other two lines appear so different from the target that you begin to think the study is silly. Sure enough, each person at the table correctly identifies the matching line on the first trial, the same thing happens on the second trial, and so on. Eventually, one of the other subjects makes an incorrect choice. "Oops," you think, "not paying attention; wrong choice." But then the second subject makes the same, wrong choice! Then the third, the fourth, and the fifth subject make the same, incorrect choice. You look at the lines again; the correct answer seems as obvious as it was in the earlier trials. Now it's your turn to respond. Would you go along with the other subjects, or would you choose what still seems obviously to be the correct response? Would you be willing to risk having the others think you are wrong? What would you do?

This situation is just one of many involving social influence; others include using power strategies, giving direct orders, and making direct requests. In many cases, reactions to social influence only involve adapting to the world. Driving on the right side of the road in the United States and Canada, for example, is a matter of safety, just as it is wise to drive on the left in Great Britain. In other cases, the wisdom of conformity behavior may be questionable, as when members of a junior high school clique determine what clothes are ac-

ceptable to wear and reject people who choose a different style of dress. The way we respond to the requests or orders of others will vary across a wide range of situations. We respond in different ways, for example, to a friend who asks us for a favor, to a door-to-door salesperson who's pressuring us to buy a gadget we don't need, and to a dictator in a repressive society.

Each time we encounter an attempt to influence our behavior or attitudes, we must decide whether to comply or resist. At the heart of this process is the issue of control—the degree to which we feel we have control over our own lives versus the degree to which others have the power to determine our behavior. This very basic issue of influence and control is the focus of this chapter. First we will consider the various forms of control—conformity, compliance, and obedience. Then we will look more carefully at why control is an important issue and how people respond to a loss of control in their lives.

▶ Conformity

Conformity means yielding to perceived group pressures when no direct request to comply with the group has been made. In the opening scenario, for example, no one directly asked that you go along with the incorrect response. Even so, you can easily imagine perceiving a considerable amount of pressure to conform your judgment to those of the other group members.

The Asch and Sherif Situations

Our opening scenario fits the basic procedure first used by Solomon Asch (1951, 1956, 1958) in his early studies of conformity. In Asch's procedure, however, the "other subjects" were actually confederates, and the real subject was always the next-to-last person to respond to the stimulus. However, the correct choices in Asch's studies usually were as simple as those depicted in Figure 8.1; in controlled tests, for example, virtually all subjects correctly matched the lines when no confederates were present. Despite its simplicity, Asch's procedure illustrates some basic characteristics of the process of influence and control.

How did Asch's subjects respond? Asch's standard procedure consisted of twelve critical trials on which

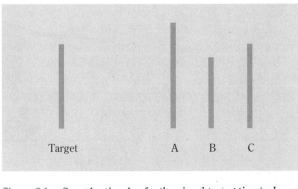

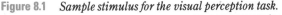

Figure 8.1 *Sample stimulus for the visual perception task.*

Target   A   B   C

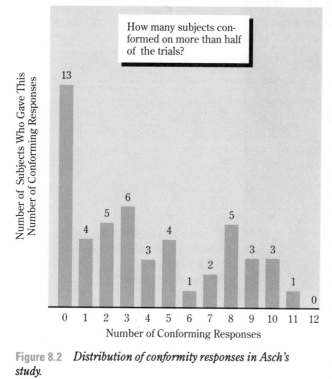

Number of Subjects Who Gave This Number of Conforming Responses

How many subjects con-formed on more than half of the trials?

Number of Conforming Responses

Figure 8.2 *Distribution of conformity responses in Asch's study.*

confederates gave the wrong response, interspersed among trials on which all confederates gave the correct answer. The conformity behavior of fifty subjects is shown in Figure 8.2. When we consider the subjects' responses on all the critical trials, we find that 32% of the responses were conforming. On the average, subjects conformed on 3.84 out of 12 possible trials. But the averages are deceiving; in Asch's study the distribution of conforming responses is important because of the great range of individual differences. Notice in Figure 8.2 that almost 75% of the subjects conformed to the majority on at least one critical trial, whereas four subjects (8%) yielded on ten or more of those trials. Although conformity was certainly prevalent, not all subjects conformed, and many of Asch's subjects conformed only occasionally.

Asch's work on conformity was influenced by the even earlier studies of Muzafer Sherif (1935) on the **au-tokinetic effect.** If you look at a stationary light in an otherwise dark room, the light will appear to move be-cause your eyes have no other reference point. Sherif

capitalized on this phenomenon to study the effects of another person's response and found that a subject's reports of movement were highly influenced by other people's estimates. Subjects who reported only a small amount of movement when tested alone, for example, later reported more movement when tested with a con-federate whose estimates were greater than the sub-ject's initial estimates. Similarly, the initially disparate estimates of a group of naive subjects tend to converge toward an average.

Conformity in the Sherif situation is not very surpris-ing; the stimulus is ambiguous, and there is no other source of information. Conformity in the Asch situa-tion, however, is slightly surprising because the correct response is so clear and the subjects were not exposed to any overt group pressure.

Why Do People Conform?

What can explain this tendency to conform to other people's opinions? Morton Deutsch and Harold Gerard (1955) proposed two different types of social influence: informational and normative. **Informational influ-ence,** as the term suggests, involves the presentation of facts or knowledge about a situation. Other people produce informational influence simply because they constitute a source of information that is unavailable to a solitary individual. Sherif's subjects, for example, were uncertain about how much the light (apparently) moved, and they relied on information from others to make their decisions. Sherif (1936) also demonstrated that subjects' estimates of movement continued to be influenced by others' estimates even when the others were no longer present. Like facts remembered from a book, the others' estimates were considered objective evidence by Sherif's subjects, evidence that they con-tinued to use in the absence of the original source of the information. Thus, informational influence provides people with a reason to comply.

In contrast, **normative influence** involves per-ceived pressure to comply, social pressure brought about by a combination of the existence of group norms and a desire to be like the group members and to avoid appearing deviant. Subjects in Asch's experiments could easily tell which line was equal to, longer than, or shorter than the standard. The confederates' opinions still exerted considerable influence, perhaps because

Maintaining group membership includes engaging in behaviors that are consistent with group norms.
Bob Clay/Clay Images

Asch's subjects did not want to risk being labeled "strange."

More recently, Dominic Abrams and Michael Hogg (1990) have proposed **self-categorization,** our spontaneous inclusion of ourselves as a member of a group, as an underlying process for both informational and normative influences. As we saw in Chapter 4, categorizing another person as a member of this or that group occurs as soon as we know enough about the person to enable some sort of group membership identification. We spontaneously think of others, for example, as "male" or "female," "young" or "old," and so forth (Fiske & Neuberg, 1990). Abrams and Hogg propose we do the same thing to ourselves; that is, once we categorize ourselves as a member of a particular group, the self-consistency processes discussed in Chapter 3 operate to maintain that membership. Belonging to the group becomes a salient characteristic of our self-concept (Tajfel, 1982), a characteristic we are as unwilling to change as any other aspect of our self-concept. Maintaining group membership includes engaging in behaviors that are consistent with group norms. Therefore, according to Abrams and Hogg, conformity occurs because it enables us to maintain our self-concept by maintaining our membership in a group with which we identify.[1]

[1] The importance of group membership as part of the self-concept will be discussed in more detail in Chapter 12.

One of the more intriguing aspects of self-categorization as an explanation of conformity is the notion that, at different times or in different places, the same person may conform to very different group norms. That is, a person's conformity to one group's norms does not necessarily prevent him or her from also accepting another group's norms. Conformity depends on which group is salient in the self-categorization process. We can easily imagine a person who does not defend rock music when she is among friends who are devoted to classical music. That same person might also dance up a storm when she is with different friends and a band begins playing Chuck Berry's "Johnny B. Goode." In each case, conformity occurs, but to the group that is salient at the time.

Self-categorization also provides an explanation for those instances in which someone appears not to conform. Consider, for example, two different types of nonconformity responses. One is **independence,** defined as behavior that is not responsive to group norms. The man who continues to wear blue jeans when "everyone else" has switched to wearing casual slacks may be demonstrating independence. Independence is also illustrated by the woman who may be the first among her friends to cut her hair short and who continues to keep her hair short after "everyone else" begins to do the same. In self-categorization terms, the group consisting of "everyone else" is not a salient dimension for maintaining one's self-concept. Thus, the independent

"I just got damn well fed up with being formal all the time"

Not everyone conforms.
Drawing by R. Taylor; © 1942, 1970 The New Yorker Magazine, Inc.

person does not conform (or perhaps does not pay attention) to the norms that define membership in that group. **Anticonformity,** in contrast, is characterized by consistent opposition to the norms of a group. The anticonformist may choose to wear blue jeans when "everyone else" is wearing dresses but to switch to dresses when blue jeans become popular. In self-categorization terms, the anticonformist categorizes himself or herself as *"not* everyone else" and actively pursues behaviors that are inconsistent with group norms so as to maintain that aspect of the self-concept.

Consider, for example, the results of two studies that illustrate the importance of self-categorization. In one study, Deutsch and Gerard (1955) made group membership explicit in a replication of the Asch procedure. As you can see in the left side of Figure 8.3, the number of errors (conformity) was considerably greater when subjects were explicitly identified as members of the same group. Presumably, being identified as part of a group—even an ad hoc group formed for the experiment—was sufficient for the subjects to incorporate membership in the group into their self-concepts. Thus, they conformed with the group in order to maintain their self-concepts.

In another study, Abrams and his colleagues (cited in Abrams & Hogg, 1990) examined anticonformity using a derivation of Sherif's autokinetic procedures. Six people were in the darkened room at the same time;

three were real subjects, and the others were confederates. To create the perception of two groups, the confederates consistently responded with an estimate that was 5 cm greater than the subjects' estimates. In the explicit group condition, Abrams and his colleagues used a competitive task in which the real subjects were pitted against the confederates. As you can see in the right side of Figure 8.3, the discrepancy between the subjects' estimates and the confederates' estimates (anticonformity) was much greater in the explicit group condition. Thus, both informational (the autokinetic effect) and normative (the Asch procedure) influences can be strengthened through self-categorization, and the process operates for conformity as well as anticonformity.

Just as it is important to recognize that people do not always conform to group pressures, it is also important to recognize that social influence in a group works both ways. As the French psychologist Serge Moscovici (1985) has frequently pointed out, not only can the majority influence an individual or a small minority, but the minority can affect the beliefs and behaviors of the majority as well. Although the phenomenon of conformity helps us understand the general regularity of social life, the frequent successes of minority groups in their efforts to influence the majority indicate that the group that sets the norms can shift its position (Kruglanski & Mackie, 1990). We will consider the influence

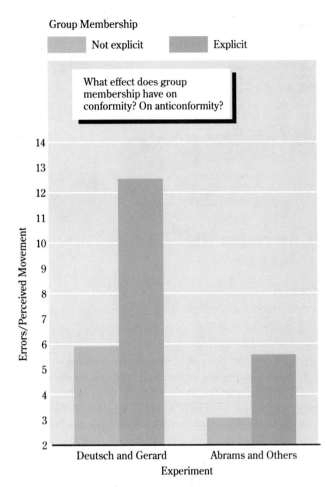

Group Membership

Not explicit   Explicit

What effect does group membership have on conformity? On anticonformity?

Figure 8.3 *The effect of explicit group membership on conformity (left) and anticonformity (right).*

Sources: "A Study of Normative and Informational Social Influences upon Individual Judgment" by M. Deutsch and H. B. Gerard, 1955, *Journal of Abnormal and Social Psychology, 51,* pp. 629–636; and "Social Identification, Self-Categorization, and Social Influence" by D. Abrams and M. A. Hogg, 1990, *European Review of Social Psychology, 1,* pp. 195–228.

of the minority in more detail in Chapter 12, when we discuss group behavior more generally.

Influences on Conformity

Many factors affect the extent to which people will conform to a group norm. As you might expect, group size is one such factor. In general, the larger the group, the more influence it exerts (Latané, 1981; Tanford & Pen-

rod, 1984; Wolf, 1987). As a group becomes larger, the greater number of members may be able to provide more reasons to comply with group norms. Also, as group size increases, so does the probability that someone in the group has the power to exert pressure to comply (Insko, Smith, Alicke, Wade, & Taylor, 1985). However, the effectiveness of greater numbers diminishes as group size grows beyond three.

An important factor in the effect of group size is the extent to which members of the group are regarded as a single unit (Wilder, 1977). Consider the difference between an Asch-type situation in which four individuals all give the wrong answer, apparently independently, and one in which those four persons are viewed as a single group or club to which the real subject does not belong. In the latter case, conformity pressures are less effective and more closely approximate the pressure exerted by a single individual. In other words, the four opinions are actually considered to represent only one voice, and hence the size of the majority becomes less important. Essentially, the question of conforming to "them" (the individuals) becomes one of conforming to "it" (the group). As we have seen, however, when the subject belongs to the group, the "unit" exerts considerably greater influence.

Thus far we have discussed conformity as though it always involves one individual among several others who think alike. What happens when the others are not unanimous, when there is a clear majority and minority? When the group is not unanimous, conformity to the majority is dramatically reduced. In this case, the minority becomes a source of influence in its own right and also exerts pressure on the individual. In a divided jury containing one person who can't decide, for example, pressure to make a decision—to join a "side"— may come from jurors who favor conviction as well as from jurors who favor acquittal. When the majority is overwhelming, its position also affects the amount of conformity shown. The more discrepant a group position is from one's own, the more pressure one will feel to move toward the group norm. And people tend to succumb to conformity pressures more readily when the group's position is increasingly different from their own than they do when the group's position becomes increasingly similar to their own (Campbell, Tesser, & Fairey, 1986). Thus, as more jurors decide in favor of conviction, for example, the juror who can't decide may experience increasing pressure to decide to convict.

Individual Differences in Conformity

The wide variation in responses to Asch's task led many investigators to explore various personality types that may be susceptible to pressures to conform. A number of differences were reported. Richard Crutchfield (1955), for example, reported that independent businessmen and military officers demonstrated "more intellectual effectiveness, ego strength, leadership ability, and maturity of social relations, together with a conspicuous absence of inferiority feelings, rigid and excessive self-control, and authoritarian attitudes," than their more conforming colleagues (p. 194). Other researchers have found that conforming subjects have a stronger need for affiliation (McGhee & Teevan, 1967) and stronger tendencies to blame themselves (Costanzo, 1970). People who are given reason to doubt their ability to judge a particular task are, not surprisingly, more likely to conform, relying on the group to supply the information that they lack (Campbell, Tesser, & Fairey, 1986).

It is generally believed, and early research supported the notion, that women are more conforming than men. More recent evidence, however, indicates that much of this apparent gender difference resulted from research settings in which men had an informational advantage (Zimbardo & Leippe, 1991). That is, women conform more when they know less than men about the topic, but men conform more when they know less than women about the topic (Cacioppo & Petty, 1980). Also, women are more likely to conform in situations that involve face-to-face interaction (Eagly & Carli, 1981). One explanation for this difference is that women are more likely than men to be socialized to consider group harmony as important. Thus, when group pressure is exerted, women are more likely to go along with the group than to assert their own judgment and risk disharmony. For example, Christine Maslach and her colleagues (Maslach, Santee, & Wade, 1987) have shown that scores on a measure of gender-role norms, including the importance of group harmony, are better predictors of conformity than whether one is male or female.

Despite the abundance of research on individual differences in conformity, the general conclusion is that such variables cannot be used to predict all conformity. If the laboratory research on conformity has demonstrated anything, it is that situational factors are of great importance in eliciting conformity behavior. It is also important to consider the reasons for individual choices. Conformity is one outcome of an attempt to solve problems and reach conclusions about one's surroundings. Such a perspective should be considered before one too quickly adopts the judgment that conformity is always bad. As Barry Collins has stated:

> It would be a mistake to oversimplify the question and ask whether conformity is good or bad. A person who refused to accept anyone's word of advice on any topic whatsoever ... would probably make just as big a botch of ... life ... as a person who always conformed and never formed a[n independent] judgment. [1970, p. 21]

▶ Compliance

The term **compliance** has often been used interchangeably with conformity. Here, however, we will use the term in a more specific sense, limiting its use to situations in which a direct request is made and the person agrees to behave in accordance with that request. Conformity, in contrast, is a response to indirect pressure, to pressure perceived by an individual in the absence of a direct request. When you decide to wear semi-formal clothes because you think everyone else will be and you don't want to appear different, that's conformity. When your friends ask you to wear semi-formal clothes because they don't want you to appear different and you agree, that's compliance. Such demands are made of us daily. A professor may ask you to stop by after class; a salesperson may suggest you buy a new vacuum cleaner; a panhandler may stop you on the street and ask for a dollar. Many experimental studies of compliance have, in fact, taken their lead from these common events.

The Foot-in-the-Door Effect

The foot-in-the-door effect is well known to salespeople. The sales lore suggests that once the seller has his or her foot in the door, a sale will be no problem. In social-psychological terms, the **foot-in-the-door effect** refers to the fact that a person who complies with one small request is likely to comply later with a larger, more substantial demand.

In an initial test of this hypothesis, Jonathan Freedman and Scott Fraser (1966) arranged for two undergraduate experimenters to contact suburban women in their homes and present them first with a small request and later with a larger one. The experimenters first asked the women either to place a small sign in their window or to sign a petition about driving safely or keeping California beautiful. Two weeks later, a different experimenter returned to each home and asked each subject to place a large, unattractive billboard promoting auto safety on her lawn for the next couple of weeks—a rather substantial request. A second group of women (the control group) was presented with the second request only. The results showed a very strong foot-in-the-door effect—those subjects who had complied with the earlier, trivial request were much more likely to comply with the larger request two weeks later. More intriguing yet was the apparent generality of the effect; signing a petition to "keep California beautiful" led to greater compliance with a different experimenter on a different issue.

What causes the foot-in-the-door effect? One explanation stresses people's self-perceptions (see Chapter 3). Having once agreed to help, a person may decide that he or she is basically a helpful person. That person may then grant a second request—even a burdensome one—because he or she wishes to maintain that image of helpfulness. Considerable evidence supports this interpretation (DeJong, 1979). However, at least two conditions are necessary to produce the effect. First, the initial request must be large enough to cause people to think about the implications of their behavior. Offhandedly telling someone the correct time, for example, might not be enough to cause you to think of yourself as a helpful person, whereas giving a set of complicated directions to someone who was lost might be sufficient. A second necessary condition is a perception of free choice. If a person feels forced to comply, then there is no reason to attribute one's compliance to any internal disposition. In fact, any external justification for the compliance will weaken or eliminate the foot-in-the-door effect (see also Chapter 7). For example, women who were offered money for agreeing to a five-minute telephone interview were no more likely to comply with a later request for a twenty-five–minute interview than women who did not receive the initial request. The money was sufficient justification for complying with the request. Demonstrating the foot-in-the-door effect, women not offered the monetary justification for granting the first request were more likely to agree to the later request (Zuckerman, Lazzaro, & Waldgeir, 1979).

What about people who refuse the initial request? The self-perception explanation suggests that these people should be *less* likely to comply with subsequent requests. In contrast to people who agree to help, these noncompliers should view themselves as unhelpful people and act accordingly on future occasions. Labels can also be provided by others, as Robert Kraut (1973) has shown. In this experiment, subjects who gave to charity were either labeled as charitable or not labeled. Subjects who gave a donation might be told, for example, "You are really a generous person. I wish more people were as charitable as you are." Similarly, subjects who refused to give to charity were either labeled as uncharitable or not labeled. All subjects were later asked by another canvasser to contribute to a second charity. Subjects who had been labeled as charitable gave more, and subjects labeled as uncharitable gave less, than their respective unlabeled peers.

Thus, consistent with sales lore, considerable evidence exists to support the foot-in-the-door effect. A "foot in" makes future compliance more likely; conversely, "no foot in" should reduce future compliance. But such a reduction in compliance does not always occur.

The Door-in-the-Face Effect

Robert Cialdini and his co-workers, who coined the term **door-in-the-face effect,** suggested that on some occasions people who refuse an initial request may be *more* likely to agree to a subsequent request (Cialdini et al., 1975). These researchers approached college students with a socially desirable but highly demanding request: Would they serve as voluntary counselors at a county juvenile detention center for two years? Virtually everyone politely refused, in effect slamming the door in the face of a demanding request for compliance. However, when the researchers made a second, smaller request—specifically, to chaperon juveniles on a trip to the zoo—many subjects readily agreed.[2]

Why wasn't there less compliance in this case, as the self-categorization explanation would predict? Apparently, investigators have concluded, the door-in-the-

[2] Interestingly, the impetus for Cialdini's research on the door-in-the-face effect came from an undergraduate in one of his social psychology classes (Cialdini, 1990).

The door-in-the-face technique.

face effect depends on a particular set of circumstances (DeJong, 1979). First, the initial request must be very large—so large that the people who refuse will make no negative inferences about themselves. Thus, the people who declined two years of voluntary service probably concluded that anyone would have declined such a large request and therefore had no reason to think of themselves as any less helpful than anyone else. Second, for the door-in-the-face effect to occur, the second request must be made by the same person who makes the first request. According to Cialdini and his colleagues, subjects view the toned-down request as a concession and then feel pressure to reciprocate that concession. If a different person makes the second request, however, such conciliatory behavior is not necessary because no concession was made.

The door-in-the-face technique has been applied in a business context as well (Mowen & Cialdini, 1980). Pedestrians selected at random were more likely to agree to fill out a brief insurance-company survey when the initial request had been for a much longer survey. In this case, however, the second request had to be part of the first request for the tactic to be successful. In other words, a door slammed in the face could be reopened only if the topic of the second survey was the same.

Closely related to the door-in-the-face technique is what Jerry Burger (1986) has called the "that's not all" technique. Imagine that you are sitting at home and

hear a knock at your door. A boy and a girl from the local high school are there, selling candles to raise money for a band trip. "We're selling the candles for $3 apiece," the boy says. Before you have a chance to say yes or no, the girl jumps in to say that they'll let you have them for only $2. Would you be more likely to buy a candle now than you would be if they had originally been offered to you at $2 apiece? Yes, according to Burger's research. Notice that the major difference between the door-in-the-face and "that's not all" is that in the former case the consumer, or subject, has the opportunity to refuse; in "that's not all," a more favorable offer is made before any refusal (or acceptance) occurs. In a comparison of the two techniques, Burger found "that's not all" to be the more effective, inducing greater compliance. Both procedures, however, are dependent on some concession from the person making the request.

The Low-Ball Procedure

Another investigation of compliance that was inspired by a practitioner's rule of thumb is the investigation of the low-ball procedure (Cialdini, Cacioppo, Bassett, & Miller, 1978). Presumably widespread (especially among new-car dealers), the technique of "throwing a low ball" consists in inducing the customer to buy a car by offering an extremely good price (for example, $500 below what competitors are offering). Then, once the

Sometimes, once a customer has agreed to buy a car, the conditions of the sale are changed.
Peter Glass/Monkmeyer Press

customer has agreed to buy the car, the conditions of the deal are changed; the end result is a higher purchase price than the customer originally agreed to. Reported techniques include a refusal by the salesperson's boss to approve the deal, a reduction in the trade-in figure given by the used-car manager, and the exclusion of various options from the purchase price offered. Thus, instead of a concession from the requester (the seller), as is made in the foot-in-the-door technique, the low-ball technique involves an extremely favorable offer that eventually requires a concession from the buyer.

As Cialdini and his colleagues demonstrated, the low-ball technique of inducing compliance works beyond the new-car showroom. University students, for example, were more likely to show up for an experiment at 7 A.M. if they had first agreed to participate in a

general way than if they were initially told of the early hour. Although this technique of inducing compliance is in many ways similar to the foot-in-the-door procedure, there is at least one important difference. In low-balling, the initial commitment is to the behavior to be performed; in the "foot" procedure, the commitment is first to a different, less demanding behavior.

Why does the low-ball technique work? Cialdini (1985) suggests that after receiving the initial offer, people make a commitment and then develop a set of justifications for that commitment. When the initial justification—the low price—is then taken away, they still have the remaining justifications to support their decision to buy the product—even if those reasons were developed late in the game.

The Lure

Yet another technique salespeople use is a derivation of low-balling called the "lure" by Robert Joule and his colleagues (Joule & Beauvois, 1987; Joule et al., 1989). The **lure technique** begins when someone is enticed by an extremely attractive offer, such as 50% off the regular price of an item. The individual decides to purchase the product, only to discover that it is no longer available or that the correct color, size, or some other quality is not available. The salesperson then displays a similar item that is available, but at regular price. The difference between the lure and low-balling is that in low-balling the cost of the desired product is raised, whereas in the lure a substitute product is offered at a higher cost. Despite the difference in technique, both low-balling and the lure take advantage of the fact that the person has already made a commitment to engage in a particular activity.

In an experimental test of the lure technique, Joule and his colleagues (1989, Experiment 1) asked students to participate in one of two different studies. Half the students were asked to volunteer for a rather boring hour-long study that involved memorizing numbers. No compensation was offered at the time of the request. As you might expect, only about 15% of those asked agreed to participate. The other half of the students were asked to volunteer for an interesting, half-hour-long study that involved watching a movie, for which they would be paid 30 francs (about U.S. $6). About 47% of the second group of students agreed to participate. When the latter subjects arrived at the laboratory, however, a different experimenter told them the interesting study had been completed the day before, and no more subjects were needed. Instead, they were offered an opportunity to participate in the boring memory study, but they would not be paid for doing so. Every one of the students who were offered the "lure" took it; they all agreed to participate in the memory study. Having committed themselves to volunteering for a study, the lured students followed through on that commitment.

The Generality of Compliance

The previous discussion concentrated on manipulative techniques for obtaining compliance, what might be considered "dirty tricks." In the course of a normal day, each of us receives many requests, and all of them certainly will not involve "dirty tricks." People use a variety of strategies in their attempts to get others to comply. Table 8.1 shows 15 possible tactics (Rule, Bisanz, & Kohn, 1985). Interestingly, the most popular tactic is a simple request.

One reason that the strategies in the list were ranked in the obtained order is provided by Penelope Brown and Stephen Levinson's (1987) theory of politeness. According to Brown and Levinson, impression management is a universal concern in social situations, and therefore social interactions invariably involve what Erving Goffman (1967) called *saving face*. Face saving involves behaving so as to prevent changing others' impressions of one, or behaving in a manner that will restore a changed impression. For example, when a man stands near the door of a women's restroom, and someone looks too often or too long at him, he is likely to offer some comment indicating that he is waiting for a specific person to emerge. No explanation is actually required, but the explanation saves face; it is designed to prevent the onlooker from forming an unwanted impression and, perhaps, from attributing deviant motivations to the behavior.

Getting someone to do something for you necessarily involves altering the intended behavior of the other person, which may threaten the "face" of that other. Attempting to obtain compliance, for example, presupposes some power or right to impose on the other or may involve an assumption that the other has the ability

Table 8.1 Strategies used to obtain compliance, ranked from most to least preferred

1. Ask (either directly or indirectly).
   Example: "Would you please . . ."
2. Invoke personal expertise.
   Example: "I read in *Consumer Reports* that . . ."
3. Offer a personal reason.
   Example: "I need . . ."
4. Invoke a role relationship.
   Example: "If you were my friend, you would . . ."
5. Bargain for a favor.
   Example: "If you'll do this for me, I promise I'll . . ."
6. Invoke a norm.
   Example: "Everyone is doing it."
7. Invoke a moral principle.
   Example: "It would be the right thing to do."
8. Invoke altruism.
   Example: "The health of other people depends on you."
9. Butter them up.
   Example: "You look so attractive today."
10. Bargain for an object (or bribe).
    Example: "I'll give you $100 if you will . . ."
11. Appeal to their emotions.
    Example: "I'm going to cry if you don't . . ."
12. Offer a personal criticism.
    Example: "You're so stingy, you probably wouldn't . . ."
13. Try deception.
    Example: "The boss told me to tell you . . ." (when the boss never said a word about it).
14. Threaten.
    Example: "I'm going to tell father if you don't . . ."
15. Use force.
    Example: "Do it right now!" (accompanied by physical shaking).

Source: "Anatomy of a Persuasion Schema: Targets, Goals, and Strategies" by B. G. Rule, G. L. Bisanz, and M. Kohn, 1985, *Journal of Personality and Social Psychology, 48,* pp. 1127–1140.

to comply. Similarly, the other's refusal to comply may result in a loss of face for the person attempting to obtain compliance. According to Brown and Levinson, requests that are more polite are less threatening to the

*"Have you determined yet whether you will
or will not eat your cereal?"*

A polite request often increases compliance.
Drawing by Koren; © 1991 The New Yorker Magazine, Inc.

faces of speaker and listener, so polite attempts to obtain compliance should be preferred over impolite attempts. An examination of the rankings in Table 8.1 supports such reasoning. A simple request, particularly one phrased "Would you mind . . .," is more polite and less face-threatening than is a statement of need, a bribe, or a threat. There is also evidence that the theory of politeness holds up well across very different cultures. Thomas Holtgraves and Joong-Nam Yang (1990), for example, asked students in Muncie, Indiana, and in Seoul, Korea, to rank the politeness of various types of requests. Although the obtained rankings were not perfectly consistent with the theory of politeness, "the ordering for perceived politeness was the same for Koreans and Americans" (p. 722).

The theory of politeness also provides insight into instances in which compliance is what Ellen Langer (1978b, 1989a) calls "mindless," involving little thought about the request. If, as Brown and Levinson propose, face saving is the primary determinant of politeness, then perhaps when the *form* of a request is consistent with saving face, we will comply more readily, even if there's no substance beneath the form.

Although compliance may sometimes be mindless, studies of power strategies suggest that at other times we are quite sensitive to the form in which compliance is requested. John French and Bertram Raven (1959) have identified five forms of power, or ways in which one person can induce another's compliance. These forms are defined in Table 8.2. You can probably think of instances when others have exercised each of these types of power in an effort to gain your compliance. The parent who promises use of the car in return for some behavior, for example, is using reward power, and the parent who threatens "grounding" is using coercive power. A professor may gain compliance through the use of expert power, whereas a friend may be powerful because he or she is someone you would like to emulate (referent power). Corporate officers and elected officials are said to have legitimate power and gain compliance because it is agreed that they have a right to expect it. Of course, it is possible that one person may have several power bases; an admired professor, for example, may be able to reward and punish by means of grades and may be an important role model and source of expertise as well. Notice, too, that the bases for expert, legitimate, and referent power result from perceptions of the target; the agent has power only as long as the target holds the relevant beliefs.

The likelihood of compliance varies with the form of power exercised, although in practice it is often difficult to isolate the effect of a single power type when multiple forms are being used (Podsakoff & Schriesheim, 1985). Coercive power may be quite effective if the power source is present but less effective if the power source is not present when the behavior is to be performed. Away from a coercive parent, for example, a child may ignore all the household rules. Further, people's explanations for compliance depend on the power strategy being used. When either referent or reward power is used, for example, compliance is generally explained by referring to characteristics of the person who performs the compliant behavior. That is, the use

Teachers often possess multiple forms of power.
Gale Zucker

of referent or reward power is not necessarily recognized as power; the target's behavior is considered to be voluntary (Wells, 1980). In contrast, when either coercive or legitimate power is used, explanations for compliance generally focus on the person who has made the request (Litman-Adizes, Raven, & Fontaine, 1978). For example, when a confession is obtained through promises of leniency (reward power), jurors perceive the confession to be voluntary and are more likely to convict the defendant than when a confession is obtained by threats (coercive power), even though the leniency offer may be more powerful and involve greater social influence (Kassin & Wrightsman, 1980, 1981). Attributions about one's own compliance follow a similar pattern and may affect the extent of future compliance once the agent who has made the request is no longer present. For example, if an individual attributes compliance to dispositional characteristics, perhaps as a result of reward or referent power, then the individual is likely to continue to perform the behavior after the power basis becomes irrelevant.

In summary, people may be willing to comply with the request of another person for many reasons. At one extreme is the mindless response: we comply almost automatically, giving little thought to the reasons we

Table 8.2 **Forms of power and their bases**

Form	Basis
Coercive power	Agent's ability to administer punishment
Reward power	Agent's ability to give rewards
Expert power	Target's belief that agent has superior knowledge, ability, or expertise
Legitimate power	Target's belief that agent is authorized by a recognized power structure to command and make decisions
Referent power	Target's identification with, attraction to, or respect for agent

Source: "The Bases of Social Power" by J. R. P. French, Jr., and B. H. Raven, in *Studies in Social Power* (pp. 150–167), ed. by D. Cartwright, 1959, Ann Arbor, MI: University of Michigan Press.

should or should not agree to carry out the behavior. This form of compliance is most likely to occur when the response is overlearned and requires little conscious monitoring and when the form of the request matches our expectations about legitimate requests. At the other extreme are situations in which we carefully weigh the reasons for compliance and act accordingly. Although rational thought enters the picture on many occasions, the sheer force of the request often determines our response. As we shall see in the case of obedience, once legitimate power has been established, a person may refuse to question the reasons for the agent's request and simply carry out orders because they are given.

▶ Obedience

A special form of compliance, in response to a direct request made in the form of an order, is **obedience.** All of us feel some degree of pressure to obey certain symbols of authority, such as parents, police officers, and traffic lights. But obedience also can lead us to take extreme actions against our better judgment and can be carried to destructive lengths. The cases of Lieutenant William Calley and Adolf Eichmann are two examples of such destructive obedience. When he was tried for killing 22 South Vietnamese villagers, U.S. Army Lieutenant Calley stated that he was simply following orders. Adolf Eichmann, in charge of exterminating six million Jews, Romany, homosexuals, political prisoners, and others deemed unacceptable by the Third Reich during World War II, also did what he was told. At his trial for war crimes, Eichmann denied any moral responsibility. He was, he said, simply doing his job.

Laboratory Studies of Destructive Obedience

Are Eichmann and Calley unusual cases? Stanley Milgram, a social psychologist, attempted to determine whether people in more normal circumstances will obey an authority even when they believe they are endangering another person's life. Through advertisements and direct-mail solicitations in New Haven, Connecticut, Milgram (1963) gathered forty men of various ages and occupations for paid participation in a re-

search project at Yale University. When each subject arrived for the experiment, he was introduced to the experimenter and an accomplice of the experimenter, who he was led to believe was another subject. The subjects were told that the purpose of the experiment was to determine the effects of punishment on learning. Subjects drew lots to determine who would be the teacher and who the learner, but the drawing was rigged so that the true subject was always the "teacher" and the accomplice was always the "learner." Then the learner was strapped to a chair in another room, electrodes were attached to his wrist, and the subject was instructed in his task.

The lesson to be "taught" by the subject was a verbal learning task. The teacher was told to administer a shock to the learner each time he gave a wrong answer, by operating a shock generator with 30 switches. The switches presumably controlled electric current that increased by 15-volt increments from 15 to 450 volts and were labeled from "Slight shock" at the low end to "Danger: severe shock" and finally an ominous "XXX" at the high end. In fact, this equipment was a dummy generator and the confederate never received an actual shock, but its appearance was quite convincing.

After each wrong answer (of which the accomplice intentionally gave many), the experimenter instructed the subject to move one level higher on the shock generator. When the subject reached 300 volts, the accomplice began to pound on the wall between the two rooms, and from that point on, he no longer answered any question posed by the subject. At this point subjects usually turned to the experimenter for guidance. In a stoic and rather stern way, the experimenter replied that a failure to answer should be treated as a wrong answer and that the learner should be shocked according to the usual schedule.

Milgram's basic question was simply how many subjects would continue to follow the experimenter's orders and administer all the shocks in the series. Figure 8.4 contains the results. Of the forty subjects, twenty-six (65%) continued to the end of the shock series. Not a single subject stopped before administering 300 volts—the point at which the learner began to pound on the wall. Five refused to obey at that point; a total of fourteen subjects defied the experimenter. Because nearly two-thirds of his subjects obeyed the experimenter's instructions even though they were led to believe they were hurting another human being, Milgram concluded that obedience to commands is a strong force in our society. In Milgram's words:

> If in this study an anonymous experimenter could successfully command adults to subdue a fifty-year-old man, and force on him painful electric shocks against his protests, one can only wonder what government, with its vastly greater authority and prestige, can command of its subjects. [1965, p. 75]

Milgram (1965, 1974) extended his research program to study some of the situational factors that may lead subjects to obey or to refuse to obey when the experimenter (the authority figure) tells them to hurt another person. He found, for example, that the closer the victim was to the subject, the more likely the subject was to refuse the experimenter's command. Thus, when the victim was in the same room as the subject and only 1½ feet away, only one-third of the subjects were willing to go to the maximum shock level. Milgram also found that obedience was less frequent when the experimenter was not physically present but issued his commands either by telephone or by tape recording. In fact, when the experimenter was absent, several subjects administered shocks of a lower voltage than

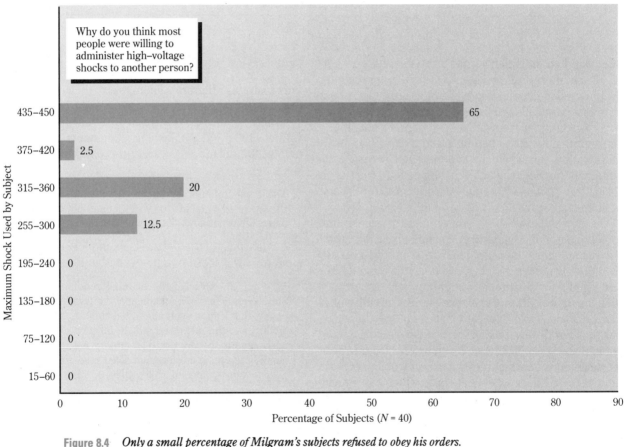

Figure 8.4 *Only a small percentage of Milgram's subjects refused to obey his orders.*
Source: "Behavioral Study of Obedience" by S. Milgram, 1963, *Journal of Abnormal and Social Psychology, 67,* pp. 371–378.

Obedience is an everyday phenomenon.
DOONESBURY, copyright 1990 G. B. Trudeau. Reprinted with permission of UNIVERSAL PRESS SYNDICATE. All rights reserved.

was required, thus defying the experimenter's authority. In an interesting reversal of the typical procedure, Milgram also demonstrated that authority could be a force for good. In this case, the learner was the one who insisted that the shocks be continued, claiming a commitment to the experiment and a challenge to his masculinity. But when the experimenter repeated his command to stop, the subjects stopped. To hurt or to help, the commands of an authority exert a strong influence.

In the years since Milgram's original demonstration of obedience in the laboratory, numerous other researchers have investigated the conditions under which obedience occurs. Similar findings have emerged from a variety of countries and age groups (Miller, 1986). Thus, obedience is not a peculiarity of the German people or of New Haven men. It is a behavior that can be observed in most of us, one that can be encouraged or discouraged by situational factors. That is, obedience is a result of social influence processes that any individual may initiate or to which any individual may succumb. As we noted earlier, we often look to others for information when we are in a novel situation. When one of those others also has legitimate power as an authority figure, and we do not have sufficient time to weigh carefully and comprehensively all possible alternatives, the result is likely to be obedience to the authority figure (Milgram, 1974).

Criticisms of the Obedience Studies

Impressive as Milgram's findings are, they have not escaped criticism. In fact, they have been a focus of considerable controversy within the social sciences (Miller, 1986). The following statements reflect the tone of the debate. First, from the psychiatrist Bruno Bettelheim:

> These experiments are so vile, the intention with which they were engaged in is so vile, that nothing these experiments show has any value. [Quoted in Miller, 1986, p. 124]

The other pole of the debate is exemplified by a statement from the social psychologist Alan Elms:

> Milgram, in exploring the external conditions that produce such destructive obedience, the psychological processes that lead to such attempted abdications of responsibility, and the means by which defiance of illegitimate authority can be promoted, seems to me to have done some of the most morally significant research in modern psychology. [Quoted in Miller, 1986, p. 132]

Two major issues are at stake in this often heated debate: the ethics of the experiments and the generalizability of their findings.

Ethics of the experiment One criticism of Milgram's obedience studies is that the subjects' rights were not protected. Subjects were not told that the experiment would arouse distressful conflict, nor did the experimenters ask them for permission to put them in such a situation. Partly because of the public reaction to these studies, experimenters are now required to give subjects more information before they consent to participate than Milgram gave his subjects. In fact, it is unlikely that the exact procedures of Milgram's studies could be replicated today (Dane, 1990).

A second criticism is that participation in these experiments could have had long-term effects. The subjects could have lost their trust in experimenters, the university, or science in general. More important, the subjects' self-concepts might also have suffered long-term effects. Until the experiment, most subjects probably saw themselves as persons who would not deliberately inflict pain unless the circumstances were extreme. After the experiment, they would have to believe otherwise. One can certainly argue that such self-education might be beneficial, but it is probably not within the province of the experimental social psychologist to force such education on anyone.

Milgram argued that debriefing at the end of the experiment was sufficient to eradicate any tensions, doubts, or resentment that subjects experienced. In describing the debriefing procedure, Milgram stated:

> After the interview, procedures were undertaken to assure that the subject would leave the laboratory in a state of well-being. A friendly reconciliation was arranged between the subject and the victim, and an effort was made to reduce any tensions that arose as a result of the experiment. [1963, p. 374]

Milgram further reported (1974) that interviews by psychiatrists and follow-up questionnaires completed by the subjects indicated no long-term deleterious effects.

Generalizability of the findings People have also questioned whether the extreme degrees of obedience found in Milgram's subjects can be generalized to the real world. For example, trust in and obedience to the authority figure may be demand characteristics that are especially salient for subjects in experiments (Orne & Holland, 1968). In other words, subjects who will do as they are told in an experiment may disobey another authority figure, such as the physician who tells them to exercise daily or the employer who tells them to fire a popular co-worker. Along with this criticism goes the claim that the prestige of Yale University contributed to the high obedience rate. Subjects may have assumed that any study carried out at Yale must be scientifically and socially acceptable, so they were more inclined to obey. However, the available evidence contradicts this last claim. Milgram repeated the experiment with another group of men in a run-down office building in a deteriorating area of Bridgeport, Connecticut. Here he found that almost 50% of the men obeyed the experimenter to the end of the shock series. Although the prestige of Yale apparently accounted for some obedience, the phenomenon still occurred in a blatantly non-university setting. Further, many would argue that the influence of authority is considerable in any organization that has a powerful hierarchy. Individuals often do agree to fire popular subordinates if their superior tells them to do so, and carry out other orders that are contrary to their own inclinations. As a further argument in support of the generalizability of the obedience experiments, one must consider the reactions of subjects in the experiment. Whereas ethical questions can surely be raised about the stress that was created, the evidence of stress testifies to the impact of the procedures and the reality of the subjects' experience (Miller, 1986).

Despite the legitimate criticisms, Milgram's work demonstrated that obedience is a much more pervasive phenomenon than had been thought. Neither a group of undergraduates nor a group of psychologists and psychiatrists, when told of the procedures, predicted that subjects would continue to obey when the high voltage levels were reached.

▶ The Sense of Control

As we have seen, people will conform to group pressure, comply with requests, and obey orders in a variety of circumstances. However, discussions about social influence processes and the situational characteristics that affect them often engender a certain amount of resistance. Many students we have taught, for example, believe they have too much control over their own behavior to fall for the door-in-the-face tactic or to obey in a situation similar to that in Milgram's studies. In contrast, other students seem willing to be-

Many people believe they can exert some control over chance outcomes such as lotteries.
Alan Carey/The Image Works

lieve they would comply in a variety of situations; they do not believe they have so much control over their own behavior.

Theorists, too, are divided on the issue of personal control. Humanistic approaches to social behavior often rest on the assumption that we have almost complete control over our behavior. B. F. Skinner and his followers, in contrast, take the position that stimuli in the environment determine our behavior—that we are controlled by external rewards and punishments and that personal control is merely a figment of our imagination (Skinner, 1971). Between these two positions lie numerous variations, which social psychologists have explored. In the remainder of this chapter, we will con-

sider the general issue of control—how we develop illusions of control, how a belief in control affects our behavior, and how we react to a loss of control in our lives.

The Illusion of Control

Magicians entertain by appearing to control events in a way we cannot explain. Although most of us cannot make rabbits appear out of hats or make people float on air, we believe in our ability to control more mundane events. We even develop an illusion of control over the outcomes of events that we know are determined purely by chance. Ellen Langer (1983) and her colleagues have presented persuasive evidence in support of these beliefs.

Participating in a lottery is one situation in which winning is determined solely by chance—the "luck of the draw" allows little room for an individual to influence the outcome. Nevertheless, many people believe they can exert some control in such situations. To illustrate the illusion of control, Langer (1975) gave people the opportunity to buy $1 lottery tickets with the chance of winning a $50 prize. To vary the illusion of control, the experimenters allowed one group of people to select the ticket they wanted. Other participants received randomly assigned lottery tickets from the experimenter (identical to those chosen by the first group). Before the random drawing of the prize ticket, the experimenter approached all subjects and asked whether they would be willing to sell their ticket to someone who would pay more than the going price for it. Subjects who had been assigned tickets were willing to sell them for an average of $1.96. In contrast, subjects who had chosen their own tickets demanded an average of $8.67 for their tickets, presumably because they believed they had a better chance of winning than did those subjects who had not exercised a choice.

Choosing one's lottery ticket is only one of many factors that can increase our belief in control. In general, the more similar a purely chance situation is in appearance to a real skill situation, the more likely we are to believe in our own ability to control the outcome. Competition, for example, increases our belief in control. We will be much more confident of our success when we are paired with a seemingly incompetent competitor than when the competitor appears competent, even though the outcome is determined purely by chance (Langer, 1975). For example, playing a slot machine when a 5-year-old is playing at the next stand would probably lead us to believe we had greater control over our outcome—even though the machines themselves are obstinately beyond our control. Similarly, involvement in the task, knowledge about the procedures involved, and practice in performing the task all lead us to believe we have more control than we in fact possess.

Success at a task may also create the illusion of control. In another study, Langer and Roth (1975) asked subjects to predict coin tosses and structured the outcome so that people experienced exactly the same rate of overall success. However, one group experienced early success and later failure, another group experienced early failure and later success, and a third group experienced a purely random outcome. People with early success were much more confident of their ability at the task, predicting more future successes for themselves and viewing themselves as more skilled. Early experience with success apparently created a belief in the ability to control the outcome, a finding that is probably quite similar to the case of the novice gambler who hits the jackpot the first time around—and then proceeds to lose far more than he or she initially won.

Belief in one's ability to control events is not limited to the realm of coin tosses and lottery tickets. People believe they have control over many events in their lives (Wright, Zautra, & Braver, 1985). Belief in control is not uniform, however. People believe they have more control over positive events than over negative events, and more control over events that seem likely to recur in the future than over events they do not expect to recur (see Figure 8.5). This pattern of belief is consistent with some of the self-enhancement behaviors discussed in Chapter 3: people take credit for positive events and deny responsibility for negative events. This pattern of belief in control is also consistent with attributions about responsibility for the behavior of others. For example, we noted earlier that people who comply under coercive power conditions are more likely to be perceived as having less control than people who comply in situations involving reward power.

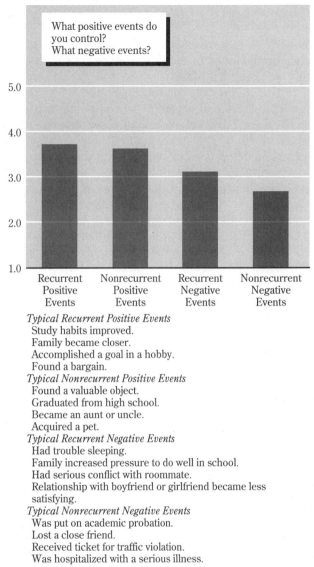

Figure 8.5 *Ratings of personal control for a variety of events.*
Source: "Distortion in Control Attributions for Real Life Events" by M. H. Wright, A. J. Zautra, and S. L. Braver, 1985, *Journal of Research in Personality, 19,* pp. 54–71.

Such findings do not mean that we never have real control over situations and outcomes. It is apparent, however, that our belief in the extent of our control may far outstrip our actual ability to determine the course of events.

Consequences of a Belief in Control

Why do we believe so strongly in our ability to influence events, often in the face of evidence suggesting that we in fact have little or no control? One reason is that a belief in such control makes the world seem more predictable. If we are expecting to interact with someone in a competitive situation, for example, we would like to be able to predict that person's behavior so we can determine our own outcomes. Experiments have shown that we may exaggerate our ability to make such predictions. In one study, for example, subjects who expected to compete with another subject were more certain that they would be able to infer the personality of their competitor than were subjects who expected only to observe the interaction (Miller, Norman, & Wright, 1978). Yet the belief in control is not solely a fantasy. Behavior, too, is altered when we believe we have control over our circumstances.

Performance on routine tasks was found to be better when people believed they could control a loud noise to which they were subjected before the performance, even when they did not actually exercise any control over it (Glass & Singer, 1972). People who can control their environment perceive conditions to be less crowded than do those who feel they have no control; further, they consider their surroundings more pleasant and their own mood more positive (Rodin, Solomon, & Metcalf, 1978). In general, over a wide range of circumstances, we react more positively when we believe we have some control than when we do not.

Perhaps one of the most dramatic demonstrations of the power of a belief in control is a study of aged people in institutions by Ellen Langer and Judith Rodin (Langer & Rodin, 1976; Rodin & Langer, 1977). These investigators suggested that one reason for the debilitated condition of many elderly residents of institutions is their perception of having no control. When these people had lived in their own homes, dozens of decisions had been required of them every day. In contrast, the typical institution is a nearly decision-free environment where control resides primarily in others. Such psychological factors may be as important as physical factors—perhaps more so—in determining well-being.

To test this hypothesis, Langer and Rodin (1976) gained the cooperation of the staff of a Connecticut nursing home, divided the residents into two groups, and administered one of two communications. Residents of one floor received a message that stressed the staff's responsibility for them and for their activities. Residents were given a plant but were told that the nurses would care for it. Similarly, they were informed that they would be allowed to see a movie but that the staff would determine what day the movie would be shown. This message minimized the residents' sense of control (and probably paralleled the situation in most nursing homes). Members of the other group, in contrast, were given a communication that emphasized their own responsibility. The message stressed the things they could do for themselves, from arranging the furniture in their room to deciding how to spend their time. Further, in the message the residents were encouraged to make their complaints known if they were not satisfied with the current arrangements. Members of this group were also given a plant, but they were allowed to pick the plant they wanted and were told that it would be their responsibility to care for it. Finally, these residents were told that a movie would be shown and that they could decide when and whether they would view it.

In many respects, the communication provided to the experimental group is quite weak. The defined areas of responsibility are, after all, ones that most of us take for granted. It may be difficult to believe that a specific reminder would have much effect. But it did. Members of the group whose message had stressed personal control reported significant increases in happiness when they were questioned three weeks later. Nurses judged the mental outlook of these residents to be improved and reported substantially increased activity among the group—talking with other patients, visiting people from outside the nursing home, and talking to the staff. Even attendance at the promised movie was greater among those residents who could decide when they would see the film.

More dramatic evidence of the effects of control was found when Rodin and Langer (1977) returned to the nursing home eighteen months later. Nurses continued to rate the group whose responsibility had been encouraged as more active, more sociable, and more vigorous. Physicians rated their health as better. Most striking of all was the difference in mortality rates. Whereas 30% of the patients in the control group had died in the intervening months, only 15% of the residents in the responsibility group had died. These results provide powerful evidence for the importance of control in a person's life.

Our perceptions of control also extend to our reactions to others' behavior. John Fleming and John Darley (1990), for example, conducted an experiment in which they asked subjects to read about people playing backgammon and to estimate the extent to which the players exerted control over the dice. Subjects attributed much greater control to those players who planned moves before rolling the dice than they did to players who did not engage in prior planning or to players whose dice were rolled by someone else. More to the point of our present discussion, Fleming and Darley's subjects were willing to put their money where their illusions of control were. Subjects were more likely to indicate they would bet money on those players who they perceived to be exercising control over the rolls of the dice. Of course, the players could not truly exert any influence over the dice, but the illusion of such influence was sufficiently strong to convince the subjects to risk money.

Individual Differences in Perceptions of Control

Situational factors can forcefully affect the extent to which we believe we have power over events. It is also true, however, that people vary widely in their general beliefs about control. Some of Fleming and Darley's subjects, for example, reported believing they could influence the outcome of a roll of dice. The general question of individual differences in behavior will be discussed much more extensively in Chapter 13. Here, however, we should give some attention to the idea of **locus of control,** originally proposed by Julian Rotter (1966). Rotter suggested that people generally tend to believe that control of the events in their lives is either primarily internal or primarily external. Internal people tend to believe in their own ability to control events; external people believe that other people or events are the primary influences on their own circumstances. (Table 8.3 shows some items from the scale Rotter developed to measure these general orientations.) Although Rotter's ideas are accurate in a general sense, they may be too simplified. A belief in external control, for example, can imply several different beliefs: in fate,

Table 8.3 Internal versus external locus of control: Sample items from the I-E scale

Rotter's internal-external (I-E) scale contains pairs of statements about both oneself and people in general. In each case, a respondent is asked to indicate which of the two statements he or she believes more strongly.

1. a. People's misfortunes result from the mistakes they make.

   b. Many of the unhappy things in people's lives are partly due to bad luck.

2. a. With enough effort we can wipe out political corruption.

   b. It is difficult for people to have much control over the things politicians do in office.

3. a. There is a direct connection between how hard I study and the grades I get.

   b. Sometimes I can't understand how teachers arrive at the grades they give.

4. a. What happens to me is my own doing.

   b. Sometimes I feel that I don't have enough control over the direction my life is taking.

Source: "Generalized Expectancies for Internal versus External Control of Reinforcement" by J. B. Rotter, 1966, *Psychological Monographs, 80*(1, Whole No. 609).

in powerful others, in a difficult world, in a politically unresponsive world (Collins, 1974; Gurin, Gurin, Lao, & Beattie, 1969; Mirels, 1970).

Although the concept of locus of control is somewhat ambiguous, considerable research has shown that people do differ, often dramatically, in their approach to the world and in their feelings of effectiveness over their environment (Phares, 1976; Strickland, 1977). People who believe their behavior is more externally controlled, for example, are more likely to comply with social influence attempts than those who believe their behavior is internally controlled. On the other hand, among people who comply with a social influence attempt, those with a more internal locus of control tend to change their attitudes to make them consistent with their behavior, through dissonance reduction or some other mechanism (see Chapter 7). Not unexpectedly, individuals with an internal locus of control also are more likely to take precautions to avoid natural disasters, such as tornados, than are people with an external locus of control (Sims & Baumann, 1972).

▶ Reactions to a Loss of Control

Whether primarily internal or external in our locus of control, most of us would like to believe we have at least some control over events. Yet such control is not always possible. Often we are faced with situations in which someone or something else appears to control our fate, and our own freedom of choice is severely limited. In some cases, this sense of another's control may simply be exasperating or frustrating. The social critic L. Rust Hills (1973), for example, concluded that several "cruel rules" govern social life in the contemporary United States. One of these rules is that "(*a*) whenever you really feel like going out you don't have an invitation; and in converse: (*b*) whenever you are invited to go out, you feel like staying at home" (p. 15). In this case, although the belief in control by others may not be overpowering, it can be a source of some annoyance—especially on a Saturday night. In other cases, a perception that others have control over our lives may be much more pervasive. Citizens living under a repressive dictatorship, for example, may feel they have little control over their daily activities, their conversations, and even their thoughts. How do people cope with such perceptions of loss of control?

A Theory of Reactance

The social psychologist Jack Brehm (1966; Brehm & Brehm, 1981) has proposed the concept of psychological reactance to explain some of our reactions to a loss of control or of freedom of choice. According to Brehm, **reactance** is a motivational state that is aroused whenever a person feels that his or her freedom has been abridged or threatened. Consider the following commonplace example:

> Picture Mr. John Smith, who normally plays golf on Sunday afternoons, although occasionally he spends Sunday afternoon watching television or puttering around his workshop. The important point is that Smith always spends Sunday afternoon doing whichever of these three things he prefers; he is free to choose which he will do. Now consider a specific Sunday morning on which Smith's wife announces that Smith will have to play golf that afternoon since she has invited several of her lady friends to the house for a party. Mr. Smith's freedom is threatened with reduction in several ways: (1) he cannot watch tele-

vision, (2) he cannot putter in the workshop, and (3) he must (Mrs. Smith says) play golf. [Brehm, 1966, p. 2]

Given this threat to his freedom, reactance theory predicts that Mr. Smith will attempt to restore his personal freedom. He might choose to stay in his workshop, for example, perhaps creating a clamor of protest in the process. Threats to freedom, according to this theory, create a psychological state of reactance, and this motivational state leads the person to take actions that will help him or her retain control and personal freedom.

The exact actions the person chooses depend on the nature of the threat and the freedom being threatened. As we saw in Chapter 7, a threatening communication may motivate someone to change an attitude in a direction opposite to that advocated, thus confirming a sense of independence and control. Another instance of reactance occurs in a situation in which certain alternatives are eliminated, so that our ability to choose freely is threatened. In one experiment, for example, subjects were initially given a choice of record albums and later told that certain albums would not be available. In reaction to this threat to their freedom, the subjects' feelings toward the threatened options became increasingly positive (Brehm, Stires, Sensenig, & Shaban, 1966). The effects of restrictions on people's feelings are seen with striking clarity in the case of limitations on the availability of pornography. According to reactance theory, material that is restricted or censored becomes increasingly appealing, which explains some musicians' willingness to go along with recent rules requiring an "explicit lyrics" label on albums, compact discs, and cassettes. In fact, censorship of a message can cause a potential audience to change its attitudes in the direction of the position advocated by the message, as well as to develop a greater desire to hear the message (Worchel, Arnold, & Baker, 1975).

Clee and Wicklund (1980) have reviewed a wide variety of areas of consumer behavior in which feelings of reactance may play a role. The high-pressure salesperson, for example, may create reactance by pushing a particular product too hard and putting down a competing brand, thus leading the consumer to prefer the competing product. Similarly, government regulations or bans may increase the desire for the prohibited product or policy.

We can imagine many other situations in which a threat to freedom or a perception of external control may lead to actions geared to restoring a sense of personal control. For example, a child who is told not to touch the stereo is likely to make a game of touching the forbidden object. Teenagers show similar behavior when they break a parent's imposed curfew, not because they lost track of time or were involved in anything of interest but simply to demonstrate that they, not their parents, control their activities. Recalling your own behavior, you can probably easily think of cases in which reactance was operating, when the sheer sense of control was more important than the particular action you took.

Of course, it is not always to our advantage to assert control of a situation. If someone pointed a gun in your face and demanded money, you probably would not try to show that you were in control by wrestling with the robber. In such cases, when an attempt to reestablish control could lead to personal injury, people are often willing to acknowledge the other person's control (Grabitz-Gneich, 1971). In still other cases, personal harm may not be likely, but the responsibility for harm to someone else may be equally discomforting. Milgram's obedience studies are a case in point. In other, similar instances, people voluntarily relinquish control in order to avoid responsibility for some unpleasant outcome (Feldman-Summers, 1977). Thus, in situations that involve negative outcomes and personal responsibility for them, we are willing to forgo a sense of control; in many other cases, however, in which outcomes are positive or simply neutral, we actively attempt to reassert control and preserve our sense of personal freedom.

Learned Helplessness

One aspect of our belief in personal control rests on the fact that outcomes are predictable—the issues of predictability and control are very closely related. Many routines in our life are based on a sense of predictability. If you live in a city that has a subway system, you have probably learned to expect that every time you put a token in the turnstile, it will click, turn, and allow you to board the next train. A failure of the stile to turn when the coin is dropped almost inevitably results in frustration. Such a break in the normal routine threatens both predictability and control. On the one hand, the turnstile did not react as you predicted it would and, on the other, its recalcitrance casts doubt on your ability to control your own outcomes.

The whole pack rose in the air.

The adventures of Alice in Wonderland: Experiences with noncontingency.

Consider the adventures of Alice in Wonderland. Finding herself in a strange environment, Alice quickly discovers that all is not as she has learned it to be. When she drinks the contents of a bottle labeled "Drink me," she quickly shrinks to a mere 10 inches high. Trying another bottle similarly labeled, Alice grows to gigantic proportions. Such fictional adventures illustrate the principle of *noncontingency:* similar actions do not lead to similar outcomes. There are many situations in life in which people experience such unexpected outcomes.

The result of experiences with noncontingent out-

Learned helplessness may be one response for people who feel they have no control over their own situations.
Mimi Forsyth/Monkmeyer Press

comes is a state that the psychologist Martin Seligman (1975) has termed **learned helplessness,** defined as a belief that one's outcomes are independent of one's actions. The first research on this problem was done with animals. It was found that animals that were first exposed to shock they could not avoid were later unable to learn how to avoid shock when it actually could be avoided. Seligman suggested that three kinds of deficits result from experiences with uncontrollable outcomes. First, motivation is lost: the animal does not *try* to learn new behaviors. Second, the failure to try leads to a cognitive deficit: the animal does not learn anything new from its experiences because it is not trying anything new. Finally, the learned-helplessness hypothesis suggests that repeated experiences of this kind lead to an emotional deficit: the animal becomes depressed by its inability to control outcomes.

Although this phenomenon would seem applicable to humans as well, we cannot make the transfer without considering one additional element—the factors to which a person attributes responsibility for his or her situation. Imagine that you have taken two biology exams and failed them both. In one case you studied hard, and in the other you just glanced at your notes. Nevertheless, you failed both times—the outcome was not contingent on your behavior. Would you experience a state of learned helplessness and depression? The answer depends on the attributions you make to explain your failure. If you made external attributions—for example, the tests were unfair and everyone else failed, too—then you might feel helpless, but you would not

take the failure personally. However, if you made an internal attribution, seeing the failure as specific to yourself and not shared by others, then your reaction would probably be more severe. Such attributions to personal helplessness lead to a fourth deficit—lowered self-esteem—and make depression more likely (Abramson, Seligman, & Teasdale, 1978; Peterson & Seligman, 1984).

Thus, the experience of learned helplessness in humans depends on a complicated pattern of explanations. Depression will be most severe if one attributes unwanted outcomes (1) to internal factors, so that helplessness becomes one's personal problem; (2) to stable factors, so that helplessness becomes chronic; and (3) to global factors, so that helplessness is generalized to other situations. If you attributed your failure in the exams to your general stupidity, your performance in other courses would also decline (Mikulincer, 1986). Eventually, you might avoid the college curriculum in general.

A crowded environment also can affect a person's ability to regulate social control and thus can contribute to a feeling of learned helplessness. Rodin (1976), for example, found that children who lived in a high-density residence were less likely to assume control of outcomes than children who lived in less densely populated settings. They also performed less well on puzzles. Patients in hospitals, who have little control over their environment, show progressively greater deficits in performance as the length of their hospitalization increases, even though their physical condition may be improving (Raps, Peterson, Jonas, & Seligman, 1982).

But why do people fall with such apparent ease into a state of learned helplessness? Why don't they react against the situation, as reactance theory suggests they should? Sometimes they do. In a situation in which the person had no initial belief in control, learned helplessness may be the immediate response. In contrast, Camille Wortman and Jack Brehm (1975) predict that "reactance will precede helplessness for individuals who originally expect control" (p. 308). The basic principle, as shown in panel *A* in Figure 8.6, is that a person who expects to be able to control a situation will experience reactance, whereas a person who does not have such expectations will experience learned helplessness. As the graph in panel *B* shows, the shift from reactance to learned helplessness may be gradual. Repeated experience with noncontingent outcomes eventually eliminates the perception of control, at which point helplessness replaces reactance as the dominant response.

In a field study of this hypothesis, Andrew Baum and his colleagues selected residents of college dormitories who lived either in large or in moderate-sized groups and for whom the architecture of the building (long- or short-corridor design) either facilitated a sense of control and predictability in their interactions or diminished such a sense of control (Baum, Aiello, & Calesnick, 1978). Baum and his colleagues brought these subjects into the laboratory to perform a standard social task that allowed either cooperation or competition and evaluated their performance as a function of the length of time they had lived in the residence halls—either one, three, or seven weeks. Students who had lived in the low-control dormitories for shorter periods (one or three weeks) reported negative feelings about their living conditions, but they also engaged in highly competitive behavior. The competitive behavior, Baum concluded, suggested an attempt to assert control. But after living in the low-control situation for several more weeks, the students seemed to abandon some of their attempts at control. They became less negative and more accepting of the conditions, and their play in the game became less competitive, less involved and motivated, and more withdrawn. Thus, the students initially appeared to experience reactance, but their unsuccessful attempts to control outcomes, regulated by the facts of the dormitory design, were replaced by feelings of resignation and helplessness. Residents of short-corridor (high-control) dormitories, in contrast, perceived no problems of control, and their behavior was more adaptive than the other residents' and did not change over the course of the study.

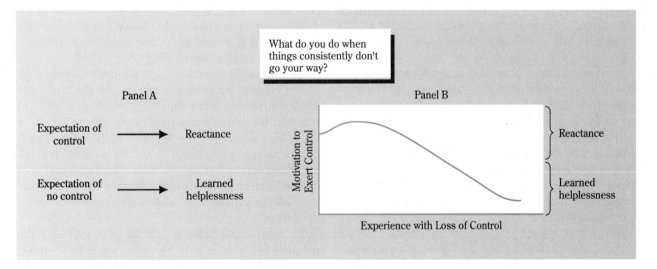

Figure 8.6 *Reactance and learned helplessness.*
Source: "Responses to Uncontrollable Outcomes: An Integration of Reactance Theory and the Learned Helplessness Model" by C. B. Wortman and J. W. Brehm, 1975, *Advances in Experimental Social Psychology, 8,* pp. 278–336.

Self-Induced Dependence

Uncontrollable outcomes are one source of feelings of a loss of control. Other situations can also create such feelings as well as creating an illusion of incompetence. For example, others may imply or suggest directly that a person is incompetent, and the person in question may incorporate that belief. Langer (1983) has suggested that part of the apparent dysfunction of the elderly may result directly from the experience of being labeled incompetent. As a society, we tend to disparage the elderly, assuming they are past their prime, incapable of any significant physical or mental activity, and generally dependent on the aid of friends, relatives, and institutional personnel. Such assumptions not only are inaccurate, Langer argues, but may create a self-fulfilling prophecy. The elderly themselves, labeled as dependent, may come to believe the label.

The reality of such self-induced dependence was made clear in a study by Langer and Benevento (1978). They gave male high school students the opportunity to perform a set of word-hunt problems and to experience success at the task. In a second phase, each student worked in a team with another male (actually a confederate of the experimenter). By a predetermined draw, the student was assigned the role of assistant, and the confederate was assigned the role of boss. After working on a second task in the role of assistant, the subjects once again worked individually on the word-hunt task they had performed earlier. As Figure 8.7 shows, the students' performance dropped by 50%—they located only half as many words—after they had experienced a dependent role. In contrast, those who had not participated in the assistant role performed as well as they had earlier.

Perhaps the most surprising aspect of this experiment is how strong the performance effects were after only a brief experience in the role of assistant. We can easily imagine how pervasive and powerful induced dependence effects can be in the elderly and in other people who are forced to adopt a dependent role. Langer (1989b) has argued that one of the positive consequences of exerting control over one's environment is an increase in **mindfulness,** "a state of alertness and lively awareness" (p. 138). According to Langer, the mindfulness required when exerting, or even attempting to exert, control enhances learning, memory, and physical health.

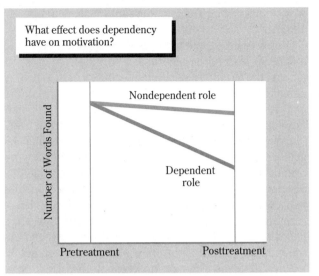

Figure 8.7 *Effect of experience in a dependent role on performance on a word-hunt task.*
Source: "Self-Induced Dependence" by E. J. Langer and A. Benevento, 1978, *Journal of Personality and Social Psychology, 36,* pp. 886–893.

▶ Summary

The issues of social influence and personal control are central to human behavior. Many social situations involve some aspect of social influence, and our beliefs about personal control affect decisions we make about ourselves as well as about others.

Conformity is a yielding to group pressure when no direct request to comply with the group has been made. Sherif and Asch separately conducted some of the earliest studies demonstrating the effect of a group's judgments on the behavior of the individual. A group can exert two kinds of influence on the individual: informational influence, based on facts, and normative influence, based on social pressure. Conformity depends, in part, on the individual's identification with the group.

Nonconformity behavior can be of two types. Independent behavior is that which occurs with no reference to the group position. A person who engages in anticonformity behavior, in contrast, does exactly the opposite of what the group does; thus, the group is still a reference point for the individual's behavior. Investigators have shown that a variety of situational factors—

such as group size, number of persons who agree with the individual, status of the group members, and type of task—can affect the degree of conformity.

Compliance is behavior that occurs in response to a direct request. The foot-in-the-door technique consists of a small request followed by a substantially larger one. Agreement with the first request increases the probability of compliance with the second request. The door-in-the-face effect works in the opposite way. In this case, the person who initially refuses a fairly large request is more likely to agree to a subsequent smaller request. A third technique for inducing compliance is the low-ball procedure, in which initial commitment to a behavior correlates with increased probability of compliance when the costs are increased. The lure technique involves enticing someone with a highly attractive offer, making the initial offer unavailable, and then substituting some other, less attractive offer.

Although compliance with some requests appears to be relatively mindless, occurring without conscious thought, other acts of compliance evidence considerable thought, as when we evaluate the kind and amount of power the agent has over our own situation. Requests generally follow the face-saving rules of one's culture.

Obedience studies show that most people readily follow orders even when their compliance may harm another person. Obedience declines when the victim is physically near to the subject and when the person who has issued the orders is not physically present.

Criticisms of the obedience studies focus on ethical questions and on their generalizability. Nevertheless, these studies provide strong demonstrations of the extent to which social influence attempts can alter another's behavior.

Despite pressures for conformity, compliance, and obedience, people maintain a pervasive belief in their own control. Even when outcomes are obviously determined by chance, people have an illusion of control. Some factors that strengthen this illusion are competition, involvement in the task, knowledge and practice, and the similarity of the situation to a task requiring skill.

Belief in personal control improves performance and makes feelings more positive. Individuals vary in their perceptions of control; some people are inclined to believe in external control, and others believe strongly in internal control.

Because belief in personal control is so pervasive, people often react strongly to a perceived or real loss of control. Psychological reactance is a motivational state that is aroused whenever a person feels that his or her freedom has been abridged. According to reactance theory, people will attempt to restore their sense of freedom when they perceive such threats. In some cases, however, as when insistence on control may bring harm to oneself or to others, people are often willing to accept the control of others.

Learned helplessness is induced by situations in which outcomes are not contingent on one's own behavior. People who experience such apparently random outcomes may develop the belief that their own responses have no effect on subsequent outcomes. A variety of deficits may result—motivational, cognitive, and emotional, as well as loss of self-esteem—depending on the factors to which one attributes one's loss of control.

Self-induced dependence may develop even when outcomes are not random. Labeling people as dependent can cause decrements in subsequent behavior, apparently because the labeled person begins to believe that the outcomes of his or her own behavior depend primarily on others' actions. Attempts to exert control tend to involve mindfulness, which generally improves performance, learning, and physical health.

▶ *Key Terms*

anticonformity
autokinetic effect
compliance
conformity
door-in-the-face effect
foot-in-the-door effect
independence
informational influence
learned helplessness
locus of control
lure technique
mindfulness
normative influence
obedience
reactance
self-categorization

Nobody loves me, well do I know,

Don't all the cold world tell me so?

Hattie Starr

Love is much nicer to be in than an

automobile accident, a tight girdle, a

higher tax bracket, or a holding pattern

over Philadelphia.

Judith Viorst

9

Affiliation, Attraction, and Love

Suppose you have been offered $50 a day to remain in a room by yourself. You are free to leave whenever you want. The room has no windows, but it has a lamp, bed, chair, table, and bathroom facilities. Food is brought at mealtime and left outside your door, but you see no one. You are allowed no companions; no telephone; no books, magazines, or newspapers; and no stereo or television. If you were to volunteer for such a project, how long could you remain in the room? More important, would you volunteer in the first place?

Remaining alone is not easy. As social animals, we need interpersonal relationships, and we need them in a variety of forms. In this chapter, we consider three forms of interpersonal relationship: acquaintanceship,

friendship, and love. Why are we sometimes lonely, wanting relationships we do not have? Why, too, do we sometimes find ourselves too involved, needing to be (temporarily) alone? Why do we like some people and dislike others? Why do some relationships last, and why do some end in boredom or distress? These are the central questions concerning interpersonal relationships, the questions we address in this chapter.

▶ Alone or Together?

Our opening scenario comes from a study conducted by Stanley Schachter (1959), a study in which five male students volunteered to place themselves in a situation

Being alone is not the same as being lonely.
Jagdish Agarwal/The Image Works

Similarly, being lonely is not the same as being alone.
Alan Carey/The Image Works

similar to the one we described. One volunteer remained in the room for only twenty minutes before experiencing an uncontrollable desire to leave. Another remained in isolation for eight days, after which he admitted that he was growing uneasy and nervous, but he appeared to suffer no serious effects from the isolation. Clearly, people have varying reactions to isolation. Some people, as Peter Suedfeld (1982) notes, seek isolation, finding it exhilarating, stimulating, or conducive to religious experience. But others find that being isolated from other people can be deeply disturbing.

Loneliness

Being alone is not the same as being lonely. Aloneness is an objective state, easily assessed by any (unseen) observer. Loneliness is a subjective experience and depends on our interpretations of events. Many definitions of loneliness have been offered (Peplau & Perlman, 1982). Although the definitions vary in subtle ways, most of them touch on three elements. First, as we have indicated, loneliness is a subjective experience; we cannot measure it by simply observing whether someone is alone or with other people. Second, loneliness generally results from perceived deficiencies in a person's social relationships. Third, loneliness is unpleasant. In an attempt to understand what "feeling lonely" meant, Carin Rubenstein and Phillip

Shaver (1982) asked people to describe in detail the feelings they experienced when they were lonely. Four general factors emerged from these descriptions: desperation, in the sense of feeling panicked and helpless; depression; impatient boredom; and self-deprecation. Although each factor taps a slightly different emotion, all of them reflect the unhappiness inherent in being lonely.

In addition to different emotional reactions to loneliness, Robert Weiss (1973) has suggested that there are two different types of loneliness: emotional and social. *Emotional loneliness* is caused by the lack of a close, intimate attachment to one particular person. Anyone—especially the recently divorced or widowed person—who does not have such a "special someone" is subject to emotional loneliness. *Social loneliness* results from an absence of friends and relatives or of some form of social network in which activities and interests can be shared. One type of loneliness can be quite independent of the other type (Russell, Cutrona, Rose, & Yurko, 1984). A student may live in a dormitory, for example, eating, studying, and having bull sessions with friends, and yet feel emotionally isolated without an intimate relationship with one special person.

What causes loneliness? We may never know for sure, primarily because obtaining certainty about the causes of loneliness would require unethical experiments involving conditions designed to make people

Some lonely people may sink into a sad passivity.
David M. Grossman

lonely. Correlational research, however, has provided several plausible causes. First, people who are lonely tend to report having poor social skills (Horowitz & French, 1979) and to be perceived by others as relatively unskilled in a variety of social domains (Sloan & Solano, 1984). Second, people who report being lonely also tend to experience higher levels of anxiety about their social skills. That is, even if one has very good social skills, anxiety about those skills may be enough to produce loneliness (Solano & Koester, 1989). Two general factors related to these causes are low self-esteem and an unwillingness to use social support resources (Vaux, 1988).

Just as the causes of loneliness vary, so do people's reactions to it. Some people, particularly those who are severely lonely, may sink into a sad passivity. Crying, sleeping, drinking, eating, taking tranquilizers, and just watching television aimlessly are typical responses. Other responses to loneliness may be more active and

in some cases, probably more helpful. Some people, despite their solitude, engage in such activities as working on a hobby, studying, exercising, or going to a movie; others (particularly those with high incomes) go on shopping sprees; still others attempt social contact, calling someone on the telephone or paying a visit (Rubenstein & Shaver, 1982).

Some types of people are more prone to loneliness than others, and some types of situations are more likely to cause feelings of loneliness than others. It is important to distinguish between *trait loneliness* and *state loneliness* (Shaver, 1982; Shaver, Furman, & Buhrmeister, 1985). Trait loneliness is a stable pattern of feeling lonely that often changes little with the situation. In general, people with low self-esteem are more likely to report trait loneliness (Jones, Freemon, & Goswick, 1981; Peplau, Miceli, & Morasch, 1982). People who report having meaningful interactions with other people are less likely to experience loneliness. Conversely, lonely people report a lack of intimate conversations with close friends (Solano, Batten, & Parish, 1982).

State loneliness is a more temporary experience that is often caused by some dramatic change in one's life. For example, students often experience state loneliness when they enter college and leave behind the familiarity of home and high school as they enter a new, often bewildering environment. The same experience can occur when one moves to a new location, obtains a new job, or begins attending a different church. This loneliness often goes away as one establishes new social networks (Shaver, Furman, & Buhrmeister, 1985).

Women and men appear to experience loneliness with about the same frequency, yet women are more likely than men to label themselves as lonely. More of the lonely men deny their loneliness. What causes this difference in honesty of self-appraisal? One reason may be that a lonely man is less acceptable and more likely to be socially rejected than is a lonely woman (Borys & Perlman, 1985). According to gender stereotypes, expressions of emotion are less appropriate for men than for women, and the man who says he is lonely defies that expectation.

Coping with loneliness depends largely on the factors to which the person attributes his or her unhappiness. Those who blame their own deficiencies for their loneliness are more likely to remain unhappy. The person who sees loneliness as only a temporary state is less likely to remain unhappy and may be more apt to take corrective action. One of the best counters to loneliness, for example, is the establishment of meaningful relationships with friends. It is the presence of friends, rather than of relatives or romantic partners, that most clearly distinguishes between the lonely college student and the contented college student (Cutrona, 1982).

Important, too, is the self-presentation strategy one employs to deal with the challenges life transitions pose. In conversations, for example, one strategy shy people employ involves acting as an "interviewer." The interview strategy keeps others talking about themselves, and shy people can thereby avoid having to talk about themselves (Snyder & Smith, 1986; Thorne, 1987). Such strategies, in addition to being protective, allow others to control situations and typically are not very effective ways to cope with loneliness. For exam-

Table 9.1 Examples of other-directed strategies toward life tasks

1. Is desirous of having structure imposed by others.
2. Judges self according to others' standards.
3. Consciously attempts to make own tasks similar to others'.
4. Uses perceived similarity of self to typical others in situations as guide to decision making.

Source: "Social Anxiety and Social Constraint: When Making Friends Is Hard" by C. A. Langston and N. Cantor, 1989, *Journal of Personality and Social Psychology, 56*, pp. 649–661.

ple, Christopher Langston and Nancy Cantor (1989) reported that college students who used a variety of other-directed strategies (see Table 9.1) for overcoming social anxiety expressed considerably less satisfaction with the social domain of their lives than did students who employed more self-directed, assertive strategies—such as setting their own standards and generating their own tasks.[1] That is, how lonely we feel in transitional circumstances depends in part on how we cope with the social anxiety that normally occurs in such circumstances. Langston and Cantor also noted that students who used the less effective, other-directed strategies reported their family members were more likely to keep emotions to themselves and to be less expressive in other ways. Like many other social skills, assertive coping with state loneliness requires experience and practice, and the students with less expressive families presumably had little of either.

Reasons for Affiliation

Contact with other people is often an antidote for loneliness. But what, aside from avoiding loneliness, are our reasons for affiliation? What do we gain from social interaction that we cannot experience alone? In his pioneering work on affiliation, Stanley Schachter (1959) proposed four possible answers to this question. First, being around other people directly reduces anxiety; simply put, there is safety in numbers. Second, the presence of others may distract us from our concerns,

[1]Interestingly, Langston and Cantor reported no differences in the academic domain; self- and other-directed students were equally satisfied with their own academic performance.

thereby indirectly reducing anxiety. Third, the reactions of other people can provide information about the situation, thus increasing one's cognitive clarity. Finally, as noted in the discussion of **social comparison theory** in Chapter 3, other people provide one means by which we evaluate ourselves. Although Schachter preferred his fourth explanation, as we consider the research on affiliation we will see that all but the distraction explanation have some merit.

We began this chapter by discussing Schachter's demonstration that one's initial reaction to isolation may be a state of extreme anxiety. In his first study on affiliation, Schachter (1959) reasoned that perhaps the reverse is also true: anxiety may lead to a desire for affiliation. To test this notion, Schachter told female introductory psychology students at the University of Minnesota that they would receive a series of electrical shocks. Subjects in the "high anxiety" condition were told that the shocks would be painful but would cause no permanent damage. Subjects in the "low anxiety" condition were led to expect virtually painless shocks that would feel, at worst, like a tickle. After receiving this description, the students were told there would be a ten-minute delay while the equipment was set up. Each subject was allowed to choose whether she would wait by herself or with some of the other subjects in the experiment. After the subjects had chosen, the experiment was over; the subjects never received the shocks. Schachter's concern was only with the choices subjects made.

As Schachter had predicted, the level of induced anxiety influenced the waiting preferences. Of the 32 subjects in the high-anxiety condition, 20 wanted to wait with other subjects; only 10 of the 30 subjects in the low-anxiety condition chose to wait with others. The adage "misery loves company" was confirmed.

As noted earlier, knowing that affiliation was desirable for highly anxious subjects was not sufficient for Schachter; he was interested in understanding why this was so. Because the study did not involve a situation in which the presence of others would enable the subjects to repel a direct attack, Schachter ruled out direct reduction of anxiety as a viable explanation of his results. That left three possible explanations: (1) the presence of others serves as a distraction, (2) others provide cognitive clarity, and (3) others enable self-evaluation through social comparison. If the distraction explanation were correct, then the company of any other person would be desirable. But if cognitive clarity or self-evaluation is critical, it would be important to seek people who were in a similar situation.

To test these explanations, Schachter (1959) conducted a second experiment. This time all subjects were told they would receive painful shocks; that is, all subjects were in a high-anxiety condition. Each subject was given the choice of waiting alone or with others, but the characteristics of the others were varied. Some subjects were given the choice of waiting alone or waiting with other students who were taking part in the same experiment. Other subjects could wait either alone or with female students who were not participating in the experiment but were waiting to see their faculty advisers.

The results of the second study were clear. Subjects who had the opportunity to wait with others in the same experiment showed a clear preference for doing so. In contrast, subjects who could wait with students not involved in the experiment showed a unanimous preference for waiting alone. These findings suggest that distraction is *not* an explanation of the link between anxiety and affiliation.

Additional research by Schachter (1959) and Wrightsman (1960) led to the conclusion that affiliation reduces anxiety by enabling individuals to engage in self-evaluation, to evaluate the propriety of their reactions and emotions through social comparison. Upon reexamining that research, however, Phillip Shaver and Mary Klinnert (1982) argued that Schachter too quickly dismissed the cognitive clarity explanation. Babies, for example, often turn to their mothers when unexpected or novel events occur. In the same manner, college students faced with electrical shock may seek the company of others in order to appraise the situation. More generally, people in a stressful situation tend to seek someone who will help them cope with the stress. In some cases, they may seek a competent, intelligent person; in others, they may prefer a warm, supportive person (Kirkpatrick & Shaver, 1988; Rofé, 1984).

Electric shocks in a psychology laboratory are far removed from most people's lives. Still, the relationship between stress and affiliative behavior can be generalized to the more ordinary circumstances of daily life. Consider, for example, the concept of **social support,** defined as useful coping resources provided by others. Carolyn Cutrona (1986) asked college students at the

University of Iowa to keep a daily record of social interactions and stressful experiences for fourteen consecutive days. When she analyzed these records, Cutrona found a significant relationship between social interaction and stress. Behaviors reflecting a perceived need for both emotional support and informational support were more likely to occur following stress than in the absence of stressful events. Thus, when people are under stress, they have good reason to seek other people. Other people and the resources they offer may serve as a *buffer* that reduces the impact of the stressful event (Cohen & Wills, 1985). Sometimes the information we obtain from others—cognitive clarity—reduces the anxiety. At other times, emotional support—self-evaluation—is the underlying mechanism for anxiety reduction. For example, Gayle Dakof and Shelley Taylor (1990) found that cancer victims have different expectations for support from different people. From some people, such as physicians, they expect informational support, and from others, such as friends and family members, they expect self-esteem and emotional support. When the type of support provided did not match the type expected, it was more likely to be perceived as unhelpful.

Thus, affiliation may reduce anxiety for several reasons. First, we often look to others for assistance in overcoming a threat; we will return to this point in Chapter 10. Second, the information we obtain from others enables us to clarify the anxiety-provoking situation. And third, emotional support from others serves to verify our own responses to stressful situations. Of course, people's reasons for affiliation include more than reducing stress and anxiety. People affiliate with others because they like them, because they enjoy the company, and because they share interests. People may also affiliate with others to gain approval or to develop an identity that can be achieved only through interaction with other people. In summary, affiliation is motivated by a variety of needs and desires, each of which increases the likelihood of social interaction.

Affiliation Patterns and Social Networks

To understand patterns of affiliation, investigators have begun in their own backyards—on the college campuses where they are located. For example, Bibb Latané and Liane Bidwell (1977) observed people in various locations on the Ohio State and University of North

Women may be more likely than men to look to social interaction as a way to deal with the initial stress of adjusting to college.
Hugh Rogers/Monkmeyer Press

Carolina campuses, and recorded whether each person observed was alone or with others. Overall, about 60% of the people Latané and Bidwell saw were with at least one other person. Interestingly, women were much more likely to be with other people than men were, suggesting that, at least in public places, women may affiliate more than men.

Looking more closely at social interaction patterns, Ladd Wheeler and John Nezlek (1977) asked first-year college students to keep track of all interactions they had during two-week periods in both the fall and the spring semesters. By limiting interactions to those that lasted ten minutes or more, the investigators hoped to focus on actual affiliation, as opposed to casual exchanges, such as getting a homework assignment or checking a book out of the library. The advantage of this strategy, called a *diary study,* over simple observation is that data could be collected for a single person over a longer period. More important, the researchers could tap private as well as public affiliation patterns and could assess reactions to the interaction and relate them to other attitude and personality measures (Nezlek, 1990). Wheeler and Nezlek found same-gender affiliation was more common among these students: 56% of their interactions were with a person of the same gender. During the first semester, the women students spent significantly more time engaged in some kind of interaction than the men; but by the second semester this difference had disappeared. As one explanation of this difference, Wheeler and Nezlek suggested that women may be more likely to look to social interaction as a way to deal with the initial stress of adjusting to college.

Patterns of affiliation are not random, of course. We systematically establish links with particular people whom we find rewarding and try to avoid people whose companionship is less enjoyable. The term **social network** refers to those persons with whom an individual is in actual contact (Berscheid, 1985), and analysis of social networks examines the question of "who" as well as "how often."

When people move to a new location, their social networks change. New people are added to the network, and others gradually may be dropped. Entering college is one such point in many people's lives, although the experience may be quite different for the student who has moved away from home and into a dormitory than for the student who remains at home and commutes to the university. Robert Hays and Diana Oxley (1986) studied these two types of experiences among first-year university students. As expected, commuters' social networks were initially more intimate, and these students maintained connections with old friends and relatives more easily. The resident students required more time to establish social networks, and the networks they eventually established included a much greater proportion of new acquaintances. Their networks were also more centered on campus activities and relaxation. The networks of male and female students differed in some respects. Men, for example, included more opposite-sex friends in their social network than did women. Women, on the other hand,

interacted more frequently and exchanged more informational and emotional support with their friends than did men, but no differences existed between males and females with respect to interactions with family members. Research with noncollege samples also indicates women have closer and more frequent contact with friends than do men (Booth, 1972).

Why do gender differences exist in social networks? Ladd Wheeler, Harry Reis, and John Nezlek (1983) concluded one reason may be that women are socialized to express their emotions more than men. Wheeler and his colleagues asked ninety-six students to record various measures of their daily interactions; some of the results are illustrated in Figure 9.1. The researchers found, for example, that both males and females scored lower on a measure of loneliness as the percentage of interactions with females and the amount of time spent with females increased. However, when the researchers examined the meaningfulness of interactions—measured by intimacy, self-disclosure, other-disclosure, and pleasantness—interactions with men and women were about equally related to reducing loneliness. That is, meaningful affiliation with either gender reduces loneliness. However, interactions with females tend to be more meaningful than interactions with males, presumably because women are socialized to be more emotionally expressive than men (Andersen & Bem, 1981; Deaux, 1976a).

These studies provide us with a picture of human social interaction. For example, although interactions between genders frequently draw more attention, affiliation with someone of the same gender is an obviously important aspect of many people's social life. To understand more fully how social networks and more intimate relationships come about, we will examine the research and theories that help us understand our choices concerning with whom we affiliate.

▶ Attraction

So far we have considered some of the reasons people choose to affiliate with others and examined some general patterns of social interaction. We must now consider, given the general need for affiliation, how people choose those with whom they will interact. Why are we friendly with or attracted to some people, whereas we

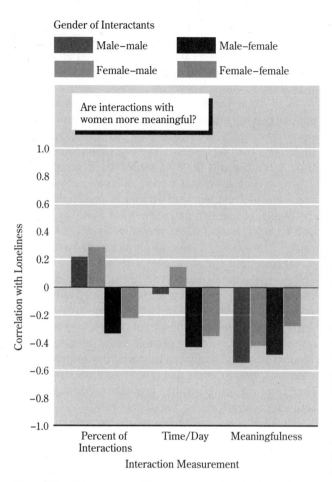

Figure 9.1 *Interactions with women are related to lower levels of loneliness.*
Source: "Loneliness, Social Interaction, and Sex Roles" by L. Wheeler, H. Reis, and J. Nezlek, 1983, *Journal of Personality and Social Psychology, 45,* pp. 943–953.

reject or dislike others? In this section we move from the general nature of affiliation to the specific reaction of attraction.

The Basis of Initial Attraction

What characteristics make people attractive to us? To understand the basis of initial attraction, psychologists have often brought strangers together in the laboratory and studied the features associated with greater or lesser liking. Despite their reliance on artificial situa-

tions, such methods enable us to avoid the confounding effects of past knowledge and experience. On the basis of this research, we can say the odds are in favor of our liking a person if that person

1. is in geographical proximity to us;
2. has similar beliefs, values, and personality characteristics;
3. satisfies our needs;
4. is pleasant or agreeable;
5. is physically attractive; and
6. reciprocates our liking.

Let us consider each of these factors in turn.

Proximity All else being equal, we tend to like people who live close to us better than those who are at some distance. This factor of **propinquity** has even been set to music, as in the song from *Finian's Rainbow* that says "When I'm not near the one I love, I love the one I'm near." More recently, Stephen Stills has advised us to love the one we're with. At a more scientific level, Festinger, Schachter, and Back (1950) found that residents of an apartment complex were more apt to like and interact with those who lived on the same floor of the building than with people who lived on other floors or in other buildings. Similarly, members of Air Force bomber crews develop closer relationships with co-workers stationed near them than with co-workers stationed a few yards away (Kipnis, 1957). Further, students in a classroom where alphabetical seating is required are more likely to report friendships with people whose names begin with the same letter than with those whose names are at some distance away in the class roll (Byrne, 1961).

Why is propinquity a factor in attraction? One obvious reason is that we are more likely to encounter people who live, work, or play near us; it is difficult to be attracted to people unless we meet them. The effect also may be partly due to simple familiarity. A mass of evidence indicates the existence of a **mere exposure effect;** that is, repeated exposure to the same stimulus leads to greater attraction to that object (Harrison, 1977; Saegert, Swap, & Zajonc, 1973). Robert Bornstein (1989) has proposed that the mere exposure effect is sociobiological. Based partly on evidence that arousal from unknown causes tends to be associated with negative emotions (Maslach, 1979), Bornstein argues that the greatest adaptive advantage results from reacting to novel stimuli with suspicion. But if one experiences the same stimuli several times and suffers no negative consequences from such experiences, suspicion or negative bias should eventually disappear. That is, increased positive affect for stimuli to which we are frequently exposed may have considerable survival value. Upon first encountering a stranger on the street or in your apartment building, for example, you might be inclined to be wary. After repeatedly passing that stranger on the street or in the hall without any negative consequences, however, you may be more willing to treat him or her as a "nodding acquaintance."

Bornstein's interpretation can also be supported by the fact that the mere exposure effect occurs for an extremely wide range of stimuli, including those presented so briefly they cannot be recognized. Also, having another person respond positively to one's behavior—the likelihood of which increases with the frequency of contact—also makes that person more attractive in our eyes (Davis, 1982). Frequency of interaction can also affect perceptions of similarity and thereby increase the attraction we feel to another (Moreland & Zajonc, 1982). The mere anticipation of interaction seems to increase our liking for another person (Darley & Berscheid, 1967), even when the person is either initially disliked (but not dangerous) or ambivalently valued. As Tyler and Sears (1977) suggest, we may even come to like obnoxious people when we know we must live with them.

Similarity of beliefs, values, and personality We like people whose attitudes and values agree with ours, and we dislike those who disagree with us (Byrne, 1971). If someone's personality is like ours, the attraction is even stronger. Most of the early studies that demonstrated this relationship were performed in the laboratory and were based on descriptions of hypothetical persons. A subject might be told, for example, that he or she would soon meet and talk with another person and that both of them should separately complete and then exchange an attitude survey to provide some basis for the discussion that eventually would take place. Upon reading the other's (fictitious) responses to the survey, the subject would discover either that the other shared his or her beliefs on 80% of the attitude issues or that the alleged similarity was only 20%. In

general, the former condition resulted in the subject's greater attraction toward the other person. Because the other person existed only as responses on an attitude survey, the subject never actually met the person to whom the responses belonged.

Field studies provide a broader view of the effects of similarity upon attraction. In an early field study, Theodore Newcomb (1961) gave male college students free housing if they agreed to fill out questionnaires about their attitudes and their liking for their housemates. The results of this massive study showed generally that men whose attitudes were similar at the beginning of the semester came to like each other more by the end of the testing period. More recently Kandel (1978) conducted an extensive questionnaire study with over 1,800 male and female adolescents aged 13 to 18. By comparing each student's attitudes and values with those of his or her best friend, she obtained strong support for the similarity relationship. Some areas of similarity were more important than others, however. For example, best friends were most apt to be similar with respect to such demographic variables as grade, sex, race, and age. Friends also tended to have similar attitudes toward drug use, but they did not always share attitudes toward parents and teachers.

Looking at a broader range of characteristics, Hill and Stull (1981) questioned college roommates representing both sexes, all years, and a variety of religious and ethnic backgrounds. Among female roommates, similarity in values was very important. Value similarity was very high among pairs who had chosen to be roommates, and it was also influential in predicting which assigned roommates decided to stay together. Sharing values with others was less important for men, for whom similarity of activities plays a greater role in attraction (Hays, 1985).

The relationship between interpersonal attraction and similarity is two-sided. On one hand, people seem to like and feel attracted to people who are similar to themselves. On the other hand, people may also dislike those who are dissimilar to themselves. Milton Rosenbaum (1986) has argued that repulsion of dissimilar others, as opposed to merely ignoring them, is sometimes the stronger force in interpersonal encounters. As we saw in Chapter 3, those who are dissimilar to us may represent threats to our self-concept; they challenge our beliefs and pose possible impediments to our

© 1982, Washington Post Writers Group. Reprinted with permission.

goals. Thus, both similarity-attraction and dissimilarity-repulsion can occur, although the majority of empirical evidence indicates similarity-attraction is the more likely process (Byrne, Clore, & Smeaton, 1986; Dane & Harshaw, 1991; Smeaton, Byrne, & Murnen, 1989).

Also, we do not always dislike people whose attitudes are dissimilar. On some occasions we even *prefer* others to have attitudes different from ours. For example, if a person is stigmatized (Novak & Lerner, 1968) or is of lower status (Karuza & Brickman, 1978), we may prefer that person's attitudes to be dissimilar to ours. Such preferences may result because too much similarity to an otherwise less desirable person threatens our self-image. In addition, even our initial tendency to dislike those dissimilar to us can be modified, often quite easily. Simply having the opportunity to predict a person's attitudes (Aderman, Bryant, & Donelsmith, 1978) or being allowed to discuss areas of disagreement (Brink, 1977) may substantially increase our liking for the initially dissimilar person. As we discussed in Chapter 4, we prefer individuals who are more easily categorized and whose behavior we can more easily predict.

Complementarity of need systems Sometimes people with different needs are attracted to each other. According to the theory of need **complementarity,** people choose relationships in which their basic needs can be mutually gratified (Winch, Ktsanes, & Ktsanes, 1954). Sometimes such a choice results in a match between very different needs, such as when a very dominant person is attracted to a very submissive partner

(Seyfried & Hendrick, 1973). Some evidence exists that the complementarity principle operates in long-term relationships (Kerckhoff & Davis, 1962); however, it probably operates only on a few behavioral dimensions, such as dominance and submission (Brehm, 1992; Levinger, Senn, & Jorgensen, 1970).

One reason for the ambiguity of findings in this area is that investigators have failed to consider the total picture of needs in a relationship. Needs exist in various domains, and the resources that one person brings to the relationship may be exchanged for very different resources brought by the other person (Foa, 1971). In an intriguing demonstration of this more complex pattern of needs, Harrison and Saeed (1977) examined 800 advertisements in the lonely-hearts column of a widely circulated weekly tabloid. By analyzing both what people offered (such as "good company" offered by a "good-looking woman of high moral standards") and what they sought ("wealthy older man with good intentions"), these investigators discovered some interesting aspects of the apparent need systems of heterosexual individuals. For example, women were more likely to offer physical attractiveness, and men were more likely to seek it. In similar fashion, men were more likely to offer financial security and women to request it.

In another study of personal advertisements, Kay Deaux and Randall Hanna (1984) gathered 800 ads representing equal numbers of heterosexual females, homosexual females, heterosexual males, and homosexual males. Each ad was coded in terms of what the person requested and what was offered. Like Harrison and Saeed (1977), Deaux and Hanna found heterosexual women were most likely to offer physical attractiveness and to seek financial security, whereas heterosexual men offered financial status and security and provided objective physical descriptors. On the other hand, physical characteristics were much less important to homosexual women than to heterosexual women; the lesbians placed greater emphasis on hobbies, interests, and sincerity in the prospective relationship. Although physical appearance was downplayed by the homosexual women, it was emphasized by the homosexual men. The latter group mentioned physical characteristics most often, and personality factors seemed to be much less important than they were for the heterosexual men. Sexuality was also a more central issue for homosexual males than for any other group.

Thus, complementarity may play some role in attraction, particularly with respect to a match between what one person wants and another has to offer. To date, however, the evidence for similarity is much stronger and more broadly based, applying to both same-sex and opposite-sex friendships in both laboratory and field settings. By contrast, complementarity has been found primarily in romantic heterosexual pairings; we do not know how important it is either in same-sex friendships or in homosexual romantic pairs.

Pleasant or agreeable characteristics   Not surprisingly, we like people who are pleasant or who do nice things. As discussed in Chapter 4, personality characteristics vary in their likability, and we are more attracted to someone who has positive traits than to someone who has negative traits (Kaplan & Anderson, 1973). Beyond evaluating the characteristics of another person in and of themselves, however, we are also concerned with the interpersonal implications of those traits (Clore & Kerber, 1978). In other words, when we evaluate another person's characteristics, we consider what those traits, and the behaviors we associate with them, mean for us. For example, "considerate" not only favorably describes another person but also implies that we ourselves will receive some positive outcome from interaction with that person. At the negative pole, we tend to be least attracted to persons who can be described in terms that not only suggest negative aspects of their personality but imply negative consequences

for us as well (such as "unappreciative" or "dishonest").

Physical attractiveness   Aristotle wrote that "beauty is a greater recommendation than any letter of introduction," and things have not changed much in the last 2,300 years. As we discussed in Chapter 4, physical appearance is one of the first things we notice about another person, and it is the basis for many of our initial impressions about others. The vast amounts of money spent on cosmetics, plastic surgery, diet foods, and contemporary fashions attest to the degree of concern people invest in presenting a favorable image.

One reason we like attractive people is aesthetic appeal—in general, we find attractive people and objects more appealing. But there is more to the connection between beauty and interpersonal attraction than aesthetics. For example, most people in our society appear to hold a stereotype that can be described as "what is beautiful is good" (Dion, Berscheid, & Walster, 1972). In a study illustrating this stereotype, Karen Dion (1972) showed college women some photographs of children who had allegedly misbehaved. Some of the children were physically attractive; others were not. Particularly when the misbehavior was severe, the beautiful children were given the benefit of the doubt. Respondents tended to disregard the misbehavior of the attractive children, whereas less beautiful children who committed the same acts were called maladjusted and deviant. Even children themselves are aware of this stereotype: children as young as 3 years prefer pretty children to less attractive peers (Dion, 1977). In general, a wide variety of positive characteristics are attributed to attractive people (Feingold, 1990; Hatfield & Sprecher, 1986).

Interestingly, the bias inherent in the stereotype also works in reverse: What is good is beautiful. Often we believe that people we like for other reasons have attractive physical features (Gross & Crofton, 1977). Junior high school students who are perceived to excel in athletic ability or academic ability, for example, are considered more attractive than their peers who are not so outstanding (Felson & Bohrnstedt, 1979).

Still another reason we are beckoned by the physically attractive is that we hope that affiliating with attractive others will enhance our own image (Waller, 1937). In same-gender pairs, this "halo" effect does occur, and it occurs for both women and men. People of average attractiveness who are with a more attractive other are perceived as more attractive, whereas individuals seen with an unattractive other are perceived as less attractive (Geiselman, Haight, & Kimata, 1984; Kernis & Wheeler, 1981). But in male-female pairs, when the presumption is that of a dating couple, the halo effect only works one way. A man makes the most favorable impression on observers when he is accompanied by a good-looking woman. He is viewed most negatively when his female companion is physically unattractive (Sigall & Landy, 1973). But women do not necessarily receive equal benefits. Daniel Bar-Tal and Leonard Saxe (1976) showed subjects slides of presumably married couples in which the man and the woman varied in physical attractiveness. The unattractive man who was paired with an attractive woman was judged to have the highest income, the greatest professional success, and the highest intelligence. In contrast, the unattractive woman paired with an attractive man gained no advantage by the pairing—she was judged solely on her own level of attractiveness.

Although the qualities associated with attractive men are not associated with the women who accompany them, physical attractiveness is not unimportant for the man himself. Harry Reis and his colleagues have found that, for both genders, attractiveness is associated with the *quality* of social interactions: highly attractive people report more satisfaction and more pleasurable interactions (Reis, Nezlek, & Wheeler, 1980; Reis et al., 1982). Also, the more attractive a man is, the more social interaction he has with women—and the less he has with other men. Among women, however, the amount of social interaction is unrelated to physical attractiveness. This surprising result makes sense when we consider the relationship between attractiveness and social skills. Reis and his colleagues (Reis et al., 1982) reported a positive correlation between physical attractiveness and social skills among men; more attractive men were more socially skilled. Among women, however, the correlation was negative; more attractive women were less socially skilled. According to Sharon Brehm (1992), this may result from others encouraging attractive women to conform more closely to the passive gender-role stereotype for women. That is, attractive women are discouraged from developing assertive social skills but still experi-

ence a high level of social interaction as a result of their attractiveness. Unattractive women, however, may not be discouraged from developing social skills, and they, too, experience a high level of social interaction as a result of their skills.

Reciprocal liking Finally, we are attracted to people who like us. Heider's (1946) balance theory, presented in Chapter 7, predicts, for example, that if Susan likes herself and Kyung likes Susan, a cognitively balanced state will result in which Susan likes Kyung in return. In other words, liking and disliking are often reciprocal. If members of a discussion group are told that other group members like them very much, they are most likely to choose those members when asked to form smaller groups later in the experimental session (Backman & Secord, 1959). Reciprocity also occurs for dislike: we tend to dislike people who have indicated negative feelings toward us. Our tendency toward balance also is not limited only to mutual reciprocity, as illustrated by the maxim "My enemy's enemy is my friend." Two persons who dislike a third person will tend to be more attracted to each other than those who do not share this bond (Aronson & Cope, 1968).

Theoretical Models of Attraction

The variety of antecedent conditions that influence interpersonal attraction can be confusing without theoretical models that create some understanding of why and how they work. Not surprisingly, psychologists have developed numerous theoretical models of attraction. Three of these models will be considered in more detail here: reinforcement/affect theory, social exchange theory, and interdependence theory.

Reinforcement/affect theory Perhaps the most basic explanation of interpersonal attraction relies on the concept of reinforcement—we like people who reward us and dislike people who punish us. Donn Byrne and Gerald Clore (1970) conceptualize interpersonal attraction as a basic learning process. This model assumes that most stimuli can be classified as rewards or punishments and that rewarding stimuli elicit positive feelings (or affect), whereas punishing stimuli elicit negative affect. Our evaluations of people or objects are, in turn, based on the degree of positive or negative affect we experience, and neutral stimuli associated with the affect will gain the capacity to produce similar feelings. Lott and Lott (1974) have proposed a similar model.

To examine this theory in more concrete terms, let us consider some factors we discussed previously. Having someone do kind things for us, for example, would undoubtedly be a positive, rewarding experience. Byrne and Clore (1970) suggest that the reward value of such an experience creates positive affect and, in turn, leads us to evaluate positively (that is, to like) the person associated with that reward. Further, Byrne and Clore would also predict that we would also tend to like other people and objects associated with that situation (for example, the place the interaction occurred and other people present at the time) more because of the conditioning process. Byrne and his colleagues (Byrne, 1971; Byrne, Clore, & Smeaton, 1986) have marshaled an impressive array of support for this apparently simple principle.

Social exchange theory Social exchange theory does not challenge the general assumption that reinforcement is an important basis of interpersonal attraction, but it goes beyond simple reinforcement theory. **Social exchange theory** involves both persons in the relationship, specifically the costs and benefits each person associates with the relationship. Attraction involves (at least) two persons; therefore, it seems reasonable to consider how the two persons interact rather than to focus on the characteristics of one person while ignoring the other.

Margaret Clark and Judson Mills, recognizing that costs and benefits may be defined differently in different relationships, suggest that an important distinction should be made between exchange and communal relationships (Clark & Mills, 1979; Mills & Clark, 1982). Some relationships, such as those between strangers, acquaintances, or business associates, are based on a strict *exchange* of benefits. Reciprocity is the rule in such relationships: what one gives to the relationship and what one gets from it are kept in balance. In *communal* relationships, such as those with family members and close friends, people are more responsive to the other person's needs and less concerned with balancing every input and outcome. This does not mean, however, that there is no concern at all about costs and

benefits. If your best friend is in trouble, for example, you may go to your friend's aid without expecting any direct compensation in return. However, if your friend ignores you except when he or she is in trouble, the lack of reciprocity will eventually alter your appraisal of the relationship.

In a clever demonstration of the difference between exchange and communal relationships, Clark (1984) scheduled pairs of students for an experiment. The pairs were either two friends or two strangers. The experimental task for the two subjects involved looking for specified sequences of numbers in a 15×26 matrix of numbers. The subjects were asked to take turns looking for a set of numbers and circling them when they were located, and the experimenter promised the participants a joint reward that they could divide as they wished. Two pens were available for the task, one with red ink and one with black, and the choice between these pens was the dependent variable of interest. In a strict exchange relationship, Clark reasoned, it would be important for the two participants to keep track of each other's contribution so they could divide the reward according to their relative contribution. How to keep track? By choosing a pen of a different color from the pen one's partner had used. This kind of record keeping should be less important in a communal relationship, and the friends would be more likely to use the same pen. As Figure 9.2 shows, that was the outcome of the study.

Whereas participants in an exchange relationship are more likely to keep track of contributions and to reciprocate in kind, participants in a communal relationship are more likely to be attuned to each other's needs. For example, people in a communal relationship will check more often to see whether a partner needs help, regardless of whether they believe the other person could reciprocate that help. On the other hand, people in exchange relationships are more likely to keep track of the other person's needs when they believe reciprocity of help is possible (Clark, Mills, & Powell, 1986).

Interdependence theory As we discussed in Chapter 1, the interdependence theory of John Thibaut and Harold Kelley is similar to social exchange theory; both conceptualize interaction in terms of costs and rewards (Kelley & Thibaut, 1978; Thibaut & Kelley, 1959). Inter-

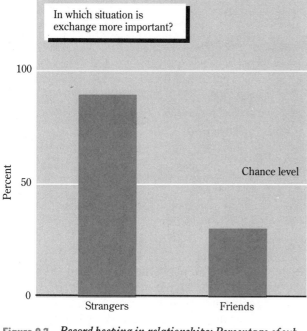

Figure 9.2 *Record keeping in relationships: Percentage of subjects who chose to use a pen of a different color from that used by their partners (either strangers or friends).*
Source: "Record Keeping in Two Types of Relationships" by M. S. Clark, 1984, *Journal of Personality and Social Psychology, 47,* pp. 549–557.

dependence theory, however, includes more detail about the interaction of two people's behaviors and frames these interdependencies in terms of an outcome matrix. Also important in interdependency theory is the concept of a **comparison level,** a standard against which the relationship is evaluated. The theory suggests that people compare the gains in a relationship with what they have come to expect. This comparison level is based on past experiences, and any present relationship will be judged satisfactory only if it exceeds the comparison level. The comparison level can change over time; for example, as you grow older, you may demand more from a relationship than you did when you were a teenager. The comparison level is also specific to situations. Your calculations of outcome value (reward minus costs), for example, may differ greatly when considering your relationship with a dentist versus your relationship with a lover.

One other factor enters into the calculations of interdependence theory—the evaluation of alternative relationships. Imagine you have been in a relationship for some time; it is an acceptable relationship that barely exceeds your comparison level. Then you meet an exciting stranger who promises far more rewards and fewer costs. What would you do? In all likelihood, you would choose the exciting stranger with little hesitation. Suppose, instead, that your current relationship is very good; it greatly exceeds your comparison level. The exciting stranger still may produce some instability, but the "pull" of the alternative relationship would not be as great.

This example illustrates how important subjective evaluations are in the social exchange process. Rewards and costs are not objective standards that can be measured with a ruler. Rather, they depend on individual beliefs, on attributions about ourselves and others, and they are subject to constant change (Kelley, 1979). As a result, it may be difficult to assess exact outcomes in a complex interaction. Still, the general idea that we consider such factors in the course of a relationship is very convincing.

Each of these three theories highlights important aspects of the attraction process. At the most basic level, reinforcement theory tells us much about the factors that will influence our attraction to another person. Most of the antecedents to attraction we discussed earlier, in fact, can be handled by a simple reinforcement model. Yet, when we consider a more active interaction between two persons, additional factors are needed to explain interpersonal attraction. Social exchange theory and interdependence theory take us in that direction, considering both partners as necessary components of the explanation. With this in mind, let us consider the ways in which relationships develop.

▶ Developing Relationships

The initial impression we form of another person, whether from verbal or nonverbal cues, is a critical starting point in any relationship. Yet it is only a starting point; a relationship between two people involves far more than an initial attraction to each other (Berscheid, 1985). One important difference is that relationships develop over time and cannot be characterized in terms of a single interaction. For this reason, the social-psychological analysis of close relationships was slow to develop. The laboratory tradition of social psychology, in which subjects participate in brief, one-time sessions contrived by researchers, lends itself to the study of initial attraction but not to the study of continuing relationships. As psychologists have added other methods to their repertoires, the study of close relationships has progressed (Fletcher & Fitness, 1990; Ickes, Bissonnette, Garcia, & Stinson, 1990). In this section we will examine more closely two types of relationships: friendship and love.

Friendship

What does it mean to be a friend? What do you expect of a friend that you would not expect from a casual acquaintance? Are some behaviors incompatible with friendship, so that their occurrence signals the end of the relationship? Such questions suggest that friendships are regulated by a set of informal rules that people recognize and to which they adhere.

Do such rules exist? To answer this question, Michael Argyle and Monika Henderson (1984) began by defining four criteria for a friendship rule:

1. People should generally agree that the behavior specified by the rule is important in a friendship.
2. The rule should be applied differently to current friends and to former friends.
3. Failure to adhere to the rule should often be cited as a reason for the breakup of a friendship.
4. The rule should differentiate behavior between close friends and not-so-close friends.

They then interviewed students in four countries— England, Italy, Japan, and Hong Kong—about their views of friendship. By applying the four criteria to the interview responses, Argyle and Henderson were able to identify six rules that people from different cultures agree are central to friendship. These rules are shown in Table 9.2, along with three other rules that met most of the criteria but failed to differentiate between close and less close friends.

Students entering college, particularly those whose attendance requires a move away from home, have

Table 9.2 The rules of friendship

1. Share news of success with a friend.
2. Show emotional support.
3. Volunteer help in time of need.
4. Strive to make a friend happy when in each other's company.
5. Trust and confide in each other.
6. Stand up for a friend in his or her absence.
7. Repay debts and favors.
8. Be tolerant of other friends.
9. Don't nag a friend.

Source: "The Rules of Friendship" by M. Argyle and M. Henderson, 1984, *Journal of Social and Personal Relationships, 1,* pp. 211–237.

ample opportunity to apply the rules identified by Argyle and Henderson (1984) to developing friendships. The assignment of a dormitory roommate, for example, often provides the first chance for a new friendship. Of course, some of these assignments are more successful than others. Little time seems to be required for roommates to decide whether a friendship will form. For example, John Berg (1984) discovered that the decision to continue to share a room during the second year could be predicted from reactions reported early in the first year. Among other factors, a student's perceived comparison level for alternatives was related to his or her later choice. Consistent with interdependence theory, students who saw their current arrangement as much better than any other they could make were more likely to seek a continued relationship.

From the beginning, pairs of people who become close friends act quite different from pairs who do not become friends (Hays, 1985). Relationships between acquaintances who do not become friends show a steady decline in contact. A developing friendship, in contrast, is characterized by an initial flurry of activity and then a gradual decline in the sheer amount of activity. This gradual decline in amount of interaction, explained in part by the probable increase in other activities during a student's first year at college, is accompanied by an *increase* in the intimacy or quality of the interaction. As we saw in the studies of affiliation, gender differences also emerge in the analysis of friendship development. Male friendships are more apt to evolve from shared activities, whereas female friendships depend more on verbal communication and self-disclosure (Hays, 1985).

Gender differences exist, too, in the extent to which nonverbal communication through touch plays a role in friendships. For example, Valerian Derlega and his colleagues (Derlega, Lewis, Harrison, Winstead, & Costanza, 1989) asked friends and dating partners to act out a scenario in which one friend was greeting the other at the airport after returning from a trip. In all, fourteen dyads were included in each of three categories of friends—male-male, female-female, and male-female—plus male-female dating partners. The greetings were photographed and later scored for the intimacy of contact, ranging from no touch at all to combinations of hugging and kissing. The results, presented in Figure 9.3, clearly demonstrated differences between men's and women's use of touch in friendships. Not unexpectedly, dating partners exclusively employed the most intimate levels of touch; all of them engaged in some combination of hugging and kissing. When both friends were male, however, the intimacy level of touching was significantly lower than for any other pair of friends. A second study involving perceptions of touching behavior led Derlega and his colleagues to conclude that men were more likely than women to perceive touching to be primarily sexual. Similarly, touching by males was more likely to be interpreted sexually than touching by females.

Characteristics other than gender also distinguish friendship patterns. For example, the individual who has a strong need for intimacy is more apt to develop friendships and is more likely to engage in self-disclosure with those friends. By contrast, individuals motivated by needs for power and dominance are more

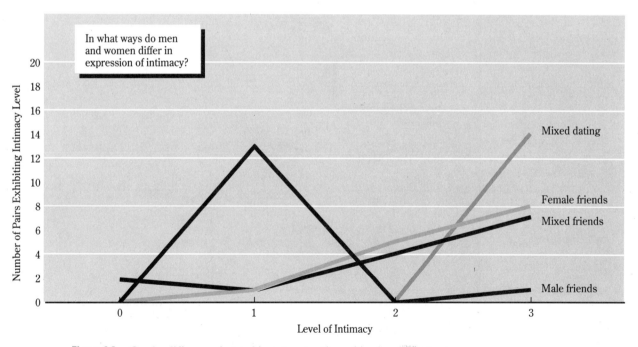

Figure 9.3 *Gender differences in touching upon greeting a friend or dating partner.*

Source: "Gender Differences in the Initiation and Attribution of Tactile Intimacy" by V. J. Derlega, R. J. Lewis, S. Harrison, B. A. Winstead, and R. Costanza, 1989, *Journal of Nonverbal Behavior, 13,* pp. 83–96.

likely to seek a large-group context for activity—affiliation rather than friendship (McAdams, Healy, & Krause, 1984).

Conceptions and Measurement of Love

Most people believe love differs from friendship. Romantic love often seems to develop quite rapidly, for example, whereas the course of friendship can be more gradual. Romantic love appears more fragile than friendship and can have more negative consequences, such as suffering and frustration (Berscheid, 1985).

The idea of caring is basic to conceptions of love. In a love relationship, behavior is often motivated by concern for the partner's interests rather than one's own. Primary concern with one's own needs seems more characteristic of casual attraction than of more intense love relationships (Steck, Levitan, McLane, & Kelley, 1982).

The social psychologist Zick Rubin (1970, 1973) has developed two questionnaires to measure the separate states of liking and loving. According to Rubin, liking is based primarily on affection and respect. Items on Rubin's liking scale deal with consensus about a friend's positive qualities and a desire to be similar to one's friend. Loving, however, relies on intimacy, attachment, and care for the other person's welfare. Items from the love scale deal with misery resulting from a loved one's absence, with forgiveness for transgressions, and with extremely high levels of self-disclosure.

These scales were presented to 158 couples at the University of Michigan who were dating but not engaged. They were asked to complete both the love scale and the liking scale with respect to their dating partner and then with respect to a close friend of the same gender. The average scores for the men and women in Rubin's study are shown in Figure 9.4. It is clear that the love scores of men and women in regard

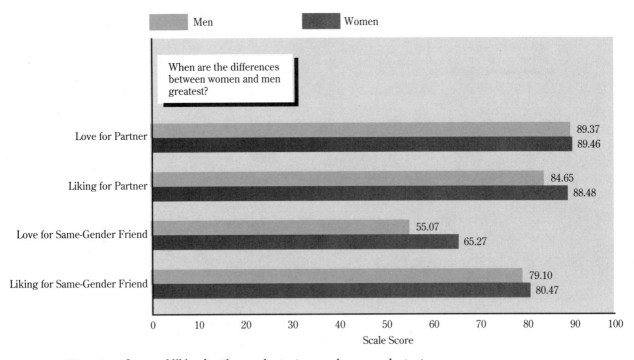

Figure 9.4 *Love and liking for other-gender partners and same-gender partners.*
Source: "Measurement of Romantic Love" by Z. Rubin, 1970, *Journal of Personality and Social Psychology, 16,* pp. 265–273.

to their respective dating partners were almost identical. However, women *liked* their dating partners significantly more than they were liked in return. This difference resulted from women rating their partners higher on such task-oriented dimensions as intelligence and leadership potential. Men and women reported liking their same-gender friends equally, but women indicated greater love toward their same-gender friends than men did. Women's deeper involvement in same-gender associations—greater self-disclosure and expressiveness, for example—is consistent with the research on affiliation patterns we discussed earlier.

Rubin's work shows that a conceptual distinction exists between liking and romantic love. Other results that suggest these measures differ include the finding that the two partners' scores were more closely related on the dimension of love than on the dimension of liking. In addition, Rubin found that the higher the partners' love scores, the more likely the partners were to expect that they would marry; liking scores, in contrast, were less strongly related to this prediction.

Although Rubin has developed a single scale for assessing love, other investigators suggest that love is not a unidimensional concept. For example, a distinction can be drawn between two types of love: *passionate* (or romantic) and *companionate* (Hatfield, 1988; Peele, 1988; Walster & Walster, 1978). Passionate love is an intensely emotional experience: ecstasy when one's partner reciprocates, agony when the partner does not. Companionate love may be a more familiar form of love, a love defined as the affection we feel for those with whom our lives are deeply intertwined. In contrast to the sometimes fleeting state of romantic love, companionate love reflects longer-term relationships and may be a later stage in a romantic relationship.

John Alan Lee (1973) has suggested that love is even more varied. He offers six types of love styles: romantic love, game-playing love, friendship love, possessive love, logical love, and selfless love. Each style is identified by a descriptive Greek or Latin label, and each can be assessed by specific questionnaire items developed by Clyde and Susan Hendrick (1986) and shown in Table 9.3. People vary in their predisposition to experience these different kinds of love; one reason, perhaps, why people may disagree about what love is.

Robert Sternberg (1986) has characterized love as a triangle consisting of three components: intimacy, pas-

Table 9.3 Love attitudes scale

Eros: Romantic, passionate love
- My partner and I were attracted to each other immediately after we first met.
- My partner fits my ideal standards of physical beauty/handsomeness.

Ludus: Game-playing love
- I try to keep my partner a little uncertain about my commitment to him/her.
- I enjoy playing the "game of love" with my partner and a number of other partners.

Storge: Friendship love
- Our love is really a deep friendship, not a mysterious, mystical emotion.
- Our love relationship is the most satisfying because it developed from a good friendship.

Pragma: Logical love
- I considered what my partner was going to become in life before I committed myself to him/her.
- One consideration in choosing my partner was how he/she would reflect on my career.

Mania: Possessive, dependent love
- When my partner doesn't pay attention to me, I feel sick all over.
- I cannot relax if I suspect that my partner is with someone else.

Agape: Selfless love
- I would rather suffer myself than let my partner suffer.
- Whatever I own is my partner's to use as he/she chooses.

Source: "A Theory and Method of Love" by C. Hendrick and S. Hendrick, 1986, *Journal of Personality and Social Psychology, 50,* pp. 392–402.

sion, and decision/commitment (see Figure 9.5). Intimacy refers to feelings of closeness in a relationship, a sense of bondedness to the other person. Passion refers to the romantic and sexual aspects of a relationship. Decision/commitment involves two aspects. In the early stages of a relationship, decision refers to one's decision about being in love with another person. Later this component refers to one's level of commitment to continue loving that person. According to Sternberg's triangular theory, different types of love result from the differential strengths of these three components. Consider, for example, the four types of love illustrated in Figure 9.5. *Liking* involves a great deal of

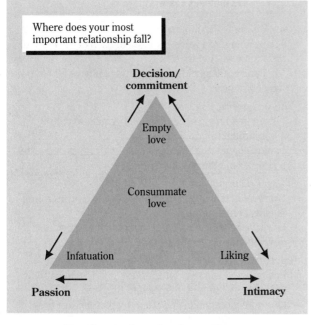

Where does your most important relationship fall?

Figure 9.5 *Sternberg's triangular theory of love.*

intimacy, but little passion or commitment. *Infatuation,* in contrast, is mostly passion, whereas *empty love* is mostly commitment. In the center of the triangle we find *consummate love*—equal parts of passion, intimacy, and decision/commitment. Romantic love (not illustrated), according to Sternberg, involves high levels of intimacy and passion, but little decision/commitment.

What is the reason for these different types of love? Cindy Hazan and Phillip Shaver (1987, 1990; Shaver & Hazan, 1987, 1988) have provided evidence that **attachment theory** can be used to explain the variety of types of love. Attachment theory was originally proposed by John Bowlby (1969, 1973, 1980) to explain the development of strong attachments to an adult observed in both human and primate infants. Bowlby proposed the development of attachment as an evolutionary mechanism that increases infants' survival by keeping them close to an adult in the face of danger. Researchers have identified three main styles of attachment: secure, anxious/ambivalent, and avoidant (Ainsworth, Blehar, Waters, & Wall, 1978). According to the theory, a *secure* attachment style results from infant-caregiver interac-

tions marked by confidence, consistency, caring, and physical contact that does not interfere overly much with an infant's ongoing activities. Such care enables the infant to explore the world and negotiate risky situations with minimal fear. When a caregiver's responses to an infant are inconsistent or interfere too much with the infant's activities, the resulting attachment style is likely to be *anxious/ambivalent.* When an infant's attempts to establish contact with a caregiver are consistently refused, the infant may develop an *avoidant* attachment style.

Hazan and Shaver reasoned that because love is a form of attachment, one's adult romantic relationships should be related to one's other attachment experiences. That is, the variety of types of love other researchers have identified may be the result of different attachment styles. Do infant attachment experiences have anything to do with adult experiences of love? Using a "love quiz" printed in the lifestyles section of a newspaper, Hazan and Shaver (1987) were able to characterize the attachment styles and obtain extensive information about the romantic experiences and reactions of over 1,200 people. Consistent with attachment theory, the respondents' reported history of their relationships with their parents differentiated their adult attachment styles (see Table 9.4).

Table 9.4   Items used by Hazan and Shaver to categorize adult attachment styles

Secure: I find it relatively easy to get close to others and am comfortable depending on them and having them depend on me. I don't often worry about being abandoned or about someone getting too close to me.

Avoidant: I am somewhat uncomfortable being close to others; I find it difficult to trust them completely, difficult to allow myself to depend on them. I am nervous when anyone gets too close, and often, love partners want me to be more intimate than I feel comfortable being.

Anxious/Ambivalent: I find that others are reluctant to get as close as I would like. I often worry that my partner doesn't really love me or won't want to stay with me. I want to merge completely with another person, and this desire sometimes scares people away.

Source: "Romantic Love Conceptualized as an Attachment Process" by C. Hazan and P. Shaver, 1987, *Journal of Personality and Social Psychology, 52,* pp. 511–524.

More directly related to our discussion are the differences in the respondents' views of love. Secure lovers, for example, believed that although romantic relationships had ups and downs, the intensity that characterizes the beginning of a relationship can reappear later in the relationship. That is, the "honeymoon," once over, can recur. They also believed that romantic love does not fade at all in some relationships. That is, they believed their "attachment" to a romantic partner was relatively secure. Those with an avoidant attachment style were considerably more pessimistic. They believed that "head-over-heels" romantic love existed only in fiction, that love doesn't last, and that people rarely find "real" love. Respondents with an anxious/ambivalent attachment style also believed "real" love was extremely rare, even though they believed it was easy to fall in love and indicated they *started* to fall in love relatively often. According to the respondents' reports about their most important romantic relationships, differences among those with different attachment styles were not limited to beliefs about love. For example, secure respondents' most important romantic relationships were characterized by happiness, friendship, trust, and an absence of fear of closeness. In contrast, avoidant respondents indicated their relationships were characterized by low levels of acceptance and high levels of jealousy, whereas anxious/ambivalent respondents described their relationships as marked by emotional extremes, excessive preoccupation, sexual attraction, desires for union and reciprocation, and love at first sight. Using a sample of 144 currently dating couples, Jeffrey Simpson (1990)

confirmed most of Hazan and Shaver's (1987) results. Simpson also found little evidence for matching attachment styles; his subjects were not necessarily dating someone whose attachment style matched their own. Instead, one's own attachment style played a much greater role in perceptions of the relationship than did the partner's attachment style.

Does this mean that how we view love, or whether we fall in love, depends entirely on our attachment experiences as an infant? Of course not. It does, however, provide evidence that love, like most social behavior, is a partial reflection of previous social experiences. Although attachment styles may originate in infancy, they are not "fixed in place" at that time or at any other. Styles continue to be influenced by new experiences, but how we perceive new experiences depends on our conceptualizations of previous experiences. Attachment theory also provides for a biological basis of love, one rooted in the survival value of infants staying close to protective adults. For example, Hazan and Shaver (1987) found only minor gender differences: "what stood out was the marked similarity of the results for men and women" (p. 517), further supporting the notion of love as attachment.

It should be noted that the gender of the lovers is not an implicit part of these definitions or theories about love. Although social psychologists have tended to focus primarily on heterosexual relationships, perhaps due to the greater availability of research participants, love between two persons does not appear to differ among sexual orientations. For example, Hazan and Shaver (1987) found no differences between heterosex-

CALVIN AND HOBBES, copyright 1986 Watterson. Dist. by UNIVERSAL PRESS SYNDICATE. Reprinted with permission. All rights reserved.

ual and homosexual individuals in their massive study (Phillip Shaver, personal communication, January 18, 1991).

Mate Selection

It is said that in the 1960s and 1970s, the prerequisites for marriage in China were "four things that go round"—a bicycle, a watch, a fan, and a sewing machine. Now, with changes in the Chinese economy, the four things are more modern—a television set, a washing machine, a stereo, and a refrigerator—according to one news report (Bennett, 1985). Economic advantages, it is claimed, are the major attraction in a marriage partner.

Less materialistic types might claim that the choice of a partner is based more on personal than on financial characteristics. In a series of replications by different researchers, for example, college students asked to rate the importance of eighteen different characteristics in a potential mate consistently included the same traits as most important: dependable character, emotional stability, pleasing disposition, and mutual attraction (Hill, 1945; Hudson & Henze, 1969; McGinnis, 1959; Silva, 1990). Similarly, a group of married persons, varying in age from 18 to 40, listed the following ten characteristics as most important: being a good companion, consideration, honesty, affection, dependa-

bility, intelligence, kindness, being understanding, being interesting to talk to, and loyalty (Buss & Barnes, 1986). Characteristics that they would not value in a mate included dominance, agnosticism, being a night owl, and being an early riser (the same people did not necessarily mention all these features).

The principle of similarity, which we discussed earlier in relation to initial impressions, plays a role in mate selection as well. In **ethology**—the study of the behavior of animals in their natural settings—the coupling of individuals based on resemblance of one or more characteristics is termed **assortative mating** (Buss, 1984). In other words, people do not mate randomly; they often seek mates who share common characteristics and who like to engage in similar activities. For example, some investigators have found that married couples are similar on such characteristics as susceptibility to boredom, desire to seek experiences, and impulsivity (Lesnik-Oberstein & Cohen, 1984). Others have found that spouses tend to be similar in their choice of activities, their willingness to display intimacy, and the level of quarrelsomeness they will tolerate (Buss, 1984). Of course, the possibility exists that couples who do not share some commonalities will be less successful and may not still be around (as a couple) when a psychologist comes to question them. However, that the degree of similarity stays constant over time indicates that it is an important factor in initial selection (Buss, 1984).

Stages in the Development of Love

Developing a close relationship takes time; no relationship becomes instantly close. As a general model, we can consider a relationship—any close relationship—to move from a fairly superficial stage to a deeper, more intimate bond (Kelley et al., 1983). In the first stage, which can be called acquaintanceship, two people begin to get to know each other. Initial impressions are made, and the two begin to interact. Many relationships never progress beyond this stage. The dental hygienist who cleans our teeth, the bus driver on our regular route, and the person we meet occasionally at a neighborhood party all exemplify this level of contact.

The movement from acquaintance to the actual building of a relationship constitutes a second stage. During this stage, increasing degrees of interdependence are established. The people involved discover aspects of each other through increasing interaction, and they become more willing to disclose information about themselves. The two partners in this stage of a relationship also begin to invest time and energy in the relationship, coordinating their activities with each other and anticipating rewarding future interactions. Students involved in dating relationships, for example, rate the physical and sexual attractiveness of opposite-sex models in advertisements lower than students not involved in a dating relationship (Simpson, Gangestad, & Lerma, 1990). Because the dating students did not differ from nondating students in their perceptions of same-gender models or models much older than themselves, it may be that these changes in perception are due to effort justification via dissonance reduction (see Chapter 7). In mixed-gender "get acquainted" sessions, for example, a large proportion of males' behavior is related to the physical attractiveness of the female (Ickes, 1990). Once in a relationship, heterosexual males may downgrade the attractiveness of women other than their partner in order to maintain the relationship.

Buildup is the third stage of a close relationship. Progress in this stage is not always smooth, as the partners face an unfolding set of circumstances and problems, some of which temporarily increase the tension between them. People in love, for example, often idealize their partners (Brehm, 1988), but eventually they discover their partners' less-than-ideal characteristics. You

"It's as though everything nice about you had been just some kind of introductory offer."
Drawing by Wm. Hamilton; © 1991 The New Yorker Magazine, Inc.

may discover that the "wonderful" person with whom you fell in love, for example, is not as bright, sensitive, or attentive as you once thought, or you may discover that your partner's plans for the future are very different from your own. Responding to a partner's needs may involve personal sacrifices, which are another major source of conflict (Holmes, 1989). One interesting result of the increased tension that accompanies the development of commitment is an alteration in patterns of deception (Metts, 1989). Early in a relationship, deception tends to be self-focused and to involve falsification; the "little white lies" we tell tend to protect our own self-concept or rewards. For example, you might say your phone was out of order rather than admit you forgot to call in order to avoid your partner's accusation of not caring. Later, deception tactics are more often used to protect the relationship itself, and they involve withholding information more than providing false information—not mentioning a birthday card from a former lover, for example, because you fear it may initiate an argument. Still later, deception by omission remains dominant, but it is primarily motivated by concern for protecting the partner's self-esteem. Despite being sure that an argument will not ensue, you still might not mention that birthday card from a former lover because you know your partner thinks the former lover is more attractive.

Another development that arises as commitment grows is jealousy. Jealousy may be almost inevitable, according to the French writer La Rochefoucauld, who stated, "Jealousy is always born together with love." Most definitions of jealousy refer to an emotional state one experiences when he or she perceives that some other person (either real or imagined) poses a threat to an ongoing relationship. Research suggests that two factors are common to most jealous reactions: a desire for an exclusive relationship and feelings of inadequacy (White, 1981; White & Mullen, 1989). These factors are found in the jealousy experienced by both men and women, but the patterns of jealousy differ.

A man's jealousy is often related to self-esteem, particularly with respect to his partner as a source of self-esteem, and to the extent to which he holds traditional gender-role beliefs. A woman's jealousy is associated mainly with a strong dependence on the relationship itself—a belief that it is more rewarding than any available alternative (White, 1981). Thus, for men jealousy seems more closely related to issues of status, whereas for women the nature of the relationship is more crucial. These different emphases also appeared in a study that asked men and women to say how they would react to situations that were likely to create jealous feelings (Shettel-Neuber, Bryson, & Young, 1978). Men were more likely to say they would become angry and involve themselves in activities that would endanger the relationship; women were more apt to say they would become depressed and do things to improve the relationship. Although jealousy may be a nearly universal threat to continued development of a relationship, it is not always experienced in the same way by women and by men.

In the fourth stage of relationship growth, real commitment develops. At this point, the advantages of the relationship clearly outweigh the disadvantages. For example, a recent review of sixty-nine studies of positive well-being provided unequivocal evidence of greater well-being among married than among non-married individuals, although the effect was stronger among women than among men (Wood, Rhodes, & Whelen, 1989). In some cases, commitment may develop as a result of love. In other cases, as in those societies in which arranged marriages are the rule, commitment may be the outcome of a formal agreement, after which emotional involvement and love can follow. Based on research by Marc Blais and his colleagues (Blais, Sabourin, Boucher, & Vallerand, 1990), the decision to commit and remain committed to a relationship may not be as critical a predictor of couples' happiness as the *motivation* behind the commitment. Individuals in long-term relationships (both married and unmarried) whose motivation to remain committed is self-determined or intrinsic—as opposed to motivated by obtaining rewards, avoiding punishment, or avoiding guilt—perceive their relationship-oriented behaviors in a more positive light. These perceptions of their behaviors, in turn, are directly related to their personal happiness with the relationship. As you might expect, each partner's perceptions of the relationship affect the other's perceptions. However, Blais and his colleagues also found that women's, but not men's, motivations affect their partner's perceptions; this indicates that women play a greater role in developing and maintaining close relationships than men. These results, obtained with couples whose average age was 38.1 and whose relationships averaged 12.6 years in length, support previous research with college-aged, dating couples whose relationships were less lengthy (Davis & Oathout, 1987; Franzoi, Davis, & Young, 1985; Rusbult, Johnson, & Morrow, 1986).

Many behaviors and feelings change, as Table 9.5 indicates. An increase in trust is one of those changes. When we talk about trust, we can consider three separate ways in which a person views his or her partner (Rempel, Holmes, & Zanna, 1985). First, trust involves predictability, the ability to estimate what the person will do. Second, trust implies dependability: a partner develops certain assumptions about the internal characteristics and dispositions of his or her mate. Both predictability and dependability are based on past evidence and experience with the partner. Beyond these two elements, trust implies faith. In this case, a partner

Table 9.5 Characteristics of a relationship

As a relationship develops and the partners become more closely involved with each other, several changes take place. Some of these changes are as follows:

1. Partners interact more often, for longer periods of time, in a widening array of settings.

2. People attempt to restore proximity when separated and feel comforted when proximity is regained.

3. People open up to each other, disclosing secrets and sharing physical intimacies.

4. People become less inhibited, more willing to share positive and negative feelings and to praise and criticize each other.

5. People develop their own communication system.

6. People increase their ability to map and anticipate each other's views.

7. People begin to synchronize their goals and behavior.

8. People increase their investment in the relationship, increasing its importance in their life space.

9. People begin to feel that their separate interests are inextricably tied to the well-being of their relationship.

10. People increase their liking, trust, and love for each other.

11. People see the relationship as irreplaceable, or at least as unique.

12. People more and more relate to others as a couple rather than as individuals.

Source: "Interpersonal Attraction" by E. Berscheid, 1985, in *Handbook of Social Psychology* (3rd ed., Vol. 2, pp. 413–484) by G. Lindzey and E. Aronson (Eds.), New York: Random House.

is looking ahead, confident that certain outcomes will occur. In a close relationship, love and happiness are closely linked to these three elements of trust.

Falling Out of Love

The movies of the 1930s usually ended with man and woman together, presumably guaranteed to live happily ever after. Although the Hollywood version of ro-

mance has changed even in Hollywood itself, it has surely never been true of all real-life relationships. People do meet, fall in love, and live together or marry. Yet some of these people fall out of love, break off engagements, and separate or divorce. Why do some relationships work and others fail? Do certain factors influence the course of a relationship, and can we predict the positive and negative outcomes? We now turn to this side of the attraction coin.

Breaking Up Is Hard to Do

Many relationships that begin with the glow of romantic or passionate love do not go on to fulfill their initial promise; others endure and lead to long marriages and golden anniversaries. Can any patterns be detected in those relationships that break up versus those that last? To answer this question, Hill, Rubin, and Peplau (1976) conducted an extensive two-year study, following the course of 231 heterosexual couples in the Boston area. At the end of the two years, 103 couples (45% of the original sample) had broken up; 65 others were still dating, 9 were engaged, 43 were married, and 11 could not be contacted.

To understand the process of breaking up, Hill and his colleagues first examined the answers to the initial questionnaire that each couple had completed at the beginning of the two-year period. Not surprisingly, those couples who reported feeling closer in 1972 were more likely to be together in 1974. Yet those reported feelings were not a perfect predictor: many couples who reported feeling close at the initial testing did break up during the subsequent two years. Consistent with our earlier discussion, scores on a love scale were more predictive than scores on a liking scale. In addition, the women's love scores were a better indicator of whether the relationship would last than the men's love scores. Perhaps because, as we noted earlier, women tend to play a greater role in maintaining relationships, the feelings of the woman in a relationship are a more sensitive index of the health of the relationship. Whether the couple had had sexual intercourse and whether they had lived together were unrelated to the future success of the relationship. Couples were equally likely to maintain a relationship whether or not they had engaged in these more intimate forms of interchange.

Similarity of the two partners, discussed earlier as an important factor in attraction, also was important among these Boston couples. As Table 9.6 indicates, similarities in education, intelligence, and attractiveness were all greater for the couples who stayed together than for those who broke up. However, similarity of religion, gender-role attitudes, and desired family size did not predict the long-term success of relationships. Nonetheless, couples were fairly well matched on each of these variables at the beginning of the study, suggesting that these factors are important in the initial selection of a partner.

Another important predictor of the success of the relationship was the man's need for power (Stewart & Rubin, 1976), which is defined as a stable tendency to influence others through direct action or more subtle means. Men who scored high in need for power in the Boston couples study were more likely to expect problems in the relationship and were more likely to express dissatisfaction with the relationship at the initial testing. True to these men's expectations, a couple in which the man had a high need for power was much less likely to be together two years later. In fact, 50% of these relationships had broken up, compared with only 15% of those in which the man's need for power was low. The women's need for power was measured as well, but their scores showed absolutely no association with the success or failure of the relationship.

To gain more understanding of the breakup process, Hill, Rubin, and Peplau used a second method of data

Table 9.6 **Relationship between similarity and breaking up: Correlations of partners' characteristics and attitudes two years later, by status**

Characteristics and attitudes of partners	All couples (N = 231)	Together couples (N = 117)	Breakup couples (N = 103)
Characteristics			
Age	.19	.38	.13
Highest degree planned	.28	.31	.17
SAT, math	.22	.31	.11
SAT, verbal	.24	.33	.15
Physical attractiveness	.24	.32	.16
Father's educational level	.11	.12	.12
Height	.21	.22	.22
Religion (% same)	51%	51%	52%
Attitudes			
Gender-role traditionalism	.47	.50	.41
Favorability toward women's liberation	.38	.36	.43
Approval of sex among "acquaintances"	.25	.27	.21
Romanticism	.20	.21	.15
Religiosity	.37	.39	.37
Number of children wanted	.51	.43	.57

Source: "Breakups before Marriage: The End of 103 Affairs" by C. T. Hill, Z. Rubin, and L. A. Peplau, 1976, *Journal of Social Issues, 32*(1), pp. 147–168.

collection: intensive interviews with some of the couples that had broken up. These interviews provided many insights into the process of breaking up, even including such facts as when the breakup occurred. In view of the fact that most of the couples in this study were college students, it may not be surprising that these relationships were most likely to break up at critical points in the school year—at the beginning of the fall term and at the ends of the fall and spring terms. These natural break points in the calendar year allowed couples to break up more easily, and the less involved partner in a relationship was more likely to take advantage of these natural break points to end the relationship. In contrast, when the partner who had reported being more involved chose to end the affair, the timing was more likely to be in the middle of the school year than at the end. For the less involved partner, the separation of a summer vacation may have provided a good excuse for ending the relationship, testifying to the truth of La Rochefoucauld's maxim "Absence diminishes mediocre passions and increases great ones."

Most of the breakups were perceived as somewhat one-sided: over 85% of both men and women reported that one person wanted to end the relationship more than the other. These perceptions were not totally accurate, however. Although there was considerable agreement in many cases, the reports also contained systematic bias to protect one's self-esteem. People were more likely to say that they were the one who wanted to break off the relationship than to say that their partner wished to do so. Such a strategy is, of course, self-protective: partners who did the breaking up were considerably happier, less lonely, and less depressed (but felt more guilty) than the partners with whom they broke up.

Who does the breaking up in the typical male-female couple? Although some cases are clearly mutual decisions, when one person initiates the split, it is more likely to be the woman. Zick Rubin and his colleagues (Rubin, Peplau, & Hill, 1978) have suggested that in our society men tend to fall in love more readily than women, and women fall out of love more readily than men. Although such an assertion contradicts many of the stereotypes of the romantic woman and the "strong, silent" man, the data support the argument. An interesting by-product of men's greater unwillingness

to end the relationship is found in the contact that the partners reported having after the breakup. If the man dissolved the relationship, the couple were very likely to remain casual friends; however, if the woman was the one to end the relationship, it was apparently much more difficult for them to stay friends, and fewer than half the couples did so.

The end of an affair is probably less traumatic than the end of a marriage. Nevertheless, the factors that contribute to the breakup of short-term relationships have something in common with those that lead to the rupture of long-term bonds.

Inequity and Impermanence

Earlier we discussed the general principles of social exchange theories. Equity theory, another version of social exchange theory, particularly applies to the dissolution of relationships. According to **equity theory,** people in a relationship consider not only their own costs and rewards but also the costs and rewards for the other person (Hatfield & Traupmann, 1981; Walster, Walster, & Berscheid, 1978). Ideally, these two ratios are balanced. Equity theory suggests that people have some notion of what they deserve from a relationship, and this notion is based partly on what the other partner in the relationship is receiving. The person who feels that the relationship is out of balance will become distressed and will try to restore the balance, either by actually altering the input and outcomes or by psychologically altering his or her perception of the gains and costs that both partners are experiencing.

One interesting prediction of equity theory is that people become dissatisfied whenever the relationship is out of balance whether they are overbenefited or underbenefited compared with their partner. Thus, great rewards coupled with small costs will not necessarily be satisfying. When one partner's outcomes are either much greater or much less than the others, that partner is likely to feel some distress. If both partners perceive inequity, both will feel distressed.

The form that distress takes depends both on the gender of the partner and on the type of inequity. Both men and women report being angry when they perceive an inequitable relationship; men, however, are more likely to report being hurt and resentful, whereas women mention sadness and frustration. When they feel they are overbenefited, men report guilt; when they feel underbenefited, they express anger. Women are more likely than men to express anger when they are overbenefited; when underbenefited, they are more likely to become depressed (Sprecher, 1986).

Relationships that both partners perceive as equitable are most likely to be successful (Davidson, 1984; Traupmann, Petersen, Utne, & Hatfield, 1981). In contrast, the perception of inequity can signal difficulty. For example, you might feel you invest a lot in a relationship, giving your partner emotional support and comfort. If at the same time you felt your partner was giving little to the relationship in exchange for your kindness, what would you do? Equity theory would predict that if the imbalance were too great, you would probably choose to end the relationship. In a test of this prediction, 511 men and women at the University of Wisconsin were interviewed about their relationships with their dating partners (Berscheid & Walster, 1978). At the initial testing each person was asked to evaluate his or her dating relationship in terms of the contributions and the benefits each partner was receiving. For example, the person was asked to consider all the things that might contribute to a relationship (such as personality, emotional support, help in making decisions) and to rate his or her own contribution on a scale from +4 to −4. Subjects were then asked to make a similar rating of their partners' contributions. Each person was also asked to rate the benefits received from the relationship, such as love, excitement, security, or a good time, again for both the self and the partner. These four estimates enabled the investigators to determine how equitable the relationship was perceived to be.

Three months later, the people were interviewed again and asked whether they were still going out with the same partner and how long they expected the relationship to last. People who had reported equitable relationships at the earlier session were more likely to be dating at the second testing period. They were also more likely to predict that the relationship would last than were those who reported a less equitable relationship. Hence, although it may be difficult to measure accurately all the factors that contribute to a relationship,

it seems clear that our willingness to stay in a relationship is directly related to our perceptions of its costs and benefits.

Marriage and Divorce

The breakup of an affair probably forestalls a marriage that would not have worked. Yet marriage is obviously not a guarantee of lifelong attraction. In the United States, for example, the divorce rate has been increasing for a number of years. What happens in these more extended relationships to cause a split?

Several personality and demographic factors have been associated with the likelihood of divorce (Newcomb & Bentler, 1981). For example, people who marry young are more likely to divorce. In terms of personality, people with high amounts of ambition and strong achievement needs tend to have less stable marriages.

Yet such static factors do not address the dynamics of a marital relationship. In fact, relationships are constantly changing, and it is in the shifting balance between two persons that marriage and divorce must be explored (Kelley et al., 1983). George Levinger (1979) has offered a descriptive analysis of marital relationships based on a combination of attractions and barriers. Some of the attractions he identifies are material rewards, such as family income; others are either symbolic (such as status) or affectional (such as companionship and sexual enjoyment). Barriers include the potential costs of divorcing, such as financial expenses, feelings toward children, and religious constraints. Finally, Levinger suggests that people also weigh the alternative attractions, a concept similar to Thibaut and Kelley's (1978) *comparison level for alternatives*. Possible alternative attractions that a husband or wife might consider are the values of independence or a preferred companion or sexual partner. This framework is helpful in identifying some of the factors that may come into play when individuals decide whether to continue or to end a relationship. In general, we can predict that when the attractions of the present relationship decrease, the barriers to escape from the relationship diminish, and the strength of alternative attractions increases; at that point an individual would choose to end the relationship.

The deterioration of a relationship is rarely sudden. Steve Duck (1982) has suggested that four distinct stages can be identified as a relationship dissolves. In the first, *intrapsychic* stage, the individual focuses on his or her partner, identifying causes of dissatisfaction and planning how to confront the partner with the problem. This confrontation occurs in the *dyadic* stage, and its outcome can be either reconciliation or a clearer determination to end the relationship. If the latter occurs, it is then publicized in the *social* stage. What was private now becomes public, and both partners will work on ways to save face, assign blame, and adjust their lives to a new status. Finally, in the "*grave-dressing*" phase, each partner devises an ending to the relationship and constructs a story about the events that led to it. The stories may or may not be accurate, but they will guide future recollections and interpretations.

Janice Gray and Roxanne Silver (1990) examined the grave-dressing stage of divorce by surveying a sample of couples who filed for divorce in Ontario, Canada. Usable questionnaires were obtained from forty-five couples who had been together an average of ten years,

Many couples do not live happily ever after.
Bob Kalman/The Image Works

and comparing the men's and women's responses provided considerable support for self-serving bias. Men and women were equally likely to protect their self-esteem by perceiving themselves and their role in the breakup more favorably than they perceived their former spouse's role. For example, one couple, together for seventeen years, had considerably different views of the "other woman," each of which reflected self-serving bias. The male reported "I met another woman that I liked better than my spouse. . . . My new wife is younger and better looking. . . ." His former spouse, however, described her as "a real bimbo" whose "elevator doesn't go quite to the top" (Gray & Silver, 1990, p. 1188). Gray and Silver found such self-serving biases were related to coping successfully with the divorce. Also, just as women appear to influence the development and maintenance of relationships more strongly than men, Gray and Silver reported that both ex-spouses indicated the woman exercised substantially more control over the separation process. Interestingly, women's greater sensitivity to interpersonal cues was also evident approximately 3½ years after the divorce. Women's perceptions of their former husbands' evaluations of them, while not very accurate, were more accurate than men's perceptions of their former wives' evaluations of them.

In 1958 the psychologist Harry Harlow wrote: "So far as love or affection is concerned, psychologists have failed in their mission. The little we know about love does not transcend simple observations, and the little we write about it has been written better by poets and novelists" (1958, p. 673). We know much more today than we did in 1958. Many more investigators have become interested in the topic of love, and the issue is no longer taboo. Further, the wider variety of methodologies that social psychologists are now using make it possible to investigate complex and long-term relationships more fully.

▶ Summary

Loneliness is a subjective experience, generally an unpleasant one. Emotional loneliness involves the absence of an intimate relationship with one person; social loneliness results from the lack of a broader social network. Inadequate social skills and anxiety about one's social skills appear to be independent causes of loneliness.

The need to affiliate, or to be with others, is exceedingly strong in most people. Reasons for affiliation include the intrinsic value of companionship and the usefulness of other people in providing a standard for social comparison and self-evaluation. Under conditions of increased situational anxiety, one feels a greater desire to be with others, particularly those in the same situation. Studies of affiliation patterns have provided descriptive data on the extent to which people choose to be alone or with others and how social networks develop over time.

Initial attraction to another person is influenced by the following factors: similarity of beliefs, values, and personality; complementarity of needs; physical attractiveness; pleasant or agreeable characteristics; reciprocal liking; and propinquity. Theories that have been proposed to explain interpersonal attraction include reinforcement/affect theory, social exchange theory, and interdependence theory.

Close relationships are far more complex than initial attraction and involve a long sequence of interactions between two people. Relationships between friends also involve a set of implicit rules that both partners are expected to follow.

Liking and loving are different emotions, and questionnaires have been developed to assess the two. Different kinds of love can also be identified and measured and are related to attachment styles that develop in early childhood. Love develops through a set of stages, from acquaintanceship through buildup to commitment.

People fall in love, and people fall out of love. Initial feelings of intimacy and similarity of interests are related to breakups, as are motivations for commitment; perceptions of inequality in the relationship are also a factor. Even after couples marry, relationships continue to change. The decision to divorce has been represented as the result of an imbalance among attractions, barriers, and alternative attractions. Like the formation of a relationship, the breakup occurs in a series of stages.

▶ Key Terms

assortative mating
attachment theory
comparison level
complementarity
equity theory
ethology

mere exposure effect
propinquity
social comparison theory
social exchange theory
social network
social support

Y ou cannot shake hands with a

clenched fist.

Indira Gandhi

O ne of television's great

contributions is that it brought murder

back into the home where it belongs.

Alfred Hitchcock

10

Aggression and Violence

During the 5,600 or so years that humans have recorded their history, more than 14,600 wars have occurred, an average of nearly 3 wars per year throughout our history (Montagu, 1976). Places such as the Falkland Islands and the Persian Gulf countries Qatar and Kuwait have become known to many people only because of warfare. Indeed, as this chapter is being written, war continues in the location credited with the beginning of civilization, the Mesopotamian Valley in Iraq. Nor are violent deaths limited to wars. Since the beginning of the twentieth century, more than 900,000 civilians in the United States have died as a result of criminal acts. In fact, among stable industrialized societies, the United States has the highest rates of homicide, assault, rape, and robbery. With great regularity one reads in the newspapers of parents abusing children, husbands and wives engaging in physical violence, and people being attacked and killed because someone wanted their fancy sneakers.

One could easily conclude from these facts that violence and aggression are integral facets of human society. Some behavioral scientists do assume that aggression is the natural result of a "killer instinct" in human nature. Claiming an evolutionary basis, the popular writer Robert Ardrey (1961) stated that a human "is a predator whose natural instinct is to kill with a weapon." Others, however, believe that aggression can be explained completely as a learned social behavior that is predictable and potentially controllable.

Interpretations of aggressive behavior are determined by theoretical viewpoints, and when we consider the nature of aggression we find more than enough theories. These theoretical perspectives differ in a variety of ways: in the extent to which they consider aggression innate or learned, in the extent to which the person, rather than situational factors, is considered influential, and in the proposed ways in which aggression might be controlled in the future. In this chapter we will examine several of these theories. In addition, we will consider some of the factors that influence aggression. For example, we will discuss how alcohol and drugs affect aggressive behavior, whether violence on television and in films affects the observer, how aggression is expressed in the home, and how violence might be controlled in the future.

▶ Aggression and Human Nature

It is difficult to argue that humans lack the capacity to behave in aggressive and antisocial ways. The reasons for human aggression and the source of that capacity, however, remain the focus of considerable disagreement. At an even more basic level, confusion exists as to just what it means to be aggressive. Although *aggression* is a term used often in everyday language, it takes on some very specific meanings when social scientists use it.

Definitions of Aggression

Numerous definitions of aggression have been suggested; these definitions often reflect the theoretical assumptions of their proponents. The psychoanalytic theory developed by Freud, for example, defines aggression as an underlying biological urge that must be expressed. From the perspective of **ethology**—the study of the behavior of animals in their natural settings—Konrad Lorenz described aggression as "the fighting instinct . . . directed against members of the same species" (1966, p. ix). Behaviorists, in contrast, define it in terms of outward behaviors rather than of inner drives and motives. In general, definitions of aggressive behavior vary on several dimensions, including the extent to which observable behaviors versus motives and intentions are stressed, the relevance of immediate versus long-term consequences, and the inclusion of psychological as well as physical effects (Baron, 1977; Krebs & Miller, 1985). For most of our discussion, however, we will rely on a definition of aggression that most social psychologists accept: **aggression is any behavior directed toward harming another living being.**

This definition includes several important features. First, it limits aggression to those forms of behavior in which the person *intends* to harm a victim. If you accidentally knock someone over while riding your bicycle, for example, that would not be considered an act of aggression. Similarly, when a nurse gives a patient a routine injection, the intention is not to do harm, although pain may be involved. But what if the patient has just insulted the nurse, who then jams the needle in with unnecessary force? Certainly there is a component of aggression in this behavior. Another important feature of the definition is that an unsuccessful attempt to harm someone—for example, throwing a punch that misses—is also considered aggressive because the intent was to inflict harm. Although it is often difficult to establish intention with complete certainty, as the proceedings of criminal trials well indicate, the concept of intentionality is important in distinguishing aggressive behavior from other forms of behavior that might lead to harm.

Often, in everyday speech, people talk about an "aggressive manager" or an "aggressive salesperson." Generally, such descriptions refer to a person who is competitive, energetic, and assertive. These behaviors do not fit our definition of aggression, however, unless the particular manager or salesperson is deliberately trying to harm another person in the process of being successful.

Our working definition doesn't limit aggression to physical harm. Verbal insults are forms of aggression, and even refusal to give a person something he or she needs can be considered a form of aggression. Our definition does, however, limit aggression to those behaviors that involve other living beings. A person who kicks a wall is probably angry, but this behavior would not be considered aggressive according to our definition. On the other hand, when that person kicks a dog, the behavior does fit our definition of aggression.

In research practice, aggressive behavior has been studied in a wide variety of forms. Ethologists have observed the physical combat of animals in the wild, and social psychologists have considered the willingness of college students to administer shock to another student. Written stories have been analyzed for evidence of themes of violence, and court records have been collected for reports of assault and battery. Not all of these behaviors fully satisfy the definition of aggression that we have offered, at least insofar as intent must be proven. However, all these forms of aggression can be offered as evidence that humans have the capacity to express violence and to cause harm to one another.

Why do people attempt to harm others? Answers fall into two categories. In one category we find theorists who have argued that aggression is so basic to human

Confusion exists as to just what it means to be aggressive.
Mark Antman/The Image Works

nature that it will inevitably find expression. Proponents of this point of view include psychoanalysts, ethologists, and sociobiologists. In the other category are theorists who take a cultural perspective and see norms, learning, and socialization as the sources of aggressive behavior. Before considering more specific determinants of aggression, we will discuss explanations in each of these categories.

Biological Explanations of Aggression

Sigmund Freud (1930) wrote: "The tendency to aggression is an innate, independent, instinctual disposition" (p. 102). According to traditional psychoanalytic theory, aggressive energy is constantly generated by our bodily processes. For example, the intake of food leads to the generation of energy, some of which is presumed to be aggressive. Aggression is thus defined as an underlying urge that must be expressed. Much like a bal-

loon being slowly overinflated, aggressive urges must be "released," and the release can be expressed directly or indirectly. Aggressive urges can be discharged either in socially acceptable ways (such as a vigorous debate or an athletic activity) or in unacceptable ways (such as insults or fights). The destructive release of aggressive urges need not be directed against other people; it may be aimed toward the self, as in suicide. However it is discharged, aggression is considered innate and inevitable. In fact, Freud believed that one function of society is to keep natural aggression in check.

Another biological view of aggression comes from ethology, a subfield of biology concerned with the instincts and action patterns common to all members of a species operating in their natural habitat (Eibl-Eibesfeldt, 1970). Ethologists observe the normal behavior of fish, birds, and other animals in the field and try to identify similarities in and causes of the behavior. Ethologists often assume that these behaviors (or "action patterns") are under innate, or instinctual, control (Crook, 1973).

Like psychoanalytic theorists, ethologists propose that the expression of any fixed action pattern depends on the accumulation of energy. But ethologists also propose that the release of energy must be triggered by an external stimulus called a *releaser* (Hess, 1962). Specifically, ethologists suggest that certain environmental cues are required before an organism expresses aggressive behavior. Threatening actions of another member of the species, such as bared teeth or an outright attack, are common releasers for aggression. This two-factor theory of the expression of aggression includes the notion that environmental changes contribute to the aggressive response. In this respect, this theory has an advantage over psychoanalytic theories because it enables one to predict when and where aggression will occur.

Aggression, according to Lorenz (1966), functions to preserve the species as well as the individual; that is, aggression has survival value. Lorenz believes that an organism is far more aggressive toward its own species than toward other species. The basic purpose of such aggression is to keep members of the species separated—to give each member enough territory to survive. Intraspecies aggression also affects sexual selection and mating; the stronger are more likely to mate and, presumably, produce stronger offspring. Thus, aggression ensures that the best and strongest animals will carry on the species.

In Lorenz's view, aggression becomes undesirable only when the species—the human species, for example—fails to develop the usual instinctual inhibitions against it. Among other animals, intraspecies fights usually do not end in death. The loser, instead, performs some act of appeasement to signal the end of aggression. For example, a wolf might indicate by the positions of her ears and tail that she submits to the dominance of another wolf, thereby ending the aggression. According to Lorenz, humans' troubles arise from

Among nonhuman animals, intraspecies fights usually do not end in death.
Charles Summers / Colorado Nature Photographic Studio / Amwest

[their] being a basically harmless, omnivorous creature, lacking in natural weapons with which to kill [their] big prey, and, therefore, also devoid of the built-in safety devices which prevent "professional" carnivores from abusing their killing power to destroy fellow members of their own species. [1966, p. 241]

That is, because humans could not kill each other naturally (without weapons), there was no survival value to developing natural signals to end aggression, such as the submissive postures of animals.

Another theory that has developed from animal studies is **sociobiology,** defined by E. O. Wilson (1975) as the "systematic study of the biological basis of all social behavior" (p. 4). Sociobiology is an extension of Darwinian evolutionary theory, and from this perspective aggression must be, or must have been, adaptive. More specifically, sociobiologists argue that a population or society will maintain such genetically based behaviors "if they increase the genetic fitness (i.e., reproductive success) of the individual or . . . close relatives who also carry the genes for that behavior" (Cunningham, 1981, p. 71). In the case of aggression, sociobiologists suggest that biological advantages of aggression include the abilities to acquire more resources, to defend the resources one has, and to protect one's relatives. If successful, the aggressive individual might thereby strengthen the position of his or her own group in relation to others. Thus, for the sociobiologist, aggressive behavior has a clear goal—to preserve one's own species and to increase its chances of future success.

At the same time, aggression as a competitive strategy has a serious disadvantage. It is a potentially costly strategy; severe injury or death can result, making it impossible for the individual to transmit genes to the next generation. Consequently, aggression may develop in a selective fashion, to be used in those circumstances where other methods of satisfying needs are not available or where the potential gains are considerable (Krebs & Miller, 1985).

Although the views of psychoanalysts, ethologists, and sociobiologists differ in some important respects, they share some basic assumptions. Most important, all three positions consider aggression to be an innate, instinctual behavior—a basic part of the human condition. Proponents of different biological theories may argue about when and where aggression will be displayed, but they all agree that it will be displayed.

Social Explanations of Aggression

Another group of theorists believes that although the aggressive behavior of lower animals can be explained by instinctual processes, the aggressive behavior of humans is not regulated by internal drives. Instead, social theorists propose aggression is learned from other people. The psychologist J. P. Scott (1958) has concluded that "all research findings point to the fact that there is no physiological evidence of any internal need or spontaneous driving force for fighting; that all stimulation for aggression comes eventually from forces present in the physical environment" (p. 98). Similarly, the International Society for the Study of Aggression determined in 1986 that there is no evolutionary or genetic basis for violence (Smith, 1991). If aggressive behavior is indeed learned, then how does such learning take place? Proponents of this viewpoint have suggested two methods: instrumental learning and observational learning (Bandura, 1973).

According to the principle of **instrumental learning,** any behavior that is reinforced or rewarded is more likely to recur in the future. Therefore, if aggressive acts are associated with a reward, the individual is more likely to act aggressively on other occasions. The possible range of reinforcements for humans is broad. For example, social approval or increased status can reinforce aggressive behavior (Geen & Stonner, 1971; Gentry, 1970). Money can be a reinforcement for adults (Buss, 1971; Gaebelein, 1973), and candy is an effective reward for children (Walters & Brown, 1963). For the person who is extremely provoked, evidence of a victim's suffering can serve as a form of reinforcement (Baron, 1974; Feshbach, Stiles, & Bitter, 1967), suggesting a mechanism whereby mass murderers are able to carry out their activities.

Although many aggressive responses can be learned through direct reinforcement, most investigators believe that **observational learning,** or social **modeling,** is a more common method of acquiring aggressive behaviors. Specifically, we can learn new behaviors by observing the actions of other people (called *models*). Consider the following situation: A child in a nursery school is brought to a room and asked by an experimenter to play a game that involves making pictures by using potato prints and colorful stickers. After showing the child how to play the game, the experimenter brings an adult into the room and takes that person to another corner, where a mallet, a set of Tinker Toys, and an inflated Bobo doll are placed.

After the experimenter leaves the room, the adult begins to play with the "adult toys." In a nonaggressive condition, the adult plays quietly with the Tinker Toys for ten minutes. In an aggressive condition, the adult spends most of the time attacking the Bobo doll, hitting it, kicking it, pounding its nose, and yelling aggressive comments such as "Sock him in the nose!" After ten minutes, the experimenter returns and takes the child to another room with another set of toys, but tells the child not to play with a favorite toy. The now-frustrated child may, however, play with any of the other toys in the room. These include aggressive toys (such as a Bobo doll, a mallet, and several dart guns) and nonaggressive toys (such as crayons, toy bears, a tea set, and plastic farm animals).

In this and similar experiments, Albert Bandura and his collaborators were interested in the ways in which the observation of an adult's aggressive behavior would affect a child's play choices (Bandura, Ross, & Ross, 1961, 1963). The adult's behavior did have an effect. Children who had watched an aggressive adult model were consistently more aggressive than children who had watched a nonaggressive model. They were also more aggressive than members of control groups, who had watched no model at all.

The behavior of these children really cannot be considered aggression according to our definition, because a Bobo doll is not a living being. Other investigations have shown, however, that attacks directed toward a Bobo doll relate to other forms of aggression. Nursery school children who behaved most violently toward the doll were also rated by their teachers and their peers as being most aggressive in general (Johnston, DeLuca, Murtaugh, & Diener, 1977).

Despite the indirect link between an attack on a Bobo doll and aggression, Bandura (1973) has argued for the importance of the experiments in demonstrating the ways in which aggressive behaviors can be acquired. He makes the important distinction between *learning* and *performance* of a response. Presumably, when children observe the attacks, they learn or acquire a response. Subsequently, when interacting with living beings, they may or may not perform the acquired response. Many studies with adults attest to the importance of modeling (Bandura, 1973). Although most adults know how to be aggressive, their willingness to do so is often based on the presence of an aggressive model. The model may not teach the person how to be aggressive, but the model can disinhibit norms that run counter to aggression and serve as an example that "It's all right to be aggressive in this situation."

Those who explain aggression as a learned response claim that societies in which no aggressive behavior is manifested are evidence that learning, rather than instinct, plays a dominant role in aggression. A few such societies do exist. For example, in the United States and Canada, members of isolated communities such as the Amish, the Mennonites, and the Hutterites strive to achieve peaceful coexistence. The Hutterites advocate a life of pacifism; aggressive acts in their society go unrewarded (Bandura & Walters, 1963). Geoffrey Gorer (1968) has reviewed anthropological evidence of societies whose goal is peaceful isolation; these societies include the Arapesh of New Guinea, the Lepchas of Sikkim, and the Pygmies of central Africa.

The societies Gorer described share several characteristics that facilitate the development and maintenance of nonaggressive behavior. First, they tend to exist in rather inaccessible places that other groups do not covet as a living area. Whenever other groups have invaded their territory, the members of these societies have responded by retreating into even more inaccessible areas. Second, members of these societies are oriented toward the concrete pleasures of life—such as eating, drinking, and sex—and an adequate supply of these pleasures apparently satisfies their needs. Achievement or power needs are not encouraged in children: "The model for the growing child is of concrete performance and frank enjoyment, not of metaphysical symbolic achievements or of ordeals to be surmounted" (Gorer, 1968, p. 34). Third, these societies make few distinctions between males and females. Although differences between the roles of men and women exist in each of these societies, no attempt is made to project (for instance) an image of brave, aggressive masculinity.

Biology and Learning

The majority of societies in the world exhibit some form of aggression (Rohner, 1976). There is, of course, no reason to assume aggression results from *either* instinctual *or* social processes. The existence of nonaggressive societies reminds us of the malleability of human nature and the great diversity in "normal" behaviors from one society to another (Eisenberg, 1972). Both within and among societies, various conditions encourage or discourage the display of aggression.

Members of any society, for example, must learn how to use what Arlo Guthrie calls "implements of destruction" and may learn to use them either aggressively or nonaggressively. Aversive stimuli, including threats, produce physiological arousal that enables the individual equally to flee and to fight (Berkowitz & Heimer, 1989). Therefore, whatever instinctual readiness to aggress may exist among humans, it can surely be modified by learning experiences.

▶ Conditions That Influence Aggression

Both the biological and the social perspectives offer explanations for the fact that people are capable of aggression. Such general perspectives, however, do not enable us to determine specifically how that capability is implemented, nor do they enable us to determine the circumstances under which an individual will engage in aggressive behavior. In this section, we ask the question, "When and under what circumstances do people actually act in an aggressive manner?" The answer is not simple; there are many conditions that increase the probability of aggressive behavior. Some of these conditions relate to the motivational or affective state that the person is experiencing. Other conditions are external to the individual, a feature of the environment or the immediate circumstances. At the end of the section, we consider a model of the processes through which the various influences may operate.

Frustration

In 1939 a group of psychologists at Yale University (Dollard, Doob, Miller, Mowrer, & Sears, 1939) hypothesized that frustration causes aggression. More specifically, the **frustration-aggression hypothesis** postulated that "the occurrence of aggression always presupposes frustration" (Miller, 1941, pp. 337–338). Although these psychologists believed that aggression is always a consequence of some frustration, frustration may have other consequences as well. Neal Miller, one of the developers of this hypothesis, noted that aggression is one possible, but not inevitable, result of frustrating events. "Frustration produces instigations to a number of different types of responses, one of which is an instigation to some form of aggression" (1941, p. 338).

In their original formulation, the Yale theorists defined **frustration** as the state that emerges when circumstances interfere with a goal response. That is, frustration is the result of an organism's inability to complete a behavior sequence. For example, a rat accustomed to running down a particular path for food might experience frustration if it finds the path blocked. Similarly, a human who expects to be able to open a door would be frustrated upon discovering the door was locked. Even if the individual had a key and was able to unlock the door, the fact that unlocking the door was an unexpected part of the behavior sequence would produce frustration (Worchel, 1974).

Nor does it seem to matter whether the frustration comes from unexpected difficulty of the task itself or from interference by others. In one experiment, Russell Geen (1968) asked subjects to work on a jigsaw puzzle and manipulated the source of frustration. In one condition the puzzle had no solution; the task itself was frustrating. In another condition the task was solvable, but the experimenter's confederate continually interfered with subjects as they worked, preventing them from completing the puzzle. In both experimental conditions, subjects were more aggressive toward the confederate than the subjects in a control condition were.

Evidence derived from studies using both human and nonhuman subjects suggests that aggression may sometimes be caused by frustration (Azrin, Hutchinson, & Hake, 1966; Rule & Percival, 1971). For example, Arnold Buss (1963) subjected college students to three types of frustration: failing a task, losing an opportunity to win money, and missing a chance to earn a better grade. Each type of frustration led to approximately the same level of aggression. Therefore, frustration, the common element in the three conditions, was the most likely cause. In each condition, the level of aggression was greater than in a control condition in which subjects did not experience frustration. Yet the level of aggression exhibited was not very great in any case.

Perhaps the aggression was minimal because it could not be used to overcome the cause of the frustration. Buss (1961, 1967) suggests that frustration and aggression may be linked only when the aggression has *instrumental value*—that is, when aggressive behavior will help override the frustration. Other studies also have reported no increase in aggression as a result of the degrees of frustration produced in human subjects in the laboratory (Gentry, 1970; Taylor & Pisano, 1971).

Fairly mild frustration is unlikely to result in aggression; in contrast, intense frustration often leads to aggressive behavior. A field study by Mary Harris (1974) suggests the importance of frustration level. Harris had her confederates purposely cut in ahead of people standing at different points in lines at theaters and grocery stores. If the confederate cut in ahead of the person who was second in line, that person tended to become quite aggressive (verbally), whereas a person who was twelfth in line exhibited substantially fewer aggressive reactions. Presumably, when you are close to the checkout counter or the ticket window, interference is much more frustrating than when you still have a considerable way to go.

Aggressive responses also depend on how arbitrary the frustration is. In one demonstration of this relationship, Burstein and Worchel (1962) created a situation in which group members had difficulty completing a task. Group members whose progress was impeded by a member who had a hearing problem were much less aggressive than group members whose difficulty was caused by one member who appeared to be deliberately blocking the group's progress.

It seems clear, on the basis of several decades of research that have followed the original Yale experiments, that frustration is not sufficient in itself to cause aggression in all cases. Anger is a most important mediator of the frustration–aggression effect (Krebs & Miller, 1985): does the frustration or the blocking of the goal cause the person to feel angry? In a further modification of the original hypothesis, Leonard Berkowitz (1965b, 1969, 1971, 1989) emphasizes the interaction between environmental cues and internal cognitive and emotional states.

Berkowitz suggests that reaction to frustration creates "only a *readiness* for aggressive acts. Previously acquired aggressiveness habits can also establish this readiness" (1965b, p. 308). In other words, Berkowitz maintains that the occurrence of aggressive behavior is not solely dependent on frustration and that an intervening variable—readiness—must be added to the chain.

According to Berkowitz, another important factor is the presence in the environment of aggressive cues that trigger the expression of aggression. Frustration creates readiness in the form of anger; stimulus cues actually elicit aggression. Further, the cues themselves can increase the strength of the aggressive response, particularly when the aggressive response is impulsive (Zillmann, Katcher, & Milavsky, 1972). Although stimulus cues are not always needed for aggression to occur, Berkowitz would argue that they increase the probability of aggressive behavior.

Aggressive Cues: The Weapons Effect

A systematic research program conducted by Berkowitz and his colleagues at the University of Wisconsin has established considerable support for the position that aggressive cues elicit aggressive behavior. In a typical experiment, a male college student is introduced to another subject, who is actually a confederate of the experimenter. The confederate either angers the subject deliberately or treats him in a neutral manner. Immediately after this phase of the experiment, both persons watch a brief film clip—either a violent prizefight scene from the film *Champion* or a neutral film showing English canal boats or a track race. After watching the film clip, the subject has an opportunity to administer electrical shocks to the accomplice. Using this basic paradigm, Berkowitz and his colleagues have developed a variety of tactics to create aggressive cues in the environment.

In one experiment, for example, the accomplice was introduced either as a nonbelligerent speech major or as a physical education major who was interested in boxing. When the confederate was introduced as a boxer, the subjects administered more severe shocks (Berkowitz, 1965a). In another experiment, the confederate was introduced either as Kirk Anderson (presumably providing an association with Kirk Douglas, the lead actor in *Champion*) or as Bob Anderson. Again, the aggressive-cue value of the confederate affected the level of aggression the subject displayed. As you can see in Figure 10.1, subjects gave the most shocks when they were angered, when they had watched a violent film, and when the accomplice had the same name as the boxer in the film. In addition, subjects who had

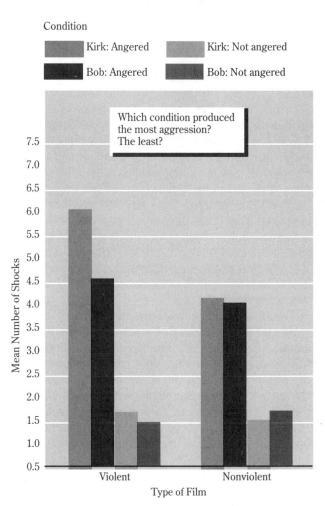

Figure 10.1 *The influence of aggressive cues on aggression.*
Source: "Some Aspects of Observed Aggression" by L. Berkowitz, 1965, *Journal of Personality and Social Psychology, 2,* pp. 359–369.

been angered were always more aggressive than those who had not been angered.

Other experiments in this series have focused on the aggressive-cue value of weapons (Berkowitz & LePage, 1967). In one such experiment, male university students received either one or seven electrical shocks from another student (confederate) and then were given an opportunity to administer shocks in return. When some subjects participated in the study, a rifle and a revolver were on a nearby table; for other subjects, no objects were present. As one might expect, the subjects who had been shocked more by the confederate were apt to administer more shocks in return. More important, the presence of the guns increased the average number of shocks administered from 4.67 to 6.07.

Critics have suggested that the weapons effect may be due to demand characteristics (see Chapter 2). There is evidence that the presence of weapons is not sufficient to produce aggression if the person fails to interpret the weapon appropriately; that is, as something designed to harm living things (Fraczek & Macaulay, 1971; Turner & Simons, 1974). Further, if the individual fears that a display of aggression will result in punishment or disapproval, the cues are less likely to be effective (Turner, Simons, Berkowitz, & Frodi, 1977). Yet beyond these qualifications, there is still evidence that the sight of weapons may increase aggressive behavior.

The weapons effect has important practical implications. One implication is that the free display of dangerous weapons poses an inherent danger. As Berkowitz has phrased it, "Guns not only permit violence, they can stimulate it as well. The finger pulls the trigger, but the trigger may also be pulling the finger" (Berkowitz, 1968, p. 22). Differences in homicide rates in Canada and the United States are consistent with Berkowitz's position. In Canada, where firearms such as revolvers and submachine guns must be registered and may not be owned for "protection," the homicide rate is considerably lower than in the United States. There are, of course, other differences between these countries, and we cannot be certain that the availability of guns is a major cause of homicides. Imprisonment, for example, is more likely in Canada than in the United States, and such policies may also be related to the frequency of homicide. However, when legislation in Jamaica included gun control and a ban on gun-related segments for television and movies, the number of violent crimes decreased considerably (Diener & Crandall, 1979).

General Arousal

The frustration-aggression model suggests that aggression is caused by a specific kind of emotion. Other models of aggression point to more general states of arousal that will increase the likelihood of aggressive behavior. These general models of arousal, which we discussed

in regard to emotional expression in Chapter 3, are typified by Dolf Zillmann's **excitation transfer theory** (Zillmann, 1979). According to this theory, arousal generated in one situation may be transferred to and intensify another emotional state. More specifically, Zillmann suggests that the expression of anger (or any other emotion, for that matter) depends on three factors: (1) the person's learned dispositions or habits; (2) some source of energization or arousal; and (3) the person's interpretation of the arousal state. Thus, the way we interpret an event is important in determining whether we act aggressively.

Zillmann has taken this analysis a step further, suggesting that energy may transfer from one situation to another. For example, imagine that you've just finished dancing to several lengthy songs. You're back at your table, cooling off from the exertion, and someone says something that *could* be considered an insult. What would you do? If you had just settled down at the table, you would probably do nothing. You might feel aroused, but you would attribute the arousal to your exercise on the dance floor. However, if the apparent insult came a few minutes later, you might no longer be thinking of the exercise—but some arousal might still remain. In this circumstance, that residual arousal could be transferred to the insulting incident, and you might react aggressively to your tormentor—more aggressively than if you had not just exerted yourself on the dance floor (Bryant & Zillmann, 1979).

Verbal and Physical Attack

Direct verbal and physical attacks are much more obvious influences on aggressive behavior. When someone yells at you for no apparent reason, are you likely to yell back? Or if someone walked up to you in the street and began to shove you, how would you react? In all probability, you would be tempted (and might well act) to retaliate with some form of verbal or physical aggression.

Attacks are a much more reliable provocation to aggressive behavior than frustration. For example, in the experiment in which Geen (1968) manipulated two types of frustration while subjects were working on a jigsaw puzzle, a third experimental condition was included in which the subjects were allowed to complete the puzzle (thus eliminating the possibility of frustra-

When someone yells at you for no apparent reason, are you likely to yell back?
David M. Grossman

tion). When the task was completed, however, the confederate proceeded to insult the subject, attacking both his intelligence and his motivation. Subsequent aggression toward the confederate was stronger in this condition than in either of the frustration conditions. In line with these findings, many laboratory investigations of aggressive behavior have included verbal attack before the assessment of aggression.

Stuart Taylor and his colleagues (Taylor, 1967; Taylor & Epstein, 1967) have also examined the effect of direct attack on subsequent aggression. In their experiments, the subjects were not asked to administer shocks to a passive learner; instead, subjects engaged in a two-person interaction in which both persons were allowed to administer shocks.[1] In general, these exper-

[1] In actuality, the subject's opponent was a confederate of the experimenter or was fictitious—the subject was told that another person was returning the shocks, but in fact the schedule of shocks was arranged by the experimenter.

iments provide clear evidence of reciprocity—subjects tended to match the level of shock their opponent delivered. If the opponent increased the level of shock, the subject also increased the intensity. Although the absolute level of shock can vary with certain factors—for example, both men and women are more reluctant to administer shock to a woman than to a man (Taylor & Epstein, 1967)—the general pattern of increases and decreases in response to the partner's pattern holds true.

We do not always retaliate immediately when another person attacks us. Remembering the discussion of attribution in Chapter 4, you may suspect that our explanations of an attacker's motives can affect our reactions. Research by Brendan Rule and her colleagues (Ferguson & Rule, 1983; Lysak, Rule, & Dobbs, 1989; Rule & Ferguson, 1984) provides strong support for the importance of such perceptions. As you might expect, perceived intent affects retaliation; we are more likely to retaliate against someone who we believe intentionally tried to harm us. Lysak, Rule, and Dobbs (1989), however, obtained evidence that perceived avoidability is an even more important determinant of blame than is perceived intent. If another causes harm, we attribute blame if we believe the other could, or should, have foreseen the consequences of the actions, even when we believe the person did not intend to cause harm.

In one demonstration of the role of attributions, college men received bursts of aversive noise from a male opponent in an experimental task (Dyck & Rule, 1978). The level of noise was described as either the typical amount administered by most people (high consensus) or an atypical amount (low consensus). A second variable that the experimenters manipulated was whether the opponent had any knowledge of the consequences of his action—whether he knew the type and level of noise he was imposing on the subject. Both factors affected the amount of aggressive behavior that subjects showed. Subjects showed less retaliation when they believed the behavior was typical (thus leading the attribution away from the particular individual) and when the subject believed that the opponent was unaware of the consequences of his actions. Beliefs about the intentions of one's attacker are important; intent implies foreseen consequences. We are more likely to retaliate if we believe an opponent intended to hurt us than if we think the person did not realize the pain he or she was causing (Greenwell & Dengerink, 1973; Ohbuchi & Kambara, 1985).

In fact, beliefs about foreseeability and intent are more influential than the actual harm suffered. Advance knowledge of mitigating circumstances is extremely effective in reducing a person's tendency to retaliate. Both verbal self-reports of anger and physiological measures of arousal show this deterrent effect. Consider an experiment by Ken-ichi Ohbuchi, Masuyo Kameda, and Nariyuki Agarie (1989), in which a laboratory assistant made mistakes that apparently caused the experimenter to believe the subjects were not very bright (thus causing intellectual harm). In one condition, the laboratory assistant apologized for the mistakes in front of the experimenter, which also removed the harmful impression the experimenter had formed. In another condition, the assistant apologized while the experimenter was out of the room, which meant the harmful impression remained. In a third condition, the assistant did not apologize, but the harm was removed by the experimenter's remark that the subject's performance was so poor that something must have gone wrong with the equipment. The subject was given an opportunity to retaliate against the assistant when completing an evaluation form by giving the assistant a low rating. Because the assistant's performance was the same in all conditions—she always made the same number of mistakes—any differences in the ratings assigned to her were presumably motivated by intent to cause her harm in the form of a loss of face with respect to her supervisor.

As you can see in Figure 10.2, the subjects retaliated more (gave lower ratings) when the assistant did not apologize. The effect for apology was obtained regardless of whether the harm caused by the assistant—the experimenter's belief that the subject was not very bright—was removed. Information regarding possible mitigating circumstances, including an apology, is less effective at reducing retaliation, though, if it comes after the pain has been experienced. At this point, attributions of intent and foreseeability may already be formed, and the later information may not effectively counter the earlier impression (Johnson & Rule, 1986).

Third-Party Instigation

Aggression doesn't always occur in isolation. Often witnesses and bystanders become involved in the interac-

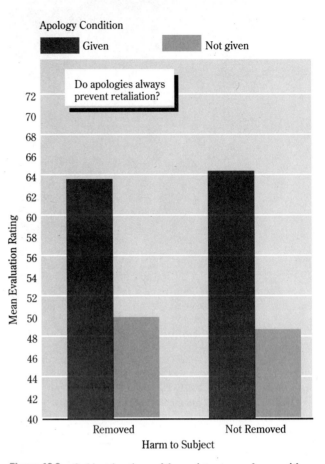

Figure 10.2 *Subjects' ratings of the assistant were lower without an apology, regardless of whether the assistant's harm was removed.*

Source: "Apology as Aggression Control: Its Role in Mediating Appraisal of and Response to Harm" by K. Ohbuchi, M. Kameda, and N. Agarie, 1989, *Journal of Personality and Social Psychology, 56,* pp. 219–227.

tion. At a prizefight, for example, members of the audience can enthusiastically urge their favorite fighter to pulverize the opponent. Newspapers frequently report incidents in which pedestrians urge a potential suicide victim to jump. What are the effects of such third-party instigations on the frequency and intensity of aggressive behavior?

In the obedience experiments described in Chapter 8, Stanley Milgram (1963, 1965, 1974) explored the effect of an experimenter's commands on the willingness of individuals (in this case, men in New Haven and Bridgeport, Connecticut) to administer shock to another person. In these studies, the effect of external pressure was clear: those who were prodded to continue delivered more, and more severe, shocks than subjects who acted alone.

Not all bystanders are as intrusive as Milgram or the crowd at a prizefight. Richard Borden (1975) found that the effect of inactive bystanders depends largely on the implicit values conveyed by the observers. For example, in one case, male subjects participating in the standard shock experiment were observed by either a male or a female student. Subjects who were observed by a man showed a significantly higher level of aggression than subjects who were observed by a woman. After the male observer left, the subjects reduced their level of aggression, whereas subjects' behaviors were relatively unaffected by the departure of the woman. Why did the gender of the observer have an effect? Borden hypothesized that the norms of our society implicitly suggest that men approve of violence, whereas women are opposed to it.

To test this hypothesis of implicit approval, Borden conducted a second experiment in which the observer belonged either to a karate club (someone who might approve aggression) or to a peace organization (someone who might not approve aggression). In the second experiment, the gender of the observer was also varied, so that both men and women assumed the aggressive and pacifistic roles. When the observer's organizational affiliation was explicit, the gender of the observer had no effect, but the organizational membership was influential. Subjects who were observed by a member of the karate club were more aggressive than subjects who were observed by a member of a peace organization, regardless of the observer's gender. Again, the departure of the aggressive instigator led to a decrease in shock levels, but the departure of the pacifist resulted in no increase in shocks.

Turning the tables slightly, it is also true that the aggressor can affect bystanders who instigate aggression. Jacqueline Gaebelein, who later published as Jacqueline White, conducted a series of studies examining the behavior of the person who instigates aggression (Gaebelein, 1973, 1978; Gaebelein & Hay, 1974; Mander & Gaebelein, 1977; White & Gruber, 1982). Her studies show that instigators will urge more aggression if their recommendations are followed. In contrast, if the target of the instigation refuses to be aggressive, the instigator will reduce or cease attempts to foster aggres-

sion. Thus, cooperation by the target of instigation leads to an increased level of violence, whereas noncooperation tends to decrease the level of hostility. Another way to reduce hostility is to involve the instigator directly in the situation by allowing the instigator both to give and to receive shocks. Instigators tend to "chill" when they themselves are vulnerable to shock (Gaebelein & Hay, 1974).

In summary, direct urging by an observer or audience member will increase the amount of aggression a person displays. Further, an observer who reflects aggressive values can cause increases in aggressive behavior, much like the weapons effect described earlier. Unlike weapons, however, the instigator is not totally removed—his or her behavior is affected by the aggressor's cooperation or noncooperation, and the instigations may wane when the recommended aggression is not forthcoming.

Deindividuation

When people can't be identified, they are more likely to perform antisocial acts. For example, Philip Zimbardo (1970) conducted an experiment in which four students believed they shared responsibility for giving another student electric shocks. Zimbardo dressed half the subjects in hoods; these students never gave their names, and they performed the experiment in the dark. The others had their identities emphasized: the experimenter greeted them by name, they wore large name tags, and they interacted on a first-name basis. All subjects were free to give as much or as little shock to the other student as they wished, but subjects in the hooded condition gave more shock than did subjects in the name-tag condition. Other experiments have used similar manipulations of anonymity and have found that people are more likely to express both physical and verbal aggression when their own identity is not stressed (Cannavale, Scarr, & Pepitone, 1970; Festinger, Pepitone, & Newcomb, 1952; Mann, Newton, & Innes, 1982).

In discussing **deindividuation,** a state of relative anonymity in which individuals cannot be singled out or identified, Zimbardo (1970) suggested that deindividuation minimizes concerns with evaluation and thus weakens the normal controls that are based on guilt, shame, and fear. More recently, investigators have pointed specifically to the concept of private self-awareness (in some respects, the opposite of anonymity; see Chapter 3). That is, when one's focus is shifted to external cues, private self-awareness decreases (Prentice-Dunn & Rogers, 1982), and standards for socially appropriate behavior are less likely to be compared with one's current behavior. No longer as tuned to their standards, people seem more willing to engage in aggressive behavior.

We noted earlier that bystanders sometimes urge on those contemplating suicide. To understand more about this aspect of group behavior, Leon Mann (1981) analyzed newspaper reports of twenty-one cases in which a crowd was present when someone was attempting to commit suicide by jumping from a building, a bridge, or a tower. In ten of these cases, the crowd had urged the person to jump. Two factors were significantly associated with the baiting crowd. First, crowds were more likely to urge the victim to jump in the evening hours—baiting was more common after 6:00 P.M. than earlier in the day. Second, baiting was less likely when the potential suicide victim was higher than the twelfth floor of the building. Both nighttime and distance from the victim are factors that increase deindividuation, and therefore aggression. (If the victim is too far away, however, potential hecklers may realize that their cries will not be heard.) Like distance, the cover of darkness increases anonymity, and, in this case, it made aggression more likely.

The concept of deindividuation can be applied to the victim as well as to the aggressor. For example, Milgram (1965) found that people were more willing to administer electric shocks when they could not see the victim and when the victim could not see them. In contrast, Mann (1981) found that in the few cases when bystanders were very close to the person, baiting did not occur. In some ways, "long distance" aggression is dehumanized—because people cannot see the consequences of their actions, these actions may be easier to perform. It is probably significant that the genocide of World War II involved gas chambers that could be controlled from a distance and that hoods are often placed over the heads of execution victims. During the Persian Gulf War that followed the Iraqi invasion of Kuwait, U.S. and other allied military spokespeople reported the number of tanks and aircraft that were destroyed or "lost," presumably to avoid arousing antiwar sentiment that might stem from the realization that people were

in those tanks and aircraft. Even when aggression is not severe, such as honking the horn at a driver whose stalled car is blocking one's path, those who cannot see the "victim" in the other car are more likely to honk (Turner, Layton, & Simons, 1975). Clearly, aggression is more probable and more tolerable when we cannot see the consequences of our actions.

Drugs

Drugs are widely used in our society. Popular wisdom suggests that alcohol facilitates aggression, and cartoons of the hostile drunk are common. The crack-cocaine user who capriciously aggresses against others has become commonplace in movies and newspapers. Similarly, many people believe that marijuana has the opposite effect—that it tends to "mellow people out" and minimize any tendencies toward aggression.

For marijuana, at least, the popular wisdom appears to be close to the mark. Stuart Taylor and his colleagues have conducted a series of studies in which various dosages of either alcohol or THC (tetrahydrocannabinol, the major active ingredient of marijuana) are administered to subjects before they participate in an aggression experiment (Myerscough & Taylor, 1985; Shuntich & Taylor, 1972; Taylor, 1986; Taylor & Gammon, 1975; Taylor, Gammon, & Capasso, 1976). In the aggression situation, subjects compete against a partner in a reaction-time experiment; each player has an opportunity to shock the player who loses on each turn. These specific conditions are important to remember because it appears that effects are found only when a person is provoked or attacked (Taylor, Gammon, & Capasso, 1976).

What happens when alcohol or THC is present in the bloodstream of a potential attacker? As Figure 10.3 shows, the two substances have quite different effects (Taylor, Vardaris, et al., 1976). Low doses of alcohol (the equivalent of one cocktail) actually reduce aggression compared with a group that has had no alcohol. Larger doses of alcohol (equivalent to three cocktails) have the opposite effect: subjects who had consumed large doses of alcohol gave substantially stronger shocks. Marijuana has a different effect. Small amounts of THC (0.1 milligram per kilogram of body weight) had no effect on aggressive behavior, and larger doses (0.3 milligrams per kilogram of body weight) tended to

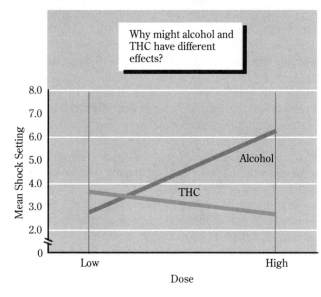

Figure 10.3 *Mean shock setting as a function of high and low doses of alcohol and THC.*

Source: "The Effects of Alcohol and Delta-9-Tetrahydrocannabinol on Human Physical Aggression" by S. P. Taylor, R. M. Vardaris, A. B. Rawtich, C. B. Gammon, J. W. Cranston, and A. I. Lubetkin, 1976, *Aggressive Behavior, 2,* pp. 153–161.

suppress aggressive behavior. Still higher doses of marijuana (0.4 milligrams per kilogram) do not facilitate aggression either, but rather decrease the individual's willingness to retaliate against an aggressor (Myerscough & Taylor, 1985). Amphetamines appear to have little effect on aggression (Taylor, 1986), but laboratory research does not take into account the possibility of aggression resulting from crimes committed to obtain illegal substances.

Environmental Conditions

Conditions in the environment often affect people's moods. For example, you may complain that you feel grouchy because the air conditioning in your room doesn't work on a hot day or because the noise of construction outside your window is distracting. Environmental conditions affect behavior as well as moods. In Chapter 14 we will consider several ways in which the environment influences behavior. Here we limit ourselves to the more specific question: Can environmental conditions such as noise, air pollution, and extreme temperatures influence the likelihood that a person will act aggressively toward others?

Unpleasant levels of noise can lead to an increase in aggressive behavior. Subjects exposed to loud bursts of noise in a laboratory experiment, for example, delivered significantly higher levels of shock to a partner than subjects exposed to either low-level noise or no noise at all (Donnerstein & Wilson, 1976). In general, these increases in aggression are found only if subjects are provoked or angered. As in the case of alcohol, the external stimulus in itself is not sufficient to produce aggression. It does lower the threshold, however, so that when an instigation to aggression is present, the aggressive behavior is displayed more readily.

Unpleasant air quality—smog, smoke, haze—also affects the tendency toward aggression. Air quality can be assessed by measuring the ozone level, an index of the level of pollutants in the air. Using this measure, James Rotton and James Frey (1985) conducted an archival study that revealed a relationship between weather and violent crime. As the ozone level increased, so did reports of family disturbances. With some regularity, days of high temperatures and low winds (which prevent the dissolution of noxious air pollutants) preceded violent episodes.

Many people have also suggested a relationship between temperature and violence. During the extensive outbreak of civil disturbances in the United States in the 1960s, the mass media frequently emphasized the "long hot summer" effect. Heat was cited as a cause of riots. Indeed, the majority of disturbances did occur in summer (U.S. Riot Commission, 1968).

The actual relationship between temperature and aggression is not quite so simple, however, and the form of the relationship varies between laboratory and field settings. In a series of experiments, Robert Baron and his colleagues (Baron, 1972; Baron & Bell, 1975, 1976; Bell & Baron, 1974, 1976) found that under some conditions, heat increases the tendency toward aggression, even in subjects who have not been angered. Under other conditions, however, higher temperatures seem to decrease the tendency toward aggression. Although the initial set of findings was somewhat confusing, Baron (1977) has provided an intriguing explanation that appears to incorporate all the findings: he suggests that aggression is mediated by the level of negative affect or discomfort that a person experiences and that the relation between this discomfort and aggression is curvilinear. In other words, at very low or very high levels of discomfort, aggression is minimized. Aggression is most likely to occur at intermediate levels of discomfort.

Other laboratory findings have supported this complex explanation. For example, Palamarek and Rule (1979) either insulted or did not insult college men in a room that was either fairly comfortable (about 73°F) or unreasonably warm (about 96°F). When they were given a choice of tasks to perform, the men who had been insulted were more likely to choose a task that allowed them to aggress against their partners when the temperature was comfortable, but they were less likely to choose the aggressive task when the room was excessively warm. Again, these results support the curvilinear interpretation: moderate arousal, caused by *either* insult or heat, leads to greater aggression, but when both factors are present *or* when both are absent, less aggression occurs.

An alternative explanation for these findings, however, has been suggested by Craig and Dona Anderson (1984). Subjects in the laboratory are, of course, aware that they are in an experiment. In most cases, they also are aware that the experiment has something to do with the effects of temperature because subjects must be informed about any risk or aversive conditions before they agree to participate. Consequently, the subject who experiences uncomfortably high temperatures and who is then given the opportunity to be aggressive toward another student may well guess what the experiment is about. Having decided that the experimenter wanted to see if they would be more aggressive, these subjects may consciously resist the aggressive choice. Thus, the curvilinear relationship Baron and his colleagues reported could be an artifact of the experimental procedure.

The debate over the relationship between temperature and aggression also has included data collected outside the laboratory. In one of the first tests of this relationship, Baron and Ransberger (1978) identified the instances of collective violence in the United States between 1967 and 1971. Then they obtained records of the average temperatures on the days when the violence occurred. Their findings supported Baron's contention that temperature and aggression are related in a curvilinear manner: riots are more likely to occur as the days get hotter—but only up to a point.

This conclusion has not gone unchallenged. Carlsmith and Anderson (1979) suggested that Baron and Ransberger did not take into account the number of days in different temperature ranges. In other words, if 80-degree days are more common than 90-degree days, simple probability would lead us to expect more riots in the 80-degree periods than in the 90-degree periods. By using simple probability theory, Carlsmith and Anderson calculated the likelihood of a riot for each temperature interval. Their results suggest a simple linear relation—the higher the temperature, the more likely a riot.

In further support for the linear argument, Craig and Dona Anderson (1984) collected data on temperatures and violent crimes—specifically, rape and murder—in Houston between 1980 and 1982. Their findings, shown in Figure 10.4, clearly support the contention that the relationship between aggression and temperature is more linear than curvilinear. To test the hypothesis further, these investigators considered the ratio of aggressive crimes to total crimes as it relates to temperature. Again they found a linear relationship, suggesting that it is aggressive crimes, rather than crimes in general, that increase when the temperature rises. There is, of course, an upper limit to this relationship. At a temperature of 130 degrees, for example, few people would want to move, let alone be aggressive. Within the normal range of temperatures, however, aggression seems to rise with the temperature.

Most recently, Craig Anderson (1989) reexamined the findings of a variety of laboratory and field studies. He concluded: "The massive body of work reviewed in this article demonstrates two main points. First, temperature effects are direct; they operate at the individual level. Second, temperature effects are important; they influence the most antisocial behaviors imaginable" (p. 94). He also concluded there is not yet sufficient information to select one particular model as the best way to explain the effects of temperature. Most of the available explanations received some empirical support, indicating that explaining why heat instigates aggression will be much more complicated than demonstrating that heat instigates aggression.

The Role of Anger in Aggression

In this section we consider the extent to which anger and its associated emotions contribute to aggression. Is

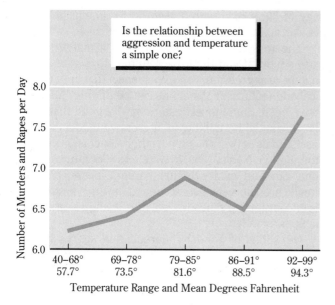

Figure 10.4 *The relationship between aggressive crime (murder and rape) and maximum daily temperature.*
Source: "Ambient Temperature and Violent Crime: Tests of the Linear and Curvilinear Hypotheses" by C. A. Anderson and D. C. Anderson, 1984, *Journal of Personality and Social Psychology, 46,* pp. 91–97.

on several factors, one of which is the network of associations between aggression and anger in memory.

Figure 10.5 depicts Berkowitz's **cognitive-neoassociationistic model** of the role of anger and aggression. According to this model, the specific emotion, anger, does not instigate aggression directly; negative affect does that. Instead, to the extent that anger occurred together with previous aggression, the experience of anger can prime (that is, make more accessible) thoughts about aggressive behaviors (Rule, Taylor, & Dobbs, 1987).

This priming effect is bi-directional; thinking about aggressive behavior can also prime feelings of anger. In a series of experiments, Berkowitz and Karen Heimer (1989) demonstrated that asking their subjects to contemplate aggressive actions while writing a brief essay in defense of punishment produced as strong an experience of anger as did an aversive stimulus (immersing one's hand in cold water). When these subjects were given an opportunity to aggress against a simulated employee by delivering blasts of noise into the employee's headphones, those who had written about the aggressive essay topic delivered more blasts than did subjects who had written an essay about cold weather and snow. In a different experiment, subjects asked to think about an annoying situation reported

anger a necessary ingredient of aggression? If not, what role does it play? To answer these questions, we rely heavily on the cognitive-neoassociationistic model developed by Leonard Berkowitz (1983a, 1983b) and his colleagues.

As we have just seen, the conditions associated with increased aggression constitute a long list. Some conditions—such as heat and air pollution—are aversive because of inherent properties, and some—such as verbal insults and interference with goals—are aversive because we have learned to associate unpleasant outcomes with them. Whatever the reason, aversive stimuli by definition produce negative affect or a general dislike. Despite this connection, not all individuals begin to beat another person, say, whenever they don't like the air or don't like someone who cuts in ahead of them in a line. According to Berkowitz, the key is that negative affect produces inclinations toward avoidance as well as toward aggression. That is, sometimes we move away from aversive stimuli, and sometimes we lash out aggressively. Which reaction prevails depends

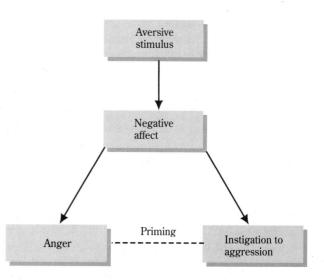

Figure 10.5 *Anger and instigation to aggression independently result from negative affect but are also associated in memory.*

more anger and were more aggressive than subjects who thought about a neutral situation.

Although thinking about aggression led to more intense feelings of anger, Berkowitz and Heimer's subjects did not always behave more aggressively when they were angrier. In line with the old adage to "count to ten" before acting, other investigators (for example, Troccoli, 1986) also have reported a decrease in willingness to aggress when individuals focus on their feelings, including anger. According to the cognitive-neoassociationistic model, the experience of anger also primes beliefs about appropriate behavior. The longer people dwell on their anger, the more likely they are to consider social constraints on aggression.

On the other hand, Thomas Johnson and Brendan Rule (1986) have shown that retaliatory aggression, with or without anger, is determined primarily by the extent to which an individual believes the other person has violated social or personal expectations for behavior. We may become angry when someone causes us to spill a drink on ourselves, but we may not retaliate if we believe that it was an accident—that the other person violated no rules for proper behavior. The anger may prime our beliefs about social constraint, which generally include the notion that punishment is an inappropriate response to an accident. In this case, anger reduces the likelihood of aggression. If, however, we believe the other's actions were intentional—a clear violation of social propriety—the anger produced by the aversive stimulus could increase aggression by priming thoughts about "teaching a lesson." Anger, though produced independent of instigation to aggression, can be associated both with increases and with decreases in aggressive behavior.

Individual Differences in Aggressive Behavior

Not all individuals are equally aggressive. Although we have been discussing conditions that will increase the probability that any individual will become more aggressive, it is also true that some people are generally more aggressive than others. In fact, evidence exists that individual differences in aggressive behavior are quite stable over time, particularly among men (Huesmann, Lagerspetz, & Eron, 1984; Olweus, 1979, 1984b). Thus, the 8-year-old boy who is named frequently by classmates as one who pushes and shoves other children is more likely than other boys to become, by the age of 30, a man with a record of criminal behavior, abuse, and traffic violations (Eron, 1987).

The reasons for this stability are a matter of disagreement. If you think back to our discussion of the nature of aggression, you may suspect that both biological and cultural explanations can be offered. And they have been. Some investigators have argued that there is substantial heritability in aggressive tendencies and use studies of twins to support their conclusions (Rushton, Fulker, Neale, Nias, & Eysenck, 1986). In contrast, one can find evidence that parents, peers, and the media provide a consistent context in which aggression is encouraged or discouraged, thus leading to stable reactions as well.

Questions of gender differences in aggressive behavior often are debated on this same ground. In an early review of the literature, Eleanor Maccoby and Carol Jacklin (1974) concluded that men are the more aggressive sex and that the behavioral differences found may result from differences in biological readiness for aggressive behavior. More recent investigators are not so sure. Alice Eagly and Valerie Steffen (1986) have also concluded that men are more aggressive than women but that the differences observed in social-psychological research are small and not always consistent. Gender differences are greater when the issue is physical aggression than when verbal and other types of psychological harm are considered. These investigators also find substantial differences between women and men in their beliefs about aggression. Women, for example, feel more guilty and anxious about behaving aggressively. They are also more concerned about the harm they may cause their victims and more worried about possible danger to themselves. These beliefs, suggest Eagly and Steffen, may mediate the extent to which men and women consciously choose to behave aggressively.

Kenneth Dodge and Nicki Crick (1990), after reviewing the literature on aggression among children, have suggested that individual differences in aggression may stem from differences in abilities for processing social information. Specifically, Dodge and Crick point to differences in individuals' abilities (1) to interpret social cues and others' behaviors, (2) to generate possible responses in social situations, and (3) to decide which response to put into action. As we noted in Chapter 4, several processes are involved in making attributions about intentions underlying others' behaviors. Some of these processes include biases, such as the **fundamental attribution bias** (Ross & Fletcher, 1985), the tendency to prefer dispositional attributions for others' actions. Aggressive children and adolescents appear to have what Dodge and Crick refer to as a "hostile attributional bias." In both simulated and actual situations, aggressive children are more likely than nonaggressive children to attribute hostile intent to others' actions. Their attributions about others' intentions also are generally less accurate than those of nonaggressive individuals (Crick & Dodge, 1989; Dodge & Coie, 1987; Dodge & Tomlin, 1987; Sancilo, Plumert, & Hartup, 1989).

In most social situations, several possible responses are available to any individual. For example, if someone bumps into us, the response alternatives include both nonaggressive actions—ignoring the incident or moving away—and aggressive actions—calling the person a name or "bumping" the person in retaliation. You may recall from the discussion of **scripts** in Chapter 4 that some alternatives are more accessible in memory (that is, more easily recalled) than others. Dodge and Crick noted that aggressive responses appear to be more accessible for aggressive children than for nonaggressive children. That is, aggressive individuals may have more difficulty in thinking of nonaggressive responses to social situations, presumably because aggressive responses are more familiar to them (Logan, 1989).

Similarly, aggressive children differ from nonaggressive children in their evaluations of aggressive responses and in their confidence in their ability to engage in nonaggressive responses. Several investigators (Asarnow & Callan, 1985; Crick & Ladd, 1989) have found that, compared with those of nonaggressive children, aggressive and rejected children's attitudes toward aggressive behaviors are more positive. At the same time, their attitudes toward nonaggressive behaviors are more negative. Crick and Dodge (1989) have also reported that aggressive children are more confident about their ability to perform aggressive behaviors successfully. On the other hand, aggressive children are less confident than nonaggressive children in their ability to withdraw from a situation involving potential conflict.

Taking into account all three aspects of social information processing adds considerably to our understanding of individual differences in aggression. For example, in studies attempting to predict aggressive behavior, investigators have been able to account for as much as 60% of individual variation in children's aggressive behavior by measuring abilities for processing social information (Dodge, Pettit, McClaskey, & Brown, 1986; Slaby & Guerra, 1988). Again, we see the importance of avoiding oversimplified explanations for aggression. In the following section, we will examine one possible source of individual differences in interpreting social cues, accessing responses, and evaluating alternative responses.

▶ Violence and the Mass Media

On March 30, 1981, John W. Hinckley, Jr., stood outside a Washington, D.C., hotel among a crowd of reporters and well-wishers waiting for President Ronald Reagan to appear. When the president came out of the hotel, Hinckley fired, wounding the president, his press secretary, and two other persons. Why did he do it? This disturbed young man apparently identified with the protagonist of the movie *Taxi Driver.* He is reported to have seen the movie more than a dozen times and to have fallen in love with an actress who had a featured role in the film. By shooting the president, Hinckley somehow thought he could make part of the film's fiction become his own reality.

Some years earlier, a 15-year-old boy in Florida killed his 82-year-old neighbor for no apparent reason. The defendant's lawyers claimed that the boy was legally insane at the time of the murder as a result of watching too much television. (Their defense was unsuccessful, however, and the boy was convicted of murder.)

David Phillips (1986) found that suicides in the United States increase dramatically during the month in which stories about suicides appear on the front page of the *New York Times.* Similarly, in California, the numbers of noncommercial airplane fatalities and motor vehicle accidents increase by as much as 35% in the week following reports of suicides in San Francisco and Los Angeles newspapers.

Do presentations of violence in the media encourage the observer to act aggressively? Is aggression in our society greater than it would be if such presentations were not available? In this section we consider answers to these questions, which have caused heated debate in academic circles as well as among the general public.

Although newspapers can be a source of influence, most of the debate has focused on two issues: (1) the influence of televised violence on aggressive behavior in children, and (2) the influence of pornographic films on aggression toward women.

Television Violence and Aggression in Children

In a small village on the Ivory Coast, an old African man watched a battery-powered television set at a local schoolhouse. After several hours of viewing mostly imported American programs, the man asked with some perplexity, "Why are whites always stabbing, shooting, and punching one another?" (Odino, 1986).

The prevalence of violence on television is indisputable. Violent acts shown on prime-time television average eight per hour. On children's Saturday morning cartoons, a violent act occurs every two minutes. It has been estimated that by age 16 the average child will have witnessed more than 13,000 killings on television (Liebert & Schwartzberg, 1977). The proliferation of cable stations and in-home videocassette recorders has further increased the availability of violence on one's television screen (Milavsky, 1988). Nor are violent acts limited to fiction. For example, in the early months of 1991 U.S. news programs regularly replayed videotapes of "smart" bombs and missiles destroying Iraqi communications centers, bunkers, and underground hangars. The videotapes were recorded by cameras in the planes that released the bombs and missiles. Though viewers could not see the violence done to the humans inside the buildings, the implication was unavoidable. What had once been the purview of computer games had become a reality.

The first evidence that witnessed aggression could lead to aggressive behavior came from Bandura's studies of children's behavior with a Bobo doll. In some of these studies, the aggressive model was a live actor who was in the room with the child; in others, the model was shown on film or in the form of a cartoon character (Bandura, Ross, & Ross, 1961, 1963). In all cases, children who watched a model acting aggressively were more likely to engage in similar aggression against the Bobo doll.

In studying the possible link between media violence and subsequent aggression, investigators adopted two strategies. First, they continued to perform experiments, but they began to use actual film and television material instead of the more artificial Bobo-doll sequences. Second, many investigators have conducted field studies of actual television viewing patterns and have used quasi-experimental designs to analyze the results.

Within the laboratory setting, investigators were able to define some of the factors related to the acquisition and display of aggressive behavior. For example, some investigators have suggested that aggressive behavior follows the viewing of filmed violence only if the film justifies the violence it shows (Berkowitz & Alioto, 1973). Other factors that appear important are the degree to which the observer identifies with the aggressor in the film, the initial aggressiveness of the observer, the degree to which the aggressor is portrayed as having some redeeming features, and the presence of cues that remind the observer of portions of the televised violence (Geen & Stonner, 1971; Josephson, 1987; Liebert & Schwartzberg, 1977; Turner & Berkowitz, 1972).

A few experiments have been conducted in more natural settings outside of the laboratory. A boarding school in Belgium was one such site. During a designated "Movie Week," investigators manipulated the amount of violent content shown on television (Leyens, Camino, Parke, & Berkowitz, 1975). Teenaged boys who lived in four small dormitories at the boarding school were observed before Movie Week started, and their aggressive behavior was recorded. Aggressive behavior tended to be high in two of the dormitories and relatively low in the other two. During Movie Week, the television sets the boys normally watched were disconnected, and special movies were shown instead. Boys in two of the dormitories (one high in aggressive behavior, one low) watched only films that were saturated with violence, including *Bonnie and Clyde* and *The Dirty Dozen*. The residents of the other two dormitories saw nonviolent films, such as *La Belle Américaine*. Observers then rated the amount of each boy's aggressive behavior during Movie Week and the week that followed it.

Physical aggression increased among the boys who saw the violent films. The authors concluded that "the films evoked among the spectators the kind of aggression they had been exposed to" (Leyens et al., 1975, p. 353). Verbal aggression, however, increased only among the residents of the aggressive dormitory who were shown violent films. Residents of the nonaggressive dormitory who saw the violent films actually exhibited a decrease in verbal aggression, perhaps because the violence in the films reminded them of the dangers of aggression. As might be expected, the effects of the films were more pronounced shortly after residents saw them than they were much later. Other studies conducted in the United States have produced similar findings (Parke, Berkowitz, Leyens, West, & Sebastian, 1977).

Field studies, as we know, sacrifice some control, but they allow investigators to consider people's natural viewing habits. The basic strategy of these studies is to obtain information about the amount and type of television programming watched and to relate those data to some measure of an individual's aggressive behavior. Despite considerable debate, the bulk of the evidence from these studies supports a relationship between media violence and aggression: children who watch more violence on television are more aggressive (Freedman, 1984, 1986; Friedrich-Cofer & Huston, 1986; Roberts & Maccoby, 1985; Singer & Singer, 1981). This relationship has been observed not only in the United States but also in Finland, Poland, and Australia (Eron, 1982).

If only this kind of correlational data were available, we could not be sure that media violence really causes aggression. Perhaps children who are more aggressive choose to watch more violent television fare. In fact, the causality is bi-directional, as sophisticated longitudinal research designs have demonstrated (Eron, 1982; Huesmann, Lagerspetz, & Eron, 1984). In these research designs, investigators first observe children as young as age 8 and assess their aggressiveness and the amount of time they spend viewing television. Then some years later (when the subjects have reached age 18 for example), the investigators again assess aggressiveness and amount of television watching. Applying statistical techniques, investigators can then determine whether the amount of television the child watches at age 8 is related to the amount of aggressive behavior shown at 18. These correlations are statistically significant, often more significant than the two measures that were assessed at the same time. In other words, the amount of time an 8-year-old watches television tells us more about how aggressive that child will be at 18 than

it does about how aggressive the child is now (Eron, 1980). Such evidence does not show that viewing televised violence is the only cause of aggression, but it has become quite clear that it is one cause.

Why does viewing televised violence have this effect? What psychological processes can explain this relationship? Observational learning is one explanation. While watching televised models, we learn a set of behaviors that we can imitate later. The degree to which these behaviors are acquired and later displayed is affected by several factors. For example, children who believe that violent TV shows portray life as it really is are more likely to demonstrate aggressive behavior. The child who identifies strongly with the aggressive characters in a show is also more likely to be aggressive (Huesmann, Lagerspetz, & Eron, 1984).

Cognitive explanations can also be offered. Frequent observation of violence on television may make aggression themes more accessible in memory. According to Berkowitz's cognitive-neoassociationistic model discussed earlier, television may be a priming device. With violent thoughts and schemas more readily available, the individual may be more likely to engage in behaviors with an aggressive tone. Nor is this effect limited to children. Brad Bushman and Russell Geen (1990) demonstrated in two experiments that male and female college students exposed to scenes that were clearly violent produced more aggressive cognitions and emotional reactions than students who were not exposed to violent scenes. Then, too, frequent exposure to violent material may cause the individual to become desensitized, less concerned and anxious about the consequences of potentially harmful actions (Berkowitz, 1984).

On the basis of evidence collected through various research methods, it seems reasonable to conclude that the viewing of television violence can increase people's tendency to be aggressive, both immediately afterward and at some distance in the future. Yet it is also important to recognize that this link is not inevitable. Not all children who watch violence on television will grow up to be aggressive adults. Wendy Josephson (1987) has found that among nonaggressive children violence may prime social norms against aggression and reduce the extent to which an individual acts out behavioral scripts learned from televised violence. Similarly, Bushman and Geen (1990) found that reactions to viewing moderate violence increased violent cognitions among individuals who scored high on a personality measure of hostility, but the same scenes decreased violent cognitions among those who scored low on the hostility scale.

Researchers also have explored ways to weaken the link between viewing violence and acting aggressively (Singer & Singer, 1983). For example, if a child watches violence on television in the presence of an adult who condemns the violence, that child is less likely to behave aggressively in later situations (Hicks, 1968; Horton & Santogrossi, 1978). On the other hand, condoning or encouraging comments made by an adult can lead to more aggressive behavior by the child. The behavior of children's peers may also be influential (Leyens, Herman, & Dunand, 1982). Leonard Eron (1982) has experimented with short training sessions in which children are helped to discriminate television fantasy from real-life events, learning, for example, how special effects are used to simulate violence. His findings are encouraging, suggesting that a year later children who had gone through the three-hour training session were less aggressive than a comparable group of children who had not had the training. Programs such as these may be important keys to the control of aggressive behavior.

Pornography and Aggression toward Women

During the past few decades, pornographic material has become much more common, including scenes of rape, coercion, and the exercise of power in both books and films. We define **pornography** as a particular type of erotic material—material that combines elements of sexuality and aggression and in which force or coercion is used to accomplish the sexual act. What effect does this kind of material have on aggressive behavior toward other people, particularly toward women, who are usually portrayed as the victims of aggression?

Freud was one of the first to suggest that sexual behavior and aggression are closely linked. He stated that "the sexuality of most men shows an admixture of aggression, of a desire to subdue" (1938, p. 659). Psychoanalytic theory has continued to argue for this connection, as exemplified in the following statement: "Hostility, overt or hidden, is what generates and enhances sexual excitement, and its absence leads to sexual indifference and boredom" (Stoller, 1976, p. 903).

The U.S. President's Commission on Obscenity and Pornography (1970), appointed to determine whether a link exists between erotic material and violence, concluded that there is no such link. Later research has modified that conclusion. A widely publicized study in Denmark, for example, considered the frequency of sex offenses before and after restrictions on the sale of pornographic materials were lifted (Kutchinsky, 1973). The initial findings of this "natural experiment" suggested that sex crimes declined markedly after the restrictions were eliminated, and the study gave rise to a "safety valve" theory (Kronhausen & Kronhausen, 1964). It was argued that because it was easier to obtain pornographic materials, potential sex offenders may have derived sufficient sexual satisfaction from such materials, thereby reducing sex crimes. However, later figures from Denmark showed an increase, rather than a decrease, in rape after pornographic materials became readily available (Bachy, 1976). Because these data are correlational, we cannot be certain that the lifting of restrictions on pornography caused the increase in sex crimes in Denmark. These findings do, however, pose questions concerning the safety-valve theory.

More conclusive answers to the question of the relationship of pornography and violence come from the extensive research program of Edward Donnerstein and his colleagues (Donnerstein, 1982; Malamuth & Donnerstein, 1982, 1984). Their findings show very consistently that men who are exposed to pornographic materials will be more aggressive toward women in subsequent interactions. Let us consider one of these experiments by Donnerstein and Berkowitz (1981) in some detail.

Male college students believed they were participating in an experiment on stress and learning, in which they would be paired with either a male or a female student. In the initial stage of the experiment, the subjects were asked to write an essay. Then each subject's partner was asked to evaluate the essay, indicating a judgment by administering shocks to the subject. The partner gave a high number of shocks, indicating a negative evaluation. In the next stage of the experiment, the subjects were exposed to one of four films: a neutral talk-show interview, an erotic film depicting sexual intercourse with no aggressive content, or one of two pornographic films that combined aggression and sexuality by depicting a woman being slapped and sexually attacked. One of these pornographic films ended with the woman smiling at her attackers. In the other pornographic film, the woman was clearly suffering at the end of the film. After viewing one of these films, the subject was returned to the "learning task" and given the opportunity to be aggressive toward (that is, to shock) his partner. Figure 10.6 shows the results of this experiment.

As Figure 10.6 shows, aggression levels varied markedly with the gender of the target. When the male subject was paired with another man, none of the sexual films aroused significantly more aggression than the neutral film. With a female partner, in contrast, both pornographic films dramatically increased the man's level of aggression. But what if the male subject had not been angered? Is a state of anger necessary for such a display of aggression against women? Donnerstein and Berkowitz (1981) conducted a second study to answer these questions. Using the same four films, they found that nonangered men did not act aggressively toward a female partner when the pornographic film ended with the woman clearly suffering. But when the pornographic film showed the woman enjoying the sexual violence, nonangered men were nearly as aggressive toward a female partner as were the men who had been angered.

Research continues to demonstrate the negative effects of pornography on attitudes and behavior toward women. Men who listen to audiotapes depicting rape, for example, are more likely to believe that women derive pleasure from being raped, are more prone to have aggressive sexual fantasies, and are more accepting of violence against women (Malamuth, 1981a, 1981b).

Men were also shown to be more accepting of interpersonal violence against women after watching commercially released violent-sexual films, such as *Swept Away* and *The Getaway* (Malamuth & Check, 1981). The same effect has been observed for music videos (Peterson & Pfost, 1989). Not all men respond this way, but for some men, including men who have been convicted of rape, scenes of rape are more arousing than scenes of mutually consenting sex (Malamuth, 1981b; Quinsey, Chaplin, & Upfold, 1984).

If a person has not been previously angered, then exposure to erotic (as opposed to pornographic) material seems to have little effect on aggression (Donnerstein, 1982). When anger is involved, however, aggression and exposure to erotica seem to be related, although the linkage is slightly complex. In some

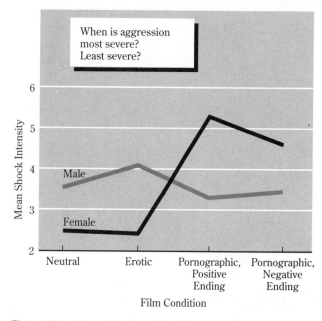

Figure 10.6 *Aggression by male subjects toward a male or female partner after viewing neutral, erotic, or pornographic films.*

Source: "Victim Reactions in Aggressive Erotic Films as a Factor in Violence against Women" by E. Donnerstein and L. Berkowitz, 1981, *Journal of Personality and Social Psychology, 41,* pp. 710–724.

cases, exposure to erotic material may actually inhibit the display of aggression. For example, Robert Baron and Paul Bell (1977) found that college men who had seen pictures of women in bathing suits, pictures of nude women, or pictures of acts of lovemaking were less aggressive than men who had seen neutral pictures of scenery. Men who read erotic literary passages, however, showed no decrease in aggression. This finding suggests that only some forms of erotica will inhibit aggression. Further research has shown that this inhibitory effect also depends on a very low level of provocation (Ramirez, Bryant, & Zillmann, 1982).

In contrast, more intense provocation or more arousing forms of erotic material—such as films depicting actual intercourse and oral and anal activities—will increase aggressive behavior (Donnerstein, Donnerstein, & Evans, 1975; Ramirez et al., 1982). Lengthy exposure to these more intense forms of erotic material has also been shown to have other effects, including more leniency in attitudes toward rape and greater cal-

Research continues to demonstrate the negative effects of pornography on attitudes and behavior toward women.
Paul Conklin / Monkmeyer Press

lousness in attitudes toward women in general (Zillmann & Bryant, 1982).

Thus, to answer our earlier question, the effects of pornography on subsequent behavior appear quite strong. Exposure to pornographic materials, but not all erotic materials, leads to more aggressive behavior. This aggression is directed primarily against women.

▶ Violence in Society

Questions about the effects of media violence have taken investigators out of the laboratory. In more naturalistic settings, they have found ample evidence of aggressive behavior. Between relatives at home, between strangers on the street, and between groups and nations in conflict, aggression is pervasive.

Violence in the Home

As the great film director Alfred Hitchcock has noted, when it comes to aggressive behavior, "there's no place like home." Well-publicized statistics on spouse and child abuse testify to the frequency with which aggression occurs. In light of this evidence, some social scientists have described the family as the "cradle of violence" (Steinmetz & Straus, 1973).

Violence between romantic partners often begins long before the marriage ceremony. More than half of 500 university students in Kentucky who were asked to describe their dating relationships said they had committed some physically abusive act toward their partners (Sigelman, Berry, & Wiles, 1984). As Table 10.1 shows, pushing and shoving were the most common forms of abuse. Women were more likely than men to slap a partner; they were also more likely to kick, hit, bite, and throw things at their partners. Despite these differences in form, the abuse in relationships was generally mutual. Those who reported being abusive also reported being abused.

Straus and his colleagues have conducted an extensive series of studies within the home setting to describe and explain the incidence of family violence (Steinmetz & Straus, 1974; Straus, 1973; Straus, Gelles, & Steinmetz, 1980). Their research shows that aggressive behavior in the family is extremely frequent, if not commonplace. In a study of more than 2,000 married couples in the United States, these investigators found that more than 25% of the couples had engaged in some form of physical violence during their married life. Both husbands and wives engaged in acts of violence, but the husbands' rates were higher for the more harmful forms of violence, such as beating or using a knife or gun.

Comparisons of social-class differences tended to challenge some popular stereotypes. Although white-collar workers indicated less approval of marital violence than blue-collar workers did, the reported frequency of actual aggressive behavior did not vary much between the two groups. The fact that aggression between spouses is so common (and that such incidents are far more frequent than physical attacks between

Table 10.1 Percentage of male and female college students reporting having abused a heterosexual partner

Action	Gender of abuser	
	Male	*Female*
Threw something	18%	27%
Pushed, shoved	42%	29%
Slapped	17%	34%
Kicked, hit, bit	9%	18%
Hit with some object (or tried)	12%	19%
Beat up	3%	1%
Threatened with knife or gun	2%	1%
Used a knife or gun	<1%	<1%

Source: "Violence in College Students' Dating Relationships" by C. K. Sigelman, C. J. Berry, and K. A. Wiles, 1984, *Journal of Applied Social Psychology, 5,* pp. 530–548.

strangers or mere acquaintances) provides support for Straus's somber description of "the marriage license as a hitting license" (Straus, 1975).

Family violence is not restricted to adults. Children, too, become victims of domestic violence. For example, a survey of university students revealed that more than half had experienced either actual or threatened physical punishment during their final year of high school (Straus, 1971). Reports of child abuse have become increasingly prominent in recent years. Although parent/child aggression is an obvious problem in itself, there are also suggestions that the consequences of such aggression extend far beyond the immediate incident. For example, Owens and Straus (1975) report that persons who experience violence as children are more likely to favor violence as a means of achieving personal and political ends as adults. In other words, through learning and role modeling, people can (but are not destined to) perpetuate the aggressive behaviors they learned as children. Like the relationship between media violence and aggression, however, the cycle of family violence is not guaranteed to occur (Widom, 1989).

Violence in the Streets

Although the home is the most common site of violence, aggressive behavior in our society is not limited to the family. Reports of homicides, rapes, and other forms of aggression appear daily in the newspapers, often as feature articles in some of the more sensational tabloids. Acts of aggression are common even in the classroom. The occurrence of bullying and harassment in the primary schools (grades 1 through 9) was declared a serious problem in Norway, and a nationwide campaign was developed to reduce the incidence of this form of aggression (Olweus, 1984a).

According to the Federal Bureau of Investigation and the Royal Canadian Mounted Police, crime rates in the United States and Canada have been increasing yearly. No single explanation accounts for these forms of aggression and violence. Although "individual criminal tendencies" may explain some occurrences, broader structural explanations are also needed. For example, Peggy Sanday (1981) has found that certain cultural groups are more likely to have a high incidence of rape than others. Looking at a sample of tribal societies, Sanday found that rape was most common in societies that (1) had a large amount of interpersonal violence, (2) generally supported male dominance, and (3) encouraged separation of males and females. In contrast, societies that fostered greater equality between genders were likely to have a very low incidence of rape. Sanday's findings, though based on cultures quite different from our own, suggest that general cultural values may be related to particular forms of aggression and violence.

Exact figures on the incidence of aggression are difficult to obtain, particularly if one wants to make comparisons across countries. Reporting procedures, for example, may exaggerate crime rates in one country while underestimating them in another. Available statistics suggest, however, that the United States has the dubious distinction of leading most of the industrialized nations of the world in crimes of violence. Such evidence certainly testifies to the importance of understanding the causes of aggression and of seeing the problem of aggression as more than an academic issue.

Collective Violence

Aggression is not confined to single individuals acting alone. Collective violence—violence between nations or between identifiable groups within a nation—has

The United States has the dubious distinction of leading most of the industrialized nations of the world in crimes of violence.
Kathy Willens/AP/Wide World Photos

played a role in most civilizations. For example, in the United States, incidents of collective violence were frequent between 1879 and 1889, whereas rates were low in the following decade (Levy, 1969). Again, in the 1960s, collective violence occurred frequently in riots involving young people, ghetto residents, and others. Canada, too, has had its share of collective violence. Canadians rioted over unemployment in the 1930s, conscription in the 1940s, and confederation in the 1960s and 1970s.

Why does collective violence occur? Davies (1962, 1969) has suggested that dissatisfaction occurs when a long period of rising prosperity is followed by a sharp drop in fortunes. The earlier increase in socioeconomic or political satisfaction leads people to expect the continuation of such improvements (thus producing a "curve of rising expectations"). When these expectations are not met, collective violence is more likely to occur. One early explanation of Iraq's invasion of Kuwait, for example, was the relative prosperity of Kuwait coupled with Iraqi perceptions of deserving a share of that prosperity. Conflicts in the Baltic republics of the former Soviet Union may stem from the failure of economic reforms to match rising expectations. Similarly, economic trends in both the United States and Canada in the late 1980s and early 1990s fit a general pattern of rising expectations, leading some to fear that collective

violence may be one result of the recession of the 1990s.

Other theorists have developed Davies's ideas further, focusing on the concept of relative deprivation. According to this general theory, people compare their conditions with those of others (Crosby, 1976). **Relative deprivation** is "a feeling of discontent based on the belief that one is getting less than one deserves" (Martin, 1980). One feels *fraternal deprivation* when one compares one's own group with another group. For example, blacks might compare their condition with that of whites, or women might make comparisons with men. One feels *egoistic deprivation* when the comparison is made on a more individual level, as when you compare your general situation with that of a more prosperous friend.

Several factors influence feelings of relative deprivation. Among them is the belief that one deserves a particular outcome and that one is not responsible for failure to achieve that outcome (Crosby, 1976). If a person feels deprived in relation to some other person or group, what does he or she do? Joanne Martin (1980) suggests that the actions depend on how optimistic or pessimistic a person is about the situation. A person who sees grounds for hope may engage in self-improvement efforts at the individual level or in constructive actions, such as voting, at the system level. If one's hopes are frustrated, however, negative outcomes may result. An individual may turn to alcohol or may take part in collective violence. Nor are such reactions limited to political or economic comparisons. The riots precipitated by fans of the losing team in major competitions, such as the World Cup in soccer, can be described as a reaction to the fact that winning is no longer an attainable goal.

Considerable support exists for this theory, ranging from laboratory experiments to historical analyses of cases as disparate as the French Revolution and the civil-rights protests in the United States. In each case, the evidence suggests that it is not those groups that are most oppressed that engage in collective violence; rather, it is those that believe they should and could have something better. Or, as Tocqueville once commented, "evils which are patiently endured when they seem inevitable become intolerable when once the idea of escape from them is suggested" (quoted in Crosby, 1976, p. 85).

▶ How Can Aggression Be Controlled?

Although some form of violence has always existed in our society, we can question whether aggression is inevitable. Can aggressive behavior be controlled or eliminated? The answer depends on the assumptions one makes about the causes of aggression.

Theorists who believe that aggression is an innate human characteristic are pessimistic about the possibilities of controlling aggressive behavior. As Freud grew older and witnessed the devastation of World War I, he became increasingly resigned to the inevitability of aggression. His postulation of a death instinct, which he called *thanatos*—a compulsion in all human beings "to return to the inorganic state out of which all living matter is formed" (Hall & Lindzey, 1968, p. 263)—represented the culmination of his pessimism. Freud saw aggression as a natural derivation of the death instinct.

Psychoanalysts who adopt this position see little chance of restraining our violent behaviors. Freud himself wrote that there is "no likelihood of our being able to suppress humanity's aggressive tendencies" (quoted in Bramson & Goethals, 1968, p. 76). However, two forms of action may provide some hope. One, at an international level, involves combining forces to restrain the aggressive actions of powerful nations. At an individual level, developing the superego can serve to restrain innate aggressive impulses. Additionally, **neo-Freudians,** theorists who accept the basic tenets of Freud's theory but who differ from Freud's specific premises, advocate participation in socially acceptable aggressive activities (sporting events, debates, and the like) as a way of releasing aggressive energy.

Ethologists and sociobiologists also believe that eliminating aggression is unlikely. To them, the task is one of channeling aggression into socially acceptable behaviors. Lorenz (1966), for example, believed that Olympic games, space races to Mars, and similar international competitions provide opportunities for directing aggressive behaviors into relatively harmless pursuits. Ethologists would encourage us to identify, and thereby control, the cues that trigger the expression of aggression.

For those who favor cultural explanations of aggressive behavior, possibilities for the control and reduction of violence are more numerous. Because they believe that environmental factors control the acquisition and maintenance of aggressive behaviors, advocates of cultural explanations argue that appropriate changes in environmental conditions decrease aggression and violence. For example, social learning theorists suggest that observing nonaggressive models leads to acquiring nonaggressive behavior. In an experiment demonstrating this effect, students watched a subject administer shocks to a "victim" before they were given their turn (Baron & Kepner, 1970). As Figure 10.7 shows, the students who had observed an aggressive model administered more shocks to the "learner" than did students who had not observed a model. In contrast, students who witnessed a restrained, nonaggressive model were less aggressive.

Other investigators have found similar results (Donnerstein & Donnerstein, 1977), although the model's success in reducing an opponent's aggression may be an important qualification (Lando & Donnerstein, 1978). Even more important, research has shown that if both types of models are present, the nonaggressive model can effectively negate the influence of the aggressive model (Baron, 1971). Therefore, even if we cannot eliminate all aggressive models from our soci-

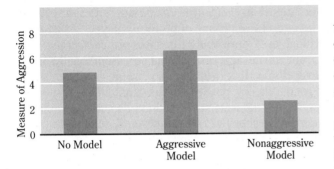

Figure 10.7 *Impact of aggressive and nonaggressive models on overt aggression.*
Source: "Model's Behavior and Attraction toward the Model as Determinants of Adult Aggressive Behavior" by R. A. Baron and C. R. Kepner, 1970, *Journal of Personality and Social Psychology, 14,* pp. 335–344.

ety, we may be able to reduce aggression by adding more nonaggressive models to the environment.

Learning theorists also advocate nonreinforcement of aggressive responses (Brown & Elliott, 1965). A person who is not rewarded for displays of aggression is less likely to acquire or maintain aggressive behaviors. Some people have also suggested that punishment or the threat of it may deter aggressive behavior, but actual punishment may be an effective deterrent only under certain conditions. Robert Baron (1977) suggests four necessary conditions: (1) the punishment must be predictable, (2) it must immediately follow the aggressive behavior, (3) it must be legitimized by existing social norms, and (4) the persons administering the punishment should not be seen as aggressive models. If these conditions are not met, punishment could encourage aggression.

The conditions under which the *threat* of punishment can reduce aggression are perhaps even more limited. A threat appears to be effective only when the person who makes it is not terribly angry, when the expected punishment is very great and the probability of its delivery is high, and when the potential aggressor has relatively little to gain by being aggressive (Baron, 1977). These apparent limitations suggest that, in general, threat of punishment is not a very effective means of reducing aggressive behavior.

David Phillips (1980) conducted an archival study that presents some relevant information. Using reports of murders and capital punishments recorded in London between 1858 and 1921, Phillips found that homicides decreased immediately after a well-publicized execution—and then they increased. As Figure 10.8 shows, homicides decreased by about 35% during the period just after an execution. During subsequent weeks, however, homicides increased above the rate that would be expected, then returned to the base rate about six weeks later. The threat of capital punishment may serve as a deterrent in the short run, but the long-term effects are not evident—at least not in nineteenth-century England.

Investigators have pointed to incompatible responses as a third means of controlling violence. Basically, they suggest that because it is difficult to do two things at once, the performance of violent acts should be reduced when conditions induce responses that are incompatible with the expression of aggression. Demonstrations of the effectiveness of this strategy have included the use of humorous cartoons (Baron & Ball, 1974) and conditions that foster empathy (Rule & Leger, 1976). In both cases subjects were less aggressive when an alternative response was available than when aggression was their only choice.

Information about mitigating circumstances can also reduce aggressive responses to an apparent threat or attack. Explaining a person's aggressive behavior—providing reasons that suggest the provocation was beyond the person's control—reduces the tendency to counterattack (Zillmann, Bryant, Cantor, & Day, 1975; Zillmann & Cantor, 1976). As we saw earlier, information about mitigating circumstances is particularly effective if it comes before the act of aggression. Of course, such explanations are not always available. To the extent that they can be introduced and accepted as reasonable, however, they allow people to choose to reduce their aggressive tendencies.

If frustration is considered a major determinant of aggression, then we might look to ways of reducing frustration as a means of controlling aggression. When Ransford (1968) interviewed blacks living in the Watts area of Los Angeles in the 1960s, he found that those with intense feelings of dissatisfaction and frustration

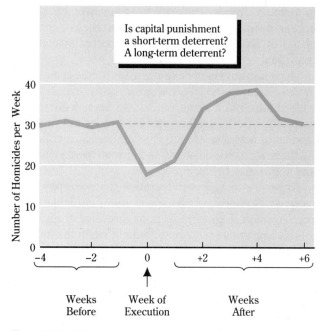

Is capital punishment a short-term deterrent? A long-term deterrent?

Figure 10.8 *The influence of a publicized execution on subsequent homicides.*
Source: "The Deterrent Effect of Capital Punishment: New Evidence on an Old Controversy" by D. P. Phillips, 1980, *American Journal of Sociology, 86,* pp. 139–148.

were more prone to violent action. The violence that accompanied Quebec's separatist movement was also attributed to social and economic frustrations. Community leaders can take numerous actions to reduce such frustrations; by providing better services, introducing human-relations training for police, and dealing directly with the causes of frustration, they could reduce aggression and violence.

Another suggested means of reducing aggression is catharsis, which has a long history (Scheff & Bushnell, 1984). Aristotle first used the concept to explain the value of theater, arguing that dramatic catharsis could purge the audience of negative emotional experiences. Later Freud applied the term to a particular method of treating neurosis. As research psychologists use the term today, **catharsis** refers to the release of aggressive energy through expression of aggressive emotions

or through alternative forms of behavior. The role of catharsis in reducing aggressive behavior is stated by Dollard and his colleagues: "The expression of any act of aggression is a catharsis that reduces the instigation to all other acts of aggression" (Dollard et al., 1939, p. 33). In other words, the concept of catharsis suggests that if you can get the anger off your chest, you will be less likely to behave aggressively on future occasions.

Proponents of the catharsis hypothesis have suggested that fantasy is one way in which aggression can be reduced. Although investigators have found that aggressive behavior can result in a decrease in aggressive fantasies (Murray & Feshbach, 1978), the more important possibility if one wishes to control aggressive behavior—that fantasies can reduce aggressive behavior—has not received much support (Hartmann, 1969; Walters & Thomas, 1963). Somewhat more support exists for the notion of behavioral catharsis—the opportunity to express aggression at the time of frustration reduces subsequent aggressive behavior (Konečni, 1975). Behavioral catharsis, however, does not reduce the overall incidence of aggressive behavior. Instead, it controls the future expression at the cost of present violence.

Berkowitz's (1989) cognitive-neoassociationistic model of aggression points toward controlling violence through measures that (1) reduce aversive stimuli, such as inadequate food and shelter; (2) strengthen social norms against aggressive actions by simultaneously rewarding nonaggressive actions and failing to reward aggressive solutions; and (3) reduce overall exposure to models of aggression in order to reduce the accessibility of aggressive actions that may be primed through experiences of anger. None of these goals are easily accomplished, but one cannot reasonably expect simple solutions to a complex problem.

A belief in innate aggressive tendencies might lead us to throw up our hands and say, "There's nothing to be done; war is inevitable and people are naturally violent." Ample evidence shows, however, that aggressive behavior can be modified. Changes in a variety of factors, such as those reviewed here, can affect the occurrence of aggression. Even if such factors do not account for all aggressive behavior, they clearly account for a portion of it. These facts should not be overlooked as we seek a more peaceful human existence.

▶ Summary

Definitions of aggression vary in accordance with one's theoretical perspective. For our discussion, we consider aggression to be any form of behavior directed toward harming or injuring another living being.

Why are human beings aggressive? Answers to this question take two general forms, one stressing biological causes and the other emphasizing social factors. Biological explanations, offered by psychoanalysts, ethologists, and sociobiologists, stress the innate character of aggression. Proponents of socialization point to learning processes, such as reinforcement and modeling, to explain how aggressive behavior develops.

Many conditions can influence the occurrence of aggressive behavior. Experiencing frustration when one is blocked from achieving a goal can lead to aggressive behavior if the frustration arouses anger. Both the level of frustration and the intentions of the frustrating agent will influence this effect. Cues in the environment, such as weapons and firearms, increase the likelihood of aggression. So, too, do direct physical and verbal attacks. Instigation by a third party also increases the tendency toward aggressive behavior.

Aggressive behavior is more likely to occur when the potential aggressor is not readily identifiable—when he or she is in a deindividuated state.

Moderate amounts of alcohol increase levels of aggressive behavior; marijuana, in contrast, acts as a deterrent. Environmental factors, such as noise, air pollution, and heat, can also affect the amount of aggression exhibited.

Individual differences in tendencies toward aggressive behavior are fairly stable over time. Men are somewhat more aggressive than women on the average, but gender differences regarding aggression vary widely in different situations. Individual differences, at least among children, are also related to ability to process social cues and evaluate outcomes associated with response alternatives.

Anger, though not itself an instigator of aggression, appears to make aggressive responses more accessible in memory. Anger can result from any aversive stimulus and from aggressive actions undertaken or contemplated by an individual as well as directed against the individual.

Depictions of violence in the mass media can lead to increases in aggressive behavior. Early experiments with children and Bobo dolls have been followed by more realistic laboratory studies and by longitudinal studies of actual television-viewing habits in children. All these studies indicate a link between media violence and aggressive behavior.

Exposure to aggressive erotica (pornography) can increase aggressive behavior in men, particularly toward women. Exposure to nonaggressive erotica can inhibit aggressive responses, but not when the individual is angry.

Considerable violence occurs in the home—between spouses, between parents and children, and among children. Other forms of violence in our society include assault, homicide, and rape. Collective violence—violence between nations and between identifiable groups within a nation—is also relatively common. The concept of relative deprivation has been used to explain why some groups decide to revolt or engage in collective violence.

Prospects for the control of aggression depend largely on one's theoretical assumptions. A belief that aggression has an innate, instinctual basis leads to a relatively pessimistic outlook. Although aggression may be diverted into socially acceptable forms, from this outlook its expression is seen as inevitable.

For those who favor social and cultural explanations of aggression, the control and eventual reduction of aggression seem more feasible. Suggested strategies for reducing aggression include provision of nonaggressive models, nonreinforcement and punishment, incompatible responses, and information about mitigating circumstances.

▶ *Key Terms*

aggression
catharsis
cognitive-neoassociationistic model

deindividuation
ethology
excitation transfer theory
frustration
frustration-aggression hypothesis
fundamental attribution bias
instrumental learning

modeling
neo-Freudians
observational learning
pornography
relative deprivation
scripts
sociobiology

A word of kindness is better than a

fat pie.

Russian Proverb

W hy do you hate me—I never even

helped you.

Indian Proverb

11

Prosocial Behavior

This chapter was written by Carol K. Sigelman.

R oger Lindsay, age 31, was spending a pleasant day fishing with his wife at a lake south of Albuquerque, New Mexico, when he spotted a young man swimming toward an island in the middle of the lake. The swimmer started to go under, and his friend started out after him but apparently could not swim. Lindsay dove in, pulled the friend to shore, and then went after the drowning man, who by now was sinking to the bottom of the lake. Lindsay pulled the man to the surface, dragged him to shore with great effort, and pressed hard on his back until water spurted out and the man finally began coughing and breathing (Kreutz, 1991).

In 1991, Lindsay was selected as one of the one hundred or so "everyday heroes" in the United States and Canada honored by the Carnegie Hero Fund Commission each year. He received $2,500, a medal, and a certificate for his efforts. What makes his heroism truly extraordinary is that he did it all wearing an artificial leg that felt like an "anchor" as he swam. He jumped into the lake so fast that he did not think to remove the heavy limb that he had worn ever since his leg had been amputated several years ago after a motorcycle accident. Nor did it cross his mind that he hadn't had a life-saving course and hadn't swum for several years (Kreutz, 1991).

This dramatic rescue raises many questions: Why do people like Lindsay help in emergencies—and why do others fail to help? What was his true motivation? What was going on inside him as he sized up the situation and decided to act? Whatever the answers, his act is a clear example of what this chapter is about: prosocial behavior. **Prosocial behavior** is behavior that benefits others or has positive social consequences (Staub, 1978; Wispé, 1972). The term *prosocial* contrasts with the term *antisocial,* which applies to the aggressive, violent behaviors discussed in Chapter 10. A host of specific behaviors can be viewed as prosocial—bystander intervention in emergencies, charity, cooperation, donation, helping, sacrifice, and sharing. *Cooperation,* or working with others for mutual benefit, is an important prosocial behavior that will be discussed in Chapter 13. Here we emphasize **helping behavior,** or prosocial behavior that benefits another person more than oneself, especially intervention in emergencies. One helping situation that arises for many college students is deciding whether to intervene when a companion is too drunk to drive. In an ethnically diverse sample of UCLA students, for example, 51% had intervened at least once in the past year to stop a potential drunk driver from driving (Rabow, Newcomb, Monto, & Hernandez, 1990).

Note that prosocial behavior has been defined in terms of its consequences; such a definition raises some questions. For example, if you unintentionally worsen the condition of an accident victim to whom you are administering first aid, have you acted in a prosocial manner? What if you clearly benefit someone by giving him or her money, but do so to get a favor in return? The act has positive social consequences, but wouldn't most of us call it a bribe rather than a prosocial act? Because of such problems, it is useful to consider not only the consequences of an act but the motives behind it.

The clearest instances of prosocial behavior merit the term *altruism.* **Altruism** is a special form of helping behavior that is voluntary, costly to the altruist, and motivated primarily by a desire to improve another person's welfare rather than by the anticipation of reward (Batson, 1987; Walster & Piliavin, 1972). Altruism, then, is selfless rather than selfish prosocial behavior and can be contrasted with helping that is motivated by **egoism,** or self-interest. One of the most intense debates among social psychologists interested in prosocial behavior centers on the question of whether true altruism even exists—on whether human beings are really capable of putting others' interests before their own.

The study of prosocial behavior started later than the study of antisocial behavior but soon became a lively area of research (Krebs & Miller, 1985). The behaviors studied have ranged from the merely considerate to the heroic—from picking up pencils and turning off the lights in parked cars to stopping thieves and helping the victims of falls and epileptic seizures. The emergencies staged by some researchers are so realistic and intense that ethical issues arise about whether such research should even be undertaken (see Chapter 2). Yet such research reveals much about human beings.

We will begin our exploration of prosocial behavior by examining the challenge that the very idea of altruism poses to our understanding of human nature, asking whether people are capable of genuinely altruistic helping and exploring the possible contributions of biology and culture to prosocial behavior. Then we will examine a model that describes what happens when an individual encounters a situation in which help is needed. This decision-making model can help us analyze a wide range of influences on prosocial behavior. Such influences include both factors in the situation, such as characteristics of the person in need and the presence of other people who could potentially help, and factors within the person, such as aspects of personality and moods of the moment. Throughout most of the chapter, we will be looking through the potential helper's eyes, but later we will shift our perspective to that of the recipient of help in order to understand why some prosocial acts are appreciated and others are not. Finally, we will apply what we have learned to the task of building a more prosocial society in the future.

▶ Are We Capable of Truly Altruistic Behavior?

There are many practical reasons for being interested in the study of prosocial behavior. Many of us believe that the world would be a better place if people were more prosocial, and we deplore the cases we read about in which individuals in desperate need of help fail to receive it. For psychologists, however, part of the fascination of prosocial behavior is theoretical rather than practical. The very existence of prosocial behavior, especially altruism, poses a challenge to psychology.

Traditional Psychological Theories and Altruism

It has long been a tradition among Western thinkers, including social scientists, to view human beings as motivated primarily by self-interest (Batson, 1987). As a result, many of the traditional psychological theories introduced in Chapter 1 have a hard time explaining altruism. Freudian **psychoanalytic theory,** for example, rests on the assumption that human nature is instinctively selfish and aggressive. How, then, can it explain altruism? Not very easily. Some psychoanalytic theorists view altruism as a means of defending ourselves against our own internal conflicts and anxieties, but this suggests that altruism is ultimately self-serving rather than motivated by a genuine concern for others. Psychoanalytic theorists acknowledge that positive socialization experiences might make us less selfish and more selfless (Ekstein, 1978), but they still view human beings as selfish at the core.

Or consider learning theories, especially those that emphasize principles of reinforcement. B. F. Skinner and other reinforcement theorists have claimed that we repeat and strengthen those behaviors that result in positive consequences for us. How, then, can altruism increase in strength, or even exist, if it is associated with negative consequences, such as loss of resources, injury, even death? It cannot, learning theorists argue; what appears to be altruism is really egoism or self-interest in disguise. People may feel better about themselves after they rush to the rescue, may expect rewards in the afterlife, or may avoid the unpleasant feelings of guilt and shame they would experience if they failed to help. Thus, even if a person cannot expect praise, recognition, or prize money in return for helping, he or she nonetheless may be motivated by more subtle rewards (Gelfand & Hartmann, 1982). Even role theorists, while they do not necessarily claim that human beings are pure egoists, suggest that people will not help others unless they are properly socialized and find themselves in roles where prosocial behavior is part of the "job description."

In fact, most theories social psychologists have developed specifically to explain prosocial behavior assume that people's motives for helping are basically egoistic rather than altruistic (Batson, 1987). For example, those of us who hand quarters to street people may do so more to relieve our own discomfort at the sight of needy people than to relieve their suffering. Fortunately, social psychologists are not content to merely argue back and forth about whether people's motives for helping are primarily altruistic or egoistic. Instead they have attempted through research to determine what really motivates people to help in various situations. The stakes are high: If psychologists demonstrate that people are capable of helping more to relieve the suffering of a fellow human being than to satisfy their own needs, it might be time to reject the dim view of human nature expressed in so many psychological theories.

The Empathy-Altruism Hypothesis

The question of whether altruism is possible has been of central concern to C. Daniel Batson and his colleagues (Batson, 1987, 1990; Batson & Oleson, 1991;

Coke, Batson, & McDavis, 1978). Much evidence shows that a relationship exists between helping and **empathy,** or the vicarious experiencing of another's emotions (Eisenberg & Miller, 1987). Thus, you may be more likely to volunteer to work at a hospice for people with AIDS if you genuinely "feel for" them and share in their emotional pain than if you can muster little sympathy. The question is why feeling empathy for others makes us more likely to help them. In his **empathy-altruism hypothesis,** Batson states that empathic emotions can produce a genuinely altruistic motivation to help aimed primarily at reducing a victim's need rather than at satisfying one's own needs.

How can one distinguish between egoistically-motivated helping and altruistically-motivated helping based in empathy? Batson and his colleagues have attempted to measure two distinct emotional reactions to people in distress: *empathic concern,* a sympathetic focus on another person's distress and a motivation to reduce it, and *personal distress,* or concern with one's own discomfort and a motivation to reduce it. On a scale these researchers have used to measure reactions to a victim's plight, adjectives reflecting empathic concern include *sympathetic, compassionate, moved, softhearted,* and *tender,* whereas reactions indicating personal distress include *alarmed, worried, disturbed,* and *upset.* Batson and his associates have tried to show that empathic concern, but not personal distress, prompts people to help even when it is not in their own best interests to do so.

In one study (Batson, Duncan, Ackerman, Buckley, & Birch, 1981), college women were told they would be participating in a learning experiment and were assigned to observe while another student, Elaine, received mild electric shocks as she attempted to recall strings of digits. Elaine soon became quite distressed, needing to stop and drink a glass of water, at which point the experimenter raised the possibility that the "observer" might be able to take the remaining shocks in her place. Through their experimental manipulations, the researchers made some women feel empathic concern and others feel personal distress in response to Elaine's plight, and made escaping the obligation to help either difficult or easy.

To manipulate emotional reactions to the victim's situation, women were given a placebo drug, "Millentana," supposedly in connection with a second experiment on memory. Half of them were told that the drug would give them a feeling of "uneasiness and discomfort," like that they might feel reading a distressing novel. This was the "empathy condition"; the researchers expected that these women would attribute any symptoms of personal distress they experienced to the drug and would therefore interpret their emotional reactions to Elaine's suffering as empathic concern for her. In the "personal distress" condition, women were told that the drug would cause empathy-like feelings of "warmth and sensitivity," like those they might feel reading a touching novel, and were therefore led to believe that their reactions to Elaine represented personal distress rather than empathy.

To separate the true altruists from the egoists, half the women experiencing empathy and half the women experiencing personal distress were given no possibility of escaping the situation; they were told they would have to stay and watch the victim take additional shocks if they failed to substitute for her. The other half were told they were free to leave and thus could escape the situation easily without helping. If empathy truly arouses an altruistic motivation to help, the researchers reasoned, individuals experiencing empathic concern rather than personal distress should be willing to rescue Elaine even when they could easily escape. After all, helping her is the only way to end her distress, even though escaping would relieve their own distress. By contrast, women experiencing personal distress were expected to behave egoistically; given a chance to escape, they could obviously reduce their own distress more easily and quickly by leaving than by subjecting themselves to electric shocks.

As Figure 11.1 shows, highly empathic women did indeed behave altruistically, helping at high rates whether escape was easy or difficult. By contrast, the women experiencing personal distress helped Elaine when escape was difficult, but abandoned her when escape was easy. Thus, empathy, but not personal distress, appeared to arouse a genuinely altruistic motivation for helping that could be satisfied only by seeing the other woman's suffering end.

Batson and his colleagues have demonstrated several times that empathically aroused individuals will help even when they could easily relieve their own distress by escaping (Batson, 1987; Batson & Oleson, 1991). But can we really conclude that empathic con-

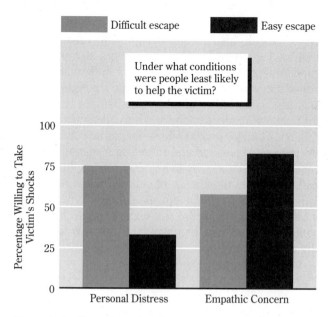

Difficult escape   **Easy escape**

Under what conditions were people least likely to help the victim?

Percentage Willing to Take Victim's Shocks

100

75

50

25

0

Personal Distress   Empathic Concern

Figure 11.1 *Empathy versus distress: Percentage of subjects who were willing to help a victim as a function of arousal experience and ease of escape.*
Source: "Is Empathic Emotion a Source of Altruistic Motivation?" by C. D. Batson, B. D. Duncan, P. Ackerman, T. Buckley, and K. Birch, 1981, *Journal of Personality and Social Psychology, 40,* pp. 290–302.

cern inspires genuinely altruistic helping? Not unless we can rule out other possible egoistic motives that empathic individuals might have for helping.

Challenging the Empathy-Altruism Hypothesis

In their initial studies, Batson and his colleagues established that empathic individuals helped for reasons other than reducing their own unpleasant arousal or distress. But perhaps these potential helpers were motivated by a desire to avoid punishment—either the social disapproval or the self-criticism that might result if they failed to help (Archer, 1984). To determine whether empathic helpers might be worried that others would evaluate them negatively if they failed to help, Batson and his colleagues compared students with high and low levels of empathic concern in situations where the potential for negative social evaluation by others was either high or low (Fultz, Batson, Fortenbach, McCarthy, & Varney, 1986). College students who empathized with a young woman who expressed

her loneliness and need for friends during a taped interview were more willing to help her than less empathic students were—even when no one, including the victim, would ever know they failed to help, not just when looking bad to others was a real threat. Self-centered concern with others' disapproval of one's failure to help could not explain why empathic concern motivates helping.

But what if highly empathic individuals help in order to avoid feeling bad about themselves if they walk away from needy victims? In testing this possibility, Batson and his colleagues (Batson et al., 1988) reasoned that if empathic people's motives were truly altruistic, they would help even if they could easily justify not helping and could therefore ignore a victim's plight with a clear conscience. For example, in one of these researchers' studies subjects were supposedly involved in a study of "auditory numeric facility" and ended up watching Batson's favorite victim, Elaine, receive shocks as she attempted to recall numbers. This time, when Elaine seemed unable to continue taking shocks, observers were told they could help her by taking the remainder of her shocks only if they performed well on a numerical task. To determine whether women who reported high levels of empathy in response to Elaine's plight were more altruistically motivated than women who reported high levels of personal distress, some women (those in the easy-qualification-standard condition) were told that seven out of ten college students pass this test; the rest (those in the difficult-standard condition) learned that only one of five college students passes. Faced with a difficult standard to qualify as a helper (and to win the right to suffer electric shocks!), women who were less than altruistically motivated might be tempted to take the easy way out, either by declining to help when the odds of qualifying appeared so low or by volunteering to help but giving the qualifying test less than their best effort. After all, one need not feel guilty about not helping if one were unable to qualify as a helper. However, if women truly wanted to end Elaine's suffering, they would want to qualify no matter what the standard.

Table 11.1 shows the percentage of empathic and nonempathic women in each condition who volunteered to help, as well as the scores these would-be helpers obtained on the qualifying test. In support of the empathy-altruism hypothesis, highly empathic women were very likely to offer to help, even when they could avoid doing so, but women feeling personal distress were less willing to volunteer when the qualification standard was difficult than when it was easy. Interestingly, among those women who volunteered to help and then took the qualification test, distressed women answered fewer questions correctly when the standard was difficult than when it was easy, whereas empathic women actually did better when qualifying was difficult than when it was easy. It seemed that these empathically concerned altruists genuinely wanted to take Elaine's remaining shocks for her even though they could dodge responsibility without feeling any shame or guilt.

These studies cast doubt on the idea that empathic people help in order to avoid any social or self-punishment that might result if they fail to help. But could it be that empathic people are instead motivated to gain rewards by helping? One leading alternative to Batson's empathy-altruism hypothesis is the **negative-state relief model** of helping offered by Robert Cialdini and his colleagues (Cialdini, Darby, & Vincent, 1973; Cialdini et al., 1987). According to this model, people learn during childhood that helping is gratifying and can help them overcome negative psychological states such as sadness and guilt. People who experience empathy for a victim also feel sad, the argument goes, and they help because they want to decrease their own sadness rather than because they feel an altruistic desire to end a victim's suffering.

Using methods much like those Batson used, Cialdini and his colleagues (Cialdini et al., 1987) gave college students, who were to watch a fellow student receive shocks, instructions designed to create either high or low empathy. The researchers also made escape from the situation either easy or difficult. But they added a new twist: They offered some students either a surprise dollar bill or lavish praise before the request for help was made. Cialdini and his colleagues thought this might make people whose empathic concern had been aroused less sad and therefore less motivated to relieve their sadness by helping. According to the empathy-altruism hypothesis, of course, highly empathic individuals should be helpful even if they experience a mood-lifting event before the opportunity to help presents itself; for them, helping is the only way to relieve the victim's distress.

In support of the negative-state relief hypothesis, highly empathic people were no more helpful than less empathic people when their moods were lifted by the surprise dollar bill, though unexpected praise for their performance did not lessen their motivation to help. In another study, the motivation of empathic students to help also diminished when they were led to believe that their moods had been "fixed" in place by a drug and that, as a result, they could not expect any relief from their gloom if they helped (Cialdini et al., 1987). In yet another study, the empathy-altruism link was broken when highly empathic (and saddened) subjects were told they would soon hear a comedy tape that could be expected to improve their moods (Schaller & Cialdini, 1988).

Here, then, is a model that appears to seriously challenge the empathy-altruism hypothesis. But other re-

Table 11.1 **Percentage of women offering help and performance on qualifying test when qualifying to help is easy or difficult**

	Percentage offering to help	Score on qualifying test
Easy qualifying standard		
High-empathy subjects	86	9.90
High-personal-distress subjects	73	11.30
Difficult qualifying standard		
High-empathy subjects	65	13.00
High-personal-distress subjects	28	8.25

Source: "Five Studies Testing Two New Egoistic Alternatives to the Empathy-Altruism Hypothesis" by C. D. Batson, J. L. Dyck, J. R. Brandt, J. G. Batson, A. L. Powell, M. R. McMaster, and C. Griffitt, 1988, *Journal of Personality and Social Psychology, 55*, pp. 52–77.

searchers have found that highly empathic individuals do not always lose their motivation to help when they have no hope of escaping their sadness by helping or when they can escape their sadness without helping (Schroeder, Dovidio, Sibicky, Matthews, & Allen, 1988). Although people often help in order to improve their own moods, it appears that sometimes people experiencing empathy help primarily to relieve the victim's suffering.

Finally, consider another possible source of egoistic reward that could explain the link between empathy and altruism. Kyle Smith, John Keating, and Ezra Stotland (1989) proposed that highly empathic people may help in order to share in the victim's joy upon being helped. They then offered evidence that students who felt empathy for a young woman having difficulty adjusting to college life were more willing to offer her advice when they thought they would later learn about the effects of their advice than when they expected no such opportunity to experience empathic joy upon learning of her improvement. Yet Batson and his colleagues (Batson et al., in press) have conducted new studies showing that people experiencing high levels of empathy did not help any less when the prospects of experiencing empathic joy were low than when they were high.

Overall, the quest to determine whether humans are capable of genuinely altruistic behavior when they feel empathy for a person in need has proven exciting and enlightening. Although the findings of different studies do not all agree, a good deal of evidence has now been marshaled to support Batson's empathy-altruism hypothesis and to suggest that human beings are not always governed by entirely egoistic motives. One by one, various egoistic explanations of why empathic people help have been challenged. Under at least some conditions, empathic people's altruism is not easily explained away as an attempt to reduce their own unpleasant arousal; to avoid punishment (for example, disapproval of others or feelings of guilt and shame associated with failing to help); or to gain subtle rewards (for example, relief from the sadness that often accompanies empathic concern or empathic joy upon seeing the victim's suffering end). It is possible, of course, that some other egoistic reason for the apparent altruism of highly empathic people will be identified or that new research methods will produce different results. It is also possible that studies designed to rule out one egoistic motive nonetheless allow other egoistic motives to operate (Cialdini, 1991). However, if research continues to indicate that empathically-aroused people often help for altruistic rather than egoistic reasons, Batson believes that ". . . we must radically revise our views about human nature and the human capacity for caring" (Batson & Oleson, 1991, p. 80).

Lest we become too carried away with this new image of humans as altruists, however, it should be noted that even highly empathic people behave egoistically on occasion, especially when helping is costly and escape from responsibility is easy (Batson, O'Quin, Fultz, Vanderplas, & Isen, 1983). When highly empathic subjects were asked to take *painful* shocks in poor Elaine's place but could easily leave instead, only 14% of them stayed to help, whereas 86% were willing to endure *mildly* unpleasant shocks on her behalf under similar circumstances (Batson et al., 1983). Thus, genuine concern for others may be "a fragile flower, easily crushed by egoistic concerns" (Batson et al., 1983, p. 718). It may be best to conclude that people help for both altruistic and egoistic reasons.

Biology, Culture, and Altruism

The argument that human beings have a greater capacity for caring than has commonly been recognized would be strengthened by evidence that empathy and altruism are biologically based. Are we biologically predisposed to behave prosocially, or are we basically selfish beasts who must be carefully taught by society to look after anyone besides ourselves? Let us examine the possible contributions of biology and culture or society to prosocial behavior.

Genes and altruism   As we saw in regard to aggressive behavior in Chapter 10, **sociobiology** relies on evolutionary theory and genetic inheritance to explain social behavior. Traditional evolutionary theory, as developed by Charles Darwin and others, has real problems accounting for altruistic behavior. Darwin's "survival of the fittest" view says that if one's genes help one to survive and thus allow one to produce more offspring than less "fit" individuals, those genes will become more common in future generations of the species. But how could genes that predispose an individual to altruism be passed on with any frequency when altruists endanger their very survival for the sake of others?

Suppose that generations ago, some birds were genetically programmed to sound warning calls when predators approached the nest and others were not. The altruists who warned the flock would attract attention to themselves and stand a good chance of being eaten. Such altruism is impossible to explain in terms of the survival of the fittest individuals; before long, with altruists dying instead of reproducing, the genes for altruism would disappear from the species. Sociobiologists have suggested, however, that such altruism can be explained in terms of survival of the fittest *genes* (W. D. Hamilton, 1964; Trivers & Hare, 1976). What is needed is the concept of **kin selection,** the selection over the course of evolution of characteristics or traits that contribute to the survival of the *kinship group's* genes. Sociobiologists argue that it is the survival of genes, which are shared with relatives or kin, rather than the survival of individuals, that matters in evolution. A bird who warns her children, or perhaps her brothers and sisters, of an approaching hawk may actually transmit more of her genetic material to future generations, through her kin, by jeopardizing her own life and potential to reproduce than by saving her own skin and letting her relatives die. Similarly, our altruistic human ancestors may have passed on more of their kinship group's genes to future generations than their selfish peers did, and therefore a genetically-based predisposition to behave prosocially may have become more widespread in our species over the course of evolution.

The sociobiological view, like many others, regards altruism as ultimately a matter of selfishness—in this case, an interest in passing on as much of the family's genetic formula as possible. Of course, no one is suggesting that birds, bees, or even humans consciously make decisions based on the probability that their actions will cause their kinship group's genes to flourish. Sociobiologists argue that prosocial tendencies could have become built into the genetic codes of humans and other animal species because they have been effective over time in ensuring the survival of kin.

If we accept sociobiological assumptions, kin selection might explain our willingness to help blood relatives, but why would we help anyone else? One answer is that we may have evolved to help those who *might* share our genes—for example, people who are physi-

cally similar to us (Krebs, 1983; Rushton, 1989). As social psychologists have long realized, similarity breeds attraction. We tend to choose friends and mates who are similar to us in everything from blood type and race to intelligence and values and who therefore resemble us genetically. Perhaps, then, we have evolved to recognize and be especially helpful toward anyone genetically similar to us (Rushton, 1989).

Still, this does not explain why people would help perfect strangers, dissimilar others, or members of outgroups. Here the concept of **reciprocal altruism** has been introduced (Taylor & McGuire, 1988; Trivers, 1971). Basically, natural selection over the course of evolution would favor those with genes that predispose them to help others because in the long run prosocial acts are reciprocated and thus benefit the individual. You might be genetically predisposed to risk your own safety to help a total stranger, the argument goes, if you anticipated some help in return—help that would compensate you for your original sacrifice and would benefit you both in the long run.

Using such concepts as kin selection, preferential treatment of genetically similar others, and reciprocal altruism, sociobiologists have argued that altruistic behavior could be rooted in the basic biological endowment of human beings, just as selfishness apparently is. But is there any evidence that altruistic tendencies are genetically influenced? Martin Hoffman (1981) thinks so and has proposed that the capacity for empathy is the genetically-influenced quality underlying altruism. In support of this hypothesis, some fascinating studies indicate that humans are designed from birth to respond to the distress of their peers. In one such study, newborns became distressed by the cries of other newborns (Martin & Clark, 1982). Importantly, not just any crying sound distressed them, for they were not similarly upset by their own tape-recorded cries or by the cries of chimpanzees. In other studies, toddlers have been observed attempting to comfort and help distressed playmates (Radke-Yarrow & Zahn-Waxler, 1984; Zahn-Waxler, Radke-Yarrow, & King, 1979). At 18 months, for example, Jenny did all she could to quiet a crying baby, offering him cookies and toys, patting him and stroking his hair, and fetching her mother to help (Radke-Yarrow & Zahn-Waxler, 1984).

In addition, differences among adults in the strength of their capacities for empathy and altruism appear to have a genetic basis (Matthews et al., 1981; Rushton et al., 1986). For example, J. Phillipe Rushton and his colleagues found that identical twins, who have identical genes, responded similarly to questionnaires designed to measure their tendencies to empathize with others and to behave altruistically. If one twin scored high on a measure, the other twin did too, as indicated by twin correlations of .54 and .53 for the empathy and altruism measures, respectively. Fraternal twins, who share about half their genes on average, were less similar (the correlations were .20 for empathy and .25 for altruism). This evidence suggests that some people are more empathic and altruistic than others partly because of the genetic makeup they inherited at conception. However, that identical twins did not have identical prosocial tendencies indicates that their unique life experiences also affected them. Overall, then, there is some evidence of a biological basis for empathy and altruism. Yet it is not at all clear exactly what is inherited, and it is very clear that social learning experiences also determine how prosocial we are.

Culture and altruism Critics of sociobiological views of human behavior suggest that *cultural* evolution may be more important than biological evolution in shaping prosocial behavior (Boyd & Richerson, 1990; Campbell, 1978). If societies have functioned better and lasted longer when they have developed ways of socializing their members to control their selfish urges and to act prosocially, societies might have evolved in prosocial directions over time. If the mechanism behind biological evolution is genetic inheritance, the mechanism behind cultural evolution is learning. Through such means as child-rearing practices, religious training, education, and even the borrowing of ideas from other cultures, some societies could have evolved to be far more prosocial than others, even if humans everywhere were biologically predisposed to be selfish (Boyd & Richerson, 1990).

Some cultures have indeed been more successful at fostering prosocial behavior than others have. Summarizing research on cross-cultural differences in children's tendencies to help and cooperate, for example, Nancy Eisenberg and Paul Mussen (1989) conclude, "Most children reared in Mexican villages, Hopi children on reservations in the Southwest, and youngsters on Israeli kibbutzim are more considerate, kind, and cooperative than their 'typical' middle-class American counterparts" (p. 66). Prosocial behavior is most strongly encouraged in **collectivist cultures,** cultures in which the good of the group (for example, the extended family) is considered more important than the desires of the individual (Triandis, McCusker, & Hui, 1990). People in many Latin American and Asian countries, as well as members of many Native American groups in North America, grow up in collectivist cultures. In **individualist cultures,** such as those of the United States and Canada, less emphasis is placed on the individual's responsibility for others' welfare, and more is placed on freedom to pursue one's own personal goals. Thus, for example, when Japanese children (from a collectivist culture) and Australian children (from an individualist culture) were asked to decide whether their own group or another group of children should have a chance to win chocolates over a series of trials, Japanese children typically favored giving everyone an equal chance to win treats, whereas Australian children selfishly claimed that their own group should have more opportunities to win (Mann, Radford, & Kanagawa, 1985).

One of the main ways in which societies influence their members is by establishing, transmitting, and enforcing *norms,* socially agreed-upon standards of behavior. Even our relatively individualist culture has norms that encourage prosocial behavior and make us feel we "must" help (Simmons, 1991). The **social-responsibility norm,** for example, states that we should help those who need help (Berkowitz & Daniels, 1963). We all learn this and are indeed likely to feel morally obligated to help those who are dependent or needy. More compelling still is the **reciprocity norm,** which states that people should help those who have helped them and should not injure those who have helped them (Gouldner, 1960). People often experience strong feelings of obligation to reciprocate when someone does them a favor, a fact well known to prisoners who attempt to "buy" and dominate newcomers by giving them gifts (McCorkle & Korn, 1954). Equity theorists (see Chapter 9) would say that helping someone creates an imbalance in the relationship that motivates the recipient of the help to restore equity.

Of course, people who have internalized societal norms that call for prosocial behavior do not always behave as they know they should (Piliavin, Dovidio, Gaertner, & Clark, 1981). Moreover, norms that would discourage helping—for example, norms that say "Mind your own business" or "Look out for Number

One"—may seem equally applicable in a particular situation. Nonetheless, the social norms of one's cultural group influence one's tendency to behave prosocially.

Most likely, biological and cultural forces work together to encourage selfless behavior (Batson, 1983; Simon, 1990b). For example, kin selection might create a biologically-based tendency to aid kin, and culture might then build on that foundation by urging us to be concerned about non-kin as well. After all, norms embodied in religious teachings encourage us to love our neighbors as ourselves and to act in a spirit of "brotherly love." Or, as Herbert Simon (1990b) has argued, the biological basis for altruism could actually be a genetic predisposition to learn society's rules and norms well, including norms of prosocial behavior. As evidence mounts that empathy can produce a truly altruistic motivation to help, and as we come to appreciate the contributions of both biology and culture to prosocial behavior, we gain new insights into why people like Roger Lindsay behave as they do.

▶ A Decision-Making Model of Helping

Whether our motivations to help other people are biological or cultural in origin, and whether they are altruistic or egoistic in nature, we still must decide whether or not to help in specific situations. Most models of helping behavior assume that people progress through steps when deciding to help or not to help (Latané & Darley, 1970; Piliavin et al., 1981; Schwartz, 1977). These models emphasize *cognitive processes,* such as interpreting a situation and weighing the consequences of alternative actions, and they emphasize *emotions* as motivators of helpful behavior (Krebs & Miller, 1985).

For example, Jane Piliavin and her associates (Piliavin et al., 1981) have proposed an **arousal/cost-reward model** of helping in emergency situations; this model can be extended to nonemergencies as well. It consists of five steps: (1) becoming aware of someone's need for help, (2) experiencing arousal, (3) interpreting cues and labeling one's arousal, (4) calculating the costs and rewards of alternative actions, and (5) making a decision and taking action of some kind.

No decision making will occur at all if you never notice that someone needs help. It is easier to become aware of the need for help if the situation is a clear-cut,

unambiguous emergency—if billowing flames rather than wisps of smoke are coming out of your neighbor's house and if you hear screaming rather than the blare of a TV inside. But many helping situations are ambiguous and may or may not be interpreted as emergencies.

The second step in the model is becoming emotionally aroused, and the third step is labeling or interpreting that arousal. You may, for example, hear what sounds like a struggle outside your apartment and feel your heart begin to thump, but you are more likely to help if you attribute your arousal to what is going on outside your door than if you attribute it to the three cups of coffee you just drank or the vampire movie you have been watching on TV. More generally, you must interpret your physiological arousal and the cues in the situation in a way that motivates you to help. Piliavin and her associates assume that arousal is distressing and that we are egoistically motivated to reduce it. However, arousal could just as well be created by empathy for a victim and might then create an altruistic motive to decrease the victim's distress, as Batson's empathy-altruism hypothesis claims.

Emergencies are indeed physiologically arousing and, more important, people who are more highly aroused are more likely to help or to help quickly (Piliavin et al., 1981). For example, Samuel Gaertner and John Dovidio (1977) staged an emergency in which a stack of chairs apparently crashed down on a woman in the next room. Bystanders who had the fastest heart rates and reported that they felt the most upset intervened more quickly than those who were less aroused. However, arousal alone was insufficient to motivate helping: it also had to be labeled as a response to the victim's plight. Bystanders who were given a placebo that they were told would arouse them were slower to help than were bystanders who were given a placebo that supposedly would give them a dull headache and related symptoms but would not arouse them. Those given the "arousing" placebo would be likely to attribute any arousal they felt when they heard the crash to the drug rather than to the crash.

The fourth step of the arousal/cost-reward model involves carrying out a cost-reward analysis in which one cognitively weighs the consequences of helping or failing to help. Emotional arousal motivates action of some kind, and cost-benefit deliberations then influence what kind of action (direct helping, indirect helping, or escape) one chooses in the fifth step of the decision-making process.

In weighing consequences, first the individual must consider the almost inevitable *costs of helping:* effort and time expended, loss of resources, the risk of harm, possible embarrassment or disapproval of others, negative emotional reactions to interacting with the victim, and so on. Costs also include rewards one has to forgo in order to help (as when helping means missing a party or a job interview). To establish the *net* costs of helping, the bystander would subtract these costs from any potential rewards for helping: monetary rewards to heroic citizens, social approval, increased self-esteem associated with being helpful and living up to one's moral values, and so on.

The individual must also weigh the *costs of not helping*. Piliavin and her colleagues (Piliavin et al., 1981) divide these costs into personal costs and empathy costs. Personal costs of failing to help include such consequences as guilt, loss of self-esteem, and social disapproval. Empathy costs are those related to the knowledge that the victim will continue to suffer without help.

We are concerned here with costs and rewards *as the individual perceives them*. Different people may calculate costs differently; the person with a black belt in karate may view tackling a mugger as a low-cost action, but others of us may figure it will be our last day on earth if we try. Moreover, people sometimes distort costs and rewards when they face difficult decisions. Such cognitive distortion offers one way out of the dilemma posed by an emergency in which the costs of helping and the costs of failure to help are both high (Piliavin et al., 1981). A person can downplay the consequences of failing to help by thinking, "It's not so serious," or "Someone else will soon be along to help." Magically, the costs of failing to help are lowered!

Many of the influences on prosocial behavior that we discuss in this chapter work by affecting perceptions of costs and rewards. Figure 11.2 summarizes the general predictions Piliavin's model makes about how a person is likely to respond when the costs of helping and the costs of not helping are either high or low. For example, the model predicts that a person is most likely to help when the costs of helping are low but the costs of not helping are very high. This might be the case if a simple tug on your child's arm could keep the child from being hit by a car. By contrast, one can expect little help if helping is likely to be very costly but failing

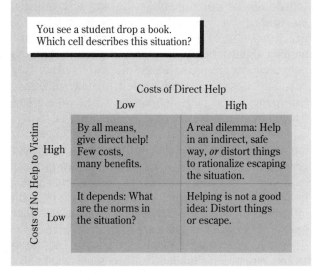

Figure 11.2 *Predicted effects of cost factors.*

to help is not, as when it might take many years of volunteer work to significantly improve the lives of homeless people in your community and no one would notice if you did nothing at all. Much research supports these predictions (Piliavin et al., 1981).

Perhaps this picture of how people decide whether to offer help seems too cold and calculating. The arousal/cost-reward model of helping views arousal or emotion as an important motivator of helping. However, potential helpers are also seen as proceeding step by step through a decision-making process that starts with the perception of a need for help and ends, after a rational consideration of costs and rewards, in a decision. Let us modify this picture a bit. Bibb Latané and John Darley (1970) emphasize that, by their very nature, emergencies are dangerous, unusual, unique, unforeseen, and pressing. As a result, emergencies produce high levels of arousal that may interfere with rational decision making and action. Indeed, some emergencies are so severe and arousing that bystanders act impulsively, ignoring many cues in the situation, failing to weigh costs and rewards, and behaving in ways that appear irrational to an outsider. For example, Roger Lindsay, the hero described at the start of the chapter, said the following about his decision making: "I didn't stop to think. . . . Something just took over me" (Kreutz, 1991, p. 2B). Decision-making models of helping do not describe impulsive helping in compelling emergencies very well. Nor do they fit situations in which we merely act out well-rehearsed routines of helping (Schwartz, 1977), as when parents routinely help their children with homework and bandage their cuts. Still, decision-making models fit many situations, emergencies and nonemergencies, when we are confronted by a new situation and are unsure what to do.

Now that we have introduced emotion (experiencing arousal, including empathic arousal) and cognition (interpreting the situation, labeling one's arousal, and calculating costs and rewards) as basic aspects of the helping response, we can look more closely at specific influences on helping behavior. Like all social behavior, prosocial behavior is influenced by characteristics of the situation, characteristics of the person, and the interaction between situational and personal factors.

▶ Situational Influences on Prosocial Behavior

The situations in which prosocial acts occur vary widely, from emergencies to nonemergencies, from ambiguous situations to clear-cut ones. Accordingly, levels of emotional arousal and cost-reward factors also vary widely from situation to situation.

The Person in Need of Help

Characteristics and behaviors of persons needing help are among the most important situational cues that potential helpers use to interpret the situation and decide whether to help. Who receives help and who does not?

The nature of the need By its very nature, helping is a response to a person in need, a person who is dependent. Dependency can be a stable characteristic of a person (for example, a mentally retarded child), the result of a temporary plight (for example, a sprained ankle), or a feature of the role relationship between two people (for example, between therapist and client). However, potential helpers look closely at the nature of and reasons behind an individual's dependency.

First, potential helpers are influenced by the clarity and legitimacy of a person's need. They are more likely to intervene when the victim's need is clear and unambiguous than when it is unclear whether the victim really needs help (Clark & Word, 1972; Krebs & Miller,

1985). If Roger Lindsay had thought the man in the lake was frolicking in the water rather than drowning, he probably would not have launched a rescue effort. A practical tip to accident victims, then: Don't make bystanders guess; yell for help!

Potential helpers also consider the legitimacy of a person's need. Imagine how you would react if a woman approached you in the supermarket and asked for a dime to buy milk. Then imagine how you would react if she instead asked for a dime for frozen cookie dough. Bickman and Kamzan (1973) found that 58% of the shoppers who were asked for milk money responded, but only 36% were willing to give money for cookie dough. The more legitimate the need, the more help is received.

The perceived cause of a person's need is also important. Suppose you are approached by a fellow student who needs your class notes. Would you be more likely to help the student who claims to be incapable of taking good notes or the student who is unmotivated and skips class for the fun of it? Typically, you are more likely to help if the need is caused by something the individual cannot control, such as a lack of ability or a family emergency, than if it arises from something more controllable, such as a lack of effort (Weiner, 1980). According to Bernard Weiner's attribution theory (Weiner, 1986; see also Chapter 4), the attributions we make about the cause of dependency or need influence the nature of our emotional responses, which in turn influence our behavior. When we attribute someone's need to uncontrollable causes, emotions such as empathy and pity are aroused, and these emotions motivate helping (Betancourt, 1990). However, when we attribute a person's need to controllable factors and hold the person responsible for his or her plight, negative emotions such as anger are aroused, and they prompt us to deny the person aid. This has unfortunate implications for people whose problems are viewed by many of us as their own fault—people who have AIDS, abuse drugs, or are overweight, for example. The person whose AIDS was apparently caused by a blood transfusion can generally expect more sympathy and help than the person whose AIDS we attribute to sexual promiscuity (Weiner, Perry, & Magnusson, 1988).

All this is quite straightforward. The people who receive help are those who are in need or dependent on others and whose needs are clear, legitimate, and uncontrollable in origin. But a puzzle arises: sometimes the people who should have the greatest claims on us for those very reasons are not given the help they deserve. In one study, for example, a person with a bandaged forearm received more help picking up dropped envelopes than a person who was not disabled, but a person with a bandaged forearm, an eye patch, and a scar received no more help than a person who was not disabled (Samerotte & Harris, 1976). The best way to account for such exceptions may be to consider the costs of helping. People often experience an aversion to disabled, disfigured, or otherwise stigmatized individuals and may be reluctant to pay the extra "costs" of interacting with such individuals, despite their clear need for help.

Relationship with the potential helper Relationships between relatives and friends imply mutual dependency and a special obligation to help (M.S. Clark, 1983). We help family members and friends more than strangers in everyday life (Amato, 1990). Even a brief acquaintance is enough to make us more likely to help someone (Latané & Darley, 1970; Pearce, 1980). Those people with whom we have some relationship are seen as part of our "we-group," as Harvey Hornstein (1976) phrases it. We become more emotionally aroused and therefore motivated to help when someone in our we-group is in trouble than when the person in need is a total stranger. We may also view the rewards of helping and the costs of not helping as greater.

More generally, we are especially helpful to anyone who is similar to ourselves in some important way (Krebs, 1975). Other attractive qualities in a victim besides similarity also influence us. For example, pleasant people are helped more than unpleasant ones (Gross, Wallston, & Piliavin, 1975), and applications for graduate school left in phone booths are more likely to be returned if a physically attractive person's photo is attached than if a physically unattractive person's photo is attached (Benson, Karabenick, & Lerner, 1976).

If we generally help people who are similar to ourselves or are otherwise attractive, are we more helpful to members of our own racial or ethnic group than to members of other groups? The evidence here is mixed (see Piliavin et al., 1981). For example, whites sometimes help blacks less than they help whites, sometimes help blacks and whites equally, and sometimes show reverse discrimination by helping blacks more

than they help whites. Similar inconsistencies are found in the helping behavior of blacks. The simple "help those who are similar" rule does not seem to hold up well here. Why not?

According to Irwin Katz (1981), the feelings of most white people toward black people are ambivalent: most whites feel sympathetic toward blacks and want to be unprejudiced, but at the same time they are uncomfortable around blacks and harbor some negative feelings toward them. These ambivalent emotional responses result in inconsistent and extreme behavioral reactions. For example, if denial of help to blacks would smack of racial prejudice, most whites would bend over backward to help. However, if whites can find an acceptable reason other than race for failing to help blacks, the negative side of their ambivalence may win out. Gaertner and Dovidio (1977) found that whites helped blacks as quickly as they helped whites in an unambiguous emergency in which a fellow research participant was apparently struck by a stack of falling chairs and screamed from the next room. In this clear emergency, failure to help the black victim would be inexcusable and would seem racist. However, whites helped blacks less quickly than they helped whites in an ambiguous emergency (the same crashing sounds, but no scream to signal injury). Here subjects may have consciously or unconsciously rationalized their failure to help along these lines: "It's not that I'm prejudiced against blacks; it's just that this person does not seem to be in any serious trouble" (see also Frey & Gaertner, 1986).

Generally, then, we can expect whites to be most helpful to blacks when a failure to help would clearly mark them as bigots and least helpful to blacks when they can avoid this cost of not helping by justifying their inaction on more acceptable grounds. Such prejudiced behavior is far more subtle than the overt racism of the past, but it is prejudice nonetheless (see Chapter 13 for a fuller discussion of racism). Similarly, ambivalent feelings toward people with disabilities may explain why we sometimes go out of our way to help them and at other times fail to give them as much help as we give people without disabilities who are in the same situation (Katz, 1981).

So who elicits help? We help those who are dependent and whose dependency is clear, legitimate, and no fault of their own. In addition, we are especially helpful to people we view as part of our we-group, people with whom we already have some relationship, people who are similar to ourselves, or people who are otherwise attractive to us. At the same time, ambivalent attitudes toward dissimilar others, such as those of another race, can cause us to help them more or less than similar others, depending on whether our sympathetic or prejudiced feelings win out.

The Influence of Other Bystanders

If you witness an emergency and other people are present, they too become part of the situation from your perspective and can influence you not only by their actions but by their very presence. Some of the first and most fascinating social-psychological research on helping behavior was inspired by a disturbing and puzzling incident in New York City in 1964. The stabbing of Kitty Genovese might have passed for "just another murder" except for some peculiar circumstances:

> For more than half an hour thirty-eight respectable, law-abiding citizens in Queens watched a killer stalk and stab a woman in three separate attacks in Kew Gardens. Twice the sound of their voices and the sudden glow of their bedroom lights interrupted him and frightened him off. Each time he returned, sought her out and stabbed her again. Not one person telephoned the police during the assault; one witness called after the woman was dead. [Gansberg, 1964, p. 1]

The New York community was appalled by this dramatic failure to help, all the more because the number of potential helpers was so large. Why did it happen? Why have similar incidents happened since? Bibb Latané and John Darley set out to find an explanation, suspecting that the very presence of so many witnesses may have contributed to Kitty Genovese's death.

In one of their early laboratory studies, Darley and Latané (1968) seated students in cubicles connected by an intercom system and asked them to discuss college life. Students were led to believe either that they were alone with another participant (who would soon be the victim of an epileptic seizure), that there was one other witness besides themselves, or that there were four other witnesses. The victim explained that he had seizures; then the next time he came on the air he had one, becoming incoherent and crying for help ("I'm gonna die-er-help-err-er-seizure-er"). Helping was both less likely and slower to occur as the number of potential helpers increased (see Figure 11.3). This, then, is the **bystander effect:** The presence of other bystanders decreases the likelihood that an individual will help.

After reviewing more than fifty studies of the bystander effect in both emergencies and nonemergencies, Latané and Nida (1981) concluded that the effect is very consistent and that the biggest difference in willingness to help is between solo bystanders and those accompanied by at least one other potential helper. In studies in which participants were either alone or in the presence of confederates of the experimenter who failed to take action, 75% of the people who were alone helped on average, but only 53% of those in the presence of others did so. But does this really mean there is no safety in numbers? Even if each individual has a lower probability of helping when he or she is part of a group, isn't it likely that *someone* in a group will provide help and that the victim will therefore be helped more often by groups than by individuals? Not really, according to Latané and Nida. In many situations, the victim is actually less likely to receive help from a group of bystanders than from a single bystander. Thus, the presence of others not only decreases the likelihood that an individual will help but can even decrease, though less consistently and powerfully, the probability that the victim will receive help.

What causes the bystander effect? Three social processes may account for it (Latané & Darley, 1970; Latané, Nida, & Wilson, 1981). Through a *social influence* process, bystanders look to others to help them interpret the situation and decide what to do, and they may conclude that the need for help is not so great if others do not seem alarmed or are not taking action. Second, *audience inhibition*, also called *evaluation apprehension,* may contribute to the bystander effect if a bystander is worried about how others will evaluate his or her behavior. The risk of embarrassing oneself—for example, by rushing around as though there were an emergency when there is not—is a cost factor that may inhibit helping. The third contributing process is *diffusion of responsibility:* when several potential helpers are available, responsibility for acting is divided, so each individual may be less likely to assume personal responsibility for acting. These three processes—social influence, audience inhibition, and diffusion of responsibility—influence whether or not the bystander effect will occur.

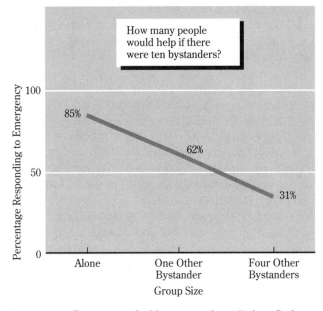

Figure 11.3 *Percentage of subjects exposed to a "seizure" who intervened before the end of the taped emergency.*
Source: "Bystander Intervention in Emergencies: Diffusion of Responsibility" by J. M. Darley and B. Latané, 1968, *Journal of Personality and Social Psychology, 8,* pp. 377–383.

Social influence processes that affect a bystander's interpretation of the situation are more important in ambiguous emergencies than in clear and severe emergencies, where there is little need to rely on cues from other people to tell you an emergency is occurring. Indeed, in one study 100% rates of helping were obtained from groups of bystanders when a maintenance man fell and cried out in pain in the next room (Clark & Word, 1972). The presence of others inhibited helping only when the emergency was more ambiguous—when bystanders heard the fall, but not the cry. If other bystanders are not passive but instead indicate by their alarmed expressions or by what they say that the situation is clearly an emergency, they can actually encourage the individual to view the situation as serious and to help (Bickman, 1979). Indeed, if someone in the group begins to help, others will follow his or her lead (Wilson & Petruska, 1984). In the language of social learning theory, then, other bystanders can be models of either action or inaction.

The audience inhibition process underlying the bystander effect depends on the individual's believing that others will disapprove if he or she treats the situation as an emergency and takes action. When other bystanders seem unconcerned, a person may conclude that the group norm in the situation is inaction and may worry about being negatively evaluated if he or she helps. However, if the group clearly views helping as appropriate, a person may worry instead about what others will think if he or she *fails* to act. Much depends on what an individual thinks the group's norm is (Schwartz & Gottlieb, 1980). If a group is cohesive or close, helping rates may actually increase when other group members are present, possibly because people know that their friends will approve if they act in socially responsible ways (Rutkowski, Gruder, & Romer, 1983). Similarly, neighborhood watch programs may increase people's sense that they can count on their neighbors' support if they report suspicious activity in the area to the police.

Finally, diffusion of responsibility appears to depend partly on whether responsibility is focused on individual bystanders and on whether they feel more competent to help than other bystanders. For example, 95% of the beach-goers in one study who noticed a thief swiping a portable radio from a beach blanket pursued the culprit if they had been specifically asked by the radio's owner to guard his or her belongings. Only 20% of those who were not singled out for responsibility in this way intervened (Moriarty, 1975). And, because they feel especially competent to help in medical emergencies, registered nurses do not seem to fall prey to the bystander effect; even when another bystander is present, they help (Carmer, McMaster, Bartell, & Dragna, 1988). Meanwhile, people without medical training feel little personal responsibility for intervening in a medical emergency when they know that someone with medical expertise is on the scene (Schwartz & Clausen, 1970).

In summary, the bystander effect is most likely to occur when all three processes underlying it are operating—when bystanders conclude from one another's impassive behavior that nothing is wrong (social influence), when they feel that the group's norm is one of inaction and fear social disapproval if they act (audience inhibition), and when they feel no personal responsibility for acting because responsibility seems to be spread among them (diffusion of responsibility). But the bystander effect can also be avoided—for example, when an event is clearly an emergency and group members react as if it were, when group norms support prosocial action, and when bystanders somehow feel personally responsible for acting, perhaps because they have been singled out for responsibility or possess needed expertise. Although the bystander effect can play itself out time and again if the conditions are right, our tendencies to help can also be influenced in more positive ways by the presence and actions of other people.

Personal Influences on Prosocial Behavior

Clearly, situational influences on prosocial behavior are important. But don't some people have traits that make them more likely than others to be Good Samaritans, regardless of the situation? Wouldn't Mother Teresa, who has devoted her life to helping needy people all over the world, be the first to return a lost wallet or give a stranger directions? How do more fleeting psychological states, such as moods of the moment, affect a person's willingness to help? In this section we will see how a potential helper's characteristics influence his or her behavior.

Searching for the Good Samaritan

The search for a prototype of the Good Samaritan has proven challenging. Consider the seemingly simple question of whether men or women are more helpful. It has not been possible to conclude that one gender is more helpful overall because it depends so much on the type of helping situation (Eagly & Crowley, 1986). For example, men are more likely than women to intervene in dangerous emergencies. In one study, all but one of a sample of people who had intervened to stop criminals was a man (Huston, Ruggiero, Connor, & Geis, 1981). Acting heroically in dangerous situations is considered part of the traditional male role (Eagly & Crowley, 1986), and men may perceive the costs of intervening in risky situations to be lower than women do because the men are stronger or are more likely to have relevant skills, such as self-defense training (Huston et al., 1981). Meanwhile, women are more likely than men to provide help and emotional support in con-

nection with their traditional gender roles as nurturers—for example, to care for children and aging parents on a day-by-day basis (Brody, 1990; Eagly & Crowley, 1986; Pleck, 1985).

People who live in rural areas or small towns have been found to be more helpful in many situations than people who live in big cities (House & Wolf, 1978; Steblay, 1987). As Figure 11.4 shows, the percentage of people who help strangers who approach them on the street decreases as population size increases in many, though not in all, helping situations (Amato, 1983). However, this difference does not mean that growing up in a small town endows people with altruistic personalities and growing up in a big city makes them callous. Instead, there is something about being in a crowded, noisy, hectic environment, wherever one grew up, that inhibits helping (Steblay, 1987). One explanation for this phenomenon is the **urban-overload hypothesis** proposed by Stanley Milgram (1970). According to Milgram, people living in big cities must be selective in the face of high levels of stimulation or they would not be able to function. That sometimes means ignoring people in need, treating people brusquely, and being choosy about whom to help. (See Chapter 14 for further discussion of this hypothesis.)

More important than where you grew up is whether your parents served as models of altruism and instilled concern for the welfare of others. When researchers have interviewed people who rescued Jews from the Nazis during World War II at great risk to their own lives, they have found that almost all these altruists identified strongly with parents who had high moral standards, were caring, and taught their children to be concerned about all human beings, not just members of their own "in-groups" (Fogelman & Wiener, 1985; London, 1970; Oliner & Oliner, 1988). For example, one rescuer said her parents taught her "not to make differences between people. We all have one God. It doesn't matter how much money you have, or anything" (Fogelman & Wiener, 1985, p. 65).

Influenced perhaps by their experiences in the family during childhood, helpful people seem to have a highly developed sense of morality. They think in sophisticated ways about moral issues, are concerned with principles of human justice, are oriented toward the needs of others, and have taken the norm of social responsibility to heart (Eisenberg, 1986; Erkut, Jaquette, & Staub, 1981; Rushton, 1984). They also have a highly developed capacity to understand others' viewpoints and to empathize with them (Eisenberg & Miller, 1987; Underwood & Moore, 1982). Either principled moral thinking or empathy for victims often motivated people who rescued Jews from the Nazis (Oliner & Oliner, 1988). One woman, for example, became involved because she was committed to the principle of human equality. Another was motivated by empathy for an escaped concentration camp inmate who begged her for shelter: "He was shivering, poor soul, and I was shivering too, with emotion" (Oliner & Oliner, 1988, p. 189).

Another factor that distinguishes helpful people from less helpful people is their sense of competence to help, as indicated by both high self-esteem and possession of the helping skills needed in particular situations (Midlarsky, 1984). People who intervene in dangerous emergencies are more likely to have had training in such relevant skills as lifesaving, first aid, and self-defense than similar individuals who do not intervene (Huston et al., 1981; Shotland & Heinold,

1985). Other skills may be more relevant in other helping situations. Thus, volunteers who succeed as telephone crisis counselors have good perspective-taking skills that allow them to understand callers' problems (Clary & Orenstein, 1991).

Finally, helpfulness in everyday life may be influenced not only by one's personality traits and competencies but by the extent of one's social involvements. Paul Amato (1990) asked college students to report how often they engaged in various forms of formal planned helping, informal planned helping, and spontaneous or unplanned helping; Table 11.2 contains examples of these three kinds of helping. Engaging in a good deal of planned helping—doing volunteer work, caring for sick relatives, and so on—was associated with scoring high on a measure of sense of social responsibility and having a strong sense of self-efficacy as a helper (believing that one's helping efforts would have a positive impact). An even stronger association existed, though, between engaging in planned helping and being involved in many social relationships. As role

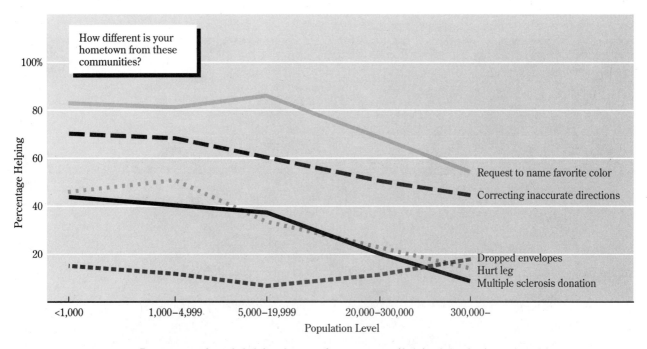

Figure 11.4 *Percentages of people helping decrease for most types of helping behavior in communities with larger populations. Different requests also elicit different rates for helping.*
Source: "Helping Behavior in Urban and Rural Environments: Field Studies Based on a Taxonomic Organization of Helping Episodes" by P. R. Amato, 1983, *Journal of Personality and Social Psychology, 45,* pp. 571–586.

theorists would predict, students very often helped as part of their roles as sons and daughters, friends, neighbors, church members, and so on. The more roles they played in life, the more prosocial acts they performed. Meanwhile, neither personal traits nor level of involvement in social roles and relationships predicted the amount of spontaneous helping an individual did, perhaps because these opportunities to help strangers—the very opportunities studied so often by social psychologists—arise unexpectedly and involve little thought or planning, and therefore may not closely reflect a person's enduring personal and social characteristics.

Relationships between prosocial tendencies and some of the personal factors emphasized here—parents who model and encourage altruism, a strong sense of morality, empathy for others, competence, and involvement in many social roles—have tended to be fairly weak and inconsistent. The problem is that helping situations vary so greatly that it may be unrealistic to expect the same traits to predict behavior in every situation. As a result, researchers have sometimes had better luck predicting helping behavior when they have

focused on personal qualities directly relevant to a specific helping situation. (This may remind you of the discussion of attitude-behavior relationships in Chapter 6.) For example, Shalom Schwartz and his colleagues (Schwartz, 1973; Schwartz & Howard, 1984) have shown that strong *personal norms,* or feelings of moral obligation to help *in a specific situation,* predict helping in that situation better than endorsement of broad norms of prosocial behavior does. Thus, if you wish to predict which people will recycle their cans, bottles, and newspapers, ask people whether they feel a sense of moral obligation to recycle waste rather than about their general sense of social responsibility.

However, to really understand why some people are more helpful than others, we must understand how situational characteristics and personal characteristics interact to influence behavior. To cite just one example, Michael White and Lawrence Gerstein (1987) presented lectures on helping behavior to introductory psychology students. Some students were given the message that norms supporting prosocial behavior are strong and that one can expect social rewards for helping and disapproval for failing to help. Others heard in-

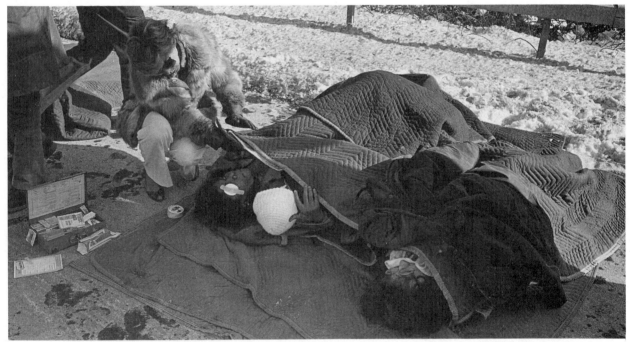

One factor that distinguishes helpful people from less helpful people is their sense of competence to help.
Alan Carey / The Image Works

Table 11.2 Examples of planned and unplanned spontaneous forms of everyday helping: How many have you engaged in this month?

Formal Planned Helping

Donated time to a charitable organization that gives assistance to needy people.

Served as a volunteer counselor through an organization or agency.

Donated blood or any other medical item.

Returned bottles, cans, or newspapers to a recycling center.

Informal Planned Helping

Lent a possession, such as a book, record, or car, to a friend or relative.

Helped someone move into a house.

Had a talk with a friend or relative about a personal problem he or she was experiencing.

Looked after a person's plants, mail, or pets while he or she was away.

Spontaneous Helping

Gave directions to a stranger.

Opened a door for someone who had his or her arms full.

Helped a stranger with a stalled car by providing jumper cables or calling for assistance.

Provided assistance to a stranger who had fallen over or appeared to be ill.

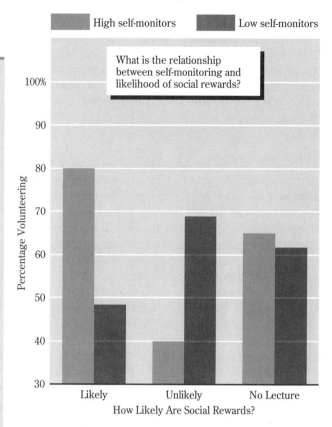

Figure 11.5 *Personal and situational factors interact to influence volunteering to help people with visual impairments.*
Source: "Helping: The Influence of Anticipated Social Sanctions and Self-Monitoring" by M. J. White and L. H. Gerstein, 1987, *Journal of Personality, 55,* pp. 41–54.

stead that prosocial norms have lost force today and that one cannot necessarily expect social rewards for helping or punishments for not helping. Still others served as controls and heard no lecture at all. The researchers also administered a scale to identify students who were high self-monitors—individuals likely to be closely attuned to information about norms of appropriate behavior—and low self-monitors, who were likely to be less concerned with "impression management" (see Chapter 3, where **self-monitoring** was discussed in more detail). Four weeks later, students received phone calls asking them to volunteer as readers for students with visual impairments.

As Figure 11.5 shows, high and low self-monitors in the control group did not differ at all in their willingness to volunteer; self-monitoring tendencies, by themselves, were unrelated to helping. However, high self-

monitors were far more likely to volunteer when they had been led to believe that helping is socially rewarding than when they had been led to believe that it is not, as if they were egoistically motivated to use the information they had received to gain social approval by volunteering. Low self-monitors were *less* likely to volunteer when reward seemed likely than when it seemed unlikely, suggesting that they may have resisted the social pressure to help contained in the "help is rewarding" lecture. In this case, a personality variable (self-monitoring) and a situational variable (information about the social rewards associated with helping) interacted to influence behavior.

If the kind of person who helps in one situation is simply not the same kind of person who helps in another situation, the search for traits that predict Good Samaritanism in all situations may indeed be futile (Piliavin & Charng, 1990). Although some people seem to be more consistently prosocial across a range of situations than others are (Rushton, 1984), we must learn much more about who helps most in which specific situations.

Moods and Helping

Just as our enduring traits influence our willingness to help, so too do our temporary states. Suppose you have had a wonderful day, with money, grades, love, and anything else your heart desires all coming your way. Would you want to spread your happiness to a beggar, or would you walk by rather than risk spoiling your good mood? What happens if your mood is bad?

Good moods   Alice Isen (1970) administered a battery of tests to teachers and college students, telling some they had scored very well, others they had performed poorly, and still others nothing at all. A fourth group did not take the tests. The "successful" subjects were more likely than the others to help a woman struggling with an armful of books. Isen therefore spoke of a "warm glow of success" that makes people more likely to help. As it turns out, good moods that have nothing to do with success also make people more helpful than they would otherwise be (Carlson, Charlin, & Miller, 1988; Isen, 1987). Students who are given free cookies are more helpful than students who have no such good fortune (Isen & Levin, 1972). Even beautiful weather can lift people's spirits and make them more helpful (Cunningham, 1979). These findings have practical implications: People who are made to feel happy are more likely to help with charity drives (Weyant, 1978), and happy salespeople are more likely than their glummer colleagues to go beyond the call of duty in serving customers and lending a hand to co-workers (George, 1991).

When are good moods most likely to motivate prosocial behavior, and why? One view is that positive emotions give rise to positive thoughts and set up a "loop" of positive cognitions about self and others. The happy person can prolong this loop by engaging in prosocial behavior (Isen, 1987). If people must do something unpleasant to be helpful—for example, if they

must participate in an experiment in which their job is to distract rather than to aid subjects—they are less likely to volunteer (Isen & Levin, 1972). Happy people often seem to be motivated to stay happy and may not want to jeopardize their happiness by doing something distasteful (Carlson et al., 1988).

Happy people are also more motivated to help when their attention is focused on their own good fortune rather than on the good fortune of someone else (Carlson et al., 1988). For example, David Rosenhan and his colleagues (Rosenhan, Salovey, & Hargis, 1981) found that happiness over the idea of being sent to Hawaii increased helping, but empathic joy at the thought of a friend's going to Hawaii actually decreased helping below the level for the control group that imagined more neutral experiences. Feeling happy for someone else rather than for oneself may create negative feelings, such as jealousy. Happy people, then, are highly motivated to help unless negative thoughts—concern that providing help might be a "downer" or resentment of a friend's good fortune, for example—intrude on their happy feelings and thoughts (Carlson et al., 1988).

Bad moods   If good moods make helping more likely, do bad moods make it less likely? Actually, most evidence suggests the opposite. People in bad moods are often more helpful than they would be otherwise (Carlson & Miller, 1987). Yet the link between bad moods and helping is not as consistent and strong as the link between good moods and helping, so there has been much interest in determining when bad moods motivate helping and when they do not.

Guilt—for example, the guilt felt after accidentally breaking someone's camera or knocking an experimenter's research materials to the floor—appears to be the negative emotion that most consistently motivates helping (Carlson & Miller, 1987; Dovidio, 1984). As emphasized by the negative-state relief model of helping discussed earlier in this chapter, sadness can also motivate helping under some conditions (Cialdini, Darby, & Vincent, 1973; Cialdini et al., 1987; Schaller & Cialdini, 1988). People feel happier and better about themselves as people after they help someone (Williamson & Clark, 1989), and this may motivate those in bad moods to help.

People who are feeling guilty may not be more helpful, however, if something good happens to them before an opportunity to help arises (Cialdini, Darby, & Vincent, 1973), and people saddened by someone else's misfortunes may lose their motivation to help if they expect they will soon be laughing at comedy tapes (Schaller & Cialdini, 1988). Helping is only one way to relieve one's guilt or sadness, and the motivation to help is sometimes lost if there is another way to improve one's mood. People in bad moods also seem to weigh the costs and rewards of helping quite carefully (Cunningham, Shaffer, Barbee, Wolff, & Kelley, 1990; Weyant, 1978). For example, they help more if helping is likely to be easy and potentially very beneficial, as in sitting in a donation booth for the American Cancer Society, than if it is likely to be costly and of more dubious value, as in going door to door collecting for Little League baseball (Weyant, 1978).

Finally, people who are highly preoccupied with their own woes are not likely to help others (Aderman & Berkowitz, 1983; Gibbons & Wicklund, 1982). If you think you've just failed an important test and ruined your career, you may not even notice that someone needs help or, if you do, you may be too wrapped up in yourself to help. Bad moods are more likely to increase helping when they involve focusing one's attention on the misfortunes of others than when they involve thinking about one's own misfortunes (Carlson & Miller, 1987). If students are instructed to imagine the feelings a dying friend might experience, they are more helpful than students instructed to imagine their own reactions to a friend's dying (Thompson, Cowan, & Rosenhan, 1980). As Figure 11.6 shows, then, happy people are most likely to help when the focus of their attention is their own happiness, but sad people are most likely to help when their thoughts are focused on someone else's sadness. In short, not just any bad mood, or for that matter any good mood, increases helping behavior. It is important to consider the thoughts that accompany the mood.

In sum, being in a good mood generally makes people more likely to help than usual, especially if they are focused on their own good fortune and if negative thoughts do not intrude on their happy reveries. Being in a bad mood can also motivate helping, though less consistently. This is especially true when people feel guilty or sad, when helping is likely to improve their mood, and when their attention is focused on someone else's misfortunes rather than their own.

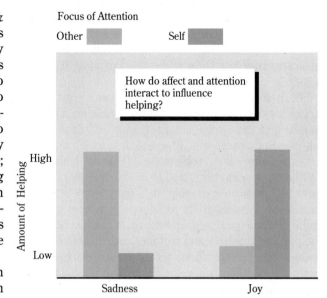

Figure 11.6 *Amount of helping as a function of mood and focus of attention.*
Source: "The Joys of Helping: Focus of Attention Mediates the Impact of Positive Affect on Altruism" by D. L. Rosenhan, P. Salovey, and K. Hargis, 1981, *Journal of Personality and Social Psychology, 40,* pp. 899–905.

▶ **Seeking and Receiving Help: The Recipient's Perspective**

So far we have been concerned with giving help rather than receiving it. Yet if our society has norms that call for giving help when it is needed, it also has norms that place a high value on self-reliance and independence. How do you feel when a back-seat driver "helps" you remember to stop at red lights? When a classmate who is no more capable than you are offers you help with your studies? Probably like screaming, "I'd rather do it myself!" Think too of the times when you have genuinely needed help but have been reluctant to seek it, as when you have driven around hopelessly lost rather than ask for directions or when you just couldn't bring yourself to ask your professor an important question. Seeking and receiving help sometimes means admitting that you are needy, incompetent, and dependent on others rather than self-reliant. It may also mean feeling indebted and pressured to reciprocate (Greenberg, 1980). The norm seems to be "Beggars can't be choosers" (Stein, 1989); no wonder receiving help has been characterized as a "mixed blessing" (Nadler & Fisher, 1986).

In their attempt to account for people's reactions to receiving help, Arie Nadler and Jeffrey Fisher have proposed that the critical determinant of whether help is appreciated or resented is the extent to which receiving it threatens one's self-esteem (Fisher, Nadler, & Whitcher-Alagna, 1982; Nadler & Fisher, 1986). As Figure 11.7 indicates, if help supports people's self-esteem—if it makes them feel loved or allows them to achieve their goals—they will react positively to the helper and the help and will feel comfortable seeking help in the future. If help threatens self-esteem, however, the recipient will generally dislike the helper and resent the help and will be motivated to regain a sense of self-respect.

What happens next depends on whether or not the help recipient feels in control of his or her life and sees possibilities for becoming more self-reliant in the future. People who have a strong sense of control will resist additional help and struggle hard to become more independent, as though they are determined to prove they can do without help. If their efforts succeed, their negative reactions to aid will give way to more positive feelings about it. However, when a help recipient's self-esteem has been threatened, and he or she perceives little opportunity to exert control, negative feelings toward the helper and the help will persist, and the individual may eventually give up and become chronically dependent on aid, resenting it all the while.

The critical question is: When is receiving help most likely to threaten people's self-esteem, make them more likely to bite than shake the hand that feeds them, and contribute to long-term dependency and helplessness? This question has special importance when we consider people who are frequently in the position of needing and receiving help—welfare recipients, homeless people, people with cancer or AIDS, and even countries heavily dependent on aid from

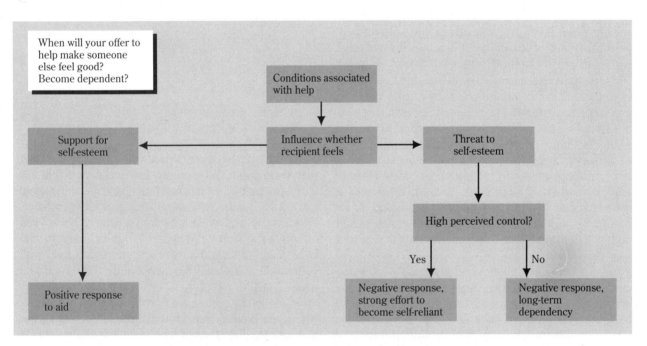

Figure 11.7 *Reactions to receiving aid depend on whether the conditions of the aid threaten self-esteem and on whether the help recipient perceives control over future performance.*
Source: "The Role of Threat to Self-Esteem and Perceived Control in Recipient Reaction to Help: Theory Development and Empirical Validation" by A. Nadler and J. D. Fisher, 1986, *Advances in Experimental Social Psychology, 19,* pp. 81–122.

Volunteers providing food to homeless people expect them to display "gratitude" rather than "attitude" and may be irritated by the occasional diner who is demanding or complains.

other nations. Characteristics of the helper, the helping situation, and the recipient can all make a difference.

To explore the effects of helper characteristics and of the helping situation, Nadler, Fisher, and Ben-Itzhak (1983) asked students to solve a mystery. Some were told that the task was a good indicator of intelligence; others, that it was a game of chance or luck. Some were then helped by a friend; others, by a stranger. When do you suppose students reacted most negatively to receiving help? In this study and others, threat to self-esteem appears greatest, and reactions to receiving help most negative, when people receive help from a similar other (a friend) on a task that is central to their self-concept (the "intelligence" test). We apparently cannot bear to feel incompetent compared with someone we regard as an equal when it is very important to us to feel competent. Needing help with a game of chance is not very ego-threatening; in situations like this, as in many everyday situations, we respond more positively to help from friends than to help from strangers.

Characteristics of the help recipient also matter: Some people simply have a harder time accepting help than others do. For example, people with high self-esteem are more likely than people with low self-esteem to view needing or receiving help as threatening, perhaps because they are less often in the position of having to admit to personal inadequacies (Nadler & Fisher, 1986; Nadler, Altman, & Fisher, 1979). People with high self-esteem may resist seeking help in the first place, especially when it means depending on someone similar to themselves to succeed at a task that is central to their sense of self-worth (Nadler, 1987). These people are also especially uncomfortable seeking help when they know they will not be able to reciprocate it and must remain in their helper's debt (Nadler, Mayseless, Peri, & Chemerinski, 1985).

Yet as the Nadler-Fisher model indicates, reacting negatively to receiving help can motivate people who have a strong sense of perceived control to become more self-reliant (Nadler & Fisher, 1986). In one study (DePaulo, Brown, Ishii, & Fisher, 1981), people with high self-esteem who were given a hint on one problem-solving task did better on a second, unrelated task than those who had not been helped. It was as though they rose to the challenge of proving that they needed no help. Meanwhile, people with low self-esteem actually did worse on the second task if they had been helped than if they had not. They may have seen receiving help as further proof of their incompetence and inability to control their lives and may have given up.

In summary, these findings explain why receiving help is a mixed blessing and have many practical implications for people in helping roles. Ideally, helpers should do all they can to reduce the threat to self-esteem associated with seeking and receiving help, to convince the people they are helping that there is no shame in needing help. Helpers can also make help readily and routinely available so people do not have to beg and humiliate themselves to get it (Broll, Gross, &

Piliavin, 1974). When help recipients experience a threat to their egos, helpers may be able to turn that into an advantage if they work to boost their clients' self-esteem, convince them that they can take control of their own lives, and actually show them how they can help themselves and become less dependent on others. When help undermines the self-worth of people with problems, and they feel powerless to change their lives, it only adds to their problems.

Some of these themes are well illustrated by the efforts of a woman named Lupe Anguiano to develop an alternative to the current welfare system (B. Berkowitz, 1987). In talks with women receiving Aid to Families with Dependent Children (AFDC), Anguiano heard them say repeatedly how much they hated being on welfare and how much they wanted to work. Yet many of these women had been through painful divorces, lacked confidence in themselves, and had no idea how to go about getting off welfare. Anguiano's approach, first tried in San Antonio, Texas, and since exported elsewhere, was simple: Give AFDC mothers job-skill training, put them in jobs that require those skills, and help them with child care and transportation expenses until they are established. The key, though, may be Anguiano's efforts to help women feel better about themselves and gain a sense of control over their lives. As she tells participants, "Hey, it's not Lupe Anguiano, or the National Women's Employment, it's you who's going to get you a job" (B. Berkowitz, 1987, p. 103).

▶ Toward a Prosocial Society

Although help is not always appreciated, and although some people believe we should value individual initiative and independence more highly than interdependence, most would agree that the world would be better if whatever prosocial tendencies people have were strengthened. How might knowledge of prosocial behavior be applied to achieve this goal?

Raising Prosocial Children

Although signs of empathy and tendencies to help and share are evident early in life, young children are still relatively egoistic at heart. As they get older, they normally become more prosocial, and their reasons for helping shift from a desire for rewards and approval to a more altruistic concern with other people's welfare (Eisenberg & Mussen, 1989). For example, most elementary school children claim that a girl who helps her father unload the car at the beach will be less happy than a girl who immediately runs to the shore to play; most adolescents believe that a helpful person is likely to be happier than a selfish one (Perry, Perry, & Weiss, 1986). This shift occurs partly because children's cognitive abilities improve and they become better able to take the perspectives of and empathize with others (Eisenberg & Mussen, 1989; Underwood & Moore, 1982). It also results from learning norms of prosocial behavior and discovering that adults approve of children who help and share (Cialdini, Baumann, & Kenrick, 1981).

How can parents contribute to this development? Parents of children who display high levels of empathy generally do not tolerate aggressive behavior and forcefully point out the consequences for others of their children's failures to share and help (Koestner, Franz, & Weinberger, 1990; Radke-Yarrow & Zahn-Waxler, 1984; Zahn-Waxler et al., 1979). In short, they teach empathy. For example, after Muffy has selfishly grabbed all the toys in the playroom, Mom might say, "Look, Muffy, Timmie is crying because you haven't left him anything to play with."

As learning theorists appreciate, children can also be encouraged to behave more prosocially if they are reinforced for their prosocial behavior—praised and told they are good, for example. Reinforcement may be especially effective with young children because they have not yet acquired internal motives for helping and sometimes need promises of external rewards to motivate them (Bar-Tal, Raviv, & Lesser, 1980). As children grow older, however, rewarding them for helping may actually undermine their intrinsic motivation to help for the sake of helping. Richard Fabes and his colleagues (Fabes, Fultz, Eisenberg, May-Plumlee, & Christopher, 1989) promised some children toys, but offered others no reward, for sorting colored paper squares so that sick children in the hospital would have a game to play. When children then were given an opportunity to continue sorting squares but stood to gain no reward, those children who had previously been rewarded and whose mothers strongly believed in using rewards to encourage good behavior at home lost interest in helping sick children.

Exposure to models of prosocial behavior also strengthens children's prosocial tendencies (Eisen-

Children can be encouraged to behave more prosocially if they are reinforced for their prosocial behavior.
Elizabeth Crews/The Image Works

berg & Mussen, 1989). As we discussed earlier, heroic altruists often grew up with parents who preached prosocial values and practiced what they preached. Preaching charity in a clear, forceful way teaches children norms of prosocial behavior and is an effective way to encourage them to behave prosocially (Eisenberg & Mussen, 1989; Grusec, Saas-Korlsaak, & Simutis, 1978). Parents are likely to have more impact, however, if they reinforce their good words with good deeds; that is, if they both preach and practice charity (Midlarsky & Bryan, 1972). Models on television can also affect children. Just as exposure to violence on television can increase aggression, exposure to prosocial behavior on television (if one can find it) can increase prosocial behavior (Liebert & Sprafkin, 1988; Roberts & Maccoby, 1985).

Finally, children can be encouraged to behave prosocially if they are given real opportunities to behave prosocially in everyday life—if they are asked to look after their younger brothers and sisters, pitch in when the house needs cleaning, or collect cans and bottles for recycling. This may be one of the main reasons that children growing up in collectivist cultures seem to behave more prosocially than children growing up in individualist cultures: they are involved from an early age in caring for younger children and contributing to the family's welfare (Graves & Graves, 1983).

Encouraging Adults to Give

How can society encourage more adults to give to worthy charities, volunteer their time to community service programs, and otherwise behave more prosocially? In an era when federal funding for many social programs has been cut, finding answers to this question is especially important.

Perhaps because our society is highly individualistic, lawmakers have been reluctant to mandate prosocial behavior (J. A. Kaplan, 1978; Shotland, 1985). Although the law requires us to pay taxes that help support services for the needy, no law says we must contribute to the United Way, donate blood, or shelter the homeless. Nor are we necessarily punished if we fail to help. Under most laws in the United States and Canada, for example, you could be sitting on a dock munching a sandwich as the person next to you falls in the water and screams for the nearby life preserver, and you would suffer no legal penalty if you continued to eat your sandwich and watch the person drown (J. A. Kaplan, 1978).

Yet our society encourages prosocial behavior through many other means. As if they were well-versed in learning principles and cost-reward models of prosocial behavior, fund-raisers for charities can and do attempt to reduce the costs and increase the rewards of donating. They make it easy for us to give at the office and highlight the fact that donations are tax-deductible. They give us little gifts, hoping we will reciprocate with bigger gifts. They hold telethons designed to put us in good moods and to expose us to a parade of stars who model charitable behavior.

But it is not always easy to budge us. Consider, for example, the challenge of motivating people to donate blood. It is estimated that only about 4% to 8% of eligible adults in the United States donate blood regularly (McCombie, 1991). People's mistaken fears that they can somehow contract AIDS by donating blood (it's not possible) have only aggravated the problem (LoBello,

Fund-raisers for charities attempt to increase the rewards of donating.
Katherine McGlynn/The Image Works

1990). What sorts of appeals are most likely to get people to the blood center or bloodmobile?

What works best seems to depend on the potential donor's likely motives for giving blood (Charng, Piliavin, & Callero, 1988; Piliavin, Evans, & Callero, 1984). Many blood donors at first seem motivated to gain social approval and are influenced by social pressures, such as being coaxed to the bloodmobile by friends who give blood themselves (Foss, 1983; McCombie, 1991). During one campus blood drive, 31% of students approached by friends agreed to give blood, but only 14% of those approached by students they did not know signed up (Jason, Rose, Ferrari, & Barone, 1984). However, after three or four donations, people who have a good experience initially are likely to begin to view giving blood as a role they play, as part of their identities (Charng et al., 1988; Piliavin et al., 1984). They become more intrinsically and altruistically motivated to give blood and are no longer influenced much by what others think.

As a result, what may work in recruiting first-time donors may not work to keep veterans returning, and vice versa. In one study, first-time donors were more likely to give blood if they were offered fast-food coupons and other prizes for doing so than if they were not (Ferrari, Barone, Jason, & Rose, 1985). Such incentives had no effect on experienced donors. In another study, pointing out to donors the benefits they themselves would derive from giving blood—a strategy that should work well with egoists concerned with cost-reward calculations—was less effective than highlighting the altruistic nature of blood donation in persuading ex-

perienced blood donors to commit themselves to further donations (Paulhus, Shaffer, & Downing, 1977). In short, those who try to induce people to part with their blood (or money) must understand that different people may have different motives for giving. Egoists may want bonus coupons, but altruists may simply want to know that someone will benefit from their actions.

Applying social-psychological research to create a more prosocial society is challenging. Altruism may be inherent in our nature, but so are selfishness and aggression. As Harvey Hornstein (1976) put it, "human beings are potentially the cruelest and kindest animals on earth" (p. 66).

▶ Summary

Prosocial behavior—behavior that benefits others or has positive social consequences—takes many forms, including helping behavior and cooperation. The term *altruism* is reserved for voluntary, costly prosocial acts whose primary motivation is to benefit another person. Altruism poses a challenge to traditional psychological theories that view people as basically selfish. Research testing the empathy-altruism hypothesis, however, suggests that empathy can motivate genuinely altruistic helping whose primary goal is to relieve another's suffering rather than to reduce one's own egoistic distress, avoid punishment, or gain subtle rewards, such as relief from sadness or empathic joy after help is received.

As sociobiologists have argued, altruistic tendencies could have been built into the human genetic code over the course of evolution through such mechanisms as kin selection, preference for genetically similar others, and reciprocal altruism. Prosocial tendencies could also be the product of culture—for example, emphasis on group welfare in collectivist cultures and transmission of norms of social responsibility and reciprocity.

The arousal/cost-reward model of helping describes a decision-making process that starts with an awareness of the need for help and involves emotional arousal, the labeling of arousal, and consideration of the costs and rewards of helping and failing to help. This model can help explain how many situational and personal factors affect the likelihood that someone will help.

Situational influences on helping behavior include characteristics of the person in need of help. Generally, the people most likely to receive help are those who are dependent or needy, whose need is clear and legitimate, and whose need is due to an uncontrollable cause. In addition, we tend to help people with whom we already have a relationship, who are similar to ourselves, or who are otherwise attractive to us. Ambivalence toward members of other ethnic or racial groups can result in some exceptions to these generalizations.

Other important situational influences are associated with the presence and actions of other bystanders. The bystander effect, which causes a person to be less likely to help when others are present than when he or she is alone, is brought about by three processes: social influence affecting interpretations of the situation, audience inhibition or fear of social disapproval, and diffusion of responsibility among potential helpers.

Personal characteristics also influence prosocial behavior. Although men and women do not differ much in overall helpfulness, they differ in the kinds of help they provide. People who live in small towns are typically more helpful than people who live in cities. Helpful people are also likely to have been raised by parents who fostered altruistic values, to be highly moral, to be highly empathic, to feel competent to help, and to have extensive social involvements. Ultimately, however, it is difficult to identify traits that predict helpful behavior in all situations because the demands of different helping situations differ greatly and because personal and situational factors interact to influence behavior.

Being in a good mood, especially while thinking about one's own good fortune, consistently increases the likelihood of helping unless negative thoughts dis-rupt a happy person's chain of positive thoughts. Being in a bad mood can also motivate helping, especially when the individual feels guilty or sad, when helping offers easy relief from one's bad mood, and when one is focused on others' woes rather than preoccupied with his or her own.

Taking the perspective of the help recipient makes us realize that it is difficult to seek and receive help because of threats to self-esteem. Threats to self-esteem and negative reactions to receiving help are most likely when a person high in self-esteem receives help from a similar other on an ego-central task. However, if ego-threatened help recipients have a strong sense of perceived control, they may be motivated to become more self-reliant.

Knowledge of prosocial behavior can be used to build a more prosocial society. For example, although children normally become more prosocially oriented with age, they can be encouraged further through judicious use of rewards, exposure to prosocial models, and everyday opportunities to behave prosocially. Similarly, we can apply social-psychological research to encourage adults to behave more prosocially if we understand their motivations.

▶ Key Terms

altruism
arousal/cost-reward model
bystander effect
collectivist culture
egoism
empathy
empathy-altruism hypothesis
helping behavior
individualist culture
kin selection
negative-state relief model
prosocial behavior
psychoanalytic theory
reciprocal altruism
reciprocity norm
self-monitoring
social-responsibility norm
sociobiology
urban-overload hypothesis

No [person] is an island, entire of itself.

John Donne

It takes two flints to make a fire.

Louisa May Alcott

Behavior in Groups

Stuck in a stalled elevator, seven strangers begin to notice one another, compare reactions and share stories of past experiences, and then develop a plan of action to get out of the elevator. Waiting in line for hours, strangers hoping to purchase concert tickets first begin to chat with their neighbors, then share food and drink, and finally pass the time discussing the discography of the performer. Both of these situations show how subtle group formation can be: individuals shift their thinking from considering themselves one of many people to considering themselves members of a group, and their actions are thereby influenced by the group. With such examples, we also shift the focus of our attention to social behavior. We are no longer focusing strictly on the individual but rather on the behavior of people in groups.

To many people, behavior in groups is the essence of social psychology, but that opinion is not shared by all. As we have seen in previous chapters, social psychologists often prefer to study social behavior at the level of the individual, stressing each person's perceptions, beliefs, and actions and ignoring the interaction that takes place in groups. Some early social psychologists even suggested that groups are not real. The late Floyd Allport used to say, "You can't stumble over a group," meaning that groups exist only in people's minds. In Allport's view, groups are merely shared sets of values, ideas, thoughts, and habits that exist simultaneously in the minds of several persons.

Others argued just as impressively that groups are real entities that should be treated as objects in our environment (Durkheim, 1898; Warriner, 1956). Such advocates renounced the suggestion that all social behaviors could be explained adequately at the individual level; rather, they stressed the unique aspects of the group process in and of itself. That is, a group is more than the coincidental coming together of people who share ideas. Consider, for example, a riot after a sporting event. Such social interactions can be understood only by analyzing behavior at the *group* level, as opposed to the individual level. Some advocates of analyzing group behavior even argue that understanding social behavior requires social psychologists to consider groups as real entities simply because group membership is an integral part of the self-concept (Tajfel, 1982).

Clearly, one can adopt any of numerous perspectives on the way a situation can be influenced by the number of people involved in it. Most of us would probably agree that many activities in our lives involve other people. Football teams, families, special project teams, and fishing crews all involve the interaction of a group of people. But groups also can be composed of individuals who do not come into close proximity with one another or see one another often. For example, the national sales manager for Frisbee™, along with his or her field representatives, may constitute a group, even though their face-to-face contact may be infrequent.

What is a group? Not every collection of people can be considered a group. The term **aggregate** refers to collections of individuals who do not interact with one another: persons standing on a street corner waiting for the light to change, members of an audience at the latest Spike Lee movie, and, in many cases, students in a large college lecture hall. Such people typically do not interact or share feelings to such a degree that they influence one another. However, as the case of the passengers in the stalled elevator illustrates, an aggregate can become a group.

Groups differ from aggregates in several respects. For example, an aggregate has no particular structure, but a group has some definite form of organization, and its members have some relationship with one another. Groups are dynamic, whereas aggregates are relatively passive. Members of groups are aware of one another; people in an aggregate are often oblivious of others who share the same space at the same time. As a working definition of groups, Joseph McGrath offers the following: "A **group** is an aggregation of two or more people who are to some degree in dynamic interrelation with one another" (1984, p. 8; emphasis added).

This definition encompasses many types of groups: a small family, a large work group, an experimental group that meets only once, a military unit that stays together for months or years. Some groups are, as McGrath (1984) has recognized, more "groupy" than others. In other words, some groups involve greater amounts of social interaction, exert more intense pressures on their members, or involve greater commitments to the group's function. In every case, however, the group process influences the behavior of the individual members.

In this chapter we consider the ways in which groups act—how they perform, how group members communicate with one another, and how groups form or break up. First, however, let us turn our attention to a simpler question—how does the presence of other people influence the behavior of the individual?

▶ The Influence of Other People

In the late nineteenth century a graduate student at Indiana University, Norman Triplett, became interested in the effects of other people on individual performance. While studying the records of the Racing Board of the League of American Wheelmen, Triplett observed that cyclists' times were faster when the cyclists were racing against each other than when they simply raced against a clock. On the basis of this observation, Triplett proposed a theory of *dynamogenesis,* the generation of action by the presence of others. To test his theory, Triplett (1898) asked children to wind fishing reels and compared their performance when they were alone with their performance when another child was present. This experiment marks the earliest attempt to understand how behaving in the presence of others—not necessarily acting as a group—can influence behavior. Triplett reported that most of the children wound reels faster when in the presence of another child, and a considerable amount of research has followed his initial venture.

The influence of other people depends on several factors. Bibb Latané (1981) has suggested three major factors in his **social impact theory:** the number of people, their immediacy, and their strength (or status). Latané uses the analogy of a light bulb to illustrate the impact of these factors. Just as the amount of light falling on a surface depends on the number of bulbs, their closeness to the surface, and the wattage, so does social impact represent the joint contribution of number, immediacy, and strength. Each of these factors affects an individual's performance in the presence of others.

As the **number** of people increases, so does their impact. Although the exact form of this relationship is a matter of dispute, most investigators would agree that the effect of an increase in the number of others exhibits diminishing returns (Latané, 1981; Tanford & Penrod, 1984). The difference between three and four others present, for example, would be much greater than the difference between nine and ten others (see Figure 12.1). At some point, Sarah Tanford and Steven Penrod

(1984) suggest, further increases in the number of others will have no incremental effect at all; an effective ceiling will have been reached.

Less powerful than the number of people, but still influential, are their immediacy and strength (Jackson, 1986; Latané, 1981; Mullen, 1985). **Immediacy** refers to the proximity of the others to the target individual. Orders from a drill instructor screaming in your face have a greater impact than do the same orders, at the same volume, issued from 10 feet away. Similarly, audiences that are physically present have more impact than those that are at some distance—for example, the "live" audience at a play has a greater impact on a stage actor than does the "future" audience for a movie actor.

Latané (1981) defines **strength** as the power, status, or resources of the influence agents. Demonstrating the influence of strength, Latané and Harkins (1976) found that students who expected to sing before an audience of high-status people reported more tension than those who expected a low-status audience. Also, recall from Chapter 8 that obedience was greater in the Milgram studies when the procedure was conducted at Yale University than at a seedy warehouse in Bridgeport (A. G. Miller, 1986).

Alone or in combination, these three factors can affect the degree of influence others exert on us. What remains to be seen, however, is the way in which number, immediacy, and strength have their impact. For example, what is it about other people that makes four of them more influential than three of them?

Before we can answer this question, we first must distinguish among situations that involve an audience, those that involve coactors, and those that involve group performance. In an audience situation, the individual is performing in the presence of people but without direct interaction; the members of the audience are passive observers of the action (Geen, 1980). Classic examples of an audience situation include a one-actor play and a stand-up comedian. Coaction, in contrast, refers to situations in which others are also performing the behavior, but each person's performance is independent. Strangers on the bank of a stream, each trying to catch fish, is one example. Students taking an exam is another example of coaction. Finally, group performance involves coordinated coaction, as in the case of a basketball team or students studying together to prepare for an examination. As we consider each type of situation, we will explore some of the mechanisms through which the presence of others affects social behavior.

The Effects of an Audience

Often we are aware that others are watching us when we act as individuals. For example, on entering a room full of strangers, we may be painfully (or gleefully) aware that many eyes are focused on us. Many people experience fear and anxiety in the presence of an audience. A survey of people's fears showed that speaking before a group is feared more than heights, darkness, loneliness, sickness, and even death (Borden, 1980). In general, the larger and the less familiar the audience is, the less willing people are to speak in front of it (McCroskey & Richmond, 1990). On some occasions, however, the presence of an audience can give us an extra "charge." Athletes report that they perform better before a crowd than in an empty stadium (Davis, 1969), and many actors comment on the difference between playing for a full house and playing in a theater that is nearly empty. Even the potential existence of an audience, as in the case of a movie actor, can affect the way someone performs a task. What effects does an audience have upon performance?

Sometimes, as Triplett observed, an audience may increase the quality of performance. In other cases, such as when a public speaker becomes frozen with fear, an audience decreases performance quality. **Social facilitation,** a term coined by Floyd Allport (1920), refers to the improvement of individual performance in the presence of other people. In contrast, **social inhibition** (also known as **social impairment**) refers to a decrease in an individual's performance in the presence of others. Some thirty years after Allport labeled

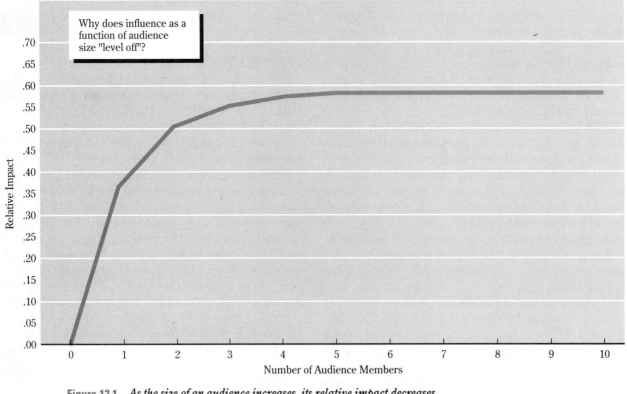

Figure 12.1 *As the size of an audience increases, its relative impact decreases.*
Source: Adapted from "The Psychology of Social Impact" by B. Latané, 1981, *American Psychologist, 36,* pp. 343–356.

The presence of an audience may either increase or decrease the quality of a performance.
Bob Clay/Clay Images

audience effects, Solomon Asch (1952) noted social psychologists had yet to deal with the apparent contradiction in audience effects. What was lacking was a theory that explained when facilitation would occur and when impairment would occur.

More than a decade later, Robert Zajonc (1965) proposed a theoretical model to account for audience effects (see Figure 12.2). Relying on a drive model of learning, Zajonc suggested that the presence of others is a source of general arousal, or drive, because other people can be unpredictable and can thereby create feelings of uncertainty in the individual. When the response required in a situation is well learned (or dominant, in the terminology of the model), the increased drive results in better performance. But when the required response is not well learned, the resulting performance is poorer because some other, better-learned response interferes with the required response (Zajonc & Sales, 1966).

Consider, for example, someone playing pool. According to Zajonc's theory, good players should play better in the presence of an audience, and not-so-good players should play worse in the presence of the same audience. James Michaels and his colleagues tested this prediction in the pool center of a college union (Michaels, Blommel, Brocato, Linkous, & Rowe, 1982). Teams of four observers first unobtrusively watched a game of eight ball until one of them could determine

whether the players were above average or below average. Then the team moved to about seven feet from the table and quietly watched the game in a manner that made it apparent to the players that an audience was present.

Six pairs of above-average players and six pairs of below-average players were observed in this manner. As is illustrated in Figure 12.3, the above-average players increased their shot accuracy when the audience's presence became apparent. In contrast, below-average players became worse; their accuracy decreased after the observation team made their presence obvious. Although the extent of the effect varies across situations, Zajonc's explanation accounts for many of the findings regarding the effects of an audience on performance (Bond & Titus, 1983; Cottrell, 1972; Geen & Gange, 1977; Guerin, 1986; Schmitt, Gilovich, Goore, & Joseph, 1986).

Zajonc assumed that the arousal properties of an audience are innate and has shown that even cockroaches are subject to social facilitation effects (Zajonc, Heingartner, & Herman, 1969). Nickolas Cottrell (1972), on the other hand, argued for a learning explanation, specifically the learned expectation that an audience will evaluate one's performance. For example, subjects performing in front of others who are blindfolded or who otherwise cannot evaluate the performance showed less arousal than when they performed before a group

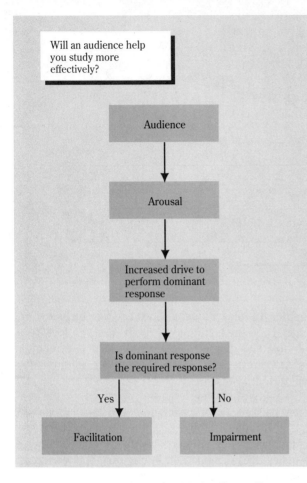

Figure 12.2 *An arousal-drive model of audience effects.*
Source: "Social Facilitation" by R. B. Zajonc, 1965, *Science, 149,* pp. 269–274.

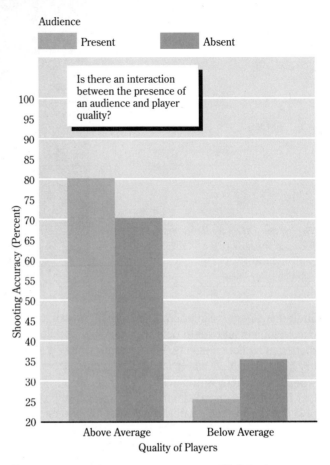

Figure 12.3 *Dominant responses are more likely in the presence of an audience.*
Source: "Social Facilitation and Inhibition in a Natural Setting" by J. W. Michaels, J. M. Blommel, R. M. Brocato, R. A. Linkous, and J. S. Rowe, 1982, *Replications in Social Psychology, 2,* pp. 21–24.

of evaluators. Cottrell and others (Cottrell, Wack, Sekerak, & Rittle, 1968; Guerin, 1986; Harkins & Szymanski, 1987) have found support for this distinction between the mere presence of an audience and expectations of evaluation by an audience. Still, it is difficult to believe cockroaches and ants exhibit the effect as a result of expected evaluation by an audience (Bond & Titus, 1983).

Robert Baron (1986) incorporated both innate and learned responses in his distraction-conflict theory. Baron argued that other members of one's species are distracting for various reasons, including the reasons offered by Zajonc for increases in arousal. But rather than assume others automatically cause arousal, Baron noted that distractions cause conflict in the performer's attention and that it is this attentional conflict that produces the increase in arousal as the organism responds to the greater need for energy to handle the conflict. The increased arousal, in turn, either facilitates or impairs performance, depending on the manner in which the individual deals with the conflict.

As illustrated in Figure 12.4, if the individual devotes too much attention to the distraction, interruption of the performance results in impairment. If, instead, the

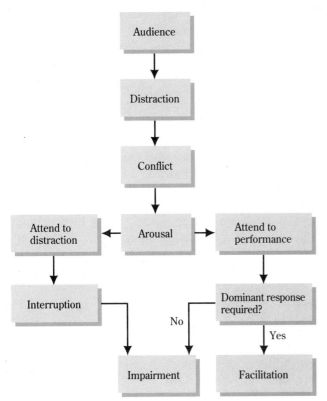

Figure 12.4 *Baron's distraction-conflict theory of social facilitation and social impairment.*

Source: "Distraction-Conflict Theory: Progress and Problems" by R. S. Baron, 1986, *Advances in Experimental Social Psychology, 19,* pp. 1–40.

person directs attention toward performance, however, the increased arousal facilitates performance of a well-learned (dominant) response and impairs performance of a poorly learned (nondominant) response. Although more complicated, distraction-conflict theory enables us to understand audience effects equally well for cockroaches (who presumably can experience attentional conflict) and for humans.

For humans, expectations about audience evaluation add to attentional conflict. For example, someone confronted with an audience may feel pressure to present a positive front (Sanders, 1984). With simple tasks, the arousal attentional conflict produces can lead to enhanced performance. On the other hand, when one is faced with a complex task, the arousal may combine with frustration from impaired performance, leading to embarrassment, withdrawal, or anxiety (Bond, 1982; Sanders, 1984).

Underscoring the importance of audience evaluation as a source of attentional conflict, Kate Szymanski and Stephen Harkins (1987; Study 1) demonstrated that the self can be included as a potential audience. In their experiment, subjects were asked to generate as many uses as possible for a single object. Some subjects were led to believe the experimenter would know how many uses they had generated, and others were led to believe the experimenter would not be able to determine how many uses they had generated. Within each of these groups, half the subjects were told they would find out the average number of uses generated by other subjects in the study, and half were told they would not discover the average number of uses so as to protect the other subjects' confidentiality.

As illustrated in Figure 12.5, social facilitation occurred (the subjects generated more uses for the object) when either the experimenter or the subjects were in a position to evaluate performance. Presumably, the prospect of one's self as a (future) audience member creates attentional conflict and produces social facilitation. Brian Mullen and Roy Baumeister (1987) have extended the distraction-conflict explanation by noting that self-awareness may bring into focus competing goals, such as speed versus accuracy. When competing goals exist for the same task, attentional conflict may result in more attention directed toward one goal at the expense of the other, leading to an overall decrement in performance. In the presence of another, for example, a typist's speed may increase, but his or her accuracy may decrease because it is too demanding to focus simultaneously on the audience, typing speed, and typing accuracy.

The Effects of Coactors

So far, we have concentrated on the effects of passive others who observe and evaluate while the actor performs. However, if we look back to Triplett's initial experiment, we see that the audience was not passive; two children were performing the task simultaneously. Because they are a kind of audience, we would expect coactors to produce the same effects as passive audiences. Because coactors are also engaged in the same

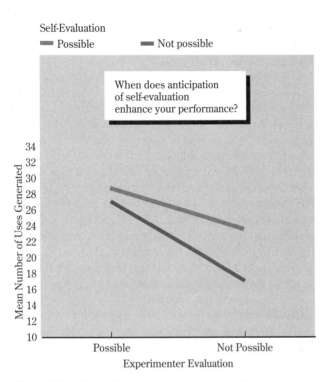

Self-Evaluation

■ Possible   ■ Not possible

When does anticipation of self-evaluation enhance your performance?

Figure 12.5 *Evaluation by another or by the self can produce social facilitation effects.*

Source: "Social Loafing and Self-Evaluation with a Social Standard" by K. Szymanski and S. G. Harkins, 1987, *Journal of Personality and Social Psychology, 53,* pp. 891–897.

activity, we might also expect them to have additional influences. For example, Triplett (1898) reasoned that the presence of coactors adds the element of competition to what we described as the basic audience situation. Many people, particularly in Western societies, would consider the situation a challenge and attempt to do better than their companion. Consistent with Mullen and Baumeister's (1987) notion of competing goals, Dashiell (1930) cited competition as an explanation when he found that people in a coactive situation performed faster but less accurately than people working alone.

Thus, a coacting audience enables **social comparison** (see Chapter 3), which represents yet another source of attentional conflict. By observing others' behavior, we can establish a basis for evaluating our own performance. If another person is doing somewhat bet-

ter than we are, we may direct our attention toward performance in order to compete, thereby producing a social facilitation effect. On the other hand, if the other person is doing about as well as, or even worse than, we are, then the coactor seems to have no more effect than a passive audience member. There is also little additional effect when the other person is vastly superior; the person's great distance from us may make him or her an invalid source of comparison (Seta, 1982).

In addition to social facilitation and impairment effects, performers in a coacting audience also use one another as a source of new information. This modeling effect, discussed in Chapter 10, suggests that a performer can learn new responses simply by observing the other participants. If the other participants are successful in their actions, a person is most likely to learn and perform these same responses (Bandura, 1965). For example, people throwing a Frisbee™ at a park or beach may attempt to imitate coactors' techniques or styles. Once a performer has observed the others, however, distraction-conflict theory would lead us to expect the performer would do better practicing the new, poorly learned technique without the presence of coactors.

The Effects of Other Group Members

As we have seen, both passive and coacting members of an audience can either enhance or impair an individual's performance, depending on the complexity of the task and how well learned the task is. It is reasonable to expect the same effects when those involved are members of a group. But group membership involves more than individuals who happen to be doing the same thing at the same time. We might expect, therefore, that interactions among group members produce effects beyond those produced by mere presence and simple coaction.

On a purely physical task, we might expect a group to perform better than an individual. For example, removal of debris from a California highway after a major mud slide should be more efficiently accomplished by five people working together than by a single person working alone or by five people working independently. But as it turns out, group performance does not always lead to increases in productivity.

When people perform in a group, a decrease in individual effort, called **social loafing,** often occurs. Investigators have known about this effect since Max Ringelmann (1913), a French professor of agricultural engineering, conducted a series of studies on workers' performance (Kravitz & Martin, 1986). Ringelmann wanted to assess the relative efficiency of humans, oxen, and machinery in pulling and pushing loads. In the course of his investigations, he had occasion to compare the performance of people working alone with those working as part of a group, and he found evidence of lesser performance in group conditions.

Ringelmann's primary explanation for this effect pointed to the lack of coordination that may exist when several individuals work concurrently. For example, some group members may be pulling in one direction while others are pulling in a different direction, resulting in an overall decrease in the amount of work performed per person. In light of research on social facilitation, more recent investigators have paid greater attention to the motivational loss that group participation may cause. Latané and his colleagues have conducted several studies to demonstrate the scope of these effects (Harkins, Latané, & Williams, 1980; Latané, Williams, & Harkins, 1979). In the typical experiment, students are asked either to cheer or to clap as loud as they can—sometimes alone, sometimes with one other student, sometimes in a group of four, and sometimes in a group of six. In each case, the investigators record the sound each individual produces. Further, subjects wear headsets and blindfolds so that they cannot tell what the other people in the group are doing. In general, groups produce social loafing: individual effort drops precipitously as group size increases.

Why does social loafing occur? One explanation concerns the lack of identifiability in a group (Williams, Harkins, & Latané, 1981). People in a group may feel that they can "hide in the crowd"—yet another example of evaluation by others as a source of attentional conflict. In support of this explanation, Kipling Williams and his colleagues found that subjects who were told their individual output would be identified did not show the social loafing effect. Similarly, **deindividuation** (discussed more fully in Chapter 10) also reduces the extent to which an individual is self-aware, further reducing attentional conflict that may result from competing goals.

One explanation for social loafing—beliefs about what others in the group will do—is unique to group performance situations. Interactions with current group members or with members of other groups may lead us to form expectations about the performance levels of the other group members. If such interactions lead us to think the others are going to loaf, then we may be led by equity considerations to reduce our effort as well (Jackson & Harkins, 1985). When other group members specifically state they plan to work as hard as they can, however, the social loafing effect is eliminated.

The contribution of individuals to the group product can be improved in other ways as well. Making the job more difficult, for example, results in increased overall performance (Harkins & Petty, 1982; Jackson & Williams, 1985). People can also counter the social loafing tendency if the task is personally involving. Thus, students who worked on a problem they believed had consequences for future academic procedures in their institution did not loaf, whereas their loafing was evident when the consequences of their effort would be felt only by students at a school in another part of the country (Brickner, Harkins, & Ostrom, 1986).

Clearly, social psychologists have answered Asch's (1952) call for work toward an explanation of audience effects. The variety of conditions that produce attentional conflict illustrates the extent to which the presence of other people complicates behavior. When we direct attention to well-learned tasks, other people usually enhance our performance. But when we direct our attention to the other people, or when the task is a relatively new one, the presence of those other people causes a decrement in performance. When we perform a task as a group member, expectations about the performance levels of other group members may also prompt social loafing. No single condition is necessarily present in all circumstances, but each has considerable empirical support. No single cause may be a necessary condition, but each points to the same phenomenon: arousal produced by others leads to an increase in the performance of well-learned or simple responses and a decrease in the performance of poorly learned or complicated responses.

▶ Group Composition and Structure

A group, as defined earlier in this chapter, is more than people performing the same activity at a particular time and place. As we saw with social loafing, groups involve interaction, shared perceptions and experiences, development of emotional or affective ties, and interdependent roles (DeLamater, 1974).

Not all groups are alike, however; they vary in at least as many ways as individuals do. One way in which groups differ is in their composition—in very loose terms, what the group "looks like," the size of the group, the gender and ethnic identity of the members, and so forth. Groups can also be characterized by their structure. **Group structure** refers to the system of roles, norms, and relationships among members that provides a framework for the group's functioning. Group structure holds a group together, accounting for some of the regularities in the behavior of group members (Forsyth, 1983). Leadership is one structural property. Others include the networks or channels of communication that are established in a group and the particular roles that certain members assume.

In this section we will consider one of the ways group composition can differ—group size—and three aspects of group structure: communication networks, leadership, and roles and norms.

Group Size

Even within the limits of the definition of group we introduced at the beginning of the chapter, it is possible to conceive of groups that range in size from a couple on their honeymoon to all the members of the U.S. Congress or the Canadian House of Commons. Most experimental research, however, has concentrated on small groups, generally varying from three to ten persons.

Some efforts have been made to specify the "ideal size" of problem-solving groups. For example, P. E. Slater (1958) concluded that groups of five were the most effective for dealing with mental tasks in which group members collect and exchange information and make a decision based on evaluation of that information. Others have suggested that the optimum size of problem-solving groups should fall between five and ten members (Osborn, 1957).

For various reasons, such conclusions regarding the ideal size of groups are inevitably oversimplifications. First, criteria for determining success are likely to vary. Smaller groups may be more satisfying to participants because the members have a chance to express their opinions fully. But the addition of a few more members may add essential skills and make it easier to accomplish the task at hand. Similarly, larger groups may lower members' participation and morale, but smaller groups are more likely to result in minorities of one. Second, task structure can interact with group size. Some tasks require only one person, whereas other tasks can be performed only by several individuals. Third, the amount of structure in the group interacts with its size. Although groups composed of more than five persons are often less satisfying than small groups, larger groups can be effective without any major loss of morale when the task is structured. Further, one must consider the circumstances and the duration of the group. In exotic and stressful environments, such as expeditionary stations in the Antarctic, larger groups appear more satisfying than smaller groups, perhaps because a larger group offers a greater variety of possibilities for interaction (Harrison & Connors, 1984).

The effects of group size are important in less exotic environments as well, such as in a jury room. The traditional jury in England, the United States, and Canada once consisted of twelve persons who had to reach a unanimous decision. In 1966 Great Britain changed its policy to require agreement by only ten of the twelve. In 1970 the U.S. Supreme Court ruled that a jury of six people could do the job just as well as a jury of twelve and cited research findings to support its decision (Wrightsman, 1991).[1]

Even when research results are interpreted correctly, the question of whether a six-person jury performs as well as a twelve-person jury is not easy to answer. For example, early research yielded inconsistent results (Hastie, Penrod, & Pennington, 1983; Wrightsman, 1991) even though models of decision making predict that the possibility of a hung jury—a jury that cannot reach a unanimous decision—increases as the number of jurors increases (for example, Tanford & Penrod, 1983). To test this possibility in controlled con-

---

[1]As we noted in Chapter 2, the Court thoroughly misinterpreted the research it cited.

ditions, Norbert Kerr and Robert MacCoun (1985b) conducted a study in which college students deliberated about a series of armed robbery cases. The subjects were randomly assigned to mock juries consisting of three, six, or twelve people and were asked to deliberate on each of the cases for a maximum of ten minutes per case. Kerr and MacCoun were also interested in the deliberation process itself, so some juries were randomly assigned to use secret ballots in their deliberations, and others used open ballots.

Although all the fictitious cases were designed to be close—prosecution and defense evidence was relatively balanced—it turned out that some of the cases were clear-cut to the mock jurors: some cases produced more acquittals, some produced more convic-

tions. Group size made a difference in this study, as is illustrated in Figure 12.6. Larger groups (twelve persons) were less likely to reach a unanimous verdict than were the six-person mock juries, which, in turn, were less likely to reach a unanimous decision than three-person groups.

Examining in a more detailed way the different types of cases and the rules concerning ballots, Kerr and MacCoun observed that the effect of using secret ballots depended on both group size and the type of case. For the close cases (Figure 12.6a), secret ballots produced more hung juries in the three-person groups, but fewer hung juries in the largest groups. When a case was clear-cut (Figure 12.6b), however, the type of ballot had no effect on the decision outcome.

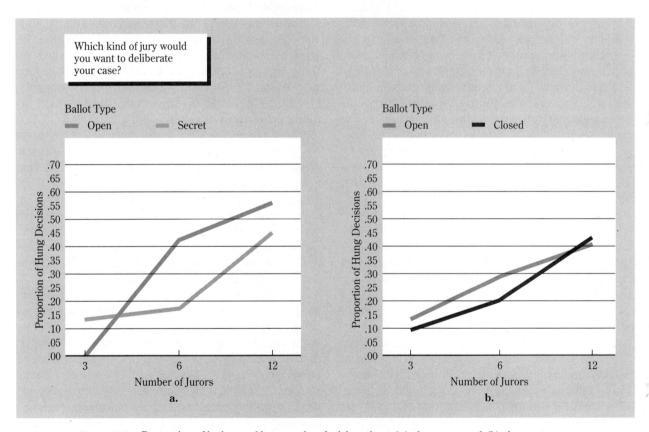

Figure 12.6 *Proportion of juries unable to reach a decision about (a) close cases and (b) clear-cut cases.*

Source: "The Effects of Jury Size and Polling Method on Process and Product of Jury Deliberation" by N. L. Kerr and R. J. MacCoun, 1985, *Journal of Personality and Social Psychology, 48,* pp. 349–363.

As the results of this jury-simulation study show, size is not merely a descriptive characteristic of a group, but also a factor that can influence group process. For example, larger groups take longer to reach unanimous decisions. When the decision is difficult, individuals in small groups are more likely to give in to the majority when decisions are public. We will return to the topic of minority and majority influence in groups after we complete our examination of group structure and composition.

Communication Networks

Group size is meaningless when group members have difficulty communicating with one another. Real-world groups, for example, sometimes establish restricted channels through which messages may go. Members of a large faculty may not be allowed to speak about problems with the university president directly but instead may have to communicate through a dean, similar to the military chain of command. Personal feelings between individuals also can affect communication channels. For example, a church's board of deacons may include two members who "haven't spoken to each other for years," a situation that requires an intermediary before any communication can take place between them. Location of some group members in a different building may inhibit communication between them.

Prescribed patterns of communication are referred to as **communication networks** (Shaw, 1964, 1978). Some communication networks are represented schematically in Figure 12.7. Although these representations are abstract, it is relatively easy to think of concrete examples of each. On a football team (a "wheel" network), for example, the quarterback is generally the center of communication. Other players direct most of their comments to the quarterback, who speaks to everyone on the team. The typical discussion group, such as a deliberating jury, follows the "comcon" pattern; everyone talks to everyone else. Organizational hierarchies represent more complex communication networks; these networks often involve hundreds of people, but they can usually be broken down into these simpler patterns. The "Y" formation is a typical hierarchy; the president communicates with the dean, who communicates with the faculty.

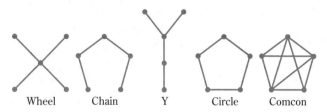

Figure 12.7 *Examples of communication networks. The dots represent people, and the connecting lines represent communication channels.*

The form of a communication network is important because it determines the way the group functions. For example, the wheel gives great control to the person in the middle; he or she can communicate with each of the other members, but they can communicate only with the central person and not with one another. If such a communication network were established by the ground rules during the formation of a new group, the person in the central position would probably emerge as the leader. In such cases, possession of information leads to power.

The Y and chain networks in Figure 12.7 also lead to centralized organization as the central person becomes pivotal. In contrast, circle networks do not facilitate the emergence of a dominant leader (Leavitt, 1951). In groups that have a circle or a comcon network, in which every member is able to communicate with everyone else, it is impossible to predict which position will lead to leadership and dominance. In these networks, the group members' individual personalities and skills are the determining factors.

What effects do communication networks have on productivity? Which networks are most satisfying to group members? The second question can be answered simply, and the answer is one we would expect on the basis of what we know about the importance of perceived control (Chapter 7 and Chapter 8). People prefer positions in which they have greater opportunities for communication and participation. "Silent" group members often do not like to remain quiet. The central position in the wheel, the chain, and the Y is considered a satisfying one, whereas the peripheral positions in these same networks are associated with poor morale (Leavitt, 1951). Networks that permit decentralized communication (comcon networks, for example) lead to higher morale for persons at all positions.

The efficiency of various communication networks depends on the task faced by the group. Centralized networks—such as a wheel or a Y—are most efficient when the task is relatively simple. The job gets done faster, and fewer errors are made. When a problem becomes more complex, however, the advantages of such centralization are diminished. Routing all information through a central person becomes time-consuming and does not take advantage of the contributions other members of the network might make. In this case, a circular network pattern is superior. A circular network also reduces the negative impact of the loss of some group members. One factor that contributed to the tragic destruction of the *Challenger* space shuttle was the departure of two staff members responsible for scheduling a meeting about the infamous O-ring seals. Without these key members in the communication network, concerns about the performance of the O-rings were not channeled to the appropriate individuals (Romzek & Dubnick, 1987).

Although we tend to think the characteristics of the people in a group are of paramount importance, research clearly shows that structural factors can influence the group process. Communication networks (and their cousin, the organization chart) have a major influence on the activities of a group, as do the tasks and problems in which a group engages. As noted earlier, some communication patterns require the person occupying a specific position to assume the leadership position.

Leadership

What makes one person a successful leader, whereas another person fails in the same position? For example, can a president be considered an effective leader in foreign, but not domestic, policy in the United States? How have some leaders, such as Iraq's Saddam Hussein, been able to control the destinies of millions of people, whereas other leaders come and go? Why does one person consistently become the class president, the director of the local city council, or the occupant of other leadership positions? Early efforts toward understanding leadership focused on the qualities and behaviors of leaders, perhaps because leadership positions are usually occupied by an individual. Historians, for example, proposed a "great man" theory of leadership—those who lead successfully do so because they have sufficient charisma, intelligence, or some other trait or ability (Hook, 1955; Wood, 1913).

As a result of such theoretical reasoning, the earliest social-psychological approach to studying leadership involved finding a group of leaders and followers, giving them a series of personality measures, and attempting to determine which characteristics distinguished the leaders from the followers. Researchers were initially enthusiastic about this approach toward a personality-based definition of leadership, partly because several personality traits were identified with leadership in one or another study. Comprehensive reviews of the research, however, provided little evidence that personality characteristics could be used to identify leaders (Bird, 1940; Jenkins, 1947; Stogdill, 1948): no single trait consistently characterizes leaders. Even intelligence did not turn out to be overwhelmingly important as a general leadership trait.

Disappointment with the results of research on leaders' characteristics, coupled with the rising influence of learning theory as outlined in Chapter 1, prompted researchers to examine what leaders do, to concentrate on leadership instead of on leaders (Stogdill, 1974). These efforts resulted in a new focus on *influence* as the salient aspect of leadership. A 150-item survey known as the Leadership Behavior Description Questionnaire (LBDQ) is one example of an attempt to identify empirically the functions of leaders (Hemphill & Coons, 1950). The LBDQ was administered to a wide variety of groups and subjected to complicated statistical analyses (Halpin & Winer, 1952; Stogdill, 1963). Two major clusters of leadership behaviors emerged: consideration and initiating structure. Other analyses of leadership have produced similar results (Bales, 1953; Gibb, 1969; Kahn & Katz, 1953), though different labels have sometimes been applied to the two functions. These two dimensions of leadership are independent of each other; in other words, a person's standing on one dimension is not related to his or her standing on the other.

Consideration reflects the extent to which the leader shows behavior "indicative of friendship, mutual trust, respect, and warmth" in relationships with the other group members (Halpin, 1966, p. 86). A leader's genuine consideration reflects an awareness of the needs of each member of the group. Leaders high in this behavioral characteristic encourage their group members to communicate with them and to share their feelings (Korman, 1966). In Halpin and Winer's (1952) study, consideration accounted for almost half of the variability in behavior among leaders.

Initiating structure refers to "the leader's behavior in delineating the relationship between [the leader] and members of the work group and in endeavoring to establish well-defined patterns of organization, channels of communication, and methods of procedure" (Halpin, 1966, p. 86). Thus, initiating structure refers to the leader's task of motivating the group to move toward its designated goal; part of this task may include identifying and agreeing on the goal. Initiating structure accounted for about one-third of the variability among leaders.

Subsequent research on consideration and initiating structure illustrated both the importance of the two leadership functions (Cartwright & Zander, 1968; Greenfield & Andrews, 1961; Halpin, 1953, 1954; Hemphill, 1955; Keeler & Andrews, 1963) and the shortcomings of an approach that focused only on the leader or the leader's behaviors (Lord, Binning, Rush, & Thomas, 1978; Rush, Thomas, & Lord, 1977; Stogdill, 1974). Consideration and initiating structure, for example, were not consistently related to such group outcomes as performance and satisfaction (Fleishman & Harris, 1962; Korman, 1966). Apparently, leadership theorists had fallen prey to **fundamental attribution bias** (see Chapter 4), overemphasizing the causal influence of dispositional characteristics and neglecting the importance of situations in which leadership occurs.

Most current investigators believe it is necessary to study both the leader's behavior and the situation in which leadership is exercised. These new models of leadership indicate that the effectiveness of any particular leadership style is contingent upon the circumstances or conditions in which a particular group finds itself. Not surprisingly, these models are called **contingency models.** Several contingency models have been developed, each emphasizing a distinctive set of leadership behaviors and situational factors (for example, House, 1971; Vroom & Yetton, 1973). Here we will focus on the model developed by Fred Fiedler (1964, 1967)—perhaps the most prominent contingency model, and the one to have received the most empirical support (Chemers, 1983, 1987; Strube & Garcia, 1981).

There are four basic components in Fiedler's contingency model. One refers to the personality of the leader; the other three describe characteristics of the situation in which the leader must lead. The personality component is represented by leadership style defined in terms of motivational objectives and characterized by the leader's liking for the least preferred co-worker (LPC). LPC is measured by a leader's ratings of the least preferred co-worker on dimensions such as friendly/unfriendly, pleasant/unpleasant, and accepting/rejecting (Fiedler, 1967). Leaders who obtain low scores on the LPC measure are highly motivated by successful outcomes, dislike their least preferred co-worker because he or she may interfere with success, and tend to direct their efforts toward initiating structure. Low LPC leaders, for example, may respond to dissatisfied group members by saying, "this isn't a popularity contest." High LPC leaders, in contrast, are highly motivated by successful interpersonal relations among group members, like their least preferred co-worker, and tend to direct their behaviors toward consideration.

The remaining three components of Fiedler's contingency model involve the extent to which the leader has control over the situation in which he or she must exercise leadership (Rice & Kastenbaum, 1983). Situational control depends on three specific factors: (1) leader/member relations, (2) task structure, and (3) leader position power.

Leader/member relations   Leader/member relations can range from very good to very poor. Some leaders are liked and respected by their group, whereas others may be disliked, distrusted, or even completely rejected. Fiedler proposes that this general group atmosphere is the most important single factor determining the leader's influence in a small group (Fiedler, 1964).

Task structure   The amount of structure in the task that the group has been assigned can vary widely. Some tasks have a great deal of goal clarity; that is, the requirements of the task are clearly known or programmed. For example, the factory team assembling a car or a refrigerator has little doubt about what it is sup-

Some tasks have a great deal of goal clarity.
Alan Carey/The Image Works

posed to do. Other tasks, such as those of ad hoc committees, policy-making groups, and creative groups, often lack goal clarity and structure—no one knows exactly what the group's purposes are or how the group should proceed. A second element of task structure concerns solution specificity—that is, whether there is more than one way to complete the task. A third element of task structure is decision verifiability, or how clearly the group can determine that a group decision is correct. All these aspects of task structure play a role in determining the effectiveness of different types of leaders.

Leader position power The third major component of situational control is the power and authority inherent in the leadership position: authority to hire and fire, authority to reward persons by raising pay or status, and support from the organization are some aspects of power. For example, the person in charge of a group of volunteer workers in a political campaign would ordinarily have little position power over the volunteers. A football coach, an owner of a small business, and a police chief will often have high degrees of position power.

The three aspects of situational control can be used to create eight different leadership situations that range from very high to very low situational control, as illustrated in Figure 12.8. In the figure, Category I represents the highest degree of control, and Category VIII represents the lowest degree of control. A low LPC style is associated with a high degree of effectiveness in situations that involve either very high or very low levels of situational control. A high LPC style, in contrast, produces maximum effectiveness only at moderate levels of situational control. In the situation characterized by poor leader/member relations, an unstructured task, and strong leader power (Category VII), neither style produces any advantage (Chemers & Skrzypek, 1972).

Fiedler's contingency model provides us with considerable hindsight about earlier failures to find consistent, empirical support for personality characteristics or behavior patterns as sole explanations for leadership effectiveness. In some situations, initiating structure is a more effective style; in others, consideration is more effective; and in at least one situation neither style is particularly effective. We will return to leadership when we consider the dynamics of groups, but let us now turn to other roles as important aspects of group structure.

Roles and Expectations

Chapter 1 introduced the concept of **role,** referring to the functions performed by a person who occupies a particular position within a particular context. Similarly, **role expectations** were defined as assumptions about the behavior of a person who occupies a particular role. When a group initially forms, the roles of individual members are often not very clearly defined. Sometimes a leader will have been designated in advance. More often, however, various roles emerge and develop in the course of group interaction—a process termed **role differentiation** (Forsyth, 1983). In a new study group, for example, one student may eventually assume the role of keeping the group on task, and another student may occupy the role of "morale officer" or "social director." In contrast, when a group or organization has been functioning for some time, the roles tend to be quite clearly defined, and a newcomer may be assigned to some previously defined position. In a newspaper office, for example, a new reporter may discover that the "new kid" always starts out as the obituary writer. In such cases, roles are associated with particular positions rather than with persons (Katz & Kahn, 1976; McGrath, 1984).

As groups continue to develop, more generalized expectations about appropriate rules and procedures (called **norms**) develop as well. In Chapter 8 we described some of Muzafer Sherif's (1935, 1936) early experiments on the **autokinetic effect**—the apparent movement of a spot of light in an otherwise darkened room. One of the most interesting aspects of Sherif's research was the findings on how group norms become established. The judgments made by subjects who were part of a group were much less variable than those made by people who were alone. Such norms

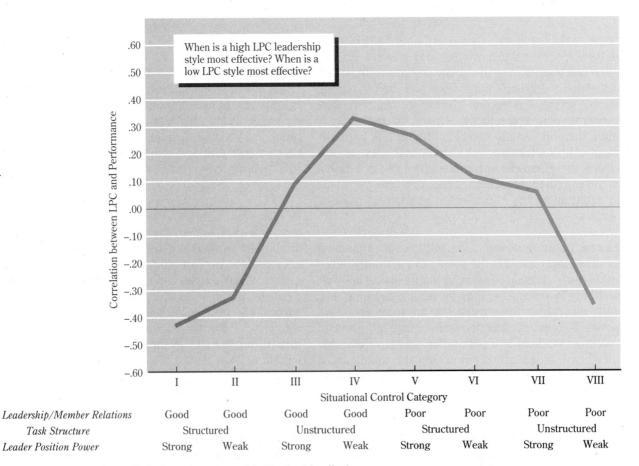

Figure 12.8 *Fiedler's contingency model of leadership effectiveness.*
Source: "Recent Developments in Research on the Contingency Model," by F. E. Fiedler. In L. Berkowitz (Ed.) *Group Processes,* 1978, San Diego: Academic Press.

persist even after the members who established the norm leave the group (Jacobs & Campbell, 1961). Your own participation in ongoing groups may provide additional insight on the persistence of norms.

Norms also enable group members to make distinctions about the relative status of group members, and hierarchies of authority almost inevitably develop. This tendency to organize on the basis of status distinctions seems a ubiquitous human tendency, even though the precise basis of the status assignment may vary from one group to another. Sociologist Joseph Berger and his colleagues have developed a model called **status characteristics theory** to explain how some of these organizing processes work (Berger, Rosenholtz, & Zelditch, 1980; Humphreys & Berger, 1981). According to this theory, differences in evaluations and beliefs about types of individuals become the basis for inequalities in social interaction. A status characteristic can be any characteristic for which one can perceive differences. For example, in a college seminar intelligence may be considered a status characteristic, and those with higher intelligence are accorded more status than those low in intelligence. In turn, certain expectations are attached to the performance of those who differ in status—someone in a college seminar might expect the more intelligent members of the seminar to be better prepared to discuss the reading assignment and to have a better understanding of the subject matter than the less intelligent members. In this instance, intelligence would be labeled a *specific* status characteristic because it is directly relevant to the group task.

Diffuse status characteristics are less directly linked to the task, but people may infer relevant characteristics on the basis of them. Race and gender operate in this fashion. People often assume, for example, that members of one identifiable group (such as men) have more skill in particular domains that could be relevant to the group task (such as mathematical or mechanical ability). A diffuse status characteristic may then be used as the basis for expectations about the performance of individuals who are members of those categories. A group working on a homecoming float, for example, may implicitly assume that the men in the group should be responsible for designing and building the infrastructure of the float without bothering to find out whether any of the women happen to be engineering majors. In turn, these expectation states lead to the development of particular hierarchies of authority within the group.

More than one type of status characteristic may exist in a group. For example, a work group might contain both women and men, and both skilled workers and unskilled workers. For the particular job, let us assume that people believe men to be better than women and skilled workers to be more talented than unskilled workers. In this case, a skilled female worker and an unskilled male worker would both represent cases of status inconsistency. In such instances, Humphreys and Berger (1981) predict that a state of relative equality is more likely to develop.

Gender is an interesting example of a diffuse status characteristic because the role expectations associated with male and female can be so pervasive. Just as people often assume that parents will contribute more effort to a family group than will children, so some people think it appropriate for men to contribute more to a group effort than women do. As the stereotype goes, men are more dominant, assertive, and competitive, whereas women are more passive, dependent, and weak. Kerr and MacCoun (1985a) reasoned that if such beliefs are common, then people working in a dyad would be more likely to take a free ride—let their partner do more of the work—if the partner is a man than if the partner is a woman. In contrast, a man should be most reluctant to let his partner "carry him," because such behavior would contradict normative role beliefs. Setting up a two-person task that involved pumping air into a container and manipulating the information that subjects had about their partner's performance, Kerr and MacCoun found strong support for their predictions. Gender beliefs affected behavior, sorting even two-person groups into a status hierarchy. We will discuss the effects of status characteristics more comprehensively in Chapter 13.

Interaction in Groups

Composition and structure are primarily static features of groups, but they can influence the dynamic processes that occur. In this section we look directly at the dynamics of group interaction: the processes that take place in groups and the performance of groups as they attempt to accomplish tasks.

Problem Solving

A major question group researchers have addressed is whether individuals working together in a group perform more successfully or efficiently than individuals working alone. Such interest is not surprising: any organization seeking to maximize its output needs to know how to plan its division of labor. Although the question may seem simple and straightforward, the answer is complex.

As stated earlier, expectations about the performance levels of other group members may result in social loafing, and the presence or potential for evaluation by other group members may produce other forms of social impairment or social facilitation. Another factor that increases the complexity of our seemingly simple question is the fact that not all group tasks are similar. Tasks differ in the kinds of behavior they require, the degree to which they encourage individual or group effort, their physical and intellectual demands, the criterion by which success is determined, and a variety of other ways (McGrath, 1984). We will examine problem solving to illustrate some of these variations and their influences on group performance.

The term *problem solving* refers to a wide variety of tasks, varying from counting dots to solving problems faced by managers of large business organizations. The requirements of these tasks frequently vary. Some tasks are easily divisible so that the overall problem can be broken down into specialized subtasks, each of which may be performed by one person. Other tasks cannot be divided into subtasks. Even when subtasks can be defined, they may or may not be obvious to the participants; if they are not obvious, considerable judgment and negotiation may precede the attempt to solve the problem (Steiner, 1972).

One problem-solving task that cannot be easily divided into subtasks is known as the *Tower of Hanoi,* an exercise in which disks of various diameters must be rearranged on a series of pegs, one move at a time. In a classic study, Marjorie E. Shaw (1932) used puzzles and problems similar to this one to compare group and individual problem solving. Subjects worked either in groups of four or as individuals. Groups were more likely to solve such problems—only 8% of the individuals produced correct solutions, compared with 53% of the groups. The groups, however, took about 1½ times

as long to solve the problems. The cost in person-hours was thus greater in the groups; they were less efficient. Shaw concluded that the major advantage of the group was its ability to recognize and reject incorrect solutions and suggestions.

Partly because groups are better at recognizing and rejecting solutions, an advertising executive named Alex Osborn (1957) began to advocate "brainstorming" as a way to devise new or creative solutions to difficult problems. The ground rules for brainstorming are shown in Table 12.1, and they can be applied to a wide range of problems. For example, an advertising agency could use brainstorming to develop a new slogan, a government agency could use it to devise a policy change, or a school board could use it to discover ways of handling a financial deficit.

Osborn claimed great success with the brainstorming procedure, but empirical evaluations indicate its success is qualified. For example, Taylor, Berry, and Block (1958) found that the number of suggestions made by groups exceeded the number made by any given individual working alone. However, when the suggestions of four separate individuals operating under brainstorming instructions were combined, they produced almost twice as many ideas per unit of time as did four-person face-to-face groups. This was also true when the subjects were research scientists who had worked together to solve problems (Dunnette, Campbell, & Jaastad, 1963). The majority of research on brainstorming indicates interacting group members generate *fewer* solutions than the same number of individuals working alone (Diehl & Stroebe, 1987; Lamm & Trommsdorff, 1973).

Much early research on brainstorming groups has been criticized because it involved bringing together individuals who do not know one another—groups created solely for experimental purposes (Bouchard, 1972). In such instances, group members might be reluctant to express some of their wild flights of fancy in front of strangers, even under ground rules that prohibit criticism of any idea. Prohibiting public criticism does not necessarily preclude others from thinking privately that a particular group member is "strange."

Transitory groups also may not be highly motivated; training and practice can improve the performance of brainstorming groups (Cohen, Whitmyre, & Funk, 1960; Parnes & Meadow, 1959). Consistent with the

Table 12.1 Rules for brainstorming

1. Given a problem to solve, all group members are encouraged to express whatever solutions and ideas come to mind, regardless of how preposterous or impractical they may seem.

2. All reactions are recorded.

3. No suggestion or solution can be evaluated until all ideas have been expressed. Ideally, participants should be led to believe that no suggestions will be evaluated at the brainstorming session.

4. The elaboration of one person's ideas by another is encouraged.

Source: Applied Imagination by A. F. Osborn, 1957, New York: Scribner.

earlier discussion of social loafing, Diehl and Stroebe (1987, Experiment 1) obtained a larger number of generated solutions when group members were told that the number of ideas each person generated would be evaluated than when they were told only that the group output would be evaluated. Despite enhanced personal accountability, however, brainstorming individuals still produced more solutions than interacting groups.

Perhaps the primary reason brainstorming groups do not generate more solutions than individuals is production blocking (Lamm & Trommsdorff, 1973). **Production blocking** reduces the number of ideas generated during brainstorming as a result of turn taking. While one person speaks, others must wait their turns while simultaneously trying to remember their ideas. Because short-term memory is limited, holding one idea in memory makes it extremely difficult to generate more ideas. Consequently, additional ideas are not generated because individuals are trying to remember what they will say about their first idea when it is their turn to speak.

In a series of experiments, Michael Diehl and Wolfgang Stroebe (1987) tested the extent to which production blocking occurred during brainstorming. As illustrated in Figure 12.9, forcing group members to take turns reduced the number of ideas they generated. It is also apparent from Figure 12.9 that individuals working alone generated the most ideas. Even when turn taking is not enforced, some production blocking occurs as a result of group members' inability to talk "all at once." Diehl and Stroebe concluded that brainstorming pro-

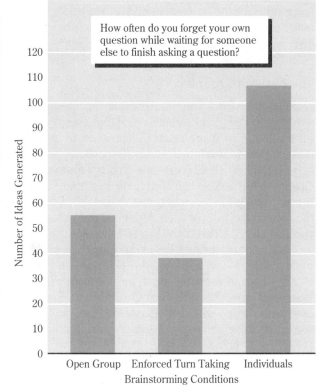

How often do you forget your own question while waiting for someone else to finish asking a question?

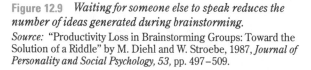

Figure 12.9 *Waiting for someone else to speak reduces the number of ideas generated during brainstorming.*
Source: "Productivity Loss in Brainstorming Groups: Toward the Solution of a Riddle" by M. Diehl and W. Stroebe, 1987, *Journal of Personality and Social Psychology, 53,* pp. 497–509.

cedures are most effective when group members first generate and record ideas individually, then discuss all the recorded ideas. With this method, new ideas stimulated by the discussion can also be offered without interfering with individually generated ideas because the latter, having been recorded, need not be held in memory.

To summarize the work on group problem solving, one must consider both the task and the nature of the individuals engaged in the task. Under many circumstances, a group may be better able than an individual to solve a problem—for example, when a task can be divided into subtasks and individuals' skills matched with those subtasks (Steiner, 1972). However, when the division of tasks is unspecified or when the members of a group lack the necessary skills, group performance may fall well below its potential (and even below the level of an individual performing the task alone).

The Perils of Groupthink

Groups, as we have described them so far, appear to be a rational creation: individuals come together, seek the best solution to a problem, and proceed to perform tasks to the best of their ability. Experience tells us, however, that such an ideal state does not always exist. Groups often make bad decisions and then defend those decisions in ways that defy rationality. Consider the dramatic effects of such decisions: the lack of preparedness on the part of the United States for the attack on Pearl Harbor during World War II, the U.S. invasion of the Bay of Pigs in Cuba, the U.S. involvement in North Korea, the escalation of the Vietnam War, the Watergate cover-up, and incitement of the Kurds to overthrow Iraq's Saddam Hussein. After analyzing some of these group-produced fiascos, Irving Janis (1972, 1982) coined the term **groupthink,** which he originally defined as "a mode of thinking that people

engage in when they are deeply involved in a cohesive in-group, when the members' striving for unanimity override[s] their motivation to realistically appraise alternative courses of action" (Janis, 1972, p. 9). More recently, Janis has simplified the definition, referring only to a tendency to seek concurrence prematurely (Janis, 1982; Janis & Mann, 1977; Longley & Pruitt, 1980).

Janis identified five conditions that are likely to foster groupthink (see Figure 12.10). The first condition, **cohesiveness,** is the total of all the forces attracting members to a group (Cartwright, 1968). From the perspective of an individual, cohesion is the extent to which one is attracted to the group. Thus, high cohesiveness occurs when most or all of the members are attracted to the group.

Highly cohesive groups are more likely than less cohesive groups to agree on a common goal (Schachter, Ellertson, McBride, & Gregory, 1951). Uniformity is stressed in cohesive groups, and members of cohesive groups are more likely to change their opinions in the direction of their fellow members' opinions than are members of less cohesive groups (Back, 1951; Lott & Lott, 1961). When you like the other members of a

Some groups, especially highly cohesive ones, may tend to seek concurrence prematurely—a situation that Janis describes as groupthink.
Spencer Grant/Monkmeyer Press

group to which you belong, you may have a greater tendency to go along with their opinions, believing that

harmony will enhance the good feelings among you. Thus, high cohesiveness increases the likelihood of both conformity—public compliance with group norms—and persuasion—internalization of group norms (Cartwright, 1968; see also Chapter 8).

More recently, Clark McCauley (1989) has argued that cohesion alone may not be a necessary condition for groupthink. In a review and reexamination of the case studies described by Janis and of other empirical tests of groupthink, McCauley proposed **uncertainty of approval** from the group as another necessary condition for groupthink. Uncertainty of approval refers to the extent to which a group member can count on acceptance by other members of the group (Longley & Pruitt, 1980; Steiner, 1982). For example, McCauley describes the child who is more obedient to neighbors and strangers than to parents because the child is more certain about approval from parents, not because the child is more attracted to strangers. Similarly, uncertainty of approval may be one reason we are likely to quietly consume cold, lumpy mashed potatoes at a friend's home but complain bitterly about the same fare when a spouse serves it (R. S. Miller, 1991).

Although cohesiveness and uncertainty of approval are probably the most important single factors that produce groupthink, other conditions also foster a tendency to seek concurrence. Add a highly directive leader trying to promote his or her views, and groupthink becomes even more likely (Courtright, 1978; Flowers, 1977; Leana, 1985). Groups that are isolated from the judgments of qualified outsiders also are likely victims. Consider, for example, two very different decisions by the same group about two very similar problems: the Bay of Pigs and Cuban Missile Crisis decisions made by U.S. President Kennedy and his advisors. The disastrous consequences of the former decision were avoided in the latter because Kennedy avoided promotional leadership by encouraging debate, appointing a "devil's advocate," and importing "outsiders" as sources of information and differing opinions (McCauley, 1989).

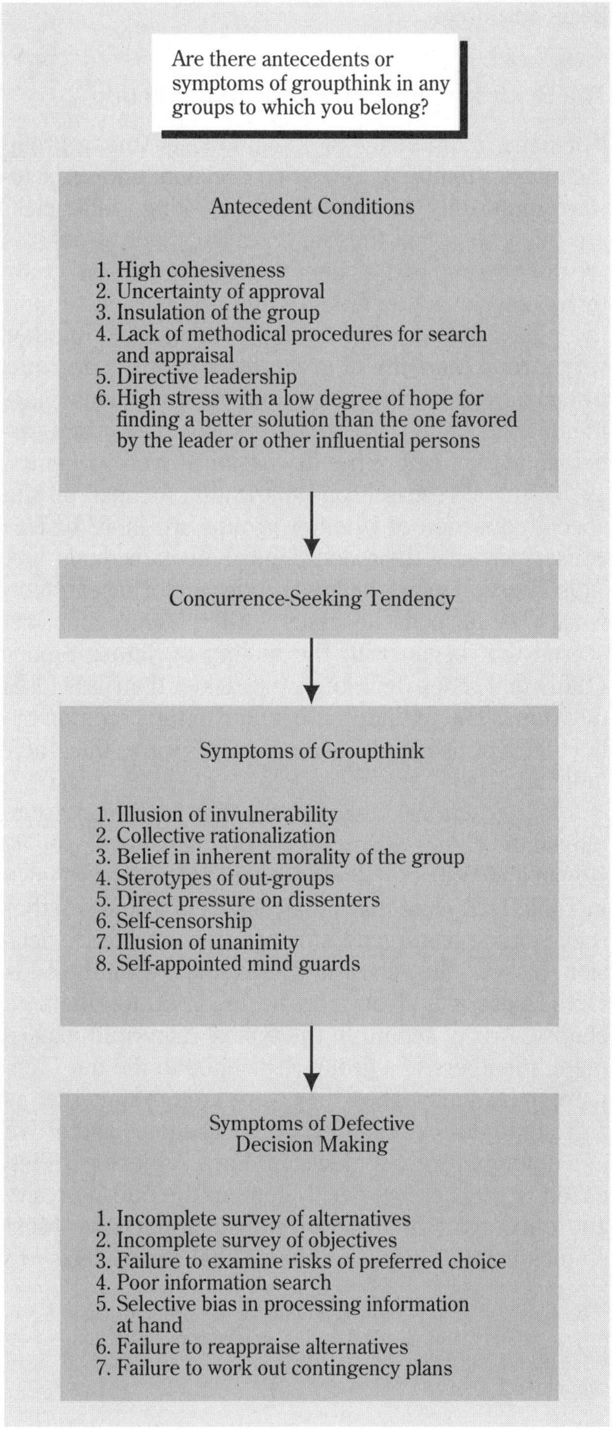

Are there antecedents or symptoms of groupthink in any groups to which you belong?

Antecedent Conditions

1. High cohesiveness
2. Uncertainty of approval
3. Insulation of the group
4. Lack of methodical procedures for search and appraisal
5. Directive leadership
6. High stress with a low degree of hope for finding a better solution than the one favored by the leader or other influential persons

↓

Concurrence-Seeking Tendency

↓

Symptoms of Groupthink

1. Illusion of invulnerability
2. Collective rationalization
3. Belief in inherent morality of the group
4. Sterotypes of out-groups
5. Direct pressure on dissenters
6. Self-censorship
7. Illusion of unanimity
8. Self-appointed mind guards

↓

Symptoms of Defective Decision Making

1. Incomplete survey of alternatives
2. Incomplete survey of objectives
3. Failure to examine risks of preferred choice
4. Poor information search
5. Selective bias in processing information at hand
6. Failure to reappraise alternatives
7. Failure to work out contingency plans

Figure 12.10 *Antecedents and consequences of groupthink.*
Sources: Decision Making: A Psychological Analysis of Conflict, Choice, and Commitment (p. 132) by I. L. Janis and L. Mann, 1977, New York: Free Press; and "The Nature of Social Influence in Groupthink: Compliance and Internalization" by C. McCauley, 1989, *Journal of Personality and Social Psychology, 57,* pp. 250–260.

Groupthink is also indicated by typical symptoms, shown in Figure 12.10. Among these symptoms is the emergence of "mind guards"—members who protect the group from information that might shatter its complacency. For example, *The Presidential Transcripts* (Washington Post, 1974) contains numerous examples of the symptoms of mindguarding as experienced by U.S. President Nixon and his staff during the Watergate cover-up that eventually led to Nixon's resignation. Other symptoms have received empirical support from an archival study of public statements by decision makers involved in five U.S. foreign-policy crises; Janis described three of these crises as examples of groupthink (Tetlock, 1979). Consistent with Janis's hypothesis, groupthink decision makers made more positive references to the United States and to its allies than did the non-groupthink participants. Moreover, groupthink policy makers were more simplistic in their perceptions of basic issues. As is also indicated in Figure 12.10, the characteristics of the decision-making process that occurs under groupthink indicate a process that generally is highly selective both in information search and in evaluation of alternatives.

In a constructive vein, Janis has suggested ways in which groupthink can be prevented. A leader should encourage dissidence, call on each member of the group to be critical, and reinforce members who voice criticism of a favored plan. Such actions would increase certainty of approval. Further, a leader should avoid promotional leadership by not presenting a favored plan at the outset. Even if the leader has a favored plan, initially he or she should describe a problem rather than recommend a solution. For larger groups, it may be possible to establish routine procedures by which several independent groups could work on the same problem. With such dispersion of energies, it is unlikely that a consensus will develop prematurely. Of course, the groups must merge to reach a final decision.

It should be noted that groupthink does not always lead to defective decisions, nor is it necessarily undesirable in all situations (Janis, 1982; Longley & Pruitt, 1980). As a tendency toward concurrence, groupthink produces defective decisions only to the extent that concurrence takes place before all worthwhile alternatives have been given adequate consideration. Similarly, not all group decisions are as important as those described in this section. When the problem confronting a group is trivial, such as a decision about where to go for coffee after the theater, speedy concurrence may be an advantage.

The Polarizing Effects of Group Interaction

Whenever a difference of opinion exists among group members attempting to reach a decision, pressures toward uniformity (or concurrence-seeking tendencies) are likely to occur (Festinger, 1950). Such pressures are often strong and, as demonstrated in a classic study by Stanley Schachter (1951), can result in a lone minority-opinion holder being treated as an outcast. Another very strong outcome of group discussions is a **group polarization** of responses; that is, consensus judgments and opinions are more extreme after group participation than before the discussion (Myers & Lamm, 1976). Initial research on polarization focused on the specific question of whether groups are more or less conservative in their decisions than individuals are. This question generated over a decade of research on what was termed the **risky shift** phenomenon, research that began with the finding by James Stoner (1961) that group decisions were riskier than individual decisions. The finding ran counter to the common belief that groups tend to be more conservative than their individual members.[2]

Most research studies that followed Stoner's employed the choice-dilemma questionnaire developed by Kogan and Wallach (1964), one item of which is shown in Table 12.2. Note that subjects are not asked whether they would recommend a risky or a conservative decision. Instead, they are asked to estimate what the odds for success would have to be in order for them to choose a risky action. In the typical risky-shift experiment, members of a group responded to the questionnaire individually. Then they were brought together as a group to discuss each hypothetical choice and arrive at a unanimous group decision. Each subject was then asked to go back over each item on the questionnaire and once again indicate an individual decision. Most studies using this method found that group decisions

---

[2]The view that groups are less productive and produce less satisfactory solutions than individuals still pervades popular wisdom—consider the description of a camel as "a horse designed by a committee."

Table 12.2 A choice-dilemma questionnaire item

Mr. A., an electrical engineer who is married and has one child, has been working for a large electronics corporation since graduating from college five years ago. He is assured of a lifetime job with a modest, though adequate, salary and liberal pension benefits upon retirement. On the other hand, it is very unlikely that his salary will increase much before he retires. While attending a convention, Mr. A. is offered a job with a small, newly founded company which has a highly uncertain future. The new job would pay more to start and would offer the possibility of a share in the ownership if the company survived the competition of the larger firms.

Imagine that you are advising Mr. A. Listed below are several probabilities or odds of the new company proving financially sound. *Please check the lowest probability that you would consider acceptable to make it worthwhile for Mr. A. to take the new job.*

_____ The chances are 1 in 10 that the company will prove financially sound.

_____ The chances are 3 in 10 that the company will prove financially sound.

_____ The chances are 5 in 10 that the company will prove financially sound.

_____ The chances are 7 in 10 that the company will prove financially sound.

_____ The chances are 9 in 10 that the company will prove financially sound.

_____ Place a check here if you think Mr. A. should *not* take the new job no matter what the probabilities.

Source: Risk-Taking: A Study in Cognition and Personality (p. 256) by N. Kogan and M. A. Wallach, 1964, New York: Holt.

were indeed riskier, and various theoretical formulations were offered to explain this initially unpredicted finding.

Eventually, investigators realized that the shift produced by group discussion was not necessarily in the direction of greater risk. If the initial opinions of the group tend toward conservatism, then the shift resulting from group discussion will be toward a more extreme conservative opinion (Fraser, 1971; Myers & Bishop, 1971). Therefore, the term group polarization has effectively replaced *risky shift* as a general description of this particular phenomenon. Given the pervasiveness of group polarization, researchers focused

their efforts on why such polarization occurs. A combination of two general types of influence, normative and informational, appears to provide an adequate explanation of group polarization (Kaplan, 1987).

According to the **normative influence** explanation, individuals in a group assess the opinions of others and move to a position of perceived agreement as a result of conformity pressures. Motives suggested for this behavior include the desire for favorable evaluation by others and a concern for self-presentation. This explanation focuses on the characteristics of the group members, not on information that might develop in the course of group discussion. One variation of this position is the "bandwagon" effect, believed to be particularly evident when group members expect future interactions with one another in other settings (Andrews & Johnson, 1971). One aspect of normative influence is that individuals consider themselves part of a specific group (Mackie, 1986; Turner, 1982). For example, there is evidence that group members often perceive attitudinal positions of their group to be more extreme than they actually are. Such perceptions, coupled with motivation to conform to group norms, constitute one mechanism accounting for polarization shifts.

In contrast, the **informational influence** explanation stresses learning that results from exposure to persuasive arguments during group discussion. Here the emphasis is on the actual content (or the "message") of discussion and on how much members are persuaded by new information other group members present. Essentially, informational influence results from persuasion processes, as described in Chapter 7. Even when all group members are exposed to the same information, such as in a jury, some "new" information may be presented during discussion, if for no other reason than that some group members may have been inattentive or have forgotten some of the information.

It is important to note that both normative and informational influence may operate in any given group at any given time, although informational influence appears to be the stronger of the two processes (Isenberg, 1986; Kaplan, 1987). Persuasion also may imply pressure to conform. For example, Myers and Bishop (1971) found that 76% of the arguments in a group supported the position held by most of the members. The abundance of persuasive messages advocating the same position may also create the impression that there is greater solidarity of opinion than actually exists. Similarly, pressure to conform may involve emphasizing the "overwhelming" weight of information supporting one's viewpoint. Normative influences, therefore, can involve presentation of information, some of which may be new to some group members.

Given that both informational and normative influence can cause group polarization, Martin Kaplan (1987) has reviewed the conditions that make one or another type of influence more likely to occur. As outlined in Table 12.3, conditions that involve "correct" answers and getting the task done tend to favor informational influence. On the other hand, conditions that involve tasks for which there is no correct answer and that focus on the group rather than on the task tend to favor normative influence. Interestingly, unanimous-decision rules favor both types of influence. Because those holding one opinion are forced to convince members holding the opposing opinion in order to achieve unanimity, greater emphasis will be placed on information when, for example, a "correct" answer exists. On the other hand, when there is no correct answer, a unanimous-decision rule also emphasizes the importance of group harmony and forces members' decisions to become public (Kaplan & Miller, 1987).

In summary, group polarization effects are indeed real. Whether polarization effects cause a group to become more conservative or more risky depends on the initial opinions of the majority of group members. As with many other group processes, exactly how polarization occurs depends on several conditions, including the nature of the task and the motivations of group members. As we shall see in the next section, however, the initial opinion held by a majority of group members does not always become the group's decision.

Minority Group Influence

Not all members of a group necessarily identify with the group as a whole. Sometimes particular policies may cause some group members to feel at odds with the group goals. The cost-conscious diner who orders a less expensive meal to conserve money may want to disagree with other group members when they suggest dividing the check evenly as a way to avoid having to reconstruct everyone's order. On other occasions, visible signs may cause one or more members of a group to stand out from the others. As discussed in Chapter 4, certain characteristics may make individuals salient—easily distinguishable from the other members of the group. For example, blacks in predominantly white organizations or women in predominantly male organizations may be viewed by members of the majority as a recognizable subgroup. Further, as noted in Chapter 3, people whom others view as different may become more aware of the characteristics that distinguish them from the majority and thus may come to define themselves as a minority.

A person may be in the minority for more than one reason. Anne Maass and her colleagues have made a distinction between "single" and "double" minorities (Maass, Clark, & Haberkorn, 1982). In their terms, a "single" minority is someone who deviates from the majority only in terms of belief, as in our earlier example of the cost-conscious diner. A "double" minority is a person who differs both in belief and in category, as

Table 12.3   **Conditions that enhance normative or informational influence during group discussion**

Conditions	Emergent mode of influence	
	Normative	*Informational*
Underlying motivations	Maintain harmony, acceptance by group, self-presentation, comparison with others	Being correct, knowing, being informed about components of a decision
Type of issue	Judgmental (value)	Intellective (factual)
Interactive goal	Group set	Task set
Personal orientation	Communal, socio-emotional	Agentic, task-oriented
Mode of response	Public	Private
Decision rule	Enhanced by unanimity	Enhanced by unanimity

Source: "The Influence Process in Group Decision Making" by M. F. Kaplan, 1987, *Review of Personality and Social Psychology, 8,* pp. 189–212.

when a cost-conscious diner is the only woman in the group.

The person who is in the minority by virtue of some ascribed characteristic, such as race or gender, has little choice about being seen as a minority, at least initially. Other members of the group will spontaneously categorize such a member and are likely to interpret the member's behavior in terms of that category (Fiske & Neuberg, 1990). When expressing their difference of belief, "double" minority members may choose to increase or decrease the distance between themselves and the dominant group. A person who is similar to the majority in ascribed characteristics but who differs in values may not be accorded minority status so quickly. That is, a "single" minority may have to "try harder" to convince the other group members that the difference of opinion is real.

Students of social influence have long recognized the possibility of discrepant views among members of a group. In Chapter 8, for example, we saw how a minority could be influenced by the majority, as the naive individuals in Asch's (1951) study frequently conformed to the confederates' judgments even though those judgments were incorrect. Recognition of the reverse, that a minority can also influence a majority, has been slower to develop (Moscovici, 1976, 1985; Mugny, 1982), and disagreement exists about the extent to which such influence involves different processes than majority influence does (Kruglanski & Mackie, 1990).

Some investigators believe minority influence processes differ from those of the majority because members of minorities need to engage in specific behavior patterns to influence the rest of the group (Levine & Russo, 1987; Maass, West, & Cialdini, 1987). According to French psychologist Serge Moscovici (1976, 1985), a leading proponent of this perspective, the success of a minority subgroup depends on the inferences other members of the group make about the subgroup and its alternative position. A small subgroup that presents a united front may cause the others to attribute strong beliefs and commitment to the minority. Having made such an inference, the majority group will be more open to the minority's arguments. Moscovici suggests the behavioral style of the subgroup members is important; they should appear to be consistent, to be invested in their position, to have autonomy, to be able to stand up for their beliefs, to be somewhat rigid, and to be fair.

A minority that states its position consistently is generally more successful in influencing the majority (Nemeth, 1979). However, particular situational factors can moderate this effect (Mugny, 1975; Wolf, 1979), and on some occasions a negotiating style may be more effective than inflexible presentation. Sometimes, for example, an active, consistent minority may appear too rigid or too consistent, thereby alienating the others and resulting in the minority's exclusion from the group (Di Giacomo, 1980; Mugny, Kaiser, Papastamou, & Perez, 1984).

Agreement with a minority position may differ from agreement with a majority in other important respects. The conformity exhibited in agreement with the majority position is more apt to be a public phenomenon. Minority influence, in contrast, sometimes has a greater effect on private, internalized attitudes and beliefs (Maass & Clark, 1984). To explain these differences, Charlan Nemeth (1986) suggests that exposure to persistent minority views causes majority members to think more about the issue. More specifically, she predicts that people who encounter a minority position are more likely to entertain divergent thoughts and consider novel solutions. Responses to a majority argument, in contrast, are believed to be more limited, converging on the proposed solution quite quickly. Testing this prediction, Nemeth and Wachtler (1983) arranged for college students to work on a creative problem-solving task in groups in which the experimenter had "planted" confederates. The task was an embedded-figures task in which one searches for figures, such as animals, that are partially hidden in a picture of, say, a jungle. In the "majority" condition, groups consisted of two subjects and four confederates; the confederates constituted a numerical majority. In the "minority" condition, the ratio was reversed, and the confederates represented a numerical minority. Although in each case the confederates offered the same solution to the problem, the responses of the subjects differed. Subjects presented with the solutions of a majority tended to go along with the confederates' solutions. In contrast, subjects who heard solutions offered by only two confederates (the minority condition) discovered many more possible solutions to the problems. It is also interesting to note that subjects in the majority condition reported feeling more awkward in a postexperimental questionnaire than did subjects in the minority condition. This finding suggests that majority pressure produced some stress on group members.

Despite the preceding information, other investigators believe that minority and majority influences operate much the same way (Latané & Wolf, 1981; Tanford & Penrod, 1984; Wolf, 1987). Recalling the model of social impact discussed earlier in this chapter, we can think of minority influence as being determined by the strength, the immediacy, and the number of minority group members. According to this view, members of a minority will be more effective when they have higher status or greater ability, when they are closer to the majority in space or time, and when there are more of them. Of course, when the number of members of one subgroup equals the number of members in another subgroup, neither can be considered a minority.

In a recent review of the research and theory concerning majority and minority influence, Arie Kruglanski and Diane Mackie (1990) concluded there is very little support for the viewpoint that two different influence processes exist. Kruglanski and Mackie argue instead that those supporting a "separate process" viewpoint have failed to distinguish between processes and outcomes that typically accompany minority influence and those that necessarily accompany minority influence. That is, minority processes are not different, but appear different as a result of the conditions under which minority influence usually occurs.

To illustrate their point, let us again consider the study by Nemeth and Wachtler (1983). In the majority condition, subjects were faced with an existing majority opinion—that of the four confederates—concerning "correct" answers for an embedded-figures task. Unless the subjects were highly motivated to search for additional solutions, we can speculate that they perceived the problem to be solved almost immediately. One can imagine a subject wondering what he or she could add if four of six people had already identified the hidden figures. Such perceptions could also create the awkward feelings noted on the postexperimental questionnaire; it is awkward to join a task-oriented group only to discover others in the group have already done all the work. In the minority condition, however, the situation was quite different. Only two members of the group proposed initial solutions, so a perception that the task was accomplished was not likely. Because the task was not immediately completed, the subjects

began to work on the task, thereby generating more solutions. Had the two confederates in the minority condition persuasively stated their solutions were the only solutions, perhaps the subjects would not have attempted to generate more solutions. That is, Nemeth and Wachtler's (1983) results do not necessarily support different *types* of influence for majorities and minorities; there may only be different *levels* of the same influence process.

Kruglanski and Mackie admit that their conclusions involve speculation and that resolution of the controversy will require considerably more research. One reason it is important to resolve the question of one versus two processes is simply that at different times the same person may be part of the minority or part of the majority. Recognition of the potential of minority influence is particularly important in exploring how social change can occur. Understanding the ways in which minority influence occurs also enhances our understanding of the processes of social change.

▶ Group Socialization

So far, most of the discussion has focused on intact groups, studied at one particular time and often brought together by a researcher for one occasion. In actuality, groups are not static. People join groups and leave them; groups accept members, including leaders, and reject them. To truly understand the nature of groups, we need to examine more closely the process of socialization and the changes that occur in the group composition and the member status.

The social psychologists Richard Moreland and John Levine (1982) have provided an insightful account of the process of group socialization, and we will rely on their model as we discuss the relation between groups and their members. Later, we will use Martin Chemers's (1987) systems-process model to examine how prior socialization affects experience within a group.

Basic Processes

People belong to many kinds of groups—sports teams, fraternities and sororities, church groups, political parties, and work groups, to name a few. Although groups differ in focus and purpose, some characteristics are common to all groups. According to Moreland and Levine (1982), three processes are basic to group socialization: evaluation, commitment, and role transitions.

Evaluation is a process by which members of the group assess group-related rewards: what benefits one derives from the group, what it costs to be a member, and how important the group goals are. Further, recalling the ideas of interdependence theory (Kelley & Thibaut, 1978; Thibaut & Kelley, 1959; see also Chapter 9), individuals also consider the comparison level for alternatives and compare the rewards of membership in one group with the possibilities for rewards in other groups: Would you rather be in sorority *A* or sorority *B*? Would you rather be a member of the chess club or of the skydiving club?

Group members also make such assessments about individual members. Does Blair really contribute to our group? Is Sonny fun to have around? These evaluation processes continue through the life of a group and can incorporate many different dimensions. Further, these evaluations take into account past rewards and costs and expected future rewards and costs. For example, Susan might look at her team and decide that although Robin has been an important contributor in the past, his ability to contribute to the next project is doubtful. Once again, these evaluations will probably take into account people now outside the group who might be recruited for membership.

Commitment is not independent of evaluation. As Moreland and Levine state, "groups are more committed to individuals who help them attain group goals, and individuals are more committed to groups that help them satisfy personal needs" (1982, p. 145). In assessing commitment, both the group and the individual again consider various temporal perspectives—past, present, and expected future rewards. For example, a relatively new member who has received little from the group will be less committed to the group than a longtime member who has benefited greatly from membership. Commitment also involves comparisons with other situations that might offer more. The more rewarding the present member or group, and the less rewarding other available groups, the greater the commitment.

Commitment has a number of consequences, some of which we discussed in describing the group interac-

tion process. Here we can consider four specific consequences: (1) consensus agreement on the group goals and values, (2) positive affective ties, both of the individual to the group and of the group to the individual, (3) a willingness to exert effort on behalf of the group or the individual, and (4) a desire for continuance of membership in the group (Moreland & Levine, 1982). Again, we examine these consequences from two perspectives—from that of the individual who is committed to the group and from that of the group that is committed to the individual member.

Groups are not stable over time, and the role of any individual within the group can change. We may think of the various roles as lying on a dimension from nonmembers at one end to full members at the other end. A nonmember of a bowling team, for example, may be either someone who has never joined or someone who quit the team last month. Full members of a group are those who are closely identified with the group and are fully established in their roles. Between these two extremes are so-called quasi-members—newcomers to the group who are not yet fully accepted or marginal members who have lost some of their former status. For example, the longtime bowling team member who shows up only occasionally may shift in status from full member to quasi-member.

As the group changes over time, individual members may have different roles within the group. Often the transition from one role to another is marked by formal ceremonies, or rites of passage. Bar mitzvahs and bat mitzvahs, for example, mark the transition of Jewish children to adulthood. Tenure marks the transition from "junior" faculty member to one upon whom the group (the university) has conferred considerable commitment. Other role transitions can be marked in more personal ways. On becoming a member of an honorary society, for example, you may be toasted by your friends at a party. After being promoted to a more desirable team in the organization, you may buy yourself a present. These and other activities may serve as markers of a social-psychological transition in the life of a group.

Stages of Group Socialization

The basic processes of group socialization give rise to a variety of levels or stages in the life of a group and its

Role transitions are sometimes marked by formal ceremonies, such as by this bat mitzvah.
Bill Aron/PhotoEdit

members. As Figure 12.11 illustrates, one can view the life span of a group as consisting of five general periods, with four specific points marking the transitions between stages. As we analyze each stage, you may want to think of your own experiences in groups as possible illustrations of the process. Bear in mind that this curve is only a general model; the exact shape of the curve may vary. Some stages may be nearly nonexistent in some groups—there is little "recruitment" in an immediate family group when the mother gives birth to a child. In other groups, the same stage may be more extensive—the "recruitment" of a prospective child through adoption can involve years.

1. Investigation Fraternity or sorority rush provides an excellent example of the investigation stage. From the perspective of the individual who wants to join a group, the rush period is one of reconnaissance: assessing the various groups, trying to decide which one would be most compatible with personal needs and values. Individuals' reasons for joining a group can vary widely, of course, as will their actual choice of a group. Some of these differences can be related to the person's prior experience with groups. For example, the reconnaissance activities of first-year college students are influenced by their positive or negative experiences with groups in high school (Pavelchak, Moreland, & Levine, 1986). Students whose high school experiences were generally positive try harder to identify potentially desirable college groups. Students who have had little past experience with groups are at a disadvantage as they try to evaluate the potential satisfaction a college group will offer. Not only are their reconnaissance activities less extensive, but they are also likely to be overly optimistic in assessing the rewards a group may offer.

While individuals are assessing the potential value of group membership, existing group members are engaging in recruitment activities, looking for persons who will "fit in" with their goals and activities. Fraternities and sororities, for example, use various criteria to gauge the suitability of a prospective member. Not all groups are as formal and closed, of course. Many groups do very little evaluation at this stage and are willing to accept anyone who wishes to be a member. Political organizations, for example, are relatively open groups. A group's willingness to accept new members may depend partly on its past success. One example of such influence is the famous study by Festinger, Riecken, and Schachter (1956), who investigated the behavior of a group that predicted the end of the world on a particular date. When the prediction proved false, members of this group became active proselytizers, seeking new recruits wherever they could find them.

2. Entry The entry stage (indicated by the first triangle in Figure 12.11) marks the role transition between investigation and socialization. At this point the individual moves from being a prospective member to being a new member of the group. In formal groups, this transition is usually marked by some kind of ceremony or initiation rite, designed in part to increase the member's commitment to the group. In less formal groups, this transition may occur without much notice, and the commitment to and by the group may be weaker as a result. As noted in Chapter 7, greater investment in an attitudinal position (for example, "I am a member") makes the attitude stronger (Aronson & Mills, 1959).

3. Socialization During the period of socialization, the individual and the group attempt to merge their respective goals and norms. The group attempts to assim-

ilate the individual, instructing the person in its ways, its rituals, its procedures, and its expectations. At the same time, the individual may attempt to shape the group so it is compatible with his or her own needs. It is in this phase that the relative influence of majorities and minorities plays a major role in group dynamics.

The socialization period varies in length and can take many forms. In the sorority or fraternity, for example, the pledge period represents a stage of socialization. Many corporations have an initial training program for prospective managers that serves much the same function. In less formal organizations, the socialization stage may be less clearly defined but still can be viewed in terms of gradual assimilation of the member to the group and gradual accommodation of the group to the new member.

4. Acceptance Acceptance marks the transition between being a new member and being a full member, or between being an outsider and an insider within the

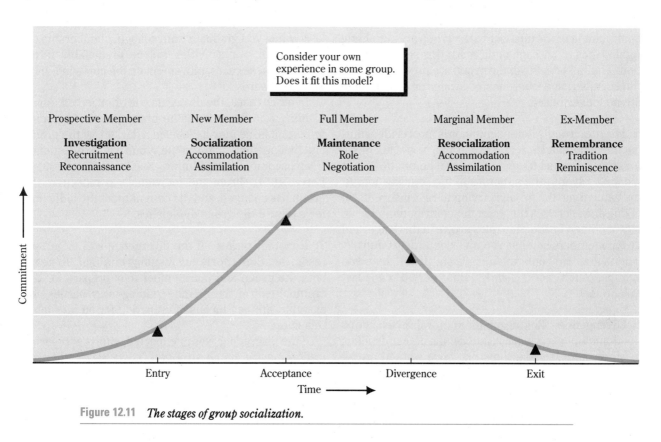

Figure 12.11 *The stages of group socialization.*

Rites of passage often accompany formal acceptance by the group.
Alan Carey/The Image Works

group. Awarding a commission to graduates of an ROTC program or military academy is one example of this step. At this point, as the curve in Figure 12.11 indicates, commitment of the group to the member and commitment of the member to the group are both high. Again, rites of passage often mark this second transition. The full benefits of the group are now available to the member, and questions of loyalty or contribution are no longer raised.

5. Maintenance Role negotiation is most evident during the maintenance period of a group. Now a full member, the individual tries to see where he or she will fit most clearly into the structure of the organization. At the same time, the group is trying to restructure itself, taking into account the potential contributions of the new member. Leadership roles evolve in this stage, and group members negotiate complex, interdependent relationships with one another (Gibb, 1969). In some groups, such as a family, this period can last indefinitely.

6. Divergence Role negotiation is not always successful. Sometimes workable relationships do not develop; in other cases, relationships that once worked are altered by the addition of new members to the group. When the group no longer satisfies the individual, or the individual no longer satisfies the group, a third transition point (termed "divergence") is marked. Some-

times this transition is expected. For example, when you graduated from high school and went to college, your departure (at least in part) from your group of high school friends was an expected divergence. Similarly, when you graduate from college, memberships in college clubs or activities will be predictably terminated. In these cases, movement on the curve in Figure 12.11 is toward exit.

In other cases, the divergence is unexpected. An individual who veers from the group position on some important issue may be labeled a deviant by the group, and that person's status in the group will be questioned (Di Giacomo, 1980; Mugny, Kaiser, Papastamou, & Perez, 1984). From the individual's perspective, the group has changed, and the commitment the individual feels toward the group diminishes.

7. Resocialization If the divergence was expected, resocialization efforts are usually minimal. Instead, both the group and the member may prepare for the eventual exit of the member. Going-away parties, for example, are one means of preparing for an inevitable transition.

If the divergence was unexpected, efforts at resocialization may be much stronger. As we saw earlier, responses to a deviant often involve a great deal of attention and communication in attempts to change the person's position so it will be more consistent with the group's (Schachter, 1951). Both the individual and the group may negotiate and compromise, trying to regain the prior levels of commitment. Should these efforts be successful, the individual will return to full membership status, essentially moving backward on the curve shown in Figure 12.11. If the efforts are unsuccessful, then this individual, like the expected divergent, will move toward the exit transition point.

8. Exit At the point of exit, the individual's and the group's commitment to each other has diminished. An evaluation of the rewards of the situation has led to a conclusion that such rewards are minimal either in themselves or in comparison with the rewards another group or another member would offer. The exit transition may occur very quickly, as when an employee resigns or is fired outright. In other cases, negotiating this transition point takes more time as both the individual and the group prepare for the new situation. The individual may show a gradual decline in his or her commitment to the group—first missing a few meetings, then failing to carry out some responsibilities, then being a member in name only. On the other side, the group will gradually shift the individual to a marginal position where the individual is less involved in decisions and interacts less with members.

Rites of passage may mark the exit transition as well. Retirement ceremonies mark the end of service for the employee. Angry public statements are sometimes made by the individual who has been expelled from the group. From the group's viewpoint, the head of an immediate family may officially declare a son or daughter "disowned." These events, like the rites that preceded them, testify to the importance of such transition points in the relationships between individuals and groups.

9. Remembrance Finally, when the relationship between the individual and the group has been severed, a period of remembrance takes place. The individual reminisces (with either favorable or unfavorable thoughts) about his or her relationship to that group and what it means for the future. From the group's perspective, recall of events involving that person often takes the form of tradition. "Remember what Todd did when we . . ." may be the basis of consolidating the memories of Todd, either favorable or unfavorable, depending on the basis of the exit. Although commitment is now weak or absent, evaluations of the member or the group persist and provide a basis for future evaluations by groups and by prospective members.

This model of group socialization can be applied to nearly every kind of group, from formal to informal, from large to small, from short-lived to long-lived. Although the lengths of various stages and the forms of various transition points vary, the model captures important aspects of the socialization process in every group.

The Influence of Culture

Groups do not exist in a vacuum, nor do individuals maintain memberships in only one group at a time. As an outgrowth of his research on leadership, Martin Chemers (1983, 1987) has developed a systems-process model of group dynamics in which he proposes that socialization at the cultural or societal level also affects dynamics at the immediate group level. Individuals reflect societal values and bring those values with them to smaller groups. For example, if a society values accomplishment and productivity, then the expectations, behaviors, and reactions of small-group members (leaders and followers) will stem from such values. Evaluation processes will be based on productivity: does Frank get the job done, can Mary work independently, and so on. In contrast, societal values emphasizing interpersonal harmony will produce small-group members whose perceptions and reactions are very different. Evaluation processes will reflect cohesion: is Tom disruptive, can Jean get along with others. The influence of situational characteristics also can begin outside the group. During a recession, for example, an employee might consider mere membership in a job-related group to be satisfying. During better economic times, however, movement "up the company ladder" may be a prerequisite for satisfaction.

Chemers and Roya Ayman have conducted several studies that support the systems-process model (Ayman, 1984; Ayman & Chemers, 1983; Chemers, 1969; Chemers & Ayman, 1985). For example, Iranians and Americans have different implicit personality theories about "good" leaders; Iranians apparently don't distinguish between initiation and consideration the same way Americans do. For Iranians, treating group members considerately is synonymous with "getting the job done." As noted earlier, Americans usually consider these two leadership duties separately. Despite these cultural differences, Iranian subjects used the same process Americans use to evaluate both American and Iranian leaders. The match between the followers' beliefs about a good leader and the global style of the leader was the key component of positive evaluations. In fact, overall leader style was a better predictor of the group members' evaluations of the leader than was any specific behavior of the leader. Thus, not only are individuals affected by other group members, but small groups are affected by norms and expectations that stem from still larger groups.

▶ Summary

A group is defined as two or more people who interrelate in some dynamic way. Groups have structure, organization, and relationships among the members. An aggregate—a collection of people who do not interrelate—is not the same as a group.

Other people may influence our behavior even when we are not part of a group. The social impact of an audience is determined by the number of people in the audience, their status, and their immediacy to the target.

The drive theory of social facilitation suggests that the presence of others is a source of general arousal that will result in increased performance of simple or well-learned responses and decreased performance of more complex tasks. Various social and cognitive concerns can lead to greater arousal. Other explanations of social facilitation point to the distractive aspects of an audience and to the self-presentation concerns of the performer.

Coacting others can add a feeling of competition to the typical audience situation. In addition, they provide a source of modeling and of social comparison.

In a true group situation, social loafing becomes yet another possible effect upon an individual's performance as a result of the individual's expectations about what other members of the group will do.

Groups vary in composition—for example, in their size and the identity of their members—and in structure—the systems of roles and norms that hold a group together. Group size is a composition variable that has attracted a great deal of interest, including interest in its practical implications for jury size.

Communication networks are one feature of group structure. These networks affect both the performance of the group and the satisfaction of its members.

There appears to be no basis for concluding that certain personality characteristics are related to effective leadership. Instead, the effects of leadership upon group performance and satisfaction are best understood as an interaction among leadership style, situational constraints, and group members' expectations concerning a leader. Under some conditions, a task-oriented leadership style is a more effective style. Under different conditions, consideration for group members is more effective.

Role expectations and norms develop in all groups, and authority hierarchies are seemingly inevitable as well. Often these hierarchies are based on status characteristics, which may or may not be related to the specific group project.

Whether a group will perform better than an individual depends both on the nature of the task and on the characteristics of individual members. Although touted as a technique in which groups outperform individuals, brainstorming in groups also results in production blocking, which effectively limits the number of ideas a group can generate through discussion.

Groupthink, defined as a tendency of members to seek concurrence, illustrates the process by which groups may come to poor decisions. Several conditions encourage the development of groupthink; perhaps the most important are a high degree of cohesiveness, or "we-feeling," and a high level of uncertainty of approval.

In general, group interaction tends to lead to a polarization of responses: opinions resulting from group discussion are more extreme than are the opinions of individuals before the group discussion. Both normative and informational influence are responsible for polarization, but different conditions make one or the other type of influence more likely to occur.

Not all members of a group feel equally committed to the group. Those who share beliefs or characteristics may form a minority subgroup within the larger group. Such subgroups can influence the majority, primarily through display of a consistent behavioral style.

It remains unclear whether minority influence is a different process from majority influence or both types of influence involve the same process.

Over the life span of a group, three processes appear particularly important: evaluation, commitment, and role transition. The socialization of a group can be described in terms of five general periods, separated by four specific transition points. These periods and transition points are investigation, entry, socialization, acceptance, maintenance, divergence, resocialization, exit, and remembrance. Both the individual and the group engage in characteristic activities at each stage of this socialization process.

Groups are also influenced by larger groups of which they are a part, such as cultures and societies. The values instilled at societal levels are brought into the group and affect the outcomes of group processes, although the processes themselves do not appear to vary among cultures.

▶ *Key Terms*

aggregate
autokinetic effect
cohesiveness
communication networks
consideration

contingency models
deindividuation
fundamental attribution bias
group
group polarization
group structure
groupthink
immediacy
informational influence
initiating structure
norm
normative influence
number
production blocking
risky shift
role
role differentiation
role expectations
social comparison
social facilitation
social impact theory
social impairment
social inhibition
social loafing
status characteristics theory
strength
uncertainty of approval

We must recognize that beneath the superficial classifications of sex and race the same potentialities exist.

Margaret Mead

You're going to find racism everyplace. In fact, I have never lived a day in my life that in some way—some small way, somewhere—someone didn't remind me that I'm black.

Henry Aaron

Behavior between Groups

Imagine a summer camp in which eleven- and twelve-year-old boys enjoy the usual mixture of activities: living in relatively primitive cabins, hiking, swimming, camping out, and so on. Ecology-minded counselors make the boys remove litter from the beach and other areas, but the kids don't mind because they are proud of their camp. Now and then, boys from one cabin compete against boys from another cabin in good-natured games such as football and tug-of-war; the winner gets a prize. Sounds wonderful, doesn't it?

Now imagine that same summer camp a little later—a summer camp gone wrong. The same boys who willingly picked up litter from the beach cheat during competitions in order to win the prize. They have nothing good to say about boys from other cabins. Indeed, boys from each cabin steal from and vandalize the other cabins. Picnics turn into food fights, and the counselors no longer schedule movies because boys brought together from different cabins have shouting matches and fistfights. The boys are determined to prove, at every opportunity and in any way possible, that they are better than the boys who live in any other cabin (Sherif, Harvey, White, Hood, & Sherif, 1961). No longer wonderful, this camp now seems to resemble any one of the international hotspots reported in the news.

Are these boys "bad"? Are they otherwise reasonable boys who have legitimate grievances? Did the camp counselors do something wrong? Is there something about the camp itself that incites conflict? Does the mere fact that the boys live in separate cabins make conflict inevitable? Is this summer-camp nightmare a reflection of human nature? More general versions of these questions are the basis for our discussion in this chapter.

When groups come in contact with each other, conflict often results. Examples of such conflict are all too numerous in literature and in reality, in history and in the present. Shakespeare's Montagues and Capulets have modern descendants in the nineteenth-century Hatfields and McCoys, who waged a fifty-year feud over the theft of some pigs. Wars between the Spartans and the Athenians are echoed in modern conflicts, between the United States and Iraq, the Palestinians and the Israelis, and numerous other parties.

In many Western countries, labor and management exemplify groups that must continually negotiate to achieve their sometimes shared and often opposing goals. Groups as diverse as professional athletes, steel and auto workers, and elementary school teachers engage in recurring negotiations with their respective managers. In other cases, negotiation may be less formal but the conflicts as great or greater, as in relations among whites, blacks, and other ethnic groups or between women and men.

These situations of conflict and potential conflict, so readily found in our society, present a real challenge to those who wish to understand human behavior. As the late British psychologist Henri Tajfel stated, "intergroup relations represent in their enormous scope one of the most difficult and complex knots of problems which we confront in our times" (1982, p. 1). It is those problems, too, that we will consider in this chapter.

First, however, we should specify exactly what is meant by the term **intergroup behavior.** Following the lead of Muzafer Sherif and Carolyn Sherif (1979, p. 9), we offer the following definition:

> Whenever individuals belonging to one group interact, collectively or individually, with another group or its members in terms of their group identification, we have an instance of intergroup behavior.

The emphasis on *group* in this definition is important, for it reflects some of the critical issues in the study of intergroup relations. If I as an individual am frustrated by my boss, our behavior involves interpersonal, not intergroup, relations. However, if I as a union member take up particular issues with my boss, conscious both of my union membership and of his or her role as a representative of management, then our behavior falls under the category of intergroup relations. In other words, individual actions are an important part of intergroup behavior *if* those actions are influenced by the stance or values of a group.

To understand the process of intergroup relations, we begin with a brief overview of cross-cultural psychology, a field that attempts to determine the generality of basic psychological principles across a variety of countries and cultural groups. Then we will analyze negative attitudes that people hold toward members of identifiable groups—in particular, racial prejudice and discrimination. We will turn next to the issue of social identity, looking at how groups define themselves in relation to other groups. Strategies of interaction between groups will be considered, including cooperation, competition, negotiation, and third-party intervention. Finally, on a more optimistic note, we will consider how conflict can be reduced, reviewing some of the strategies that have been successful in different arenas.

▶ Similarities and Differences among Groups

In *Gulliver's Travels* (Swift, 1726/1960), the wandering Captain Gulliver visits a series of imaginary societies, including the Lilliputians, the Blefuscudeans, and the Houyhnhnms. In each case, he finds a group of people whose appearance, values, and behaviors differ radically from those of the other groups and from his own. Do these kinds of differences among groups represent mere fictional license, or can each of us find in Swift's descriptions some reflection of our beliefs about groups? How we can determine the extent to which these beliefs reflect reality is one of the general questions addressed in this section.

Throughout recorded history, people have compared their own racial or geographical group with other groups. For example, Aristotle believed that Greece's benign climate enabled the Greeks to develop physical and mental characteristics superior to those of other Europeans. Such bias is certainly not unique to Aristotle. When people compare their own country with other countries, their own gender with the other gender, or their own class with other classes, they tend to imply that their country, gender, and so on are superior. The possibility of such biases is one issue with which the investigator of group differences must be concerned. People often fail to recognize how strongly their own experience influences what they see.

When we consider possible differences among groups, several important issues arise. First, as a backdrop, there is the tradition of social psychology, which gives far more attention to situational factors than to personal factors. A second issue is the nature of differences—are they differences in kind or in degree? Third, and perhaps most important, we must consider the causes of any differences that are found. Let us review these issues in more detail before moving on to specific comparisons among groups.

The Social-Psychological Tradition

Modern social psychology is strongly rooted in the interactionist perspective of Kurt Lewin, who stressed the person's present psychological life space as a source of behavior (Lewin, 1935, 1936; see also Chapter 1) and disdained past determinants. Lewin's original formulation—$B = f(P,E)$, where B, P, and E represent behavior, the person, and the environment, respectively—clearly shows that he considered personality and individual differences to be as important as environmental differences.

Most of Lewin's followers, however, have tended to stress the environment as the stronger of the two sources of influence. As Robert Helmreich (1975) has pungently stated, "classic, laboratory social psychology has generally ignored individual differences, choosing to consider subjects as equivalent black boxes or as two-legged (generally white) rats from the same strain" (p. 551). In other words, social psychologists did not give much thought to possible differences among individuals or groups. What was true of one group, they assumed, would probably be true of any other group.

This assumption has been challenged, however, as more and more social psychologists have begun to explore the nature of group differences at a variety of levels. Cross-cultural psychologists ask whether behaviors observed in the United States can be generalized to people in other cultures. Within the United States, many people have begun to examine the role of gender, often questioning earlier assumptions that what was true of men must also be true of women. Personality variables have begun to appear more frequently in the theories of social psychologists, and debates on the importance of these variables have been waged with increasing fervor.

Thus, the assumption that the empirical relationships discovered in one laboratory, from work with one kind of subject in one country or culture, will be found among all people is no longer so widely held as it once was (Gergen, 1985). Some social psychologists still hold to the "universal" position, but many others agree that the patterns of variation among groups are important keys to understanding human social behavior.

Overlapping Distributions

Terms such as *cultural differences* and *gender differences* can be misleading. They invoke an implicit assumption that differences must exist, waiting to be found, and encourage questions concerning the size and nature of differences. We should, of course, first ask whether differences exist. Only after such differences have been empirically demonstrated should we begin to address the nature and importance of differences (Eagly & Wood, 1991).

When looking for differences we assume exist, we can become blind to similarities between members of different groups. Anthropologists, for example, use the term **exotic bias** to refer to the investigators' tendencies to focus only on those aspects of a group or society that differ from their own society. North American social scientists visiting a South Seas island may first notice differences in style of dress and diet. If the island's society is matrilineal, with status descending through women's lineage, this feature also may command the attention of investigators who are accustomed to a patrilineal system. However, aspects of the culture that correspond to the investigators' culture may go unnoticed—because these aspects are not exotic or different, they may be taken for granted. The effects of exotic biases are not restricted to anthropological field studies. Whenever we set out to explore the ways in which two groups differ (blacks and whites, or women and men, for example), we risk ignoring the groups' similarities, which may far outweigh their differences.

Even when we do observe differences between two identifiable groups, we must take precautions. For example, if you found a statistically significant gender difference in aggression, you could not assume all men are more aggressive than all women. There may be many women who are more aggressive than many men, and many men and many women who are about equally aggressive. This concept of *overlapping distributions* is illustrated in Figure 13.1. Each curve represents a fictitious distribution of aggressiveness scores for females and males, assuming an arbitrary range of scores from 0 to 100. The group averages, indicated by the Greek letter μ (mu), clearly indicate that the average male is more aggressive than the average female. However, many females have higher scores than some males, and some females are more aggressive than the average male. Also, many males and females show similar degrees of aggressiveness. Most psychological traits and social behaviors exhibit this kind of overlap when two groups are compared, whether the groups are defined by gender, race, or culture. We tend to think in terms of categories (see Chapter 4), which leads to comparisons such as "all men" versus "all women." However, we must also realize that categories

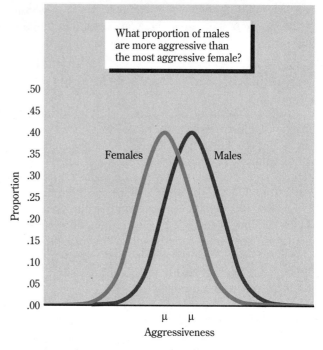

Figure 13.1 *The concept of overlapping distributions.*

are more likely to result from our perceptions of others than from the way others actually are.

Questions of Causality

Perhaps the most difficult problem in the study of possible differences between groups is that of determining why differences occur. Recall from Chapter 2 that in an experiment, the experimenter manipulates the independent variable, and subjects are randomly assigned to the different conditions created by the manipulation. With adequate controls for extraneous variables, the experimenter can be relatively confident that the independent variable is the cause of any differences noted among subjects with respect to the dependent variable. On the other hand, gender, race, culture, and similar characteristics cannot be manipulated; subjects cannot be randomly assigned, for example, to be males or females. With such quasi-independent variables, then, we cannot be confident about the cause of observed differences. In Figure 13.1, for example, the apparent gender difference in aggression allows us to conclude only that some systematic difference exists between men and women, but we have no way of knowing what causes that difference.

Traditionally, investigators have three general options for explaining possible causes of group differences: hereditary factors, environmental factors, or some combination of both. In trying to assess the relative contribution of heredity and environment, psychologists have encountered innumerable obstacles and have often become embroiled in controversy.

Hereditary explanations stress the importance of genetic factors and often assume the inevitability of observed group differences (Scarr & McCartney, 1983). Sociobiology provides one example of the hereditary perspective. Sociobiologists assume that gender differences in such behaviors as aggression and caring for children are genetically based. Other investigators with a biological bent have pointed to a variety of possible genetic and hormonal determinants of postulated differences between women and men in various intellectual behaviors, such as verbal abilities and skill in problem solving (for example, Broverman, Klaiber, Kobayashi, & Vogel, 1968).

Most questions of genetic determinants have related to the issue of intelligence. During the 1970s, for example, considerable controversy surrounded the issue of racial differences in intelligence. Numerous studies indicate that on the average, black children score approximately 15 points lower than white children on standard IQ measures (Loehlin, Lindzey, & Spuhler, 1975). Although both "hereditarians" and "environmentalists" recognized the existence of such differences in test scores, they did not agree on how the differences should be interpreted. Genetically based interpreters concluded such differences were evidence of innate racial differences (Herrnstein, 1973; Jensen, 1973). Environmentally based interpreters noted the influence of home environment upon intelligence (Bradley & Caldwell, 1980) and pointed toward cultural bias in the tests themselves (Bernal, 1984; Cole, 1981).

Hereditary arguments also have been posed to explain assumed gender differences in intelligence and were particularly popular in the early part of the twentieth century. As Stephanie Shields (1975) has vividly shown, these investigations were problematic. Shifts in theory regarding which area of the brain controlled intelligence were often followed by dramatic reversals in

findings concerning which gender possessed more of that particular area of the brain. According to turn-of-the-century investigators, male dominance in social life was paralleled by, and indeed resulted from, male superiority in intelligence. In subsequent years some investigators took a different stance and assumed that gender differences in intelligence did not exist. In fact, the standard Stanford-Binet test of intelligence was constructed to include only items that showed no gender differences (McNemar, 1942).

Other investigators have looked to socialization experiences for the causes of observed differences between groups. These explanations cover a broad range of factors, including economic and environmental conditions, specific socialization practices of parents, and more general issues of racism and sexism. Thus, one may see cultural differences as the result of different norms and cultural beliefs. Racial and ethnic differences may be explained by patterns of socialization, economic and social-class differences, or differences in reactions to the testing situation itself. Similarly, gender differences may be attributed to differences in boys' and girls' learning experiences and to the continued pervasiveness of **gender-role norms**—beliefs about appropriate behavior for women and men (Eagly, 1987; Eagly & Wood, 1991).

Rather than focus exclusively on either heredity or environment, many investigators prefer to consider the possible influence of both factors—although they may still differ considerably in the weight they attach to each factor. As just one example of this strategy, from hundreds that could be considered, we can look at a study by Richard Price and his colleagues (Price, Vandenberg, Iyer, & Williams, 1982). These researchers studied 138 pairs of Swedish twins, as well as the spouses and children of those twins. Height, clearly a genetically based physical characteristic, was measured, as were a variety of personality traits. The twins and their relatives were much less similar in personality than in height. In fact, the authors suggest that personality was influenced mainly by environment, especially by influences outside the home (experiences not shared by the family as a whole).

Other studies have shown a stronger effect of heredity. Overall, however, it is probably safe to conclude that although both heredity and environment may be influential, environment and experience have more to do than heredity with determining the kinds of social behaviors discussed in this book.

Cross-Cultural Comparisons

Much of the research reported in this book has been based on samples of U.S. citizens. Social psychology is, in the words of one critic, both "culture bound and culture blind" (Berry, 1978). This focus may be attributed partly to an ethnocentric bias and partly to the fact that most social psychologists are located in the United States. At one point it was estimated that 80% of all psychologists who were living or who ever had lived were from the United States (Triandis & Lambert, 1980). Such overwhelming representation prompted Jos Jaspers (1986) to call for greater intellectual independence among European social psychologists, a call most recently answered with the publication of an annual series entitled *European Review of Social Psychology* (Stroebe & Hewstone, 1991).

Investigators from the United States too often generalized their findings to other cultures without much thought. For cxample, it is frequently assumed that people in the United States and Canada are quite similar in attitudes, behaviors, and values. However, the governments of these two countries differ, as do their basic constitutional premises and many of their social customs. Canadians pointed out that such differences exist and that past generalizations are not warranted (Berry, 1974; Sadava, 1978). If important differences exist between these two neighboring countries, then it is easy to see how cultural differences can be quite substantial if we compare the United States with countries in Europe, Asia, Latin America, and other parts of the globe. For example, Michael Harris Bond in Hong Kong has pointed out "psychology . . . is translated into Chinese characters using the character for heart rather than the character for mind" (Levine, 1991, p. 80).

The aim of cross-cultural psychology is to study and understand these potential differences. More specifically, in the words of Harry Triandis (1980), "cross-cultural psychology is concerned with the systematic study of behavior and experience as it occurs in different cultures, is influenced by culture, or results in changes in existing cultures" (p. 1). We cannot fully cover the discipline of cross-cultural psychology, nor is that our intention in this section. Instead, we offer enough information to demonstrate the importance of including cultural differences in any attempt to understand social behavior.

Universal or Culture-Specific?

Investigators outside the United States have often questioned how applicable the theories and principles of American social psychology are to their own countries. For example, French psychologist Serge Moscovici (1972) has argued that equity theory (see Chapter 8) applies particularly to capitalistic systems and plays only a small role in the interpersonal behavior of people who live under other forms of government. Similar arguments have been voiced regarding other U.S.-derived principles, such as the relationship between similarity and attraction discussed in Chapter 9 (Brislin, 1980).

Recognizing these potential problems, social scientists distinguish between what they call etic constructs and emic constructs. **Etic constructs** concern universal factors—those that hold across all the cultures we know or have investigated. For example, the concept of the family can be considered an etic construct, even though the forms of family life vary across cultures (Triandis, 1977). Similarly, the use of heuristics, shortcuts in problem solving (see Chapter 4), appears universal (Simon, 1990a). In contrast, **emic constructs** are culture-specific—they exist or have meaning only within a particular cultural framework. For example, concepts such as "Southern hospitality" and "a New York minute" probably have meaning only in the United States. The problem arises when truly emic constructs are assumed to be etic—in other words, when findings from one culture, such as the pervasiveness of equity concerns in close relationships, are assumed to apply to the larger society. The term *pseudoetic* has been applied to this type of conclusion.

One of the challenges confronting cross-cultural psychologists is that of distinguishing the etic from the pseudoetic. How does the cross-cultural psychologist make this distinction? There are no easy answers to this question, but some strategies are more productive than others. Of course, research has to be carried out in more than one culture to determine what the cultures have in common and what is different (Segall,

1986). We must also recognize that how one interprets the results of a cross-cultural investigation will be determined partly by one's own cultural background (Gergen, 1985).

It is important for the investigator exploring another culture to become familiar with that culture. Through familiarization, the investigator may realize that certain concepts taken for granted in one's own country are not assumed in the other country. For example, people in many cultures know the Disney Studios' character Mickey Mouse. However, the pejorative label attached to the character's name—as in "This is a mickey-mouse course"—may not be understood in all cultures familiar with the character. For much the same reason, an experimenter cannot always take a methodology and apply it intact in another setting. Procedures may have different meanings in other countries; for example, conditions designed to represent "crowding" in the United States, might be considered luxurious space in a more heavily populated country.

Although the problems of cross-cultural research are considerable, the rewards may also be great. Cultures themselves may be considered as independent variables, so the investigator has a far greater range of conditions than would be possible within a single setting (Mann, 1980). For example, investigators have studied patterns of gender-role development by examining cultures that vary widely in the degree to which physical strength is required in the society's activities (Whiting & Edwards, 1973). With this range of variation, investigators have been able to conclude that gender roles of boys and girls become more divergent when physical strength is an important issue in a society. More recently, Hugh Lytton and David Romney (1991) were able to demonstrate that in the United States, but not in other Western countries, parents tend to socialize children toward gender-stereotyped activities. Thus, by extending our horizons to include culture as an object of study, we can increase our understanding of human behavior.

Some Research Examples

Cross-cultural psychologists have explored a wide range of issues, from perception to cognition to emotion (Triandis & Lonner, 1980). Let us consider a few examples.

As we noted in Chapter 5, facial expressions are an important form of nonverbal communication. Do such expressions constitute an etic principle? Extensive research suggests that expressions of some emotions are indeed innate and universal (Izard, 1980). However, the **display rules** that govern the particular expression of an emotion vary widely among cultures, indicating emic principles are at work with regard to a particular expression.

The social-distance literature shows a similar combination of etic and emic principles. **Social distance** refers to the degree of acceptance or rejection of social interaction between members of diverse groups (Westie, 1953). Measures of social distance are often used to assess prejudice: investigators ask a person whether he or she would accept members of group X as close friends, as neighbors, as co-workers, and so forth. The more negatively people evaluate a particular group, the more social or psychological distance they will want to place between themselves and members of that group. Harry Triandis and his colleagues have found that citizens throughout the world use information about occupation, race, religion, and nationality when they evaluate other people. The relative importance of these cues, however, varies among cultures. For example, in the United States a person's race was found to be more important to people than someone's occupation or religion; in Germany, occupation and religion were more important influences than race (Triandis, Davis, & Takezawa, 1965).

Kenneth Gergen and his colleagues have suggested that social exchange is a basic principle of human interaction (Gergen, Morse, & Gergen, 1980). Yet the actual resources that are exchanged and the principles by which fairness is assessed can vary widely among cultures. Edna Foa and Uriel Foa (1974) suggest that there are six basic classes of resources: status, love, services, information, money, and goods. These classes vary on two dimensions, as illustrated in Figure 13.2. First, a resource can be more or less concrete (or symbolic). Goods and services are considered concrete, for example, whereas status and information are relatively symbolic. Second, resources can vary in the degree to which they are particularized, or identified with a particular individual. Love, for example, is a resource that is usually connected with a particular person, whereas money is a more generalized type of resource. Accord-

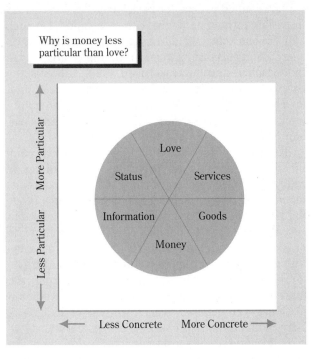

Figure 13.2 *Basic classes of resources in social exchange.*
Source: Social Structure of the Mind, by E. B. Foa and U. G. Foa,
1974, Springfield, IL: Charles C Thomas.

ing to Foa and Foa, resources that are adjacent to each other in the diagram in Figure 13.2 should be most easily interchangeable, and research supports this prediction (Brinberg & Castell, 1982; Foa & Foa, 1980). If we move to other cultures, however, we will probably find shifts in the preferences for certain sectors of the exchange pattern. Some societies stress the concreteness of rewards; others stress particularism. Thus, patterns of preference can vary, but the overall structure of resources can probably be considered an etic construct.

The principles by which fairness is assessed in a culture relate to more general patterns within that culture, such as emphasis on collectivism versus individualism. Societies with a Chinese background, such as those of Hong Kong, Singapore, and Taiwan, tend to have a collectivist orientation, emphasizing the social environment. In contrast, such countries as the United States stress individualism and self-interest. Kwok Leung and Michael Bond (1984) suspected that people of these contrasting societies would use different principles in

allocating rewards for performance. They predicted further that the recipient's status as a friend or stranger would affect the reward patterns. To test their predictions, Leung and Bond asked Chinese and U.S. students to evaluate the fairness of allocations a worker made to either a friend or a stranger. In the scenario that students received, the worker used a principle either of equity (rewarding the person according to relative performance) or of equality (sharing the reward equally, with no reference to performance). As predicted, Chinese students were much more sensitive to the distinction between friend and stranger. They used the equality principle for friends but the equity principle for strangers. In contrast, the U.S. students favored equity rather than equality with friends, showing less concern for the collectivism that was important to the Chinese.

These Chinese and U.S. students may have been using different cultural scripts to interpret the interaction. As Harry Triandis and his colleagues define it, a **cultural script** is a pattern of social interaction that is characteristic of a particular cultural group (Triandis, Marin, Lisansky, & Betancourt, 1984). As an example, Triandis points to the black South African concept of *ubuntu,* a concern for the dignity of others and an obligation to give sympathy and help to those who need it. Among Hispanics, Triandis suggests, the concept of *simpatía* is a dominant cultural script. According to this script, people are generally perceived to be likable, attractive, and fun to be with. They are expected to be able to share in others' feelings and to strive for harmony in interpersonal relations. Operating on the basis of a *simpatía* script, Hispanics would be expected to be more positively oriented toward social interaction and to be more optimistic about the good tone of such interaction.

To test this prediction, Triandis and his colleagues gave a set of questionnaires to Hispanic and non-Hispanic naval recruits and asked them to estimate the likelihood of a wide range of behaviors in various interactive situations. As the investigators had predicted, Hispanics expected much more positive interactions. Triandis and his colleagues did not examine actual behavior in this study. However, if behavior follows the attitudes, one can expect Hispanics to approach interactions with more positive expectations and to be less prone to competitive or critical interchanges.

Differences in cultural scripts can be very important for the person traveling to another country. Like the social psychologist, the traveler should not assume all concepts are etic but should be on the lookout for the emic. Sometimes, however, cultural differences are presumed rather than empirically demonstrated. The consequence of such presumptions is the topic of the following section.

▶ **Prejudice and Discrimination**

Consider the following case:

Ann Hopkins, an Associate in the large accounting firm of Price Waterhouse, was proposed for a promotion to Partner. Having brought in business worth $25 million, she was responsible for more billable hours than any other Associate proposed that year. She was not promoted, nor was she proposed for promotion the following year. The reason? Some of her evaluators claimed she had problems with interpersonal skills. She was described in terms such as macho, needing a charm-school course, and overcompensating for her gender. She was advised that she would do better if she was more feminine, if she would walk, talk, and dress more appropriately for a woman, and wear make-up, styled hair, and jewelry.

In this example, behavior toward a particular individual is being influenced by general attitudes that are held about groups of people.

Prejudice, discrimination, and *stereotype* are often used interchangeably, but they are three distinct concepts. **Prejudice** refers to a negative affective or emotional response to a particular group of people resulting from intolerant, unfair, or unfavorable attitudes toward that group (Brewer & Kramer, 1985; Harding, Proshansky, Kutner, & Chein, 1969). Feeling uncomfortable because the person sitting next to you in class is a member of another race is one example of prejudice, as is becoming angry because the couple moving in next door appears to have a different sexual orientation from your own. Feeling indignation because a competent woman doesn't act "like a girl" is also prejudice.

Discrimination refers to specific behaviors toward members of a group that are unfair in comparison with behavior toward members of other groups. Examples of discrimination that parallel the previous examples of prejudice include making an excuse to avoid sharing your class notes with a member of another race when you have shared notes with members of your own race, calling the police to report the "loud party" hosted by neighbors with a different sexual orientation when similar parties of other neighbors are not reported, and refusing to promote a woman while promoting an equally qualified man. More violent discrimination also occurs in the form of *hate crimes* or *bias crimes,* crimes directed at individuals because of their membership in a particular group. Some surveys indicate as many as 92% of gay men and lesbians report being victimized by threats and other forms of verbal abuse, and almost one-fourth have been physically attacked (Herek, 1989).

Stereotypes, as we saw in Chapter 4, are beliefs about the characteristics of members of an identifiable group. Stereotypes can be either positive or negative (Jussim, Coleman, & Lerch, 1987). Although stereotypes are the foundation upon which prejudice and discrimination are built (Bersoff & Verrilli, 1988; Fiske, Bersoff, Borgida, Deaux, & Heilman, 1990; *Price Waterhouse v. Hopkins,* 1989), the fact that someone has stereotypic beliefs about a group does not necessarily mean that person will exhibit prejudice or engage in discrimination (Oakes & Turner, 1990).

Patricia Devine (1989) has developed a model of prejudice in which she separates the automatic and controlled components of a prejudicial response. As is illustrated in Figure 13.3, encountering a member of a group for which one holds stereotypic beliefs spontaneously activates those beliefs. Even those who are not prejudiced toward a group will experience this process, provided they know about the stereotype. If the individual does nothing to inhibit the negative beliefs contained in the stereotype, prejudicial responses will occur. On the other hand, an active attempt to inhibit or disregard the negative beliefs will not produce prejudice. Such inhibition may also reduce the strength of the stereotype, although elimination of the stereotype is likely to be a protracted process. Thus, the primary difference between prejudiced and unprejudiced people involves the extent to which they inhibit whatever negative stereotypes they may have learned about the target group.

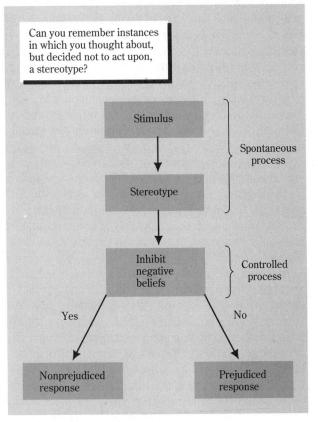

Can you remember instances in which you thought about, but decided not to act upon, a stereotype?

Figure 13.3 *Activation of a stereotype is spontaneous. Inhibiting the stereotypic beliefs to prevent a prejudiced response is a controlled process.*
Source: "Stereotypes and Prejudice: Their Automatic and Controlled Components" by P. G. Devine, 1989, *Journal of Personality and Social Psychology, 56,* pp. 5–18.

Prejudice and discrimination can be directed toward any group: women, men, blacks, Native Americans, Asians, Hispanics—unfortunately, the list is endless. To illustrate more fully the ways in which prejudice and discrimination operate, we will focus on two of the most pervasive "isms": racism and sexism. In doing so, we will also consider the various causes of prejudice and discrimination.

Racism

The U.S. Commission on Civil Rights (1969) has defined **racism** as "any attitude, action, or institutional structure which subordinates a person because of his or her color" (p. 1). Such a definition incorporates both negative attitudes (prejudice) and discriminatory behavior, and it acknowledges that racism can exist on either an individual or an institutional level.

Examples of racism are unfortunately all too numerous. In February 1987 the *New York Times* reported that in the previous two years there had been forty-five cases of arson and cross burning in the United States after minority families had moved into mostly white neighborhoods (Williams, 1987). Hundreds of acts of vandalism and intimidation were reported as well. In 1991 millions of television viewers saw a videotape recording of Rodney King being brutally beaten by members of the Los Angeles Police Department.

Examples of institutional racism are also numerous. Early in 1942 the U.S. government forced more than 110,000 Japanese Americans to move to hastily constructed, heavily guarded camps where they were detained for three years because they were perceived as a threat to national security. Similarly, thousands of Japanese Canadians in British Columbia were uprooted and resettled in the interior. Most of them lost their homes, farms, and businesses in the process. During the Persian Gulf War, Palestinians living in Israel were confined to their homes. They were allowed excursions to buy food only at specified times and in small groups.

In both Great Britain and Canada, attitudes and behaviors toward settlers from India and Pakistan frequently reflect extreme prejudice and discrimination. In South Africa, a minority of whites descended from Europeans live in domination over a majority of Africans whose ancestors once ruled the region. The government did not allow newspapers to print articles critical of the ruling party, and until 1975 the government did not permit television in South Africa. Segregation of the races was virtually total before the last of the *apartheid* laws were repealed in 1991.

Although examples of racism are numerous throughout the world, we will focus on the research dealing with blacks and whites in the United States because this situation has been studied most extensively. However, such an emphasis does not imply that other ethnic groups do not also experience prejudice and discrimination. For example, Hispanics and Native Americans experience many of the same consequences as blacks, though the larger society is generally less aware of their problems (Ramirez, 1988).

Some forms of prejudice and discrimination have been reduced or eliminated in recent years. For example, in the historic *Brown* v. *Board of Education* (1954) decision, the U.S. Supreme Court ruled school segregation unconstitutional, and equal rights policies in the United States and elsewhere have mandated equal treatment regardless of color. Nevertheless, the long history of racism in the United States has laid a firm foundation of racial stereotypes. It may be less socially acceptable to show blatant racism than it once was, but that doesn't mean that racism has disappeared. Instead, racism is expressed in related issues such as housing, employment, and law and order. **Symbolic racism,** from this perspective, is a mixture of negative affect and traditional moral values (Kinder & Sears, 1981). Also known as **modern racism,** it is rooted in early-learned racial fears and stereotypes and in fundamental feelings about social morality and propriety (Kinder & Sears, 1981; Sears & Kinder, 1985). For example, individuals who hold such deep-seated attitudes still oppose issues that promise equality for the races. However, they express their opposition in more socially acceptable ways, such as framing opposition to equal-opportunity hiring in terms of the impropriety of quotas. Thus, modern racists can simultaneously maintain attitudes that oppose racial equality and attitudes that oppose prejudice and discrimination (Sears, 1988).

As one might expect, measuring the attitudes associated with modern racism requires more subtle measurement instruments than those associated with blatant racism (Crosby, Bromley, & Saxe, 1980). One such measure is the Modern Racism Scale (McConahay, Hardee, & Batts, 1981), a nonreactive measure of negative attitudes toward blacks. Various other measures have been borrowed from the methodologies of cognitive psychology. One technique involves pairing adjectives with racial labels, such as *black* and *white,* and asking subjects to decide rapidly whether the pairs are meaningful or "fit together" (Dovidio et al., 1986; Gaertner & McLaughlin, 1983). The underlying premise is that people will respond more rapidly if the adjective-race pair represents an existing attitude and less rapidly if the trait is not typically associated with the racial group. When such measures have been employed, white subjects generally have responded more quickly to pairings of positive adjectives with the label *white* and to negative adjectives paired with *black.* Consistent with Devine's model concerning the spontaneous acti-

vation of stereotypes, such measures often do not produce differences between subjects who score high on a measure of prejudice and those who score low. That is, both prejudiced and unprejudiced individuals appear equally familiar with stereotypes about blacks and whites (Devine, 1989).

In what ways do prejudiced individuals differ from those who are not prejudiced? As is illustrated in Figure 13.4, differences become apparent when people of all races are asked to report their personal thoughts about blacks. According to Devine's model, people who are not prejudiced will not report stereotypical negative

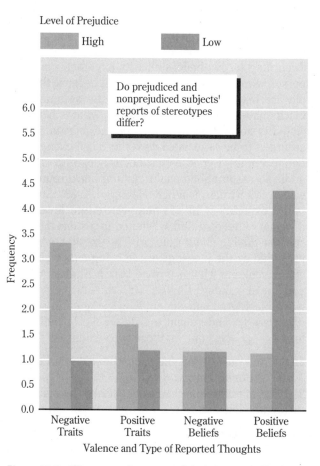

Figure 13.4 *When reporting personal thoughts, prejudiced whites report different thoughts from whites who score low on a nonreactive measure of prejudice.*

Source: "Prejudice with and without Compunction" by P. G. Devine, M. J. Monteith, J. R. Zuwerink, and A. J. Elliot, 1991, *Journal of Personality and Social Psychology, 60,* pp. 817–830.

qualities that they believe to be false. Thus, despite equal knowledge of stereotypes about blacks, whites who obtain high scores on the Modern Racism Scale are most likely to list negative traits—hostile, lazy, stupid—when asked to list all their thoughts concerning black Americans. On the other hand, those who score low on the same scale are most likely to list positive beliefs—blacks and whites are equal, for example—in response to the same instructions. Similarly, white students who score low on the Modern Racism Scale report feeling guilty when they fail to inhibit spontaneously activated, negative stereotypes, whereas those who obtain high scores do not report feeling guilty (Devine, Monteith, Zuwerink, & Elliot, 1991).

Some investigators have argued that prejudice or rejection results largely from perceived dissimilarity in values (Rokeach, 1968, 1979; Rokeach & Mezei, 1966). According to this belief-similarity hypothesis, a white person who rejects blacks does so not because the people are black, but because he or she assumes that blacks have different values. That is, what is being rejected is not the person's race per se, but the values assumed to be associated with the racial category. In one test of this hypothesis, speech styles were used as a cue to assumptions about cultural background and values (McKirnan, Smith, & Hamayan, 1983). Subjects in this experiment, all of whom were white, lower-middle-class college students, listened to a short tape of a speaker talking about Chicago. The speaker, who was identified by the investigators as being either black or white, spoke in what is termed "black English vernacular" or in standard English. (In actuality, the speaker was a black graduate student who spoke easily in both dialects.) To understand the difference in these two forms of speech, contrast these two sentences:

1. Sports would be my thang, but the teams in Chicago ain't 'bout nothing.
2. I like to follow sports, except Chicago teams are always so bad.

After listening to the tape, subjects gave the speaker an overall evaluation and rated the speaker on perceived similarity and desirability of social contact in various degrees of social distance. Analysis of these ratings supported the belief-similarity hypothesis. Specifically, the speaker was rated more positively when he sounded like the subjects themselves—all of whom, it

For some behaviors, such as accepting a person as close kin by marriage, race is more influential than beliefs.
Michael Siluk / The Image Works

should be recalled, were white—and the effect of racial label was minimal.

Although these results support the contention that belief similarity outweighs racial attitudes, other investigators are not so sure. Using the terminology of the early 1960s, the social psychologist Harry Triandis (1961) forcefully stated, "People do not exclude other people from their neighborhood . . . because the other people have different [values], but they do exclude them because they are Negroes" (p. 186).

Both views have some merit, as prejudice and discrimination depend on the type of behavior being considered (Jussim et al., 1987). For some issues, such as whether one is willing to work with a person, evidence suggests that beliefs are more important than the person's race. For other behaviors, such as accepting a person as close kin by marriage, race is more influential than beliefs (Moe, Nacoste, & Insko, 1981). Social pressure accounts for some of these effects: when social pressure favors discrimination, the effect of race is stronger than the effect of beliefs. In contrast, when such pressure is weak, beliefs may be a more important determinant of attitudes.

Not everyone agrees that racism exists, despite substantial evidence that the phenomenon is persistent and real. In a survey of more than 1,800 U.S. citizens conducted by James Kluegel and Eliot Smith (1986), 44% of whites reported the chances of getting ahead are the same for blacks and other racial minorities as they are for the average American. Another 29% reported the same chances for blacks and other racial minorities were better than, or much better than, those of the average American. In apparent contradiction, about the same percentages of respondents indicated they believed some or a lot of discrimination against blacks occurs. How can acknowledgment of racial discrimination coexist with beliefs about other races' better-than-average chances of getting ahead? An overwhelming 82% of the respondents endorsed the notion that blacks and other racial minorities receive some or a lot of preferential treatment that improves their chances for getting ahead.

Consistent with the concept of modern racism, Kluegel and Smith argued that beliefs about economic equality are heavily influenced by the country's dominant ideology. In the United States, ideology includes the belief that individual effort can create opportunity. Thus, those who work hard will profit, and, in a reversal of the argument, those who are economically deprived must not have worked so hard. (This is consistent with a belief in a just world; see Chapter 4.) Many white citizens see their own opportunities as plentiful and regard the U.S. opportunity structure as a fair one. Whites therefore tend to deny structural causes for a state such as poverty. Consequently, whites often believe that any other person's position in the stratification system is the result of individual ability and effort—or the lack thereof. As a result, whites may feel that specific equal-opportunity programs benefit members of other races too much. As might be expected, black respondents were (more correctly) less likely to believe that opportunities for blacks are substantial. Almost twice as many blacks as whites (50% versus 26%) believe they have not had a fair chance to make the most of themselves.

Racism is not just a matter of individual prejudices and attitudes. At the national level, the laws and practices of a society can enforce and perpetuate discrimination against one group by another. In South Africa, as we noted earlier, wide-ranging laws and restrictions kept black South Africans separate from the ruling white minority. Less recently, the Untouchables in India were controlled by a similar set of policies and long-standing norms; members of that group were not allowed to participate freely in the society. In the United States, numerous policies have kept blacks "separate but equal" and perpetuated institutional racism. Although many of these policies have changed in recent years, it is clear that racism still exists and that the larger social structure is as important a factor in racism as individual attitudes of prejudice (Wellman, 1977).

Sexism

Sexism, like racism, incorporates attitudes and actions that treat one group as subordinate to another. In the case of **sexism,** however, prejudice and discrimination are directed against people because of gender rather than color or ethnic identity. Sexism is also different from racism in many respects, and its history is considerably longer. The amount of daily interaction between genders is, at least in Western countries, much greater than the interaction between races. For example, most people live next to, share or have shared a household with, and have intimate relationships with members of the opposite sex. Despite these differences, gender-based prejudice and discrimination follow much the same pattern as racism.

As in the case of beliefs about blacks and whites, people generally associate different characteristics with women and men. Many investigators have asked groups of people to describe what the average man and the average woman are like. As noted in Chapter 4, the personality characteristics ascribed to men and women typically fall into two general groups—one collection of traits representing competence and independence (men) and a second group focusing on warmth and expressiveness (women) (Broverman, Vogel, Broverman, Clarkson, & Rosenkrantz, 1972; Spence, Helmreich, & Stapp, 1974). Gender stereotypes also include beliefs about the role behaviors in which men and women can be expected to engage and the physical characteristics they possess (Deaux & Lewis, 1983). As with stereotypes about race, stereotypes about men and women represent differences in degrees, not either-or certainties. These beliefs, too, have considerable generality across cultures, having been observed in both North and South America, Europe, Australia, and parts of the Middle East (Williams & Best, 1982).

Although one might argue that these two patterns—competence and expressiveness—are different but do not represent more favorable or less favorable impressions, other evidence suggests that the picture is not so optimistic. Consider the results of a study by Inge Broverman and her colleagues (Broverman, Broverman, Clarkson, Rosenkrantz, & Vogel, 1970). These authors asked seventy-nine practicing mental health clinicians (clinical psychologists, psychiatrists, and social workers) to describe the characteristics of one of three types of persons: a normal adult male, a normal adult female, and a normal adult person (no specified gender). The clinicians were asked to characterize the healthy, mature, socially competent person in each category. The results, not particularly encouraging if sexual equality is our goal, were quite clear-cut. Both male and female clinicians saw the healthy adult male and the healthy adult person as nearly synonymous; in contrast, their view of the healthy adult female differed significantly from their view of the healthy adult person. For example, the clinicians described both the healthy adult person and the healthy adult male with adjectives from the competency cluster—independent, active, competitive—whereas they saw the healthy adult female as possessing far less of each of these characteristics. The clinicians viewed the healthy adult female as more submissive, more concerned about her appearance, and more excitable in minor crises—a set of characteristics not attached to either the healthy adult or the healthy male.

Representations of women and men in the media also can reflect stereotypic beliefs. In a fascinating exploration of media presentations, Dane Archer and his colleagues (Archer, Iritani, Kimes, & Barrios, 1983) explored the phenomenon of "face-ism," or the degree of facial prominence in visual representations. In any photograph or artistic portrait, one can calculate the percentage of the vertical dimension occupied by the subject's head to obtain an index of relative facial prominence. Several types of visual images, including newspaper and magazine photographs, classic art, and drawings by college students, were measured in this way. In nearly every case, the measurements showed greater facial prominence accorded to men than to women. In other words, depictions of men show relatively more of the head, whereas representations of women show relatively more of the body. As Archer and his colleagues suggest, these visual representations may indicate the relative emphasis our culture places on mental life for men and physical appearance for women.

Face-ism is a rather subtle form of discrimination between the sexes; other actions are much more blatant, and the evidence of differential treatment is more substantial. In a study of performance evaluation, for example, subjects who viewed a man's successful performance attributed that performance to ability, whereas subjects observing a woman perform at an equivalent level believed luck to be more responsible for the outcome (Deaux & Emswiller, 1974). Clerks in a department store have been observed to give priority to a man if both a male and a female customer are waiting for service (Zinkhan & Stoiadin, 1984).

In employment categories, women are underrepresented in nearly all professional and prestige occupations. The kinds of behaviors women often encounter as they attempt to prepare themselves for these occupations constitute one obstacle. For example, women applying for doctoral work were subjected to men's comments that generally questioned the women's seriousness about their profession. One man commented, "Why don't you find a rich husband and give this all up?" (Harris, 1970, p. 285). Numerous studies have documented the existence of bias in hiring women. For example, Fidell (1970) sent a number of academic résumés to psychology department chairs at major U.S. universities. Each was asked to evaluate the applicant as a potential professor in that department. Two forms—identical except for gender of applicant—were used, each form going to half the selected chairs. The results showed that men were generally offered a higher position than women (that is, associate professor rather than assistant professor) despite the equality of their backgrounds. Lest we infer that only psychologists are biased, it should be noted that Lewin and Duchan (1971) found similar results in physics departments.

Once hired, women also face substantial obstacles for promotion, as illustrated by the experience of Ann

Hopkins, described earlier. Citing psychological research on gender stereotyping for the first time, the U.S. Supreme Court ruled that the accounting firm of Price Waterhouse had discriminated against Hopkins on the basis of gender (*Price Waterhouse* v. *Hopkins,* 1989). Susan Fiske, whose testimony about research on stereotyping in the original trial continued to be cited through the appeals process, outlined the conditions under which stereotypes about gender are likely to result in prejudice and discrimination (Fiske et al., 1990). Among these conditions is a lack of incentives to prohibit the controllable aspects of prejudice. Price Waterhouse, for example, had no policy concerning sexism or racism; a senior partner's opinion that women could not function as senior managers, expressed as a complaint about having to review credentials of women proposed for partnership, was never challenged by any of the other partners. Women also face work environments that impede their advancement in the form of sexual harassment, ranging from outright sexual advances to sexually suggestive calendars displayed in the workplace (Cecil & Wiggins, 1991).

Beliefs about women's opportunities, like beliefs about opportunities for blacks and other ethnic minorities, are linked to more general values and ideologies (Kluegel & Smith, 1986). In the case of women, gender-role traditionalism plays a major role, together with the dominant ideology that links effort and rewards (Eagly, 1987). These beliefs have more influence on a person's judgment of discrimination and opportunity structures than do more immediate issues, such as one's own self-interest. Married men, for example, are not more supportive of policies that would reduce job discrimination than are single men, despite the financial advantages they would gain. Again, these findings testify to the pervasiveness of both racism and sexism as general values.

People are more aware of discrimination and limited opportunities in the case of women than they are in the case of blacks. They tend to see more evidence of discrimination against women than against blacks and believe blacks receive more preferential treatment than women (Kluegel & Smith, 1986). However, available statistics on such indicators as unemployment and education belie these beliefs. Then why do such beliefs persist? One reason, Kluegel and Smith suggest, is the segregation of U.S. society. Many whites know little about the life of blacks and may have very little day-to-day contact with them. Thus, their information about opportunity for blacks is based on accounts from media and friends rather than on direct experience. As noted earlier, the lives of men and women are generally intermeshed, and information is probably more readily available. Discrimination against women is therefore much more likely to be observed than discrimination against blacks.

Perhaps the greatest difference between sexism and racism is that gender-based discrimination begins earlier in life and begins with those who first interact with us. In a recent meta-analysis of research on parental practices, Hugh Lytton and David Romney (1991) demonstrated that North American parents both encourage gender-typed activities for their children and are likely to perceive their children in stereotypic ways. Such discrimination creates gender differences in personality development through adolescence (Cohn, 1991) and perpetuates gender-role stereotypes (Eagly, 1987; Eagly & Wood, 1991).

Racism and sexism are not the only examples of prejudice and discrimination shown by members of one group toward members of another group. In Canada, for example, views of the dominant English-speaking groups toward the French Canadians are often prejudicial, and evidence of discrimination has been shown. Studies of the career advancement of civil servants have shown that on the average, French-speaking Canadians make less money than English-speaking Canadians when factors of age, education, and seniority are equivalent (Beattie & Spencer, 1971). In the United States, one study showed that observers tend to discriminate against Vietnam veterans in hiring recommendations, citing a higher likelihood of psychological problems (Bordieri & Drehmer, 1984). And in many societies, ageism—discrimination against the elderly—is both a social reality and a political issue. Older people are evaluated more negatively, particularly on measures of competence (Kite & Johnson, 1987), and are the targets of discrimination in employment and other arenas.

Causes of Prejudice and Discrimination

Many theories have been advanced to explain why prejudice and discrimination occur. Gordon Allport, in his

Ageism is both a social reality and a political issue.
Paul Conklin/Monkmeyer Press

Some historically oriented theories of prejudice emphasize economic factors. For example, advocates of the theories of Karl Marx see prejudice as a way of allowing the rulers to exploit the laboring class. As Cox (1948) has stated, "race prejudice is a social attitude propagated among the public by an exploiting class for the purpose of stigmatizing some group as inferior so that the exploitation of . . . the group itself or its resources may both be justified" (p. 393). In the treatment of black slaves before the U.S. Civil War, of Asian immigrants in California at the turn of the century, and of Chinese laborers brought in to build the Canadian Pacific Railroad we see classic examples of the "haves" vilifying the "have-nots."

Sociocultural emphasis Sociologists and anthropologists emphasize sociocultural factors as determinants of prejudice and discrimination. These factors include characteristics of the society or culture that increase the likelihood of discrimination, such as a cultural emphasis on competence and training in combination with scarcity of jobs and competition for jobs. Other sociocultural factors include the following:

1. Increased urbanization, mechanization, and complexity
2. The upward mobility of certain groups
3. Population increases in the face of a limited amount of usable land and a lack of adequate housing
4. The inability of many people to develop internal standards, leading to reliance on others and a conforming type of behavior
5. Changes in the role and function of the family, with concomitant changes in standards of morality

These explanations all emphasize the effects that social change can have on a society and suggest that the uncertainty experienced in times of change is expressed in hostility toward groups whose values and customs seem different from one's own.

In emphasizing broad patterns, the historical, economic, and sociocultural explanations provide useful background and contribute to our understanding of the prevalence of prejudice and discrimination at the cultural or social level. Social psychologists, however, prefer more "micro" explanations, such as the ways in which broad patterns are expressed interpersonally.

classic book *The Nature of Prejudice* (1958), identified six levels of analysis that theorists continue to apply to efforts to understand the causes of "isms." These levels of explanation include historical and economic, sociocultural, situational, psychodynamic, phenomenological, and earned reputation.

Historical and economic emphasis Historians remind us that we cannot fully understand the causes of prejudice without studying the background of the relevant conflicts, and it is a sad fact that most prejudices have a long history. Anti-black prejudice in the United States, for example, has its roots in slavery and the slave owner's treatment of black families, in the exploitation of blacks by carpetbaggers, and in the failure of Reconstruction in the South after the Civil War.

Situational emphasis Let us now turn to explanations that operate at a more individual level—those that attempt to show why some people are prejudiced but others are not. The situational emphasis is the most social-psychological one. It focuses on current forces in the environment as the cause of prejudice. Within this emphasis, conformity to others strongly influences prejudice. During the 1960s in the U.S. South, for example, many restaurant owners claimed that they themselves were not prejudiced but that their customers would object if they allowed blacks to be served.

Changes over time in stereotypes of racial or national groups often reflect this situational emphasis. During World War II, U.S. citizens were exposed to government propaganda that led to Americans' adopting negative stereotypes of the Japanese and the Germans and favorable stereotypes of allies, including the Russians. Early in the war most U.S. citizens described the Russians as hard-working and brave. In 1948, as postwar conflicts between the two great powers emerged, the stereotypes changed considerably. Although "hard-working" was still considered an appropriate description of Russians, more people in the United States in 1948 believed Russians were cruel. In a world where the Soviet Union was no longer an ally but an adversary, assumptions about the nature of Russians had changed. In recent years another change has begun to occur in the assumptions many U.S. citizens have held about Russians: negative attitudes are moderating with the advent of a freely elected president of the Russian Republic, the attempt to shift to a capitalist economy, and the dissolution of the Soviet Union.

Psychodynamic emphasis The psychodynamic view sees prejudice as a result of the prejudiced person's own conflicts and maladjustments. Psychodynamic theories of prejudice take two approaches. One assumes that prejudice is rooted in the human condition because frustration is inevitable in human life. Frustration and deprivation lead to hostile impulses, "which if not controlled are likely to discharge against ethnic minorities" (Allport, 1958, p. 209). In this interpretation, we can see the role the frustration-aggression hypothesis (discussed in Chapter 10) plays in explaining discrimination. Theorists hypothesize that **scapegoating**—the displacement of hostility onto less powerful groups—results from frustration when the actual source of the frustration is not available or can-

not be attacked for other reasons. Lynching of blacks, burning of synagogues, and other assaults on members of minority groups are instances of such behavior. Blaming the loss of employment or the stagnation of one's upward mobility on other races or ethnic groups is another example of scapegoating.

A second approach assumes that prejudice develops only in people who have a personality defect or a weak character structure. This approach does not accept prejudice as normal; it postulates that prejudice results from the strong anxieties and insecurities of neurotic persons.

The original research on the authoritarian personality was based on this type of psychoanalytic model. According to T. W. Adorno and his colleagues (Adorno et al., 1950), the authoritarian personality results from a strict and rigid superego, a primitive id, and a weak ego structure (Sanford, 1956), which lead to predictable patterns of behavior toward minority groups. The hundreds of studies conducted on the concept have given us a picture of the authoritarian person as one who is generally conservative in political and social attitudes, deferent to authority, and prone to look askance at deviations from the conventional moral order (Altemeyer, 1988). The combination of institutional structures that support discrimination, a strong motivation to maintain what authority has established, and an intolerance for "different" cultures or lifestyles makes authoritarians likely to engage in prejudice and discrimination.

Phenomenological emphasis According to the phenomenological emphasis, the individual's perception of the world is more important than any objective features of that world. Unlike the psychodynamic view, which stresses more durable personality characteristics, the phenomenological emphasis stresses the immediate perceptions of a person. As we saw in Chapter 4, a single event can be interpreted in many ways. A variety of events can influence interpretations: past experience, the behavior of other people in the same situation, selective attention to certain aspects of the situation. For example, the assertive behavior of a woman, seen in the context of more passive women, may be interpreted as "too aggressive" and "pushy," even though the behavior may be comparable to that of a man in the same situation. As a result, discriminatory behavior may follow. In contrast, previous experience with that woman, or comparison of her behavior with that of others in a similar situation, might result in very different behavior on our part. In other words, the phenomenological interpretation of prejudice and discrimination emphasizes immediate influences and pays little attention to broad historical factors.

Emphasis on earned reputation All the previous approaches have localized the source of prejudice in the observer. They have failed to consider that minority groups, by their behavior or characteristics, may precipitate the negative feelings that are directed toward them. The earned reputation theory postulates that minority groups possess characteristics that provoke dislike and hostility. Some evidence exists to support this theory. For example, Triandis and Vassiliou (1967), in a study of people from Greece and the United States, conclude: "The present data suggest that there is a 'kernel of truth' in most stereotypes *when they are elicited from people who have firsthand knowledge of the group being stereotyped*" (p. 324). A careful review by Brigham (1971) concludes that ethnic stereotypes can contain a "kernel of truth" in the sense that different groups of respondents agree on which traits identify a particular object group.

Further, at least in some cases these beliefs about the characteristics of members of another group may be relatively accurate (McCauley & Stitt, 1978; Oakes & Turner, 1990). For example, Asians and whites do have different display rules regarding facial affect (Ekman et al., 1987). Asians are generally less likely to display emotions. Similarly, blacks tend to make less eye contact with someone who is speaking to them than do whites (LaFrance & Mayo, 1976). Of course, these "kernels of truth" do not justify stereotypes concerning deceptiveness, but they enable us to understand the source of some stereotypes and the prejudice that results from them.

Each of these explanations of prejudice has some merit, but no single one is sufficient for us to understand prejudice and discrimination. The pervasiveness of both prejudice and discrimination indicates that each has more than one source. If we are to understand prejudice and discrimination, we must avoid the presumption that a single explanation can account for all instances of such behavior. Therefore, we turn to a discussion of the processes of intergroup perceptions.

▶ In-Groups and Out-Groups

Prejudice and discrimination are two general consequences of intergroup relations. We have considered how people react to certain identifiable groups by emphasizing *outcomes* of intergroup relations. In this section we consider some of the specific *processes* that inevitably emerge when groups come in contact with one another. These processes generally involve distinctions between an **in-group**—any group to which an individual belongs—and an **out-group**—any group to which an individual does not belong. In-group, then, does not necessarily refer to the group in power or the majority group; both in-groups and out-groups are determined by an individual's membership. Thus, Henry Aaron's racial in-group is black, and Margaret Mead's racial in-group is white.

Categorization and Social Identity

Many of the cognitive processes (discussed in Chapters 3 and 4) that concern how people translate experience into mental representations have been used to explain how groups gain a definition (Stephan, 1985). As David Wilder (1986) has stated, "on the simplest level, groups may be defined as categories of persons subject to the same principles of organization and inference attributed to any category" (p. 293). From this perspective, the processes of attention, encoding, and retrieval explain how a group comes to associate certain characteristics with itself and, similarly, how certain attributes come to be associated with other groups.

Categorization itself leads people to assume similarity among the members of a category. Even when the distinctions between groups are arbitrary, people outside a group tend to minimize the differences they see among members of the same group and to accentuate the differences between members of different groups (Brewer & Kramer, 1985; Wilder, 1986).

Although an outside observer tends to see group membership as relatively homogeneous, those inside the group find more heterogeneity among themselves. For example, when members of a sorority were asked to describe members of their own sorority and members of another sorority, they saw much greater similarity among members of the other sorority. In other words, they were more willing to use a common stereo-

"I'm surprised, Marty. I thought you were one of us."
Categorization precipitates perceptions of group differences.
Drawing by Ziegler; © 1983 The New Yorker Magazine, Inc.

typic category in judging members of the other sorority while seeing greater diversity among the members of their own group (Linville, 1982).

Differences between views of in-groups and out-groups may reflect different levels of categorization (Park & Rothbart, 1982; van Knippenberg & Ellemers, 1990). When we consider members of our own group, people we know rather well, we may use a finer level of categorization to distinguish among different members of the group. For example, when everyone, including yourself, is a member of a social psychology class, that knowledge does not add to your ability to discriminate among class members. Additional categories, such as "good versus poor student" or "tall versus short," are required to organize and interpret the differences apparent from your knowledge of class members' behavior. When judging members of a group that we do not know very well, we may see them all mainly as members of "group X," with a common set of attributes. Our

relatively limited knowledge of these group members is subjectively expanded by the stereotypic information that results from categorization (Oakes & Turner, 1990).

The mere presence of another group can make members more aware of their own group identity. Students at Rutgers University, for example, reacted very similarly in a verbal learning task to either a Rutgers pennant or a pennant from rival school Princeton. Compared with a New York Yankees pennant or no pennant at all, both school pennants increased awareness of words related to Rutgers (Wilder & Shapiro, 1984). More recently, Charles Perdue, John Dovidio, Michael Gurtman, and Richard Tyler (1990) demonstrated that this activation of group identity is a spontaneous cognitive process that occurs at the most general level of categorization: us versus them. Perdue and his colleagues asked subjects to decide whether or not adjectives flashed on a computer screen could be used to describe a person. Some of the adjectives were positive and could be applied to people (*good, kind, trustworthy*), some were equally applicable to people but negative (*bad, cruel, untrustworthy*), and some control traits were not applicable to people (*drafty, brick*). Before each adjective appeared, one of three primes (*we, they, XXX*) was displayed in a procedure called masked priming: the prime is presented so rapidly that a subject does not have time to consciously process its meaning. Even though no conscious perception occurs, masked priming spontaneously increases the cognitive accessibility of related concepts for a brief period (Fowler, Wolford, Slade, & Tassinary, 1981).

As illustrated in Figure 13.5, the results Perdue and his colleagues obtained clearly show that, when primed with *we,* subjects took less time to decide positive traits were applicable and more time to decide negative traits were applicable than when the subjects were primed with *they* or *XXX.* Even general references to one's group identity (*we*) activate positive association in memory and make it easier to decide that positive adjectives are applicable. The reaction times for *they* and *XXX* did not differ; this indicates that references to one's own group are the important part of the cognitive process. The results also indicate that one consequence of being reminded of one's group identity is a positivity bias, a means of favorably discriminating between one's own and another group. This process is related to BIRGing (see Chapter 3), in which individuals attempt to associate themselves with high-status others. In this case, however, the individual is already a member of the group in question.

Why should an automatic positivity bias exist toward members of one's own group? One answer can be found in social identity theory, proposed by Tajfel (1978, 1982; Tajfel & Turner, 1986). According to social identity theory, the groups to which we belong are an integral part of our self-concept. Thus, discrimination between groups results from individual group members' motivations to enhance or maintain self-esteem. For example, if the status of group *X* is higher than the status of group *Y,* then I, as a member of *X,* share in that higher status (van Knippenberg & Ellemers, 1990).

Positivity bias is particularly likely when a group member has experienced some personal failure (Meindl & Lerner, 1984). In one experiment, for exam-

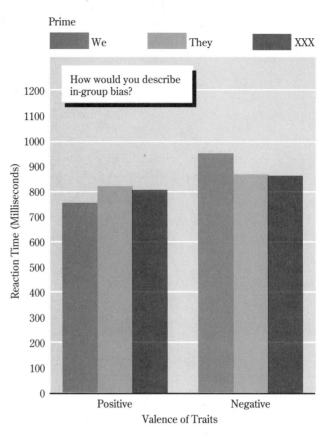

Figure 13.5 *When primed with the word* we, *subjects respond more quickly to positive traits and more slowly to negative traits.*

Source: "Us and Them: Social Categorization and the Process of Intergroup Bias" by C. W. Perdue, J. F. Dovidio, M. B. Gurtman, and R. B. Tyler, 1990, *Journal of Personality and Social Psychology, 59,* pp. 475–486.

ple, Michael Hogg and Jane Sunderland (1991) temporarily manipulated self-esteem by telling subjects they had done either well or poorly on a test of "interpersonal empathy." Subjects were then asked to assign rewards to individuals identified by code numbers. Subjects in the *group* condition were told the code numbers represented distinct groups to which the subject and others had been randomly assigned. Subjects in the *individual* condition were told the code numbers similar to their own simply represented other individuals in the study. The results, illustrated in Figure 13.6, show that only subjects in the group condition who had experienced failure assigned rewards using strategies that maximized differences between the "groups." That is, despite the fact that group membership was based on random assignment, subjects whose self-esteem was temporarily reduced took the opportunity to boost their self-esteem by elevating the status of their group relative to that of another group.

Views of the In-Group and Out-Group

In intergroup relations, the views of the in-group often serve as a reference point for judging an out-group. This phenomenon is known as **ethnocentrism,** originally defined by the sociologist William Sumner (1906) as the "view of things in which one's own group is the center of everything, and all others are scaled and rated with reference to it" (quoted in Brewer, 1986, p. 88). In a descriptive passage, Sumner goes on to say:

> Each group nourishes its own pride and vanity, boasts itself superior, exalts its own divinities, and looks with contempt on outsiders. Each group thinks its own folkways the only right ones, and if it observes that other groups have other folkways, these excite its scorn. [quoted in Brewer, 1986, p. 88]

According to Sumner, many behaviors were associated with ethnocentrism: some of these behaviors are summarized in Table 13.1. For the in-group, evaluations are positive, and behaviors indicate loyalty to the group goals. In marked contrast, values and behaviors

The groups to which we belong are an integral part of our self-concept.
Alan Carey/The Image Works

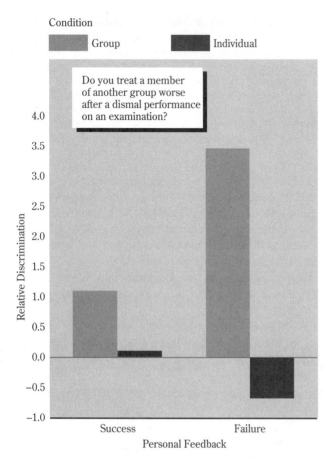

Figure 13.6 *Even in groups without a history of interaction, discrimination is greatest after a failure experience.*
Source: "Self-Esteem and Intergroup Discrimination in the Minimal Group Paradigm" by M. A. Hogg and J. Sunderland, 1991, *British Journal of Social Psychology, 300,* pp. 51–62.

regarding the out-group indicate negative evaluations, rejection, and fear. Subsequent research, however, has shown ethnocentrism to be somewhat more complex than Sumner so eloquently described it. Sometimes a decided in-group bias exists, reflecting Sumner's position. Cross-cultural studies, for example, have shown that there appears to be a universal tendency to view one's own group as morally superior and more worthy of trust (Brewer, 1986). On other dimensions, however, in-groups do not describe the out-group in more negative terms than those they use to describe themselves

(Brewer, 1986; Tajfel, 1982). In some cases, members of an in-group recognize that their own position is less favorable than the out-group's. Rather than deny that distinction, the in-group either (1) minimizes the difference between the two groups, seeing them as less dissimilar than outsiders perhaps would; or (2) devalues the dimension on which the out-group is superior (van Knippenberg & Ellemers, 1990).

Because an in-group recognizes that it is not necessarily better on every dimension, there is often a tendency to choose for comparison those dimensions that favor one's in-group over the out-group. Whites, for example, may prefer to compare their academic prowess with that of blacks (who score lower on standardized tests) but may prefer to compare their height with that of Asians (who tend to score higher than whites on standardized tests). In concluding her discussion of this issue, Brewer (1986) accordingly suggests that "perhaps the essence of ethnocentrism is this tendency to expect that the out-group will share the in-group's definition of the conflict or distinction between them and will be willing to make comparisons in terms that favor the in-group" (p. 101). That is, each of us expects members of other groups to see things the same way we see them, even if that view is disadvantageous to the members of the other group.

Ethnocentric views lead not only to negative evaluations of an out-group but also to biased explanations for the out-group members' actions. As a general rule, group members are guilty of what Thomas Pettigrew (1979) has termed the *ultimate attribution error.* Like the fundamental attribution bias of individuals (discussed in Chapter 4), the **ultimate attribution bias** involves in-group members attributing their own desirable behaviors to internal, stable factors and citing transitory factors to explain desirable behaviors of the out-group. The reverse pattern is evident when undesirable behaviors are at issue.

Members of different groups also offer different explanations for their basis of differentiation. For example, students at two universities in Hong Kong offered different explanations for the differences between their two schools (Hewstone, Bond, & Wan, 1983). Asked to explain why graduates of Hong Kong University are placed more highly in the city's work force, Hong Kong University students suggested that they were more adaptable to the needs of Hong Kong society. In contrast, students at the Chinese University of Hong Kong believed that Hong Kong University students had more connections that outweighed simple merit. In Great Britain, Hewstone and Jaspars (1982) found a similar pattern of explanations for differences between blacks and whites in arrests, unemployment, educational opportunities, and other areas. Asked to choose between racism and dispositional differences as explanations, black subjects tended very strongly to see white representatives of "the system" as the chief cause of racial discrimination. White subjects tended to divide the blame evenly, although they saw blacks as more responsible and whites as less responsible than the black subjects did.

In Chapter 8 we discussed forms of power that may be in effect between two individuals. In intergroup relations, power issues also come into play (Apfelbaum, 1979). Often, though not always, two groups confront each other with different levels of power and potential influence or with different kinds of power. In labor-management conflicts, for example, management typically has the financial resources, but labor can shut down operations. Unequal power has certain effects on each

of the groups in question, perhaps more notably on the group with lesser power. Often the group with lesser power is more aware of the power and status differentials (Tajfel, 1982).

Early in the study of intergroup relations, Lewin observed that "the privileged group . . . usually offers its members more and hinders them less than does the less privileged group" and further noted that "the member of the underprivileged group is more hampered by . . . group belongingness" (quoted in Apfelbaum, 1979, pp. 194–195). More recent research has suggested that differences in status between two groups will increase the tendency in both groups toward in-group bias—particularly if the difference in status is perceived as unreasonable, illegitimate, or unstable (Tajfel, 1982; van Knippenberg & Ellemers, 1990). Power differences between groups may affect one's perceptions both of one's own group and of the other group, typically accentuating actual differences that exist between two interacting groups. Lucie Cheng and Yen Espiritu (1989) used this concept to explain why Korean businesses in Los Angeles encounter considerably more hostility in black neighborhoods than in Hispanic neighborhoods. Blacks, as native-born Amer-

Table 13.1   **Facets of ethnocentrism**

Orientations toward in-group	Orientations toward out-group
See selves as virtuous and superior	See out-group as contemptible, immoral, and inferior
See own standards of value as universal, intrinsically true	Rejection of out-group values
See selves as strong	See out-group as weak
Sanctions against theft	Sanctions for theft
Sanctions against murder	Sanctions for murder
Cooperative relations with other group members	Absence of cooperation
Obedience to authorities	Absence of obedience
Willingness to retain membership in group	Rejection of membership
Willingness to fight and die for group	Virtue in killing out-group members in warfare
	Maintenance of social distance
	Negative affect, hate
	Use as bad examples in training children
	Blame for in-group troubles
	Distrust and fear

Source: Folkways by W. G. Sumner, 1906, Boston: Ginn.

icans, categorize Koreans as members of an out-group—immigrants—who receive advantages that have been denied to blacks through racism. Because many Hispanics are immigrants from Mexico, they are more likely to categorize Koreans as members of the in-group—immigrants—and consider successful Korean business owners as role models.

▶ Strategies of Interaction

Groups can deal with each other in a variety of ways. The situation itself may foster certain approaches; for example, certain situations encourage cooperation be-tween groups, whereas others, where resources are limited, engender competition. Often groups approach situations with very different goals in mind, and one group's success may mean the other group's failure. In such situations, negotiation and bargaining—aimed at resolving conflicts in such a way that both groups will be at least partly satisfied with the outcome—often become necessary. Groups cannot always resolve their conflicts, however, and sometimes must bring a third party into the situation to work for a resolution.

In this section we will discuss these various strategies of interaction. Some of the studies of these strategies and processes have been performed with a minimal situation—with two-person "groups," called dyads. While such studies do not match the complexity of in-

Cooperation involves working together for mutual benefit.
Dan Childester / The Image Works

tergroup relations, they can indicate some fundamental aspects of the interaction process.

Cooperation and Competition

Whether we consider the interaction between two individuals or two groups, cooperation and competition are two very different approaches to interaction. **Cooperation** involves working together for mutual benefit. **Competition,** in contrast, is activity directed toward achieving a goal at the expense of another individual or group. Whether an individual or group chooses to cooperate or to compete depends largely on the reward structures inherent in the situation because reward structures "set the stage" for the kinds of actions that will be taken. There are three basic types of reward structures: cooperative, competitive, and individualistic.

In the **cooperative reward structure,** the goals of the situation are linked so that one individual or group can attain its goals only if the other individuals or groups attain theirs. Emphasizing the interdependence of group members under this reward structure, Morton Deutsch (1973) has used the term *promotive interdependence* to describe this kind of situation. In the contrasting **competitive reward structure,** the participants' goals are negatively linked so that the success of one party necessarily means failure for the other; Deutsch's term for this situation is *contrient interdependence.* More graphically describing the distinction between these two situations, Deutsch (1973) has stated: "In a cooperative situation the goals are so linked that everybody 'sinks or swims' together, while in the competitive situation if one swims, the other must sink" (p. 20). A third type of reward structure, the **individualistic reward structure,** operates when individual or group goals are independent of one another—that is, what one group does has no influence on what the other group does.

The distinctions among these three reward structures may be clearer if we shift to the familiar situation of the college classroom and grading procedures. If a professor announces that grades will be determined on a curve and that 15% of the students will receive an "A" no matter what the absolute scores are, that professor is setting up a competitive reward structure. Every "A" attained by one student is an "A" that cannot be attained by another. The most extreme competitive reward structure in this context occurs when the professor says that only one "A" will be given. In contrast, a cooperative reward structure can be established by developing team projects in which all team members share the same grade. If the group does well, everyone in the group receives an "A," and if the group does poorly, everyone in the group suffers accordingly. Finally, as an example of the individualistic reward structure, the professor might say, "I reward competent work. If your assignments are excellent, you will receive an 'A.' There are no curves or quotas; in fact, I would be happy to see all of you produce high-quality work and would award an 'A' to everyone." In this case students' outcomes are not interdependent because reward attainment by one does not affect the probability of reward attainment by another.

The prevailing reward structure can sharply alter the behavior of people in a situation. Numerous researchers, convinced of the advantages of cooperation, have tried to impose cooperative reward structures in desegregated public schools (N. Miller & Davidson-Podgorny, 1987). These researchers are concerned that desegregation might produce two separate groups, racial minorities and whites, competing for the same rewards. One attempt to prevent this outcome is the *jigsaw method* of learning developed by Elliot Aronson and his colleagues (Aronson, Blaney, Stephan, Sikes, & Snapp, 1978).

In one application of this method, fifth-graders were divided into heterogeneous, multiethnic teams and assigned to study the biography of Joseph Pulitzer. Each child on the team was given one section of the material on Pulitzer (one piece of the jigsaw puzzle). All team members assigned to the same section then met and worked together to master their assigned material, after which each child returned to the original group to teach the material to the other members of the team. Thus, children cooperated with members of other teams and were dependent upon others in their own team for parts of the "jigsaw." In studies conducted over six-week periods, the method was tested by comparing jigsaw classes with traditional classes taught by instructors identified by their colleagues as good teachers. The studies were preceded by workshops to train teachers and by "team building" exercises to help students put aside their competitive motives. The teams met for about forty to forty-five minutes a day, at least three times a week.

At the end of the six-week period, comparisons between jigsaw classes and control classes showed the following results: (1) jigsaw students grew to like their groupmates; (2) white and black children, but not Mexican American children, developed more favorable attitudes toward school in the jigsaw classes; (3) jigsaw students' self-esteem increased; (4) black and Mexican American jigsaw students tended to master more material, and white students did no worse in the jigsaw classes than in traditional ones; and (5) children in the jigsaw groups were more likely to express cooperative attitudes and to see their classmates as learning resources. Thus, by changing the reward structure in the class, the jigsaw method avoided what might have been intergroup rivalry and enhanced the performance of minority students.

Very different outcomes result when competitive reward structures are used to foster intergroup rivalry. A graphic example of these consequences was described in the opening scenario of this chapter, the classic field study at Robber's Cave conducted by Sherif and his associates (Sherif, 1966; Sherif et al., 1961).

The boys at Robber's Cave were a normal group of 11- and 12-year-olds attending a summer camp. What was different about this camp—and what the boys did not know, but their parents did—was that it was staffed by researchers who observed the boys' behavior and specifically structured the situation. Two groups of boys were brought to separate cabins on the first day of camp, each group unaware that the other group existed. To develop cohesiveness within each group, the researchers planned activities that required the boys to cooperate for mutual benefit (for example, camping out or cleaning up a beach). The boys soon came to recognize one another's strengths and weaknesses, and leaders emerged on the basis of their contributions to the group. Each group developed a name for itself (the "Rattlers" and the "Eagles"), group jokes, standards for behavior, and sanctions for those who "got out of line."

Thus, during this phase, the reward structure within each group was cooperative, whereas the reward structure between groups was essentially individualistic. What one group did had no effect on the other group, and each group was unaware of the other.

Then the researchers made each group aware of the other group's existence and shifted to a competitive reward structure by creating situations in which only one group would win. One way this was accomplished involved setting up tournaments with desirable prizes for only one group, thus stimulating considerable intergroup conflict. When the groups were brought together for this series of contests, fair play was replaced by an ethic akin to that of the former Green Bay Packer coach Vince Lombardi: "Winning isn't everything, it's the only thing." The groups began to call each other derogatory names, pick fights, and raid each other's camp. "Rattlers" downgraded all "Eagles," and vice versa, to the extent that neither group desired further contact with the other group. Sherif (1966) remarked that a neutral observer who had no knowledge of what had happened would have assumed that the boys were "wicked, disturbed and vicious bunches of youngsters" (p. 58).

We will return to the boys of Robber's Cave later in this chapter. For the moment, however, it is important to point out how easily intergroup conflict can begin. Competitive reward structures often foster the development of such conflict by mandating that rewards given to one group will automatically be unavailable to the other. Social psychologist Morton Deutsch (1973), who has extensively studied the workings of cooperative and competitive groups, has identified three likely consequences of the competitive situation.

First, communication between competitive groups is unreliable and impoverished. Groups either do not use available communication channels or use them to deliberately mislead the other group. Consequently, neither group trusts the information it receives from the other. The use of propaganda and "misinformation" during wars and election campaigns is a classic example of such communication.

Second, perceptions of the other group are distorted, as the discussion of in-groups and out-groups suggested. Groups see their own behavior toward the

*The 1991–1992 Mideast Peace Talks are
one example of negotiation.*
Greg Gibson/AP/Wide World Photos

other group as benevolent while viewing the actions of the other group as hostile and ill intentioned. Suspicion of the other's motives may lead in turn to a negative response to any request the other group makes and to a greater willingness to exploit the other group's needs. One group's request for a reconciliation meeting, for example, is more likely to be perceived as a "trap" than as a valid offer.

Finally, groups in competition develop the belief that the only way to resolve the conflict is for one side to impose a solution through the use of superior force. Each side tries to enhance its own power and minimize the legitimacy of the other group. In this process, the scope of the conflict is often expanded, moving from a specific issue to a concern with moral principles and general superiority.

On the surface, it sounds easy to avoid intergroup conflict: simply substitute a cooperative reward structure for a competitive one, and groups will work in harmony. But the solution is not that simple. Often a real conflict exists between group interests, such as when a shortage of resources makes it impossible for both groups to achieve what they want. In industry, labor unions often want higher wages, whereas managers want to lower costs. In warfare, both nations may want

a single piece of territory. In other cases, religious or cultural values may be inherently contradictory.

Bargaining and Negotiation

Most conflicts between groups are mixed-motive situations in which elements of both cooperation and competition are present. The parties must cooperate with each other to achieve at least a portion of their own goals, and bargaining and negotiation become the means for attempting resolution and compromise. *Bargaining* and *negotiation* are familiar terms that are used often in conversation, media reports, and a variety of contexts. For example, we may speak of bargaining with a car dealer for a good price, or reporters may keep us abreast of the latest negotiations in the Mideast. Although there is some tendency to use the term *bargaining* when we speak of interactions between individuals and *negotiation* when we speak of interactions between groups, we will consider the terms interchangeable. **Bargaining** (or negotiation) is defined as "the process whereby two or more parties attempt to settle what each shall give and take, or perform and receive, in a transaction between them" (Rubin & Brown, 1975, p. 2).

The core of a bargaining relationship is the involvement of at least two parties whose interests conflict with regard to one or more issues (Rubin & Brown, 1975). In labor-management negotiations, for example, the two parties may disagree on several issues—wages, fringe benefits, work hours, or job security, to name a few. To begin to negotiate, both parties must voluntarily enter into the bargaining relationship. If one group refuses to negotiate, then no bargaining can take place. For example, if a teachers' union goes on strike but the board of education refuses to hear the union's demands, then intergroup conflict is at a stalemate, and bargaining cannot begin.

In labor-management conflicts, labor often uses a strike, a work-to-rule policy, or a similar work action to coerce management to negotiate. For example, the U.S. auto industry has a coordinated collective bargaining arrangement whereby a strike is held at only one of the "big three" automakers (Ford, General Motors, and Chrysler), but the agreement reached in that settlement generally applies to all three companies. The existence of such an arrangement allowed Ross Stagner and Boaz Eflal (1982) to conduct a quasi-experimental study of the effects of a strike on attitudes of union members in which Stagner and Eflal compared workers at the plant that went on strike with those at the plants that did not. Being on strike made a substantial difference. Strikers evaluated both their union and their leadership more positively than nonstrikers did, and they were more willing to engage in union activities. During the strike, the striking workers showed more militant and negative attitudes toward management; after the strike, they were more satisfied with the settlement package.

A study by Shirom (1982) gives us some insight into the reactions of managers to a strike settlement and their beliefs about its influence on the resolution of the conflict. In this study, Shirom questioned fifty-one management negotiators, each of whom had been involved in a strike in which at least one hundred workers participated. Somewhat surprisingly, the duration of the strike did not appear to influence managers' opinions about the eventual settlement. The two factors that were related to managers' perceptions of a positive outcome—the size of the striking work force and the ability of management to keep the plant operating during the strike—provide some insight into why this may be so. Larger work forces make it more difficult for the union to support workers while they are on strike, which causes greater hardship for labor than for management. Similarly, the ability to maintain operations, and thereby maintain income for the company, reduces the burden on management. Thus, strike duration per se may not be a factor from management's viewpoint when operations continue and labor shares the greater portion of the burden.

Once both parties have agreed to negotiate, the give-and-take process of bargaining can begin. If the issues that separate the two parties are numerous, the bargaining process can be extremely complex, although the stages in the process may be predictable. Dean Pruitt (1981) has outlined six steps in the negotiating process, which are listed in Table 13.2. Examples of international negotiation, whether the lengthy process of nuclear arms reduction or the relatively rapid reunification of Germany, typically follow the stages outlined by Pruitt. A variety of activities occur during each stage in the course of bargaining. Each side presents demands or proposals, which in turn are evaluated by the other party. Often counterproposals follow, accompanied perhaps by some concessions, and the process is characterized by a sequence of such exchanges (Rubin & Brown, 1975). Usually some division or exchange of resources occurs. For example, in a labor-management dispute, labor may agree to accept a somewhat lower wage increase in return for greater job security.

Like many social processes, the basic bargaining process can be described rather simply, but many factors affect its outcome. Social scientists have exerted considerable effort toward understanding more about particular characteristics of the bargaining process (see, for example, Druckman, 1977; C. Miller & Crandall, 1980; Pruitt, 1981; Rubin & Brown, 1975). We will examine some of these factors.

Both the size and the timing of demands can affect the ultimate outcome of the bargaining process. For example, if an agreement is eventually reached, the party that makes larger initial demands and smaller concessions generally achieves a larger outcome (Pruitt, 1981). However, if both parties make smaller initial demands and faster concessions, they usually achieve resolution more rapidly. There are some exceptions to this

Table 13.2 **The six steps of the negotiating process**

1. Agreeing about the need to negotiate.
2. Agreeing on a set of objectives and principles (for example, in arms-control negotiations, the principle that the agreement should permit neither side to coerce the other).
3. Agreeing on certain rules of conduct.
4. Defining the issues and setting up an agenda.
5. Agreeing on a formula for resolving the conflict; reaching an agreement in principle.
6. Agreeing on implementing details.

Source: Negotiation Behavior by D. G. Pruitt, 1981, New York: Academic Press.

seemingly obvious statement. If one party makes extremely low demands or concedes very quickly, agreement is more difficult to reach (Bartos, 1974; Hamner, 1974). Presumably the other party merely waits for additional concessions without feeling a need to make any concessions of its own (Pruitt, 1981).

In formal bargaining situations, each group is often represented by one selected individual, a representative bargainer. For example, the union president may represent the total union membership, and management may similarly appoint one individual to represent the broader management group. In general, studies of this process show that representative bargainers are more competitive, make smaller concessions, and are less likely to reach agreements than individual bargainers who represent only themselves (Davis, Laughlin, & Komorita, 1976). Surveillance of the representative bargainer by his or her constituents intensifies this effect. In a laboratory study of bargaining, some bargainers were told that their behavior would be constantly observed by the "owner" of the company, who was seated behind a one-way mirror (Carnevale, Pruitt, & Britton, 1979). In other cases, bargainers were told that the "owners" would receive only a final report on the negotiated agreement. When they believed they were being observed, bargainers made more statements about their own role, made more threats and putdowns of the other negotiator, and were less likely to indicate an understanding of the other bargainer's priorities.

Surveillance also affected the outcome of the negotiations. Bargainers under surveillance settled for lower profits than bargainers who were not being observed.

Accountability to one's constituents can have similar effects. Knowing that one is accountable may make a bargainer reluctant to give in, fearing that the constituency will perceive him or her as a loser. "Saving face" becomes more important than achieving a good agreement (Brown, 1977). Bargainers who are held accountable engage in more pressure tactics and gain lower outcomes (Carnevale, Pruitt, & Seilheimer, 1981). Interestingly, however, this pattern holds only when the bargainers meet face to face. Perhaps the greater range of nonverbal communication possible in the face-to-face encounter (see Chapter 5) creates stronger messages of dominance and thus impedes the bargaining process.

Many other factors can affect the bargaining process. The personalities of individual bargainers, for example, can facilitate or hinder the process (Rubin & Brown, 1975). Different kinds of strategies and different types of communication will alter the process as well (Putnam & Jones, 1982). Events external to the bargainers themselves that create stress and tension make bargaining more difficult and outcomes less favorable (Hopmann & Walcott, 1977). Publicity in the mass media, for example, can "leak" critical information, narrowing bargainers' options.

At least two general kinds of agreements can be reached in a bargaining process (Pruitt, 1982). In a compromise, both parties concede to a middle ground on some obvious dimension. For example, if a teachers' union wants starting salaries of $20,000 per year and the school board offers only $16,000, a settlement at $18,000 would represent a compromise agreement. Alternatively, compromise agreements may involve trade-offs whereby one party concedes in one area and the other concedes in another. For example, the school board might hold fast on salaries while agreeing to the teachers' demands for job security.

A second type of agreement is the **integrative agreement,** one that reconciles both parties' interests and thus yields a high payoff for both groups. In general, the basis for integrative agreements is initially less obvious and may require development of new alternatives. For example, instead of higher wages, labor and management might both benefit from a profit-sharing plan. In this respect, integrative agreements are like creative problem solving (Pruitt, 1982). Both compromise and integrative agreements have been termed "win/win" outcomes (Filley, 1975) because both parties in the conflict may gain in the eventual resolution.

Third-Party Intervention

Conflicting groups frequently fail to reach an agreement. In such cases, a third party may be brought in to reconcile or to mediate their differences. **Mediation** is defined as "third-party assistance to two or more disputing parties who are trying to reach agreement" (Pruitt & Kressel, 1985, p. 1). Sometimes a mediator has the power to force both sides to accept a particular solution, in which case the process is usually called **arbitration.** Mediators or arbitrators are found in divorce and small-claims courts, labor-management negotiations, community disputes, and many other situations. The technique has become more frequent since the founding in 1973 of the Society for Professionals in Dispute Resolution (Pruitt & Kressel, 1985).

Once mediation is expected, the bargaining process often slows down. In what has been described as a "chilling effect," bargainers tend to resist making additional concessions until the third party has arrived. One reason for this is that bargaining groups may lose face. Any losses as a result of mediation can be blamed on the mediator, an external attribution that enables each group to save face. More practically, bargaining groups may expect an arbitrator to "split the difference"— hence, any concession that weakens either position will reduce the group's outcome in the mediated settlement. Both reasons may help explain why, when third-party intervention is expected, movement toward an agreement is slower for larger conflicts (Hiltrop & Rubin, 1982)—there is less "face" to be lost and more payoff to be gained by moving slowly.

Mediation is not likely to be effective when the relationship between the two bargaining groups is poor. Nor are the chances for successful resolution very high when resources are scarce. Under such conditions, the likelihood of finding a mutually acceptable compromise is not very high. Conversely, mediation is most likely to be successful when both parties are highly motivated to settle the case and when they are committed to the mediation process. In general, however, clients are likely to be satisfied with the mediation process; most studies show satisfaction rates of 75% or higher (Kressel & Pruitt, 1985).

To create pressure toward agreement, a successful mediator needs to possess certain characteristics and to adopt particular strategies. Most important among the personal characteristics are trustworthiness and perceived ability (Rubin & Brown, 1975)—traits that have been found to be effective source characteristics in research on attitude change (see Chapter 7). Deborah Kolb (1985) suggests that successful mediators use specific techniques of impression management, such as those discussed in Chapter 3. Thus, the mediator attempts to convey an impression of legitimacy, social position, and expertise in order to gain both parties' confidence and to win acceptance for the proposed solution. A good mediator will also tailor tactics to the particular situational demands, consistent with interaction principles introduced by contingency theories of leadership (Chapter 12). For example, a mediator may use humor and directive tactics to approach a group that is experiencing considerable hostility; a mediator will use nondirective techniques when bargainers are inexperienced and lack expertise (Carnevale & Pegnetter, 1985). In summary, no single set of mediation tactics guarantees success.

▶ Reduction of Intergroup Conflict

Bargaining and negotiation are formal procedures that can be used to reduce intergroup conflict when both parties recognize the disagreement and are willing to negotiate to resolve the conflict. These procedures work best when specific issues can be defined and the parties are interested in resolving those issues.

Other cases of intergroup conflict are less easily resolved, such as the centuries-old conflict between Ireland and Britain (Heskin, 1980). The division of Ireland in 1921 into the predominantly Catholic southern Republic of Ireland and the predominantly Protestant Northern Ireland exacerbated conflict between political factions and religious denominations. Northern Ireland is among the poorest of countries, plagued by poverty, unemployment, and poor housing (Trew & McWhirter, 1982). The modern conflict in Northern Ireland is often dated from 1969, when reactions to housing discrimination led to riots and the subsequent intervention of the British Army. Terrorism has since become a major issue (Alexander & O'Day, 1984). The conflict is extremely complex, partly because religious affiliation is a source of social identity in Northern Ireland. As we discussed earlier, visible signs, such as gender and race, facilitate in-group/out-group distinctions. In Northern Ireland, the basis of distinguishing Catholic from Protestant is more subtle, and even facial structure comes into play. For example, given only surnames, location of residence, and school attended, both Protestant and Catholic students in Ulster (Northern Ireland) agreed on the categorization of individuals described to them (Stringer & Cook, 1985).

As in Northern Ireland, sometimes the issues cannot be limited in such a way that bargaining may proceed. At other times the groups may have no formal relationship with each other, so specific negotiation is very difficult. In the case of black-white relations in the United States, for example, intergroup conflict is both less defined and more general than a bargaining situation could handle. For those concerned with intergroup relations, it is important to identify situations that will prevent conflict as well as to develop means for conflict reduction when bargaining is not immediately applicable. In this section we will consider several principles and procedures that have been found effective in decreasing intergroup conflict.

Superordinate Goals

Recall that when we left the boys at Robber's Cave, they were "wicked, disturbed and vicious"—the outcome of a competitive reward structure created by the researchers. The investigators did not wish to let the state of intergroup conflict persist, and they tried by various methods to reduce the hostilities (Sherif, 1966; Sherif et al., 1961). Several strategies were tried and found wanting. The boys attended religious services that emphasized love and cooperation, but this appeal to moral values did not stop them from going right back to their warlike strategies when the services ended. Introduction of a third group, which served as "a common enemy," only widened the scope of conflict. Conferences between the leaders of the two groups were rejected because concessions by the leaders would be in-

terpreted by their followers as traitorous sellouts of the groups' interests. Essentially, the Eagles and Rattlers had become like any other groups with a long-standing history of conflict.

The resolution of this conflict was finally made possible through the introduction of a **superordinate goal**—an important goal that could be achieved only through cooperation. First, the researchers arranged for a breakdown in the water-supply line. The boys joined forces to find the leak, but they resumed their conflict when the crisis had passed. The researchers then instigated a series of such joint efforts to achieve a superordinate goal: the groups pooled their money to rent a movie, and they used a rope to pull and start the food-supply truck. As a cumulative effect of these joint projects, the groups became friendlier with each other, began to see strengths in each other, and developed friendships across group lines. In fact, the majority of the boys chose to return home on the same bus, and the group that had won $5 as a prize used the money to treat the other group.

One result of a superordinate goal is a change in the salient group identity. Rather than identifying themselves as "Rattlers" or "Eagles," the boys at Robber's Cave presumably began to consider themselves members of a common group—"boys without water" or "boys without food." Within the laboratory, Roderick Kramer and Marilynn Brewer (1984) have shown that people are more cooperative when a superordinate group identity is emphasized than when differentiating group memberships are stressed.

An important element in the effectiveness of superordinate goals is the group's success in achieving that goal. Groups with a previous history of competition who work together on a project and fail may like each other less than they did before work on the superordinate project began. As Stephen Worchel (1986) cautions, "anyone wishing to reduce intergroup conflict through intergroup cooperation must pay careful attention to the conditions surrounding the cooperative encounter" (p. 297).

Intergroup Contact

Many people have optimistically assumed that if two racial or religious groups could be brought together, the antagonism expressed by each group toward the other would erode, and positive attitudes would develop. This, in essence, is the **intergroup contact hypothesis.**

The optimism expressed in this hypothesis must be qualified. Contact between groups does not always reduce conflict; on some occasions, intergroup contact can increase antagonism. Before conflict can be reduced through contact, several conditions must be met (Amir, 1976; Cook, 1970; N. Miller & Brewer, 1984; Stephan, 1985). First, the situation must provide what can be called "acquaintance potential." In other words, people need to have the opportunity to interact with one another and thus to discover that some of their beliefs may be erroneous. Casual or superficial contact—such as between two persons who work on the same floor of a building but have no real interaction—has little effect on intergroup attitudes.

Second, the interaction must provide disconfirming information about the negative traits believed to be characteristic of the other group. If one has contact with a typical or representative member of the other group who simply confirms the stereotypes that were held, then positive change is unlikely (Wilder, 1984).

Third, the relative status of participants in a contact situation is important (Norvell & Worchel, 1981). Positive change is more likely to occur when members of the two groups occupy the same social status or level of power (Ramirez, 1977). In the school setting, for example, Albert Ramirez (1988) found that Hispanic high school students report much less prejudice and discrimination when Hispanics occupy some of the leadership positions in the school than when administrative positions are dominated by whites.

Finally, institutional support for intergroup contact must exist (E. Cohen, 1980). For example, early studies of the short-term effects of school desegregation, when there was often no support or there was outright antagonism from school authorities, revealed few, if any, reductions in racial conflict. More recent studies, however, indicate the contact achieved through school desegregation produces a substantial decrease in prejudice and discrimination among blacks and whites (Stephan, 1990).

Investigators today are generally far more cautious about claiming positive effects for the intergroup contact hypothesis than they were twenty-five years ago. As Tajfel (1982) has stated, the change may reflect a "loss of innocence." More complex models of intergroup contact indicate its potential for both positive and negative results, depending on the conditions that surround the contact (Stephan, 1987). Equal status, a need for cooperation, a social climate that favors intergroup contact, and rewards from the contact itself all work to support the intergroup contact hypothesis. In contrast, situations that foster competition, produce frustration, or emphasize status differences between participants tend to strengthen rather than reduce prejudice between two groups. Individuals' perceptions of the procedures through which intergroup contact has been achieved also affect the outcome of the contact.

Through a series of studies on affirmative action, Rupert Nacoste (1985, 1987a, 1987b, 1989; Nacoste & Lehman, 1987) has demonstrated that perceptions of procedural fairness are also extremely important. When affirmative action procedures are perceived as fair, both majority and minority group members react positively to affirmative action. When procedures are perceived as unfair, however, prejudice and discrimination by majority members do not decrease, and the beneficiaries of affirmative action are likely to feel stigmatized as a result of the ambiguity concerning their qualifications and anxiety concerning future evaluations of their performance. Nacoste (in press) has argued that affirmative action programs that concentrate on outcomes, such as achieving certain proportions of group representation, are less likely to be perceived as fair than are programs that concentrate on establishing procedures to reduce or to eliminate categorical bias in selection.

Reduction of Threat

In international relations, interactions between major powers are more appropriately described at the level of perceived balance of power rather than at the level of individual contact between nations. Conflict between Israel and its neighbors concerning the "occupied territories," and between the United States and Japan concerning trade policies are but two examples of such

Table 13.3   The basic principles of GRIT

1. Publicly state intentions to reduce tension through conciliatory acts, indicating the advantages for the other party in reciprocating.

2. Announce each unilateral initiative in advance, indicating that it is part of a general strategy, and invite some form of reciprocation.

3. Carry out each initiative as announced and continue the initiatives for some time even in the absence of reciprocation.

4. Make each initiative unambiguous and open to verification.

5. Initiatives should be risky and vulnerable to exploitation, but they should not reduce the capacity to retaliate if attacked.

6. Once the other party begins to reciprocate, the initiator should reciprocate as well, exposing itself to at least as much, or slightly more, vulnerability.

7. Diversify unilateral initiatives by type of action and geographical location.

Source: Perspective in Foreign Policy by C. E. Osgood, 1966, Palo Alto, CA: Pacific Books.

conflict. Psychologist Charles Osgood (1966, 1979) has offered one strategy for reducing such conflicts. Osgood calls this strategy **GRIT**—**g**raduated and **r**eciprocated **i**nitiatives in **t**ension reduction. The basic principles of this strategy are outlined in Table 13.3.

Osgood's GRIT strategy was designed explicitly to be applied to the nuclear arms race, although the technique can be applied to any conflict for which bargaining is not an immediate possibility. His recommended procedure is a gradual one, with the initiating party maintaining strength while gradually reducing the level of conflict. During the initial stages of this sequence, the aim is to put pressure on the target party both through one's own actions and, presumably, through a buildup of world public support. Later stages in the sequence (for example, steps 3, 4, and 5) are intended to establish an image of credibility and predictability and to incorporate a mixture of resistance and yielding.

The ultimate success of this model cannot be tested experimentally; it must await the actions of world leaders. Nonetheless, considerable laboratory experimentation has supported the validity of many of the strategy's points (Lindskold, 1986), and aspects of GRIT can be identified in the process that led to nuclear arms reductions accomplished by the United States and the former Soviet Union. Svenn Lindskold and Gyuseog Han (1988) have also demonstrated that the use of GRIT in one situation facilitates positive outcomes for subsequent bargaining sessions. However, other laboratory research indicates that participants in intense conflict are often reluctant to use conciliatory techniques and prefer to rely on threat instead (Deutsch, Canavan, & Rubin, 1971). Thus, whether GRIT will be the chosen method of conflict resolution in Northern Ireland, the Middle East, and other areas of conflict remains to be seen.

▶ **Summary**

Intergroup behavior occurs whenever individuals belonging to one group interact, collectively or individually, with another group or its members in terms of their group identification. Examples of intergroup behavior are numerous, including ethnic relations, labor-management negotiations, and international conflict.

Social psychologists have traditionally been more interested in situational determinants of behavior than in individual differences among people. In recent years, however, interest in group differences, such as race and gender, has increased. When one compares members of different groups, one should not lose sight of the extent to which the groups' characteristics also overlap.

Issues of causality involve both hereditary and environmental explanations, although the latter are generally weighted more heavily. Gender differences in social behavior, for example, are more likely to result from gender-role norms than from biological differences between genders.

Cross-cultural research attempts to determine how general our knowledge of human behavior is—whether our constructs are etic (truly universal) or emic (specific to a particular culture). Certainly it is evident that patterns of behavior vary in some ways from one culture to another, and the cultural script of a culture may be a key to understanding that variation.

Prejudice refers to an intolerant attitude toward a group of people; discrimination refers to specific unfair behaviors toward members of that group. Both may be independent of stereotypes. Although stereotypes may be spontaneously activated by stimuli, both prejudice and discrimination are controllable.

Racism is a particular form of prejudice and discrimination, directed toward an ethnic group. Although overt discrimination on the basis of race has been reduced, modern racism is still expressed in symbolic forms. Attitudes toward minority groups and the opportunities available to them are influenced by belief similarity and by endorsement of the dominant ideology that relates hard work to rewards.

Sexism is a similar form of prejudice, but in this case the behavior is directed against a person by virtue of gender rather than race. Prejudice toward women is related to stereotypic beliefs about the characteristics that men and women typically possess. Much more than blacks and other groups, however, women are widely perceived as suffering discrimination.

Many theories have attempted to explain prejudice. These theories, differing in their level of analysis and the factors considered relevant, emphasize historical and economic factors, sociocultural factors, situational factors, psychodynamic characteristics, phenomenological perceptions, and the earned reputation of the target group.

Cognitive principles of categorization explain some of the phenomena that characterize in-group/out-group relations. In-groups and out-groups have predictable views of one another and demonstrate an ethnocentrism that emphasizes the moral superiority of the in-group and the failings and dangerousness of the out-group. Characterized primarily by a positive bias for the in-group, ethnocentrism is linked to group members' maintenance of self-esteem.

There are three basic types of reward structures—cooperative, competitive, and individualistic—each of which affects interactions between groups. Competitive reward structures are most apt to lead to intergroup conflict. Cooperative reward structures, particularly when they foster interdependence, lead to reductions in intergroup conflict.

Bargaining is a process used to reduce conflict and resolve differences between groups. A variety of conditions can affect the outcome of the bargaining process, including the timing and size of demands, the accountability of a representative bargainer to his or her constituents, and surveillance by the constituency. Often a third party must be called in when bargaining parties cannot resolve their differences.

Other strategies also have been used to reduce or avoid intergroup conflict. Establishing a superordinate goal is one such strategy. Recent models of the intergroup contact hypothesis suggest that contact will reduce antagonism only under certain conditions. These include equal status, sufficient intimacy to disconfirm stereotypes, institutional support, and perceived fairness of procedures.

GRIT (graduated and reciprocated initiatives in tension reduction) is one strategy that has been suggested for resolving the problem of arms control and other international conflicts.

▶ *Key Terms*

arbitration
bargaining
competition
competitive reward structure
cooperation
cooperative reward structure
cultural script
discrimination
display rules
emic constructs
ethnocentrism
etic constructs
exotic bias
gender-role norm
GRIT
individualistic reward structure
in-group
integrative agreement
intergroup behavior
intergroup contact hypothesis
mediation
modern racism

out-group
prejudice
racism
scapegoating
sexism

social distance
stereotype
superordinate goal
symbolic racism
ultimate attribution bias

We shape our buildings and

afterwards our buildings shape us.

Winston Churchill

There are places I'll remember all my

life, though some have changed . . .

John Lennon and
Paul McCartney

14

Social Behavior in the Physical Environment

Michael Conn assisted in the preparation of this chapter.

Look around. Look at, listen, feel, and smell all that is around you begin to read this chapter. Are other people in the vicinity? What color are the walls? What kind of chair are you sitting on, and how does it feel? What other furniture is in the room? Can you hear music playing, birds singing, or some other sound, such as the hum of an air conditioner? What do you smell? Is there enough light, or too much light? More important, do any of these aspects of the environment distract you? Do any seem to make studying easier? These types of questions will be addressed in this chapter.

More generally, the basic question we address deals with the ways in which the physical environment affects social behavior. Psychologists, philosophers, and experts from other disciplines have been debating the answers for some time. One early answer was the notion of **environmental determinism,** the view that aspects of the environment have a powerful, decisive influence on human behavior. One proponent of this view used the phrase "stony skeleton of social life" (Youtz, 1929, p. 60) to express the idea that buildings are molds to which organized social processes must conform. Some early research on propinquity and interpersonal attraction (for example, Festinger et al., 1950) represents the social-psychological interpretation of this view.

Critics of environmental determinism have argued that we do not react passively to our physical surroundings. Instead, we mold our settings to suit our purposes or actively alter our behavior to cope with our environments (Franck, 1984; Lipman, 1969). After all, they reason, inert buildings cannot actively influence our behavior. And because physical environments are only part of a wider context, they represent just a few of the many factors that figure in our perceptions, choices, and decisions. According to these views, physical environments do not determine behavior, but they indirectly influence it.

More recently, environmental psychologists have considered social behavior in the physical environment from the viewpoint of **transactionalism,** the perspective that the person and the environment are integral aspects of a unitary system of change (Altman & Rogoff, 1987; Saegert & Winkel, 1990). Like Lewin's (1936; 1938) concept of **life space,** the transactional perspective includes the assumption that the individual, the social environment, and the physical environment all exist and influence one another simultaneously at any given time and place. That is, the confluence of the physical environment and the individual produces conditions from which social behavior emerges, much like the path of someone walking through an uncultivated forest develops as the walk progresses. Whether one walks around large rocks and trees or breaks through some of the underbrush, neither the individual nor the forest remains unchanged by the walk.

In this chapter we explore some of the theory and research concerning the interplay between physical settings and interpersonal behavior. In the first section we examine the relationship between the ambient environment and the experience of stress. In the remaining three sections we consider the regulation of privacy and crowding, the environment as a context for interpersonal interaction, and the symbolic aspects of the physical environment in terms of attachment to places. As a whole, the chapter suggests that the physical environment alters and is altered by interpersonal behavior in many ways. Physical settings emerge as sources of stress, contexts for conversation, constraints on personal accessibility, symbols of self-identity and status, sources of distraction, resources for privacy, boundaries around neighborhoods, and more.

▸ Ambient Stress

The **ambient environment** includes aspects of the physical setting that are chronic, that can be perceived but generally go unnoticed, and that cannot be altered easily—if at all—by an individual (Campbell, 1983). Temperature, sound, air quality, and natural illumination are a few of the aspects of ambient environment that alter interpersonal behavior.

In what ways does the ambient environment affect behavior? One possible effect of the ambient environment is increased **arousal,** a generalized state of physiological and psychological excitation. Exposure to uncomfortably warm temperatures or to moderately loud noises, for example, can temporarily increase a person's arousal (Sundstrom, 1986a). Arousal, you may recall from Chapter 3, is an integral component of emotion, which affects a variety of social processes. For example, positive moods can inhibit aggression or make attitude change easier. Here, however, we are concerned with the arousal associated with the experience of stress.

Stress can be defined as an imbalance between environmental demands and an organism's response capabilities (Evans & Cohen, 1987). That is, stress is the body's response to excessive change, either too much change or too many changes (Selye, 1971; Sundstrom, 1986a). How many and what kind of responses are mobilized depend on the perceived threat associated with a change (S. Cohen, 1980b). For example, the distraction produced by a loud noise might cause you to spill a glass of water, or it might cause you to lose control of your car on a busy freeway. A spilled glass of water is not particularly threatening and does not generate many responses. Although annoying, the stress one experiences from spilling a glass of water is not very great. The greater threat associated with losing control of one's car on a freeway, however, engenders a host of physical and psychological responses and therefore is considerably more stressful. In general, sources of stress are most disturbing when they are intense and uncontrollable (Baum, Singer, & Baum, 1981). However, Monica Paciuk (1990) has demonstrated that the process of exerting control over sources of stress reduces one's satisfaction with the environment. Joan Campbell (1983) used the term **ambient stressors** to refer to those aspects of the environment that contribute to the experience of stress.

How do ambient stressors affect social behavior? Based on their review of research, Carolyn Aldwin and Daniel Stokols (1988) have argued that ambient stress can produce either negative or positive outcomes at several different levels (see Table 14.1). There is not enough research yet for us to predict when ambient stress may precipitate positive versus negative effects. However, Aldwin and Stokols suggest that strong relationships among life domains—work, school, marriage, parenting, and so on—may make positive outcomes more likely. The timing of the stressor event is also important. As we noted, hearing a loud noise while holding a glass of water will precipitate different outcomes than hearing the same noise while driving on the freeway.

Consider, for example, the different ways in which ambient stress can diminish an individual's cognitive capacity (S. Cohen, 1980a). Reduced ability to process information under stress can produce enhanced sensitivity to some social cues and insensitivity to others. People under stress sometimes exhibit a **narrowing of attention;** they focus on the cues most salient to their immediate goals and overlook others (Hockey, 1970; Solly, 1969). Thus, a person on a busy sidewalk whose focus is on meeting a friend may overlook or ignore a person nearby who has just dropped a load of packages. Another person whose focus is on a personal problem may arrive at a creative solution through enhanced concentration on the problem.

Ambient stress also may create cognitive overload, an amount of stimulation or information that exceeds the individual's processing capacities. To cope with overload a person may set priorities and then ignore the "low-priority stimuli" (Milgram, 1970; J. G. Miller, 1964). Overwhelmed by the sights and sounds of a busy sidewalk, a tourist might ignore the jostling crowd and, consequently, would not notice the subtle, specific jostling of a pickpocket. On the other hand, a police of-

Table 14.1 **Outcomes precipitated by ambient stressors**

Level of analysis	Negative	Positive
Physiological	Decrements in neuroendocrine functioning	Increments in neuroendocrine functioning
Cognitive	Narrowing of attention	Creativity, heightened awareness
Affective	Motivational deficits	Sense of challenge, positive self-esteem
Behavioral	Negative aftereffects on performance	Enhanced performance following setbacks
Social	Derogation of victims, stigmatization	Strengthened social identity
Cultural	Cultural upheaval and disintegration	Cultural innovation

Source: "The Effects of Environmental Change on Individuals and Groups: Some Neglected Issues in Stress Research" by C. Aldwin and D. Stokols, 1988, *Journal of Environmental Psychology, 8,* pp. 57–75.

Overwhelmed by the sights and sounds of a busy sidewalk, a tourist might ignore the jostling crowd and, consequently, not notice the subtle, specific jostling of a pickpocket.
Irene Bayer/Monkmeyer Press

ficer might ignore people moving with the crowd and be more likely to notice the pickpocket's attempts to move into position next to the tourist.

Stress resulting from chronic aspects of the environment also produces **adaptation,** responses that allow organisms to adjust to their environments (Dubos, 1980). One such response is *perceptual adaptation,* a change in perception after continued exposure to an environment (Wohlwill, 1974). For someone who lives near a busy freeway, for example, the constant din of passing traffic becomes part of the background and is no longer consciously noticed. Similarly, most people become accustomed to even strong odors after a short time. As a result of such adaptation, ambient stressors may seem most intense to newcomers to a physical setting.

Through perceptual adaptation, each of us establishes a personal standard for evaluating environments, called an **adaptation level.** The urbanite who visits a suburb, for example, may find it uncomfortably quiet, but a visitor from a farm, accustomed to more peaceful surroundings, may experience the same suburb as noisy. Adaptation levels develop through continued exposure to an environment (Helson, 1964). In one study, for example, individuals residing in small, medium, and large cities rated the amount of crowding and congestion they perceived in a series of photographs. The photographs depicted scenes from communities of many different sizes. As is illustrated in Figure 14.1, residents of larger cities consistently rated the scenes as less crowded and congested than did residents of smaller cities, regardless of the size of the community in which the photograph was taken (Wohlwill & Kohn, 1973).

Our ability to adapt to potentially stressful environments also can produce aftereffects. That is, we may experience effects after the source of ambient stress is gone. One experiment showed that people working in the presence of loud, unpredictable, uncontrollable noise were able to adapt to the noise; they performed clerical tasks with unimpaired speed and accuracy. When they went to a different, quiet room to work, however, they identified fewer errors when proofreading a manuscript and showed less persistence on a frustrating task (Glass & Singer, 1972). Later research confirmed the adverse aftereffects of unpredictable, uncontrollable noise and found that other stressors had similar effects (S. Cohen, 1980a). However, Nagar, Pandey, and Paulus (1988) have reported that adaptation to one ambient stressor (crowding) does not affect individuals' ability to cope with a different stressor (noise).

Thus, ambient stress influences interpersonal behavior through a variety of mechanisms and with a variety of outcomes. To explore ambient stress more fully, we consider some specific sources of stress.

Temperature

Heat can create discomfort, arousal, or stress, depending on the ambient temperature, the relative humidity, and other factors (Sundstrom, 1986a). As a consequence of discomfort or mild arousal due to heat, peo-

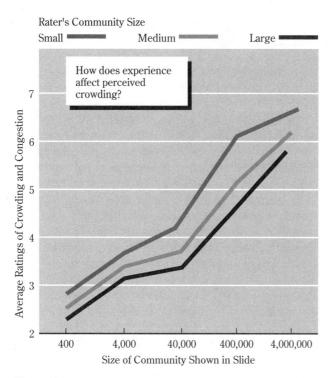

Rater's Community Size
Small ▬▬▬ Medium ▬▬▬ Large ▬▬▬

How does experience affect perceived crowding?

Figure 14.1 *Perceived crowding as a function of size of the target community and size of rater's community.*
Source: "The Environment as Experienced by the Migrant: An Adaptation-Level View" by H. Wohlwill and I. Kohn, 1973, *Representative Research in Social Psychology, 4,* pp. 135–164.

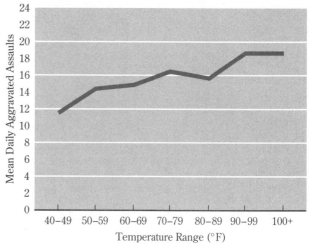

Figure 14.2 *The linear relationship between temperature and aggravated assaults in Dallas, Texas.*
Source: "Heat and Violence: New Findings from the Dallas Field Data, 1980–1981" by K. D. Harries and S. J. Stadler, 1988, *Journal of Applied Social Psychology, 18,* pp. 129–138.

ple may react with unusual violence to provocation or frustration (see the discussion in Chapter 10).

Research on violent crime corroborates the folk wisdom that links high temperatures with aggression. When geographers Keith Harries and Stephen Stadler (1983) reviewed research on the connection between weather and crime, they found that studies on the topic had been published as early as 1833. More recently, Harries and Stadler (1988) analyzed almost 10,000 cases of aggravated assault reported to the Dallas police from March 1980 through October 1981 in conjunction with weather reports from the Dallas–Fort Worth Airport. A daily index of "thermal discomfort" based on ambient temperature and humidity was significantly correlated with the frequency of aggravated assault in Dallas (see Figure 14.2). Assaults became more frequent as the temperature and humidity climbed. Similar trends for responses ranging from homicide to horn honking have been observed across a variety of cultures, locations, and time periods, leaving little doubt that high ambient temperatures are related to increased aggression (Anderson, 1989).

Harries and Stadler (1988) also observed that although wealthier neighborhoods exhibited the usual effect of more assaults on weekends, no relationship existed between the discomfort index and assaults in the wealthiest neighborhoods. The absence of a link between temperature and violent crime in wealthy neighborhoods, where air conditioning is more prevalent, is consistent with Berkowitz's (1983a, 1983b) cognitive-neoassociationistic model of aggression (discussed in Chapter 10). According to Berkowitz, high temperatures produce discomfort (negative affect), which is directly linked to aggression. At extremely high temperatures, however, discomfort is more likely to precipitate escape than aggression.

Paul Bell and Marc Fusco (1989), upon reanalyzing the data Harries and Stadler (1988) obtained, also noted that the variation among daily assault frequencies was related to temperature. Figure 14.3 again illustrates the mean number of assaults in Dallas as a function of temperature, but with the addition of the

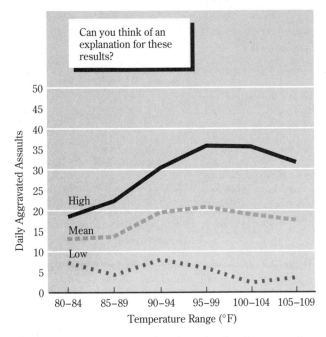

Figure 14.3 *The number of assaults on hot days is more variable than the number of assaults on cooler days.*

Source: "Heat and Violence: New Findings from the Dallas Field Data, 1980–1981" by K. D. Harries and S. J. Stadler, 1988, *Journal of Applied Social Psychology, 18,* pp. 129–138.

dition (Griffitt, 1970; Griffitt & Veitch, 1971). However, when participants believed the stranger was in the next room and had just either complimented or insulted them, liking for the other was based on the other's behavior instead of the ambient temperature (Bell & Baron, 1974, 1976).

Other research suggests a **shared stress effect:** people who share stressful environments feel attracted to one another. In one experiment on reactions to an actual person instead of a hypothetical stranger, researchers used loud noise as the stressor and exposed volunteers to stressful or comfortable conditions (Kenrick & Johnson, 1979). Half the participants in each condition indicated how much they liked an actual person in the same room; half responded to a dossier of an absent stranger. Consistent with the shared stress hypothesis, a real person was liked better by participants in the stressful environment than by participants in the comfortable environment. As in the earlier studies, participants liked the stranger they never met less in stressful conditions than in comfortable ones. (This study lasted less than an hour, so it does not indicate whether the shared stress effect occurs during longer exposures to stressful environments.)

Noise

As we have seen, **noise,** or unwanted sound, can influence interpersonal interactions through its capacity to create arousal, stress, or overload (Sundstrom, 1986a). Like other ambient stressors, noise is also subject to adaptation (Glass & Singer, 1972).

In a study conducted on the streets of Paris, Gabriel Moser (1988) demonstrated that noise can add to the effects of another ambient stressor, congestion. Congestion was defined in terms of traffic and pedestrian flow and the number of shops on the street. Moser compared responses of pedestrians to several situations under conditions of low congestion, high congestion, and high congestion plus noise from ongoing road construction. Some pedestrians were asked for directions to the nearest subway station, others were asked to complete a questionnaire, and some were not approached but were observed to determine whether they noticed or picked up a set of keys that a confederate walking ahead of them had dropped. As is illustrated in Figure 14.4, congestion (and the usual amount

minimum and maximum number of assaults recorded in a given temperature range. As you can see, the number of assaults committed varied more on hot days than on cooler days. The minimum recorded number of assaults does not change much, but the maximum increases with higher temperatures. Bell and Fusco (1989) interpreted this result to mean that "under some circumstances heat produces more aggression, and under others it yields more escape attempts" (p. 1480).

If high ambient temperatures can precipitate aggravated assault, it should come as little surprise that uncomfortable heat also influences more subtle forms of interpersonal relations. In two similar studies, groups of volunteers performed simple tasks for 45 minutes in either a comfortable or a "hot" environmental chamber (100°F with 60% relative humidity). Subjects read the dossier of a stranger, including a picture, a biographical sketch, and an attitude scale the stranger had supposedly completed. Participants liked the absent stranger less in the "hot" condition than in the comfortable con-

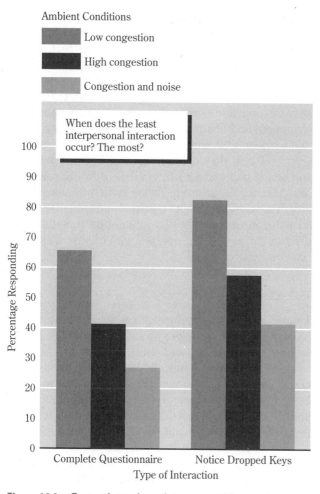

Low congestion

High congestion

Congestion and noise

When does the least interpersonal interaction occur? The most?

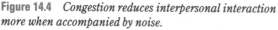

Figure 14.4 *Congestion reduces interpersonal interaction more when accompanied by noise.*

Source: "Urban Stress and Helping Behavior: Effects of Environmental Overload and Noise on Behavior" by G. Moser, 1988, *Journal of Environmental Psychology, 8,* pp. 287–298.

of noise associated with congestion) reduced pedestrians' responses to both explicit and implicit opportunities for prosocial behavior. The extra noise from the road construction further reduced both types of prosocial behavior.

In contrast, nearly all the pedestrians who were asked for directions provided them. The differences in Figure 14.4, therefore, are probably not due to a reduction in helpfulness. Instead, the more likely cause appears to be a reduction in cognitive capacity (Cohen,

1978). Pedestrians experiencing additional ambient stress were less likely to notice the keys, and perhaps were less likely to devote attention to the interviewer's questions. Several other studies concerning the effects of noise on helping lend credence to this cognitive-capacity explanation (Mathews & Canon, 1975; Page, 1977; Sherrod & Downs, 1974; Wiener, 1976; Yinon & Bizman, 1980).

Noise reduces attention to social cues, and its effects are not limited to cues concerning prosocial behavior. For example, Sheldon Cohen and Anne Lezak (1977) showed color slides to students as the students learned lists of nonsense syllables in either quiet or noisy conditions. The slides depicted people in everyday activities—a man paying for oil at a gas station—or in dangerous situations—a man trying to rob the same gas station. When unexpectedly quizzed about the slides, participants in the noisy conditions described fewer of the dangerous situations. In another experiment, researchers placed "novel objects," including a female research assistant holding a large yellow teddy bear, near a sidewalk. Pedestrians who had passed two such objects when traffic was either quiet or noisy were then interviewed. Fewer pedestrians noticed the novel objects in noisy conditions. Pedestrians also walked faster when the traffic was noisy (Korte & Grant, 1980).

Noise, like most ambient stressors, also increases the chances of aggression. In one study, volunteers saw a film depicting violent or nonviolent acts, then were given an opportunity to administer electric shocks to another person (an accomplice who did not actually receive the shocks). Some participants experienced noisy conditions during the latter part of the experiment, whereas others experienced quiet conditions. As you might expect, participants in the noisy conditions gave more shocks (Geen & O'Neal, 1969). Other studies found similar effects of noise (Geen, 1978; Konečni, 1975).

Does noise always produce negative reactions? Not necessarily. Donnerstein and Wilson (1976), for example, added control as an independent variable to the typical noise-aggression laboratory study and found that loud noise increased aggression only when subjects could not control the noise. Volunteers heard random bursts of noise that was either loud or soft; other subjects had access to a button they believed would stop the noise, so they had a sense of control. The subjects who had access to a control button did not evidence more aggression in the noisy conditions even though they never used the button to control the noise. More recently, Margaret Topf (1989) reported that individual differences in sensitivity to noise and commitment to one's occupation are also related to individuals' reactions to ambient noise. Topf studied nurses working in hospital critical-care units; nurses generally cannot control noise produced by heart monitors, respirators, and other hospital equipment. Despite the lack of control, nurses who were less sensitive to noise experienced less stress, as did nurses who reported a greater commitment to their work.

Illumination

Like noise, ambient light has also been associated with arousal levels. In one experiment, Sanders, Gustanski, and Lawton (1976) varied the lighting intensity outside classrooms and recorded the noise level of conversations as students gathered before and after classes. They discovered that conversational volume was directly correlated with illumination level. People apparently hushed their voices in low levels of illumination and spoke more loudly as lighting became brighter. Louder talk may reflect the effects of arousal by the bright light. Similarly, Gifford (1988) found that students writing letters to friends engaged in more self-disclosure under bright lighting than under dim lighting. Cunningham (1979) reported that the number of survey questions pedestrians were willing to answer was also positively correlated with the level of ambient sunlight.

One exception to the link between illumination and arousal occurs in situations involving sexual or romantic intimacy. Paul Biner and his colleagues (Biner, Butler, Fischer, & Westergren, 1989) asked males and females to rate the preferred level of illumination for various activities shared with a platonic friend, a romantic partner, and a group of friends present. Both men and women preferred significantly lower levels of lighting for activities shared with a romantic partner than with one friend or with a group of friends.

In a more extreme experiment, Ken Gergen and his colleagues (Gergen, Gergen, & Barton, 1973) placed some participants in a well-lit room and others in a completely dark room. The participants in the dark-room condition were told that each would leave separately and never see the others. All groups included both men and women; they were given no special instructions except that they would remain together in the room for an hour. Tape recordings and interviews revealed very different behavior when the room was dark than when it was illuminated. Those in the dark explored their environment and chatted at first. But conversation eventually faded as the students began to interact physically. Over 90% said they deliberately touched one another, and nearly half said they hugged. Most (80%) said they became sexually aroused. Those in the well-lit room, in contrast, stayed at a polite distance and talked sedately. As noted in Chapter 10, dim lighting precipitates deindividuation, in which people act with relative lack of inhibition (Zimbardo, 1970).

Pollution

Air pollution is an ambient stressor encountered in most of the world's major cities. In addition, few waterways are truly clean, and there may be as many as 100,000 toxic waste sites in the United States alone (Edelstein & Wandersman, 1987). Compared with the extensive medical research on pollution, however, our knowledge of the effects of pollution on interpersonal behavior is relatively scant (Evans & Jacobs, 1982).

Like other ambient stressors, pollution may influence social behavior through physiological effects or psychological stress. For example, air pollution in the form of cigarette smoke produced degraded performance on tests of cognitive abilities (Oborne, 1983). As we discussed earlier, such degradations may be manifested as decreased sensitivity to social cues. Air pollution also influences social activities through the tendency to discourage outdoor recreation (Chapko & Solomon, 1976) and, in the case of cigarette smoke, indoor activities (Bleda & Bleda, 1978). Similarly, air pollution appears to precipitate aggression to the same extent that high temperatures do (J. W. Jones & Bogat, 1978; Rotton & Frey, 1985).

In a study comparing women from two different cities in Germany, Monika Bullinger (1989) obtained evidence that adaptation may not alleviate the effects of air pollution on stress and mood. Although the two cities differed in amount of pollution, particularly sulphur dioxide, pollution levels in both cities were well below levels associated with health effects such as respiratory distress. Despite these relatively low levels of pollution, Bullinger found residents of the more polluted city reported significantly more stress and greater emotional impairment than residents of the less polluted city. Performance levels on various cognitive tasks also differed between residents of the two cities. In both cities, levels of sulphur dioxide were directly related to temporary experiences of stress and emotional impairment. All the subjects had resided in their respective cities for at least two years, indicating that adaptation to even low levels of pollution may not prevent stress and mood alterations. Laboratory studies also provide evidence of mood changes precipitated by ambient air pollution, including cigarette smoke (Zillman, Baron, & Tamborini, 1981).

The effects of a noxious odor on liking another person are similar to those of uncomfortable heat or noise. In a series of studies, James Rotton and his colleagues asked subjects, who were in a room that either had or did not have an extremely unpleasant odor, to rate how much they liked a stranger (Rotton, Barry, Frey, & Soler, 1978). In the first of two studies, participants believed the stranger was in the next room. Those exposed to the odor, presumably believing the stranger was experiencing the same odor, liked the stranger more (a shared stress effect). In the second study, the experimenter told each participant that he or she was "the only person being interviewed that evening" (p. 64) and would probably never meet the stranger. Participants exposed to the noxious odor in these circumstances liked the stranger less than those exposed to no odor, a result similar to those obtained with other ambient stressors.

Even less research has been conducted on psychological reactions to other types of pollution, with the exception of the discovery of toxic waste. In their review of the effects of discovering toxic waste dumps in communities, Michael Edelstein and Abraham Wandersman (1987) noted that identifying the boundaries of the pollution precipitates social identification processes (see Chapter 13). Those affected by the pollution begin to perceive themselves as a group and often experience the effects of being stigmatized by those who live out-

Air pollution is an ambient stressor encountered in most of the world's major cities.
David M. Grossman

side the polluted area. The media exposure that accompanies identification of a toxic waste site also triggers difficulties with privacy regulation for those living in the identified area.

▶ Privacy and Crowding

Privacy is the extent to which one perceives control over contact with or information about one's self or group (Altman, 1975, 1976). According to this definition, invasion of privacy can occur when we receive unwanted contact from other people (Altman & Chemers, 1980; Sundstrom, 1986b) or when others are able to obtain information about us that we prefer not to be revealed (Margulis, 1977; Westin, 1967). As a result of the Family Educational Rights and Privacy Act (1974), for example, instructors in the United States are no longer allowed to use students' names or social security numbers to identify publicly posted grades. Regulating privacy often involves manipulating the physical environment to limit accessibility. For example, students in dormitories can either leave their doors open to invite visitors or close them to retreat; people lock file cabinets and desk drawers to limit access to information.

"Hello, I'm taking a poll on how people feel about invasion of their privacy . . ."
Reprinted with special permission of North America Syndicate, Inc.

Privacy Regulation

Some theorists propose that privacy contributes to our personal autonomy (Beardsley, 1971). For example, access to self-relevant information can be used to exert control over an individual, as in the crime of blackmail. Erving Goffman's theory of self-presentation (1959) suggests that when we have an audience, we maintain appearances and try to manage the impressions of ourselves that others form (see Chapter 3). From this viewpoint, privacy allows us to relax and pay less attention to impression management. Kelvin (1973) theorized that privacy insulates us from unwanted audiences who might hold us accountable to standards of acceptable behavior. By exerting control over others' knowledge of our actions, privacy enables us to limit others' power over us.

According to Irwin Altman's (1975) theory of **privacy regulation**, privacy allows us to control our involvement in social interaction. Altman points out that our desire for social interaction changes from time to time, but we try to maintain an optimal level of social contact. Altman proposes we experience privacy as a continuum, the endpoints of which include total isolation and complete openness:

> [W]hat is too much, too little, or ideal shifts with time and circumstances, so what is optimum depends on where one is on the continuum of desired privacy. If I want to be alone, a colleague who comes into my office and talks for fifteen minutes is intruding and staying too long. If I want to interact with others, then the same fifteen minute conversation may be far too brief. [1975, p. 25]

According to this theory, whenever we want more or less interaction than we are experiencing, we regulate privacy in several ways. These ways include interpersonal distance, territorial markers (discussed later in this chapter), verbal and nonverbal behavior, and uses of the physical environment. For example, students in dormitories in which rooms were arranged around a lounge area took advantage of the design to regulate privacy. They invited social contact by studying in the lounges, where social encounters often occurred. When they wanted to limit accessibility, they retreated into their rooms and shut the doors (Baum & Valins, 1977).

What happens when we cannot regulate privacy? The general result is stress, which can be manifested in many ways. For example, Vinsel, Brown, Altman, and Voss (1980) examined the privacy regulation tactics of first-year students living in dormitories at the University of Utah. Students who left school within eighteen months for nonacademic reasons had failed to adopt the strategies of privacy regulation successful students used. These first-year students were asked whether they did such things as shut the door to their room, find a quiet place, arrange the room for privacy, or use the communal bathroom at a quiet time. Students who left used fewer means of regulating interaction than students who stayed in school, and those who dropped out found the techniques they did use to be less effective than those of students who remained in school.

One way to categorize social spaces is by the extent to which they allow individuals to regulate privacy (Zimring, 1982). *Public spaces*—such as sidewalks, plazas, and malls—have few barriers to public access and serve as thoroughfares. Privacy regulation is almost impossible in such areas. *Semipublic spaces*—such as stores, restaurants, and reception areas of hotels—have physical boundaries to differentiate them and regulate privacy, but users can easily gain access to them. *Semiprivate spaces*—such as social clubs, office buildings, and dormitories—have physical barriers to limit public access. Walls, fences, doors, or gates regulate privacy by restricting access to authorized people, although the number of authorized individuals is relatively large. *Private spaces*—such as bedrooms, private offices, and private bathrooms—provide access for a very small number of people, and access is usually controlled by a single individual. Architecture is used to create areas of varying accessibility that provide a range of settings to match the needs of individuals or groups for control over interaction. Secluded spaces allow solitary or intimate activities free from observation or interruption (Westin, 1967); accessible spaces permit many public activities (Jacobs, 1970). Problems arise especially where private spaces open directly into public spaces, as in dormitories in which rooms open into long corridors, or where few private spaces exist, as in open-plan offices.

Privacy in Open-Plan Offices

Open-plan offices evolved from the German concept of *Bürolandschaft,* or "office landscape," in which employees of all ranks work in large, open areas with few walls. Work spaces are separated mainly by office furniture, potted plants, and shoulder-high partitions. Advocates claimed that workers communicate best when they can easily see one another, especially if they are located near counterparts in the flow of work. They criticized conventional offices, arguing that walls impede communication, unnecessarily emphasize status, and erode motivation (Pile, 1978; Wineman, 1986).

Do open-plan offices facilitate communication? In one survey of 519 employees in 15 open offices, a majority said open offices aided "personal contacts" and made communication easier (Nemecek & Grandjean, 1973). On the other hand, two-thirds of the workers complained of disturbance in concentration; other complaints included noise, lack of privacy, and difficulty holding confidential conversations. In another study, employees at a corporate office completed a survey before and after moving into a new open-plan facility (Sundstrom, Herbert, & Brown, 1982). These employees, too, reported a decline in privacy. Managers, who need privacy for confidential conversations, were particularly sensitive to the loss of privacy, which was confirmed by acoustical measurements. Other studies also found open-plan offices deficient in privacy (Boyce, 1974; Hedge, 1982; Hundert & Greenfield, 1969).

Eric Sundstrom and his colleagues (Sundstrom, 1986a; Sundstrom, Burt, & Kamp, 1980; Sundstrom, Town, Brown, Forman, & McGee, 1982) have found that, in general, informal conversation may be easier in an open-plan office, but confidential conversation and feedback from supervisors may suffer. They also report a positive correlation between the number of sides of the work space—bounded by walls, partitions, or barriers at least 6 feet high—and perceived privacy.

Walled offices with doors were seen as most private; work spaces without barriers were perceived as least private. Privacy, in turn, is associated with job satisfaction (Ferguson & Weisman, 1986).

Open-plan offices also created problems at community colleges, where faculty had either private offices, two-person offices, or open-plan offices (Becker, Gield, Gaylin, & Sayer, 1983). Of the professors in open-plan offices, 84% expressed dissatisfaction with their privacy, compared with 11% in private offices. Complaints about open-plan offices included interruption, distraction, restrictions in topics that could be discussed, and an inability to praise or criticize students. More professors in open-plan than in other types of offices said they worked elsewhere. Students also felt less free to drop in at open-plan offices and said professors were less likely to be there when students did visit.

On the basis of research on social facilitation (see Chapter 12), Lisa Block and Garnett Stokes (1989) reasoned that performance in an open-plan office should depend upon the type of task in which a worker is engaged. The arousal resulting from officemates should facilitate performance on simple tasks but impair performance on complex tasks. To test their hypothesis, they asked students to complete either simple or complex tasks in one of two different rooms. The simple task involved using paper clips to attach different sections of tax forms together; the complex task involved actually completing tax forms. In the private room, students worked alone at a desk. The nonprivate room contained four desks, but each student in the nonprivate room had the same amount of work space as a student in the private room.

The results of the experiment, illustrated in Figure 14.5, confirmed the hypothesis. Students performed better on the simple task in the open-plan office, but those working on the complex task performed better in the private office. Interestingly, the type of office plan did not affect satisfaction with the work environment among students working on the simple task. Those working on the complex task, however, reported being much less satisfied with the open-plan office than with the private office. Thus, before predicting reactions to various types of office plans, one must consider both the type of task and the trade-off between worker satisfaction and performance.

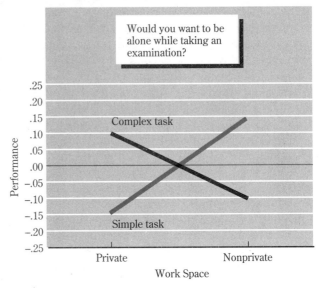

Figure 14.5 *Privacy facilitates performance on complex tasks but impairs performance on simple tasks.*
Source: "Performance and Satisfaction in Private versus Nonprivate Work Settings" by L. K. Block and G. S. Stokes, 1989, *Environment and Behavior, 21,* pp. 277–297.

Theories of Crowding

In some ways, the opposite of privacy is **crowding,** a form of stress resulting from excessive, unwanted social interaction that may accompany densely populated environments. You can experience crowding in an elevator jammed with passengers, on a downtown sidewalk at rush hour, near a bargain table at a department store, or in the theater lobby at a popular movie. As a form of stress, crowding is subjective; one person's reactions may differ from another person's reactions to the same environment. Thus, high **population density,** the amount of space per person, is not necessarily the same as crowding. Indeed, we often seek densely populated environments—cocktail parties, football games, concerts, and so on—for pleasure and stimulation. Nevertheless, high population density is one precursor to the experience of crowding, primarily because high population density may intensify emotional reactions (Freedman, 1975). The presence of a crowd may enhance an already positive experience, such as watching the home team in a championship, or it may

We often seek densely populated environments, such as soccer games, for pleasure and stimulation.
Topham/The Image Works

make an unpleasant experience (such as failure to regulate privacy) worse.

Early research and theory concerning crowding focused on the notion that high population density caused a variety of social pathologies. In one of the best-known studies, John Calhoun (1962) placed forty-eight Norway rats in a pen with four chambers, provided sufficient food and water, and allowed the population to reproduce without restriction. The colony increased to eighty animals, and the rats began to exhibit serious abnormalities in nest building, courting, mating, rearing of their young, and social organization. Some males became aggressive and disregarded the ritualized signals of submission that usually end a fight. Individuals maintained territories by force. Females often neglected their young, and up to 75% of the infant rats died. Autopsies revealed such signs of prolonged stress as enlarged adrenal glands. Other studies also found evidence of a link between population density and behavioral problems in deer (Christian, Flyger, & Davis, 1960) and humans (Galle, Gove, & McPherson, 1972; Winsborough, 1965).

To account for the negative effects of crowding, researchers have directed their attention to the same explanatory concepts used for other ambient stressors: arousal (Aiello, Epstein, & Karlin, 1975), cognitive overload (Baum & Paulus, 1987), perceived control (Rodin & Baum, 1978), and privacy regulation (Altman, 1975). Support for all these concepts has been obtained in a variety of research settings, but no one approach has emerged as the dominant explanation.

Gary Evans and his colleagues have argued that the importance of social support has not received sufficient attention in theories concerning crowding (Evans, Palsane, Lepore, & Martin, 1989). As we noted in Chapter 9, social support—assistance from friends and family, particularly with respect to problem solving—is one of the main mechanisms for coping with many stressors. Evans and his colleagues note, however, that social support is incompatible with the predominant response to crowding, social withdrawal. They propose that individuals' successful use of withdrawal when coping with crowding may cause them to overgeneralize withdrawal; that is, to use withdrawal for coping with stressors other than crowding (Cohen, Evans, Stokols, & Krantz, 1986; Evans, 1978; Evans & Cohen, 1987). Thus, the psychological problems associated with crowding may not result directly from crowding per se, but from the disruption of one's social support network that may accompany crowding.

To test their hypothesis, Evans and his colleagues interviewed 175 male heads of household in India. They obtained information about the number of people per room in the houses and about socioeconomic

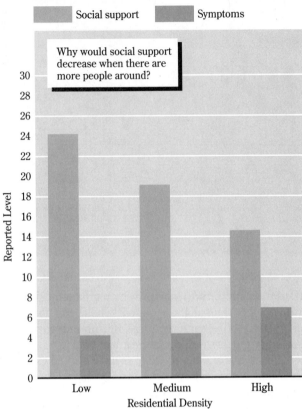

Measure

Social support   Symptoms

Figure 14.6 *As density increases and social support decreases, the number of psychological symptoms increases.*

Source: "Residential Density and Psychological Health: The Mediating Effects of Social Support" by G. W. Evans, M. N. Palsane, S. J. Lepore, and J. Martin, 1989, *Journal of Personality and Social Psychology, 57,* pp. 994–999.

status, as well as responses to a series of questions about perceived crowding, social support, and psychological symptoms. As is illustrated in Figure 14.6, social support decreased with rising density, and the number of reported psychological symptoms increased. After controlling for socioeconomic status, Evans and his colleagues found density was correlated with psychological symptoms. However, when the researchers also controlled for amount of social support, density was no longer related to symptomatology. The link between crowding and social withdrawal leads to the seemingly

paradoxical effect of reduced social support in the presence of a large number of people.

The link between crowding and social support may explain why student residents of two- to four-story dormitories reported having more friends in their dormitories than residents of a ten-story "megadorm" that housed 1,000 students (Holahan & Wilcox, 1978). Not surprisingly, megadorm residents also reported lower satisfaction with their living environments.

As Daniel Stokols (1976) has noted, people experience crowding most intensely in primary environments, such as residences or workplaces, where "an individual spends much time, relates to others on a personal basis, and engages in a wide range of personally important activities" (p. 73). To explore the link between crowding and behavioral problems more fully, we next consider the influence of residential design on the experience of crowding.

Crowding and Residential Design

As you might expect, residents of large apartment buildings are likely to experience crowding (McCarthy & Saegert, 1979), but size is not the only consideration in the experience of residential crowding. Consider, for example, the design aspects of two different college dormitories studied by Andrew Baum and Stuart Valins (1977). As shown in Figure 14.7, double-occupancy rooms in one dormitory were on either side of a long corridor. The thirty-four students who lived along the corridor shared the bathroom and the lounge. In the other dormitory, a suite of three double-occupancy rooms were situated around a central lounge and a bathroom; six students lived in each suite. In both dormitories, the bedrooms had about 150 square feet of floor space per person, and the buildings housed about the same numbers of students per floor.

Baum and Valins found that residents of corridor dormitories complained of more unwanted social contact and expressed a greater desire to avoid people than those in the suite dorms. Corridor residents also spent less time in the dormitories than suite residents. Suite residents, in contrast, did much of their studying in the dorms and carried on other nonsocial activities there. Suite residents were often seen in hallways and lounges, where most social encounters occurred; cor-

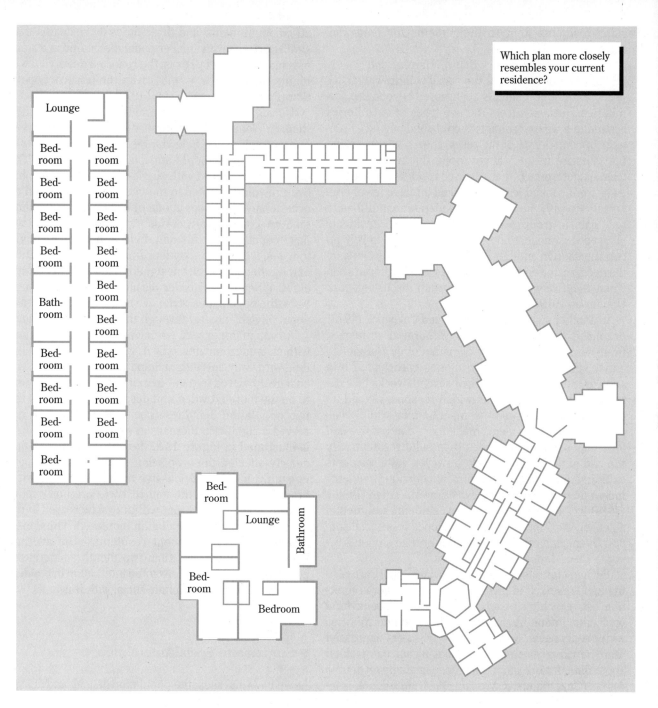

Figure 14.7 *The floor plans of corridor and suite dormitories.*
Source: Architecture and Social Behavior: Psychological Studies of Social Density by A. Baum and S. Valins, 1977, Hillsdale, NJ: Erlbaum.

ridor residents kept to their rooms for nonsocial activities.

In a laboratory study, Baum, Harpin, and Valins (1975) demonstrated that the social withdrawal tactics used by corridor residents generalized beyond the dormitories. Residents from the two types of dormitories arrived in a waiting room that contained one other student (a confederate of the researchers). By observing the behavior in the waiting room, Baum and his colleagues determined that corridor residents sat farther away from, looked less toward, and initiated fewer conversations with the waiting confederate than did suite residents. In group discussion tasks, corridor residents showed less inclination than suite residents to rely on consensus. (On another campus, corridor residents indicated greater comfort when they were ignored than when they were included in a group discussion task [Reichner, 1979].)

In another study, Baum, Aiello, and Calesnick (1978) examined the development of withdrawal strategies. First-year students who had been randomly assigned to either suite or corridor dormitories participated in a game during their first, third, or seventh weeks on campus. The game was one in which responses could include either cooperation, competition, or withdrawal. At first, corridor residents made more competitive and fewer cooperative responses than suite residents. By the end of the seventh week, however, suite residents exhibited primarily cooperation, but corridor residents increasingly resorted to withdrawal. Brian Lakey (1989) has also reported first-year students assigned to a denser, corridor dormitory developed less social support by the end of their first semester than students living in a less dense, suite dormitory.

Perhaps because sources of social support are also minimal, research in prisons shows a stronger connection between high population density and behavioral problems. Prison inmates housed in open dormitories with twenty-seven or more other prisoners expressed more negative reactions to the housing and complained about illness more often than those in single or double rooms (Cox, Paulus, & McCain, 1984). In Atlanta, complaints of illness increased as the number of prisoners per cell rose from one to six. In Texas, maximum-security prisons with large populations (an average of 1,700) had ten times more suicides, 78% more psychi-

atric commitments, and three times more deaths than similar prisons with smaller populations. And at a small psychiatric prison in Texas, the reported death rate was highly correlated ($r = +.81$) with the prison's population (Paulus, McCain, & Cox, 1978).

During an evaluation of a federal detention center, Richard Wener and Christopher Keys (1988) observed changes in inmates' behavior resulting from changes in sleeping arrangements and population density. The center was designed with single-occupancy rooms, but overcrowding resulted in the use of bunk beds and an occasional hallway cot in one of two units "resembling modern college dormitories" (p. 854). The average daily population in this unit, built to house forty-eight inmates, was about sixty-four inmates. The population of the other, identically designed unit was held at forty-eight. When a court order disallowed the use of bunk beds, the populations of the two units were equalized at about fifty-six inmates through the use of hallway cots.

As you might expect, perceived crowding in the unit with sixty-four inmates, unit A, was greater than in the unit with only forty-eight inmates, unit B. After the change, however, inmates in unit B perceived their unit to be the more crowded unit despite the equality of the two population densities. The researchers also observed a significant increase in sick calls in unit B. As is illustrated in Figure 14.8, the change in population density affected the proportion of time inmates spent engaging in isolated, passive activities. Social withdrawal decreased in the unit that was originally more densely populated (A), but withdrawal increased in the other unit (B) as its population increased. Thus, even among relatively transient residents—the average length of stay was less than two months—increased population density and unwanted interaction in residential structures can precipitate social withdrawal.

► Spaces and Social Interaction

As we have just seen, the population density and design of residences precipitate various behaviors among residents. In this section, we consider the appearance and layout of a room as they affect behavior through mood, comfort, or interpersonal distance. Specifically, we will

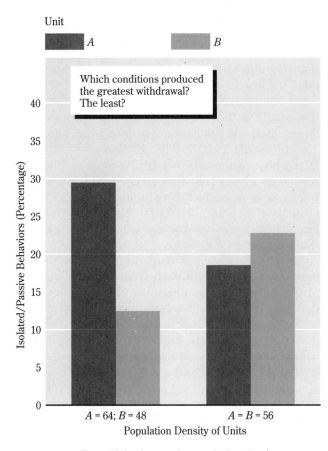

Unit
A   B

Which conditions produced the greatest withdrawal? The least?

Figure 14.8 *Even slight changes in population density can precipitate social withdrawal.*
Source: "The Effects of Changes in Jail Population Densities on Crowding, Sick Call, and Spatial Behavior" by R. E. Wener and C. Keys, 1988, *Journal of Applied Social Psychology, 18,* pp. 852–866.

examine pleasant settings for conversation, seating arrangements for dyads and small groups, psychological barriers between conversants, the layout of classrooms, and the link between proximity and attraction.

Pleasant Places

In one of the first tests of the hypothesis that pleasant settings lead to positive responses, Maslow and Mintz (1956) had volunteers provide ratings of "fatigue versus energy," "displeasure versus well-being," and other properties for ten negative-print photographs of faces. The study took place in one of three different rooms. The "average" room, a professor's office, appeared well kept but showed signs of the occupant's work. The "beautiful" room had carpeted floors, ample lighting, attractive furniture, and tasteful decorations. At the other extreme, the "ugly" room looked like an unkempt storeroom. It had gray walls, windows half covered with dirty shades, and lighting from an unshaded overhead bulb. Pails, mops, and brooms lined the walls, and the bare floor badly needed cleaning. Consistent with the hypothesis, subjects provided the most positive ratings in the "beautiful" room and the most negative ratings in the "ugly" room. One of the researchers unobtrusively observed the two experimenters, who were unaware of the hypothesis being tested, and reported that they finished their sessions more quickly in the "ugly" room (Mintz, 1956).

More recent research by Dennis Wilmot (1990), however, indicates the effects of a pleasant place may not be as simple as first hypothesized. According to Wilmot's data, room decor may affect moods only when one's attention is drawn to the decor. In two replications of the original experiment, Wilmot obtained a positive correlation between rated pleasantness of a room and evaluations of negative-print photographs only in rooms that were not typical settings for psychological research. For example, the "beautiful" room Maslow and Mintz used was uncommonly well decorated for a research laboratory and therefore was as atypical as the storeroom they used in the "ugly room" condition. In Wilmot's replications, the influence of decor on mood declined as subjects spent more time in the different rooms. Presumably the novelty of the decor, and therefore its influence, eventually faded.

In a study involving renovated classrooms, Wollin and Montagne (1981) obtained similar effects for attending to room decor. Initially, two identical forty-seat classrooms had gray walls, white chairs, and a sterile appearance. Then one was painted in attractive colors and decorated with posters, area rugs, plants, and other items. Each of two introductory psychology classes used one of the rooms for half a term, then switched. The students earned higher grades in the (novel) remodeled room, and the two teachers (who were unaware of the hypothesis) received higher ratings. In another study, D. E. Campbell (1979) had subjects examine color slides of professors' offices in which the appearance and decoration varied. When an office contained such items as a potted plant and aquarium, the students indicated they would feel more welcome and more comfortable in that office. Participants in yet another project listed either the positive or the negative features of their residences. Upon leaving the session, they encountered a confederate who asked for help in a project that involved doing arithmetic problems. Those who had focused on positive features of their residences helped more. A second experiment revealed a similar effect on altruism after participants viewed color slides of attractive or unattractive settings (Sherrod et al., 1977).

The effects of attending to settings are not limited to room decor. Robert A. Baron (1990) manipulated the presence or absence of pleasant odors by using commercially available air fresheners. Compared to subjects in rooms without air fresheners, subjects in scented rooms set higher goals for themselves, were more likely to use an efficient strategy on a coding task, were more likely to make concessions in a negotiation task, and reported being in a better mood. Consistent with the hypothesis that ambience effects require focused attention, Baron (1990) reported the level of pleasant odor "was immediately detectable upon entry into the experimental rooms" (pp. 373–374).

Rather than manipulate room decor, David Campbell and Toni Campbell (1988) noted design features in lounges used by faculty, staff, and students in various departments within a university. These features were then correlated with number of users, activity variation, and the amount of informal communication that occurred in the lounges. All three measures of lounge use were correlated with features such as proximity to primary traffic patterns within the building; the presence of vending machines, coffee makers, chairs, tables, and reading materials; and the ability of passersby to see into the lounge. The latter design characteristic emphasizes the influence of the presence of other people as a pleasant feature, a point also made by Robert Sommer and Barbara Sommer (1989). Sommer and Sommer found that groups, particularly groups joined by others, stayed longer in coffeehouses than did lone individuals. Not unexpectedly, groups also spent more of their time engaged in conversation than did individuals.

Seating Arrangements

Just as the appearance, occupants, and location of a room can affect interpersonal interactions, the arrangement of furniture within a room can precipitate certain types of interactions. You may recall from Chapter 5 that people in the United States and Canada seem to prefer interpersonal distances of $1\frac{1}{2}$ to 4 feet for everyday conversation (Hall, 1959, 1966). Robert Sommer (1959) has noted that people talking while seated at tables prefer adjacent chairs at the corners. The resulting 90-degree angle enables them to choose whether or not to make eye contact. Similarly, people prefer face-to-face over side-by-side arrangements for conversations (Sommer, 1962a, 1962b).

Such preferences make some seating arrangements more conducive to conversation than others. Osmond (1957) called these **sociopetal spaces** and suggested that such environments increase the chances of conversation. In places where people typically seek conversation, such as in cafeterias and cocktail lounges, groups of chairs are usually arranged around small tables or in circles. In contrast, **sociofugal spaces** discourage conversation among people by making eye contact difficult (Osmond, 1957). Waiting areas usually force side-by-side seating. Chairs facing each other are typically too far apart for comfortable conversation. Other sociofugal spaces include bus depots, some classrooms, and reception areas in clinics, personnel offices, and hospitals. These arrangements may represent deliberate attempts to deter unwanted conversation among strangers and to allow occupants to go about their business without feeling compelled to talk to neighbors.

Sommer and Ross (1958) demonstrated the difference between sociofugal and sociopetal spaces in a study conducted in a new geriatrics ward for women at a Saskatchewan hospital. The cheerfully decorated, newly furnished wardroom was the showplace of the hospital, but the chairs were lined up along the walls, side by side, all facing the center of the large room. In that sociofugal space, the patients seemed depressed and sat in their new chairs staring morosely into space. The staff then rearranged the chairs into circles around small tables. The patients protested at first, but after a few weeks the frequency of their conversations had nearly doubled. In more formal experiments, Mehrabian and Diamond (1971a, 1971b) demonstrated that seating arrangements that allowed more convenient eye contact precipitated more informal conversation while students waited for the experiment to begin.

The ability to make eye contact as a characteristic of sociopetal space is also evident in small groups. Steinzor (1950), for example, recorded the initiator of each comment and the next person to speak among groups of ten people seated around a circular table. Responses usually came from across the table and tended to involve people who could easily make eye contact. Seldom were responses made by people one or two seats away from the speaker. Other studies obtained similar results in a natural setting (Silverstein & Stang, 1976) and in the laboratory (Baker, 1984; Howells & Becker, 1962; Ward, 1968).

Sociopetal arrangements also influence participation in larger group settings, such as a classroom. For example, Sommer and Olsen (1980), found that an arrangement in which student seats were curved so that all students directly faced the center-front part of the room resulted in 79% of the students participating in class discussions, compared with a 37% participation rate obtained with the traditional straight-row arrangement found in most classrooms.

Ease of eye contact may also affect participation rates in traditionally arranged classrooms. As shown in Figure 14.9, Sommer (1967) observed higher participation among students seated near the front-center area of the classroom than among those seated in the rear corners. Daniel Montello's (1988) review of research concerning the effects of seating arrangements in classrooms identified substantial empirical support for the participation pattern depicted in Figure 14.9. However, despite some studies indicating similar effects upon course grades (for example, Sommer, 1974), Montello's review of the research indicates there is no consistent effect of seating arrangement on course achievement as measured by examinations. Given the variety of variables that can affect course grades—motivation, preparation, intellectual ability, and so on—it is not surprising that seating per se has little effect on overall measures of performance.

Seating arrangements can influence the roles adopted by individuals within a group. Mock jurors, for example, typically chose as foreperson one of the two people occupying the end chairs at a rectangular table (Strodtbeck & Hook, 1961). At the end of the delibera-

Classroom seating arrangements have a major impact on participation in class discussions.
D. Mahon/Monkmeyer Press

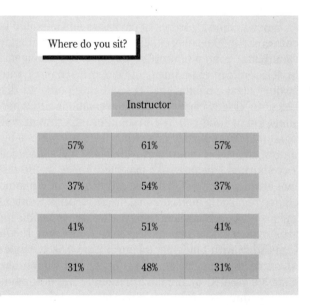

Where do you sit?		
	Instructor	
57%	61%	57%
37%	54%	37%
41%	51%	41%
31%	48%	31%

Figure 14.9 *Participation rates as a function of seating position in a typical classroom.*
Source: "Classroom Ecology" by R. Sommer, 1967, *Journal of Applied Behavioral Science, 3,* pp. 489–503.

tion, those seated at the ends of the table received higher ratings of influence in the group and participated more than other members of the mock jury. In other studies, observers attributed greater influence to the occupants of seats at the end of a table (Pelligrini, 1971), and occupants of end seats at rectangular tables received most nominations as leader (Altemeyer & Jones, 1974) and highest ratings on leadership (Bass & Klubeck, 1952). However, when group members are seated at a circular table, the differences between leaders and other group members decrease considerably (Lécuyer, 1976).

Like most roles, leadership results from the confluence of person and environment variables (see Chapter 12). Therefore, group members who aspire to leadership roles are also more likely to choose seats consistent with their aspirations (Heckel, 1973). Similarly, people who choose visible positions score relatively high in personality traits such as dominance (Hare & Bales, 1963) and internal locus of control (Hiers & Heckel, 1977). Those who do not want a leadership role are likely to avoid locations such as the head of the table. For example, Lécuyer (1976) also reported that groups for whom a leader had been designated typically reserved the end or corner seat for the leader.

When people try to talk in environments unsuited to conversation, they may experience discomfort and may even blame each other for the discomfort. Participants in a laboratory experiment indicated discomfort with seating arrangements that created interpersonal distances of 12 feet, especially for conversations about personal topics (Scott, 1984). In another experiment, volunteers held conversations either from uncomfortably distant chairs—11 feet apart—or from chairs placed at a comfortable distance. As expected, those in the distant arrangement felt ill at ease. Although they had no choice regarding interpersonal distance, participants in the distant condition held their partners responsible for their own negative feelings (Aiello & Thompson, 1980). Consistent with fundamental attribution bias (Chapter 4), subjects in the sociofugal settings misattributed the distance created by the environment to the occupants and presumably interpreted the distance as aloofness.

Even at short physical distances, a table or desk can create psychological distance. For example, subjects who viewed color slides of offices said they would feel less comfortable and less welcome in an office in which the desk was between the occupant and the visitor than in open arrangements and rated the occupant as less friendly (Campbell, 1979; Morrow & McElroy, 1981). Similarly, students rated professors who used a desk-between arrangement in their offices as less available and less attentive than professors whose offices had open arrangements (Zweigenhaft, 1976). The professors with the desk-between arrangement were also older and had higher rank; their offices apparently mirrored social distance.

Sometimes visitors may prefer the greater psychological distance of a desk-between arrangement. One physician, for example, reported patients were more likely to feel "ill at ease" on the same side of the desk than with the desk between them and the physician (Coleman, 1968). Similarly, anxious interviewees in another study rated the interviewer as more friendly when they were separated by a desk; the less anxious ones saw the interviewer as more pleasant and agreeable with no desk in between (Widgery & Stackpole, 1972).

Proximity and Attraction

Beyond the appearance and arrangement of rooms, the physical environment may affect social behavior through the layout and design of buildings and the resulting accessibility of residences and workplaces. As we discussed in Chapter 9, physical proximity, or **propinquity,** is often related to interpersonal attraction. Consider the results of a field study Leon Festinger, Stanley Schachter, and Kurt Back (1950) conducted concerning friendships in a housing complex for married students. The complex consisted of two-story buildings containing five similar apartments on each floor, with all doors facing the same direction. Couples on the waiting list received apartments as vacancies arose, so they had no choice in their location. When couples were asked to name the three people with whom they socialized most, they generally named residents of the same floor in the same building. They named 41% of all the next-door neighbors they could have mentioned, but only 22% of the possible choices two doors away. Couples on the second floor often named couples who lived near the stairs on the first floor. In general, friends were people whom residents encountered most often.

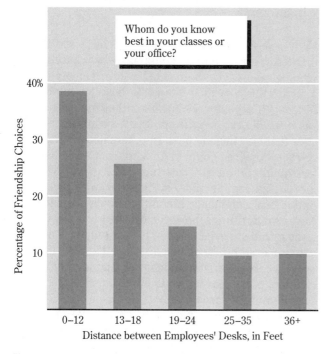

Figure 14.10 *Friendships in an office building decrease as the distance between desks increases.*
Source: "The Psycho-Social Influence of Building Environments: Sociometric Findings in Large and Small Office Spaces" by B. W. P. Wells, 1965, *Building Science, 1,* pp. 153–165.

Proximity is correlated with interaction and friendship in other settings as well. Wells (1965), for example, assessed friendships among 297 office employees who worked on the same floor of a high-rise office building. The results, illustrated in Figure 14.10, clearly indicate that friends were much more likely to occupy desks closer to each other. Among residents of suburbs, gatherings and friendships typically involve neighbors from the same block (Gans, 1967; Whyte, 1956). Residents of apartment buildings generally have acquaintances or friends in nearby apartments (Bochner, Duncan, Kennedy, & Orr, 1976; Ebbesen, Kjos, & Konečni, 1976; Nahemow & Lawton, 1975). Office workers tend to choose conversation partners and friends from among co-workers at nearby work stations (Conrath, 1973; Gullahorn, 1952; Homans, 1954), and students usually select friends from neighboring seats in classrooms (Byrne, 1961; Segal, 1974). Similarly,

Schiavo (1988) reported that adolescents attending the only high school in their community were more likely to have friends who lived outside their neighborhood than were children who attended neighborhood-based elementary schools.

People new to their environments seem especially likely to select friends on the basis of proximity. Newcomers can easily become acquainted with their neighbors and may initially choose them for friends. Students who moved into a dormitory, for example, formed friendships on the basis of proximity during the first few weeks but later sought friends with similar attitudes (Newcomb, 1961). In populations similar in age, education, socioeconomic background, or other characteristics, neighbors may be compatible enough for sustained friendship. In heterogeneous populations people may have to go farther to find others with similar outlooks. For example, friendships in an established neighborhood in Ann Arbor became more frequent with increasing proximity of residences but also involved people with similar backgrounds and preferences (Athanasiou & Yoshioka, 1973). Most of the residents of three high-rise buildings had friends in the same building, usually of similar age and race (Nahemow & Lawton, 1975). However, proximity also creates the possibility of conflict. When residents of an apartment complex in California named the couples they liked least and most, it was found that those they liked least lived even closer than those they liked most (Ebbesen et al., 1976). Similarly, Chin (1988) reported married students' overall satisfaction with their housing was negatively correlated with the extent to which they encountered other residents at the entrances to their homes.

The relationship between proximity and interaction is itself affected by architecture. For instance, houses in courts or cul-de-sacs face toward one another, and residents come and go via the same pathways, so the residents have many opportunities to become acquainted. Married students who lived in U-shaped courts tended to choose friends in their own courts; they rarely had friends in adjacent courts whose houses faced the opposite direction (Festinger et al., 1950). In two other studies, residents of cul-de-sacs knew a greater proportion of their neighbors than residents of through streets (Brown & Werner, 1985; Mayo, 1979). Indoor cul-de-sacs seem to operate the same way. Clerical workers in open-plan offices worked either in a large area with 200 co-workers or in smaller, walled areas containing about 30 workers. Two-thirds of friendship choices in smaller areas were reciprocated, compared with 38% in the large area (Wells, 1965). Occupants of U.S. Air Force barracks in which partitions divided the bunks into clusters of six spent more of their time talking with a smaller number of people than did occupants in otherwise identical buildings that did not have partitions (Blake, Rhead, Wedge, & Mouton, 1956).

Sommer and Steiner (1988) report that the basis upon which offices are assigned also affects the relationship between proximity and friendship. In a study of legislators in the California Capitol, wherein office locations are based on committee assignments and other indicators of status, office proximity was not related to friendships. Here, too, however, we find evidence that frequency of contact is the basis for the effects of propinquity. As one legislator commented, "They could put my arch-enemy next door . . . but we'd have no reason to come into contact" (Sommer & Steiner, 1988, p. 568).

▶ Attachment to Places

The confluence of the individual and the environment may be best exemplified by **place-identity,** environment-related cognitions that are incorporated into the self-concept (Proshansky, 1978; Proshansky, et al., 1983). That is, *where* we choose to behave has as much to do with how we present ourselves to others as does the behavior in which we choose to engage (Kenrick, McCreath, Govern, King, & Bordin, 1990). As Proshansky, Fabian, and Kaminoff (1983) put it: "the subjective sense of self is defined and expressed not simply by one's relationship to other people, but also by one's relationships to the various physical settings that define and structure day-to-day life" (p. 58). Place-identity, like other components of the self, has functions that range from serving as a reference for new experiences through coping with threats to the self (see Chapter 3). In this section we explore the concept of place-identity and its relationship to social behavior. We begin with territories in general and then discuss the specific places of home, workplace, and neighborhood.

Territories

Early research on **territory**—a specific place that is marked or identified with some sign—was based on an ethological model of human behavior. To an ethologist, a territory is a nesting site and a base for hunting or foraging (Carpenter, 1958). If another member of the same species crosses the boundary, a confrontation ensues that may include posturing, threatening gestures, or even ritualized combat. An ethologist who observed free-ranging domestic cats noted that when two cats met outside their territories, the animal with lower rank in the local dominance hierarchy usually retreated. In their own territories, however, cats nearly always drove away intruders, even those of higher rank in the dominance hierarchy (Leyhausen, 1965). However, not all species exhibit territorial behavior, and territorial species vary greatly in their instinctive patterns of behavior (see Wynne-Edwards, 1962).

Are humans territorial? In the strict sense of instinctive responses to encroachment, the answer is no. Humans are, for example, the only species to entertain guests (Edney, 1974). We do, of course, claim places, and the behavior of involuntarily housed individuals often resembles territoriality and dominance hierarchies (Altman, Taylor, & Wheeler, 1971). In several groups confined to institutions, the ways the members used the environment reflected the dominance hierarchy of the group. For example, in prisons, reform schools, and psychiatric wards, high-ranking or otherwise dominant residents tend to have greater freedom of movement and more desirable spaces and furniture. Episodes of aggression often accompany disruptions of such hierarchies (Austin & Bates, 1974; Esser, Chamberlain, Chapple, & Kline, 1964; Sundstrom & Altman, 1974).

However, the mechanisms that govern the use of space among humans are more complex than the instinctive reactions of nonhuman species. According to place-identity theory, the apparent territorial behavior of humans results from the inclusion of places and things in the self-concept (Belk, 1991). As extensions of the self, places are therefore subject to the same cognitive processes as those discussed in Chapter 3, including attempts to alter both our own and others' behavior to increase consistency between our self-concept and the current situation.

Even in public areas, we often may engage in some sort of "marking" behavior to let others know about these temporary extensions of our place identity. As we move about, we seem to prefer a polite distance between ourselves and others. Sommer (1966), for example, noted that students who entered libraries alone usually sat at tables by themselves (64%). Those who did sit at tables occupied by other students usually took the most distant chair. Similarly, library users stay longest at tables where nobody else sits (Becker, 1973). In a study in a game arcade, newcomers claimed machines by touching or manipulating them. When others seemed to be waiting to use a machine, the current user reacted with prolonged touching of the machine (Werner, Brown, & Damron, 1981).

Identification with a public place, however, does not occur spontaneously. When a confederate approached people who had been seated for varying lengths of time in a campus snack bar and said, "Excuse me, but you are sitting in my seat," those who had been seated for only a few minutes tended to leave apologetically. On the other hand, those who had been there longer resisted displacement (Sommer, 1969). The more time one invests in a particular place, the stronger one's identification with that place (Becker & Mayo, 1971). On a beach, for example, the longer a party of people had been there, the larger the area they viewed as "theirs" (Edney & Jordan-Edney, 1974). Similarly, the likelihood of defending a particular public place depends on its importance to our self-concept. Haber (1980) conducted a study during a break in a lengthy class in which a confederate took a seat that another student had occupied. Only 27% of the students confronted the confederate and asked for their seats back. However, students who had been sitting in the center of the room were more likely to confront the confederate, perhaps because more active students "express themselves" by sitting in the center of the room (Koneya, 1976).

That we can recognize public spaces as an extension of another's self was very clearly demonstrated in a study by Sommer and Becker (1969). In a crowded study hall, the researchers observed how much time elapsed before someone sat in either a marked chair or a randomly chosen unmarked chair. As is illustrated in Figure 14.11, unmarked chairs and those at which periodicals were scattered on the table were clearly "fair

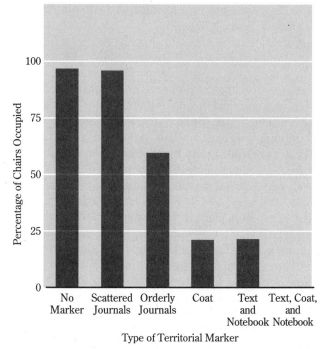

Figure 14.11   *The more personal the items used to mark a public place, the less likely others were to use the space.*
Source: "Territorial Defense and the Good Neighbor" by R. Sommer and F. D. Becker, 1969, *Journal of Personality and Social Psychology, 11,* pp. 85–92.

game." On average, an unmarked chair became occupied within twenty minutes. The more personalized the markers were, the less likely someone was to occupy the vacant chair. The combination of a sport coat, notebook, and textbook, for example, reserved a chair for the whole evening. In another study that took place in a bar where all tables were occupied and people were waiting, a jacket with a briefcase or book bag deterred users from taking a temporarily vacant table. Such personal possessions deterred would-be users at peripheral tables more than at tables with "high interaction potential" and were more effective if they appeared to belong to a man than if they appeared to belong to a woman (Shaffer & Sadowski, 1975; see also Becker & Conglio, 1975). Even empty space may be recognized as another's if it exists between individuals. People usually hesitate to walk through such spaces, and those who do show signs of discomfort and submissiveness (Lyman & Scott, 1967).

Homes

Perhaps more than any other place, homes express our identities and relationships with the larger community. The location, size, design, and other features of the buildings in which we live symbolize social status (Duncan, 1986), group membership (Altman & Gauvain, 1981), and self-identity (Dovey, 1986). Homes embody our connections with past and future (Werner, Altman, & Oxley, 1986). For example, Susan Saegert (1989) reported place-identity was one of the characteristics typical of tenants who were successful at managing their buildings after landlords had abandoned the buildings to avoid paying taxes in the Harlem area of New York City. One tenant who began looking for a house on Long Island because her apartment had no heat eventually decided to stay: "So I said to myself, why am I coming all the way here [Long Island]? I don't know anybody in the neighborhood. I don't drive. I'll be completely isolated. So I said no" (Saegert, 1989, p. 306).

Attempts to more clearly indicate the boundaries of one's residence are also related to attachment. Edney (1972) compared residents of houses surrounded by fences, hedges, retaining walls, and other borders with those whose property boundaries were less clearly defined. Edney found that residents whose boundaries were more clearly marked had lived there longer, intended to stay longer, and answered their doorbells faster. Other research indicates such differences probably result from cohesiveness with other residents as opposed to an overriding concern with security. For example, decorations on houses and in yards are correlated with social ties to the neighborhood (Greenbaum & Greenbaum, 1981). Barbara Brown and Carol Werner (1985) reported that greater affiliation and contact among residents also were correlated with holiday decorations, such as those used for Halloween and Christmas. Equally important, when photographs of homes with Christmas decorations were compared with those without decorations, residents of decorated homes were perceived to be more open and sociable (Werner, Peterson-Lewis, & Brown, 1989).

The impact of attachment to home upon other social behavior is not limited to permanent residences. Hansen and Altman (1976) examined **personalization**— use of the physical environment to express self-identity—among residents of dormitories at a large university. They counted such things as posters, rugs, stereos, and other personal objects and found that dropouts had displayed fewer personal items than students who remained on campus. Another study in the same dormitories found dropouts' rooms contained more objects referring to other localities, such as former residences (Vinsel et al., 1980). That is, identifying with another place, as opposed to expressing one's identity within the current residence, reduced the likelihood of remaining in the current residence.

Perhaps one reason that incorporating one's current residence into one's place-identity increases the likelihood of remaining in that residence is that individuals are more effective and influential under such circumstances. Martindale (1971) conducted an experiment in which pairs of students debated in one student's room about the appropriate jail sentence for a fictional criminal. One argued for the prosecution, the other for the defense. Whether they prosecuted or defended, students in their own rooms argued more persuasively and spent more time talking than their visitors. Similarly, students working on problem-solving tasks in groups of three were more influential when working in their own room than in one of the other students' rooms regardless of their relative score on a measure of dominance (Taylor & Lanni, 1982).

In Chapter 9 we discussed the relationship between interpersonal attraction and interpersonal intimacy; we share more detail about ourselves with people we like. The same relationship also applies to sharing our place-identity. Within a home, for example, rooms such as bedrooms and studies are recognized as the "private property" of those who occupy them (Sebba & Churchman, 1983). Some families exhibit this effect with respect to visitors; they receive acquaintances in the living room and allow friends in the dining room but invite only close friends and relatives into the kitchen (Fisher, Bell, & Baum, 1984). The use of common rooms such as the kitchen and living room also reflects some of the gender-role stereotypes discussed throughout other chapters. For example, Ahrentzen, Levine, and Michel-

Homeworkers usually set aside a distinct space as the work area.
Bob Clay/Clay Images

son (1989) reported men are more likely to use such rooms for individual pursuits, whereas women are more likely to be engaged in communal activities in these rooms.

Workplaces

Offices and factories do not always have places for workers to call their own. In some factories, for example, employees go to different work stations each day; their only place to personalize space at work is a locker. But in some offices people have as much control over their workplace as they do over their home (Sundstrom, 1986a, 1987). Evidence of place-identity can usually be found at **work spaces,** individually assigned work stations. Higher satisfaction with the work environment is associated with personalization of the work space—display of photographs, posters, rugs, and other personal belongings (Brill, 1984).

Personalization can serve as a **status marker,** or a physical feature of a work space that signals the occupant's standing or formal rank in the organization (Konar & Sundstrom, 1986). The offices of corporate executives often reflect their status; a promotion brings a larger office with more and better furniture. In general, bigger and better offices and greater freedom to personalize offices are more prevalent among people with supervisory responsibility (Konar, Sundstrom,

Brady, Mandel, & Rice, 1982). Paul Cherulnik and Richard Koenig (1989) have also shown that perceptions of the occupant of a work space are correlated with the quality of the work space. Not surprisingly, then, managerial employees consider the physical environment in their work space, an indicator of status, to be more important than the social environment (Zalesny & Farace, 1988). On the other hand, clerical employees consider social environment more important, perhaps because variation in status is not as great within clerical ranks.

Technological advances have made it possible for millions of individuals, called **homeworkers,** to engage in paid work at home. Although research on work spaces in homes has yet to reach the amount devoted to traditional work spaces, some tentative conclusions can be drawn. One of these is that most homeworkers use space *within* the home. That is, homeworkers usually set aside a distinct space as the work area, although such separation does not translate into exclusive use of the space (Ahrentzen, 1988). Like work spaces outside homes, those within homes reflect place-identity; one homeworker noted separate space was necessary "just to have a sense of myself" (Gottlieb, 1988, p. 151). Gottlieb also discovered in her interviews that the extent to which domestic duties reflected gender-role stereotypes did not change when either the father or mother in a nuclear family began working in the home. More recently, Sherry Ahrentzen (1990) reported that although overlap between domestic and work roles did occur, homeworkers rarely experience conflict between these roles. Basing her conclusions on an extensive survey of homeworkers, Ahrentzen stated that multiple roles in a single space precipitate no more, and perhaps less, conflict than multiple roles in multiple spaces. Ahrentzen's respondents considered many of the changes they made to cope with the overlap in domestic and work roles to be positive ones.

Neighborhoods

As social animals, humans live and behave in communities. There are, of course, many different kinds of communities, ranging from entire towns or cities to collections of a few homes in a suburban development. Similarly, the defining features of a community may differ among its residents. What **neighborhoods** have in common, however, are perceived boundaries and personal meaning to those who reside in them (Rivlin, 1987).

Place-identity with respect to neighborhoods has considerable impact on social behavior. For example, Roberta Feldman (1990) has demonstrated that personal identification with a specific type of neighborhood is strongly related to evaluations of one's current neighborhood. Feldman categorized her survey respondents on the basis of their self-descriptions as a downtown, city neighborhood, suburban, small-town, or country/mountain person. As is shown in Figure 14.12, individuals whose current neighborhood matched their self-descriptions rated their current neighborhood more positively on a wide variety of dimensions than did people whose current neighborhood did not match their self-description. Neighborhood attachment, as opposed to economic necessity, appears to be the primary reason why people in New York City used community gardens to grow flowers and vegetables (Clark & Manzo, 1988).

Feldman (1990) also found that those whose current neighborhoods did not match their self-descriptions were more likely to indicate plans to move in the near future. In the same vein, Norris-Baker and Scheidt (1990) have reported that even in a small town in Kan-

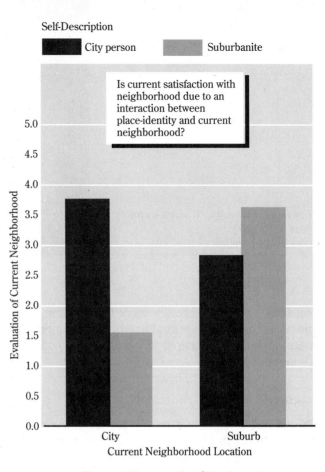

Figure 14.12 *The match between place-identity and current neighborhood is related to evaluations of the current neighborhood.*
Source: "Settlement-Identity: Psychological Bonds with Home Places in a Mobile Society" by R. M. Feldman, 1990, *Environment and Behavior, 22,* pp. 183–229.

sas that was about to become a "ghost town" as a result of economic hardship, place-identity was the primary reason residents were willing to remain in the neighborhood. The researchers noted that preventing the disappearance of such small towns will be one of the major economic and social challenges of the 1990s, as will providing neighborhoods for millions of homeless people (Rivlin, 1987).

Another challenge for the 1990s is crime reduction. Unfortunately, it appears that one of the drawbacks of place-identity at the neighborhood level may be increased fear of crime, and perhaps actual increases in crime. Cohesion among neighbors often results from perceived similarity, but Janice Bastlin Normoyle and Jeanne Foley (1988) have demonstrated that similarity may be related to increased fear of crime. Their survey of elderly residents in public housing indicated that in high-rise buildings, greater fear of crime was reported by residents whose buildings were segregated by age than by residents in unsegregated buildings. Because this relationship was unaffected by actual crime rates or victimization experiences, Bastlin Normoyle and Foley explained their results by suggesting that "crime-related judgments of older high-rise tenants become exaggerated or distorted as a consequence of being housed apart from younger families" (p. 66).

Similarly, Macdonald and Gifford (1989) obtained evidence that the well-kept appearance of houses normally associated with higher levels of neighborhood attachment may make homes more susceptible to burglaries. In their study, Macdonald and Gifford showed photographs of various types of houses to convicted burglars, who rated each house on a scale of vulnerability. As expected, houses with higher levels of visibility from the road were rated as less vulnerable, a result consistent with defensible space theory (Newman, 1972). However, better-kept houses and houses with barriers such as fences and shrubbery were rated as more vulnerable, a result inconsistent with defensible space theory. The explanations burglars gave for the vulnerability ratings indicated that they were likely to perceive better-kept houses as containing more valuable contents. Also, the burglars did not consider barriers such as fences or shrubs to be obstacles to entry. On the contrary, the burglars explained that, once crossed, such barriers worked to their advantage by reducing public visibility. The burglars' perceptions of "easy targets" seem to contradict the beliefs of many homeowners (Brower, Dockett, & Taylor, 1983; Patterson, 1978; Pollock & Patterson, 1980). In addition to visibility, the only single characteristic that resulted in lower ratings of vulnerability was a solid front door without glass.

▶ Summary

Climate, geography, and architecture are an integral part of the environment of social behavior. The transactionalist viewpoint includes the assumption that the individual, the social environment, and the physical environment all exist and influence one another simultaneously at any given time and place.

One's environment may contain any number of ambient stressors—including temperature, air quality, sound, and light—that precipitate higher levels of arousal. Increased levels of arousal can produce narrowed attention and cognitive overload, both of which can inhibit or facilitate behavior, depending upon other conditions. Some degree of adaptation usually occurs with continued exposure to ambient stressors, but aftereffects are also likely.

Uncomfortably warm temperatures are associated with increased rates of violent crime and other expressions of hostility. Loud, uncontrollable noise decreases altruism and attention to some social cues and increases responsiveness to provocation. Low levels of light are generally associated with decreased sociability, except in situations with romantic potential. Like other ambient stressors, air pollution tends to be associated with negative moods. Toxic waste in one's neighborhood is also associated with experiences of stigma.

The physical environment provides a resource for regulating and organizing interpersonal interaction and for obtaining privacy. Privacy contributes to autonomy and control over self-presentation through regulating involvement with other people. Inability to regulate privacy is often experienced as stress.

Privacy in offices is associated with physical enclosure of work spaces. Workers in open-plan offices have reported dissatisfaction with the lack of privacy. Effects of open-plan offices on performance, however, depend on the type of task being performed. Performance of simple tasks appears to be enhanced in open-plan settings, but performance of complex tasks suffers.

Crowding, a form of stress resulting from unwanted social interaction, can occur in conditions of high population density. One means of coping with the stress of crowding—withdrawal from social situations—may be the primary reason for the psychological problems associated with crowding. People who retreat from their social network are less likely to receive support when they try to cope with stress. For example, occupants of corridor-design dormitories who report unwanted interaction also demonstrate social withdrawal. In prison settings, where social support is minimal, crowding has been associated with illness, psychiatric commitments, and even death rates.

Architectural features designed to create pleasing environments appear to be effective only when one's attention is focused on the pleasing features. The presence of other people may also contribute to the perceived pleasantness of space.

Sociopetal spaces encourage conversation through seating arrangements that bring people into comfortable conversational distance and allow them to face each other directly enough to maintain eye contact. Sociofugal spaces, in contrast, decrease conversation by making eye contact difficult. For example, participation in classrooms is greatest in the front and center seats, where eye contact between student and instructor is most likely. However, seating arrangement in classrooms has little influence on performance measures such as examination scores. A desk or table between conversants adds psychological distance to an encounter.

People usually choose friends from among those whose residences or work spaces are closest to their own, apparently because propinquity provides convenient opportunities for interaction. Proximity can also increase enmity when we come into frequent contact with people we dislike.

We form attachments to places when their characteristics become meaningful as a result of some event or association. Place-identity refers to the extent to which places become incorporated into our self-concept.

The apparent territorial behavior of humans results from mechanisms that are considerably more complex than the instinctive reactions of other species. For example, the use and recognition of markers to indicate ownership depend on social and cultural norms.

Home environments signal our past, present, and future relationships with the community through exterior appearance, decoration, and demarcation of boundaries. Individual identity is expressed through personalization, which in turn is related to levels of attachment to the community.

In work environments, status markers and characteristics of an individual work space signal the occupant's rank or standing in the organization. Technological advances have increased the number of homeworkers, individuals whose primary work space is in their home. The separation of work space from domestic space appears to reduce role conflict among homeworkers, although considerably less research has been conducted on home work space than on traditional work space.

Neighborhoods are areas in which residents have developed place-identities and perceive boundaries. The type of neighborhood one prefers is related to one's evaluation of the current neighborhood as well as to one's intentions of remaining in the neighborhood. Unfortunately, the characteristics of neighborhoods that are associated with high levels of attachment are also considered cues of vulnerability by prospective burglars.

▶ Key Terms

adaptation
adaptation level
ambient environment
ambient stressors
arousal
crowding
environmental determinism
homeworker
life space
narrowing of attention
neighborhood
noise
open-plan office
personalization
place-identity
population density
privacy
privacy regulation

propinquity
shared stress effect
sociofugal space
sociopetal space
status marker
stress
territory
transactionalism
work space

Glossary

Actor–observer effect The tendency for actors to weigh the situation more heavily when explaining their behavior, whereas observers weigh the actor's dispositions more heavily when explaining the same behavior. (4)

Adaptation Processes that allow people to adjust to their surroundings, including shifts in perception of an environment with continued exposure, such as decreased sensitivity to loud noise. (14)

Adaptation level Personal standard of comparison used to evaluate noise, crowding, and other properties of the physical and social environment. (14)

Aggregate A collection of individuals who do not interact with one another. (12)

Aggression Any behavior directed toward hurting another living being. (2, 10)

Altruism A special form of helping behavior that is voluntary, costly, and motivated by a desire to improve another person's welfare rather than by the anticipation of reward. (11)

Ambient environment Changeable qualities of one's immediate surroundings, including temperature, humidity, air quality, sounds, and light. (14)

Ambient stressors Aspects of the environment that contribute to the experience of stress. (14)

Anchor A reference point used in making judgments. In social judgment theory, it is the point corresponding to the center of the latitude of acceptance. (7)

Anticonformity Behavior that is directly antithetical to group norms. Also called *counterconformity*. (8)

Arbitration Third-party assistance to two or more groups trying to reach an agreement in which the third party has the power to force the groups to accept a particular solution. (13)

Archival research The general term applied to any study in which the information or records being analyzed were not produced for the purpose of the study itself. (2)

Arousal A generalized state of physiological and psychological excitation. (14)

Arousal/cost-reward model (of helping) A model that predicts that people will help if they become aware of a need for help, experience physiological arousal, label that arousal as a response to the victim, and decide that cost and reward factors favor intervention. (11)

Assimilation effects In social judgment theory, shifts in judgments toward an anchor point. (7)

Assortative mating The nonrandom coupling of individuals based on resemblance of one or more characteristics. (9)

Attachment theory A theory of the formation and characterization of relationships based on the progress and outcomes of one's experiences as an infant in relation to the primary caregiver. (9)

Attitude An evaluation of objects, people, or issues about which an individual has some knowledge. (6)

Augmentation principle In Kelley's attribution theory, the notion that the existence of difficulties in performing a behavior results in a stronger conclusion that the actor is the cause of the event. (4)

Autokinetic effect The tendency for a stationary light, when viewed in an otherwise completely dark room, to appear to be moving. (8, 12)

Availability heuristic The tendency to be biased by events that are readily accessible in our memory. (4)

Balance theory A theory of attitude change based on the principle of consistency among elements in a relationship. Heider, who proposed this model, stated that unbalanced states produce tension, which a person will try to reduce by changing some attitude. (7)

Bargaining The process whereby two or more parties try to settle what each shall give and take, or perform and receive, in a transaction between them. (13)

Behaviorism A theoretical perspective, made prominent by John B. Watson, in which explanations of behavior emphasize external stimuli and learning processes. (1)

Belief in a just world A belief that there is an appropriate fit between what people do and what happens to them. (4)

Bystander effect The finding that a person is less likely to provide help when in the presence of witnesses than when alone. (11)

Catharsis Release of aggressive energy through the expression of aggressive emotions or through alternative forms of behavior. (10)

Causal attribution The process of explaining events or making inferences about their causes. (3, 4)

Causal schema A conception of the way two or more causal factors interact in relation to a particular kind of effect; an assumed pattern of data in a complete analysis-of-variance framework. (4)

Central tendency A statistical term for the average. (2)

Central trait A personal characteristic that strongly influences a perceiver's impressions of the person possessing it. (4)

Circumscribed accuracy The correctness of impressions that are based on specific traits that a person displays in specific situations. (4)

Cognitive dissonance theory A theory of attitude change developed by Leon Festinger and based on the principle of consistency. Cognitive dissonance exists when two cognitions contradict each other. Such dissonance is uncomfortable, and it is predicted that a person will reduce dissonance by one of several means—for example, by changing an attitude. (7)

Cognitive structure A set of principles and processes that organizes the use of knowledge and its storage in memory. (1)

Cognitive–neoassociationistic model A model of aggression in which the experience of anger and aggressive behavior are considered independent. Each, however, can prime the other, making the other more likely to occur. (10)

Cohesiveness The attraction that a group has for its members and that the members have for one another; the force that holds a group together. (12)

Collectivist culture A culture in which individuals subordinate their own desires to the good of the social group; contrasted with *individualist culture*. (11)

Communication networks Representations of the acceptable paths of communication between persons in a group or organization. (12)

Comparison level In interdependence theory, the standard against which the costs and rewards of a current relationship are evaluated. (9)

Competition Activity directed toward achieving a goal that only one person or group can obtain. (13)

Competitive reward structure A reward structure in which not all people striving for a reward can attain it and in which movement toward the goal by one person decreases the chance that others will attain that goal. (13)

Complementarity A principle to explain interpersonal attraction; refers to a pairing of different (and sometimes opposite) needs, such as dominance and submission. (9)

Compliance Behavior in accordance with a direct request. (8)

Confirmatory bias The tendency to obtain information that is consistent with our beliefs. (3, 4)

Conformity Yielding to perceived group pressures when no direct request to comply has been made. (8)

Connotation The implicit associations conveyed by a word. (5)

Consensus In Kelley's attribution theory, the extent to which the behavior of an actor is similar to that of others in the same situation. (4)

Consideration A dimension of leadership; the leader's concern with relationships between himself or herself and other group members and the maintenance of group morale and cohesiveness. (12)

Consistency In Kelley's attribution theory, the extent to which an actor's behavior is similar on other occasions. (4)

Construct A concept, defined in terms of observable events, used in a theory to account for regularities or relationships in data. (1, 4)

Contingency models In leadership theory, a collection of models based on the assumption that leadership effectiveness is dependent (contingent) upon a variety of situational factors. (12)

Contrast effect In social judgment theory, a shift in judgment away from an anchor point. (7)

Controllability In Weiner's attribution theory, the extent to which an individual has the power to change a cause of behavior. (4)

Conversational implicature An unexpected response that prompts the questioner to consider its relevance or its indirect meaning. (5)

Cooperation Working together for mutual benefit; a prosocial behavior. (13)

Cooperative principle In communication, the assumption that both parties will be informative, truthful, relevant, and concise. (5)

Cooperative reward structure A reward structure in which everyone in the group must achieve the reward for any one participant to attain it. Each person's efforts advance the group's chances. (13)

Correlation A statistical term for the degree of relatedness or association between two or more variables. The existence of a correlation does not allow conclusions about the causal relation between the two variables. (2)

Crowding A form of stress resulting from excessive, unwanted social interaction that may accompany densely populated environments. (14)

Cultural script A pattern of social interaction that is characteristic of a particular cultural group. (13)

Debriefing Discussion conducted at the end of a study in which the researcher reveals the complete procedures to the subject and explains the reasons for any deception that may have occurred. (2)

Deindividuation A state of relative anonymity in which a group member does not feel singled out or identifiable. (10, 12)

Demand characteristics The perceptual cues, both explicit and implicit, that communicate what behavior is expected in a situation. (2, 6)

Denotation The explicit meaning or definition of a word. (5)

Dependent variable A measure of participants' responses in the research situation. In an experiment, changes in the dependent variable are presumed to be caused by the independent variable. (2)

Discounting In Kelley's attribution theory, the tendency to reduce the importance of any one cause when other, plausible causes are present. (4)

Discrimination Any behavior that reflects acceptance or rejection of a person solely on the basis of membership in a particular group. (13)

Display rules Socially, personally, or culturally defined rules for controlling the expression of emotions. (5, 13)

Distinctiveness In Kelley's attribution theory, the extent to which the actor's behavior differs with respect to different targets. (4)

Distributive justice A proposition of social exchange theory in which one's rewards should be proportional to one's investments. (1)

Door-in-the-face effect A technique in which compliance with a request follows an initial refusal of a larger request. (8)

Egoism Self-interest or behavior that is motivated by selfish concerns; contrasted with *altruism*. (11)

Emblems Body gestures that substitute for the spoken word. (5)

Emic constructs Culture-specific concepts that have meaning only within a particular cultural framework. (13)

Empathy The vicarious experiencing of another person's perceptions and feelings. (11)

Empathy–altruism hypothesis The view that empathic concern for another person can produce a truly altruistic motivation to help aimed primarily at reducing a victim's need rather than at satisfying one's own needs. (11)

Environmental determinism The view that environmental characteristics, such as the climate or the layout of a city, can influence behavior. (14)

Equity theory A theory that specifies how people evaluate relative contributions to a relationship. Specifically, the theory suggests that ratios of input and outcomes should be equal for both participants. (9)

Ethnocentrism The tendency to judge other people or groups by the standards of one's own group. (13)

Ethology The study of the behavior of animals in their natural settings. (9, 10)

Etic constructs Universal factors; concepts that are not culture-specific. (13)

Evaluation apprehension An individual's concern about performing correctly and being positively evaluated by observers. A potential problem in studies in which subjects are aware that they are being observed. (2, 6)

Excitation transfer theory A theory that suggests that arousal generated in one situation may transfer to and intensify a subsequent emotional state. (10)

Exotic bias A tendency, in observing another group or society, to focus on aspects that differ from one's own group or society and to ignore similarities. (13)

Expectancy confirmation sequence A process through which perceivers' expectancies about a target are met by the target's behavior in reaction to the expectancies. See also *self-fulfilling prophecy*. (5)

Experiment A study in which the independent variable is manipulated in order to test a causal hypothesis; experiments also involve randomly assigning subjects to the different conditions of the independent variable. (2)

Experimental realism Arrangement of the events of an experiment so they will seem convincing and have the maximum possible impact on the subjects. This is sometimes accomplished through deception. (2)

Experimenter expectancies The researcher's beliefs about what should happen in a study. These beliefs can influence the outcome of the research. (2)

External validity The extent to which research situations represent situations that occur in everyday life; the extent to which any explanation for behavior can be applied to circumstances different from the research from which the explanation was derived. (2)

Facial affect program The connection between an emotional experience and a particular pattern of facial muscles. (5)

Facial feedback hypothesis The belief that the physical act of forming a facial display associated with an emotion may make one experience the emotion, even if the reason for display has nothing to do with the emotional experience. (5)

False consensus bias The belief that others share one's attitudes and behaviors. (4)

Field theory A social-psychological theory developed by Kurt Lewin in which he proposed that one's social behavior is a function not only of one's own attitudes, personality, and other intrapersonal factors, but also of one's environment, or "field." (1)

Foot-in-the-door effect A psychological effect whereby a person's compliance with a small request makes it more likely that the person will comply with a larger (and less desirable) request. (8)

Frustration The experience of having something or someone interfere with one's goal. (2, 10)

Frustration–aggression hypothesis A theory that assumes that aggression is always motivated by frustration, although frustration may have other consequences as well. (10)

Functional theory Any theory of attitude change that emphasizes the extent to which attitudes fulfill different individual needs. To change someone's attitude, one must understand why that attitude is held. (7)

Fundamental attribution bias The tendency to emphasize dispositional causes for the behavior of others. (4, 10, 12)

Gender identity One's self-awareness of being male or female. (3)

Gender-role norms Beliefs about appropriate behavior for women and men. (1, 13)

Global accuracy The correctness of impressions that are applied to many different situations and on many occasions. (4)

GRIT Graduated and reciprocated initiatives in tension reduction; a strategy of arms reduction proposed by psychologist Charles Osgood. (13)

Group Two or more people who are to some degree in dynamic interrelation with one another. (12)

Group polarization A shift in opinions by members of a group toward a more extreme position. (12)

Group structure The system of roles, norms, and relationships among members that exist in a group. (12)

Groupthink A mode of thinking in which group members' striving for unanimity overrides their motivation to realistically appraise alternative courses of action; a tendency to seek premature concurrence. (12)

Helping behavior A form of prosocial behavior that benefits another person more than oneself; as distinct from prosocial cooperation, in which mutual benefit is gained. (11)

Heuristics Shortcuts or rules of thumb used to make judgments for which we have insufficient or uncertain information. See also *availability heuristic* and *representativeness heuristic*. (4, 7)

Homeworkers Individuals who engage in paid work at home. (14)

Hypothesis A tentative description of a relationship between variables, or a supposition that a relationship may exist. Usually some scientific method (such as an experiment) is used to test (that is, attempt to confirm or disprove) a hypothesis. (1)

Ideal self The self-concept we desire to attain; hopes, wishes, and aspirations concerning different facets of our self. (3)

Illocution The intended meaning of a sentence. (5)

Illusory correlation An overestimation of the strength of a relationship between two variables when in fact the variables may not be related at all, or the relationship may be much weaker than believed. (4)

Illustrators Nonverbal behaviors that are directly linked with spoken language. (5)

Immediacy In social impact theory, the salience, or psychological "nearness," of an influence agent. (12)

Implicit personality theories Assumptions people make that two or more personality traits are related so that, if a person has one of the traits, it is believed that he or she will have the other trait (or traits) as well. (4)

Impression management The conscious or unconscious attempt to control images of oneself that are projected in real or imagined social interactions. (3)

Independence Behavior that is not responsive to group norms; neither conformity nor anticonformity. (8)

Independent variable A variable that is manipulated in an experiment; a variable whose changes are considered to cause changes in another (dependent) variable. (2)

Individualist culture A culture in which individuals are relatively free to pursue their own goals rather than to subordinate those goals to the needs of the group; contrasted with *collectivist culture*. (11)

Individualistic reward structure A reward structure in which one participant's goal attainment has no effect on the probability of goal attainment by others. (13)

Informational influence The process of changing another's attitude by presenting relevant facts, usually in a group setting. (8, 12)

In-group Any group to which an individual belongs. (13)

Initiating structure A dimension of leadership; the leader's behavior in identifying the group's goal and moving the group toward its goal. (12)

Instrumental learning A type of learning in which a response is followed by a reward or reinforcement, resulting in an increase in the frequency of the response. (10)

Integrative agreement An agreement that reconciles the interests of both parties in a negotiation, thus yielding a high payoff for both groups. (13)

Interaction A statistical term referring to the situation in which the effect of one independent variable depends on the level or state of the other independent variable. (2)

Intergroup behavior The interaction of members of one group with members of another group, where such interaction is based on group identification. (13)

Intergroup contact hypothesis The assumption that prejudice will be reduced and favorable attitudes will develop when members of two groups with negative attitudes toward each other are brought together. (13)

Internal validity The extent to which the results of an experiment can be conclusively linked to the independent variables, as opposed to the possibility that some other, uncontrolled variable or variables might have caused the observed results. (2)

Interview A survey research technique in which the researcher asks another person a set of questions according to a predetermined schedule and records the answers. (2)

Kin selection In sociobiology, the concept that genes will become more common in a species if they contribute to the survival of relatives, even if those genes decrease the individual's chances of survival. (11)

Kinesics A scheme developed by Ray Birdwhistell for classifying body motions, intended to parallel linguistic categories. (5)

Latitude of acceptance In social judgment theory, the area of an evaluative dimension that includes an individual's current attitude and defines the range of positions considered consistent with that attitude. (7)

Latitude of noncommitment In social judgment theory, the area of an evaluative dimension that defines the range of positions that are considered to be different from an individual's attitude, but not so different as to be considered unacceptable. (7)

Latitude of rejection In social judgment theory, the area of an evaluative dimension that defines the range of positions that are considered to be unacceptable. (7)

Learned helplessness The belief that one's outcomes are independent of one's actions; this belief is learned through exposure to situations in which outcomes are noncontingent and results in behavior deficits and feelings of depression. (8)

Life space A construct in field theory that includes the person plus his or her environment. The person and the environment combine to form one set of factors that operate together to influence behavior. (14)

Likert scale A method of attitude measurement in which people indicate their agreement or disagreement with a set of declarative statements. (6)

Locus of causality In Weiner's attribution theory, the extent to which an individual's behavior results from dispositional (internal) or situational (external) influences. (4)

Locus of control A person's belief that events are within his or her own control (internal) or that outside forces are in control (external). (8)

Locution Words expressed in a particular sequence, such as a sentence that conveys a specific meaning. (5)

Lure technique A compliance technique in which an enticing offer, once made and accepted, is replaced by a different, less attractive offer. (8)

Main effect The effect produced by one independent variable, without considering the impact of any other independent variable. (2)

Manipulation check A dependent measure used specifically to assess the extent to which the different conditions associated with the independent variable in an experiment really are different. (2)

Mediation Third-party assistance to two or more disputing parties who are trying to reach an agreement. (13)

Mere exposure effect The finding that repeated exposure to an object results in greater attraction to that object. (9)

Meta-analysis A type of archival research in which researchers analyze the statistical results of individual studies. (2)

Mindfulness A state of alert, active information processing that includes drawing distinctions and creating new cognitive categories. (8)

Modeling The tendency for a person to reproduce the action, attitudes, and emotional responses exhibited by a real-life or symbolic model. Also called *observational learning.* (10)

Modern racism A more subtle form of racism in which discrimination is justified in socially acceptable ways; see also *symbolic racism.* (13)

Mundane realism Arrangement of the events in an experiment so they seem as similar as possible to normal, everyday occurrences. (2)

Narrowing of attention A phenomenon in which individuals focus on the cues most salient to their immediate goals and overlook others; usually the result of arousal. (14)

Negative-state relief model A hypothesis explaining the relation between negative moods and helping behavior as a learned way of escaping negative psychological states. (11)

Neighborhood Perceived boundaries that have personal meaning to those who reside in them. (14)

Neo-Freudians Followers of Freud who depart in various ways from some of Freud's doctrines. (10)

Noise Unwanted sound, which can be stressful if it is loud, unpredictable, and uncontrollable. (14)

Noncommon effect In Jones's attribution theory, a consequence that could be achieved only by the specific manner in which the behavior was performed. (4)

Norm A socially defined and enforced standard of behavior that defines or limits the way a person should interpret the world, behave in it, or both. (1, 12)

Normative influence The process of changing another's attitude through conformity pressure or through stressing the importance of adhering to values or norms. (8, 12)

Number In social impact theory, the number of influence agents, or the frequency with which a single agent attempts to exert influence. (12)

Obedience A special form of compliance in which behavior is performed in response to a direct order. (8)

Observational learning A type of learning in which one acquires new behaviors simply by observing the actions of others. (10)

Open-plan office A style of office design in which work spaces occupy large areas that are undivided by walls but separated by furniture, plants, and movable partitions. (14)

Ought self Facets of the self-concept that should exist; duties, obligations, responsibilities, and so on. (3)

Out-group Any group of which an individual is aware but of which he or she is not a member. (13)

Paralanguage Vocalizations that are not language but that convey meaning; examples include pitch and rhythm, laughing, and yawning. (5)

Participant observer An investigator in a field study who participates in ongoing activities while observing and maintaining records of the behaviors of others in the situation. (2)

Personalization Deliberate adornment, decoration, or modification of an environment by its occupants to reflect their identities or personalities. (14)

Phenomenological approach A point of view in social psychology that includes the proposition that a person's subjective perception of the environment is a more important influence on his or her behavior than some other person's perception or an objective description of the environment. (1)

Philosophies of human nature Expectations that people possess certain qualities and will behave in certain ways. (4)

Place-identity The collection of environment-related cognitions that are incorporated into one's self-concept. (14)

Population density The number of persons or other animals per unit of space or the number of units of space per person; for example, people per acre in a city or square feet per person in a room. (14)

Pornography Erotic material that combines elements of sexuality and aggression and in which force or coercion is used to accomplish the sexual act. (10)

Prejudice An unjustified evaluative reaction to a member of a racial, ethnic, or other group, which results solely from the person's membership in that group; an intolerant, unfair, or unfavorable attitude toward another group of people. (13)

Priming A process by which situational cues activate certain memories; for example, a candle may remind you that it's your friend's birthday. (3, 4, 6)

Privacy Selective control over access to oneself or one's group, including control over information and personal accessibility to other people. (14)

Privacy regulation The use of verbal and nonverbal behaviors, including use of the physical environment, to optimize one's level of involvement with other people. (14)

Private self-consciousness A focus on personal aspects of the self, such as bodily sensations, beliefs, moods, and feelings. (3)

Production blocking An artifact of group discussion by which the number of ideas any given member generates is limited by the member's capacity to remember what he or she was going to say while another is talking. (12)

Propinquity Proximity or geographical closeness. (9, 14)

Prosocial behavior Behavior that has positive social consequences and improves the physical or psychological well-being of another person or persons. (11)

Prototype A set of abstract features commonly associated with members of a category. (4)

Psychoanalytic theory A theory of personality and social behavior developed by Sigmund Freud on the basis of psychotherapeutic experiences. (1, 11)

Public self-consciousness Concern about how one is projecting the self to the social world and awareness of how one is seen as a social object by others. (3)

Questionnaire A survey research technique in which the researcher supplies written questions to the subject, who provides written answers. (2)

Racial identity One's sense of belonging to a particular racial or ethnic group. (3)

Racism Any attitude, action, or institutional structure that subordinates a person because of his or her color or race. (13)

Randomization Assignment of conditions (for instance, assignment of subjects to treatment conditions) in a completely random manner—that is, a manner determined entirely by chance—such that each subject has an equal chance of experiencing any one particular condition. (2)

Reactance A motivational state that is aroused whenever a person feels that his or her freedom to choose an object is severely limited, resulting in the object's increased desirability. (7, 8)

Reciprocal altruism In sociobiology, the concept that natural selection would favor those with genes predisposing them to altruism because altruistic acts are eventually reciprocated and thus benefit the individual. Used to argue that altruism might be biologically based. (11)

Reciprocity norm A standard of behavior that states that people should help, and should refrain from injuring, those who have helped them. (11)

Reinforcement Any consequence of a response that increases the probability that the same response will be made again under the same stimulus conditions; often called a reward. (1)

Relative deprivation A feeling of discontent based on the belief that one is getting less than one deserves, particularly in comparison with what others are getting. (10)

Reliability Consistency with which a concrete variable, or measure, represents a theoretical concept. Also, in reference to measurement scales, stability of scores over time, equivalence of scores on two forms of a test, or similarity of two raters' scoring of the same behavior. (2)

Representativeness heuristic The tendency to consider events more representative of the total population than they are. (4)

Response Any alteration in a person's behavior that results from an external or internal stimulus. (1)

Risky shift An early term for *group polarization,* coined before research indicated polarization also occurs toward conservative positions. (12)

Role The functional aspects associated with a specific position in a social context, such as spouse, student, or baseball umpire. (1, 12)

Role differentiation The emergence and development of roles in the course of group interaction. (12)

Role expectations Assumptions about the behavior of a person who holds a particular role. (1, 12)

Scapegoating The displacement of hostility onto less powerful groups when the source of frustration is not available or cannot be attacked for other reasons. (13)

Schema An organized pattern of knowledge, derived from past experience, that we use to interpret our current experience. (1, 3, 4)

Script The conceptual representation of a stereotyped sequence of events. (4, 10)

Selective exposure Seeking information that supports one's attitudes and beliefs and avoiding information that is inconsistent with one's attitudinal position. (6, 7)

Self-affirmation A phenomenon in which one responds to a threat to self-esteem by enhancing some (perhaps unrelated) facet of the self-concept. (7)

Self-awareness A psychological state in which individuals focus their attention on and evaluate aspects of their self-concepts, which can range from physical experiences to discrepancies between "real" self and "ideal" self. (3)

Self-categorization The process by which an individual spontaneously includes himself or herself as a member of a group. (8)

Self-concept The totality of an individual's thoughts and feelings having reference to the self as an object. (3)

Self-consciousness A disposition to focus attention on the self. Two forms are private self-consciousness, which is related to self-awareness, and public self-consciousness, which deals with others' views of the self. (3)

Self-disclosure The revealing of information about the self; self-revelation. (5)

Self-esteem The overall evaluation of oneself in either positive or negative terms. (3)

Self-fulfilling prophecy The process whereby a perceiver's beliefs about a target person can elicit behavior from the target person that will confirm the expectancy. See also *expectancy confirmation sequence.* (5)

Self-handicapping strategy Any action or choice of performance setting that enhances the opportunity to avoid blame for failure and to accept credit for success. (3)

Self-monitoring The use of cues from other people's self-presentations in controlling one's own self-presentation. High self-monitoring individuals use their well-developed self-presentational skills for purposes of impression management in social relations. (1, 3, 11)

Self-perception theory A theory that proposes that we infer our attitudes, emotions, and other internal states from observations of our own behavior. (3, 6, 7)

Self-schema A set of cognitive generalizations about the self. A self-schema organizes and guides the processing of self-related information. (3)

Self-serving attribution bias The tendency to infer causes for events so as to confirm the self-concept, usually by accepting greater personal responsibility for positive outcomes than for negative outcomes. (3)

Semantic differential technique A method of attitude measurement in which people rate a concept on a series of bipolar adjective scales. (6)

Sexism Prejudice and discrimination directed against people by virtue of their gender. (13)

Shared stress effect A tendency for people who are together in a stressful environment to feel attracted to one another. (14)

Simulation A research method that attempts to imitate some crucial aspects of a real-world situation in order to gain more understanding of the underlying mechanisms that operate in that situation. (2)

Social comparison theory A theory that proposes we use other people as sources for comparison to evaluate our own attitudes and abilities. (3, 9, 12)

Social distance The degree of physical, social, or psychological closeness to members of an ethnic, racial, or religious group that a person finds acceptable. (13)

Social exchange theory A general theoretical model within the learning perspective in which interpersonal relationships are considered in terms of rewards and costs to the participants. (1, 9)

Social facilitation The state in which the presence of others improves an individual's performance. (1, 12)

Social impact theory A theory of social influence that includes the number, immediacy, and strength of influence agents. (12)

Social impairment Another name for *social inhibition.* (12)

Social inhibition A decline in individual performance in the presence of other people. (12)

Social judgment theory A theory of attitude change that emphasizes the individual's perception and judgment of a persuasive communication. Central concepts in this theory are anchors, assimilation and contrast effects, and latitudes of acceptance, rejection, and noncommitment. (7)

Social learning theory A theory that includes the proposition that social behavior develops as a result of observing others and of being reinforced for certain acts. (1, 6)

Social loafing A decrease in individual effort when people work in groups as compared to when they work alone. (12)

Social network The set of people with whom an individual is in actual contact. (9)

Social register A way of expressing a message addressed to a particular type of listener, such as the higher-pitched, simplified speech used when addressing a baby. (5)

Social-responsibility norm A standard of behavior that dictates that people should help persons who are dependent or in need of help. (11)

Social support Useful coping resources provided by others. (9)

Social theory A belief about how and in what ways variables in the social environment go together. (4)

Socialization A process of acquiring behaviors that are considered appropriate by society. (1)

Sociobiology A discipline concerned with identifying biological and genetic bases for social behavior in animals and humans. (10, 11)

Sociofugal spaces Settings that discourage conversation among people by making eye contact difficult. (14)

Sociopetal spaces Physical settings that encourage interpersonal interaction through seating arrangements that place people within comfortable conversation distances facing one another. (14)

Stability In Weiner's attribution theory, a dimension concerning the extent to which the cause of a behavior can change. (4)

Status characteristics theory A theory of group process proposing that differences in evaluations and beliefs about types of individuals become the basis for inequalities in social interaction. (12)

Status marker Physical symbol or indication of an individual's rank in an organization or relative standing in a social system, especially in work environments; one example is the size of one's office. (14)

Stereotype A schema about members of an identifiable group. (4, 13)

Stimulus Any event, internal or external to the person, that may bring about an alteration in that person's behavior. (1)

Stimulus discrimination   The process of making distinctions between similar stimuli. (1)

Stimulus generalization   A process in which a person, after learning a response to one stimulus, will produce the same response when exposed to some other, similar stimulus, even if the person has never experienced the other stimulus. (1)

Strength   In social impact theory, the power, status, or resources associated with a social influence agent. (12)

Stress   An imbalance between environmental demands and an organism's response capabilities; the body's response to excessive change. (14)

Superego   In psychoanalytic theory, the part of personality oriented toward doing what is morally proper; the conscience. The superego includes a person's ideal self-image. (1)

Superordinate goal   An important goal that can be achieved only through cooperation among different individuals or groups. (13)

Symbolic racism   A blend of negative affect and traditional moral values embodied in the Protestant ethic; underlying attitudes that support racist positions. (13)

Territory   A physical zone of control and influence. In nonhuman species, a specific region that an animal marks with scents or calls, uses for nesting or foraging, and defends against intruders of the same species. (14)

Theory   A description of relationships among abstract symbols used to represent reality. (1)

Trait   A term used to describe regularities in behavior, particularly with reference to someone's, or one's own, personality. (4)

Transactionalism   The perspective that the person and the environment are integral aspects of a unitary system of change. (14)

Ultimate attribution bias   The tendency for in-group members to attribute their own desirable behaviors to internal and stable factors while citing transitory factors to explain desirable behaviors of the out-group. (13)

Uncertainty of approval   The extent to which a member of a group is concerned about receiving acceptance from other members of the group. (12)

Unobtrusive measure   A measurement that can be made without the knowledge of the person being studied. An unobtrusive measure reduces the problem of evaluation apprehension. (2)

Urban-overload hypothesis   The idea that city dwellers react to excessive stimulation by avoiding interpersonal involvement. (11)

Validity   The extent to which a measure represents what it is supposed to represent; see also *internal validity* and *external validity.* (2)

Variability   A statistical term for the dispersion of scores, the extent to which scores are "spread out" or are highly similar. (2)

Visual dominance behavior   The tendency of people in high-status positions to look at lower-status people more fixedly when speaking than when listening. (5)

Vividness   The intensity or emotional interest of a stimulus. (4)

Work space   Work station in an office or factory assigned to a single individual. (14)

Working self-concept   The specific aspects of one's identity that are activated by the role one is playing at any particular moment. (3)

References

Abbey, A., Dunkel-Schetter, C., & Brickman, P. (1983). Handling the stress of looking for a job in law school: The relationship between intrinsic motivation, internal attributions, relations with others, and happiness. *Basic and Applied Social Psychology, 4,* 263–278.(3)

Abdalla, I. A. (1991). Social support and gender responses to job stress in an Arab culture. *Journal of Social Behavior and Personality, 6*(7), 273–288.(2)

Abelson, R. P. (1981). Psychological status of the script concept. *American Psychologist, 36,* 715–729.(4)

Abelson, R. P., & Prentice, D. A. (1989). Beliefs as possessions—a functional perspective. In A. R. Pratkanis, S. J. Breckler, & A. G. Greenwald (Eds.), *Attitude structure and function* (pp. 361–381). Hillsdale, NJ: Erlbaum.(7)

Abelson, R. P., & Rosenberg, M. J. (1958). Symbolic psycho-logic: A model of attitudinal cognition. *Behavioral Science, 3,* 1–13.(7)

Abrams, D., & Hogg, M. A. (1990). Social identification, self-categorization, and social influence. *European Review of Social Psychology, 1,* 195–228.(8)

Abramson, L. Y., Seligman, M. E. P., & Teasdale, J. D. (1978). Learned helplessness in humans: Critique and reformulation. *Journal of Abnormal Psychology, 87,* 49–74.(8)

Adelmann, P. K., & Zajonc, R. B. (1989). Facial efference and the experience of emotion. *Annual Review of Psychology, 40,* 249–280.(5)

Aderman, D., & Berkowitz, L. (1983). Self-concern and the unwillingness to be helpful. *Social Psychology Quarterly, 46,* 293–301.(11)

Aderman, D., Bryant, F. B., & Donelsmith, D. E. (1978). Prediction as a means of inducing tolerance. *Journal of Research in Personality, 12,* 172–178.(9)

Adorno, T. W., Frenkel-Brunswik, E., Levinson, D., & Sanford, N. (1950). *The authoritarian personality.* New York: Harper.(4, 13)

Ahrentzen, S. B. (1988). There's no (work) place like home. In D. Lawrence, R. Habe, A. Hacker, & D. Sherrod (Eds.), *People's needs/planet management: Paths to co-existence* (pp. 155–162). Washington, DC: Environmental Design Research Association.(14)

Ahrentzen, S. B. (1990). Managing conflict by managing boundaries: How professional homeworkers cope with multiple roles at home. *Environment and Behavior, 22,* 723–752.(14)

Ahrentzen, S. B., Levine, D. W., & Michelson, W. (1989). Space, time, and activity in the home: A gender analysis. *Journal of Environmental Psychology, 9,* 89–101.(14)

Aiello, J. R. (1977a). A further look at equilibrium theory: Visual interaction as a function of interpersonal distance. *Environmental Psychology and Nonverbal Behavior, 1,* 122–140.(5)

Aiello, J. R. (1977b). Visual interaction at extended distances. *Personality and Social Psychology Bulletin, 3,* 83–86.(5)

Aiello, J. R., Epstein, Y. M., & Karlin, R. A. (1975). Effects of crowding on electrodermal activity. *Sociological Symposium, 14,* 43–57.(14)

Aiello, J. R., & Thompson, D. E. (1980). When compensation fails: Mediating effects of sex and locus of control at extended interaction distances. *Basic and Applied Social Psychology, 1,* 65–82.(14)

Ainsworth, M. D. S., Blehar, M. C., Waters, E., & Wall, S. (1978). *Patterns of attachment: A psychological study of the strange situation.* Hillsdale, NJ: Erlbaum.(9)

Ajzen, I. (1985). From intentions to actions: A theory of planned behavior. In J. Kuhl & J. Beckman (Eds.), *Action-control: From cognition to behavior* (pp. 11–39). New York: Springer. (6)

Ajzen, I. (1987). Attitudes, traits, and actions: Dispositional prediction of behavior in personality and social psychology. *Advances in Experimental Social Psychology, 20,* 1–63. (6)

Ajzen, I., & Fishbein, M. (1980). *Understanding attitudes and predicting social behavior.* Englewood Cliffs, NJ: Prentice-Hall. (6)

Ajzen, I., & Madden, T. (1986). Prediction of goal-directed behavior: Attitudes, intentions, and perceived behavioral control. *Journal of Experimental Social Psychology, 22,* 453–474. (6)

Aldwin, C., & Stokols, D. (1988). The effects of environmental change on individuals and groups: Some neglected issues in stress research. *Journal of Environmental Psychology, 8,* 57–75. (14)

Alexander, Y., & O'Day, A. (1984). *Terrorism in Ireland.* London: Croom Helm. (13)

Alley, T. R. (1990). The ecological approach to person perception. *Contemporary Social Psychology, 14,* 153–158. (4)

Allport, F. H. (1920). The influence of the group upon association and thought. *Journal of Experimental Psychology, 3,* 159–182. (12)

Allport, F. H. (1924). *Social psychology.* Boston: Houghton Mifflin. (1)

Allport, G. W. (1935). Attitudes. In C. M. Murchison (Ed.), *Handbook of social psychology* (pp. 798–844). Worcester, MA: Clark University Press. (6)

Allport, G. W. (1958). *The nature of prejudice.* Garden City, NY: Doubleday Anchor. (Originally published in 1954.) (13)

Allport, G. W. (1985). The historical background of social psychology. In G. Lindzey & E. Aronson (Eds.), *Handbook of social psychology* (3rd ed., Vol. 1, pp. 1–46). New York: Random House. (1)

Altemeyer, B. (1988). *Enemies of freedom: Understanding right-wing authoritarianism.* San Francisco: Jossey-Bass. (13)

Altemeyer, R. A., & Jones, K. (1974). Sexual identity, physical attractiveness, and seating position as determinants of influence in discussion groups. *Canadian Journal of Behavioural Science, 6,* 357–375. (14)

Altman, I. (1973). Reciprocity of interpersonal exchange. *Journal for the Theory of Social Behaviour, 3,* 249–261. (5)

Altman, I. (1975). *The environment and social behavior: Privacy, personal space, territory, and crowding.* Pacific Grove, CA: Brooks/Cole. (14)

Altman, I. (1976). Privacy: A conceptual analysis. *Environment and Behavior, 8,* 7–29. (14)

Altman, I., & Chemers, M. (1980). *Culture and environment.* Pacific Grove, CA: Brooks/Cole. (14)

Altman, I., & Gauvain, M. (1986). A cross-cultural and dialectic analysis of homes. In L. Liben, A. Patterson, & N. Newcombe (Eds.), *Spatial representation and behavior across the life span* (pp. 283–319). New York: Academic Press. (14)

Altman, I., & Rogoff, B. (1987). World views in psychology: Trait, interactional, organismic, and interactional perspectives. In D. Stokols & I. Altman (Eds.), *Handbook of environmental psychology: Volume 1* (pp. 7–40). New York: Wiley. (14)

Altman, I., Taylor, D., & Wheeler, L. (1971). Ecological aspects of group behavior in isolation. *Journal of Applied Social Psychology, 1,* 76–100. (14)

Amato, P. R. (1983). Helping behavior in urban and rural environments: Field studies based on a taxonomic organization of helping episodes. *Journal of Personality and Social Psychology, 45,* 571–586. (11)

Amato, P. R. (1990). Personality and social network involvement as predictors of helping behavior in everyday life. *Social Psychology Quarterly, 53,* 31–43. (11)

American Psychological Association. (1973). *Ethical principles in the conduct of research with human participants.* Washington, DC: Author. (2)

American Psychological Association. (1990). Ethical principles of psychologists. *American Psychologist, 45,* 390–395. (2)

Amir, Y. (1976). The role of intergroup contact in change of prejudice and ethnic relations. In P. A. Katz (Ed.), *Towards the elimination of racism.* New York: Pergamon Press. (13)

Andersen, S. M., & Bem, S. L. (1981). Sex typing and androgyny in dyadic interaction: Individual differences in responsiveness to physical attractiveness. *Journal of Personality and Social Psychology, 41,* 74–86. (9)

Andersen, S. M., & Klatzky, R. L. (1987). Traits and social stereotypes: Levels of categorization in person perception. *Journal of Personality and Social Psychology, 53,* 235–246. (4)

Andersen, S. M., Lazowski, L. E., & Donisi, M. (1986). Salience and self-inference: The role of biased recollections in self-inference processes. *Social Cognition, 4,* 75–95. (3)

Anderson, C. A. (1989). Temperature and aggression: Ubiquitous effects of heat on occurrence of human violence. *Psychological Bulletin, 106,* 74–96. (10, 14)

Anderson, C. A., & Anderson, D. C. (1984). Ambient temperature and violent crime: Tests of the linear and curvilinear hypotheses. *Journal of Personality and Social Psychology, 46,* 91–97. (10)

Anderson, C. A., Lepper, M. R., & Ross, L. (1980). Perseverance of social theories: The role of explanation in the persistence of discredited information. *Journal of Personality and Social Psychology, 39,* 1030–1049.(4)

Anderson, C. A., & Sechler, E. S. (1986). Effects of explanation and counterexplanation on the development and use of social theories. *Journal of Personality and Social Psychology, 50,* 24–34.(4)

Anderson, N. H. (1965). Averaging versus adding as a stimulus-combination rule in impression formation. *Journal of Experimental Psychology, 70,* 394–400.(4)

Anderson, N. H. (1968). Likableness ratings of 555 personality-trait words. *Journal of Personality and Social Psychology, 9,* 272–279.(4)

Anderson, N. H. (1974). Cognitive algebra: Integration theory applied to social attribution. *Advances in Experimental Social Psychology, 7,* 2–102.(4)

Andrews, I. R., & Johnson, D. L. (1971). Small-group polarization of judgments. *Psychonomic Science, 24,* 191–192.(12)

Apfelbaum, E. (1979). Relations of domination and movements for liberation: An analysis of power between groups. In W. G. Austin & S. Worchel (Eds.), *The social psychology of intergroup relations.* Pacific Grove, CA: Brooks/Cole.(13)

Archer, D., Iritani, B., Kimes, D. D., & Barrios, M. (1983). Face-ism: Five studies of sex differences in facial prominence. *Journal of Personality and Social Psychology, 45,* 725–735.(13)

Archer, R. L. (1984). The farmer and the cowman should be friends: An attempt at reconciliation with Batson, Coke, and Pych. *Journal of Personality and Social Psychology, 46,* 709–711.(11)

Ardrey, R. (1961). *African genesis.* New York: Delta Books.(10)

Argyle, M., & Dean, J. (1965). Eye contact, distance, and affiliation. *Sociometry, 28,* 289–304.(5)

Argyle, M., & Henderson, M. (1984). The rules of friendship. *Journal of Social and Personal Relationships, 1,* 211–237.(9)

Argyle, M., & Ingham, R. (1972). Gaze, mutual gaze, and proximity. *Semiotica, 6,* 32–49.(5)

Arkin, R., Cooper, H., & Kolditz, T. (1980). A statistical review of the literature concerning the self-serving attribution bias in interpersonal influence situations. *Journal of Personality, 48,* 435–448.(3)

Aron, A., & Aron, E. N. (1989). *The heart of social psychology: A backstage view of a passionate science.* Lexington, MA: Lexington Books.(1)

Aronson, E., Blaney, N., Stephan, C., Sikes, J., & Snapp, M. (1978). *The jigsaw classroom.* Beverly Hills, CA: Sage.(13)

Aronson, E., Brewer, M., & Carlsmith, J. M. (1985). Experimentation in social psychology. In G. Lindzey & E. Aronson (Eds.), *Handbook of social psychology* (3rd ed., Vol. 1, pp. 441–486). New York: Random House.(2)

Aronson, E., & Cope, V. (1968). My enemy's enemy is my friend. *Journal of Personality and Social Psychology, 8,* 8–12.(9)

Aronson, E., & Mills, J. (1959). The effect of severity of initiation on liking for a group. *Journal of Abnormal and Social Psychology, 59,* 177–181.(7, 12)

Asarnow, J. R., & Callan, J. W. (1985). Boys with peer adjustment problems: Social cognitive processes. *Journal of Consulting and Clinical Psychology, 53,* 291–298.(10)

Asch, S. E. (1946). Forming impressions of personality. *Journal of Abnormal and Social Psychology, 41,* 258–290.(4)

Asch, S. E. (1951). Effects of group pressure upon the modification and distortion of judgments. In H. Guetzkow (Ed.), *Groups, leadership, and men.* Pittsburgh, PA: Carnegie Press.(8, 12)

Asch, S. E. (1952). *Social psychology.* New York: Holt, Rinehart & Winston.(12)

Asch, S. E. (1956). Studies of independence and conformity: A minority of one against a unanimous majority. *Psychological Monographs, 70*(9, Whole No. 416).(8)

Asch, S. E. (1958). Effects of group pressure upon modification and distortion of judgments. In E. E. Maccoby, T. M. Newcomb, & E. L. Hartley (Eds.), *Readings in social psychology* (3rd ed., pp. 174–182). New York: Holt, Rinehart & Winston.(8)

Athanasiou, R., & Yoshioka, G. A. (1973). The spatial character of friendship formation. *Environment and Behavior, 5,* 43–65.(14)

Atkins, A., Deaux, K., & Bieri, J. (1967). Latitude of acceptance and attitude change: Empirical evidence for a reformulation. *Journal of Personality and Social Psychology, 6,* 47–54.(7)

Au, T. K. (1986). A verb is worth a thousand words: The causes and consequences of interpersonal events implicit in language. *Journal of Memory and Language, 25,* 104–122.(5)

Austin, J. L. (1962). *How to do things with words.* Oxford: Oxford University Press.(5)

Austin, W. T., & Bates, F. L. (1974). Ethological indicators of dominance and territory in a human captive population. *Social Forces, 52,* 447–455.(14)

Axsom, D., & Cooper, J. (1985). Cognitive dissonance and psychotherapy: The role of effort justification in inducing weight loss. *Journal of Experimental Social Psychology, 21,* 149–160.(7)

Ayman, R. (1984, August). The effects of leadership characteristics and situational control on leadership effectiveness. In M. M. Chemers (Chair), *Leadership effectiveness* *in Mexico.* Symposium conducted at the International Congress of Psychology, Acapulco.(12)

Ayman, R., & Chemers, M. M. (1983). The relationship of supervisory behavior ratings to work group effectiveness and subordinate satisfaction among Iranian managers. *Journal of Applied Psychology, 68,* 338–341.(12)

Azrin, N. H., Hutchinson, R. R., & Hake, D. F. (1966). Attack, avoidance, and escape reactions to aversive shock. *Journal of Experimental Analysis of Behavior, 9,* 191–204.(10)

Bachy, V. (1976). Danish "permissiveness" revisited. *Journal of Communication, 26,* 40–43.(10)

Back, K. W. (1951). Influence through social communication. *Journal of Abnormal and Social Psychology, 46,* 9–23.(12)

Backman, C. W., & Secord, P. F. (1959). The effect of perceived liking on interpersonal attraction. *Human Relations, 12,* 379–384.(9)

Baker, P. M. (1984). Seeing is behaving: Visibility and participation in small groups. *Environment and Behavior, 16,* 159–184.(14)

Bales, R. F. (1953). The equilibrium problem in small groups. In T. Parsons, R. F. Bales, & E. A. Shils (Eds.), *Working papers in the theory of action.* Glencoe, IL: Free Press.(12)

Bandura, A. (1965). Vicarious processes: A case of no-trial learning. In L. Berkowitz (Ed.), *Advances in experimental social psychology* (Vol. 2). New York: Academic Press.(12)

Bandura, A. (1973). *Aggression: A social-learning analysis.* Englewood Cliffs, NJ: Prentice-Hall.(1, 10)

Bandura, A. (1977). *Social learning theory.* Englewood Cliffs, NJ: Prentice-Hall.(1)

Bandura, A., Ross, D., & Ross, S. (1961). Transmission of aggression through imitation of aggressive models. *Journal of Abnormal and Social Psychology, 63,* 575–582.(10)

Bandura, A., Ross, D., & Ross, S. (1963). Imitation of film-mediated aggressive models. *Journal of Abnormal and Social Psychology, 66,* 3–11.(10)

Bandura, A., & Walters, R. (1963). *Social learning and personality development.* New York: Holt, Rinehart & Winston.(10)

Bargh, J. A. (1989). Conditional automaticity: Varieties of automatic influence in social perception and cognition. In J. S. Uleman & J. A. Bargh (Eds.), *Unintended thought* (pp. 3–51). New York: Guilford Press.(4)

Barker, R. G., & Schoggen, P. (1973). *Qualities of community life.* San Francisco: Jossey-Bass.(2)

Baron, R. A. (1971). Reducing the influence of an aggressive model: The restraining effects of discrepant modeling cues. *Journal of Personality and Social Psychology, 20,* 240–245.(10)

Baron, R. A. (1972). Aggression as a function of ambient temperature and prior anger arousal. *Journal of Personality and Social Psychology, 21,* 183–189.(10)

Baron, R. A. (1974). Aggression as a function of victim's pain cues, level of prior anger arousal, and exposure to an aggressive model. *Journal of Personality and Social Psychology, 29,* 117–124.(10)

Baron, R. A. (1977). *Human aggression.* New York: Plenum.(2, 10)

Baron, R. A. (1990). Environmentally induced positive affect: Its impact on self-efficacy, task performance, negotiation, and conflict. *Journal of Applied Social Psychology, 20,* 368–384.(14)

Baron, R. A., & Ball, R. L. (1974). The aggression-inhibiting influence of nonhostile humor. *Journal of Experimental Social Psychology, 10,* 23–33.(10)

Baron, R. A., & Bell, P. A. (1975). Aggression and heat: Mediating effects of prior provocation and exposure to an aggressive model. *Journal of Personality and Social Psychology, 31,* 825–832.(10)

Baron, R. A., & Bell, P. A. (1976). Aggression and heat: The influence of ambient temperature, negative affect, and a cooling drink on physical aggression. *Journal of Personality and Social Psychology, 33,* 245–255.(10)

Baron, R. A., & Bell, P. A. (1977). Sexual arousal and aggression by males: Effects of type of erotic stimuli and prior provocation. *Journal of Personality and Social Psychology, 35,* 79–87.(10)

Baron, R. A., & Kepner, C. R. (1970). Model's behavior and attraction toward the model as determinants of adult aggressive behavior. *Journal of Personality and Social Psychology, 14,* 335–344.(10)

Baron, R. A., & Ransberger, V. M. (1978). Ambient temperature and the occurrence of collective violence: The "long hot summer" revisited. *Journal of Personality and Social Psychology, 36,* 351–360.(10)

Baron, R. M. (1990). Towards an ecological specification of the nature of the effective stimulus for social knowing and action. *Contemporary Social Psychology, 14,* 136–144.(4)

Baron, R. S. (1986). Distraction-conflict theory: Progress and problems. *Advances in Experimental Social Psychology, 19,* 1–40.(12)

Bar-Tal, D., Raviv, A., & Lesser, T. (1980). The development of altruistic behavior: Empirical evidence. *Developmental Psychology, 16,* 516–524.(11)

Bar-Tal, D., & Saxe, L. (1976). Perceptions of similarly and dissimilarly attractive couples and individuals. *Journal of Personality and Social Psychology, 33,* 772–781.(9)

Bartlett, F. A. (1932). *A study in experimental and social psychology.* New York: Cambridge University Press.(4)

Bartos, O. J. (1974). *Process and outcome in negotiation.* New York: Columbia University Press.(13)

Bass, B., & Klubeck, S. (1952). Effects of seating arrangement on leaderless group discussions. *Journal of Abnormal and Social Psychology, 47,* 724–727.(14)

Bastlin Normoyle, J., & Foley, J. N. (1988). The defensible space model of fear and elderly public housing residents. *Environment and Behavior, 20,* 50–74.(14)

Batson, C. D. (1983). Sociobiology and the role of religion in promoting prosocial behavior: An alternative view. *Journal of Personality and Social Psychology, 45,* 1380–1385.(11)

Batson, C. D. (1987). Prosocial motivation: Is it ever truly altruistic? *Advances in Experimental Social Psychology, 20,* 65–122.(11)

Batson, C. D. (1990). How social an animal? The human capacity for caring. *American Psychologist, 45,* 336–346.(11)

Batson, C. D., Batson, J. G., Slingsby, J. K., Harrell, K. L., Peekna, H. M., & Todd, R. M. (in press). Empathic joy and the empathy-altruism hypothesis. *Journal of Personality and Social Psychology.*(11)

Batson, C. D., Duncan, B. D., Ackerman, P., Buckley, T., & Birch, K. (1981). Is empathic emotion a source of altruistic motivation? *Journal of Personality and Social Psychology, 40,* 290–302.(11)

Batson, C. D., Dyck, J. L., Brandt, J. R., Batson, J. G., Powell, A. L., McMaster, M. R., & Griffitt, C. (1988). Five studies testing two new egoistic alternatives to the empathy-altruism hypothesis. *Journal of Personality and Social Psychology, 55,* 52–77.(11)

Batson, C. D., & Oleson, K. C. (1991). Current status of the empathy-altruism hypothesis. *Review of Personality and Social Psychology, 12,* 62–85.(11)

Batson, C. D., O'Quin, K., Fultz, J., Vanderplas, M., & Isen, A. M. (1983). Influence of self-reported distress and empathy on egoistic versus altruistic motivation to help. *Journal of Personality and Social Psychology, 45,* 706–718.(11)

Bauer, R. A. (1970). Self-confidence and persuasibility: One more time. *Journal of Marketing Research, 7,* 256–258.(7)

Baum, A., Aiello, J. R., & Calesnick, L. E. (1978). Crowding and personal control: Social density and the development of learned helplessness. *Journal of Personality and Social Psychology, 36,* 1000–1011.(8, 14)

Baum, A., Harpin, R. E., & Valins, S. (1975). The role of group phenomena in the experience of crowding. *Environment and Behavior, 7,* 185–198.(14)

Baum, A., & Paulus, P. (1987). Crowding. In D. Stokols & I. Altman (Eds.), *Handbook of environmental psychology.* New York: Wiley.(14)

Baum, A., Singer, J., & Baum, C. (1981). Stress and the environment. *Journal of Social Issues, 37*(1), 4–35.(14)

Baum, A., & Valins, S. (1977). *Architecture and social behavior: Psychological studies of social density.* Hillsdale, NJ: Erlbaum.(14)

Baumeister, R. F. (1987). How the self became a problem: A psychological review of historical research. *Journal of Personality and Social Psychology, 52,* 163–176.(3)

Baumeister, R. F., & Jones, E. E. (1978). When self-presentation is constrained by the target's knowledge: Consistency and compensation. *Journal of Personality and Social Psychology, 36,* 608–618.(3)

Beaman, A. L., Klentz, B., Diener, E., & Svanum, S. (1979). Self-awareness and transgression in children: Two field studies. *Journal of Personality and Social Psychology, 37,* 1835–1846.(3)

Beardsley, E. L. (1971). Privacy: Autonomy and selective disclosure. In J. R. Pennock & J. W. Chapman (Eds.), *Privacy* (pp. 56–70). New York: Atherton.(14)

Beattie, C., & Spencer, B. G. (1971). Career attainment in Canadian bureaucracies: Unscrambling the effects of age, seniority, education, and ethnic linguistic factors in salary. *American Journal of Sociology, 77,* 472–490.(13)

Becker, F. D. (1973). Study of spatial markers. *Journal of Personality and Social Psychology, 26,* 439–445.(14)

Becker, F. D., & Conglio, C. (1975). Environmental messages: Personalization and territory. *Humanitas, 11,* 55–74.(14)

Becker, F. D., Gield, B., Gaylin, K., & Sayer, S. (1983). Office design in a community college: Effect on work and communication patterns. *Environment and Behavior, 15,* 699–726.(14)

Becker, F. D., & Mayo, C. (1971). Delineating personal distance and territoriality. *Environment and Behavior, 3,* 375–381.(14)

Belk, R. W. (1991). The ineluctable mysteries of possessions. In F. W. Rudmin (Ed.), To have possessions: A handbook on ownership and property. [Special Issue.] *Journal of Social Behavior and Personality, 6*(6), 17–55.(14)

Bell, P. A., & Baron, R. A. (1974). Effects of heat, noise, and provocation on retaliatory evaluative behavior. *Bulletin of the Psychonomic Society, 4,* 479–481.(10, 14)

Bell, P. A., & Baron, R. A. (1976). Aggression and heat: The mediating role of negative affect. *Journal of Applied Social Psychology, 6,* 18–30.(10, 14)

Bell, P. A., & Fusco, M. E. (1989). Heat and violence in the Dallas field data: Linearity, curvilinearity, and heteroscedasticity. *Journal of Applied Social Psychology, 19,* 1479–1482.(14)

Bem, D. J. (1967). Self-perception: An alternative interpretation of cognitive dissonance phenomena. *Psychological Review, 74,* 183–200.(3, 7)

Bem, D. J. (1972). Self-perception theory. *Advances in Experimental Social Psychology, 6,* 2–62.(3, 7)

Bem, S. L. (1987). Gender schema theory and the romantic tradition. *Review of Personality and Social Psychology, 7,* 251–271.(3)

Bennett, A. (1985, October 4). In today's China, road to romance begins at the bank. *The Wall Street Journal,* pp. 1, 7.(9)

Benson, P. L., Karabenick, S. A., & Lerner, R. M. (1976). Pretty pleases: The effects of physical attractiveness, race, and sex on receiving help. *Journal of Experimental Social Psychology, 12,* 409–415.(11)

Berg, J. H. (1984). Development of friendship between roommates. *Journal of Personality and Social Psychology, 46,* 346–356.(9)

Berger, J., Rosenholtz, S. J., & Zelditch, M., Jr. (1980). Status organizing processes. *Annual Review of Sociology, 6,* 479–508.(12)

Berglas, S., & Jones, E. E. (1978). Drug choice as an externalization strategy in response to noncontingent success. *Journal of Personality and Social Psychology, 36,* 405–417.(3)

Berkowitz, B. (1987). *Local heroes.* Lexington, MA: Lexington Books.(11)

Berkowitz, L. (1965a). The concept of aggressive drive: Some additional considerations. In L. Berkowitz (Ed.), *Advances in experimental social psychology* (Vol. 2). New York: Academic Press.(10)

Berkowitz, L. (1965b). Some aspects of observed aggression. *Journal of Personality and Social Psychology, 2,* 359–369.(10)

Berkowitz, L. (1968, September). Impulse, aggression, and the gun. *Psychology Today,* pp. 18–22.(10)

Berkowitz, L. (1969). The frustration-aggression hypothesis revisited. In L. Berkowitz (Ed.), *Roots of aggression: A reexamination of the frustration-aggression hypothesis.* New York: Atherton.(10)

Berkowitz, L. (1971). The contagion of violence: An S-R mediational analysis of some effects of observed aggression. In W. Arnold & M. Page (Eds.), *Nebraska Symposium on Motivation* (Vol. 18). Lincoln, NE: University of Nebraska Press.(10)

Berkowitz, L. (1983a). Aversively stimulated aggression. *American Psychologist, 38,* 1135–1144.(10, 14)

Berkowitz, L. (1983b). The experience of anger as a parallel process in the display of impulsive, "angry" aggression. In R. Green & E. Donnerstein (Eds.), *Aggression: Theoretical and empirical reviews.* New York: Academic Press.(10, 14)

Berkowitz, L. (1984). Some effects of thoughts on anti- and prosocial influences of media events: A cognitive-neoassociation analysis. *Psychological Bulletin, 95,* 410–427.(10)

Berkowitz, L. (1989). Frustration-aggression hypothesis: Examination and reformulation. *Psychological Bulletin, 106,* 59–73.(10)

Berkowitz, L., & Alioto, J. T. (1973). The meaning of an observed event as a determinant of its aggressive consequences. *Journal of Personality and Social Psychology, 28,* 206–217.(10)

Berkowitz, L., & Daniels, L. R. (1963). Responsibility and dependency. *Journal of Abnormal and Social Psychology, 66,* 664–669.(11)

Berkowitz, L., & Heimer, K. (1989). On the construction of the anger experience: Aversive events and negative priming in the formation of feelings. *Advances in Experimental Social Psychology, 22,* 1–37.(10)

Berkowitz, L., & LePage, A. (1967). Weapons as aggression-eliciting stimuli. *Journal of Personality and Social Psychology, 7,* 202–207.(10)

Bernal, E. M. (1984). Bias in mental testing: Evidence for an alternative to the hereditary-environment controversy. In C. R. Reynolds & R. T. Brown (Eds.), *Perspectives on bias in mental testing.* New York: Plenum.(13)

Berry, D. S. (1990a). The perceiver as naive scientist or the scientist as naive perceiver?: An ecological view of social knowledge acquisition. *Contemporary Social Psychology, 14,* 145–153.(4)

Berry, D. S. (1990b). What can a moving face tell us? *Journal of Personality and Social Psychology, 58,* 1004–1014.(4)

Berry, D. S., & Brownlow, S. (1989). Were the physiognomists right?: Personality correlates of facial babyishness. *Personality and Social Psychology Bulletin, 15,* 266–279.(4)

Berry, D. S., & McArthur, L. Z. (1985). Some components and consequences of a babyface. *Journal of Personality and Social Psychology, 48,* 312–323.(4)

Berry, D. S., & McArthur, L. Z. (1986). Perceiving character in faces: The impact of age-related craniofacial changes on social perception. *Psychological Bulletin, 100,* 3–18.(4)

Berry, J. W. (1974). Canadian psychology: Some social and applied emphases. *Canadian Psychologist, 15,* 132–139.(13)

Berry, J. W. (1978). Social psychology: Comparative, societal, and universal. *Canadian Psychological Review, 19,* 93–104.(13)

Berscheid, E. (1966). Opinion change and communicator-communicatee similarity and dissimilarity. *Journal of Personality and Social Psychology, 4,* 670–680.(7)

Berscheid, E. (1985). Interpersonal attraction. In G. Lindzey & E. Aronson (Eds.), *Handbook of social psychology,* (3rd ed., Vol. 2, pp. 413–484). New York: Random House.(9)

Berscheid, E., Graziano, W., Monson, T., & Dermer, M. (1976). Outcome dependency: Attention, attribution, and attraction. *Journal of Personality and Social Psychology, 34,* 978–989.(3)

Berscheid, E., & Walster, E. (1978). *Interpersonal attraction* (2nd ed.). Reading, MA: Addison-Wesley.(9)

Bersoff, D. N., & Verrilli, D. B. (1988). *Brief for* amicus curiae *American Psychological Association in support of respondent.* Washington, DC: Wilson-Epes.(13)

Betancourt, H. (1990). An attribution-empathy model of helping behavior: Behavioral intentions and judgments of help-giving. *Personality and Social Psychology Bulletin, 16,* 573–591.(11)

Beveridge, W. I. B. (1964). *The art of scientific investigation.* London: Mercury.(2)

Bickman, L. (1979). Interpersonal influence and the reporting of a crime. *Personality and Social Psychology Bulletin, 5,* 32–35.(11)

Bickman, L., & Kamzan, M. (1973). The effect of race and need on helping behavior. *Journal of Social Psychology, 89,* 73-77.(11)

Biddle, B. J., & Thomas, E. J. (Eds.). (1966). *Role theory: Concepts and research.* New York: Wiley.(1)

Biner, P. M., Butler, D. L., Fischer, A. R., & Westergren, A. J. (1989). An arousal optimization model of lighting level preferences: An interaction of social situation and task demands. *Environment and Behavior, 21,* 3–16.(14)

Bird, C. (1940). *Social psychology.* New York: Appleton-Century-Crofts.(12)

Birdwhistell, R. L. (1978). *Kinesics and context.* Philadelphia: University of Pennsylvania Press.(5)

Birnbaum, M. H. (1972). Morality judgments: Tests of an averaging model. *Journal of Experimental Psychology, 93,* 35–42.(4)

Birnbaum, M. H. (1973). Morality judgment: Test of an averaging model with differential weights. *Journal of Experimental Psychology, 99,* 395–399.(4)

Birnbaum, M. H. (1974). The nonadditivity of person impressions. *Journal of Experimental Psychology, 102,* 543–561.(4)

Blais, M. R., Sabourin, S., Boucher, C., & Vallerand, R. J. (1990). Toward a motivational model of couple happiness. *Journal of Personality and Social Psychology, 59,* 1021–1031.(9)

Blake, R., Rhead, C., Wedge, B., & Mouton, J. (1956). Housing architecture and social interaction. *Sociometry, 19,* 133–139.(14)

Blascovich, J., & Kelsey, R. M. (1990). Using electrodermal and cardiovascular measures of arousal in social psychological research. *Review of Personality and Social Psychology, 11,* 45–73.(6)

Bleda, P., & Bleda, E. (1978). Effects of sex and smoking on reactions to spatial invasion at a shopping mall. *Journal of Social Psychology, 104,* 311–312.(14)

Bless, H., Bohner, G., Schwartz, N., & Strack, F. (1990). Mood and persuasion: A cognitive response analysis. *Personality and Social Psychology Bulletin, 16,* 331–345.(7)

Block, L. K., & Stokes, G. S. (1989). Performance and satisfaction in private versus nonprivate work settings. *Environment and Behavior, 21,* 277–297.(14)

Blumoff, T. Y. (1990). The third best choice: An essay on law and history. *The Hastings Law Journal, 41,* 537–576.(7)

Bochner, S., Duncan, R., Kennedy, E., & Orr, F. (1976). Acquaintance links between residents of a high rise building: An application of the "small world" method. *Journal of Social Psychology, 100,* 277–284.(14)

Bohrnstedt, G. W., & Fisher, G. A. (1986). The effects of recalled childhood and adolescent relationships compared to current role performances on young adults' affective functioning. *Social Psychology Quarterly, 49,* 19–32.(3)

Bond, C. F., Jr. (1982). Social facilitation: A self-presentational view. *Journal of Personality and Social Psychology, 42,* 1042–1050.(12)

Bond, C. F., Jr., & Titus, L. J. (1983). Social facilitation: A meta-analysis of 241 studies. *Psychological Bulletin, 94,* 265–292.(12)

Bond, M. H., & Cheung, T.-S. (1983). College students' spontaneous self-concept: The effect of culture among respondents in Hong Kong, Japan, and the United States. *Journal of Cross-Cultural Psychology, 14,* 153–171.(3)

Booth, A. (1972). Sex and social participation. *American Sociological Review, 37,* 183–192.(9)

Borden, R. J. (1975). Witnessed aggression: Influence of an observer's sex and values on aggressive responding. *Journal of Personality and Social Psychology, 31,* 567–573.(10)

Borden, R. J. (1980). Audience influence. In P. B. Paulus (Ed.), *Psychology of group influence.* Hillsdale, NJ: Erlbaum.(12)

Bordieri, J. E., & Drehmer, D. E. (1984). Vietnam veterans: Fighting the employment war. *Journal of Applied Social Psychology, 14,* 341–347.(13)

Bornstein, R. F. (1989). Exposure and affect: Overview and meta-analysis of research, 1968–1987. *Psychological Bulletin, 106,* 265–289.(9)

Borys, S., & Perlman, D. (1985). Gender differences in loneliness. *Personality and Social Psychology Bulletin, 11,* 63–74.(9)

Bouchard, T. J., Jr. (1972). Training, motivation, and personality as determinants of the effectiveness of brainstorming groups and individuals. *Journal of Applied Psychology, 56,* 324–331.(12)

Bowlby, J. (1969). *Attachment and loss: Vol. 1. Attachment.* New York: Basic Books.(9)

Bowlby, J. (1973). *Attachment and loss: Vol. 2. Separation: Anxiety and anger.* New York: Basic Books.(9)

Bowlby, J. (1980). *Attachment and loss: Vol. 3. Loss.* New York: Basic Books.(9)

Bowsher v. Synar. 478 U.S. 714 (1986).(7)

Boyce, P. (1974). Users' assessments of a landscaped office. *Journal of Architectural Research, 3*(3), 44–62.(14)

Boyd, R., & Richerson, P. J. (1990). Culture and cooperation. In J. J. Manbridge (Ed.), *Beyond self-interest* (pp. 111–132). Chicago: University of Chicago Press.(11)

Bradley, R. H., & Caldwell, B. M. (1980). The relation of home environment, cognitive competence, and IQ among males and females. *Child Development, 51,* 1140–1148.(13)

Bramson, L., & Goethals, G. W. (Eds.). (1968). *War* (rev. ed.). New York: Basic Books.(10)

Bray, R. M., & Kerr, N. L. (1982). Methodological considerations in the study of the psychology of the courtroom. In N. L. Kerr & R. M. Bray (Eds.), *The psychology of the courtroom.* New York: Academic Press.(2)

Breckler, S. J., & Wiggins, E. C. (1989). Affect versus evaluation in the structure of attitudes. *Journal of Experimental Social Psychology, 25,* 253–271.(6)

Brehm, J. W. (1966). *A theory of psychological reactance.* New York: Academic Press.(7, 8)

Brehm, J. W., Stires, L. K., Sensenig, J., & Shaban, J. (1966). The attractiveness of an eliminated choice alternative. *Journal of Experimental Social Psychology, 2,* 301–313.(8)

Brehm, S. S. (1988). Passionate love. In R. J. Sternberg & M. L. Barnes (Eds.), *The psychology of love* (pp. 232–263). New Haven, CT: Yale University Press.(9)

Brehm, S. S. (1992). *Intimate relationships* (2nd ed.). New York: McGraw-Hill.(9)

Brehm, S. S., & Brehm, J. W. (1981). *Psychological reactance: A theory of freedom and control.* New York: Academic Press.(7, 8)

Brenner, M., Branscomb, H. H., & Schwartz, G. E. (1979). Psychological Stress Evaluator: Two tests of a vocal measure. *Psychophysiology, 16*(4), 351–357.(5)

Brewer, M. B. (1986). The role of ethnocentrism in intergroup conflict. In S. Worchel & W. G. Austin (Eds.), *Psychology of intergroup relations* (2nd ed., pp. 88–102). Chicago: Nelson-Hall.(13)

Brewer, M. B., Dull, V., & Lui, L. (1981). Perceptions of the elderly: Stereotypes as prototypes. *Journal of Personality and Social Psychology, 41,* 656–670.(4)

Brewer, M. B., & Kramer, R. M. (1985). The psychology of intergroup attitudes and behavior. *Annual Review of Psychology, 36,* 219–243.(13)

Brickner, M. A., Harkins, S. G., & Ostrom, T. M. (1986). Effects of personal involvement: Thought-provoking implications for social loafing. *Journal of Personality and Social Psychology, 51,* 763–769.(12)

Briggs, S. R. (1985). A trait account of social shyness. *Review of Personality and Social Psychology, 6,* 35–64.(4)

Brigham, J. C. (1971). Ethnic stereotypes. *Psychological Bulletin, 76,* 15–38.(13)

Brill, M. (1984). *Using office design to increase productivity* (Vol. 1). Buffalo, NY: Workplace Design and Productivity.(14)

Brinberg, D., & Castell, P. (1982). A resource exchange theory approach to interpersonal interactions: A test of Foa's theory. *Journal of Personality and Social Psychology, 43,* 260–269.(13)

Brink, J. H. (1977). Effect of interpersonal communication on attraction. *Journal of Personality and Social Psychology, 35,* 783–790.(9)

Brislin, R. W. (1980). Introduction to social psychology. In H. C. Triandis & R. W. Brislin (Eds.), *Handbook of cross-cultural psychology: Social psychology* (Vol. 5). Boston: Allyn & Bacon.(13)

Brody, E. M. (1990). *Women-in-the-middle: Their parent care years.* New York: Springer.(11)

Broll, L., Gross, A. E., & Piliavin, I. M. (1974). Effects of offered and requested help on help-seeking and reactions to being helped. *Journal of Applied Social Psychology, 4,* 244–258.(11)

Broverman, D. M., Klaiber, E. L., Kobayashi, Y., & Vogel, W. (1968). Roles of activation and inhibition in sex differences in cognitive abilities. *Psychological Review, 75,* 23–50.(13)

Broverman, I. K., Broverman, D. M., Clarkson, F. E., Rosenkrantz, P. S., & Vogel, S. R. (1970). Sex-role stereotypes and clinical judgements of mental health. *Journal of Consulting and Clinical Psychology, 34,* 1–7.(13)

Broverman, I. K., Vogel, S. R., Broverman, D. M., Clarkson, F. E., & Rosenkrantz, P. S. (1972). Sex-role stereotypes: A current appraisal. *Journal of Social Issues, 28*(2), 59–78.(13)

Brower, S., Dockett, K., & Taylor, R. B. (1983). Residents' perceptions of territorial features and perceived local threat. *Environment and Behavior, 15,* 419–437.(14)

Brown v. Board of Education, 347 U.S. 483 (1954).(13)

Brown, B. B., & Werner, C. (1985). Social cohesiveness, territoriality, and holiday decorations: The influence of cul-de-sacs. *Environment and Behavior, 17,* 539–565.(14)

Brown, B. R. (1977). Face-saving and face-restoration in negotiation. In D. Druckman (Ed.), *Negotiations: Social-psychological perspectives.* Beverly Hills, CA: Sage.(13)

Brown, P., & Elliott, R. (1965). Control of aggression in a nursery school class. *Journal of Experimental Child Psychology, 2,* 103–107.(10)

Brown, P., & Levinson, S. (1987). *Politeness: Some universals in language use.* Cambridge, England: Cambridge University Press.(8)

Brown, R. (1986). *Social psychology: The second edition.* New York: Free Press.(5)

Brown, R., & Fish, D. (1983). The psychological causality implicit in language. *Cognition, 14,* 237–273.(5)

Brown, R., & Van Kleeck, M. H. (1989). Enough said: Three principles of explanation. *Journal of Personality and Social Psychology, 57,* 590–604.(5)

Bryant, J., & Zillmann, D. (1979). The effect of the intensification of annoyance through residual excitation from unrelated prior stimulation on substantially delayed hostile behavior. *Journal of Experimental Social Psychology, 15,* 470–480.(10)

Buck, R. (1980). Nonverbal behavior and the theory of emotion: The facial feedback hypothesis. *Journal of Personality and Social Psychology, 38,* 811–824.(5)

Bugental, D. E., Kaswan, J. E., & Love, L. R. (1970). Perception of contradictory meanings conveyed by verbal and nonverbal channels. *Journal of Personality and Social Psychology, 16,* 647–655.(5)

Bugental, D. E., Love, L. R., & Gianetto, R. M. (1971). Perfidious feminine faces. *Journal of Personality and Social Psychology, 17,* 314–318.(5)

Bullinger, M. (1989). Psychological effects of air pollution on healthy residents—A time-series approach. *Journal of Environmental Psychology, 9,* 103–118.(14)

Burger, J. M. (1986). Increasing compliance by improving the deal: The that's-not-all technique. *Journal of Personality and Social Psychology, 51,* 277–283.(8)

Burke, M. C., & Edell, J. A. (1989). The impact of feelings on ad-based affect and cognition. *Journal of Marketing Research, 26,* 69–83.(6, 7)

Burstein, E., & Worchel, P. (1962). Arbitrariness of frustration and its consequences for aggression in a social situation. *Journal of Personality, 30,* 528–540.(10)

Bushman, B. J., & Geen, R. G. (1990). Role of cognitive-emotional mediators and individual differences in the effects of media violence. *Journal of Personality and Social Psychology, 58,* 156–163.(10)

Buss, A. H. (1961). *The psychology of aggression.* New York: Wiley.(10)

Buss, A. H. (1963). Physical aggression in relation to different frustrations. *Journal of Abnormal and Social Psychology, 67,* 1–7.(10)

Buss, A. H. (1967). Instrumentality of aggression, feedback, and frustration as determinants of physical aggression. *Journal of Personality and Social Psychology, 3,* 153–162.(10)

Buss, A. H. (1971). Aggression pays. In J. L. Singer (Ed.), *The control of aggression and violence* (pp. 7–18). New York: Academic Press.(10)

Buss, D. M. (1984). Toward a psychology of the person-environment (PE) correlation: The role of spouse selection. *Journal of Personality and Social Psychology, 47,* 361–377.(9)

Buss, D. M., & Barnes, M. (1986). Preferences in human mate selection. *Journal of Personality and Social Psychology, 50,* 559–570.(9)

Buss, D. M., & Craik, K. H. (1983). Contemporary worldviews: Personal and policy implications. *Journal of Applied Social Psychology, 13,* 259–280.(6)

Byrne, D. (1961). The influence of propinquity and opportunities for interaction on classroom relationships. *Human Relations, 14,* 63–70.(9, 14)

Byrne, D. (1971). *The attraction paradigm.* New York: Academic Press.(9)

Byrne, D., & Clore, G. L. (1970). A reinforcement model of evaluative responses. *Personality: An International Journal, 1,* 103–128.(9)

Byrne, D., Clore, G. L., & Smeaton, G. (1986). The attraction hypothesis: Do similar attitudes affect anything? *Journal of Personality and Social Psychology, 51,* 1167–1170.(9)

Cacioppo, J. T., & Petty, R. E. (1980). Sex differences in influenceability: Toward specifying the underlying process. *Personality and Social Psychology Bulletin, 6,* 651–656.(8)

Cacioppo, J. T., & Petty, R. E. (1982). The need for cognition. *Journal of Personality and Social Psychology, 42,* 116–131.(7)

Cacioppo, J. T., Petty, R. E., & Kao, C. (1984). The efficient assessment of need for cognition. *Journal of Personality and Assessment, 48,* 306–307.(7)

Cacioppo, J. T., Petty, R. E., & Marshall-Goodell, B. (1984). Electromyographic specificity during simple physical and attitudinal tasks: Location and topographical features of integrated EMG responses. *Biological Psychology, 18,* 85–121.(6)

Cacioppo, J. T., Petty, R. E., & Tassinary, L. G. (1989). Social psychophysiology: A new look. *Advances in Experimental Social Psychology, 22,* 39–91.(6)

Caldwell, D. F., & O'Reilly, C. A., III. (1982). Boundary spanning and individual performance: The impact of self-monitoring. *Journal of Applied Psychology, 67,* 124–127.(3)

Calhoun, J. B. (1962). Population density and social pathology. *Scientific American, 206*(2), 139–148.(14)

Campbell, A., Converse, P. E., & Rogers, W. L. (1976). *The quality of American life: Perceptions, evaluations, and satisfactions.* New York: Russell Sage Foundation.(2)

Campbell, D. E. (1979). Interior office design and visitor response. *Journal of Applied Psychology, 64,* 648–653.(14)

Campbell, D. E., & Campbell, T. A. (1988). A new look at informal communication: The role of the physical environment. *Environment and Behavior, 20,* 211–226.(14)

Campbell, D. T. (1978). On the genetics of altruism and the counter-hedonic components of human culture. In L. Wispé (Ed.), *Altruism, sympathy, and helping: Psychological and sociological principles.* New York: Academic Press.(11)

Campbell, D. T., & Stanley, J. C. (1966). *Experimental and quasi-experimental designs for research.* Chicago: Rand McNally.(2)

Campbell, J. D., Tesser, A., & Fairey, P. J. (1986). Conformity and attention to the stimulus: Some temporal and contextual dynamics. *Journal of Personality and Social Psychology, 51,* 315–324.(8)

Campbell, J. M. (1983). Ambient stressors. *Environment and Behavior, 15,* 355–380.(14)

Cannavale, F. J., Scarr, H. A., & Pepitone, A. (1970). Deindividuation in the small group: Further evidence. *Journal of Personality and Social Psychology, 16,* 141–147.(10)

Cantor, N. (1981). A cognitive-social approach to personality. In N. Cantor & J. F. Kihlstrom (Eds.), *Personality, cognition, and social interaction* (pp. 23–44). Hillsdale, NJ: Erlbaum.(4)

Cantor, N., Mischel, W., & Schwartz, J. C. (1982). A prototype analysis of psychological situations. *Cognitive Psychology, 14,* 45–77.(4)

Caporael, L. R. (1981). The paralanguage of caregiving: Baby talk to the institutionalized aged. *Journal of Personality and Social Psychology, 40,* 876–884.(5)

Capshew, J. H. (1986). Networks of leadership: A quantitative study of SPSSI presidents, 1936–1986. *Journal of Social Issues, 42*(1), 75–106.(1)

Carli, L. L. (1990). Gender, language, and influence. *Journal of Personality and Social Psychology, 59,* 941–951.(5)

Carlsmith, J. M., & Anderson, C. A. (1979). Ambient temperature and the occurrence of collective violence: A new analysis. *Journal of Personality and Social Psychology, 37,* 337–344.(10)

Carlsmith, J. M., Ellsworth, P. C., & Aronson, E. (1976). *Methods of research in social psychology.* Reading, MA: Addison-Wesley.(2)

Carlson, M., Charlin, V., & Miller, N. (1988). Positive mood and helping behavior: A test of six hypotheses. *Journal of Personality and Social Psychology, 55,* 211–229.(11)

Carlson, M., & Miller, N. (1987). Explanation of the relation between negative mood and helping. *Psychological Bulletin, 102,* 91–108.(11)

Carmer, R. E., McMaster, M. R., Bartell, P. A., & Dragna, M. (1988). Subject competence and minimization of the bystander effect. *Journal of Applied Social Psychology, 18,* 1133–1148.(11)

Carnevale, P. J. D., & Pegnetter, R. (1985). The selection of mediation tactics in public sector disputes: A contingency analysis. *Journal of Social Issues, 41*(2), 65–81.(13)

Carnevale, P. J. D., Pruitt, D. G., & Britton, S. D. (1979). Looking tough: The negotiator under constituent surveillance. *Personality and Social Psychology Bulletin, 5,* 118–121.(13)

Carnevale, P. J. D., Pruitt, D. G., & Seilheimer, S. D. (1981). Looking and competing: Accountability and visual access in integrative bargaining. *Journal of Personality and Social Psychology, 40,* 111–120.(13)

Caron, A. H. (1979). First-time exposure to television: Effects on Inuit children's cultural images. *Communication Research, 6,* 135–154.(6)

Carpenter, C. R. (1958). Territoriality: A review of concepts and problems. In A. Roe & G. Simpson (Eds.), *Behavior and evolution.* New Haven, CT: Yale University Press.(14)

Carr, S. J., & Dabbs, J. M., Jr. (1974). The effects of lighting, distance, and intimacy of topic on verbal and visual behavior. *Sociometry, 37,* 592–600.(5)

Cartwright, D. (1968). The nature of group cohesiveness. In D. Cartwright & A. Zander (Eds.), *Group dynamics: Research and theory* (3rd ed.). New York: Harper & Row.(12)

Cartwright, D., & Zander, A. (Eds.). (1968). *Group dynamics: Research and theory* (3rd ed.). New York: Harper & Row.(12)

Carver, C. S. (1979). A cybernetic model of self-attention processes. *Journal of Personality and Social Psychology, 37,* 1251–1281.(3)

Cary, M. S. (1978). The role of gaze in the initiation of conversation. *Social Psychology, 41,* 269–271.(5)

⚬ Cash, T. F., Begley, P. J., McCown, D. A., & Weise, B. C. (1975). When counselors are seen but not heard: Initial impact of physical attractiveness. *Journal of Counseling Psychology, 22,* 273–279.(4)

⚬ Cash, T. F., Kehr, J. A., Polyson, J., & Freeman, V. (1977). Role of physical attractiveness in peer attribution of psychological disturbance. *Journal of Consulting and Clinical Psychology, 45,* 987–993.(4)

Castelfranchi, C., & Poggi, I. (1990). Blushing as a discourse: Was Darwin wrong? In R. Crozier (Ed.), *Shyness and embarrassment: A social psychological perspective* (pp. 230–251). New York: Cambridge University Press.(5)

Castore, C. H., & DeNinno, J. A. (1977). Investigations in

the social comparison of attitudes. In J. M. Suls & R. L. Miller (Eds.), *Social comparison processes: Theoretical and empirical perspectives.* Washington, DC: Halsted.(3)

Cecil, J. S., & Wiggins, E. C. (1991). Defining sexual harassment in the workplace. *APA Monitor, 22*(5), 42.(13)

Chaiken, S. (1979). Communicator physical attractiveness and persuasion. *Journal of Personality and Social Psychology, 37,* 1387–1397.(7)

Chaiken, S., & Eagly, A. H. (1976). Communication modality as a determinant of message persuasiveness and message comprehensibility. *Journal of Personality and Social Psychology, 34,* 605–614.(7)

Chaiken, S., & Eagly, A. H. (1983). Communication modality as a determinant of persuasion: The role of communicator salience. *Journal of Personality and Social Psychology, 45,* 241–256.(7)

Chaiken, S., Liberman, A., Eagly, A. H. (1989). Heuristic and systematic information processing within and beyond the persuasion context. In J. S. Uleman & J. A. Bargh (Eds.), *Unintended thought* (pp. 212–252). New York: Guilford Press.(7)

Chaiken, S., & Stangor, C. (1987). Attitudes and attitude change. *Annual Review of Psychology, 38,* 575–630.(6, 7)

Chapko, M. K., & Solomon, H. (1976). Air pollution and recreational behavior. *Journal of Social Psychology, 100,* 149–150.(14)

Chapman, L. J. (1967). Illusory correlation in observational report. *Journal of Verbal Learning and Verbal Behavior, 6,* 151–155.(4)

Charng, H., Piliavin, J. A., & Callero, P. L. (1988). Role identity and reasoned action in the prediction of repeated behavior. *Social Psychology Quarterly, 51,* 303–317.(11)

Chemers, M. M. (1969). Cross-cultural training as a means for improving situational favorableness. *Human Relations, 22,* 531–546.(12)

Chemers, M. M. (1983). Leadership theory and research: A systems-process integration. In P. B. Paulus (Ed.), *Basic group processes* (pp. 9–39). New York: Springer-Verlag.(12)

Chemers, M. M. (1987). Leadership processes: Intrapersonal, interpersonal, and societal influences. *Review of Personality and Social Psychology, 8,* 252–277.(12)

Chemers, M. M., & Ayman, R. (1985). Leadership orientation as a moderator of the relationship between job performance and job satisfaction for Mexican managers. *Personality and Social Psychology Bulletin, 11,* 359–367.(12)

Chemers, M. M., & Skrzypek, G. J. (1972). Experimental test of the contingency model of leadership effectiveness. *Journal of Personality and Social Psychology, 24,* 172–177.(12)

Cheng, L., & Espiritu, Y. (1989). Korean businesses in black and Hispanic neighborhoods: A study of intergroup relations. *Sociological Perspectives, 32,* 521–534.(13)

Cherulnik, P. D., & Koenig, R. L. (1989). Perceptions of the workplace and perceptions of the worker: A potentially practical example of the influence of environmental setting on personal identity. In G. Hardie, R. Moore, & H. Sanoff (Eds.), *Changing paradigms* (pp. 309–312). Oklahoma City, OK: Environmental Design Research Association.(14)

Chin, Y. (1988). Residents' perceptions of neighbors in married student housing: An empirical test of a conceptual model. In D. Lawrence, R. Habe, A. Hacker, & D. Sherrod (Eds.), *People's needs/planet management: Paths to co-existence* (pp. 179–185). Washington, DC: Environmental Design Research Association.(14)

Christian, J. J., Flyger, V., & Davis, D. E. (1960). Factors in the mass mortality of a herd of Sika deer, *Cervus nippon. Chesapeake Science, 1,* 79–95.(14)

Cialdini, R. B. (1985). *Influence: Science and practice.* Glenview, IL: Scott, Foresman.(8)

Cialdini, R. B. (1990). Perspectives on research classics: A door opens. *Contemporary Social Psychology, 14,* 50–52.(1, 8)

Cialdini, R. B. (1991). Altruism or egoism? That is (still) the question. *Psychological Inquiry, 2,* 124–126.(11)

Cialdini, R. B., Baumann, D. J., & Kenrick, D. T. (1981). Insights from sadness: A three-step model of the development of altruism as hedonism. *Developmental Review, 1,* 207–223.(11)

Cialdini, R. B., Borden, R. J., Thorne, A., Walker, M. R., & Freeman, S. (1976). Basking in reflected glory: Three (football) field studies. *Journal of Personality and Social Psychology, 34,* 366–375.(3)

Cialdini, R. B., Cacioppo, J. T., Bassett, R., & Miller, J. A. (1978). Low-ball procedure for producing compliance: Commitment then cost. *Journal of Personality and Social Psychology, 36,* 463–476.(8)

Cialdini, R. B., Darby, B. L., & Vincent, J. E. (1973). Transgression and altruism: A case for hedonism. *Journal of Experimental Social Psychology, 9,* 502–516.(11)

Cialdini, R. B., Levy, A., Herman, P., & Evenbeck, S. (1973). Attitudinal politics: The strategy of moderation. *Journal of Personality and Social Psychology, 25,* 100–108.(7)

Cialdini, R. B., Levy, A., Herman, P., Kozlowski, L., & Petty, R. E. (1976). Elastic shifts of opinion: Determinants of direction and durability. *Journal of Personality and Social Psychology, 34,* 663–672.(7)

Cialdini, R. B., Schaller, M., Houlihan, D., Arps, K., Fultz, J., & Beaman, A. L. (1987). Empathy-based helping: Is it selflessly or selfishly motivated? *Journal of Personality and Social Psychology, 52,* 749–758. (11)

Cialdini, R. B., Vincent, J. E., Lewis, S. K., Catalan, J., Wheeler, D., & Darby, B. L. (1975). A reciprocal concessions procedure for inducing compliance: The door-in-the-face technique. *Journal of Personality and Social Psychology, 21,* 206–215. (8)

Clark, H., & Manzo, L. (1988). Community gardens: Factors that influence participation. In D. Lawrence, R. Habe, A. Hacker, & D. Sherrod (Eds.), *People's needs/planet management: Paths to co-existence* (pp. 57–61). Washington, DC: Environmental Design Research Association. (14)

Clark, H. H. (1985). Language use and language users. In G. Lindzey and E. Aronson (Eds.), *Handbook of social psychology* (3rd ed., Vol. 2, pp. 179–231). New York: Random House. (5)

Clark, K. B., & Clark, M. P. (1947). Racial identification and preference in Negro children. In T. M. Newcomb & E. L. Hartley (Eds.), *Readings in social psychology.* New York: Holt. (3)

Clark, M. S. (1983). Reactions to aid in communal and exchange relationships. In J. D. Fisher, A. Nadler, & B. M. DePaulo (Eds.), *New directions in helping (Vol. 1): Recipient reactions to aid.* New York: Academic Press. (11)

Clark, M. S. (1984). Record keeping in two types of relationships. *Journal of Personality and Social Psychology, 47,* 549–557. (9)

Clark, M. S., & Mills, J. (1979). Interpersonal attraction in exchange and communal relationships. *Journal of Personality and Social Psychology, 37,* 12–24. (9)

Clark, M. S., Mills, J., & Powell, M. C. (1986). Keeping track of needs in communal and exchange relationships. *Journal of Personality and Social Psychology, 51,* 333–338. (9)

Clark, R. D., III, & Word, L. E. (1972). Why don't bystanders help? Because of ambiguity? *Journal of Personality and Social Psychology, 24,* 392–400. (11)

Clary, E. G., & Orenstein, L. (1991). The amount and effectiveness of help: The relationship of motives and abilities to helping behavior. *Personality and Social Psychology Bulletin, 17,* 58–64. (11)

Clee, M. A., & Wicklund, R. A. (1980). Consumer behavior and psychological reactance. *Journal of Consumer Research, 6,* 389–405. (8)

Cline, R. J. W. (1989). The politics of intimacy: Costs and benefits determining disclosure intimacy in male-female dyads. *Journal of Social and Personal Relationships, 6,* 5–20. (5)

Clore, G. L., & Kerber, K. W. (1978). *Toward an affective theory of attraction and trait attribution.* Unpublished manuscript, University of Illinois, Champaign. (9)

Clore, G. L., Wiggins, N. H., & Itkin, S. (1975). Gain and loss in attraction: Attributions from nonverbal behavior. *Journal of Personality and Social Psychology, 31,* 706–712. (5)

Cohen, D., Whitmyre, J. W., & Funk, W. H. (1960). Effect of group cohesiveness and training upon creative thinking. *Journal of Applied Psychology, 44,* 319–322. (12)

Cohen, E. (1980). Design and redesign of the desegregated school: Problems of status, power, and conflict. In W. G. Stephan & J. Feagin (Eds.), *School desegregation* (pp. 251–280). New York: Plenum. (13)

Cohen, S. (1978). Environmental load and the allocation of attention. In A. Baum, J. E. Singer, & S. Valins (Eds.), *Advances in environmental psychology.* Hillsdale, NJ: Erlbaum. (14)

Cohen, S. (1980a). The aftereffects of stress on human performance and social behavior: A review of research and theory. *Psychological Bulletin, 88,* 82–108. (14)

Cohen, S. (1980b). Cognitive processes as determinants of environmental stress. In I. Sarason & C. Spielberger (Eds.), *Stress and anxiety* (Vol. 7). Washington, DC: Hemisphere. (14)

Cohen, S., Evans, G. W., Stokols, D., & Krantz, D. S. (1986). *Behavior, health, and environmental stress.* New York: Plenum. (14)

Cohen, S., & Lezak, A. (1977). Noise and attentiveness to social cues. *Environment and Behavior, 9,* 559–572. (14)

Cohen, S., & Wills, T. A. (1985). Stress, social support, and the buffering hypothesis. *Psychological Bulletin, 98,* 310–357. (9)

Cohn, L. D. (1991). Sex differences in the course of personality development: A meta-analysis. *Psychological Bulletin, 109,* 252–266. (13)

Coke, J. S., Batson, C. D., & McDavis, K. (1978). Empathic mediation of helping: A two-stage model. *Journal of Personality and Social Psychology, 36,* 752–766. (11)

Cole, N. S. (1981). Bias in testing. *American Psychologist, 36,* 1067–1077. (13)

Coleman, A. D. (1968). Territoriality in man: A comparison of behavior in home and hospital. *American Journal of Orthopsychiatry, 38,* 464–468. (14)

Collins, B. E. (1970). *Social psychology.* Reading, MA: Addison-Wesley. (8)

Collins, B. E. (1974). Four components of the Rotter Internal-External scale: Belief in a difficult world, a just world, a predictable world, and a politically responsive world. *Journal of Personality and Social Psychology, 29,* 381–391. (8)

Conrath, D. W. (1973). Communication patterns, organizational structure, and man: Some relationships. *Human Factors, 15,* 459–470.(14)

Cook, S. W. (1970). Motives in a conceptual analysis of attitude-related behavior. In W. J. Arnold & D. Levine (Eds.), *Nebraska symposium on motivation.* Lincoln, NE: University of Nebraska Press.(13)

Cook, S. W. (1976). Ethical issues in the conduct of research in social relations. In C. Selltiz, L. S. Wrightsman, & S. W. Cook (Eds.), *Research methods in social relations* (3rd ed.). New York: Holt, Rinehart & Winston.(2)

Cook, T. D., & Campbell, D. T. (Eds.). (1979). *The design and analysis of quasi-experiments for field settings.* Chicago: Rand McNally.(2)

Cooley, C. H. (1964). *Human nature and the social order.* New York: Schocken Books. (Originally published in 1902).(1, 3)

Cooper, H. M. (1979). Statistically combining independent studies: A meta-analysis of sex differences in conformity research. *Journal of Personality and Social Psychology, 37,* 131–146.(2)

Cooper, H. M. (1990). Meta-analysis and the integrative research review. *Review of Personality and Social Psychology, 11,* 142–163.(2)

Cooper, H. M., & Lemke, K. M. (1991). On the role of meta-analysis in personality and social psychology. *Personality and Social Psychology Bulletin, 17,* 245–251.(2)

Cooper, J. (1976). Deception and role playing: In telling the good guys from the bad guys. *American Psychologist, 31,* 605–610.(2)

Cooper, J., & Fazio, R. H. (1984). A new look at dissonance theory. *Advances in Experimental Social Psychology, 17,* 229–266.(7)

Costanzo, P. R. (1970). Conformity development as a function of self-blame. *Journal of Personality and Social Psychology, 14,* 366–374.(8)

Cota, A. A., & Dion, K. L. (1986). Salience of gender and sex composition of ad hoc groups: An experimental test of distinctiveness theory. *Journal of Personality and Social Psychology, 50,* 770–776.(3)

Cottrell, N. B. (1972). Social facilitation. In C. G. McClintock (Ed.), *Experimental social psychology.* New York: Holt.(12)

Cottrell, N. B., Wack, D. L., Sekerak, G. J., & Rittle, R. H. (1968). Social facilitation of dominant responses by the presence of an audience and the mere presence of others. *Journal of Personality and Social Psychology, 9,* 245–250.(12)

Courtright, J. A. (1978). A laboratory investigation of groupthink. *Communications Monographs, 45,* 229–246.(12)

Cox, O. C. (1948). *Caste, class, and race.* New York: Doubleday.(13)

Cox, V. C., Paulus, P. B., & McCain, G. (1984). Prison crowding research. *American Psychologist, 39,* 1148–1160.(14)

Cozby, P. C. (1973). Self-disclosure: A literature review. *Psychological Bulletin, 79,* 73–91.(5)

Crandall, C. S. (1991a). AIDS-related stigma and the lay sense of justice. *Contemporary Social Psychology, 15,* 66–67.(4)

Crandall, C. S. (1991b). *AIDS-related stigmatization: Social and illness stigma.* Manuscript submitted for publication.(4)

Crick, N. R., & Dodge, K. A. (1989). *Social information processing mechanisms of reactive and proactive aggressive behavior in children.* Unpublished manuscript.(10)

Crick, N. R., & Ladd, G. W. (1989). *Children's perceptions of the outcomes of social strategies: Do the ends justify the means?* Manuscript submitted for publication.(10)

Crocker, J., & Major, B. (1989). Social stigma and self-esteem: The self-protective properties of stigma. *Psychological Review, 96,* 608–630.(3)

Crook, J. H. (1973). The nature and function of territorial aggression. In M. F. A. Montagu (Ed.), *Man and aggression* (2nd ed.). New York: Oxford University Press.(10)

Crosby, F. (1976). A model of egoistical relative deprivation. *Psychological Review, 83,* 85–113.(10)

Crosby, F., Bromley, S., & Saxe, L. (1980). Recent unobtrusive studies of black and white discrimination and prejudice: A literature review. *Psychological Bulletin, 87,* 546–563.(13)

Cross, W. E. (1978). The Cross and Thomas models of psychological Nigrescence. *Journal of Black Psychology, 5*(1), 13–19.(3)

Croyle, R. T., & Cooper, J. (1983). Dissonance arousal: Physiological evidence. *Journal of Personality and Social Psychology, 45,* 782–791.(7)

Crusco, A. H., & Wetzel, C. G. (1984). The Midas touch: The effects of interpersonal touch on restaurant tipping. *Personality and Social Psychology Bulletin, 10,* 512–517.(5)

Crutchfield, R. S. (1955). Conformity and character. *American Psychologist, 10,* 191–198.(8)

Csikszentmihalyi, M., & Figurski, T. J. (1982). Self-awareness and aversive experience in everyday life. *Journal of Personality, 50,* 15–28.(3)

Cunningham, M. R. (1979). Weather, mood, and helping behavior: Quasi-experiments with the Sunshine Samaritan. *Journal of Personality and Social Psychology, 37,* 1947–1956.(11, 14)

Cunningham, M. R. (1981). Sociobiology as a supplementary paradigm for social psychological research. *Review of Personality and Social Psychology, 2,* 69–106.(10)

Cunningham, M. R., Shaffer, D. R., Barbee, A. P., Wolff, P. L., & Kelley, D. J. (1990). Separate processes in the relation of elation and depression to helping: Social versus personal concerns. *Journal of Experimental Social Psychology, 26,* 13–33.(11)

Curtis, R. C., & Miller, K. (1986). Believing another likes or dislikes you: Behaviors making the beliefs come true. *Journal of Personality and Social Psychology, 51,* 284–290.(5)

Cutrona, C. E. (1982). Transition to college: Loneliness and the process of social adjustment. In L. A. Peplau & D. Perlman (Eds.), *Loneliness: A sourcebook of current theory, research, and therapy.* New York: Wiley.(9)

Cutrona, C. E. (1986). Behavioral manifestations of social support: A microanalytic investigation. *Journal of Personality and Social Psychology, 51,* 201–208.(9)

Cutting, J. E., & Proffitt, D. R. (1981). Gait perception as an example of how we perceive events. In R. D. Walk & H. L. Pick (Eds.), *Intersensory perception and sensory integration* (pp. 249–273). New York: Plenum.(4)

Dakof, G. A., & Taylor, S. E. (1990). Victims' perceptions of social support: What is helpful from whom? *Journal of Personality and Social Psychology, 58,* 80–89.(9)

Dane, F. C. (1990). *Research methods.* Pacific Grove, CA: Brooks/Cole.(2, 8)

Dane, F. C., & Harshaw, R. (1991, March). *Similarity-attraction versus dissimilarity-repulsion: The establishment wins, again.* Paper presented at meeting of the Southeastern Psychological Association, New Orleans, LA.(9)

Dane, F. C., & Storms, M. D. (1977, August). *Intensified reactions to the physical proximity of another: Support for an arousal model.* American Psychological Association, San Francisco.(5)

Dane, F. C., & Wrightsman, L. S. (1982). Effects of defendants' and victims' characteristics on jurors' verdicts. In N. L. Kerr & R. M. Bray (Eds.), *The psychology of the courtroom.* New York: Academic Press, pp. 83–115.(4)

Danheiser, P. R., & Graziano, W. G. (1982). Self-monitoring and cooperation as a self-presentational strategy. *Journal of Personality and Social Psychology, 42,* 497–505.(3)

Darley, J. M., & Berscheid, E. (1967). Increased liking as a result of the anticipation of personal contact. *Human Relations, 20,* 29–39.(9)

Darley, J. M., & Fazio, R. H. (1980). Expectancy confirmation processes arising in the social interaction sequence. *American Psychologist, 35,* 867–881.(5)

Darley, J. M., & Gross, P. H. (1983). A hypothesis-confirming bias in labeling effects. *Journal of Personality and Social Psychology, 44,* 20–33.(2, 4, 5)

Darley, J. M., & Latané, B. (1968). Bystander intervention in emergencies: Diffusion of responsibility. *Journal of Personality and Social Psychology, 8,* 377–383.(11)

Darwin, C. (1872). *The expression of the emotions in man and animals.* London: John Murray.(5)

Dashiell, J. F. (1930). An experimental analysis of some group effects. *Journal of Abnormal and Social Psychology, 25,* 190–199.(12)

Davidson, B. (1984). A test of equity theory for marital adjustment. *Social Psychology Quarterly, 47,* 36–42.(9)

Davidson, L. R., & Duberman, L. (1982). Friendship: Communication and interactional patterns in same-sex dyads. *Sex Roles, 8,* 809–822.(5)

Davies, J. C. (1962). Toward a theory of revolution. *American Sociological Review, 27,* 5–19.(10)

Davies, J. C. (1969). The J-curve of rising and declining satisfactions as a cause of great revolutions and a contained rebellion. In H. D. Graham & T. R. Gurr (Eds.), *Violence in America.* New York: New American Library.(10)

Davis, D. (1982). Determinants of responsiveness in dyadic interactions. In W. Ickes & E. S. Knowles (Eds.), *Personality, roles, and social behavior.* New York: Springer-Verlag.(9)

Davis, J. H. (1969). *Group performance.* Reading, MA: Addison-Wesley.(12)

Davis, J. H., Laughlin, P. R., & Komorita, S. S. (1976). The social psychology of small groups: Cooperative and mixed motive interaction. In M. R. Rosenzweig & L. W. Porter (Eds.), *Annual Review of Psychology, 27,* 501–542.(13)

Davis, M. H., & Oathout, H. A. (1987). Maintenance of satisfaction in romantic relationships: Empathy and relational competence. *Journal of Personality and Social Psychology, 53,* 397–410.(9)

Dawes, R. M., & Smith, T. L. (1985). Attitude and opinion measurement. In G. Lindzey & E. Aronson (Eds.), *Handbook of social psychology* (3rd ed., Vol. 1, pp. 509–566). New York: Random House.(6)

Dean, L. M., Willis, F. N., & Hewitt, J. (1975). Initial interaction distance among individuals equal and unequal in military rank. *Journal of Personality and Social Psychology, 32,* 294–299.(5)

Deaux, K. (1968). Variations in warning, information preference, and anticipatory attitude change. *Journal of Personality and Social Psychology, 9,* 157–161.(7)

Deaux, K. (1976a). *The behavior of women and men.* Pacific Grove, CA: Brooks/Cole.(9)

Deaux, K. (1976b). Sex: A perspective on the attribution process. In J. H. Harvey, W. J. Ickes, & R. F. Kidd (Eds.), *New directions in attribution research* (Vol. 1, pp. 335–352). Hillsdale, NJ: Erlbaum.(4)

Deaux, K., & Emswiller, T. (1974). Explanations of successful performance on sex-linked tasks: What is skill for the male is luck for the female. *Journal of Personality and Social Psychology, 29,* 80–85.(4, 13)

Deaux, K., & Hanna, R. (1984). Courtship in the personals column: The influence of gender and sexual orientation. *Sex Roles, 11,* 363–375.(9)

Deaux, K., & Lewis, L. (1984). The structure of gender stereotypes: Interrelationships among components and gender label. *Journal of Personality and Social Psychology, 46,* 991–1004.(4)

Deaux, K., & Lewis, L. L. (1983). Components of gender stereotypes. *Psychological Documents, 13,* 25. (Ms. No. 2583)(4, 13)

Deaux, K., & Major, B. (1987). Putting gender into context: An interactive model of gender-related behavior. *Psychological Review, 94,* 369–389.(3, 5)

Deaux, K., Winton, W., Crowley, M., & Lewis, L. L. (1985). Level of categorization and content of gender stereotypes. *Social Cognition, 3,* 145–167.(4)

DeGree, C. E., & Snyder, C. R. (1985). Adler's psychology (of use) today: Personal history of traumatic life events as a self-handicapping strategy. *Journal of Personality and Social Psychology, 48,* 1512–1519.(3)

DeJong, W. (1979). An examination of self-perception mediation of the foot-in-the-door effect. *Journal of Personality and Social Psychology, 37,* 2221–2239.(8)

• DeJong, W., & Kleck, R. E. (1986). The social psychological effects of overweight. In C. P. Herman, M. P. Zanna, & E. T. Higgins (Eds.), *Physical appearance, stigma, and social behavior: The Ontario Symposium, Volume 3* (pp. 65–87). Hillsdale, NJ: Erlbaum.(4)

DeLamater, J. (1974). A definition of "group." *Small Group Behavior, 5,* 30–44.(12)

Dembroski, T. M., Lasater, T. M., & Ramirez, A. (1978). Communicator similarity, fear arousing communications, and compliance with health care recommendations. *Journal of Applied Social Psychology, 8,* 254–269.(7)

DePaulo, B. M., Brown, P. L., Ishii, S., & Fisher, J. D. (1981). Help that works: The effects of aid on subsequent task performance. *Journal of Personality and Social Psychology, 41,* 478–487.(11)

DePaulo, B. M., Lanier, K., & Davis, T. (1983). Detecting the deceit of the motivated liar. *Journal of Personality and Social Psychology, 45,* 1096–1103.(5)

DePaulo, B. M., Rosenthal, R., Eisenstat, R. A., Rogers, P. L., & Finkelstein, S. (1978). Decoding discrepant nonverbal cues. *Journal of Personality and Social Psychology, 36,* 313–323.(5)

DePaulo, B. M., Stone, J. I., & Lassiter, G. D. (1985). Telling ingratiating lies: Effects of target sex and target attractiveness on verbal and nonverbal deceptive success. *Journal of Personality and Social Psychology, 48,* 1191–1203.(5)

Derlega, V. J., Lewis, R. J., Harrison, S., Winstead, B. A., & Costanza, R. (1989). Gender differences in the initiation and attribution of tactile intimacy. *Journal of Nonverbal Behavior, 13,* 83–96.(9)

Deutsch, M. (1973). *The resolution of conflict: Constructive and destructive processes.* New Haven, CT: Yale University Press.(13)

Deutsch, M., Canavan, D., & Rubin, J. (1971). The effects of size of conflict and sex of experimenter on interpersonal bargaining. *Journal of Experimental Social Psychology, 7,* 258–267.(13)

Deutsch, M., & Gerard, H. B. (1955). A study of normative and informational social influences upon individual judgment. *Journal of Abnormal and Social Psychology, 51,* 629–636.(8)

Devine, P. G. (1989). Stereotypes and prejudice: Their automatic and controlled components. *Journal of Personality and Social Psychology, 56,* 5–18.(2, 4, 13)

Devine, P. G., Monteith, M. J., Zuwerink, J. R., & Elliot, A. J. (1991). Prejudice with and without compunction. *Journal of Personality and Social Psychology, 60,* 817–830.(13)

Diehl, M., & Stroebe, W. (1987). Productivity loss in brainstorming groups: Toward the solution of a riddle. *Journal of Personality and Social Psychology, 53,* 497–509.(12)

Diener, E., & Crandall, R. (1979). An evaluation of the Jamaican anticrime program. *Journal of Applied Social Psychology, 9,* 135–146.(10)

Di Giacomo, J.-P. (1980). Intergroup alliances and rejections within a protest movement (analysis of the social representations). *European Journal of Social Psychology, 10,* 329–344.(12)

Dion, K. K. (1972). Physical attractiveness and evaluation of children's transgressions. *Journal of Personality and Social Psychology, 24,* 207–213.(9)

Dion, K. K. (1977). The incentive value of physical attractiveness for young children. *Personality and Social Psychology Bulletin, 3,* 67–70.(9)

Dion, K. K. (1986). Stereotyping based on physical attractiveness: Issues and conceptual perspectives. In C. P. Herman, M. P. Zanna, & E. T. Higgins (Eds.), *Physical appearance, stigma, and social behavior: The Ontario Symposium, Volume 3* (pp. 7–21). Hillsdale, NJ: Erlbaum.(4)

Dion, K. K., Berscheid, E., & Walster, E. (1972). What is beautiful is good. *Journal of Personality and Social Psychology, 24,* 285–290.(9)

☙ Dipboye, R. L., Arvey, R. D., & Terpstra, D. E. (1977). Sex and physical attractiveness of raters and applicants as determinants of resume evaluations. *Journal of Applied Psychology, 62,* 288–294.(4)

Dipboye, R. L., Fromkin, H. L., & Wiback, K. (1975). Relative importance of applicant sex, attractiveness, and scholastic standing in evaluation of job applicant resumes. *Journal of Applied Psychology, 60,* 39–45.(4)

Dodge, K. A., & Coie, J. D. (1987). Social information processing factors in reactive and proactive aggression in children's peer groups. *Journal of Personality and Social Psychology, 53,* 1146–1158.(10)

Dodge, K. A., & Crick, N. R. (1990). Social information-processing bases of aggressive behavior in children. *Personality and Social Psychology Bulletin, 16,* 8–22.(10)

Dodge, K. A., Pettit, G. S., McClaskey, C. L., & Brown, M. (1986). Social competence in children. *Monographs of the Society for Research in Child Development, 51*(2, Serial No. 213).(10)

Dodge, K. A., & Tomlin, A. (1987). Cue-utilization as a mechanism of attributional bias in aggressive children. *Social Cognition, 5,* 280–300.(10)

Dollard, J., Doob, L. W., Miller, N. E., Mowrer, O. H., & Sears, R. R. (1939). *Frustration and aggression.* New Haven, CT: Yale University Press.(10)

Donnerstein, E. (1982). Erotica and human aggression. In R. G. Geen & E. Donnerstein (Eds.), *Aggression: Theoretical and empirical reviews.* New York: Academic Press.(10)

Donnerstein, E., & Berkowitz, L. (1981). Victim reactions in aggressive erotic films as a factor in violence against women. *Journal of Personality and Social Psychology, 41,* 710–724.(10)

Donnerstein, E., Donnerstein, M., & Evans, R. (1975). Erotic stimuli and aggression: Facilitation or inhibition. *Journal of Personality and Social Psychology, 32,* 237–244.(10)

Donnerstein, E., & Wilson, D. W. (1976). The effects of noise and perceived control upon ongoing and subsequent aggressive behavior. *Journal of Personality and Social Psychology, 34,* 774–781.(10, 14)

Donnerstein, M., & Donnerstein, E. (1977). Modeling in the control of interracial aggression: The problem of generality. *Journal of Personality, 45,* 100–116.(10)

Doob, A. N., & Gross, A. E. (1968). Status of frustrator as an inhibitor of horn-honking responses. *Journal of Social Psychology, 76,* 213–218.(2)

Doob, L. W. (1947). The behavior of attitudes. *Psychological Review, 54,* 135–156.(6)

Dovey, K. (1986). Home and homelessness. In I. Altman & C. Werner (Eds.), *Home environments. Human behavior and environment: Advances in theory and research* (Vol. 8, pp. 33–64). New York: Plenum.(14)

Dovidio, J. F. (1984). Helping behavior and altruism: An empirical and conceptual overview. In L. Berkowitz (Ed.), *Advances in experimental social psychology* (Vol. 17). Orlando, FL: Academic Press.(11)

Dovidio, J. F., Evans, N., & Tyler, R. B. (1986). Racial stereotypes: The contents of their cognitive representations. *Journal of Experimental Social Psychology, 22,* 22–37.(4, 13)

Dreiser, T. (1929). *A gallery of women.* New York: Boni and Liveright.(4)

Druckman, D. (Ed.). (1977). *Negotiation: A social psychological perspective.* New York: Halsted.(13)

Dubos, R. (1980). *Man adapting* (2nd ed.). Haven, CT: Yale University Press.(14)

Duck, S. (1982). A topography of relationship disengagement and dissolution. In S. W. Duck (Ed.), *Personal relationships 4: Dissolving personal relationships.* New York: Academic Press.(9)

Duncan, J. S. (1986). The house as symbol of social structure: Notes on the language of objects among collectivistic groups. In I. Altman & C. Werner (Eds.), *Home environments. Human behavior and environment: Advances in theory and research* (Vol. 8, pp. 133–151). New York: Plenum.(14)

Duncan, S. (1969). Nonverbal communication. *Psychological Bulletin, 72,* 118–137.(5)

Duncan, S., Jr., & Fiske, D. W. (1977). *Face-to-face interaction.* Hillsdale, NJ: Erlbaum.(5)

Dunnette, M. D., Campbell, J., & Jaastad, K. (1963). The effect of group participation on brainstorming effectiveness for two industrial samples. *Journal of Applied Psychology, 47,* 30–37.(12)

Durkheim, E. (1898). Représentations individuelles et représentations collectives. *Revue de Métaphysique, 6,* 274–302. (In D. F. Pocock [Trans.], *Sociology and philosophy.* New York: Free Press, 1953.)(12)

Duval, S., & Wicklund, R. A. (1972). *A theory of objective self-awareness.* New York: Academic Press.(3)

Dyck, R. J., & Rule, B. G. (1978). Effect of retaliation on causal attributions concerning attack. *Journal of Personality and Social Psychology, 36,* 521–529.(10)

Eagly, A. H. (1987). *Sex differences in social behavior: A social-role interpretation.* Hillsdale, NJ: Erlbaum.(1, 13)

Eagly, A. H., & Carli, L. L. (1981). Sex of researchers and sex-typed communications as determinants of sex differences in influenceability: A meta-analysis of social influence studies. *Psychological Bulletin, 90,* 1–20.(2, 7, 8)

Eagly, A. H., & Chaiken, S. (1984). Cognitive theories of persuasion. *Advances in Experimental Social Psychology, 17,* 267–359.(7)

Eagly, A. H., Chaiken, S., & Wood, W. (1981). An attribution analysis of persuasion. In J. Harvey, W. J. Ickes, & R. F. Kidd (Eds.), *New directions in attribution research* (Vol. 3, pp. 41–65). Hillsdale, NJ: Erlbaum.(7)

Eagly, A. H., & Crowley, M. (1986). Gender and helping behavior: A meta-analytic review of the social psychological literature. *Psychological Bulletin, 100,* 283–308.(11)

Eagly, A. H., & Steffen, V. J. (1986). Gender and aggressive behavior: A meta-analytic review of the social psychological literature. *Psychological Bulletin, 100,* 309–330.(10)

Eagly, A. H., & Telaak, K. (1972). Width of the latitude of acceptance as a determinant of attitude change. *Journal of Personality and Social Psychology, 23,* 388–397.(7)

Eagly, A. H., & Warren, R. (1976). Intelligence, comprehension, and opinion change. *Journal of Personality, 44,* 226–242.(7)

Eagly, A. H., & Wood, W. (1991). Explaining sex differences in social behavior: A meta-analytic perspective. *Personality and Social Psychology Bulletin, 17,* 306–315.(1, 2, 13)

Ebbesen, E., Kjos, G., & Konečni, V. (1976). Spatial ecology: Its effects on the choice of friends and enemies. *Journal of Experimental Social Psychology, 12,* 505–518.(14)

Edelstein, M. R., & Wandersman, A. (1987). Community dynamics in coping with toxic contaminants. In I. Altman & A. Wandersman (Eds.), *Neighborhood and community environments* (pp. 69–112). New York: Plenum.(14)

Edney, J. J. (1972). Property, possession, and performance: A field study in human territoriality. *Journal of Applied Social Psychology, 2,* 275–282.(14)

Edney, J. J. (1974). Human territoriality. *Psychological Bulletin, 81,* 959–975.(14)

Edney, J. J., & Jordon-Edney, N. L. (1974). Territorial spacing on a beach. *Sociometry, 37,* 92–104.(14)

Eibl-Eibesfeldt, I. (1970). *Ethology: The biology of behavior* (E. Klinghammer, Trans.). New York: Holt, Rinehart & Winston.(10)

Eisenberg, L. (1972). The *human* nature of human nature. *Science, 176,* 123–128.(10)

Eisenberg, N. (1986). *Altruistic emotion, cognition, and behavior.* Hillsdale, NJ: Erlbaum.(11)

Eisenberg, N., & Miller, P. A. (1987). The relation of empathy to prosocial and related behaviors. *Psychological Bulletin, 101,* 91–119.(11)

Eisenberg, N., & Mussen, P. H. (1989). *The roots of prosocial behavior in children.* New York: Cambridge University Press.(11)

Eiser, J. R., & van der Pligt, J. (1984). Attitudinal and social factors in adolescent smoking: In search of peer group influence. *Journal of Applied Social Psychology, 14,* 348–363.(6)

Ekman, P. (1972). Universals and cultural differences in facial expressions of emotion. In J. K. Cole (Ed.), *Nebraska symposium on motivation* (Vol. 19). Lincoln, NE: University of Nebraska Press.(5)

Ekman, P. (Ed.) (1982). *Emotion in the human face* (2nd ed.). Cambridge, England: Cambridge University Press.(5)

Ekman, P. (1985). *Telling lies.* New York: Berkley.(5)

Ekman, P., & Friesen, W. V. (1971). Constants across cultures in the face and emotion. *Journal of Personality and Social Psychology, 17,* 124–129.(5)

Ekman, P., & Friesen, W. V. (1972). Hand movements. *Journal of Communication, 22,* 353–374.(5)

Ekman, P., & Friesen, W. V. (1974). Detecting deception from body or face. *Journal of Personality and Social Psychology, 29,* 288–298.(5)

Ekman, P., & Friesen, W. V. (1975). *Unmasking the face.* Englewood Cliffs, NJ: Prentice-Hall.(5)

Ekman, P., Friesen, W. V., O'Sullivan, M., Chan, A., Diacoyanni-Tarlatzis, I., Heider, K., Krause, R., LeCompte, W. A., Pitcairn, T., Ricci-Bitti, P. E., Scherer, K., & Tomita, M. (1987). Universals and cultural differences in the judgments of facial expressions of emotion. *Journal of Personality and Social Psychology, 53,* 712–717.(5, 13)

Ekman, P., Friesen, W. V., & Scherer, K. B. (1976). Body movement and voice pitch in deceptive interaction. *Semiotica, 16,* 23–27.(5)

Ekman, P., Levenson, R. W., & Friesen, W. V. (1983). Autonomic nervous system activity distinguishes among emotions. *Science, 221,* 1208–1210.(5)

Ekstein, R. (1978). Psychoanalysis, sympathy, and altruism. In L. Wispé (Ed.), *Altruism, sympathy, and helping: Psychological and sociological principles.* New York: Academic Press.(11)

Ellis, R. A., & Taylor, M. S. (1983). Role of self-esteem within the job search process. *Journal of Applied Psychology, 68,* 632–640.(3)

Ellsworth, P. C. (1977). From abstract ideas to concrete instances: Some guidelines for choosing natural research settings. *American Psychologist, 32,* 604–615.(2)

Ellsworth, P. C., Carlsmith, J. M., & Henson, A. (1972). The stare as a stimulus to flight in human subjects: A series of field experiments. *Journal of Personality and Social Psychology, 21,* 302–311.(5)

Erkut, S., Jaquette, D. S., & Staub, E. (1981). Moral judgment-situation interaction as a basis for predicting prosocial behavior. *Journal of Personality, 49,* 1–14.(11)

Eron, L. D. (1980). Prescription for reduction of aggression. *American Psychologist, 35,* 244–252.(10)

Eron, L. D. (1982). Parent-child interaction, television violence, and aggression of children. *American Psychologist, 37,* 197–211.(10)

Eron, L. D. (1987). The development of aggressive behavior from the perspective of a developing behaviorism. *American Psychologist, 42,* 435–442.(10)

Esser, A. H., Chamberlain, A. S., Chapple, E., & Kline, N. S. (1964). Territoriality of patients on a research ward. In J. Wortis (Ed.), *Recent advances in biological psychiatry.* New York: Plenum. (14)

Evans, G. W. (1978). Crowding and the developmental process. In A. Baum & Y. Epstein (Eds.), *Human response to crowding* (pp. 117–140). Hillsdale, NJ: Erlbaum. (14)

Evans, G. W., & Cohen, S. (1987). Environmental stress. In D. Stokols & I. Altman (Eds.), *Handbook of environmental psychology* (pp. 571–610). New York: Wiley. (14)

Evans, G. W., & Jacobs, S. V. (1982). Air pollution and human behavior. *Journal of Social Issues, 37*(1), 95–125. (14)

Evans, G. W., Palsane, M. N., Lepore, S. J., & Martin, J. (1989). Residential density and psychological health: The mediating effects of social support. *Journal of Personality and Social Psychology, 57,* 994–999. (14)

Evans, R. I. (1976). *The making of psychology: Discussions with creative contributors.* New York: Knopf. (1)

Exline, R. V. (1971). Visual interaction: The glances of power and preference. In J. K. Cole (Ed.), *Nebraska symposium on motivation* (Vol. 19). Lincoln, NE: University of Nebraska Press. (5)

Exline, R. V., Ellyson, S. L., & Long, B. (1975). Visual behavior as an aspect of power role relationships. In P. Pliner, L. Krames, & T. Alloway (Eds.), *Nonverbal communication of aggression* (Vol. 2). New York: Plenum. (5)

Exline, R., & Winters, L. (1965). Affective relations and mutual glances in dyads. In S. Tomkins & C. Izard (Eds.), *Affect, cognition, and personality.* New York: Springer. (5)

Fabes, R. A., Fultz, J., Eisenberg, N., May-Plumlee, T., & Christopher, F. S. (1989). Effects of rewards on children's prosocial motivation: A socialization study. *Developmental Psychology, 25,* 509–515. (11)

Family Educational Rights and Privacy Act, 20 U.S.C. § 1232(g). (1974). (14)

Fazio, R. H. (1986). How do attitudes guide behavior? In R. M. Sorrentino & E. T. Higgins (Eds.), *Handbook of motivation and cognition: Foundations of social behavior* (pp. 204–243). New York: Guilford Press. (6)

Fazio, R. H. (1990). Multiple processes by which attitudes guide behavior: The MODE model as an integrative framework. *Advances in Experimental Social Psychology, 23,* 75–109. (6)

Fazio, R. H., Herr, P. M., & Olney, T. J. (1984). Attitude accessibility following a self-perception process. *Journal of Personality and Social Psychology, 47,* 277–286. (6)

Fazio, R. H., Lenn, T. M., & Effrein, E. A. (1983/1984). Spontaneous attitude formation. *Social Cognition, 2,* 217–234. (6)

Fazio, R. H., Powell, M. C., & Williams, C. J. (1989). The role of attitude accessibility in the attitude-to-behavior process. *Journal of Consumer Research, 16,* 280–288. (6)

Fazio, R. H., Sherman, S. J., & Herr, P. M. (1982). The feature-positive effect in the self-perception process: Does not doing matter as much as doing? *Journal of Personality and Social Psychology, 42,* 404–411. (3)

Fazio, R. H., & Williams, C. J. (1986). Attitude accessibility as a moderator of the attitude-perception and attitude-behavior relations: An investigation of the 1984 presidential election. *Journal of Personality and Social Psychology, 51,* 505–514. (6)

Fazio, R. H., Zanna, M. P., & Cooper, J. (1977). Dissonance and self perception: An integrative view of each theory's proper domain of application. *Journal of Experimental Social Psychology, 13,* 464–479. (7)

Feild, H. S. (1978). Attitudes toward rape: A comparative analysis of police, rapists, crisis counselors, and citizens. *Journal of Personality and Social Psychology, 36,* 156–179. (4)

Feingold, A. (1990). Gender differences in effects of physical attractiveness on romantic attraction: A comparison across five research paradigms. *Journal of Personality and Social Psychology, 59,* 981–993. (9)

Feldman, R. M. (1990). Settlement-identity: Psychological bonds with home places in a mobile society. *Environment and Behavior, 22,* 183–229. (14)

Feldman-Summers, S. (1977). Implications of the buck-passing phenomenon for reactance theory. *Journal of Personality, 45,* 543–553. (8)

Felson, R. B. (1985). Reflected appraisal and the development of self. *Social Psychology Quarterly, 48,* 71–78. (3)

Felson, R. B., & Bohrnstedt, G. W. (1979). "Are the good beautiful or the beautiful good?" The relationship between children's perceptions of ability and perceptions of physical attractiveness. *Social Psychology Quarterly, 42,* 386–392. (9)

Felson, R. B., & Reed, M. D. (1986). Reference groups and self-appraisals of academic ability and performance. *Social Psychology Quarterly, 49,* 103–109. (3)

Fenigstein, A. (1979). Self-consciousness, self-attention, and social interaction. *Journal of Personality and Social Psychology, 37,* 75–86. (3)

Fenigstein, A., Scheier, M., & Buss, A. (1975). Public and private self-consciousness: Assessment and theory. *Journal of Consulting and Clinical Psychology, 43,* 522–527. (3)

Ferguson, G. S., & Weisman, G. D. (1986). Alternative approaches to the assessment of employee satisfaction within the office environment. In J. Wineman (Ed.), *Behavioral issues in office design* (pp. 85–108). New York: Van Nostrand Reinhold. (14)

Ferguson, T. J., & Rule, B. G. (1983). An attributional perspective on anger and aggression. In E. Donnerstein & R. G. Geen (Eds.), *Aggression: Theoretical and empirical reviews.* New York: Academic Press. (10)

Ferrari, J. R., Barone, R. C., Jason, L. A., & Rose, T. (1985). The use of incentives to increase blood donations. *Journal of Social Psychology, 125,* 791–793. (11)

Feshbach, S., Stiles, W. B., & Bitter, E. (1967). The reinforcing effect of witnessing aggression. *Journal of Experimental Research in Personality, 2,* 133–139. (10)

Festinger, L. (1950). Informal social communication. *Psychological Review, 57,* 271–282. (7, 12)

Festinger, L. (1954). A theory of social comparison processes. *Human Relations, 7,* 117–140. (3)

Festinger, L. (1957). *A theory of cognitive dissonance.* Stanford, CA: Stanford University Press. (7)

Festinger, L., & Carlsmith, J. M. (1959). Cognitive consequences of forced compliance. *Journal of Abnormal and Social Psychology, 58,* 203–210. (7)

Festinger, L., Pepitone, A., & Newcomb, T. (1952). Some consequences of deindividuation in a group. *Journal of Abnormal and Social Psychology, 47,* 382–389. (10)

Festinger, L., Riecken, H., & Schachter, S. (1956). *When prophecy fails.* Minneapolis: University of Minnesota Press. (2, 12)

Festinger, L., Schachter, S., & Back, K. (1950). *Social pressures in informal groups: A study of human factors in housing.* New York: Harper. (9, 14)

Fidell, L. S. (1970). Empirical verification of sex discrimination in hiring practices in psychology. *American Psychologist, 25,* 1094–1098. (13)

Fiedler, F. E. (1964). A contingency model of leadership effectiveness. In L. Berkowitz (Ed.), *Advances in experimental social psychology* (Vol. 1). New York: Academic Press. (12)

Fiedler, F. E. (1967). *A theory of leadership effectiveness.* New York: McGraw-Hill. (12)

Filley, A. (1975). *Interpersonal conflict resolution.* Glenview, IL: Scott, Foresman. (13)

Fine, M., & Bowers, C. (1984). Racial self-identification: The effects of social history and gender. *Journal of Applied Social Psychology, 14,* 136–146. (3)

Fishbein, M., & Ajzen, I. (1975). *Belief, attitude, intention, and behavior: An introduction to theory and research.* Reading, MA: Addison-Wesley. (6)

Fishbein, M., & Lange, R. (1990). The effects of crossing the midpoint on belief change: A replication and extension. *Personality and Social Psychology Bulletin, 16,* 189–199. (7)

Fisher, J. D., Bell, P. A., & Baum, A. (1984). *Environmental psychology* (2nd ed). New York: Holt, Rinehart & Winston. (14)

Fisher, J. D., Nadler, A., & Whitcher-Alagna, S. (1982). Recipient reactions to aid. *Psychological Bulletin, 91,* 27–54. (11)

Fisher, J. D., Rytting, M., & Heslin, R. (1976). Hands touching hands: Affective and evaluative effects of an interpersonal touch. *Sociometry, 39,* 416–421. (5)

Fiske, S. T., Bersoff, D. N., Borgida, E., Deaux, K., & Heilman, M. E. (1990). *Social science research on trial: The use of sex stereotyping research in* Price Waterhouse v. Hopkins. Manuscript submitted for publication. (13)

Fiske, S. T., Fischhoff, B., & Milburn, M. A. (1983). Images of nuclear war: An introduction. *Journal of Social Issues, 39*(1), 1–6. (6)

Fiske, S. T., & Neuberg, S. L. (1990). A continuum of impression formation, from category-based to individuating processes: Influences of information and motivation on attention and interpretation. *Advances in Experimental Social Psychology, 23,* 1–74. (1, 4, 6, 8, 12)

Fiske, S. T., & Taylor, S. E. (1984). *Social cognition.* Reading, MA: Addison-Wesley. (1, 4)

Fleishman, E. A. & Harris, E. F. (1962). Patterns of leadership related to employee grievances and turnover. *Personnel Psychology, 15,* 43–56. (12)

Fleming, J. H., & Darley, J. M. (1990). The purposeful-action sequence and the "illusion of control": The effects of foreknowledge and target involvement on observers' judgments of others' control over random events. *Personality and Social Psychology Bulletin, 16,* 346–357. (8)

Fletcher, G. J. O., & Fitness, J. (1990). Occurrent social cognition in close relationship interaction: The role of proximal and distal variables. *Journal of Personality and Social Psychology, 59,* 464–474. (9)

Flowers, M. L. (1977). A laboratory test of some implications of Janis's groupthink hypothesis. *Journal of Personality and Social Psychology, 35,* 888–896. (12)

Foa, E. B., & Foa, U. G. (1974). *Social structure of the mind.* Springfield, IL: Charles C Thomas. (13)

Foa, E. B., & Foa, U. G. (1980). Resource theory: Interpersonal behavior as exchange. In K. J. Gergen, M. S. Greenberg, & R. H. Willis (Eds.), *Social exchange: Advances in theory and research.* New York: Plenum. (13)

Foa, U. G. (1971). Interpersonal and economic resources. *Science, 171,* 345–351. (9)

Fogelman, E., & Wiener, V. L. (1985, August). The few, the brave, the noble. *Psychology Today,* pp. 61–65. (11)

Fong, G. T., & Markus, H. (1982). Self-schemas and judgments about others. *Social Cognition, 1,* 191–204. (4)

Forsyth, D. R. (1983). *An introduction to group dynamics.* Pacific Grove, CA: Brooks/Cole. (12)

Forward, J., Canter, R., & Kirsch, N. (1976). Role-enactment and deception methodologies: Alternative paradigms? *American Psychologist, 31,* 595–604. (2)

Foss, R. D. (1983). Community norms and blood donation. *Journal of Applied Social Psychology, 13,* 281–290.(11)

Fowler, C. A., Wolford, G., Slade, R., & Tassinary, L. (1981). Lexical access with and without awareness. *Journal of Experimental Psychology: General, 110,* 341–362.(13)

Fraczek, A., & Macaulay, J. R. (1971). Some personality factors in reaction to aggressive stimuli. *Journal of Personality, 39,* 163–177.(10)

Franck, K. A. (1984). Exorcising the ghost of physical determinism. *Environment and Behavior, 16,* 411–435.(14)

Franzoi, S. L. (1983). Self-concept differences as a function of private self-consciousness and social anxiety. *Journal of Research in Personality, 17,* 275–287.(3)

Franzoi, S. L., & Brewer, L. C. (1984). The experience of self-awareness and its relation to level of self-consciousness: An experiential sampling study. *Journal of Research in Personality, 18,* 522–540.(3)

Franzoi, S. L., Davis, M. H., & Young, R. D. (1985). The effects of private self-consciousness and perspective taking on satisfaction in close relationships. *Journal of Personality and Social Psychology, 48,* 1584–1594.(9)

Fraser, C. (1971). Group risk-taking and group polarization. *European Journal of Social Psychology, 1,* 493–510.(12)

Freedman, J. L. (1975). *Crowding and behavior.* San Francisco: W. H. Freeman.(14)

Freedman, J. L. (1984). Effect of television violence on aggressiveness. *Psychological Bulletin, 96,* 227–246.(10)

Freedman, J. L. (1986). Television violence and aggression: A rejoinder. *Psychological Bulletin, 100,* 372–378.(10)

Freedman, J. L., & Fraser, S. C. (1966). Compliance without pressure: The foot-in-the-door technique. *Journal of Personality and Social Psychology, 4,* 195–202.(8)

Freedman, R. (1986). *Beauty bound.* Lexington, MA: Lexington Books.(4)

French, J. R. P., Jr., & Raven, B. H. (1959). The bases of social power. In D. Cartwright (Ed.), *Studies in social power* (pp. 150–167). Ann Arbor, MI: University of Michigan Press.(8)

Frenkel, O. J., & Doob, A. N. (1976). Post-decision dissonance at the polling booth. *Canadian Journal of Behavioural Science, 8,* 347–350.(7)

Freud, S. (1930). *Civilization and its discontents.* London: Hogarth Press.(10)

Freud, S. (1938). Three contributions to the theory of sex. In A. A. Brill (Ed.), *The basic writings of Sigmund Freud.* New York: Random House.(10)

Freud, S. (1959). Fragment of an analysis of a case of hysteria. In *Collected papers* (Vol. 3). Authorized translation by Alix and James Strachey. New York: Basic Books. (Original work published 1905)(1)

Frey, D. (1986). Recent research on selective exposure to information. *Advances in Experimental Social Psychology, 19,* 41–80.(7)

Frey, D. L., & Gaertner, S. L. (1986). Helping and the avoidance of inappropriate interracial behavior: A strategy that perpetuates a nonprejudiced self-image. *Journal of Personality and Social Psychology, 50,* 1083–1090.(11)

Fridlund, A. J. (1991). Sociality of solitary smiling: Potentiation by an implicit audience. *Journal of Personality and Social Psychology, 60,* 229–240.(5)

Friedman, A. (1979). Framing pictures: The role of knowledge in automatized encoding and memory for gist. *Journal of Experimental Psychology: General, 108,* 316–355.(4)

Friedrich-Cofer, L., & Huston, A. C. (1986). Television violence and aggression: The debate continues. *Psychological Bulletin, 100,* 364–371.(10)

Froming, W. J., Walker, G. R., & Lopyan, K. J. (1982). Public and private self-awareness: When personal attitudes conflict with societal expectations. *Journal of Experimental Social Psychology, 18,* 476–487.(3)

Fultz, J., Batson, C. D., Fortenbach, V. A., McCarthy, P. M., & Varney, L. L. (1986). Social evaluation and the empathy-altruism hypothesis. *Journal of Personality and Social Psychology, 50,* 761–769.(11)

Gaebelein, J. W. (1973). Third party instigation of aggression: An experimental approach. *Journal of Personality and Social Psychology, 27,* 389–395.(10)

Gaebelein, J. W. (1978). Third party instigated aggression as a function of attack pattern and a nonaggressive response option. *Journal of Research in Personality, 12,* 274–283.(10)

Gaebelein, J. W., & Hay, W. M. (1974). Third party instigation of aggression as a function of attack and vulnerability. *Journal of Research in Personality, 7,* 324–333.(10)

Gaertner, S. L., & Dovidio, J. F. (1977). The subtlety of white racism, arousal, and helping behavior. *Journal of Personality and Social Psychology, 35,* 691–707.(11)

Gaertner, S. L., & McLaughlin, J. P. (1983). Racial stereotypes: Associations and ascriptions of positive and negative characteristics. *Social Psychology Quarterly, 46,* 23–30.(13)

Galle, O. R., Gove, W. R., & McPherson, J. M. (1972). Population density and pathology: What are the relations for man? *Science, 176,* 23–30.(14)

Gans, H. J. (1967). *The Levittowners: Ways of life and politics in a new suburban community.* New York: Pantheon.(14)

Gansburg, M. (1964, March 27). Thirty-seven who saw murder didn't call the police. *The New York Times,* pp. 1, 38.(11)

Geen, R. G. (1968). Effects of frustration, attack, and prior training in aggressiveness upon aggressive behavior. *Journal of Personality and Social Psychology, 9,* 316–321.(10)

Geen, R. G. (1978). Effects of attack and uncontrollable noise on aggression. *Journal of Research in Personality, 12,* 15–29.(14)

Geen, R. G. (1980). The effect of being observed on performance. In P. B. Paulus (Ed.), *Psychology of group influence.* Hillsdale, NJ: Erlbaum.(12)

Geen, R. G., & Gange, J. J. (1977). Drive theory of social facilitation: Twelve years of theory and research. *Psychological Bulletin, 84,* 1267–1288.(12)

Geen, R. G., & O'Neal, E. C. (1969). Activation of cue-elicited aggression by general arousal. *Journal of Personality and Social Psychology, 11,* 289–292.(14)

Geen, R. G., & Stonner, D. (1971). Effects of aggressiveness habit strength on behavior in the presence of aggression-related stimuli. *Journal of Personality and Social Psychology, 17,* 149–153.(10)

Geiselman, R. E., Haight, N. A., & Kimata, L. G. (1984). Context effects in the perceived physical attractiveness of faces. *Journal of Experimental Social Psychology, 20,* 409–424.(9)

Gekas, V. (1982). The self-concept. *Annual Review of Sociology, 8,* 1–33.(3)

Gekas, V., & Schwalbe, M. L. (1983). Beyond the looking-glass self: Social structure and efficacy-based self-esteem. *Social Psychology Quarterly, 46,* 77–88.(3)

Gelfand, D. M., & Hartmann, D. P. (1982). Response consequences and attributions: Two contributors to prosocial behavior. In N. Eisenberg (Ed.), *The development of prosocial behavior.* New York: Academic Press.(11)

Geller, D. M. (1978). Involvement in role-playing simulations: A demonstration with studies on obedience. *Journal of Personality and Social Psychology, 36,* 219–235.(2)

Gentry, W. D. (1970). Effects of frustration, attack, and prior aggressive training on overt aggression and vascular processes. *Journal of Personality and Social Psychology, 16,* 718–725.(10)

George, J. M. (1991). State or trait: Effects of positive mood on prosocial behaviors at work. *Journal of Applied Psychology, 76,* 299–307.(11)

Georgoudi, M., & Rosnow, R. L. (1985). Notes toward a contextualist understanding of social psychology. *Personality and Social Psychology Bulletin, 11,* 5–22.(1)

Gergen, K. J. (1985). The social constructionist movement in modern psychology. *American Psychologist, 40,* 266–275.(1, 13)

Gergen, K. J., Gergen, M. M., & Barton, W. H. (1973, October). Deviance in the dark. *Psychology Today,* pp. 129–130.(14)

Gergen, K. J., Morse, S. J., & Gergen, M. M. (1980). Behavior exchange in cross-cultural perspective. In H. C. Triandis & W. W. Lambert (Eds.), *Handbook of cross-cultural psychology: Social psychology* (Vol. 5). Boston: Allyn & Bacon.(13)

Gibb, C. A. (1969). Leadership. In G. Lindzey & E. Aronson (Eds.), *Handbook of social psychology* (2nd ed., Vol. 4). Reading, MA: Addison-Wesley.(12)

Gibbons, F. X. (1990). Self-attention and behavior: A review and theoretical update. *Advances in Experimental Social Psychology, 23,* 249–303.(3, 4)

Gibbons, F., & Wicklund, R. (1982). Self-focused attention and helping behavior. *Journal of Personality and Social Psychology, 43,* 462–474.(11)

Gibbons, F. X., & Wright, R. A. (1983). Self-focused attention and reactions to conflicting standards. *Journal of Research in Personality, 17,* 263–273.(3)

Gifford, R. (1988). Light, decor, arousal, comfort, and communication. *Journal of Environmental Behavior, 8,* 177–189.(14)

Gilbert, D. T. (1989). Thinking lightly about others: Automatic components of the social inference process. In J. S. Uleman & J. A. Bargh (Eds.), *Unintended thought* (pp. 189–211). New York: Guilford Press.(4)

Gilbert, D. T., & Jones, E. E. (1986). Perceiver-induced constraint: Interpretations of self-generated reality. *Journal of Personality and Social Psychology, 50,* 269–280.(4)

Gilbert, D. T., & Krull, D. S. (1988). Seeing less and knowing more: The benefits of perceptual ignorance. *Journal of Personality and Social Psychology, 54,* 193–202.(4)

Gilbert, D. T., Krull, D. S., & Pelham, B. W. (1988). Of thoughts unspoken: Social inference and the self-regulation of behavior. *Journal of Personality and Social Psychology, 55,* 685–694.(4)

Gilbert, D. T., Pelham, B. W., & Krull, D. S. (1988). On cognitive busyness: When person perceivers meet persons perceived. *Journal of Personality and Social Psychology, 54,* 733–740.(4)

Glass, D. C., & Singer, J. E. (1972). *Urban stress.* New York: Academic Press.(8, 14)

Godfrey, D. K., Jones, E. E., & Lord, C. G. (1986). Self-promotion is not ingratiating. *Journal of Personality and Social Psychology, 50,* 106–115.(3)

Goethals, G. R. (1986). Social comparison theory: Psychology from the lost and found. *Personality and Social Psychology Bulletin, 12,* 261–278.(3)

Goethals, G. R., & Darley, J. M. (1977). Social comparison theory: An attributional approach. In J. M. Suls & R. L. Miller (Eds.), *Social comparison processes: Theoretical and empirical perspectives,* Washington, DC: Halsted-Wiley.(3)

Goffman, E. (1955). On face-work: An analysis of ritual elements in social interaction. *Psychiatry, 18,* 213–231.(3)

Goffman, E. (1959). *The presentation of self in everyday life.* Garden City, NY: Doubleday.(3, 14)

Goffman, E. (1967). *Interaction ritual: Essays on face-to-face behavior.* Garden City, NY: Doubleday.(3, 8)

Gorer, G. (1968). Man has no "killer" instinct. In M. F. A. Montagu (Ed.), *Man and aggression.* New York: Oxford University Press.(10)

Gottlieb, N. M. (1988). Women and men working at home: Environmental experiences. In D. Lawrence, R. Habe, A. Hacker, & D. Sherrod (Eds.), *People's needs/planet management: Paths to co-existence* (pp. 149–154). Washington, DC: Environmental Design Research Association.(14)

Gouldner, A. W. (1960). The norm of reciprocity: A preliminary statement. *American Sociological Review, 25,* 161–178.(11)

Grabitz-Gneich, G. (1971). Some restrictive conditions for the occurrence of psychological reactance. *Journal of Personality and Social Psychology, 19,* 188–196.(8)

Grady, K. E. (1977). *Sex as a social label: The illusion of sex differences.* Unpublished doctoral dissertation, City University of New York.(4)

Graham, J. A., & Heywood, S. (1975). The effects of elimination of hand gestures and of verbal codability on speech performance. *European Journal of Social Psychology, 5,* 189–195.(5)

Granberg, D., & Brent, E. (1983). When prophecy bends: The preference-expectation link in U.S. presidential elections, 1952–1980. *Journal of Personality and Social Psychology, 45,* 477–491.(7)

Graves, N. B., & Graves, T. D. (1983). The cultural context of prosocial development: An ecological model. In D. L. Bridgeman (Ed.), *The nature of prosocial development: Interdisciplinary theories and strategies.* New York: Academic Press.(11)

Gray, J. D. & Silver, R. C. (1990). Opposite sides of the same coin: Former spouses' divergent perspectives in coping with their divorce. *Journal of Personality and Social Psychology, 59,* 1180–1191.(9)

Greenbaum, P. E., & Greenbaum, D. S. (1981). Territorial personalization: Group identity and social interaction in a Slavic-American neighborhood. *Environment and Behavior, 13,* 574–589.(14)

Greenberg, J., & Musham, C. (1981). Avoiding and seeking self-focused attention. *Journal of Research in Personality, 15,* 191–200.(3)

Greenberg, J., & Pyszczynski, T. (1985). The effect of an overheard ethnic slur on evaluations of the target: How to spread a social disease. *Journal of Experimental Social Psychology, 21,* 61–72.(4)

Greenberg, M. S. (1980). A theory of indebtedness. In K. J. Gergen, M. S. Greenberg, & R. H. Willis (Eds.), *Social exchange: Advances in theory and research.* New York: Plenum.(11)

Greenfield, T. B., & Andrews, J. H. M. (1961). Teacher leader behavior. *Alberta Journal of Educational Research, 7,* 92–102.(12)

Greenwald, A. G., & Pratkanis, A. R. (1984). The self. In R. S. Wyer & T. K. Srull (Eds.), *The handbook of social cognition* (Vol. 3). Hillsdale, NJ: Erlbaum.(3)

Greenwell, J., & Dengerink, H. A. (1973). The role of perceived versus actual attack in human physical aggression. *Journal of Personality and Social Psychology, 26,* 66–71.(10)

Greenwood, J. D. (1983). Role-playing as an experimental strategy in social psychology. *European Journal of Social Psychology, 13,* 235–254.(2)

Grice, H. P. (1975). Logic and conversation. In P. Cole & J. L. Morgan (Eds.), *Syntax and semantics 3: Speech acts* (pp. 41–58). New York: Academic Press.(5)

Griffitt, W. (1970). Environmental effects on interpersonal affective behavior: Ambient effective temperature and attraction. *Journal of Personality and Social Psychology, 15,* 240–244.(14)

Griffitt, W., & Veitch, R. (1971). Hot and crowded: Influences of population density on interpersonal affective behavior. *Journal of Personality and Social Psychology, 17,* 92–98.(14)

Gross, A. E., & Crofton, C. (1977). What is good is beautiful. *Sociometry, 40,* 85–90.(9)

Gross, A. E., & Fleming, I. (1982). Twenty years of deception in social psychology. *Personality and Social Psychology Bulletin, 8,* 402–408.(2)

Gross, A. E., Wallston, B. S., & Piliavin, I. M. (1975). Beneficiary attractiveness and cost as determinants of responses to routine requests for help. *Sociometry, 38,* 131–140.(11)

Grujic, L., & Libby, W. L., Jr. (1978, September). *Nonverbal aspects of verbal behavior in French Canadian French-English bilinguals.* Paper presented at meeting of the American Psychological Association, Toronto.(5)

Grusec, J. E., Saas-Korlsaak, P., & Simutis, Z. M. (1978). The role of example and moral exhortation in the training of altruism. *Child Development, 49,* 920–923.(11)

Grush, J. E., McKeough, K. L., & Ahlering, R. F. (1978). Extrapolating laboratory exposure research to actual political elections. *Journal of Personality and Social Psychology, 36,* 257–270.(7)

Guerin, B. (1986). Mere presence effects in humans: A review. *Journal of Experimental Social Psychology, 22,* 38–77.(12)

Gullahorn, J. T. (1952). Distance and friendship as factors in the gross interaction matrix. *Sociometry, 15,* 123–134. (14)

Gurin, P., Gurin, G., Lao, R. C., & Beattie, M. (1969). Internal-external control in the motivational dynamics of Negro youth. *Journal of Social Issues, 25* (3), 29–53. (8)

Haber, G. M. (1980). Territorial invasion in the classroom. *Environment and Behavior, 12,* 17–31. (14)

Hall, C. S., & Lindzey, G. (1968). The relevance of Freudian psychology and related viewpoints for the social sciences. In G. Lindzey & E. Aronson (Eds.), *Handbook of social psychology* (2nd ed., Vol. 1). Reading, MA: Addison-Wesley. (10)

Hall, C. S., & Lindzey, G. (1978). *Theories of personality* (3rd ed.). New York: Wiley. (1)

Hall, E. T. (1959). *The silent language.* New York: Doubleday. (5, 14)

Hall, E. T. (1966). *The hidden dimension.* Garden City, NY: Doubleday. (5, 14)

Hall, J. A., & Veccia, E. M. (1990). More "touching" observations: New insights on men, women, and interpersonal touch. *Journal of Personality and Social Psychology, 59,* 1155–1162. (2, 5)

Halpin, A. W. (1953). Studies in aircrew composition: III. In *The combat leader behavior of B-29 aircraft commanders.* Washington, DC: Bolling Air Force Base, Human Factors Operations Research Laboratory. (12)

Halpin, A. W. (1954). The leadership behavior and combat performances of airplane commanders. *Journal of Abnormal and Social Psychology, 49,* 19–22. (12)

Halpin, A. W. (1966). *Theory and research in administration.* New York: Macmillan. (12)

Halpin, A. W., & Winer, B. J. (1952). *The leadership behavior of the airplane commander.* Columbus, OH: Ohio State University, Research Foundation. (Mimeographed.) (12)

Hamilton, D. L. (1979). A cognitive-attributional analysis of stereotyping. *Advances in Experimental Social Psychology, 12,* 53–85. (4)

Hamilton, D. L. (Ed.). (1981). *Cognitive processes in stereotyping and intergroup behavior.* Hillsdale, NJ: Erlbaum. (4)

Hamilton, D. L., Dugan, P. M., & Trolier, T. K. (1985). The formation of stereotypic beliefs: Further evidence for distinctiveness-based illusory correlation. *Journal of Personality and Social Psychology, 48,* 5–17. (4)

Hamilton, D. L., & Gifford, R. K. (1976). Illusory correlation in interpersonal perception: A cognitive basis of stereotypic judgments. *Journal of Experimental Social Psychology, 12,* 392–407. (4)

Hamilton, W. D. (1964). The genetical evolution of social behavior, I & II. *Journal of Theoretical Biology, 7,* 1–52. (11)

Hamner, W. C. (1974). Effects of bargaining strategy pressure to reach agreement in a stalemated negotia *Journal of Personality and Social Psychology,* ? 458–467. (13)

Haney, C., Banks, C., & Zimbardo, P. (1973). Inter sonal dynamics in a simulated prison. *International Jo nal of Criminology and Penology, 1,* 69–97. (2)

Hansen, C. H., & Hansen, R. D. (1988). Finding the face in the crowd: An anger superiority effect. *Journal of Personality and Social Psychology, 54,* 917–924. (4, 5)

Hansen, W. B., & Altman, I. (1976). Decorating personal places: A descriptive analysis. *Environment and Behavior, 8,* 491–504. (14)

Harding, J., Proshansky, H., Kutner, B., & Chein, I. (1969). Prejudice and ethnic relations. In G. Lindzey & E. Aronson (Eds.), *Handbook of social psychology* (2nd ed., Vol. 5). Reading, MA: Addison-Wesley. (13)

Hare, A. P., & Bales, R. F. (1963). Seating position in small group discussion. *Sociometry, 26,* 480–486. (14)

Harkins, S. G., Latané, B., & Williams, K. (1980). Social loafing: Allocating effort or taking it easy. *Journal of Experimental Social Psychology, 16,* 457–465. (12)

Harkins, S. G., & Petty, R. E. (1982). Effects of task difficulty and task uniqueness on social loafing. *Journal of Personality and Social Psychology, 43,* 1214–1229. (12)

Harkins, S. G., & Szymanski, K. (1987). Social loafing and social facilitation: New wine in old bottles. *Review of Personality and Social Psychology, 9,* 167–188. (12)

Harlow, H. F. (1958). The nature of love. *American Psychologist, 13,* 673–685. (9)

Harries, K. D., & Stadler, S. J. (1983). Determinism revisited: Assault and heat stress in Dallas, 1980. *Environment and Behavior, 15,* 235–256. (14)

Harries, K. D., & Stadler, S. J. (1988). Heat and violence: New findings from the Dallas field data, 1980–1981. *Journal of Applied Social Psychology, 18,* 129–138. (14)

Harris, A. S. (1970). The second sex in academe. *American Association of University Professors Bulletin, 56,* 283–295. (13)

Harris, M. B. (1974). Mediators between frustration and aggression in a field experiment. *Journal of Experimental Social Psychology, 10,* 561–571. (10)

Harris, M. J., & Rosenthal, R. (1985). Mediation of interpersonal expectancy effects: 31 meta-analyses. *Psychological Bulletin, 97,* 363–386. (5)

Harrison, A. A. (1977). Mere exposure. In L. Berkowitz (Ed.), *Advances in experimental social psychology.* New York: Academic Press. (9)

Harrison, A. A., Clearwater, Y. A., & McKay, C. P. (Eds.). *From Antarctica to outer space: Life in isolation and confinement.* New York: Springer-Verlag. (2)

.. A., & Connors, M. M. (1984). Groups in environments. *Advances in Experimental Social Psy-18*, 49–87.(12)

, A. A., & Saeed, L. (1977). Let's make a deal: An is of revelations and stipulations in lonely hearts advertisements. *Journal of Personality and Social Psychology, 35*, 257–264.(9)

Hartmann, D. (1969). Influence of symbolically modeled instrumental aggression and pain cues on aggressive behavior. *Journal of Personality and Social Psychology, 11*, 280–288.(10)

Hass, R. G. (1975). Persuasion or moderation? Two experiments on anticipatory belief change. *Journal of Personality and Social Psychology, 31*, 1155–1162.(7)

Hass, R. G. (1984). Perspective taking and self-awareness: Drawing an *E* on your forehead. *Journal of Personality and Social Psychology, 46*, 788–798.(3)

Hass, R. G., & Mann, R. W. (1976). Anticipatory belief change: Persuasion or impression management? *Journal of Personality and Social Psychology, 34*, 105–111.(7)

Hastie, R. (1981). Schematic principles in human memory. In E. T. Higgins, C. P. Herman, & M. P. Zanna (Eds.), *Social cognition: The Ontario Symposium, Volume 1* (pp. 39–88). Hillsdale, NJ: Erlbaum.(4)

Hastie, R. (1984). Causes and effects of causal attributions. *Journal of Personality and Social Psychology, 46*, 44–56.(4, 7)

Hastie, R., Penrod, S. D., & Pennington, N. (1983). *Inside the jury*. Cambridge, MA: Harvard University Press.(12)

Hatfield, E. (1988). Passionate and companionate love. In R. J. Sternberg & M. L. Barnes (Eds.), *The psychology of love* (pp. 191–217). New Haven, CT: Yale University Press.(9)

Hatfield, E., & Sprecher, S. (1986). *Mirror, mirror: The importance of looks in everyday life*. Albany: State University of New York Press.(9)

Hatfield, E., & Traupmann, J. (1981). Intimate relationships: A perspective from equity theory. In S. Duck & R. Gilmour (Eds.), *Personal relationships I: Studying personal relationships*. New York: Academic Press.(9)

Hayduk, L. A. (1983). Personal space: Where we now stand. *Psychological Bulletin, 94*, 293–335.(5)

Hays, R. B. (1985). A longitudinal study of friendship development. *Journal of Personality and Social Psychology, 48*, 909–924.(9)

Hays, R. B., & Oxley, D. (1986). Social network development and functioning during a life transition. *Journal of Personality and Social Psychology, 50*, 305–313.(9)

Hazan, C., & Shaver, P. (1987). Romantic love conceptualized as an attachment process. *Journal of Personality and Social Psychology, 52*, 511–524.(9)

Hazan, C., & Shaver, P. R. (1990). Love and work: An attachment-theoretical perspective. *Journal of Personality and Social Psychology, 59*, 270–280.(9)

Heckel, R. V. (1973). Leadership and voluntary seating choice. *Psychological Reports, 32*, 141–142.(14)

Hedge, A. (1982). The open-plan office: A systematic investigation of employee reactions to their work environment. *Environment and Behavior, 14*, 519–542.(14)

Heider, F. (1944). Social perception and phenomenal causality. *Psychological Review, 51*, 358–374.(3)

Heider, F. (1946). Attitudes and cognitive organization. *Journal of Psychology, 21*, 107–112.(7, 9)

Heider, F. (1958). *The psychology of interpersonal relations*. New York: Wiley.(3, 4, 7)

Heilman, M. E., & Guzzo, R. A. (1978). The perceived cause of work success as a mediator of sex discrimination in organizations. *Organizational Behavior and Human Performance, 21*, 346–357.(4)

Helmreich, R. (1975). Applied social psychology: The unfulfilled promise. *Personality and Social Psychology Bulletin, 1*, 548–560.(13)

Helson, H. (1964). *Adaptation-level theory: An experimental and systematic approach to behavior*. New York: Harper & Row.(14)

Hemphill, J. K. (1955). Leadership behavior associated with the administrative reputation of college departments. *Journal of Educational Psychology, 46*, 385–401.(12)

Hemphill, J. K., & Coons, A. E. (1950). *Leader behavior description*. Columbus: Ohio State University, Personnel Research Board.(12)

Hendrick, C. (1977). Role-playing as a methodology for social research: A symposium. *Personality and Social Psychology Bulletin, 3*, 454.(2)

Hendrick, C., & Hendrick, S. (1986). A theory and method of love. *Journal of Personality and Social Psychology, 50*, 392–402.(9)

Hendrick, C., & Jones, R. A. (1972). *The nature of theory and research in social psychology*. New York: Academic Press.(1)

Henley, N. M. (1977). *Body politics: Power, sex, and nonverbal communication*. Englewood Cliffs, NJ: Prentice-Hall.(5)

Herek, G. M. (1986). The instrumentality of attitudes: Toward a neofunctional theory. *Journal of Social Issues, 42*(2), 99–114.(7)

Herek, G. M. (1989). Hate crimes against lesbians and gay men. *American Psychologist, 44*, 948–955.(13)

Herman, C. P., Zanna, M. P., & Higgins, E. T. (Eds.). (1986). *Physical appearance, stigma, and social behavior: The Ontario Symposium, Volume 3*. Hillsdale, NJ: Erlbaum.(3)

Herrnstein, R. (1973). *IQ in the meritocracy*. Boston: Atlantic Monthly Press and Little, Brown.(13)

Heskin, K. (1980). *Northern Ireland: A psychological analysis.* New York: Columbia University Press.(13)

Hess, E. H. (1962). Ethology. In R. Brown, E. Galanter, E. H. Hess, & G. Mandler (Eds.), *New directions in psychology.* New York: Holt.(10)

Hewstone, M., Bond, M. H., & Wan, K.-C. (1983). Social facts and social attributions: The explanation of intergroup differences in Hong Kong. *Social Cognitions, 2,* 142–157.(13)

Hewstone, M., & Jaspars, J. (1982). Explanations for racial discrimination: The effect of group discussion on intergroup attributions. *European Journal of Social Psychology, 12,* 1–16.(13)

Hicks, D. (1968). Short- and long-term retention of affectively-varied modeled behavior. *Psychonomic Science, 11,* 369–370.(10)

Hiers, J. M., & Heckel, R. V. (1977). Seating choice, leadership, and locus of control. *Journal of Social Psychology, 103,* 313–314.(14)

Higbee, K. L. (1969). Fifteen years of fear arousal: Research on threat appeals: 1953–1968. *Psychological Bulletin, 72,* 426–444.(7)

Higgins, E. T. (1981). The "communication game": Implications for social cognition and persuasion. In. E. T. Higgins, C. P. Herman, & M. P. Zanna (Eds.), *Social cognition: The Ontario Symposium, Volume 1* (pp. 343–392). Hillsdale, NJ: Erlbaum.(5)

Higgins, E. T. (1987). Self-discrepancy: A theory relating self and affect. *Psychological Review, 94,* 319–340.(3)

Higgins, E. T. (1989). Self-discrepancy theory: What patterns of self-belief cause people to suffer? *Advances in Experimental Social Psychology, 22,* 93–136.(3)

Higgins, E. T., & Bargh, J. A. (1987). Social cognition and social perception. *Annual Review of Psychology, 38,* 369–425.(4)

Higgins, E. T., & King, G. (1981). Accessibility of social constructs: Information-processing consequences of individual and contextual variability. In N. Cantor & J. F. Kihlstrom (Eds.), *Personality, cognition, and social interaction* (pp. 69–121). Hillsdale, NJ: Erlbaum.(3, 4)

Higgins, E. T., & McCann, C. D. (1984). Social encoding and subsequent attitudes, impressions, and memory: "Context-driven" and motivational aspects of processing. *Journal of Personality and Social Psychology, 47,* 26–39.(4)

Higgins, E. T., Rholes, C. R., & Jones, C. R. (1977). Category accessibility and impression formation. *Journal of Experimental Social Psychology, 13,* 141–154.(4)

Hill, C. T., Rubin, Z., & Peplau, L. A. (1976). Breakups before marriage: The end of 103 affairs. *Journal of Social Issues, 32*(1), 147–168.(9)

Hill, C. T., & Stull, D. E. (1981). Sex differences in effects of social and value similarity in same-sex friendship. *Journal of Personality and Social Psychology, 41,* 488–502.(9)

Hill, R. (1945). Campus values in mate selection. *Journal of Home Economics, 37,* 554–558.(9)

Hill, T., Lewicki, P., Czyzewska, M., & Boss, A. (1989). Self-perpetuating development of encoding biases in person perception. *Journal of Personality and Social Psychology, 57,* 373–387.(4)

Hills, L. R. (1973, October 1). The cruel rules of social life. *Newsweek,* p. 15.(8)

Hilton, J. L., & Darley, J. M. (1985). Constructing other persons: A limit on the effect. *Journal of Experimental Social Psychology, 21,* 1–18.(5)

Hilton, J. L., & Fein, S. (1989). The role of typical diagnosticity in stereotype-based judgments. *Journal of Personality and Social Psychology, 57,* 201–211.(4)

Hiltrop, J. M., & Rubin, J. Z. (1982). Effects of intervention mode and conflict of interest on dispute resolution. *Journal of Personality and Social Psychology, 42,* 665–672.(13)

Himmelfarb, S., & Eagly, A. H. (1974). Orientations to the study of attitudes and their change. In S. Himmelfarb & A. H. Eagly (Eds.), *Readings in attitude change* (pp. 2–51). New York: Wiley.(6)

Hockey, G. R. (1970). Effect of loud noise on attentional selectivity. *Quarterly Journal of Experimental Psychology, 22,* 28–36.(14)

Hoelter, J. W. (1984). Relative effects of significant others on self-evaluation. *Social Psychology Quarterly, 47,* 255–262.(3)

Hoelter, J. W. (1986). The relationship between specific and global evaluations of self: A comparison of several models. *Social Psychology Quarterly, 49,* 129–141.(3)

Hoffman, M. L. (1981). Is altruism part of human nature? *Journal of Personality and Social Psychology, 40,* 121–137.(11)

Hoge, D. R., & McCarthy, J. D. (1984). Influence of individual and group identity salience in the global self-esteem of youth. *Journal of Personality and Social Psychology, 47,* 403–414.(3)

Hogg, M. A., & Sunderland, J. (1991). Self-esteem and intergroup discrimination in the minimal group paradigm. *British Journal of Social Psychology, 300,* 51–62.(13)

Holahan, C. J., & Wilcox, B. L. (1978). Residential satisfaction and friendship formation in high- and low-rise student housing: An interactional analysis. *Journal of Educational Psychology, 70,* 237–241.(14)

Holmes, J. G. (1989). Trust and the appraisal process in close relationships. In W. H. Jones & D. Perlman (Eds.), *Advances in personal relationships* (Vol. 2). Greenwich, CT: JAI Press.(9)

Holtgraves, T. (1991). Interpreting questions and replies: Effects of face-threat, question form, and gender. *Social Psychology Quarterly, 54*, 15–24.(5)

Holtgraves, T., & Srull, T. K. (1989). The effects of positive self-descriptions on impressions: General principles and individual differences. *Personality and Social Psychology Bulletin, 15*, 452–462.(3)

Holtgraves, T., Srull, T. K., & Socall, D. (1989). Conversation memory: The effects of speaker status on memory for the assertiveness of conversation remarks. *Journal of Personality and Social Psychology, 56*, 149–160.(5)

Holtgraves, T., & Yang, J. (1990). Politeness as universal: Cross-cultural perceptions of request strategies and inferences based on their use. *Journal of Personality and Social Psychology, 59*, 719–729.(5, 8)

Homans, G. C. (1954). The cash posters. *American Sociological Review, 19*, 724–733.(14)

Homans, G. C. (1958). Social behavior and exchange. *American Journal of Sociology, 63*, 597–606.(1)

Homans, G. C. (1974). *Social behavior: Its elementary forms* (rev. ed.). New York: Harcourt Brace Jovanovich.(1)

Homer, P. M., & Kahle, L. R. (1988). A structural equation test of the value-attitude-behavior hierarchy. *Journal of Personality and Social Psychology, 54*, 638–646.(6)

Hook, S. (1955). *The hero in history*. Boston: Beacon Press.(12)

Hopmann, P. T., & Walcott, C. (1977). The impact of external stresses and tensions on negotiations. In D. Druckman (Ed.), *Negotiations: Social-psychological perspectives*. Beverly Hills, CA: Sage.(13)

Hornstein, G. A. (1985). Intimacy in conversational style as a function of the degree of closeness between members of a dyad. *Journal of Personality and Social Psychology, 49*, 671–681.(5)

Hornstein, H. A. (1976). *Cruelty and kindness: A new look at aggression and altruism*. Englewood Cliffs, NJ: Prentice-Hall.(11)

Horowitz, L., & French, R. (1979). Interpersonal problems of people who describe themselves as lonely. *Journal of Consulting and Clinical Psychology, 47*, 762–764.(9)

Horton, R. W., & Santogrossi, D. A. (1978). The effect of adult commentary on reducing the influence of televised violence. *Personality and Social Psychology Bulletin, 4*, 337–340.(10)

House, J. S., & Wolf, S. (1978). Effects of urban residence on interpersonal trust and helping behavior. *Journal of Personality and Social Psychology, 36*, 1029–1043.(11)

House, R. J. (1971). A path-goal theory of leader effectiveness. *Administrative Science Quarterly, 16*, 321–338.(12)

Hovland, C., Harvey, O. J., & Sherif, M. (1957). Assimilation and contrast effects in reactions to communication

and attitude change. *Journal of Abnormal and Social Psychology, 55*, 244–252.(7)

Hovland, C., Janis, I., & Kelley, H. H. (1953). *Communication and persuasion*. New Haven, CT: Yale University Press.(7)

Hovland, C. I., & Weiss, W. (1951). The influence of source credibility on communication effectiveness. *Public Opinion Quarterly, 15*, 635–650.(7)

Howells, L. T., & Becker, S. W. (1962). Seating arrangement and leadership emergence. *Journal of Abnormal and Social Psychology, 64*, 148–150.(14)

Hudson, J. W., & Henze, L. F. (1969). Campus values in mate selection: A replication. *Journal of Marriage and the Family, 31*, 772–775.(9)

Huesmann, L. R., Lagerspetz, K., & Eron, L. D. (1984). Intervening variables in the TV violence-aggression relation: Evidence from two countries. *Developmental Psychology, 20*, 746–775.(10)

Hui, C. H., Triandis, H. C., & Yee, C. (1991). Cultural differences in reward allocation: Is collectivism the explanation? *British Journal of Social Psychology, 30*, 145–157.(2)

Humphreys, P., & Berger, J. (1981). Theoretical consequences of the status characteristics formulation. *American Journal of Sociology, 86*, 953–983.(12)

Hundert, A. J., & Greenfield, N. (1969). Physical space and organizational behavior: A study of an office landscape. *Proceedings, 77th annual convention, American Psychological Association, 4*, 601–602.(14)

Hunt, M. (1985). *Profiles of social research: The scientific study of human interactions*. New York: Russell Sage Foundation.(2)

Huston, T. L., Ruggiero, M., Conner, R., & Geis, G. (1981). Bystander intervention into crime: A study based on naturally-occurring episodes. *Social Psychology Quarterly, 44*, 14–23.(11)

Hymes, R. W. (1986). Political attitudes as social categories: A new look at selective memory. *Journal of Personality and Social Psychology, 51*, 233–241.(6)

Ickes, W. J. (1990, November). *Correlates of shyness and physical attractiveness in mixed-sex dyads*. Paper presented at the meeting of the Society of Southeastern Social Psychologists, Raleigh, NC.(9)

Ickes, W. J., Bissonnette, V., Garcia, S., & Stinson, L. L. (1990). Implementing and using the dyadic interaction paradigm. *Review of Personality and Social Psychology, 11*, 16–44.(9)

Insko, C. A. (1965). Verbal reinforcement of attitude. *Journal of Personality and Social Psychology, 2*, 621–623.(6)

Insko, C. A. (1981). Balance theory and phenomenology. In R. Petty, T. Ostrom, & T. Brock (Eds.), *Cognitive responses in persuasion* (pp. 309–338). Hillsdale, NJ: Erlbaum.(7)

Insko, C. A. (1984). Balance theory, the Jordan paradigm, and the Wiest tetrahedron. *Advances in Experimental Social Psychology, 18,* 89–140.(7)

Insko, C. A., Smith, R. H., Alicke, M. D., Wade, J., & Taylor, S. (1985). Conformity and group size: The concern with being right and the concern with being liked. *Personality and Social Psychology Bulletin, 11,* 41–50.(8)

Isen, A. M. (1970). Success, failure, attention, and reactions to others: The warm glow of success. *Journal of Personality and Social Psychology, 15,* 294–301.(11)

Isen, A. M. (1987). Positive affect, cognitive processes, and social behavior. *Advances in Experimental Social Psychology, 20,* 203–253.(11)

Isen, A. M., & Daubman, K. A. (1984). The influence of affect on categorization. *Journal of Personality and Social Psychology, 47,* 1206–1217.(4)

Isen, A. M., & Levin, P. F. (1972). Effect of feeling good on helping: Cookies and kindness. *Journal of Personality and Social Psychology, 21,* 384–388.(11)

Isenberg, D. J. (1986). Group polarization: A critical review and meta-analysis. *Journal of Personality and Social Psychology, 50,* 1141–1151.(12)

Iyengar, S., Kinder, D. R., Peters, M. D., & Krosnick, J. A. (1984). The evening news and presidential evaluations. *Journal of Personality and Social Psychology, 46,* 778–787.(6)

Izard, C. E. (1969). The emotions and emotion constructs in personality and culture research. In R. B. Cattell (Ed.), *Handbook of modern personality theory.* Chicago: Aldine.(5)

Izard, C. E. (1977). *Human emotions.* New York: Plenum.(5)

Izard, C. E. (1980). Cross-cultural perspectives on emotion and emotion communication. In H. C. Triandis & W. Lonner (Eds.), *Handbook of cross-cultural psychology: Basic processes* (Vol. 3). Boston: Allyn & Bacon.(13)

Jaccard, J., Helbig, D. W., Wan, C. K., Gutman, M. A., & Kritz-Silverstein, D. C. (1989). Individual differences in attitude-behavior consistency: The prediction of contraceptive behavior. *Journal of Applied Social Psychology, 20,* 575–617.(6)

Jackson, J. M. (1986). In defense of social impact theory: Comment on Mullen. *Journal of Personality and Social Psychology, 50,* 511–513.(12)

Jackson, J. M., & Harkins, S. G. (1985). Equity in effort: An explanation of the social loafing effect. *Journal of Personality and Social Psychology, 49,* 1199–1206.(12)

Jackson, J. M., & Williams, K. D. (1985). Social loafing on difficult tasks: Working collectively can improve performance. *Journal of Personality and Social Psychology, 49,* 937–942.(12)

Jacobs, J. (1970). The uses of sidewalks: Contact. In H. Proshansky, W. Ittelson, & L. Rivlin (Eds.), *Environmental psychology* (pp. 312–319). New York: Holt, Rinehart & Winston.(14)

Jacobs, R. C., & Campbell, D. T. (1961). The perpetuation of an arbitrary tradition through several generations of a laboratory microculture. *Journal of Abnormal and Social Psychology, 62,* 649–658.(12)

James, W. (1890). *The principles of psychology* (Vols. 1 and 2). New York: Holt.(3)

Janis, I. L. (1972). *Victims of groupthink.* Boston: Houghton Mifflin.(12)

Janis, I. L. (1982). *Groupthink* (2nd ed.). Boston: Houghton Mifflin.(12)

Janis, I. L., & Feshbach, S. (1953). Effects of fear-arousing communications. *Journal of Abnormal and Social Psychology, 48,* 78–92.(7)

Janis, I. L., & Field, P. B. (1959). Sex differences and personality factors related to persuasibility. In I. L. Janis, C. I. Hovland, P. B. Field, H. Linton, E. Graham, A. R. Cohen, D. Rife, R. P. Abelson, G. S. Lesser, & B. T. King (Eds.), *Personality and persuasibility* (pp. 55–68). New Haven, CT: Yale University Press.(7)

Janis, I. L., & Mann, L. (1977). *Decision making: A psychological analysis of conflict, choice, and commitment.* New York: Free Press.(12)

Jason, L. A., Rose, T., Ferrari, J. R., & Barone, R. (1984). Personal versus impersonal methods of recruiting blood donors. *Journal of Social Psychology, 123,* 139–140.(11)

Jaspers, J. (1986). Forum and focus: A personal view of European social psychology. *European Journal of Social Psychology, 16,* 3–16.(13)

Jellison, J. M., & Green, J. (1981). A self-presentation approach to the fundamental attribution error: The norm of internality. *Journal of Personality and Social Psychology, 40,* 643–649.(4)

Jellison, J. M., Jackson-White, R., Bruder, R. A., & Martyna, W. (1975). Achievement behavior: A situational interpretation. *Sex Roles, 1,* 369–384.(3)

Jenkins, W. O. (1947). A review of leadership studies with particular reference to military problems. *Psychological Bulletin, 44,* 54–79.(12)

Jensen, A. R. (1973). *Educability and group differences.* New York: Basic Books.(13)

Johnson, H. G., Ekman, P., & Friesen, W. V. (1975). Communicative body movements: American emblems. *Semiotica, 15,* 335–353.(5)

Johnson, T. E., & Rule, B. G. (1986). Mitigating circumstance information, censure, and aggression. *Journal of Personality and Social Psychology, 50,* 537–542.(10)

Johnston, A., DeLuca, D., Murtaugh, K., & Diener, E. (1977). Validation of a laboratory play measure of child aggression. *Child Development, 48,* 324–327.(10)

Jones, E. E. (1985). Major developments in social psychology during the past five decades. In G. Lindzey & E. Aronson (Eds.), *Handbook of social psychology* (3rd ed., Vol. 1, pp. 47–107). New York: Random House. (1)

Jones, E. E. (1986). Interpreting interpersonal behavior: The effects of expectancies. *Science, 234,* 41–46. (5)

Jones, E. E., & Baumeister, R. (1976). The self-monitor looks at the ingratiator. *Journal of Personality, 44,* 654–674. (3)

Jones, E. E., & Davis, K. E. (1965). From acts to dispositions: The attribution process in person perception. *Advances in Experimental Social Psychology, 2,* 219–266. (4, 7)

Jones, E. E., Davis, K. E., & Gergen, K. (1961). Role playing variations and their informational value for person perception. *Journal of Abnormal and Social Psychology, 63,* 302–310. (4)

Jones, E. E., Farina, A., Hastorf, A. H., Markus, H., Miller, D. T., & Scott, R. A. (1984). *Social stigma: The psychology of marked relationships.* New York: W. H. Freeman. (3)

Jones, E. E., Gergen, K. J., & Jones, R. G. (1963). Tactics of ingratiation among leaders and subordinates in a status hierarchy. *Psychological Monographs, 77* (Whole No. 566). (3)

Jones, E. E., & Harris, V. A. (1967). The attribution of attitudes. *Journal of Experimental Social Psychology, 3,* 1–24. (4)

Jones, E. E., Kanouse, D. E., Kelley, H. H., Nisbett, R. E., Valins, S., & Weiner, B. (Eds.). (1972). *Attribution: Perceiving the causes of behavior.* Morristown, NJ: General Learning Press. (3)

Jones, E. E., & McGillis, D. (1976). Correspondent inferences and the attribution cube: A comparative reappraisal. In J. H. Harvey, W. J. Ickes, & R. F. Kidd (Eds.), *New directions in attribution research* (Vol. 1, pp. 389–420). Hillsdale, NJ: Erlbaum. (4)

Jones, E. E., & Nisbett, R. E. (1972). The actor and the observer: Divergent perceptions of the causes of behavior. In E. E. Jones, D. Kanouse, H. H. Kelley, R. E. Nisbett, S. Valins, & B. Weiner (Eds.), *Attribution: Perceiving the causes of behavior* (pp. 79–94). Morristown, NJ: General Learning Press. (4)

Jones, E. E., & Pittman, T. S. (1982). Toward a general theory of strategic self presentation. In J. Suls (Ed.), *Psychological perspectives on the self.* Hillsdale, NJ: Erlbaum. (3)

Jones, E. E., Rhodewalt, F., Berglas, S., & Skelton, J. A. (1981). Effects of strategic self-presentation on subsequent self-esteem. *Journal of Personality and Social Psychology, 41,* 407–421. (3)

Jones, E. E., & Wortman, C. B. (1973). *Ingratiation: An attributional approach.* Morristown, NJ: General Learning Press. (3)

Jones, J. W., & Bogat, A. (1978). Air pollution and human aggression. *Psychological Reports, 43,* 721–722. (14)

Jones, R. A., Howard, P. H., & Haley, J. V. (1984). Probability distortions and outcome desirability: Experimental verification of medical folklore. *Journal of Applied Social Psychology, 14,* 319–333. (4)

Jones, S. S., Collins, K., & Hong, H.-W. (1991). An audience effect on smile production in 10-month-old infants. *Psychological Science, 2,* 45–49. (5)

Jones, S. S., & Raag, R. (1989). Smile production in older infants: The importance of a social recipient for facial signal. *Child Development, 60,* 811–818. (5)

Jones, W. H., Freemon, J. E., & Goswick, R. A. (1981). The persistence of loneliness: Self and other determinants. *Journal of Personality, 49,* 27–48. (9)

Josephson, W. L. (1987). Television violence and children's aggression: Testing the priming, social script, and disinhibition predictions. *Journal of Personality and Social Psychology, 53,* 882–890. (10)

Joule, R. V., & Beauvois, J. L. (1987). *Petit traité de manipulation à l'usage des honnêtes gens* [Handbook on manipulation for use by honest people]. Grenoble, France: Presses Universitaires de Grenoble. (8)

Joule, R. V., Gouilloux, F., & Weber, F. (1989). The lure: A new compliance technique. *Journal of Social Psychology, 129,* 741–749. (2, 8)

Jourard, S. M. (1971). *Self-disclosure.* New York: Wiley. (5)

Judd, C. M., & Kulik, J. A. (1980). Schematic effects of social attitudes on information processing and recall. *Journal of Personality and Social Psychology, 38,* 569–578. (6)

Jussim, L. (1986). Self-fulfilling prophecies: A theoretical and integrative review. *Psychological Review, 93,* 429–445. (4, 5)

Jussim, L., Coleman, L. M., & Lerch, L. (1987). The nature of stereotypes: A comparison and integration of three theories. *Journal of Personality and Social Psychology, 52,* 536–546. (13)

Kahn, R. L., & Katz, D. (1953). Leadership practices in relation to productivity and morale. In D. W. Cartwright & A. Zander (Eds.), *Group dynamics* (pp. 554–570). New York: Harper & Row. (12)

Kandel, D. B. (1978). Similarity in real-life adolescent friendship pairs. *Journal of Personality and Social Psychology, 36,* 306–312. (9)

Kanter, R. M. (1977). *Men and women of the corporation.* New York: Basic Books. (3)

Kantola, S. J., Syme, G. J., & Campbell, N. A. (1984). Cognitive dissonance and energy conservation. *Journal of Applied Psychology, 69,* 416–421. (7)

Kaplan, J. A. (1978). A legal look at prosocial behavior: What can happen if one tries to help or fails to help another. In L. Wispé (Ed.), *Altruism, sympathy, and helping: Psychological and sociological principles*. New York: Academic Press.(11)

Kaplan, M. F. (1987). The influence process in group decision making. *Review of Personality and Social Psychology, 8,* 189–212.(12)

Kaplan, M. F., & Anderson, N. H. (1973). Information integration theory and reinforcement theory as approaches to interpersonal attraction. *Journal of Personality and Social Psychology, 28,* 301–312.(9)

Kaplan, M. F., & Miller, C. E. (1987). Group decision making and normative versus informational influence: Effects of type of issue and assigned decision rule. *Journal of Personality and Social Psychology, 53,* 306–313.(12)

Karlins, M., & Abelson, H. I. (1970). *How opinions and attitudes are changed* (2nd ed.). New York: Springer.(7)

Karuza, J., Jr., & Brickman, P. (1978, May). *Preference for similar and dissimilar others as a function of status.* Paper presented at meeting of the Midwestern Psychological Association, Chicago.(9)

Kassin, S. M., & Wrightsman, L. S. (1980). Prior confessions and mock jury verdicts. *Journal of Applied Social Psychology, 10,* 133–146.(8)

Kassin, S. M., & Wrightsman, L. S. (1981). Coerced confessions, judicial instruction, and mock juror verdicts. *Journal of Applied Social Psychology, 11,* 489–506.(8)

Katz, D. (1960). The functional approach to the study of attitudes. *Public Opinion Quarterly, 24,* 163–204.(7)

Katz, D., & Kahn, R. L. (1976). *The social psychology of organizations* (2nd ed.). New York: Wiley.(12)

Katz, D., & Stotland, E. (1959). A preliminary statement to a theory of attitude structure and change. In S. Koch (Ed.), *Psychology: A study of a science* (Vol. 3). New York: McGraw-Hill.(6)

Katz, I. (1981). *Stigma: A social psychological analysis.* Hillsdale, NJ.: Erlbaum.(11)

Katz, P. A. (1986). Gender identity: Development and consequences. In R. D. Ashmore & F. K. Del Boca (Eds.), *The social psychology of female-male relations* (pp. 21–67). New York: Academic Press.(3)

Kauffman, D. R., & Steiner, I. D. (1968). Conformity as an ingratiation technique. *Journal of Experimental Social Psychology, 4,* 404–414.(3)

Kaufmann, H. (1973). *Social psychology: The study of human interaction.* New York: Holt, Rinehart & Winston.(1)

Keeler, B. T., & Andrews, J. H. M. (1963). Leader behavior of principals, staff morale, and productivity. *Alberta Journal of Educational Research, 9,* 179–191.(12)

Kelley, H. H. (1950). The warm-cold variable in first impressions of persons. *Journal of Personality, 18,* 431–439.(4)

Kelley, H. H. (1967). Attribution theory in social psychology. *Nebraska Symposium on Motivation, 15,* 192–240.(4)

Kelley, H. H. (1972). Causal schemata and the attribution process. In E. E. Jones, D. Kanouse, H. H. Kelley, R. E. Nisbett, S. Valins, & B. Weiner (Eds.), *Attribution: Perceiving the causes of behavior* (pp. 151–174). Morristown, NJ: General Learning Press.(4)

Kelley, H. H. (1973). The process of causal attribution. *American Psychologist, 28,* 107–128.(4)

Kelley, H. H. (1979). *Personal relationships: Their structures and processes.* Hillsdale, NJ: Erlbaum.(9)

Kelley, H. H., Berscheid, E., Christensen, A., Harvey, J. H., Huston, T. L., Levinger, G., McClintock, E., Peplau, L. A., & Peterson, D. R. (1983). *Close relationships.* New York: Freeman.(9)

Kelley, H. H., & Michela, J. L. (1980). Attribution theory and research. *Annual Review of Psychology, 31,* 457–501.(4)

Kelley, H. H., & Thibaut, J. W. (1978). *Interpersonal relations: A theory of interdependence.* New York: Wiley-Interscience.(1, 9, 12)

Kelly, G. A. (1955). *A theory of personality: The psychology of personal constructs* (2 vols.). New York: Norton.(4)

Kelman, H. C. (1968). *A time to speak: On human values and social research.* San Francisco: Jossey-Bass.(2)

Kelvin, P. (1973). A social-psychological examination of privacy. *British Journal of Social and Clinical Psychology, 12,* 248–261.(14)

Kenrick, D. T., & Johnson, G. A. (1979). Interpersonal attraction in aversive environments: A problem for the classical conditioning paradigm? *Journal of Personality and Social Psychology, 37,* 572–579.(14)

Kenrick, D. T., McCreath, H. E., Govern, J., King, R., & Bordin, J. (1990). Person-environment intersections: Everyday settings and common trait dimensions. *Journal of Personality and Social Psychology, 58,* 685–698.(14)

Kerckhoff, A. C., & Davis, K. E. (1962). Value consensus and need complementarity in mate selection. *American Sociological Review, 27,* 295–303.(9)

Kernis, M. H., & Wheeler, L. (1981). Beautiful friends and ugly strangers: Radiation and contrast effects in perceptions of same-sex pairs. *Personality and Social Psychology Bulletin, 7,* 617–620.(9)

Kerr, N. L., & MacCoun, R. J. (1985a). The effects of jury size and polling method on process and product of jury deliberation. *Journal of Personality and Social Psychology, 48,* 349–363.(12)

Kerr, N. L., & MacCoun, R. J. (1985b). Role expectations in social dilemmas: Sex roles and task motivation in groups. *Journal of Personality and Social Psychology, 49,* 1547–1556.(12)

Kessler, S. J., & McKenna, W. (1978). *Gender: An ethnomethodological approach.* New York: Wiley.(4)

Kihlstrom, J. F., & Cantor, N. (1984). Mental representations of the self. *Advances in Experimental Social Psychology, 17,* 2–47.(3)

Kimble, C. E., & Forte, R. (1978, May). *Simulated and real eye contact as a function of emotional intensity and message positivity.* Paper presented at meeting of the Midwestern Psychological Association, Chicago.(5)

Kimble, G. A. (1961). *Hilgard and Marquis's conditioning and learning.* New York: Appleton-Century-Crofts.(1)

Kinder, D. R. (1978). Political person perception: The asymmetrical influence of sentiment and choice on perceptions of political candidates. *Journal of Personality and Social Psychology, 36,* 859–871.(7)

Kinder, D. R., & Sears, D. O. (1981). Prejudice and politics: Symbolic racism versus racial threats to the good life. *Journal of Personality and Social Psychology, 40,* 414–431.(13)

Kipnis, D. M. (1957). Interaction between members of bomber crews as a determinant of sociometric choice. *Human Relations, 10,* 263–270.(9)

Kirkpatrick, L. A., & Shaver, P. R. (1988). Fear and affiliation reconsidered from a stress and coping perspective: The importance of cognitive clarity and fear reduction. *Journal of Social and Clinical Psychology, 7,* 214–233.(9)

Kite, M., & Johnson, B. (1987). *Comparative stereotypes of younger and older adults: A meta-analysis.* Unpublished manuscript, Purdue University, West Lafayette, IN.(13)

Kleinke, C. L. (1986). Gaze and eye contact: A research review. *Psychological Bulletin, 100,* 78–100.(5)

Kleinke, C. L., Bustos, A. A., Meeker, F. B., & Staneski, R. A. (1973). Effects of self-attributed and other-attributed gaze on interpersonal evaluations between males and females. *Journal of Experimental Social Psychology, 9,* 154–163.(5)

Kluegel, J. R., & Smith, E. R. (1986). *Beliefs about inequality.* New York: Aldine de Gruyter.(13)

Knapp, M. L. (1978). *Nonverbal communication in human interaction* (2nd ed.). New York: Holt, Rinehart & Winston.(5)

Knapp, M. L., Hart, R. P., & Dennis, H. S. (1974). An exploration of deception as a communication construct. *Human Communication Research, 1,* 15–29.(5)

Knox, R. E., & Inkster, J. A. (1968). Postdecision dissonance at post time. *Journal of Personality and Social Psychology, 8,* 319–323.(7)

Koestner, R., Franz, C., & Weinberger, J. (1990). The family origins of empathic concern: A 26-year longitudinal study. *Journal of Personality and Social Psychology, 58,* 709–717.(11)

Kogan, N., & Wallach, M. A. (1964). *Risk-taking: A study in cognition and personality.* New York: Holt.(12)

Kolb, D. M. (1985). To be a mediator: Expressive tactics in mediation. *Journal of Social Issues, 41*(2), 11–26.(13)

Konar, E., & Sundstrom, E. (1986). Status demarcation and office design. In J. Wineman (Ed.), *Behavioral issues in office design* (pp. 203–223). New York: Van Nostrand Rinehold.(14)

Konar, E., Sundstrom, E., Brady, K., Mandel, D., & Rice, R. (1982). Status demarcation in the office. *Environment and Behavior, 14,* 561–580.(14)

Konečni, V. J. (1975). Annoyance, type and duration of postannoyance activity, and aggression: The "cathartic" effect. *Journal of Experimental Psychology: General, 104,* 76–102.(10, 14)

Koneya, M. (1976). Location and interaction in row-and-column seating arrangements. *Environment and Behavior, 8,* 265–282.(14)

Korman, A. K. (1966). "Consideration," "initiating structure," and organizational criteria—A review. *Personnel Psychology, 19,* 349–361.(12)

Korte, C., & Grant, R. (1980). Traffic noise, environmental awareness, and pedestrian behavior. *Environment and Behavior, 12,* 408–420.(14)

Kramer, G. P., Kerr, N. L., & Carroll, J. S. (1990). Pretrial publicity, judicial remedies, and jury bias. *Law and Human Behavior, 14,* 409–438.(2)

Kramer, R. M., & Brewer, M. B. (1984). Effects of group identity on resource use in a simulated commons dilemma. *Journal of Personality and Social Psychology, 46,* 1044–1057.(13)

Krauss, R. M., Curran, N. M., & Ferleger, N. (1983). Expressive conventions and the cross-cultural perception of emotion. *Basic and Applied Social Psychology, 4,* 295–305.(5)

Krauss, R. M., & Glucksberg, S. (1977). Social and non-social speech. *Scientific American, 236,* 100–105.(5)

Kraut, R. E. (1973). Effects of social labeling on giving to charity. *Journal of Experimental Social Psychology, 9,* 551–562.(8)

Kraut, R. E., & Johnston, R. (1979). Social and emotional messages of smiling: An ethological approach. *Journal of Personality and Social Psychology, 37,* 1539–1553.(5)

Kraut, R. E., & Poe, D. (1980). On the line: The deception judgments of customs inspectors and laymen. *Journal of Personality and Social Psychology, 39,* 784–798.(5)

Kravitz, D. A., & Martin, B. (1986). Ringelmann rediscovered: The original article. *Journal of Personality and Social Psychology, 50,* 936–941.(12)

Krebs, D. (1975). Empathy and altruism. *Journal of Personality and Social Psychology, 32,* 1134–1146.(11)

Krebs, D. (1983). Commentary and critique: Sociobiological approaches to prosocial development. In D. L. Bridgeman (Ed.), *The nature of prosocial development: Interdisciplinary theories and strategies.* New York: Academic Press.(11)

Krebs, D. L., & Miller, D. T. (1985). Altruism and aggression. In G. Lindzey & E. Aronson (Eds.), *Handbook of social psychology* (3rd ed., Vol. 2, pp. 1–71). New York: Random House.(10, 11)

Kressel, K., & Pruitt, D. G. (1985). Themes in the mediation of social conflict. *Journal of Social Issues, 41*(2), 179–198.(13)

Kreutz, D. (1991, May 1). Tucsonian who saved drowning man honored for act transcending heroism. *Arizona Daily Star,* pp. 1B–2B.(11)

Kronhausen, E., & Kronhausen, P. (1964). *Pornography and the law* (rev. ed.). New York: Ballantine.(10)

Krosnick, J. A., Li, F., & Lehman, D. R. (1990). Conversational conventions, order of information acquisition, and the effect of base rates and individuating information on social judgments. *Journal of Personality and Social Psychology, 59,* 1140–1152.(5)

Kruglanski, A. W. (1980). Lay epistomologic—Process and content: Another look at attribution theory. *Psychological Review, 87,* 70–87.(6)

Kruglanski, A. W. (1989). *Lay epistemics and human knowledge: Cognitive and motivational bases.* New York: Plenum.(6)

Kruglanski, A. W., & Mackie, D. M. (1990). Majority and minority influence: A judgmental process analysis. *European Review of Social Psychology, 1,* 229–261.(8, 12)

Kutchinsky, B. (1973). The effect of easy availability of pornography on the incidence of sex crimes: The Danish experience. *Journal of Social Issues, 29*(3), 163–181.(10)

Kutner, B., Wilkins, C., & Yarrow, P. R. (1952). Verbal attitudes and overt behavior involving racial prejudice. *Journal of Abnormal and Social Psychology, 47,* 649–652.(6)

LaFrance, M. (1990). Advancing social psychology through teaching. *Contemporary Social Psychology, 14,* 32–34.(1)

LaFrance, M., & Mayo, C. (1976). Racial differences in gaze behavior during conversations: Two systematic observational studies. *Journal of Personality and Social Psychology, 33,* 547–552.(5)(13)

LaFrance, M., & Mayo, C. (1978). *Moving bodies: Nonverbal communication in social relationships.* Pacific Grove, CA: Brooks/Cole.(5)

Laird, C. (1974). *Webster's new world thesaurus.* New York: Popular Library.(5)

Laird, J. D. (1974). Self-attribution of emotion: The effects of expressive behavior on the quality of emotional experi-ence. *Journal of Personality and Social Psychology, 29,* 475–486.(5)

Lakey, B. (1989). Personal and environmental antecedents of perceived social support developed at college. *American Journal of Community Psychology, 17,* 503–519.(14)

Lalljee, M., Watson, M., & White, P. (1982). Explanations, attributions, and the social context of unexpected behavior. *European Journal of Social Psychology, 12,* 17–29.(4, 7)

Lamm, H., & Trommsdorff, G. (1973). Group versus individual performance on tasks requiring ideational proficiency (brainstorming): A review. *European Journal of Social Psychology, 3,* 361–388.(12)

Landman, J., & Manis, M. (1983). Social cognition: Some historical and theoretical perspectives. *Advances in Experimental Social Psychology, 16,* 49–123.(1)

Lando, H. A., & Donnerstein, E. (1978). The effects of a model's success or failure on subsequent aggressive behavior. *Journal of Research in Personality, 12,* 225–234.(10)

Landy, D., & Sigall, H. (1974). Beauty is talent: Task evaluation as a function of the performer's physical attractiveness. *Journal of Personality and Social Psychology, 29,* 299–304.(4)

Langer, E. J. (1975). The illusion of control. *Journal of Personality and Social Psychology, 32,* 311–328.(8)

Langer, E. J. (1978a). The psychology of chance. *Journal for the Theory of Social Behaviour, 7,* 185–207.(3)

Langer, E. J. (1978b). Rethinking the role of thought in social interaction. In J. H. Harvey, W. J. Ickes, & R. F. Kidd (Eds.), *New directions in attribution research* (Vol. 2, pp. 35–58). Hillsdale, NJ: Erlbaum.(8)

Langer, E. J. (1983). *The psychology of control.* Beverly Hills, CA: Sage.(8)

Langer, E. J. (1989a). *Mindfulness.* Reading, MA: Addison-Wesley.(3, 8)

Langer, E. J. (1989b). Minding matters: The consequences of mindlessness–mindfulness. *Advances in Experimental Social Psychology, 22,* 137–174.(3, 8)

Langer, E. J., & Benevento, A. (1978). Self-induced dependence. *Journal of Personality and Social Psychology, 36,* 886–893.(8)

Langer, E. J., & Rodin, J. (1976). The effects of choice and enhanced personal responsibility for the aged: A field experiment in an institutional setting. *Journal of Personality and Social Psychology, 34,* 191–198.(8)

Langer, E. J., & Roth, J. (1975). Heads I win, tails it's chance: The illusion of control as a function of the sequence of outcomes in a purely chance task. *Journal of Personality and Social Psychology, 32,* 951–955.(8)

Langlois, J. H. (1986). From the eye of the beholder to behavioral reality: Development of social behaviors and social relations as a function of physical attractiveness. In C. P. Herman, M. P. Zanna, & E. T. Higgins (Eds.), *Physical appearance, stigma, and social behavior: The Ontario Symposium, Volume 3* (pp. 23–51). Hillsdale, NJ: Erlbaum. (4)

Langston, C. A., & Cantor, N. (1989). Social anxiety and social constraint: When making friends is hard. *Journal of Personality and Social Psychology, 56,* 649–661. (9)

LaPiere, R. T. (1934). Attitude and actions. *Social Forces, 13,* 230–237. (6)

Latané, B. (Ed.). (1966). Studies in social comparison. *Journal of Experimental Social Psychology,* Supplement No. 1. (3)

Latané, B. (1981). The psychology of social impact. *American Psychologist, 36,* 343–356. (8, 12)

Latané, B., & Bidwell, L. D. (1977). Sex and affiliation in college cafeterias. *Personality and Social Psychology Bulletin, 3,* 571–574. (9)

Latané, B., & Darley, J. (1970). *The unresponsive bystander: Why doesn't he help?* New York: Appleton-Century-Crofts. (2, 11)

Latané, B., & Harkins, S. (1976). Cross-modality matches suggest anticipated stage fright as multiplicative function of audience size and status. *Perception and Psychophysics, 20,* 482–488. (12)

Latané, B., & Nida, S. A. (1981). Ten years of research on group size and helping. *Psychological Bulletin, 89,* 308–324. (11)

Latané, B., Nida, S. A., & Wilson, D. W. (1981). The effects of group size on helping behavior. In J. P. Rushton & R. M. Sorrentino (Eds.), *Altruism and helping behavior: Social, personality, and developmental perspectives.* Hillsdale, NJ: Erlbaum. (11)

Latané, B., Williams, K., & Harkins, S. (1979). Many hands make light the work: The causes and consequences of social loafing. *Journal of Personality and Social Psychology, 37,* 822–832. (12)

Latané, B., & Wolf, S. (1981). The social impact of majorities and minorities. *Psychological Review, 88,* 438–453. (12)

Leana, C. R. (1985). A partial test of Janis' groupthink model: Effects of group cohesiveness and leader behavior on defective decision making. *Journal of Management, 11,* 5–17. (12)

Leary, M. R., & Meadows, S. (1991). Predictors, eliciters, and concomitants of social blushing. *Journal of Personality and Social Psychology, 60,* 254–262. (5)

Leary, M. R., Wheeler, D. S., & Jenkins, T. B. (1986). Aspects of identity and behavioral preference: Studies of occupational and recreational choice. *Social Psychology Quarterly, 49,* 11–18. (3)

Leavitt, H. J. (1951). Some effects of certain communication patterns on group performance. *Journal of Abnormal and Social Psychology, 46,* 38–50. (12)

Lécuyer, R. (1976). Social organization and spatial organization. *Human Relations, 29,* 1045–1060. (14)

Lee, J. A. (1973). *The colors of love: An exploration of the ways of loving.* Don Mills, Ontario: New Press. (9)

Lerner, M. J. (1966, September). *The unjust consequences of the need to believe in a just world.* Paper presented at meeting of the American Psychological Association, New York. (4)

Lerner, M. J. (1975). The justice motive in social behavior. *Journal of Social Issues, 31*(3), 1–19. (4)

Lerner, M. J. (1977). The justice motive: Some hypotheses as to its origins and forms. *Journal of Personality, 45,* 1–52. (4)

Lerner, M. J., Miller, D. T., & Holmes, J. G. (1976). Deserving and the emergence of forms of justice. *Advances in Experimental Social Psychology, 9,* 133–162. (4)

Lesnik-Oberstein, M., & Cohen, L. (1984). Cognitive style, sensation seeking, and assortative mating. *Journal of Personality and Social Psychology, 46,* 112–117. (9)

Leung, K., & Bond, M. H. (1984). The impact of cultural collectivism on reward allocation. *Journal of Personality and Social Psychology, 47,* 793–804. (13)

Leventhal, H. (1970). Findings and theory in the study of fear communications. *Advances in Experimental Social Psychology, 5,* 119–186. (7)

Levine, J. M., & Russo, E. M. (1987). Majority and minority influence. *Review of Personality and Social Psychology, 8,* 13–54. (12)

Levine, R. (1991). Social psychology outside the United States—Hong Kong: An interview with Michael Harris Bond. *Contemporary Social Psychology, 15,* 78–83. (13)

Levinger, G. (1979). A social psychological perspective on marital dissolution. In G. Levinger & O. C. Moles (Eds.), *Divorce and separation.* New York: Basic Books. (9)

Levinger, G., Senn, D. J., & Jorgensen, B. W. (1970). Progress toward permanence in courtship: A test of the Kerckhoff-Davis hypotheses. *Sociometry, 33,* 427–443. (9)

Levy, S. G. (1969). A 150-year study of political violence in the United States. In H. D. Graham & T. R. Gurr (Eds.), *Violence in America.* New York: New American Library. (10)

Lewin, A. Y., & Duchan, L. (1971). Women in academia. *Science, 173,* 892–895. (13)

Lewin, K. (1935). *A dynamic theory of personality.* New York: McGraw-Hill. (13)

Lewin, K. (1936). *Principles of topological psychology.* New York: McGraw-Hill. (13, 14)

Lewin, K. (1938). The conceptual representation and measurement of psychological forces. *Contributions to Psychological Theory* (Vol. 1, No. 4). Durham, NC: Duke University Press. (14)

Lewin, K. (1951). *Field theory in social science.* New York: Harper. (1)

Leyens, J.-P., Camino, L., Parke, R. D., & Berkowitz, L.

(1975). Effects of movie violence on aggression in a field setting as a function of group dominance and cohesion. *Journal of Personality and Social Psychology, 32,* 346–360.(10)

Leyens, J.-P., Herman, G., & Dunand, M. (1982). The influence of an audience upon the reactions to filmed violence. *European Journal of Social Psychology, 12,* 131–142.(10)

Leyhausen, P. (1965). The communal organization of solitary mammals. *Symposium of the Zoological Society of London, 14,* 249–253.(14)

Lieberman, S. (1956). The effects of changes in roles on the attitudes of role occupants. *Human Relations, 9,* 385–402.(1, 2, 6)

Liebert, R. M., & Schwartzberg, N. S. (1977). Effects of mass media. In M. R. Rosenzweig & L. W. Porter (Eds.), *Annual review of psychology* (Vol. 28). Palo Alto, CA: Annual Reviews.(10)

Liebert, R. M., & Sprafkin, J. (1988). *The early window: Effects of television on children and youth* (3rd ed.). New York: Pergamon Press.(11)

Likert, R. (1932). A technique for the measurement of attitudes. *Archives of Psychology,* No. 140.(6)

Lindskold, S. (1986). GRIT: Reducing distrust through carefully introduced conciliation. In S. Worchel & W. G. Austin (Eds.), *Psychology of intergroup relations* (2nd ed., pp. 305–322). Chicago: Nelson-Hall.(13)

Lindskold, S., & Han, G. (1988). GRIT as a foundation for integrative bargaining. *Personality and Social Psychology Bulletin, 14,* 335–345.(13)

Linville, P. W. (1982). The complexity-extremity effect and age-based stereotyping. *Journal of Personality and Social Psychology, 42,* 193–211.(13)

Linville, P. W. (1985). Self-complexity and affective extremity: Don't put all of your eggs in one cognitive basket. *Social Cognition, 3,* 94–120.(3)

Linville, P. W. (1987). Self-complexity as a cognitive buffer against stress-related illness and depression. *Journal of Personality and Social Psychology, 52,* 663–676.(3)

Lipman, A. (1969). The architectural belief system and social behavior. *British Journal of Sociology, 20,* 190–204.(14)

Lippa, R. (1976). Expressive control and the leakage of dispositional introversion-extraversion during role-played teaching. *Journal of Personality, 44,* 541–559.(3)

Lippa, R. (1978). The effect of expressive control on expressive consistency and on the relation between expressive behavior and personality. *Journal of Personality, 46,* 438–461.(3)

Lippmann, W. (1922). *Public opinion.* New York: Harcourt, Brace & World.(4)

Litman-Adizes, T., Raven, B. H., & Fontaine, G. (1978). Consequences of social power and causal attribution for compliance as seen by powerholder and target. *Personality and Social Psychology Bulletin, 4,* 260–264.(8)

LoBello, S. G. (1990). Differences between blood donors and nondonors in AIDS-related attitudes. *Psychological Reports, 66,* 867–870.(11)

Locksley, A., Hepburn, C., & Ortiz, V. (1982). Social stereotypes and judgments of individuals: An instance of the base-rate fallacy. *Journal of Experimental Social Psychology, 18,* 23–42.(4)

Loehlin, J., Lindzey, G., & Spuhler, J. N. (1975). *Race differences in intelligence.* San Francisco: W. H. Freeman.(13)

Loftus, E. F. (1979). *Eyewitness testimony.* Cambridge, MA: Harvard University Press.(4)

Loftus, E. F., Loftus, G. R., & Messo, J. (1987). Some facts about "weapon focus." *Law and Human Behavior, 11,* 55–62.(4)

Logan, G. D. (1989). Automaticity and cognitive control. In J. S. Uleman & J. A. Bargh (Eds.), *Unintended thought* (pp. 52–74). New York: Guilford Press.(3, 10)

London, P. (1970). The rescuers: Motivational hypotheses about Christians who saved Jews from the Nazis. In J. Macaulay & L. Berkowitz (Eds.), *Altruism and helping behavior: Social psychological studies of some antecedents and consequences.* New York: Academic Press.(11)

Longley, J., & Pruitt, D. G. (1980). Groupthink: A critique of Janis's theory. *Review of Personality and Social Psychology, 1,* 74–93.(12)

Lord, R. G., Binning, J. F., Rush, M. C., & Thomas, J. C. (1978). The effect of performance cues and leader behavior on questionnaire ratings of leadership behavior. *Organizational Behavior and Human Performance, 21,* 27–39.(12)

Lorenz, K. (1966). *On aggression.* New York: Harcourt, Brace & World.(10)

Lott, A. J., & Lott, B. E. (1961). Group cohesiveness, communication level, and conformity. *Journal of Abnormal and Social Psychology, 62,* 408–412.(12)

Lott, A. J., & Lott, B. E. (1974). The role of reward in the formation of positive interpersonal attitudes. In T. L. Huston (Ed.), *Foundations of interpersonal attraction.* New York: Academic Press.(9)

Lott, B. E., & Lott, A. J. (1985). Learning theory in contemporary social psychology. In G. Lindzey & E. Aronson (Eds.), *Handbook of social psychology* (3rd ed., Vol. 1, pp. 109–135). New York: Random House.(1)

Lott, D. F., & Sommer, R. (1967). Seating arrangements and status. *Journal of Personality and Social Psychology, 7,* 90–94.(5)

Lumsdaine, A., & Janis, I. (1953). Resistance to counterpropaganda produced by a one-sided versus a two-sided propaganda presentation. *Public Opinion Quarterly, 17,* 311–318.(7)

Lydon, J., Zanna, M. P., & Ross, M. (1988). Bolstering attitudes by autobiographical recall: Attitude persistence and selective memory. *Personality and Social Psychology Bulletin, 14,* 78–86.(7)

Lyman, S. M., & Scott, M. B. (1967). Territoriality: A neglected sociological dimension. *Social Problems, 15,* 236–249.(14)

Lysak, H., Rule, B. G., & Dobbs, A. R. (1989). Conceptions of aggression: Prototype or defining features? *Personality and Social Psychology Bulletin, 15,* 233–243.(10)

Lytton, H., & Romney, D. M. (1991). Parents' differential socialization of boys and girls: A meta-analysis. *Psychological Bulletin, 109,* 267–296.(13)

Maass, A., & Clark, R. D., III. (1984). Hidden impact of minorities: Fifteen years of minority influence research. *Psychological Bulletin, 95,* 428–450.(12)

Maass, A., Clark, R. D., III, & Haberkorn, G. (1982). The effects of differential ascribed category membership and norms on minority influence. *European Journal of Social Psychology, 12,* 89–104.(12)

Maass, A., West, S. G., & Cialdini, R. B. (1987). Minority influence and conversion. *Review of Personality and Social Psychology, 8,* 55–80.(12)

Maccoby, E. E., & Jacklin, C. N. (1974). *The psychology of sex differences.* Stanford: Stanford University Press.(2, 10)

Macdonald, J. E., & Gifford, R. (1989). Territorial cues and defensible space theory: The burglar's point of view. *Journal of Environmental Psychology, 9,* 193–205.(14)

Mackie, D. M. (1986). Social identification effects in group polarization. *Journal of Personality and Social Psychology, 50,* 720–728.(12)

Maddux, J. E., & Rogers, R. W. (1983). Protection motivation and self-efficacy: A revised theory of fear appeals and attitude change. *Journal of Experimental Social Psychology, 19,* 469–479.(7)

Major, B. (1980). Information acquisition and attribution processes. *Journal of Personality and Social Psychology, 39,* 1010–1023.(4)

Major, B. (1981). Gender patterns in touching behavior. In C. Mayo & N. M. Henley (Eds.), *Gender and nonverbal behavior.* New York: Springer-Verlag.(5)

Major, B., & Heslin, R. (1982). Perceptions of same-sex and cross-sex reciprocal touch: It's better to give than to receive. *Journal of Nonverbal Behavior, 3,* 148–163.(5)

Malamuth, N. M. (1981a). Rape fantasies as a function of exposure to violent sexual stimuli. *Archives of Sexual Behavior, 10,* 33–47.(10)

Malamuth, N. M. (1981b). Rape proclivity among males. *Journal of Social Issues, 37*(4), 138–157.(10)

Malamuth, N. M., & Check, J. V. P. (1981). The effects of mass media exposure on acceptance of violence against women: A field experiment. *Journal of Research in Personality, 15,* 436–446.(10)

Malamuth, N. M., & Donnerstein, E. (1982). The effects of aggressive-pornographic mass media stimuli. In L. Berkowitz (Ed.), *Advances in experimental social psychology* (Vol. 15, pp. 103–106). New York: Academic Press.(10)

Malamuth, N. M., & Donnerstein, E. (Eds.). (1984). *Pornography and sexual aggression.* New York: Academic Press.(10)

Mander, A. M., & Gaebelein, J. W. (1977). Third party instigation of aggression as a function of noncooperation and veto power. *Journal of Research in Personality, 11,* 475–486.(10)

Mann, L. (1980). Cross-cultural studies of small groups. In H. C. Triandis & R. W. Brislin (Eds.), *Handbook of cross-cultural psychology: Social psychology* (Vol. 5). Boston: Allyn & Bacon.(13)

Mann, L. (1981). The baiting crowd in episodes of threatened suicide. *Journal of Personality and Social Psychology, 41,* 703–709.(10)

Mann, L., Newton, J. W., & Innes, J. M. (1982). A test between deindividuation and emergent norm theories of crowd aggression. *Journal of Personality and Social Psychology, 42,* 260–272.(10)

Mann, L., Radford, M., & Kanagawa, C. (1985). Cross-cultural differences in children's use of decision rules: A comparison between Japan and Australia. *Journal of Personality and Social Psychology, 49,* 1557–1564.(11)

Margulis, S. T. (1977). Conceptions of privacy: Current status and next steps. *Journal of Social Issues, 33*(3), 5–21.(14)

Marks, G., & Miller, N. (1988). Perceptions of attitude similarity: Effect of anchored versus unanchored positions. *Personality and Social Psychology Bulletin, 14,* 92–102.(7)

Markus, H. (1977). Self-schemata and processing information about the self. *Journal of Personality and Social Psychology, 35,* 63–78.(3)

Markus, H., & Kunda, Z. (1986). Stability and malleability of the self-concept. *Journal of Personality and Social Psychology, 51,* 858–866.(3)

Markus, H., & Nurius, P. (1986). Possible selves. *American Psychologist, 41,* 954–969.(3)

Markus, H., Smith, J., & Moreland, R. L. (1985). Role of the self-concept in the perception of others. *Journal of Personality and Social Psychology, 49,* 1494–1512.(4)

Markus, H., & Zajonc, R. B. (1985). The cognitive perspective in social psychology. In G. Lindzey & E. Aronson (Eds.), *Handbook of social psychology* (3rd ed., Vol. 1, pp. 137–230). New York: Random House.(1, 4)

Marsh, H. W. (1986). Global self-esteem: Its relation to specific facets of self-concept and their importance. *Journal of Personality and Social Psychology, 51,* 1224–1236.(3)

Martin, G. B., & Clark, R. D., III. (1982). Distress crying in neonates: Species and peer specificity. *Developmental Psychology, 18,* 3–9.(11)

Martin, J. (1980). Relative deprivation: A theory of distributive injustice for an era of shrinking resources. In *Research in organizational behavior* (Vol. 3). Greenwich, CT: JAI Press.(10)

Martindale, D. A. (1971). Territorial dominance behavior in dyadic verbal interactions. *Proceedings, 79th Annual Convention, American Psychological Association, 6,* 305–306.(14)

Maslach, C. (1979). Negative emotional biasing of unexplained arousal. *Journal of Personality and Social Psychology, 37,* 953–969.(9)

Maslach, C., Santee, R. T., & Wade, C. (1987). Individuation, gender role, and dissent: Personality mediators of social forces. *Journal of Personality and Social Psychology, 53,* 1088–1093.(8)

Maslow, A. H., & Mintz, N. L. (1956). Effects of esthetic surroundings: I. Initial effects of three esthetic conditions upon perceiving "energy" and "well-being" in faces. *Journal of Psychology, 41,* 247–254.(14)

Mathews, K. E., Jr., & Canon, L. K. (1975). Environmental noise level as a determinant of helping behavior. *Journal of Personality and Social Psychology, 32,* 571–577.(14)

Matthews, K. A., Batson, C. D., Horn, J., & Rosenman, R. H. (1981). "Principles in his nature which interest him in the fortune of others . . .": The heritability of empathic concern for others. *Journal of Personality, 49,* 237–247.(11)

Maynard, D. W., & Zimmerman, D. H. (1984). Topical talk, ritual, and the social organization of relationships. *Social Psychology Quarterly, 47,* 301–316.(5)

Mayo, J. M. (1979). Effects of street forms on suburban neighboring behavior. *Environment and Behavior, 11,* 375–397.(14)

McAdams, D. P., Healy, S., & Krause, S. (1984). Social motives and patterns of friendship. *Journal of Personality and Social Psychology, 47,* 828–838.(9)

McArthur, L. A. (1972). The how and what of why: Some determinants of consequences of causal attribution. *Journal of Personality and Social Psychology, 22,* 171–193.(4)

McArthur, L. Z. (1982). Judging a book by its cover: A cognitive analysis of the relationship between physical appearance and stereotyping. In A. H. Hastorf & A. M. Isen (Eds.), *Cognitive social psychology* (pp. 149–211). New York: Elsevier/North Holland.(4)

• McArthur, L. Z., & Apatow, K. (1983/1984). Impressions of baby-faced adults. *Social Cognition, 2,* 315–342.(4)

• McArthur, L. Z., & Baron, R. M. (1983). Toward an ecological theory of social perception. *Psychological Review, 90,* 215–238.(4)

McCarthy, D., & Saegert, S. (1979). Residential density, social overload, and social withdrawal. *Human Ecology, 6,* 253–272.(14)

McCauley, C. (1989). The nature of social influence in groupthink: Compliance and internalization. *Journal of Personality and Social Psychology, 57,* 250–260.(12)

McCauley, C., Durham, M., Copley, J. B., & Johnson, J. P. (1985). Patients' perceptions of treatment for kidney failure: The impact of personal experience on population predictions. *Journal of Experimental Social Psychology, 21,* 138–148.(2)

McCauley, C., & Stitt, C. L. (1978). An individual and quantitative measure of stereotypes. *Journal of Personality and Social Psychology, 36,* 929–940.(13)

McClintock, C. G. (1958). Personality syndromes and attitude change. *Journal of Personality, 26,* 479–493.(7)

McCombe, R. P., & Stires, L. K. (1990). The effects of changes in roles on the attitudes of role occupants: A conceptual replication. *Contemporary Social Psychology, 14,* 11–14.(6)

McCombie, R. P. (1991). Blood donation patterns of undergraduate students: Family and friendship correlated. *Journal of Community Psychology, 19,* 161–165.(11)

McConahay, J. G., Hardee, B. B., & Batts, V. (1981). Has racism declined? It depends on who's asking and what is asked. *Journal of Conflict Resolution, 25,* 563–579.(13)

McCorkle, L. W., & Korn, R. R. (1954). Resocialization within walls. *Academy of Political and Social Science, 293,* 88–98.(11)

McCroskey, J. C., & Richmond, V. P. (1990). Willingness to communicate: A cognitive view. In M. Booth-Butterfield (Ed.), *Communication, cognition, and anxiety.* [Special issue]. *Journal of Social Behavior and Personality, 5,* 19–37.(12)

McGhee, P. E., & Teevan, R. C. (1967). Conformity behavior and need for affiliation. *Journal of Social Psychology, 72,* 117–121.(8)

McGinnis, R. (1959). Campus values in mate selection: A repeat study. *Social Forces, 36,* 283–291.(9)

McGinniss, J. (1970). *The selling of the president, 1968.* New York: Pocket Books.(7)

McGrath, J. E. (1980). What are the social issues? Timeliness and treatment of topics in the *Journal of Social Issues. Journal of Social Issues, 36*(4), 98–108.(1)

McGrath, J. E. (1984). *Groups: Interaction and performance.* Englewood Cliffs, NJ: Prentice-Hall.(12)

McGrath, J. E., Martin, J., & Kulka, R. A. (1982). *Judgment calls in research.* Beverly Hills, CA: Sage.(2)

McGuire, W. J. (1964). Inducing resistance to persuasion. *Advances in Experimental Social Psychology, 1,* 191–229.(2, 7)

McGuire, W. J. (1968a). Personality and attitude change: A theoretical housing. In A. G. Greenwald, T. C. Brock, & T. M. Ostrom (Eds.), *Psychological foundations of attitudes* (pp. 171–196). New York: Academic Press. (7)

McGuire, W. J. (1968b). Personality and susceptibility to social influence. In E. F. Borgatta & W. W. Lambert (Eds.), *Handbook of personality theory and research*. Chicago: Rand McNally. (7)

McGuire, W. J. (1973). The yin and yang of progress in social psychology: Seven koan. *Journal of Personality and Social Psychology, 26,* 446–456. (2)

McGuire, W. J. (1984). Perspectivism: A look back at the future. *Contemporary Social Psychology, 10,* 19–39. (1)

McGuire, W. J. (1985). Attitudes and attitude change. In G. Lindzey & E. Aronson (Eds.), *Handbook of social psychology* (3rd ed., Vol. 2, pp. 233–346). New York: Random House. (6, 7)

McGuire, W. J., & McGuire, C. V. (1981). The spontaneous self-concept as affected by personal distinctiveness. In M. D. Lynch, A. A. Norem-Hebeisen, & K. J. Gergen (Eds.), *Self-concept: Advances in theory and research*. Cambridge, MA: Ballinger. (3)

McGuire, W. J., McGuire, C. V., & Winton, W. (1979). Effects of household sex composition on the salience of one's gender in the spontaneous self-concept. *Journal of Experimental Social Psychology, 15,* 77–90. (3)

McGuire, W. J., & Millman, S. (1965). Anticipatory belief lowering following forewarning of a persuasive attack. *Journal of Personality and Social Psychology, 2,* 471–479. (7)

McGuire, W. J., & Padawer-Singer, A. (1976). Trait salience in the spontaneous self-concept. *Journal of Personality and Social Psychology, 33,* 743–754. (3)

McGuire, W. J., & Papageorgis, D. (1962). Effectiveness of forewarning in developing resistance to persuasion. *Public Opinion Quarterly, 26,* 24–34. (7)

McKirnan, D. J., Smith, C. E., & Hamayan, E. V. (1983). A sociolinguistic approach to the belief-similarity model of racial attitudes. *Journal of Experimental Social Psychology, 19,* 434–447. (13)

McNemar, Q. (1942). *The revision of the Stanford-Binet scale: An analysis of the standardization data*. Boston: Houghton Mifflin. (13)

Mead, G. H. (1934). *Mind, self, and society* (C. W. Morris, Ed.). Chicago: University of Chicago Press. (1, 3)

Medcof, J. W. (1990). PEAT: An integrative model of attribution processes. *Advances in Experimental Social Psychology, 23,* 111–209. (4)

Mehlman, R. C., & Snyder, C. R. (1985). Excuse theory: A test of the self-protective role of attributions. *Journal of Personality and Social Psychology, 49,* 994–1001. (3)

Mehrabian, A. (1969a). Significance of posture and position in the communication of attitude and status relationships. *Psychological Bulletin, 71,* 359–372. (5)

Mehrabian, A. (1969b). Some referents and measures of nonverbal behavior. *Behavioral Research Methods and Instrumentation, 1,* 203–207. (5)

Mehrabian, A. (1972). *Nonverbal communication*. Chicago: Aldine-Atherton. (5)

Mehrabian, A., & Diamond, S. (1971a). Effects of furniture arrangement, props, and personality on social interaction. *Journal of Personality and Social Psychology, 20,* 18–30. (14)

Mehrabian, A., & Diamond, S. (1971b). Seating arrangement and conversation. *Sociometry, 34,* 281–289. (14)

Mehrabian, A., & Weiner, M. (1967). Decoding of inconsistent communications. *Journal of Personality and Social Psychology, 6,* 109–114. (5)

Meindl, J. R., & Lerner, M. J. (1984). Exacerbation of extreme responses to an out-group. *Journal of Personality and Social Psychology, 47,* 71–84. (13)

Metts, S. (1989). An exploratory investigation of deception in close relationships. *Journal of Social and Personal Relationships, 6,* 159–179. (9)

Meyer, W.-U., & Starke, E. (1982). Own ability in relation to self-concept of ability: A field study of information-seeking. *Personality and Social Psychology Bulletin, 8,* 501–507. (3)

Meyerowitz, B. E., & Chaiken, S. (1987). The effect of message framing on breast self-examination attitudes, intentions, and behavior. *Journal of Personality and Social Psychology, 52,* 500–510. (7)

Michaels, J. W., Blommel, J. M., Brocato, R. M., Linkous, R. A., & Rowe, J. S. (1982). Social facilitation and inhibition in a natural setting. *Replications in Social Psychology, 2,* 21–24. (12)

Midlarsky, E. (1984). Competence and helping: Notes toward a model. In E. Staub, D. Bar-Tal, J. Karylowski, & J. Reykowski (Eds.), *The development and maintenance of prosocial behavior: International perspectives*. New York: Plenum. (11)

Midlarsky, E., & Bryan, J. H. (1972). Affect expressions and children's imitative altruism. *Journal of Experimental Research on Personality, 6,* 195–203. (11)

Mikulincer, M. (1986). Attributional processes in the learned helplessness paradigm: Behavioral effects of global attributions. *Journal of Personality and Social Psychology, 51,* 1248–1256. (8)

Milavsky, J. R. (1988). Television and aggression once again. *Applied Social Psychology Annual, 8,* 163–170. (10)

Milgram, S. (1963). Behavioral study of obedience. *Journal of Abnormal and Social Psychology, 67,* 371–378. (8, 10)

Milgram, S. (1965). Some conditions of obedience and disobedience to authority. *Human Relations, 18,* 57–76. (8, 10)

Milgram, S. (1970). The experience of living in cities. *Science, 167,* 1461–1468.(11, 14)

Milgram, S. (1974). *Obedience to authority.* New York: Harper & Row.(8, 10)

Milgram, S., Mann, L., & Harter, S. (1965). The lost-letter technique of social research. *Public Opinion Quarterly, 29,* 437–438.(6)

Millar, M. G., & Millar, K. U. (1990). Attitude change as a function of attitude type and argument type. *Journal of Personality and Social Psychology, 59,* 217–228.(7)

Millar, M. G., & Tesser, A. (1986). Effects of affective and cognitive focus on the atitude-behavior relation. *Journal of Personality and Social Psychology, 51,* 270–276.(6)

Miller, A. G. (1972). Role playing: An alternative to deception? A review of the evidence. *American Psychologist, 27,* 623–636.(2)

Miller, A. G. (1986). *The obedience experiments: A case study of controversy in social science.* New York: Praeger.(8, 12)

Miller, A. G., & Lawson, T. (1989). The effect of an information option on the fundamental attribution error. *Personality and Social Psychology Bulletin, 15,* 194–204.(4)

Miller, C., & Crandall, R. (1980). Bargaining and negotiation. In P. B. Paulus (Ed.), *Psychology of group influence.* Hillsdale, NJ: Erlbaum.(13)

Miller, D. T., Norman, S. A., & Wright, E. (1978). Distortion in person perception as a consequence of the need for effective control. *Journal of Personality and Social Psychology, 36,* 598–607.(8)

Miller, D. T., & Turnbull, W. (1986). Expectancies and interpersonal processes. *Annual Review of Psychology, 37,* 233–256.(5)

Miller, J. G. (1964). Adjusting to overloads of information. In R. Waggoner & D. Carek (Eds.), *Disorders of communication* (Vol. 42, pp. 87–100). Baltimore, MD: Williams & Wilkins.(14)

Miller, J. G. (1984). Culture and the development of everyday social explanation. *Journal of Personality and Social Psychology, 46,* 961–978.(3, 4)

Miller, J. K. (1988). Damned if you do, damned if you don't: Religious shunning and the free exercise clause. *University of Pennsylvania Law Review, 137,* 271–302.(5)

Miller, L. E., & Grush, J. E. (1986). Individual differences in attitudinal versus normative determination of behavior. *Journal of Experimental Social Psychology, 22,* 190–202.(6)

Miller, N. (1965). Involvement and dogmatism as inhibitors of attitude change. *Journal of Experimental Social Psychology, 1,* 121–132.(7)

Miller, N., & Brewer, M. B. (Eds.). (1984). *Groups in contact: The psychology of desegregation.* Orlando, FL: Academic Press.(13)

Miller, N., & Cooper, H. M. (Eds). (1991). Special issue: Meta-analysis in personality and social psychology. *Personality and Social Psychology Bulletin, 17*(3).(2)

Miller, N., & Davidson-Podgorny, G. (1987). Theoretical models of intergroup relations and the use of cooperative teams as an intervention for desegregated settings. *Review of Personality and Social Psychology, 9,* 41–67.(13)

Miller, N. E. (1941). The frustration-aggression hypothesis. *Psychological Review, 48,* 337–342.(10)

Miller, N. E., & Dollard, J. (1941). *Social learning and imitation.* New Haven, CT: Yale University Press.(1)

Miller, R. S. (1991). On decorum in close relationships: Why aren't we polite to those we love? *Contemporary Social Psychology, 15,* 63–65.(12)

Mills, J., & Clark, M. S. (1982). Exchange and communal relationships. *Review of Personality and Social Psychology, 3,* 121–144.(9)

Mintz, N. L. (1956). Effects of esthetic surroundings: II. Prolonged and repeated experience in a "beautiful" and an "ugly" room. *Journal of Psychology, 41,* 459–466.(14)

Mirels, H. L. (1970). Dimensions of internal versus external control. *Journal of Consulting and Clinical Psychology, 34,* 226–228.(8)

Mittal, B. (1988). Achieving higher seat belt usage: The role of habit in bridging the attitude-behavior gap. *Journal of Applied Social Psychology, 18,* 993–1016.(6)

Moe, J. L., Nacoste, R. W., & Insko, C. A. (1981). Belief versus race as determinants of discrimination: A study of Southern adolescents in 1966 and 1979. *Journal of Personality and Social Psychology, 41,* 1031–1050.(13)

Montagu, A. (1976). *The nature of human aggression.* New York: Oxford University Press.(10)

Montello, D. R. (1988). Classroom seating location and its effect on course achievement, participation, and attitudes. *Journal of Environmental Psychology, 8,* 149–157.(14)

Moreland, R. L., & Levine, J. M. (1982). Socialization in small groups: Temporal changes in individual-group relations. *Advances in Experimental Social Psychology, 15,* 137–192.(12)

Moreland, R. L., & Zajonc, R. B. (1982). Exposure effects in person perception: Familiarity, similarity, and attraction. *Journal of Experimental Social Psychology, 18,* 395–415.(9)

Morgan, M. (1982). Television and adolescents' sex role stereotypes: A longitudinal study. *Journal of Personality and Social Psychology, 43,* 947–955.(6)

Moriarty, T. (1975). Crime, commitment, and the responsive bystander: Two field experiments. *Journal of Personality and Social Psychology, 31,* 370–376.(11)

Morris, D., Collett, P., Marsh, P., & O'Shaughnessy, M. (1979). *Gestures, their origins and distribution.* New York: Stein & Day.(5)

Morrow, P. C., & McElroy, J. C. (1981). Interior office design and visitor response: A constructive replication. *Journal of Applied Psychology, 66,* 646–650.(14)

Morton, T. L. (1978). Intimacy and reciprocity of exchange: A comparison of spouses and strangers. *Journal of Personality and Social Psychology, 36,* 72–81.(5)

Moscovici, S. (1972). Society and theory in social psychology. In J. Israel & H. Tajfel (Eds.), *The context of social psychology: A critical assessment.* New York: Academic Press.(13)

Moscovici, S. (1976). *Social influence and social change.* New York: Academic Press.(12)

Moscovici, S. (1985). Social influence and conformity. In G. Lindzey & E. Aronson (Eds.), *Handbook of social psychology* (3rd ed., Vol. 2, pp. 347–412). New York: Random House.(8, 12)

Moser, G. (1988). Urban stress and helping behavior: Effects of environmental overload and noise on behavior. *Journal of Environmental Psychology, 8,* 287–298.(14)

Mosteller, F., & Bush, R. R. (1954). Selected quantitative techniques. In G. Lindzey (Ed.), *Handbook of social psychology* (Vol. 1, pp. 280–334). Reading, MA: Addison-Wesley.(2)

Mowen, J. C., & Cialdini, R. B. (1980). On implementing the door-in-the-face compliance technique in a business context. *Journal of Marketing Research, 17,* 253–258.(8)

Mueller, J. H. (1982). Self-awareness and access to material rated as self-descriptive or nondescriptive. *Bulletin of the Psychonomic Society, 19,* 323–326.(3)

Mugny, G. (1975). Negotiations, image of the other, and the process of minority influence. *European Journal of Social Psychology, 5,* 209–229.(12)

Mugny, G. (1982). *The power of minorities.* London: Academic Press.(12)

Mugny, G., Kaiser, C., Papastamou, S., & Perez, J. A. (1984). Intergroup relations, identification, and social influence. *British Journal of Social Psychology, 23,* 317–322.(12)

Mullen, B. (1985). Strength and immediacy of sources: A meta-analytic evaluation of the forgotten elements of social impact theory. *Journal of Personality and Social Psychology, 48,* 1458–1466.(12)

Mullen, B., Atkins, J. L., Champion, D. S., Edwards, C., Hardy, D., Story, J. E., & Vanderklok, M. (1985). The false consensus effect: A meta-analysis of 115 hypothesis tests. *Journal of Experimental Social Psychology, 21,* 262–283.(4)

Mullen, B., & Baumeister, R. F. (1987). Group effects on self-attention and performance: Social loafing, social facilitation, and social impairment. *Review of Personality and Social Psychology, 9,* 189–206.(12)

Mullen, B., Futrell, D., Stairs, D., Tice, D. M., Baumeister, R. F., Dawson, K. E., Riordan, C. A., Radloff, C. E., Goethals, G. R., Kennedy, J. G., & Rosenfeld, P. (1986). Newscasters' facial expressions and voting behavior of viewers: Can a smile elect a president? *Journal of Personality and Social Psychology, 51,* 291–295.(6)

Mullen, B., Salas, E., & Miller, N. (1991). Using meta-analysis to test theoretical hypotheses in social psychology. *Personality and Social Psychology Bulletin, 17,* 258–264.(2)

Mullen, B., & Suls, J. (1982). "Know thyself": Stressful life changes and the ameliorative effect of private self-consciousness. *Journal of Experimental Social Psychology, 18,* 43–55.(3)

Münsterberg, H. (1913). *On the witness stand.* New York: Doubleday, Page.(2)

Murchison, C. M. (Ed.). (1935). *Handbook of social psychology.* Worcester, MA: Clark University Press.(1)

Murray, J., & Feshbach, S. (1978). Let's not throw the baby out with the bathwater: The catharsis hypothesis revisited. *Journal of Personality, 46,* 462–473.(10)

Myers, D. G., & Bishop, G. D. (1971). Enhancement of dominant attitudes in group discussion. *Journal of Personality and Social Psychology, 20,* 386–391.(12)

Myers, D. G., & Lamm, H. (1976). The group polarization phenomenon. *Psychological Bulletin, 83,* 602–627.(12)

Myerscough, R., & Taylor, S. (1985). The effects of marijuana on human physical aggression. *Journal of Personality and Social Psychology, 49,* 1541–1546.(10)

Nacoste, R. B. (formerly R. W.). (in press). Sources of stigma: Analyzing the psychology of affirmative action. *Law and Policy.*(13)

Nacoste, R. W. (1985). Selection procedure and responses to affirmative action: The case of favorable treatment. *Law and Human Behavior, 9,* 225–242.(13)

Nacoste, R. W. (1987a). Affirmative action in American politics: Strength or weakness? *Political Behavior, 9,* 291–304.(13)

Nacoste, R. W. (1987b). But do they care about fairness? The dynamics of preferential treatment and minority interest. *Basic and Applied Social Psychology, 8,* 177–191.(13)

Nacoste, R. W. (1989). Affirmative action and self-evaluation. In F. A. Blanchard & F. J. Crosby (Eds.), *Affirmative action in perspective* (pp. 103–109). New York: Springer-Verlag.(13)

Nacoste, R. W., & Lehman, D. (1987). Procedural stigma. *Representative Research in Social Psychology, 17,* 25–38.(13)

Nadler, A. (1987). Determinants of help-seeking behaviour: The effects of helper's similarity, task centrality, and recipient's self-esteem. *European Journal of Social Psychology, 17,* 57–67.(11)

Nadler, A., Altman, A., & Fisher, J. D. (1979). Helping is not enough: Recipient's reactions to aid as a function of positive and negative information about self. *Journal of Personality, 47,* 615–628.(11)

Nadler, A., & Fisher, J. D. (1986). The role of threat to self-esteem and perceived control in recipient reaction to help: Theory development and empirical validation. *Advances in Experimental Social Psychology, 19,* 81–122.(11)

Nadler, A., Fisher, J. D., & Ben-Itzhak, S. (1983). With a little help from my friend: Reaction to receiving prolonged vs. one-act help from a friend or stranger, as a function of centrality. *Journal of Personality and Social Psychology, 44,* 310–321.(11)

Nadler, A., Mayseless, O., Peri, N., & Chemerinski, A. (1985). Effects of opportunity to reciprocate and self-esteem on help-seeking behavior. *Journal of Personality, 53,* 23–35.(11)

Nagar, D., Pandey, J., & Paulus, P. B. (1988). The effects of residential crowding experience on reactivity to laboratory crowding and noise. *Journal of Applied Social Psychology, 18,* 1423–1442.(14)

Nahemow, L., & Lawton, M. P. (1975). Similarity and propinquity in friendship formation. *Journal of Personality and Social Psychology, 33,* 205–213.(14)

Nemecek, J., & Grandjean, E. (1973). Results of an ergonomic investigation of large-space offices. *Human Factors, 15,* 111–224.(14)

Nemeth, C. (1979). The role of an active minority in intergroup relations. In W. G. Austin & S. Worchel (Eds.), *The social psychology of intergroup relations.* Pacific Grove, CA: Brooks/Cole.(12)

Nemeth, C., & Endicott, J. (1976). The midpoint as an anchor: Another look at discrepancy of position and attitude change. *Sociometry, 39,* 11–18.(7)

Nemeth, C. J. (1986). Differential contributions of majority and minority influence. *Psychological Review, 93,* 23–32.(12)

Nemeth, C. J., & Wachtler, J. (1983). Creative problem solving as a result of majority vs. minority influence. *European Journal of Social Psychology, 13,* 45–55.(12)

Newcomb, M. D. (1986). Nuclear attitudes and reactions: Associations with depression, drug use, and quality of life. *Journal of Personality and Social Psychology, 50,* 906–920.(6)

Newcomb, M. D., & Bentler, P. M. (1981). Marital breakdown. In S. Duck & R. Gilmour (Eds.), *Personal relationships 3: Personal relationships in disorder.* New York: Academic Press.(9)

Newcomb, T. M. (1961). *The acquaintance process.* New York: Holt, Rinehart & Winston.(9, 14)

Newman, O. (1972). *Defensible space: Crime prevention through urban design.* New York: Macmillan.(14)

Newtson, D. (1974). Dispositional inference from effects of actions: Effects chosen and effects foregone. *Journal of Experimental Psychology, 10,* 489–496.(4)

Nezlek, J. B. (1990). Self report diaries in the study of social interaction. *Contemporary Social Psychology, 14,* 205–210.(9)

Nisbett, R. E., Krantz, D. H., Jepson, C., & Kunda, Z. (1983). The use of statistical heuristics in everyday inductive reasoning. *Psychological Review, 90,* 339–363.(4)

Nisbett, R. E., & Kunda, Z. (1985). Perception of social distributions. *Journal of Personality and Social Psychology, 48,* 297–311.(4)

Nizer, L. (1973). *The implosion conspiracy.* New York: Doubleday.(5)

Noller, P. (1984). *Nonverbal communication and marital interaction.* Oxford, England: Pergamon.(5)

Norris-Baker, C., & Scheidt, R. J. (1990). Place attachment among older residents of a "ghost town": A transactional approach. In R. I. Selby, K. H. Anthony, J. Choi, & B. Orland (Eds.), *Coming of age* (pp. 333–342). Oklahoma City, OK: Environmental Design Research Association.(14)

Norvell, N., & Worchel, S. (1981). A reexamination of the relation between equal status contact and intergroup attraction. *Journal of Personality and Social Psychology, 41,* 902–908.(13)

Novak, D., & Lerner, M. J. (1968). Rejection as a consequence of perceived similarity. *Journal of Personality and Social Psychology, 9,* 147–152.(9)

Oakes, P. J., & Turner, J. C. (1990). Is limited information processing capacity the cause of social stereotyping? *European Review of Social Psychology, 1,* 111–135.(4, 13)

Oborne, D. J. (1983). Cognitive effects of passive smoking. *Ergonomics, 26,* 1163–1171.(14)

Odino, J. (1986, December 28). African nations struggle to make television their own. *New York Times,* p. E-3.(10)

O'Hair, D., & Cody, M. J. (1987). Gender and vocal stress differences during truthful and deceptive information sequences. *Human Relations, 40*(1), 1–13.(5)

O'Hair, D., Cody, M. J., & Behnke, R. R. (1985). Communication apprehension and vocal stress as indices of deception. *Western Journal of Speech Communication, 49*(4), 286–300.(5)

Ohbuchi, K., & Kambara, T. (1985). Attacker's intent and awareness of outcome, impression management, and retaliation. *Journal of Experimental Social Psychology, 21,* 321–330.(10)

Ohbuchi, K., Kameda, M., & Agarie, N. (1989). Apology as aggression control: Its role in mediating appraisal of and response to harm. *Journal of Personality and Social Psychology, 56,* 219–227.(10)

Oliner, S. P., & Oliner, P. M. (1988). *The altruistic personality: Rescuers of Jews in Nazi Europe.* New York: Free Press.(11)

Olweus, D. (1979). Stability of aggressive reaction patterns in males: A review. *Psychological Bulletin, 86,* 852–875.(10)

Olweus, D. (1984a). *Bullying and harassment among school children in Scandinavia: Research and a nationwide campaign in Norway.* Unpublished manuscript.(10)

Olweus, D. (1984b). Development of stable aggressive reaction patterns in males. In R. Blanchard & C. Blanchard (Eds.), *Advances in aggression research* (Vol. 1, pp. 103–137). New York: Academic Press.(10)

Orne, M. T. (1969). Demand characteristics and the concept of quasi-controls. In R. Rosenthal & R. Rosnow (Eds.), *Artifact in behavior research.* New York: Academic Press.(2)

Orne, M. T., & Holland, C. C. (1968). On the ecological validity of laboratory deceptions. *International Journal of Psychiatry, 6,* 282–293.(8)

Orvis, B. R., Cunningham, J. D., & Kelley, H. H. (1975). A closer examination of causal inference: The role of consensus, distinctiveness, and consistency information. *Journal of Personality and Social Psychology, 29,* 426–434.(4)

Osborn, A. F. (1957). *Applied imagination.* New York: Scribner.(12)

Osgood, C. E. (1966). *Perspective in foreign policy.* Palo Alto, CA: Pacific Books.(13)

Osgood, C. E. (1979). GRIT for MBFR: A proposal for unfreezing force-level postures in Europe. *Peace Research Reviews, 8*(2), 77–92.(13)

Osgood, C. E., Suci, G. J., & Tannenbaum, P. H. (1957). *The measurement of meaning.* Urbana, IL: University of Illinois Press.(5, 6)

Oskamp, S. (1977). *Attitudes and opinions.* Englewood Cliffs, NJ: Prentice-Hall.(6)

Oskamp, S. (Ed.). (1988). Television as a social issue. *Applied Social Psychology Annual, 8.*(6)

Osmond, H. (1957). Function as the basis of psychiatric ward design. *Mental Hospitals, 8,* 23–30.(14)

O'Sullivan, M., Ekman, P., Friesen, W., & Scherer, K. (1985). What you say and how you say it: The contribution of speech content and voice quality to judgments of others. *Journal of Personality and Social Psychology, 48,* 54–62.(5)

Owens, D. J., & Straus, M. A. (1975). The social structure of violence in childhood and approval of violence as an adult. *Aggressive Behavior, 1,* 193–211.(10)

Paciuk, M. (1990). The role of personal control of the environment in thermal comfort and satisfaction at the workplace. In R. I. Selby, K. H. Anthony, J. Choi, & B. Orland (Eds.), *Coming of age* (pp. 303–312). Oklahoma City, OK: Environmental Design Research Association.(14)

Page, M. M. (1974). Demand characteristics and the classical conditioning of attitudes experiment. *Journal of Personality and Social Psychology, 30,* 468–476.(6)

Page, R. (1977). Noise and helping behavior. *Environment and Behavior, 9,* 311–334.(14)

Palamarek, D. L., & Rule, B. G. (1979). The effects of ambient temperature and insult on the motivation to retaliate or escape. *Motivation and Emotion, 3,* 83–92.(10)

Parham, T. A. (1989). Cycles of psychological Nigrescence. *The Counseling Psychologist, 17,* 187–226.(3)

Park, B., & Rothbart, M. (1982). Perception of out-group homogeneity and levels of social categorization: Memory for the subordinate attributes of in-group and out-group members. *Journal of Personality and Social Psychology, 42,* 1051–1068.(13)

Parke, R. D., Berkowitz, L., Leyens, J.-P., West, S. G., & Sebastian, R. J. (1977). Some effects of violent and nonviolent movies on the behavior of juvenile delinquents. In L. Berkowitz (Ed.), *Advances in experimental social psychology* (Vol. 10). New York: Academic Press.(10)

Parnes, S. J., & Meadow, A. (1959). Effects of "brainstorming" instructions on creative problem solving by trained and untrained subjects. *Journal of Educational Psychology, 50,* 171–176.(12)

Patterson, A. H. (1978). Territorial behavior and fear of crime in the elderly. *Environmental Psychology and Nonverbal Behavior, 2,* 131–144.(14)

Patterson, M. L. (1976). An arousal model of interpersonal intimacy. *Psychological Review, 83,* 235–245.(5)

Patterson, M. L. (1982). A sequential function model of verbal exchange. *Psychological Review, 89,* 231–249.(5)

Patterson, M. L. (1983). *Nonverbal behavior: A functional perspective.* New York: Springer-Verlag.(5)

Patterson, M. L., Mullens, S., & Romano, J. (1971). Compensatory reactions to spatial intrusion. *Sociometry, 34,* 114–121.(5)

Patzer, G. L. (1985). *The physical attractiveness phenomena.* New York: Plenum.(4)

Paulhus, D. L., Shaffer, D. R., & Downing, L. L. (1977). Effects of making blood donor motives salient upon donor retention: A field experiment. *Personality and Social Psychology Bulletin, 3,* 99–102.(11)

Paulus, P., McCain, G., & Cox, V. (1978). Death rates, psychiatric commitments, blood pressure, and perceived crowding as a function of institutional crowding. *Environmental Psychology and Nonverbal Behavior, 3,* 107–116.(14)

Pavelchak, M. A., Moreland, R. L., & Levine, J. M. (1986). Effects of prior group memberships on subsequent reconnaissance activities. *Journal of Personality and Social Psychology, 50,* 56–66.(12)

Pearce, P. L. (1980). Strangers, travelers, and Greyhound terminals: A study of small-scale helping behaviors. *Journal of Personality and Social Psychology, 38,* 935–940.(11)

Peele, S. (1988). Fools for love: The romantic ideal, psychological theory, and addictive love. In R. J. Sternberg & M. L. Barnes (Eds.), *The psychology of love* (pp. 159–188). New Haven, CT: Yale University Press.(9)

Pelligrini, R. J. (1971). Some effects of seating position on social perception. *Psychological Reports, 28,* 887–893.(14)

Pennebaker, J. W. (1989). Stream of consciousness and stress: Levels of thinking. In J. S. Uleman & J. A. Bargh (Eds.), *Unintended thought* (pp. 327–350). New York: Guilford Press.(2)

Pepitone, A. (1981). Lessons from the history of social psychology. *American Psychologist, 36,* 972–985.(1)

Peplau, L. A., Miceli, M., & Morasch, B. (1982). Loneliness and self-evaluation. In L. A. Peplau & D. Perlman (Eds.), *Loneliness: A sourcebook of current theory, research, and therapy.* New York: Wiley.(9)

Peplau, L. A., & Perlman, D. (Eds.). (1982). *Loneliness: A sourcebook of current theory, research, and therapy.* New York: Wiley.(9)

Perdue, C. W., Dovidio, J. F., Gurtman, M. B., & Tyler, R. B. (1990). Us and them: Social categorization and the process of intergroup bias. *Journal of Personality and Social Psychology, 59,* 475–486.(13)

Perry, L. C., Perry, D. G., & Weiss, R. J. (1986). Age differences in children's beliefs about whether altruism makes the actor feel good. *Social Cognition, 4,* 263–269.(11)

Peterson, C., & Seligman, M. E. P. (1984). Causal explanations as a risk factor for depression: Theory and evidence. *Psychological Review, 91,* 347–374.(8)

Peterson, D. I., & Pfost, K. S. (1989). Influence of rock videos on attitudes of violence toward women. *Psychological Reports, 64,* 319–322.(10)

Peterson, P. D., & Koulack, D. (1969). Attitude change as a function of latitudes of acceptance and rejection. *Journal of Personality and Social Psychology, 11,* 309–311.(7)

Pettigrew, T. F. (1979). The ultimate attribution error: Extending Allport's cognitive analysis of prejudice. *Personality and Social Psychology Bulletin, 5,* 461–476.(13)

Petty, R. E., & Brock, T. C. (1976). Effects of responding or not responding to hecklers on audience agreement with a speaker. *Journal of Applied Social Psychology, 6,* 1–17.(7)

Petty, R. E., & Cacioppo, J. T. (1977). Forewarning, cognitive responding, and resistance to persuasion. *Journal of Personality and Social Psychology, 35,* 645–655.(7)

Petty, R. E., & Cacioppo, J. T. (1981). *Attitudes and persuasion: Classic and contemporary approaches.* Dubuque, IA: William C. Brown.(7)

Petty, R. E., & Cacioppo, J. T. (1986). The elaboration likelihood model of persuasion. *Advances in Experimental Social Psychology, 19,* 123–205.(7)

Petty, R. E., Wells, G. L., & Brock, T. C. (1976). Distraction can enhance or reduce yielding to propaganda: Thought disruption versus effort justification. *Journal of Personality and Social Psychology, 34,* 874–884.(7)

Phares, E. J. (1976). *Locus of control in personality.* Morristown, NJ: General Learning Press.(8)

Phillips, D. P. (1970). *Dying as a form of social behavior* (Doctoral dissertation, Princeton University). Ann Arbor, MI: University Microfilms, No. 70–19, 799.(1)

Phillips, D. P. (1972). Deathday and birthday: An unexpected connection. In J. M. Tanur (Ed.), *Statistics: A guide to the unknown.* San Francisco: Holden-Day.(1)

Phillips, D. P. (1980). The deterrent effect of capital punishment: New evidence on an old controversy. *American Journal of Sociology, 86,* 139–148.(10)

Phillips, D. P. (1986). Natural experiments on the effects of mass media violence on fatal aggression: Strengths and weaknesses of a new approach. *Advances in Experimental Social Psychology, 19,* 207–250.(10)

Pile, J. (1978). *Open office planning: A handbook for interior designers and architects.* New York: Whitney Library of Design.(14)

Piliavin, J. A., & Charng, H. (1990). Altruism: A review of recent theory and research. *Annual Review of Sociology, 16,* 27–65.(11)

Piliavin, J. A., Dovidio, J. F., Gaertner, S. L., & Clark, R. D., III. (1981). *Emergency intervention.* New York: Academic Press.(11)

Piliavin, J. A., Evans, D. E., & Callero, P. (1984). Learning to "give to unnamed strangers": The process of commitment to regular blood donation. In E. Staub, D. Bar-Tal, J. Karylowski, & J. Reykowski (Eds.), *The development and maintenance of prosocial behavior: International perspectives.* New York: Plenum.(11)

Pittenger, J. B., & Baskett, L. M. (1984). Facial self-perception: Its relation to objective appearance and self-concept. *Bulletin of the Psychonomic Society, 22,* 167–170.(3)

Pleck, J. H. (1985). *Working wives/working husbands.* Beverly Hills, CA: Sage.(11)

Podsakoff, P. M., & Schriesheim, C. A. (1985). Field studies of French and Raven's bases of power: Critique, reanalysis, and suggestions for future research. *Psychological Bulletin, 97,* 387–411.(8)

Pollock, L. M., & Patterson, A. H. (1980). Territoriality and fear of crime in elderly and nonelderly homeowners. *Journal of Social Psychology, 111,* 119–129.(14)

Post, D. L. (1980). Floyd H. Allport and the launching of modern social psychology. *Journal of the History of the Behavioral Sciences, 16,* 369–376.(1)

Pratkanis, A. R., Breckler, S. J., & Greenwald, A. G. (Eds.). (1979). *Attitude structure and function.* Hillsdale, NJ: Erlbaum.(7)

Pratkanis, A. R., & Greenwald, A. G. (1989). A sociocognitive model of attitude structure and function. *Advances in Experimental Social Psychology, 22,* 245–285.(6, 7)

Prentice, D. A. (1987). Psychological correlates of possessions, attitudes, and values. *Journal of Personality and Social Psychology, 53,* 993–1003.(7)

Prentice-Dunn, S., & Rogers, R. W. (1982). Effects of public and private self-awareness on deindividuation and aggression. *Journal of Personality and Social Psychology, 43,* 505–513.(10)

Price, R. A., Vandenberg, S. G., Iyer, H., & Williams, J. S. (1982). Components of variation in normal personality. *Journal of Personality and Social Psychology, 43,* 328–340.(13)

Price Waterhouse v. *Hopkins,* 109 S. Ct. 1775 (1989).(13)

Proshansky, H. M. (1978). The city and self-identity. *Environment and Behavior, 10,* 147–169.(3, 14)

Proshansky, H. M., Fabian, A. K., & Kaminoff, R. (1983). Place-identity: Physical world socialization of the self. *Journal of Environmental Psychology, 3,* 57–83.(3, 14)

Pruitt, D. G. (1981). *Negotiation behavior.* New York: Academic Press.(13)

Pruitt, D. G. (1982). *Integrative agreements: Nature and antecedents.* Unpublished manuscript.(13)

Pruitt, D. G., & Kressel, K. (1985). The mediation of social conflict: An introduction. *Journal of Social Issues, 41*(2), 1–10.(13)

Pryor, J. B., & Merluzzi, T. V. (1985). The role of expertise in processing social interaction scripts. *Journal of Experimental Social Psychology, 21,* 362–379.(4)

Putnam, L. L., & Jones, T. S. (1982). The role of communication in bargaining. *Human Communication Research, 8,* 262–280.(13)

Quinsey, V. L., Chaplin, T. C., & Upfold, D. (1984). Sexual arousal to nonsexual violence and sadomasochistic themes among rapists and non-sex-offenders. *Journal of Consulting and Clinical Psychology, 52,* 651–657.(10)

Rabow, J., Newcomb, M. D., Monto, M. A., & Hernandez, A. C. R. (1990). Altruism in drunk driving situations: Personal and situational factors in intervention. *Social Psychology Quarterly, 53,* 199–213.(11)

Radke-Yarrow, M., & Zahn-Waxler, C. (1984). Roots, motives, and patterns in children's prosocial behavior. In E. Staub, D. Bar-Tal, J. Karylowski, & J. Reykowski (Eds.), *The development and maintenance of prosocial behavior: International perspectives.* New York: Plenum.(11)

Radloff, R., & Helmreich, R. (1968). *Groups under stress: Psychological research in SEALAB II.* New York: Irvington.(2)

Ramirez, A. (1977). Chicano power and interracial group relations. In J. L. Martinez (Ed.), *Chicano psychology.* New York: Academic Press.(13)

Ramirez, A. (1988). Racism towards Hispanics: The culturally monolithic society. In P. Katz & D. Taylor (Eds.), *Toward the elimination of racism: Profiles in controversy.* New York: Plenum.(13)

Ramirez, J., Bryant, J., & Zillmann, D. (1982). Effects of erotica on retaliatory behavior as a function of level of prior provocation. *Journal of Personality and Social Psychology, 43,* 971–978.(10)

Ransford, H. E. (1968). Isolation, powerlessness, and violence: A study of attitudes and participation in the Watts riot. *American Journal of Sociology, 73,* 581–591.(10)

Raps, C. S., Peterson, C., Jonas, M., & Seligman, M. E. P. (1982). Patient behavior in hospitals: Helplessness, reactance, or both? *Journal of Personality and Social Psychology, 42,* 1036–1041.(8)

Reeder, G. D., & Brewer, M. B. (1979). A schematic model of dispositional attribution in interpersonal perception. *Psychological Review, 86,* 61–79.(4)

Reichner, R. F. (1979). Differential responses to being ignored: The effects of architectural design and social density on interpersonal behavior. *Journal of Applied Social Psychology, 9,* 13–26.(14)

Reis, H. T., Nezlek, J., & Wheeler, L. (1980). Physical attractiveness in social interaction. *Journal of Personality and Social Psychology, 38,* 604–617.(9)

Reis, H. T., Wheeler, L., Spiegel, N., Kernis, M., Nezlek, J., & Perri, M. (1982). Physical attractiveness in social interaction, II: Why does appearance affect social experience? *Journal of Personality and Social Psychology, 43,* 979–996.(9)

Rempel, J. K., Holmes, J. G., & Zanna, M. P. (1985). Trust in close relationships. *Journal of Personality and Social Psychology, 49,* 95–112.(9)

Rhodewalt, F. (1986). Self-presentation and the phenomenal self: On the stability and malleability of self-conceptions. In R. F. Baumeister (Ed.), *Public self and private self.* New York: Springer-Verlag.(3)

Rhodewalt, F., & Agustsdottir, S. (1986). Effects of self-presentation on the phenomenal self. *Journal of Personality and Social Psychology, 50,* 47–55.(3)

Rhodewalt, F., Saltzman, A. T., & Wittmer, J. (1984). Self-handicapping among competitive athletes: The role of practice in self-esteem protection. *Basic and Applied Social Psychology, 5,* 197–209.(3)

Rice, R. W., & Kastenbaum, D. R. (1983). The contingency model of leadership: Some current issues. *Basic and Applied Social Psychology, 4,* 373–392.(12)

Ringelmann, M. (1913). Recherches sur les moteurs animés: Travail de l'homme. *Annales de l'Institut National Agronomique*, 2e série, tome *XII*, 1–40.(12)

Rinn, W. E. (1984). The neuropsychology of facial expression: A review of the neurological and psychological mechanisms for producing facial expressions. *Psychological Bulletin, 95*, 52–77.(5)

Rips, L. J. (1990). Reasoning. *Annual Review of Psychology, 41*, 321–353.(3)

Rivlin, L. G. (1987). The neighborhood, personal identity, and group affiliations. In I. Altman & A. Wandersman (Eds.), *Neighborhood and community environments* (pp. 1–34). New York: Plenum.(14)

Roberts, D. F., & Maccoby, N. (1985). Effects of mass communication. In G. Lindzey & E. Aronson (Eds.), *Handbook of social psychology* (3rd ed., Vol. 2, pp. 539–598). New York: Random House.(6, 10, 11)

Roberts, J. V. (1985). The attitude-memory relationship after 40 years: A meta-analysis of the literature. *Basic and Applied Social Psychology, 6*, 221–241.(6)

Roberts, J. V., & Herman, C. P. (1986). The psychology of height: An empirical review. In C. P. Herman, M. P. Zanna, & E. T. Higgins (Eds.), *Physical appearance, stigma, and social behavior: The Ontario Symposium, Volume 3* (pp. 113–140). Hillsdale, NJ: Erlbaum.(4)

Rodin, J. (1976). Density, perceived choice, and response to controllable and uncontrollable outcomes. *Journal of Experimental Social Psychology, 12*, 564–578.(8)

Rodin, J., & Baum, A. (1978). Crowding and helplessness: Potential consequences of density and loss of control. In A. Baum & Y. Epstein (Eds.), *Human response to crowding*. Hillsdale, NJ: Erlbaum.(14)

Rodin, J., & Langer, E. J. (1977). Long-term effects of a control-relevant intervention with the institutionalized aged. *Journal of Personality and Social Psychology, 35*, 897–902.(8)

Rodin, J., Solomon, S. K., & Metcalf, J. (1978). Role of control in mediating perceptions of density. *Journal of Personality and Social Psychology, 36*, 988–999.(8)

Rofé, Y. (1984). Stress and affiliation: A utility theory. *Psychological Review, 91*, 235–250.(9)

Rogers, L. E., & Farace, R. V. (1975). Analysis of relational communication in dyads: New measurement procedures. *Human Communication Research, 1*, 222–239.(5)

Rogers, R. W. (1975). A protection motivation theory of fear appeals and attitude change. *Journal of Psychology, 91*, 93–114.(7)

Rogers, R. W. (1983). Cognitive and physiological processes in fear appeals and attitude change: A revised theory of protection motivation. In J. Cacioppo & R. Petty (Eds.), *Social psychophysiology* (pp. 153–176). New York: Guilford Press.(7)

Rohner, R. P. (1976, April). *A worldwide study of sex differences in aggression: A universalist perspective*. Paper presented at a meeting of the Eastern Psychological Association, New York.(10)

Rokeach, M. (1968). *Beliefs, attitudes, and values*. San Francisco: Jossey-Bass.(13)

Rokeach, M. (1970, April). Faith, hope, bigotry. *Psychology Today*, pp. 33–37, 58.(4)

Rokeach, M. (1973). *The nature of human values*. New York: Free Press.(6)

Rokeach, M. (1979). Some unresolved issues in theories of beliefs, attitudes, and values. *Nebraska Symposium on Motivation, 27*, 261–304.(13)

Rokeach, M., & Mezei, L. (1966). Race and shared belief as factors in social choice. *Science, 151*, 167–172.(13)

Romzek, B. S., & Dubnick, M. J. (1987). Accountability in the public sector: Lessons from the *Challenger* tragedy. *Public Administration Review, 47*, 227–238.(12)

Rosenbaum, M. E. (1986). The repulsion hypothesis: On the nondevelopment of relationships. *Journal of Personality and Social Psychology, 51*, 1156–1166.(9)

Rosenberg, M. (1979). *Conceiving the self*. New York: Basic Books.(3)

Rosenberg, S., & Gara, M. A. (1985). The multiplicity of personal identity. *Review of Personality and Social Psychology, 6*, 87–113.(3)

Rosenberg, S., & Jones, R. A. (1972). A method for investigating and representing a person's implicit theory of personality: Theodore Dreiser's view of people. *Journal of Personality and Social Psychology, 22*, 372–386.(4)

Rosenberg, S., Nelson, C., & Vivekananthan, P. S. (1968). A multidimensional approach to the structure of personality impressions. *Journal of Personality and Social Psychology, 39*, 283–294.(4)

Rosenberg, S., & Sedlak, A. (1972). Structural representations of implicit personality theory. *Advances in Experimental Social Psychology, 6*, 235–297.(4)

Rosenfeld, H. M. (1965). Effect of an approval-seeking induction on interpersonal proximity. *Psychological Reports, 17*, 120–122.(5)

Rosenhan, D. L., Salovey, P., & Hargis, K. (1981). The joys of helping: Focus of attention mediates the impact of positive affect on altruism. *Journal of Personality and Social Psychology, 40*, 899–905.(11)

Rosenthal, R. (1966). *Experimenter effects in behavioral research*. New York: Appleton-Century-Crofts.(2)

Rosenthal, R., & Jacobson, L. (1968). *Pygmalion in the classroom: Teacher expectation and intellectual development*. New York: Holt, Rinehart & Winston.(5)

Rosnow, R. L. (1991). Inside rumor: A personal journey. *American Psychologist, 46*, 484–496.(5)

Ross, L., Greene, D., & House, P. (1977). The "false consensus effect": An egocentric bias in social perception and attribution processes. *Journal of Experimental Social Psychology, 13,* 279–301.(4)

Ross, L. D., Amabile, T. M., & Steinmetz, J. L. (1977). Social roles, social control, and biases in social-perception processes. *Journal of Personality and Social Psychology, 35,* 485–494.(4)

Ross, M., & Fletcher, G. J. O. (1985). Attribution and social perception. In G. Lindzey & E. Aronson (Eds.), *Handbook of social psychology* (3rd ed., Vol. 2). New York: Random House.(4, 10)

Ross, M., McFarland, C., Conway, M., & Zanna, M. P. (1983). Reciprocal relation between attitudes and behavior recall: Committing people to newly formed attitudes. *Journal of Personality and Social Psychology, 45,* 257–267.(7)

Roth, D. L., Snyder, C. R., & Pace, L. M. (1986). Dimensions of favorable self-presentation. *Journal of Personality and Social Psychology, 51,* 867–874.(3)

Rothbart, M., & Park, B. (1986). On the confirmability and disconfirmability of trait concepts. *Journal of Personality and Social Psychology, 50,* 131–142.(4)

Rotter, J. B. (1966). Generalized expectancies for internal versus external control of reinforcement. *Psychological Monographs, 80*(1, Whole No. 609).(8)

Rotton, J., Barry, T., Frey, J., & Soler, E. (1978). Air pollution and interpersonal attraction. *Journal of Applied Social Psychology, 8,* 57–71.(14)

Rotton, J., & Frey, J. (1985). Air pollution, weather, and violent crimes: Concomitant time-series analysis of archival data. *Journal of Personality and Social Psychology, 49,* 1207–1220.(10, 14)

Rubenstein, C., & Shaver, P. (1982). The experience of loneliness. In L. A. Peplau & D. Perlman (Eds.), *Loneliness: A sourcebook of current theory, research, and therapy.* New York: Wiley.(9)

Rubin, J. Z., & Brown, B. R. (1975). *The social psychology of bargaining and negotiation.* New York: Academic Press.(13)

Rubin, Z. (1970). Measurement of romantic love. *Journal of Personality and Social Psychology, 16,* 265–273.(5, 9)

Rubin, Z. (1973). *Liking and loving: An invitation to social psychology.* New York: Holt, Rinehart & Winston.(9)

Rubin, Z., Peplau, L. A., & Hill, C. T. (1978). *Loving and leaving: Sex differences in romantic attachments.* Unpublished manuscript, Brandeis University, Waltham, MA.(9)

Rugg, E. A. (1975). *Social research practices opinion survey: Summary of results.* Unpublished paper, George Peabody College, Nashville.(2)

Rule, B. G., Bisanz, G. L., & Kohn, M. (1985). Anatomy of a persuasion schema: Targets, goals, and strategies. *Journal of Personality and Social Psychology, 48,* 1127–1140.(7, 8)

Rule, B. G., & Ferguson, T. J. (1984). The relations among attributions, moral evaluation, anger, and aggression in children and adults. In A. Mummendey (Ed.), *Social psychology of aggression: From individual behavior toward social interaction.* New York: Springer.(10)

Rule, B. G., & Leger, G. J. (1976). Pain cues and differing functions of aggression. *Canadian Journal of Behavioural Science, 8,* 213–222.(10)

Rule, B. G., & Percival, E. (1971). The effects of frustration and attack on physical aggression. *Journal of Experimental Research in Personality, 5,* 111–118.(10)

Rule, B. G., Taylor, B., & Dobbs, A. R. (1987). Priming effects of heat on aggressive thoughts. *Social Cognition, 5,* 131–144.(10)

Runkel, P. J., & McGrath, J. E. (1972). *Research on human behavior: A systematic guide to method.* New York: Holt, Rinehart & Winston.(1)

Rusbult, C. E., Johnson, D. J., & Morrow, G. D. (1986). Impact of couple patterns of problem solving on distress and nondistress in dating relationships. *Journal of Personality and Social Psychology, 50,* 744–753.(9)

Rush, M. C., Thomas, J. C., & Lord, R. G. (1977). Implicit leadership theory: A potential threat to the internal validity of leader behavior questionnaires. *Organizational Behavior and Human Performance, 20,* 93–110.(12)

Rushton, J. P. (1984). The altruistic personality: Evidence from laboratory, naturalistic, and self-report perspectives. In E. Staub, D. Bar-Tal, J. Karylowski, & J. Reykowski (Eds.), *The development and maintenance of prosocial behavior: International perspectives.* New York: Plenum.(11)

Rushton, J. P. (1989). Genetic similarity, human altruism, and group selection. *Behavioral and Brain Sciences, 12,* 503–518.(11)

Rushton, J. P., Fulker, D. W., Neale, M. C., Nias, D. K. B., & Eysenck, H. J. (1986). Altruism and aggression: The heritability of individual differences. *Journal of Personality and Social Psychology, 50,* 1192–1198.(10, 11)

Russell, D. (1982). The causal dimension scale: A measure of how individuals perceive causes. *Journal of Personality and Social Psychology, 42,* 1137–1145.(4)

Russell, D., Cutrona, C. E., Rose, J., & Yurko, K. (1984). Social and emotional loneliness: An examination of Weiss's typology of loneliness. *Journal of Personality and Social Psychology, 46,* 1313–1321.(9)

Russo, N. F. (1975). Eye contact, interpersonal distance, and the equilibrium theory. *Journal of Personality and Social Psychology, 31,* 497–502.(5)

Rutkowski, G. K., Gruder, C. L., & Romer, D. (1983). Group cohesiveness, social norms, and bystander intervention. *Journal of Personality and Social Psychology, 44,* 545–552.(11)

Ryan, W. (1971). *Blaming the victim.* New York: Pantheon.(4)

● **Ryckman, R. M., Robbins, M. A., Kaczor, L. M., & Gold, J. A.** (1989). Male and female raters' stereotyping of male and female physiques. *Personality and Social Psychology Bulletin, 15,* 244–251.(4)

Sacks, H., Schegloff, E., & Jefferson, G. (1974). A simplest systematics for the organization of turn-taking in conversation. *Language, 50,* 696–735.(5)

Sadava, S. W. (1978). Teaching social psychology: A Canadian dilemma. *Canadian Psychological Review, 19,* 145–151.(13)

Saegert, S. (1989). Unlikely leaders, extreme circumstances: Older black women building community households. *American Journal of Community Psychology, 17,* 295–316.(14)

Saegert, S., & Winkel, G. H. (1990). Environmental psychology. *Annual Review of Psychology, 41,* 441–477.(14)

Saegert, S. C., Swap, W., & Zajonc, R. B. (1973). Exposure, context, and interpersonal attraction. *Journal of Personality and Social Psychology, 25,* 234–242.(9)

Saks, M. J. (1977). *Jury verdicts: The role of group size and social decision rule.* Lexington, MA: Lexington Books.(2)

Saks, M. J., & Hastie, R. (1978). *Social psychology in court.* New York: Van Nostrand Reinhold.(2)

Salinger, J. D. (1953). *The catcher in the rye.* New York: Signet.(9)

Samerotte, G. C., & Harris, M. B. (1976). Some factors influencing helping: The effects of a handicap, responsibility, and requesting help. *Journal of Social Psychology, 98,* 39–45.(11)

Sancilo, M. F. M., Plumert, J. M., & Hartup, W. W. (1989). Friendship and aggressiveness as determinants of conflict outcomes in middle childhood. *Developmental Psychology, 25,* 812–819.(10)

Sanday, P. R. (1981). The socio-cultural context of rape: A cross-cultural study. *Journal of Social Issues, 37*(4), 5–27.(10)

Sanders, G. S. (1984). Self-presentation and drive in social facilitation. *Journal of Experimental Social Psychology, 20,* 312–322.(12)

Sanders, M., Gustanski, J., & Lawton, M. (1976). Effect of ambient illumination on noise level of groups. *Journal of Applied Psychology, 59,* 527–528.(14)

Sanford, N. (1956). The approach of the authoritarian personality. In J. L. McCary (Ed.), *Psychology of personality.* New York: Grove Press.(13)

Saxe, L. (1985). Liars and lie detection: Umpiring controversy. *Transaction/Society, 22*(6), 39–42.(5)

Saxe, L. (1991). Lying: Thoughts of an applied social psychologist. *American Psychologist, 46,* 409–415.(5)

Scarr, S., & McCartney, K. (1983). How people make their own environments: A theory of genotype-environment effects. *Child Development, 54,* 424–435.(13)

Schachter, S. (1951). Deviation, rejection, and communication. *Journal of Abnormal and Social Psychology, 46,* 190–207.(12)

Schachter, S. (1959). *The psychology of affiliation.* Stanford, CA: Stanford University Press.(9)

Schachter, S., Christenfeld, N., Ravina, B., & Bilous, F. (1991). Speech disfluency and the structure of knowledge. *Journal of Personality and Social Psychology, 60,* 362–367.(5)

Schachter, S., Ellertson, N., McBride, D., & Gregory, D. (1951). An experimental study of cohesiveness and productivity. *Human Relations, 4,* 229–238.(12)

Schachter, S., & Singer, J. (1962). Cognitive, social, and physiological determinants of emotional state. *Psychological Review, 69,* 379–399.(3)

Schaller, M., & Cialdini, R. B. (1988). The economics of empathic helping: Support for a mood management motive. *Journal of Experimental Social Psychology, 24,* 163–181.(11)

Scheff, T. J., & Bushnell, D. D. (1984). A theory of catharsis. *Journal of Research in Personality, 18,* 238–264.(10)

Scheier, M. F., & Carver, C. S. (1980). Individual differences in self-concept and self-process. In D. M. Wegner & R. R. Vallacher (Eds.), *The self in social psychology.* New York: Oxford University Press.(3)

Scheier, M. F., & Carver, S. C. (1981). Private and public aspects of self. *Review of Personality and Social Psychology, 2,* 189–216.(3)

Scheier, M. F., Carver, C. S., & Gibbons, F. X. (1979). Self-directed attention, awareness of bodily states, and suggestibility. *Journal of Personality and Social Psychology, 37,* 1576–1588.(3)

Scheier, M. F., Carver, C. S., & Gibbons, F. X. (1981). Self-focused attention and reactions to fear. *Journal of Research in Personality, 15,* 1–15.(3)

Scher, S. J., & Cooper, J. (1989). Motivational basis of dissonance: The singular role of behavioral consequences. *Journal of Personality and Social Psychology, 56,* 899–906.(7)

Schiavo, R. S. (1988). Age differences in assessment and use of a suburban neighborhood among children and adolescents. *Children's Environments Quarterly, 5,* 4–9.(14)

Schiffrin, D. (1977). Opening encounters. *American Sociological Review, 42,* 679–691.(5)

Schlenker, B. R. (1980). *Impression management: The self-concept, social identity, and interpersonal relations.* Pacific Grove, CA: Brooks/Cole.(3, 7)

Schlenker, B. R., & Forsyth, D. R. (1977). On the ethics of psychological research. *Journal of Experimental Social Psychology, 13,* 369–396.(2)

Schlosberg, H. (1954). Three dimensions of emotion. *Psychological Review, 61,* 81–88.(5)

Schmitt, B. H., Gilovich, T., Goore, N., & Joseph, L. (1986). Mere presence and social facilitation: One more time. *Journal of Experimental Social Psychology, 22,* 242–248.(12)

Schneider, D. J. (1973). Implicit personality theory: A review. *Psychological Bulletin, 79,* 294–309.(4)

Schroeder, D. A., Dovidio, J. F., Sibicky, M. E., Matthews, L. L., & Allen, J. L. (1988). Empathic concern and helping behavior: Egoism or altruism? *Journal of Experimental Social Psychology, 24,* 333–353.(11)

Schulz, R., & Barefoot, J. (1974). Nonverbal responses and affiliative conflict theory. *British Journal of Social and Clinical Psychology, 13,* 237–243.(5)

Schuman, H., & Kalton, G. (1985). Survey methods. In G. Lindzey & E. Aronson (Eds.), *Handbook of social psychology* (3rd ed., Vol. 1, pp. 635–697). New York: Random House.(2)

Schuman, J., & Presser, S. (1981). *Questions and answers in attitude surveys: Experiments in question form, wording, and context.* New York: Academic Press.(6)

Schutte, N. S., Kenrick, D. T., & Sadalla, E. K. (1985). The search for predictable settings: Situational prototypes, constraint, and behavioral variation. *Journal of Personality and Social Psychology, 49,* 121–128.(4)

Schwartz, G. E. (1982). Psychophysiological patterning and emotion revisited: A systems perspective. In C. Izard (Ed.), *Measuring emotion in infants and children.* Cambridge, England: Cambridge University Press.(5)

Schwartz, S. H. (1973). Normative explanations of helping behavior: A critique, proposal, and empirical test. *Journal of Experimental Social Psychology, 9,* 349–364.(11)

Schwartz, S. H. (1977). Normative influences on altruism. In L. Berkowitz (Ed.), *Advances in experimental social psychology* (Vol. 10). New York: Academic Press.(11)

Schwartz, S. H., & Bilsky, W. (1990). Toward a theory of the universal content and structure of values: Extensions and cross-cultural replications. *Journal of Personality and Social Psychology, 58,* 878–891.(4)

Schwartz, S. H., & Clausen, G. T. (1970). Responsibility, norms, and helping in an emergency. *Journal of Personality and Social Psychology, 16,* 299–310.(11)

Schwartz, S. H., & Gottlieb, A. (1980). Bystander anonymity and reactions to emergencies. *Journal of Personality and Social Psychology, 39,* 418–430.(11)

Schwartz, S. H., & Gottlieb, A. (1981). Participants' postexperimental reactions and the ethics of bystander research. *Journal of Experimental Social Psychology, 17,* 396–407.(2)

Schwartz, S. H., & Howard, J. A. (1984). Internalized values as motivators of altruism. In E. Staub, D. Bar-Tal, J. Karylowski, & J. Reykowski (Eds.), *The development and maintenance of prosocial behavior: International perspectives.* New York: Plenum.(11)

Scott, J. A. (1984). Comfort and seating distance in living rooms: The relationship of interactants and topic of conversation. *Environment and Behavior, 16,* 35–54.(14)

Scott, J. P. (1958). *Aggression.* Chicago: University of Chicago Press.(10)

Scott, R. L. (1977). Communication as an intentional, social system. *Human Communication Research, 3,* 258–267.(5)

Searle, J. (1979). *Expression and meaning: Studies in the theory of speech acts.* Cambridge: Cambridge University Press.(5)

Sears, D. O. (1986). College sophomores in the laboratory: Influences of a narrow data base on social psychology's view of human nature. *Journal of Personality and Social Psychology, 51,* 515–530.(2)

Sears, D. O. (1988). Symbolic racism. In P. E. Katz & D. A. Taylor (Eds.), *Eliminating racism: Profiles in controversy* (pp. 31–52). New York: Plenum.(13)

Sears, D. O., & Kinder, D. R. (1985). Whites' opposition to busing: On conceptualizing and operationalizing group conflict. *Journal of Personality and Social Psychology, 48,* 1141–1147.(13)

Sebba, R., & Churchman, A. (1983). Territories and territoriality in the home. *Environment and Behavior, 15,* 191–210.(14)

Segal, M. W. (1974). Alphabet and attraction: An unobtrusive measure of the effect of propinquity in a field setting. *Journal of Personality and Social Psychology, 30,* 654–657.(14)

Segall, M. H. (1986). Culture and behavior: Psychology in global perspective. *Annual Review of Psychology, 37,* 523–564.(13)

Selby, J. W., Calhoun, L. G., & Brock, T. A. (1977). Sex differences in the social perception of rape victims. *Personality and Social Psychology Bulletin, 3,* 412–415.(4)

Seligman, C., Finegan, J. E., Hazlewood, J. D., & Wilkinson, M. (1985). Manipulating attributions for profit: A field test of the effects of attributions on behavior. *Social Cognition, 3,* 313–321.(2)

Seligman, M. E. P. (1975). *Helplessness: On depression, development, and death.* San Francisco: W. H. Freeman.(8)

Seligman, M. E. P., & Schulman, P. (1986). Explanatory style as a predictor of productivity and quitting among life insurance sales agents. *Journal of Personality and Social Psychology, 50,* 832–838.(3)

Selye, H. (1971). The evolution of the stress concept. In L. Levi (Ed.), *Society, stress, and disease* (Vol. I). London: Oxford University Press. (14)

Seta, J. J. (1982). The impact of comparison processes on coactor's task performance. *Journal of Personality and Social Psychology, 42,* 281–291. (12)

Seyfried, B. A., & Hendrick, C. (1973). When do opposites attract? When they are opposite in sex and sex-role attitudes. *Journal of Personality and Social Psychology, 25,* 15–20. (9)

Shaffer, D. R., & Sadowski, C. (1975). This table is mine: Respect for marked barroom tables as a function of gender of spatial marker and desirability of locale. *Sociometry, 38,* 408–419. (14)

Shamir, B. (1986). Self-esteem and the psychological impact of unemployment. *Social Psychology Quarterly, 49,* 61–72. (3)

Shannon, C., & Weaver, W. (1949). *The mathematical theory of communication.* Urbana, IL: University of Illinois Press. (5)

Shaver, P. (1982). *State and trait loneliness during the transition into college.* Paper presented at Nags Head Conference on Social Interaction, North Carolina. (9)

Shaver, P., Furman, W., & Buhrmeister, D. (1985). Transition to college: Network changes, social skills, and loneliness. In S. Duck & D. Perlman (Eds.), *Understanding personal relationships: An interdisciplinary approach* (pp. 193–219). London: Sage. (9)

Shaver, P., & Hazan, C. (1987). Being lonely, falling in love: Perspectives from attachment theory. *Journal of Social Behavior and Personality, 2,* 105–124. (9)

Shaver, P. R., & Hazan, C. (1988). A biased overview of the study of love. *Journal of Social and Personal Relationships, 5,* 473–501. (9)

Shaver, P., & Klinnert, M. (1982). Schachter's theories of affiliation and emotion: Implications of developmental research. In L. Wheeler (Ed.), *Review of personality and social psychology* (Vol. 3). Beverly Hills, CA: Sage. (9)

Shaw, M. E. (1932). A comparison of individuals and small groups in the rational solution of complex problems. *American Journal of Psychology, 44,* 491–504. (12)

Shaw, M. E. (1964). Communication networks. In L. Berkowitz (Ed.), *Advances in experimental social psychology* (Vol. 1). New York: Academic Press. (12)

Shaw, M. E. (1978). Communication networks fourteen years later. In L. Berkowitz (Ed.), *Group processes.* New York: Academic Press. (12)

Shaw, M. E., & Costanzo, P. R. (1982). *Theories of social psychology* (2nd ed.). New York: McGraw-Hill. (1)

Sherif, C. W., Sherif, M., & Nebergall, R. E. (1965). *Attitude and attitude change: The social judgment approach.* Philadelphia: Saunders. (7)

Sherif, M. (1935). A study of some social factors in perception. *Archives of Psychology, 27*(187), 1–60. (8, 12)

Sherif, M. (1936). *The psychology of social norms.* New York: Harper. (8, 12)

Sherif, M. (1966). *In common predicament: Social psychology of intergroup conflict and cooperation.* Boston: Houghton Mifflin. (13)

Sherif, M., Harvey, O. J., White, B. J., Hood, W. E., & Sherif, C. W. (1961). *Intergroup conflict and cooperation: The Robber's Cave experiment.* Norman, OK: University of Oklahoma Book Exchange. (13)

Sherif, M., & Hovland, C. (1961). *Social judgment.* New Haven, CT: Yale University Press. (7)

Sherif, M., & Sherif, C. W. (1979). Research on intergroup relations. In W. G. Austin & S. Worchel (Eds.), *The social psychology of intergroup relations.* Pacific Grove, CA: Brooks/Cole. (13)

Sherrod, D. R., Armstrong, D., Hewitt, J., Madonia, B., Speno, S., & Teruya, D. (1977). Environmental attention, affect, and altruism. *Journal of Applied Social Psychology, 7,* 359–371. (14)

Sherrod, D. R., & Downs, R. (1974). Environmental determinants of altruism: The effects of stimulus overload and perceived control on helping. *Journal of Experimental Social Psychology, 10,* 468–479. (14)

Shettel-Neuber, J., Bryson, J. B., & Young, L. E. (1978). Physical attractiveness of the "other person" and jealousy. *Personality and Social Psychology Bulletin, 4,* 612–615. (9)

Shields, S. A. (1975). Functionalism, Darwinism, and the psychology of women. *American Psychologist, 30,* 739–754. (13)

Shinn, M., & Weitzman, B. C. (1990). Research on homeless: An introduction. *Journal of Social Issues, 46*(4), 1–11. (3)

Shirom, A. (1982). Strike characteristics as determinants of strike settlements: A chief negotiator's viewpoint. *Journal of Applied Psychology, 67,* 45–52. (13)

Shotland, R. L. (1985, June). When bystanders just stand by. *Psychology Today,* pp. 50–55. (11)

Shotland, R. L., & Heinold, W. D. (1985). Bystander response to arterial bleeding: Helping skills, the decision-making process, and differentiating the helping response. *Journal of Personality and Social Psychology, 49,* 347–356. (11)

Shuntich, R. J., & Taylor, S. P. (1972). The effects of alcohol on human physical aggression. *Journal of Experimental Research in Personality, 6,* 34–38. (10)

Siegman, A. W., & Reynolds, M. A. (1983). Self-monitoring and speech in feigned and unfeigned lying. *Journal of Personality and Social Psychology, 45,* 1325–1333. (5)

Sigall, H. E., Aronson, E., & Van Hoose, T. (1970). The cooperative subject: Myth or reality? *Journal of Experimental Social Psychology, 6,* 1–10.(2)

Sigall, H., & Landy, D. (1973). Radiating beauty: The effects of having a physically attractive partner on person perception. *Journal of Personality and Social Psychology, 28,* 218–224.(9)

Sigelman, C. K., Berry, C. J., & Wiles, K. A. (1984). Violence in college students' dating relationships. *Journal of Applied Social Psychology, 5,* 530–548.(10)

Silva, M. L. (1990). *Mate selection criteria.* Unpublished manuscript, Mercer University, Macon, GA.(9)

Silverman, I. (1977). Why social psychology fails. *Canadian Psychological Review, 18,* 353–358.(2)

Silverstein, C. H., & Stang, D. J. (1976). Seating position and interaction in triads. *Sociometry, 39,* 166–170.(14)

Silverthorne, C. P., & Mazmanian, L. (1975). The effects of heckling and media of presentation on the impact of a persuasive communication. *Journal of Social Psychology, 96,* 229–236.(7)

Simmons, R. G. (1991). Presidential address on altruism and sociology. *Sociological Quarterly, 32,* 1–22.(11)

Simon, H. A. (1990a). Invariants of human behavior. *Annual Review of Psychology, 41,* 1–19.(13)

Simon, H. A. (1990b). A mechanism for social selection and successful altruism. *Science, 250,* 1665–1668.(11)

Simpson, J. A. (1990). Influence of attachment styles on romantic relationships. *Journal of Personality and Social Psychology, 59,* 971–980.(9)

Simpson, J. A., Gangestad, S. W., & Lerma, M. (1990). Perception of physical attractiveness: Mechanisms involved in the maintenance of romantic relationships. *Journal of Personality and Social Psychology, 59,* 1192–1201.(9)

Sims, J. H., & Baumann, D. D. (1972). The tornado threat: Coping styles of the North and South. *Science, 17,* 1386–1392.(8)

Singer, J. L., & Singer, D. G. (1981). *Television, imagination, and aggression: A study of preschoolers' play.* Hillsdale, NJ: Erlbaum.(10)

Singer, J. L., & Singer, D. G. (1983). Psychologists look at television: Cognitive, developmental, personality, and social policy implications. *American Psychologist, 38,* 826–834.(10)

Skinner, B. F. (1971). *Beyond freedom and dignity.* New York: Knopf.(8)

Skowronski, J. J., & Carlston, D. E. (1989). Negativity and extremity biases in impression formation: A review of explanations. *Psychological Bulletin, 105,* 131–142.(4)

Slaby, R. G., & Guerra, N. G. (1988). Cognitive mediators of aggression in adolescent offenders: 1. Assessment. *Developmental Psychology, 24,* 580–588.(10)

Slater, P. E. (1958). Contrasting correlates of group size. *Sociometry, 25,* 129–139.(12)

Sloan, L. R., Love, R. E., & Ostrom, T. M. (1974). Political heckling: Who really loses? *Journal of Personality and Social Psychology, 30,* 518–525.(7)

Sloan, W., & Solano, C. H. (1984). The conversational styles of lonely males with strangers and roommates. *Personality and Social Psychology Bulletin, 10,* 293–301.(9)

Smeaton, G., Byrne, D., & Murnen, S. K. (1989). The repulsion hypothesis revisited: Similarity irrelevance or dissimilarity bias? *Journal of Personality and Social Psychology, 56,* 54–59.(9)

Smith, K. D., Keating, J. P., & Stotland, E. (1989). Altruism reconsidered: The effect of denying feedback on a victim's status to empathic witnesses. *Journal of Personality and Social Psychology, 57,* 641–650.(11)

Smith, M. B. (1947). The personal setting of public opinions: A study of attitudes toward Russia. *Public Opinion Quarterly, 11,* 507–523.(7)

Smith, M. B. (1991). Political psychology and world order. *Contemporary Social Psychology, 15,* 150–152.(10)

Smith, M. B., Bruner, J. S., & White, R. W. (1956). *Opinions and personality.* New York: Wiley.(7)

Smith, R. E., Keating, J. P., Hester, R. K., & Mitchell, H. E. (1976). Role and justice considerations in the attribution of responsibility to a rape victim. *Journal of Research in Personality, 10,* 346–357.(4)

Snell, W. E., Jr. (1989). Willingness to self-disclose to male and female friends as a function of social anxiety and gender. *Personality and Social Psychology Bulletin, 15,* 113–125.(5)

Snyder, C. R., Higgins, R. L., & Stucky, R. J. (1983). *Excuses: Masquerades in search of grace.* New York: Wiley/Interscience.(3)

Snyder, C. R., Lassegard, M., & Ford, C. E. (1986). Distancing after group success and failure: Basking in reflected glory and cutting off reflected failure. *Journal of Personality and Social Psychology, 51,* 382–388.(3)

Snyder, C. R., & Smith, T. W. (1986). On being "shy like a fox": A self-handicapping analysis. In W. H. Jones, J. M. Cheek, & S. R. Briggs (Eds.), *Shyness: Perspectives on research and treatment* (pp. 161–172). New York: Plenum.(9)

Snyder, M. (1979). Self-monitoring processes. *Advances in Experimental Social Psychology, 12,* 85–128.(3)

Snyder, M. (1984). When belief creates reality. *Advances in Experimental Social Psychology, 18,* 247–305.(5)

Snyder, M. (1987). *Public and private realities: The psychology of self-monitoring.* New York: W. H. Freeman.(1, 3)

Snyder, M., & DeBono, K. G. (1985). Appeals to image and claims about quality: Understanding the psychology of advertising. *Journal of Personality and Social Psychology, 49,* 586–597.(7)

Snyder, M., & DeBono, K. G. (1987). A functional approach to attitudes and persuasion. In M. P. Zanna, J. M. Olson, & C. P. Herman (Eds.), *Social influence: The Ontario Symposium, Volume 5* (pp. 107–125). Hillsdale, NJ: Erlbaum.(7)

Snyder, M., & DeBono, K. G. (1989). Understanding the functions of attitudes: Lessons from personality and social behavior. In A. R. Pratkanis, S. J. Breckler, & A. G. Greenwald (Eds.), *Attitude structure and function* (pp. 339–359). Hillsdale, NJ: Erlbaum.(7)

Snyder, M., & Gangestad, S. (1986). On the nature of self-monitoring: Matters of assessment, matters of validity. *Journal of Personality and Social Psychology, 51,* 125–139.(3)

Snyder, M., & Monson, T. C. (1975). Persons, situations, and the control of social behavior. *Journal of Personality and Social Psychology, 32,* 637–644.(3)

Snyder, M., & Swann, W. B., Jr. (1978). Behavioral confirmation in social interaction: From social perception to social reality. *Journal of Experimental Social Psychology, 14,* 148–162.(5)

Snyder, M., Tanke, E. D., & Berscheid, E. (1977). Social perception and interpersonal behavior: On the self-fulfilling nature of social stereotypes. *Journal of Personality and Social Psychology, 35,* 656–666.(5)

Solano, C. H., Batten, P. G., & Parish, E. A. (1982). Loneliness and patterns of self-disclosure. *Journal of Personality and Social Psychology, 43,* 524–531.(9)

Solano, C. H., & Koester, N. H. (1989). Loneliness and communication problems: Subjective anxiety or social skills. *Personality and Social Psychology Bulletin, 15,* 126–133.(9)

Solly, C. M. (1969). Effects of stress on perceptual attention. In B. P. Rourke (Ed.), *Explorations in the psychology of stress and anxiety.* Toronto: Longmans Canada.(14)

Sommer, R. (1959). Studies in personal space. *Sociometry, 22,* 247–260.(14)

Sommer, R. (1962a). The distance for comfortable conversation: A further study. *Sociometry, 25,* 111–116.(14)

Sommer, R. (1962b). Personal space. *American Institute of Architects Journal, 38*(6), 81–83.(14)

Sommer, R. (1966). The ecology of privacy. *Library Quarterly, 36,* 234–248.(14)

Sommer, R. (1967). Classroom ecology. *Journal of Applied Behavioral Science, 3,* 489–503.(14)

Sommer, R. (1969). *Personal space: The behavioral basis of design.* Englewood Cliffs, NJ: Prentice-Hall.(14)

Sommer, R. (1974). *Tight spaces.* Englewood Cliffs, NJ: Prentice-Hall.(14)

Sommer, R., & Becker, F. D. (1969). Territorial defense and the good neighbor. *Journal of Personality and Social Psychology, 11,* 85–92.(14)

Sommer, R., & Olsen, H. (1980). The soft classroom. *Environment and Behavior, 12,* 3–16.(14)

Sommer, R., & Ross, H. (1958). Social interaction on a geriatrics ward. *International Journal of Social Psychiatry, 4,* 128–133.(14)

Sommer, R., & Sommer, B. A. (1989). Social facilitation effects in coffeehouses. *Environment and Behavior, 21,* 651–666.(14)

Sommer, R., & Steiner, K. (1988). Office politics in a state legislature. *Environment and Behavior, 20,* 550–575.(14)

Sommers, S. (1984). Reported emotions and conventions of emotionality among college students. *Journal of Personality and Social Psychology, 46,* 207–215.(3)

Sorrentino, R. M., & Boutilier, R. G. (1974). Evaluation of a victim as a function of fate similarity/dissimilarity. *Journal of Experimental Social Psychology, 10,* 84–93.(4)

Spears, R., & Manstead, A. S. R. (1990). Consensus estimation in the social context. *European Review of Social Psychology, 1,* 81–109.(7)

Spears, R., van der Pligt, J., & Eiser, J. R. (1985). Illusory correlation in the perception of group attitudes. *Journal of Personality and Social Psychology, 48,* 863–875.(4)

Spence, J. T. (1985). Gender identity and its implications for concepts of masculinity and femininity. In T. Sondregger (Ed.), *Nebraska Symposium on Motivation.* Lincoln, NE: University of Nebraska Press.(3)

Spence, J. T., Helmreich, R., & Stapp, J. (1974). The Personal Attributes Questionnaire: A measure of sex-role stereotypes and masculinity-femininity. *JSAS Catalog of Selected Documents in Psychology, 4,* 127.(13)

Sprecher, S. (1986). The relation between inequity and emotions in close relationships. *Social Psychology Quarterly, 49,* 309–321.(9)

Staats, A. W. (1967). An outline of an integrated learning theory of attitude formation and function. In M. Fishbein (Ed.), *Readings in attitude theory and measurement* (pp. 373–376). New York: Wiley.(6)

Stagner, R., & Eflal, B. (1982). Internal union dynamics during a strike: A quasi-experimental study. *Journal of Applied Psychology, 67,* 37–44.(13)

Stapp, J., & Fulcher, R. (1981). The employment of APA members. *American Psychologist, 36,* 1263–1314.(1)

Stasser, G. (1988). Computer simulation as a research tool: The DISCUSS model of group decision making. *Journal of Experimental Social Psychology, 24,* 393–422.(5)

Stasser, G. (1990). Computer simulation of social interaction. *Review of Personality and Social Psychology, 11,* 120–141.(2, 5)

Stasser, G., & Taylor, L. A. (1991). Speaking turns in face-to-face discussions. *Journal of Personality and Social Psychology, 60,* 675–684.(5)

Staub, E. (Ed.). (1978). *Positive social behavior and morality (Vol. 1): Social and personal development.* New York: Academic Press.(11)

Steblay, N. M. (1987). Helping behavior in rural and urban environments: A meta-analysis. *Psychological Bulletin, 102,* 346–356.(11)

Steck, L., Levitan, D., McLane, D., & Kelley, H. H. (1982). Care, need, and conceptions of love. *Journal of Personality and Social Psychology, 43,* 481–491.(9)

Steele, C. M. (1988). The psychology of self-affirmation: Sustaining the integrity of the self. *Advances in Experimental Social Psychology, 21,* 261–302.(3, 4, 7)

Steele, C. M., Southwick, L. L., & Critchlow, B. (1981). Dissonance and alcohol: Drinking your troubles away. *Journal of Personality and Social Psychology, 41,* 831–846.(7)

Stein, M. (1989). Gratitude and attitude: A note on emotional welfare. *Social Psychology Quarterly, 52,* 242–248.(11)

Steiner, I. D. (1972). *Group process and productivity.* New York: Academic Press.(12)

Steiner, I. D. (1982). Heuristic models of groupthink. In H. Brandstatter, J. H. Davis, & G. Stocker-Kreichgauer (Eds.), *Group decision making* (pp. 503–524). New York: Academic Press.(12)

Steinmetz, S. K., & Straus, M. A. (1973). The family as cradle of violence. *Society* (formerly *Trans/Action*)*, 10,* 50–56.(10)

Steinmetz, S. K., & Straus, M. A. (Eds). (1974). *Violence in the family.* New York: Dodd, Mead.(10)

Steinzor, B. (1950). The spatial factor in face-to-face discussion groups. *Journal of Abnormal and Social Psychology, 45,* 522–555.(14)

Stephan, W. G. (1985). Intergroup relations. In G. Lindzey & E. Aronson (Eds.), *Handbook of social psychology* (3rd ed., Vol. 2, pp. 599–658). New York: Random House.(13)

Stephan, W. G. (1987). The contact hypothesis in intergroup relations. *Review of Personality and Social Psychology, 9,* 13–40.(13)

Stephan, W. G. (1990). School desegregation: Short-term and long-term effects. In H. Knopke (Ed.), *Opening doors: An appraisal of race relations in America.* Tuscaloosa, AL: University of Alabama Press.(13)

Sternberg, R. J. (1986). A triangular theory of love. *Psychological Review, 93,* 119–135.(9)

Stewart, A. J., & Rubin, Z. (1976). The power motive in dating couples. *Journal of Personality and Social Psychology, 34,* 305–309.(9)

Stewart, R. A. (1988). Habitability and behavioral issues of space flight. *Small Group Behavior, 19,* 434–451.(2)

Stier, D. S., & Hall, J. A. (1984). Gender differences in touch: An empirical and theoretical review. *Journal of Personality and Social Psychology, 47,* 440–459.(5)

Stogdill, R. M. (1948). Personal factors associated with leadership. *Journal of Psychology, 23,* 36–71.(12)

Stogdill, R. M. (1963). *Manual for the Leader Behavior Description Questionnaire—Form XII.* Columbus: Ohio State University, Bureau of Business Research.(12)

Stogdill, R. M. (1974). *Handbook of leadership: A survey of theory and research.* New York: Free Press.(12)

Stokols, D. (1976). The experience of crowding in primary and secondary environments. *Environment and Behavior, 8,* 49–86.(14)

Stoller, R. J. (1976). Sexual excitement. *Archives of General Psychiatry, 33,* 899–909.(10)

Stoner, J. A. F. (1961). *A comparison of individual and group decisions involving risk.* Unpublished Master's thesis, Massachusetts Institute of Technology, School of Industrial Management, Cambridge.(12)

Storms, M. D. (1973). Videotape and the attribution process: Reversing actors' and observers' points of view. *Journal of Personality and Social Psychology, 27,* 165–175.(4)

Strack, F., Martin, L. L., & Stepper, S. (1988). Inhibiting and facilitating conditions of the human smile: A nonobtrusive test of the facial feedback hypothesis. *Journal of Personality and Social Psychology, 54,* 768–777.(5)

Straus, M. (1971). Some social antecedents of physical punishment: A linkage theory interpretation. *Journal of Marriage and the Family, 33,* 658–663.(10)

Straus, M. A. (1973). A general systems theory approach to a theory of violence between family members. *Social Science Information, 12,* 105–125.(10)

Straus, M. A. (1975, September). *The marriage license as a hitting license: Social instigation of physical aggression in the family.* Paper presented at meeting of the American Psychological Association, Chicago.(10)

Straus, M. A., Gelles, R. J., & Steinmetz, S. K. (1980). *Behind closed doors: Violence in the American family.* New York: Doubleday.(10)

Streufert, S., Castore, C. H., & Kliger, S. C. (1967). *A tactical and negotiations game: Rationale, method, and analysis* (Technical Report No. 1). West Lafayette, IN: Purdue University, Office of Naval Research.(2)

Strickland, B. R. (1977). Internal-external control of reinforcement. In T. Blass (Ed.), *Personality variables in social behaviors* (pp. 219–279). Hillsdale, NJ: Erlbaum.(8)

Stringer, M., & Cook, N. M. (1985). The effects of limited and conflicting stereotypic information on group categorization in Northern Ireland. *Journal of Applied Social Psychology, 15,* 399–407.(13)

Strodtbeck, F., & Hook, H. (1961). The social dimensions of a 12-man jury table. *Sociometry, 24,* 397–415.(14)

Stroebe, W., & Hewstone, M. (1991). Preface. *European Review of Social Psychology, 1,* ix–xi.(13)

Strube, M. J., & Garcia, J. E. (1981). A meta-analytic investigation of Fiedler's contingency model of leadership effectiveness. *Psychological Bulletin, 90,* 307–321.(12)

Stryker, S. (1982). Identity salience and role performance: The relevance of symbolic interaction theory for family research. In M. Rosenberg & H. B. Kaplan (Eds.), *Social psychology of the self-concept* (pp. 200–208). Arlington Heights, IL: Harlan Davidson.(3)

Stryker, S., & Statham, A. (1985). Symbolic interaction and role theory. In G. Lindzey & E. Aronson (Eds.), *Handbook of social psychology* (3rd ed., Vol. 1, pp. 311–378). New York: Random House.(1)

Suedfeld, P. (1982). Aloneness as a healing experience. In L. A. Peplau & D. Perlman (Eds.), *Loneliness: A sourcebook of current theory, research, and therapy.* New York: Wiley.(9)

Sullivan, H. S. (1953). *The interpersonal theory of psychiatry.* New York: Norton.(3)

Suls, J., Gaes, G., & Gastorf, J. (1979). Evaluating a sex-related ability: Comparison with same-, opposite-, and combined-sex norms. *Journal of Research in Personality, 13,* 294–304.(3)

Suls, J. M., & Miller, R. L. (Eds.). (1977). *Social comparison processes: Theoretical and empirical perspectives.* Washington, DC: Halsted-Wiley.(3)

Sumner, W. G. (1906). *Folkways.* Boston: Ginn.(13)

Sundstrom, E. (1986a). Privacy in the office. In J. Wineman (Ed.), *Behavioral issues in office design* (pp. 177–201). New York: Van Nostrand Rinehold.(14)

Sundstrom, E. (1986b). *Work places: The psychology of the physical environment in offices and factories.* New York: Cambridge University Press.(14)

Sundstrom, E. (1987). Work environments: Offices and factories. In D. Stokols and I. Altman (Eds.), *Handbook of environmental psychology.* New York: Wiley.(14)

Sundstrom, E., & Altman, I. (1974). Field study of territorial behavior and dominance. *Journal of Personality and Social Psychology, 30,* 115–124.(14)

Sundstrom, E., Burt, R., & Kamp, D. (1980). Privacy at work: Architectural correlates of job satisfaction and job performance. *Academy of Management Journal, 23*(1), 101–117.(14)

Sundstrom, E., Herbert, R. K., & Brown, D. (1982). Privacy and communication in an open plan office: A case study. *Environment and Behavior, 14,* 379–392.(14)

Sundstrom, E., Town, J., Brown, D., Forman, A., & McGee, C. (1982). Physical enclosure, type of job, and privacy in the office. *Environment and Behavior, 14,* 543–559.(14)

Swann, W. B., Jr. (1984). Quest for accuracy in person perception: A matter of pragmatics. *Psychological Review, 91,* 457–477.(3, 4)

Swann, W. B., Jr. (1986). The self as architect of social reality. In R. B. Schlenker (Ed.), *The self and social life* (pp. 100–125). New York: McGraw-Hill.(3)

Swann, W. B., Jr., & Ely, R. J. (1984). A battle of wills: Self-verification versus behavioral confirmation. *Journal of Personality and Social Psychology, 46,* 1287–1302.(5)

Sweeney, P. D., Anderson, K., & Bailey, S. (1986). Attributional style in depression: A meta-analytic review. *Journal of Personality and Social Psychology, 50,* 974–991.(3)

Sweeney, P. D., & Gruber, K. L. (1984). Selective exposure: Voter information preferences and the Watergate affair. *Journal of Personality and Social Psychology, 46,* 1208–1221.(6)

Swift, J. (1960). *Gulliver's travels.* New York: New American Library. (Original work published 1726)(13)

Symonds, M. (1975). Victims of violence: Psychological effects and aftereffects. *American Journal of Psychoanalysis, 35,* 19–26.(4)

Szent-Györgyi, A. (1971). Looking back. *Perspectives in Biology and Medicine, 15,* 1–6.(2)

Szybillo, G. J., & Heslin, R. (1973). Resistance to persuasion: Inoculation theory in a marketing context. *Journal of Marketing Research, 10,* 396–403.(7)

Szymanski, K., & Harkins, S. G. (1987). Social loafing and self-evaluation with a social standard. *Journal of Personality and Social Psychology, 53,* 891–897.(12)

Tajfel, H. (Ed.). (1978). *Differentiation between social groups.* London: Academic Press.(13)

Tajfel, H. (1982). Social psychology of intergroup relations. *Annual Review of Psychology, 33,* 1–39.(8, 12, 13)

Tajfel, H., & Turner, J. C. (1986). The social identity theory of intergroup behavior. In S. Worchel & W. G. Austin (Eds.), *Psychology of intergroup relations* (2nd ed., pp. 7–24). Chicago: Nelson-Hall.(13)

Tanaka, J. S., Panter, A. T., Winborne, W. C., & Huba, G. J. (1990). Theory testing in personality and social psychology with structural equation models: A primer in 20 questions. *Review of Personality and Social Psychology, 11,* 217–242.(2)

Tanford, S., & Penrod, S. (1983). Computer modeling of influence in the jury: The role of the consistent juror. *Social Psychology Quarterly, 46,* 200–212.(12)

Tanford, S., & Penrod, S. (1984). Social influence model: A formal integration of research on majority and minority influence processes. *Psychological Bulletin, 95,* 189–225.(8, 12)

Taras, H. L., Sallis, J. F., Patterson, T. L., Nadar, P. R., & Nelson, J. A. (1989). Television's influence on children's diet and physical activity. *Journal of Developmental and Behavioral Pediatrics, 10*(4), 176–180.(6)

Tarde, G. de. (1898). *Etudes de psychologie sociale.* Paris: Giard & Briére.(1)

Taylor, C. E., & McGuire, M. T. (1988). Introduction. Reciprocal altruism: 15 years later. *Ethology and Sociobiology, 9,* 67–72.(11)

Taylor, D. W., Berry, P. C., & Block, C. H. (1958). Does group participation when using brainstorming facilitate or inhibit creative thinking? *Administrative Science Quarterly, 3,* 23–47.(12)

Taylor, R. B., & Lanni, J. C. (1982). Territorial dominance: The influence of the resident advantage in triadic decision making. *Journal of Personality and Social Psychology, 41,* 909–915.(14)

Taylor, S. E., & Lobel, M. (1989). Social comparison activity under threat: Downward evaluation and upward contacts. *Psychologial Review, 96,* 569–575.(3)

Taylor, S. P. (1967). Aggressive behavior and physiological arousal as a function of provocation and the tendency to inhibit aggression. *Journal of Personality, 35,* 297–310.(10)

Taylor, S. P. (1986). The regulation of aggressive behavior. In R. J. Blanchard & D. C. Blanchard (Eds.), *Advances in the study of aggression.* Orlando, FL: Academic Press.(10)

Taylor, S. P., & Epstein, S. (1967). Aggression as a function of the interaction of sex of the aggressor and the sex of the victim. *Journal of Personality, 35,* 474–486.(10)

Taylor, S. P., & Gammon, C. B. (1975). Effects of type and dose of alcohol on human physical aggression. *Journal of Personality and Social Psychology, 32,* 169–175.(10)

Taylor, S. P., Gammon, C. B., & Capasso, D. R. (1976). Aggression as a function of the interaction of alcohol and threat. *Journal of Personality and Social Psychology, 34,* 938–941.(10)

Taylor, S. P., & Pisano, R. (1971). Physical aggression as a function of frustration and physical attack. *Journal of Social Psychology, 84,* 261–267.(10)

Taylor, S. P., Vardaris, R. M., Rawtich, A. B., Gammon, C. B., Cranston, J. W., & Lubetkin, A. I. (1976). The effects of alcohol and delta–9–tetrahydrocannabinol on human physical aggression. *Aggressive Behavior, 2,* 153–161.(10)

Taynor, J., & Deaux, K. (1973). When women are more deserving than men: Equity, attribution, and perceived sex differences. *Journal of Personality and Social Psychology, 28,* 360–367.(2)

Teske, J. A. (1988). Seeing her looking at you: Acquaintance and variation in the judgment of gaze depth. *American Journal of Psychology, 101,* 239–257.(5)

Tesser, A. (1988). Toward a self-evaluation maintenance model of social behavior. *Advances in Experimental Social Psychology, 21,* 181–227.(1, 3, 4)

Tesser, A., & Campbell, J. (1983). Self-definition and self-evaluation maintenance. In J. Suls & A. Greenwald (Eds.), *Social psychological perspectives on the self* (Vol. 2). Hillsdale, NJ: Erlbaum.(3)

Tesser, A., & Shaffer, D. R. (1990). Attitudes and attitude change. *Annual Review of Psychology, 41,* 479–523.(6, 7)

Tetlock, P. E. (1979). Identifying victims of groupthink from public statements of decision makers. *Journal of Personality and Social Psychology, 37,* 1314–1324.(12)

Tetlock, P. E. (1981). Pre-to-post election shifts in presidential rhetoric: Impression management or cognitive adjustment? *Journal of Personality and Social Psychology, 41,* 207–212.(3)

Tetlock, P. E. (1984). Cognitive style and political belief systems in the British House of Commons. *Journal of Personality and Social Psychology, 46,* 365–375.(6)

Tetlock, P. E. (1986). A value pluralism model of ideological reasoning. *Journal of Personality and Social Psychology, 50,* 819–827.(6)

Tetlock, P. E., Bernzweig, J., & Gallant, J. L. (1985). Supreme Court decision making: Cognitive style as a predictor of ideological consistency of voting. *Journal of Personality and Social Psychology, 48,* 1227–1239.(2)

Tetlock, P. E., & Manstead, A. S. R. (1985). Impression management versus intrapsychic explanations in social psychology: A useful dichotomy? *Psychological Review, 92,* 59–77.(3)

Thibaut, J. W., & Kelley, H. H. (1959). *The social psychology of groups.* New York: Wiley.(1, 9, 12)

Thompson, W. C., Cowan, C. L., & Rosenhan, D. L. (1980). Focus of attention mediates the impact of negative affect on altruism. *Journal of Personality and Social Psychology, 38,* 291–300.(11)

Thorne, A. (1987). The press of personality: A study of conversations between introverts and extroverts. *Journal of Personality and Social Psychology, 53,* 718–726.(9)

Tomkins, S. S. (1962). *Affect, imagery, and consciousness.* New York: Springer.(5)

Tooley, V., Brigham, J. C., Maass, A., & Bothwell, R. K. (1987). Facial recognition: Weapon effect and attentional focus. *Journal of Applied Social Psychology, 17,* 845–859.(4)

Topf, M. (1989). Sensitivity to noise, personality hardiness, and noise-induced stress in critical care patients. *Environment and Behavior, 21,* 717–733.(14)

Tourangeau, R., & Rasinski, K. A. (1988). Cognitive processes underlying context effects in attitude measurement. *Psychological Bulletin, 103,* 299–314.(6)

Tourangeau, R., Rasinski, K. A., Bradburn, N., & D'Andrade, R. (1989). Belief accessibility and context effects in attitude measurement. *Journal of Experimental Social Psychology, 25,* 401–421.(6)

Trager, G. L. (1958). Paralanguage: A first approximation. *Studies in Linguistics, 13,* 1–12.(5)

Traupmann, J., Petersen, R., Utne, M., & Hatfield, E. (1981). Measuring equity in intimate relationships. *Applied Psychological Measurement, 5,* 467–480.(9)

Trew, K., & McWhirter, L. (1982). Conflict in Northern Ireland: A research perspective. In P. Stringer (Ed.), *Confronting social issues: Applications of social psychology* (Vol. 2, pp. 195–214). London: Academic Press.(13)

Triandis, H. C. (1961). A note on Rokeach's theory of prejudice. *Journal of Abnormal and Social Psychology, 62,* 184–186.(13)

Triandis, H. C. (1977, August). *Some universals of social behavior.* Address presented at meeting of the American Psychological Association, San Francisco.(13)

Triandis, H. C. (1980). Introduction. In H. C. Triandis & W. W. Lambert (Eds.), *Handbook of cross-cultural psychology: Perspectives* (Vol. 1). Boston: Allyn & Bacon.(13)

Triandis, H. C., Davis, E. E., & Takezawa, S. I. (1965). Some determinants of social distance among American, German, and Japanese students. *Journal of Personality and Social Psychology, 2,* 540–551.(13)

Triandis, H. C., & Lambert, W. W. (Eds.). (1980). *Handbook of cross-cultural psychology: Perspectives* (Vol. 1). Boston: Allyn & Bacon.(13)

Triandis, H. C., & Lonner, W. (Eds.). (1980). *Handbook of cross-cultural psychology: Basic processes* (Vol. 3). Boston: Allyn & Bacon.(13)

Triandis, H. C., Marin, G., Lisansky, J., & Betancourt, H. (1984) *Simpatía* as a cultural script of Hispanics. *Journal of Personality and Social Psychology, 47,* 1363–1375.(13)

Triandis, H. C., McCusker, C., & Hui, C. H. (1990). Multimethod probes of individualism and collectivism. *Journal of Personality and Social Psychology, 59,* 1006–1020.(11)

Triandis, H. C., & Vassiliou, V. (1967). Frequency of contact and stereotyping. *Journal of Personality and Social Psychology, 7,* 316–328.(13)

Triplett, N. (1898). The dynamogenic factors in pacemaking and competition. *American Journal of Psychology, 9,* 507–533.(1, 12)

Trivers, R. L. (1971). The evolution of reciprocal altruism. *Quarterly Review of Biology, 46,* 35–57.(11)

Trivers, R. L., & Hare, H. (1976). Haplodiploidy and the evolution of the social insects. *Science, 191,* 249–263.(11)

Troccoli, B. (1986). *Mood induction and feelings awareness in the expression of hostility.* Unpublished doctoral dissertation, University of Wisconsin–Madison.(10)

Trope, Y., & Ben-Yair, E. (1982). Task construction and persistence as means for self-assessment of abilities. *Journal of Personality and Social Psychology, 42,* 637–645.(3)

Tucker, L. A. (1983). Muscular strength and mental health. *Journal of Personality and Social Psychology, 45,* 1355–1360.(3)

Turner, C. W., & Berkowitz, L. (1972). Identification with film aggressor (covert role taking) and reactions to film violence. *Journal of Personality and Social Psychology, 21,* 256–264.(10)

Turner, C. W., Layton, J. F., & Simons, L. S. (1975). Naturalistic studies of aggressive behavior: Aggressive stimuli, victim visibility, and horn honking. *Journal of Personality and Social Psychology, 31,* 1098–1107.(10)

Turner, C. W., & Simons, L. S. (1974). Effects of subject sophistication and evaluation apprehension on aggressive responses to weapons. *Journal of Personality and Social Psychology, 30,* 341–348.(10)

Turner, C. W., Simons, L. S., Berkowitz, L., & Frodi, A. (1977). The stimulating and inhibiting effects of weapons on aggressive behavior. *Aggressive Behavior, 3,* 355–378.(10)

Turner, J. C. (1982). Toward a cognitive redefinition of the social group. In H. Tajfel (Ed.), *Social identity and intergroup relations* (pp. 15–40). Cambridge, England: Cambridge University Press.(12)

Tversky, A., & Kahneman, D. (1974). Judgment under uncertainty: Heuristics and biases. *Science, 815,* 1124–1131.(4)

Tversky, A., & Kahneman, D. (1980). Causal schemas in judgments under uncertainty. In M. Fishbein (Ed.), *Progress in social psychology: Volume 1.* Hillsdale, NJ: Erlbaum.(4)

Tyler, T. R., & Sears, D. O. (1977). Coming to like obnoxious people when we must live with them. *Journal of Personality and Social Psychology, 35,* 200–211.(9)

Uleman, J. S., & Bargh, J. A. (Eds.). (1989). *Unintended thought.* New York: Guilford Press.(1)

Underwood, B., & Moore, B. (1982). Perspective-taking and altruism. *Psychological Bulletin, 91,* 143–173.(11)

U.S. Commission on Civil Rights. (1969). *Racism in America and how to combat it.* Washington, DC: U.S. Government Printing Office.(13)

U.S. President's Commission on Obscenity and Pornography. (1971). *Report.* Washington, DC: U.S. Government Printing Office.(10)

U.S. Riot Commission. (1968). *Report of the National Advisory Commission on Civil Disorders.* New York: Bantam Books.(10)

Valle, V. A., & Frieze, I. H. (1976). Stability of causal attributions in changing expectations for success. *Journal of Personality and Social Psychology, 33,* 579–587.(4)

Vallerand, R. J., & Richer, F. (1988). On the use of the causal dimension scale in a field setting: A test with confirmatory factor analysis in success and failure situations. *Journal of Personality and Social Psychology, 54,* 704–712.(4)

Van Kleeck, M. H., Hillger, L., & Brown, R. (1988). Pitting verbal schemas against information variables in attribution. *Social Cognition, 6,* 89–106.(5)

van Knippenberg, A., & Ellemers, N. (1990). Social identity and intergroup differentiation processes. *European Review of Social Psychology, 1,* 137–169.(13)

Vaux, A. (1988). Social and emotional loneliness: The role of social and personal characteristics. *Personality and Social Psychology Bulletin, 14,* 722–734.(9)

Vinsel, A., Brown, B. B., Altman, I., & Foss, C. (1980). Privacy regulation, territorial displays, and effectiveness of individual functioning. *Journal of Personality and Social Psychology, 39,* 1104–1115.(14)

von Baeyer, C. L., Sherk, D. L., & Zanna, M. P. (1981). Impression management in the job interview: When the female applicant meets the male (chauvinist) interviewer. *Personality and Social Psychology Bulletin, 7,* 45–51.(3)

Vroom, V. H., & Yetton, P. W. (1973). *Leadership and decision-making.* Pittsburgh, PA: University of Pittsburgh Press.(12)

Waller, W. W. (1937). The rating and dating complex. *American Sociological Review, 2,* 727–737.(9)

Walster, E., Aronson, E., & Abrahams, D. (1966). On increasing the persuasiveness of a low prestige communicator. *Journal of Experimental Social Psychology, 2,* 325–342.(7)

Walster, E., & Piliavin, J. A. (1972). Equity and the innocent bystander. *Journal of Social Issues, 28*(3), 165–189.(11)

Walster, E., & Walster, G. W. (1978). *Love.* Reading, MA: Addison-Wesley.(9)

Walster, E., Walster, G. W., & Berscheid, E. (1978). *Equity: Theory and research.* Boston: Allyn & Bacon.(9)

Walters, R., & Thomas, E. (1963). Enhancement of punitiveness by visual and audiovisual displays. *Canadian Journal of Psychology, 17,* 244–255.(10)

Walters, R. H., & Brown, M. (1963). Studies of reinforcement of aggression. III. Transfer of responses to an interpersonal situation. *Child Development, 34,* 536–571.(10)

Ward, C. (1968). Seating arrangement and leadership emergence in small group discussions. *Journal of Social Psychology, 74,* 83–90.(14)

Warriner, C. H. (1956). Groups are real: A reaffirmation. *American Sociological Review, 21,* 549–554.(12)

Washington Post. (Ed.). (1974). *The presidential transcripts.* New York: Dell.(12)

Watson, J. B. (1913). Psychology as the behaviorist views it. *Psychological Review, 20,* 158–177.(1)

Webb, E. J., Campbell, D. T., Schwartz, R. D., & Sechrest, L. (1966). *Unobtrusive measures: Nonreactive research in the social sciences.* Chicago: Rand McNally.(2)

Weber, R., & Crocker, J. (1983). Cognitive processes in the revision of stereotypic beliefs. *Journal of Personality and Social Psychology, 45,* 961–977.(4)

Wegner, D. M., & Vallacher, R. R. (1977). *Implicit psychology: An introduction to social cognition.* New York: Oxford University Press.(4)

Weigel, R. H., Vernon, D. T. A., & Tognacci, L. N. (1974). Specificity of the attitude as a determinant of attitude-behavior congruence. *Journal of Personality and Social Psychology, 30,* 724–728.(6)

Weiner, B. (Ed.). (1974). *Achievement motivation and attribution theory.* Morristown, NJ: General Learning Press.(4)

Weiner, B. (1979). A theory of motivation for some classroom experiences. *Journal of Educational Psychology, 71,* 3–25.(4)

Weiner, B. (1980). A cognitive (attribution)-emotion-action model of motivated behavior: An analysis of judgments of help-giving. *Journal of Personality and Social Psychology, 39,* 186–200.(11)

Weiner, B. (1985a). An attributional theory of achievement motivation and emotion. *Psychological Review, 92,* 548–573.(4)

Weiner, B. (1985b). "Spontaneous" causal thinking. *Psychological Bulletin, 97,* 74–84.(4)

Weiner, B. (1986). *An attributional theory of motivation and emotion.* New York: Springer-Verlag.(11)

Weiner, B., Frieze, I., Kukla, A., Reed, L., Rest, S., & Rosenbaum, R. M. (1972). Perceiving the causes of success and failure. In E. E. Jones, D. E. Kanouse, H. H. Kelley, R. E. Nisbett, S. Valins, & B. Weiner, *Attribution: Perceiving the causes of behavior* (pp. 95–120). Morristown, NJ: General Learning Press.(4)

Weiner, B., Perry, R. P., & Magnusson, J. (1988). An attributional analysis of reactions to stigmas. *Journal of Personality and Social Psychology, 55,* 738–748.(11)

Weiss, R. S. (1973). *Loneliness: The experience of emotional and social isolation.* Cambridge, MA: MIT Press.(9)

Wellman, D. T. (1977). *Portraits of white racism.* New York: Cambridge University Press.(13)

Wells, B. W. P. (1965). The psycho-social influence of building environments: Sociometric findings in large and small office spaces. *Building Science, 1,* 153–165.(14)

Wells, G. L. (1980). Asymmetric attributions for compliance: Reward vs. punishment. *Journal of Experimental Social Psychology, 16,* 47–60.(8)

Wener, R. E., & Keys, C. (1988). The effects of changes in jail population densities on crowding, sick call, and spatial behavior. *Journal of Applied Social Psychology, 18,* 852–866.(14)

Werner, C., Altman, I., & Oxley, D. (1986). Temporal aspects of homes: A transactional perspective. In I. Altman & C. Werner (Eds.), *Home environments. Human behavior and environment: Advances in theory and research* (Vol. 8, pp. 8–32). New York: Plenum.(14)

Werner, C., Brown, B. B., & Damron, G. (1981). Territorial marking in a game arcade. *Journal of Personality and Social Psychology, 41,* 1094–1104.(14)

Werner, C. M., Peterson-Lewis, S., & Brown, B. B. (1989). Inferences about homeowners' sociability: Impact of Christmas decorations and other cues. *Journal of Environmental Psychology, 9,* 279–296.(14)

West, S. G., & Gunn, S. P. (1978). Some issues of ethics and social psychology. *American Psychologist, 33,* 30–38.(2)

Westie, F. R. (1953). A technique for the measurement of race attitudes. *American Sociological Review, 18,* 73–78.(13)

Westin, A. (1967). *Privacy and freedom.* New York: Atheneum.(14)

Weyant, J. M. (1978). Effects of mood states, costs, and benefits on helping. *Journal of Personality and Social Psychology, 36,* 1169–1176.(11)

Wheeler, L., Koestner, R., & Driver, R. E. (1982). Related attributes in the choice of comparison others: It's there, but it isn't all there is. *Journal of Experimental Social Psychology, 18,* 489–500.(3)

Wheeler, L., & Nezlek, J. (1977). Sex differences in social participation. *Journal of Personality and Social Psychology, 35,* 742–754.(9)

Wheeler, L., Reis, H., & Nezlek, J. (1983). Loneliness, social interaction, and sex roles. *Journal of Personality and Social Psychology, 45,* 943–953.(9)

Wheeler, L., Shaver, K. G., Jones, R. A., Goethals, G. R., Cooper, J., Robinson, J. E., Gruder, C. L., & Butzine, K. W. (1969). Factors determining the choice of a comparison other. *Journal of Experimental Social Psychology, 5,* 219–232.(3)

Whitcher, S. J., & Fisher, J. D. (1979). Multidimensional reaction to therapeutic touch in a hospital setting. *Journal of Personality and Social Psychology, 37,* 87–96.(5)

White, G. L. (1981). Some correlates of romantic jealousy. *Journal of Personality, 49,* 129–147.(9)

White, G. L. & Mullen, P. E. (1989). *Jealousy: Theory, research, and clinical strategies.* New York: Guilford Press.(9)

White, J. W., & Gruber, K. J. (1982). Instigative aggression as a function of past experience and target characteristics.

Journal of Personality and Social Psychology, 42, 1069–1075.(10)

White, M. J., & Gerstein, L. H. (1987). Helping: The influence of anticipated social sanctions and self-monitoring. *Journal of Personality, 55,* 41–54.(11)

Whitehead, G. I., III, Smith, S. H., & Eichhorn, J. A. (1982). The effect of subject's race and other's race on judgments of causality for success and failure. *Journal of Personality, 50,* 193–202.(4)

Whiting, B., & Edwards, C. P. (1973). A cross-cultural analysis of sex differences in the behavior of children aged three through eleven. *Journal of Social Psychology, 91,* 171–188.(13)

Whyte, W. H., Jr. (1956). *The organization man.* New York: Simon & Schuster.(14)

Wicker, A. W. (1969). Attitudes versus actions: The relationship of verbal and overt behavioral responses to attitude objects. *Journal of Social Issues, 25,* 41–78.(6)

Wicklund, R. A. (1975). Objective self-awareness. *Advances in Experimental Social Psychology, 8,* 233–275.(3)

Wicklund, R. A., & Frey, D. (1980). Self-awareness theory: When the self makes a difference. In D. M. Wegner & R. R. Vallacher (Eds.), *The self in social psychology.* New York: Oxford University Press.(3)

Widgery, R., & Stackpole, C. (1972). Desk position, interview anxiety, and interviewer credibility: An example of cognitive balance. *Journal of Counseling Psychology, 19,* 173–177.(14)

Widom, C. S. (1989). Does violence beget violence? A critical examination of the literature. *Psychological Bulletin, 106,* 3–28.(10)

Wiemann, J. M., & Knapp, M. L. (1975). Turn-taking in conversations. *Journal of Communication, 25,* 75–92.(5)

Wiener, F. (1976). Altruism, ambience, and action: The effects of rural and urban rearing on helping behavior. *Journal of Personality and Social Psychology, 34,* 112–124.(14)

Wilder, D. A. (1977). Perception of groups, size of opposition, and social influence. *Journal of Experimental Social Psychology, 13,* 253–268.(8)

Wilder, D. A. (1984). Intergroup contact: The typical member and the exception to the rule. *Journal of Experimental Social Psychology, 20,* 177–194.(13)

Wilder, D. A. (1986). Social categorization: Implications for creation and reduction of intergroup bias. *Advances in Experimental Social Psychology, 19,* 291–355.(13)

Wilder, D. A., & Shapiro, P. N. (1984). Role of out-group cues in determining social identity. *Journal of Personality and Social Psychology, 47,* 342–348.(13)

Williams v. Florida, 399 U.S. 78 (1970).(2)

Williams, J. E., & Best, D. L. (1982). *Measuring sex stereotypes: A thirty nation study.* Beverly Hills, CA: Sage.(13)

Williams, K., Harkins, S., & Latané, B. (1981). Identifiability as a deterrent to social loafing: Two cheering experiments. *Journal of Personality and Social Psychology, 40,* 303–311.(12)

Williams, L. (1987, February 15). Report traces 45 cases of attacks on minorities. *New York Times,* p. 22.(13)

Williams, M., & Lissner, H. R. (1962). *Biomechanics of human motion.* Philadelphia: Saunders.(6)

Williamson, G. M., & Clark, M. S. (1989). Providing help and desired relationship type as determinants of changes in moods and self-evaluations. *Journal of Personality and Social Psychology, 56,* 722–734.(11)

Wills, T. A. (1981). Downward comparison principles in social psychology. *Psychological Bulletin, 90,* 245–271.(3)

Wills, T. A. (1983). Social comparison in coping and help-seeking. In B. M. DePaulo, A. Nadler, & J. D. Fisher (Eds.), *New directions in helping* (Vol. 2, pp. 109–141). New York: Academic Press.(3)

Wilmot, D. (1990). Maslow and Mintz revisited. *Journal of Environmental Psychology, 10,* 293–312.(14)

Wilson, E. O. (1975). *Sociobiology: The new synthesis.* Cambridge, MA: Belknap Press of Harvard University Press.(10)

Wilson, J. P., & Petruska, R. (1984). Motivation, model attributes, and prosocial behavior. *Journal of Personality and Social Psychology, 46,* 458–468.(11)

Wilson, T. D., & Dunn, D. S. (1986). Effects of introspection on attitude-behavior consistency: Analyzing reasons versus focusing on feelings. *Journal of Experimental Social Psychology, 22,* 249–263.(6)

Wilson, T. D., Kraft, D., & Dunn, D. S. (1989). The disruptive effects of explaining attitudes: The moderating effects of knowledge about the attitude object. *Journal of Experimental Social Psychology, 25,* 379–400.(6)

Wilson, T. D., & Linville, P. W. (1985). Improving the performance of college freshmen with attributional techniques. *Journal of Personality and Social Psychology, 49,* 287–293.(3)

Winch, R. F., Ktsanes, I., & Ktsanes, V. (1954). The theory of complementary needs in mate selection: An analytic and descriptive study. *American Sociological Review, 19,* 241–249.(9)

Wineman, J. D. (Ed.). (1986). *Behavioral issues in office design.* New York: Van Nostrand Reinhold.(14)

Winsborough, H. (1965). The social consequences of high population density. *Law and Contemporary Problems, 30,* 120–126.(14)

Wishner, J. (1960). Reanalysis of "impressions of personality." *Psychological Review, 67,* 96–112.(4)

Wispé, L. G. (1972). Positive forms of social behavior: An overview. *Journal of Social Issues, 28,* 1–19.(11)

Wohlwill, H., & Kohn, I. (1973). The environment as experienced by the migrant: An adaptation-level view. *Representative Research in Social Psychology, 4,* 135–164.(14)

Wohlwill, J. F. (1974). Human adaptation to levels of environmental stimulation. *Human Ecology, 2,* 127–147.(14)

Wolf, S. (1979). Behavioural style and group cohesiveness as sources of minority influence. *European Journal of Social Psychology, 9,* 381–395.(12)

Wolf, S. (1987). Majority and minority influence: A social impact analysis. In M. P. Zanna, J. M. Olson, and C. P. Herman (Eds.), *Social influence: The Ontario Symposium, Volume 5* (pp. 207–235). Hillsdale, NJ: Erlbaum.(8, 12)

Wollin, D. D., & Montagne, M. (1981). College classroom environment. *Environment and Behavior, 13,* 707–716.(14)

Wood, F. A. (1913). *The influence of monarchs.* New York: Macmillan.(12)

Wood, J. V. (1989). Theory and research concerning social comparisons of personal attributes. *Psychological Bulletin, 106,* 231–248.(3)

Wood, W. (1982). The retrieval of attitude-relevant information from memory: Effects on susceptibility to persuasion and on intrinsic motivation. *Journal of Personality and Social Psychology, 42,* 798–810.(7)

Wood, W., & Kallgren, C. A. (1988). Communicator attributes and persuasion: Recipients' access to attitude-relevant information in memory. *Personality and Social Psychology Bulletin, 14,* 172–182.(7)

Wood, W., Rhodes, N., & Whelen, M. (1989). Sex differences in positive well-being: A consideration of emotional style and marital status. *Psychological Bulletin, 106,* 249–264.(9)

Worchel, S. (1974). The effect of three types of arbitrary thwarting on the instigation to aggression. *Journal of Personality, 42,* 301–318.(10)

Worchel, S. (1986). The role of cooperation in reducing intergroup conflict. In S. Worchel & W. G. Austin (Eds.), *Psychology of intergroup relations* (2nd ed., pp. 288–304). Chicago: Nelson-Hall.(13)

Worchel, S., Arnold, S., & Baker, M. (1975). The effects of censorship on attitude change: The influence of censor and communication characteristics. *Journal of Applied Social Psychology, 5,* 227–239.(8)

Wortman, C. B., & Brehm, J. W. (1975). Responses to uncontrollable outcomes: An integration of reactance theory and the learned helplessness model. *Advances in Experimental Social Psychology, 8,* 278–336.(8)

Wright, M. H., Zautra, A. J., & Braver, S. L. (1985). Distortion in control attributions for real life events. *Journal of Research in Personality, 19,* 54–71.(8)

Wrightsman, L. S. (1960). Effects of waiting with others on changes in level of felt anxiety. *Journal of Abnormal and Social Psychology, 61,* 216–222.(9)

Wrightsman, L. S. (1964). Measurement of philosophies of human nature. *Psychological Reports, 14,* 743–751.(4)

Wrightsman, L. S. (1974). *Assumptions about human nature: A social-psychological approach.* Pacific Grove, CA: Brooks/Cole.(4)

Wrightsman, L. S. (1991). *Psychology and the legal system* (2nd ed.). Pacific Grove, CA: Brooks/Cole.(2, 12)

Wyer, R. S., Jr., & Srull, T. K. (1981). Category accessibility: Some theoretical and empirical issues concerning the processing of social stimulus information. In E. T. Higgins, C. P. Herman, & M. P. Zanna (Eds.), *Social cognition: The Ontario Symposium, Volume 1* (pp. 161–198). Hillsdale, NJ: Erlbaum.(3, 4)

Wynne-Edwards, V. (1962). *Animal dispersion in relation to social behavior.* New York: Hafner.(14)

Yarkin, K. L., Town, J. P., & Wallston, B. S. (1982). Blacks and women must try harder: Stimulus person's race and sex attributions of causality. *Personality and Social Psychology Bulletin, 8,* 21–24.(4)

Yarmey, A. D., & Johnson, J. (1982). Evidence for the self as an imaginal prototype. *Journal of Research in Personality, 16,* 238–243.(3)

Yinon, Y., & Bizman, A. (1980). Noise, success, and failure as determinants of helping behavior. *Personality and Social Psychology Bulletin, 6,* 125–130.(14)

Youtz, P. N. (1929). *Sounding stones of architecture.* New York: Norton.(14)

Zahn-Waxler, C., Radke-Yarrow, M., & King, R. A. (1979). Child rearing and children's prosocial initiations toward victims of distress. *Child Development, 50,* 319–330.(11)

Zajonc, R. B. (1960). The concepts of balance, congruity, and dissonance. *Public Opinion Quarterly, 24,* 280–296.(7)

Zajonc, R. B. (1965). Social facilitation. *Science, 149,* 269–274.(12)

Zajonc, R. B. (1980). Cognition and social cognition: A historical perspective. In L. Festinger (Ed.), *Retrospections on social psychology* (pp. 180–204). New York: Oxford University Press.(1)

Zajonc, R. B., Heingartner, A., & Herman, E. M. (1969). Social enhancement and impairment of performance in the cockroach. *Journal of Personality and Social Psychology, 13,* 83–92.(12)

Zajonc, R. B., Murphy, S. T., & Inglehart, M. (1989). Feeling and facial efference: Implications of the vascular theory of emotion. *Psychological Review, 96,* 395–416.(5)

Zajonc, R. B., & Sales, S. (1966). Social facilitation of dominant subordinate responses. *Journal of Experimental Social Psychology, 2,* 160–168.(12)

Zalesny, M. D., & Farace, R. V. (1988). Job function, sex, and environment as correlates of work perceptions and attitudes. *Journal of Applied Social Psychology, 18,* 179–202.(14)

Zanna, M., Goethals, G., & Hill, J. (1975). Evaluating a sex-related ability: Social comparison with similar others and standard setters. *Journal of Experimental Social Psychology, 11,* 86–93.(3)

Zanna, M. P., & Rempel, J. K. (1988). Attitudes: A new look at an old concept. In D. Bar-Tel & A. W. Kriglanski (Eds.), *The social psychology of knowledge* (pp. 315–334). New York: Cambridge University Press.(6)

Zillmann, D. (1978). Attribution and misattribution of excitatory reactions. In J. H. Harvey, W. J. Ickes, & R. F. Kidd (Eds.), *New directions in attribution research* (Vol. 2). Hillsdale, NJ: Erlbaum.(3)

Zillmann, D. (1979). *Hostility and aggression.* Hillsdale, NJ: Erlbaum.(10)

Zillmann, D., Baron, R. A., & Tamborini, R. (1981). Social costs of smoking: Effects of tobacco smoke on hostile behavior. *Journal of Applied Social Psychology, 11,* 548–561.(14)

Zillmann, D., & Bryant, J. (1982). Pornography, sexual callousness, and the trivialization of rape. *Journal of Communication, 32*(4), 10–21.(10)

Zillmann, D., Bryant, J., Cantor, J. R., & Day, K. D. (1975). Irrelevance of mitigating circumstances in retaliatory behavior at high levels of excitation. *Journal of Research in Personality, 9,* 282–293.(10)

Zillmann, D., & Cantor, J. R. (1976). Effect of timing of information about mitigating circumstances on emotional responses to provocation and retaliatory behavior. *Journal of Experimental Social Psychology, 12,* 38–55.(10)

Zillmann, D., Katcher, A., & Milavsky, B. (1972). Excitation transfer from physical exercise to subsequent aggressive behavior. *Journal of Experimental Social Psychology, 8,* 247–259.(10)

Zimbardo, P. G. (1970). The human choice: Individuation, reason, and order versus deindividuation, impulse, and chaos. In W. J. Arnold & D. Levine (Eds.), *Nebraska Symposium on Motivation, 1969.* Lincoln, NE: University of Nebraska Press.(10, 14)

Zimbardo, P. G., & Leippe, M. R. (1991). *The psychology of attitude change and social influence.* New York: McGraw-Hill.(8)

Zimring, C. (1982). The built environment as a source of psychological stress: Impacts of buildings and cities on satisfaction and behavior. In G. Evans (Ed.), *Environmental stress* (pp. 151–178). New York: Cambridge University Press.(14)

Zinkhan, G. M., & Stoiadin, L. F. (1984). Impact of sex role stereotypes on service priority in department stores. *Journal of Applied Psychology, 69,* 691–693.(13)

Zuckerman, M. (1979). Attribution of success and failure revisited, or: The motivational bias is alive and well in attribution theory. *Journal of Personality, 47,* 245–287.(3)

Zuckerman, M., DePaulo, B. M., & Rosenthal, R. (1981). Verbal and nonverbal communication of deception. In L. Berkowitz (Ed.), *Advances in experimental social psychology* (Vol. 14). New York: Academic Press.(5)

Zuckerman, M., Lazzaro, M. M., & Waldgeir, D. (1979). Undermining effects of the foot-in-the-door technique with extrinsic rewards. *Journal of Applied Social Psychology, 9,* 292–296.(8)

Zur, O. (1990). On nuclear attitudes and psychic numbing: Overview and critique. *Contemporary Social Psychology, 14,* 96–119.(6)

Zweigenhaft, R. L. (1976). Personal space in the faculty office: Desk placement and the student-faculty interaction. *Journal of Applied Psychology, 61,* 529–532.(14)

Name Index

Wright, E., 212
Wright, M. H., 211
Wright, R. A., 62
Wrightsman, L. S., 30, 88, 111, 205, 226, 322
Wyer, R. S., Jr., 55, 98
Wynne-Edwards, V., 404

Yang, J., 133
Yang, Joong-Nam, 204
Yarkin, K. L., 110
Yarmey, A. D., 55
Yarrow, P. R., 154
Yee, C., 27, 45
Yee, Candice, 35
Yetton, P. W., 326

Yinon, Y., 389
Yoshioka, G. A., 403
Young, L. E., 244
Young, R. D., 244
Youtz, P. N., 384
Yurko, K., 223

Zahn-Waxler, C., 292, 308
Zaichkowsky, 136
Zajonc, Robert B., 15, 17, 92, 124, 229, 230, 317
Zalesny, M. D., 407
Zander, A., 326
Zanna, Mark P., 57, 67, 73, 145, 171, 189, 244
Zautra, A. J., 211

Zelditch, M., Jr., 329
Zillman, Dolf, 66, 261, 262, 275, 276, 280, 391
Zimbardo, P., 48
Zimbardo, P. G., 199, 390
Zimbardo, Philip, 41, 265
Zimmerman, D. H., 132
Zimring, C., 393
Zinkhan, G. M., 360
Zuckerman, M., 136, 200
Zuckerman, Miron, 68
Zur, O., 153
Zuwerink, J. R., 358
Zweigenhaft, R. L., 402

Subject Index

Text Credits

Chapter 1: p. 11, Figure 1.2 from "Explaining Sex Differences in Social Behavior: A Meta-Analytic Perspective," by A. H. Eagly and W. Wood, *Personality and Social Psychology Bulletin*, 1991, *17*, 306–315. Copyright © 1991 by Sage Publications, Inc. Reprinted by permission. **Chapter 2: p. 39,** Figure 2.5 from "Supreme Court Decision Making: Cognitive Style as a Predictor of Ideological Consistency of Voting," by P. E. Tetlock, J. Bernzweig, and J. L. Gallant, *Journal of Personality and Social Psychology*, 1985, *48*, 1227–1239. Copyright 1985 by the American Psychological Association. Reprinted by permission. **p. 43,** Figure 2.6 from *The Quality of American Life: Perceptions, Evaluations, and Satisfactions*, by A. Campbell, P. E. Converse, and W. L. Rogers. Copyright 1976 by the Russell Sage Foundation. **Chapter 3: p. 56,** Figure 3.2 from "Stability and Malleability of the Self-Concept," by H. Markus and Z. Kunda, *Journal of Personality and Social Psychology*, 1986, *51*, 858–866. Copyright 1986 by the American Psychological Association. Reprinted by permission. **p. 58,** Figure 3.3 from "Effects of Household Sex Composition on the Salience of One's Gender in the Spontaneous Self-Concept," by W. J. McGuire, C. V. McGuire, and W. Winton, *Journal of Experimental Social Psychology*, 1979, *15*, 77–90. Used by permission of the authors and Academic Press. **p. 70,** Figure 3.8 from "Improving the Performance of College Freshmen with Attributional Techniques," by T. D. Wilson and P. W. Linville, *Journal of Personality and Social Psychology*, 1985, *49*, 287–293. Copyright 1985 by the American Psychological Association. Reprinted by permission. **p. 78,** Figure 3.11 from "Persons, Situations, and the Control of Social Behavior," by M. Snyder and T. C. Monson, *Journal of Personality and Social Psychology*, 1975, *32*, 637–644. Copyright 1985 by the American Psychological Association. Reprinted by permission. **Chapter 4: p. 83,** Figure 4.1 from "Impressions of Baby-Faced Adults," by L. Z. McArthur and K. Apatow, *Social Cognition*, 1983/1984, *2*, 315–342. Reprinted by permission. **p. 85,** Table 4.1 adapted from "Ratings of Likableness, Meaningfulness, and Likableness Variances for 555 Common Personality Traits Arranged in Order of Decreasing Likableness," by N. H. Anderson, *Journal of Personality and Social Psychology*, 1968, *9*, 272–279. Copyright 1968 by the American Psychological Association. Reprinted by permission. **p. 87,** Figure 4.2 from "What Can A Moving Face Tell Us?" by D. S. Berry, *Journal of Personality and Social Psychology*, 1990, *58*, 1004–1014. Copyright 1990 by the American Psychological Association. Reprinted by permission. **p. 89,** Table 4.2 from "A Method for Investigating and Representing a Person's Implicit Theory of Personality," by S. Rosenberg and R. Jones. In *Journal of Personality and Social Psychology*, 1972, *22*, 372–386. Copyright 1972 by the American Psychological Association. Reprinted by permission. **p. 95,** Figure 4.4 from "Self-Perpetuating Development of Encoding Biases in Person Perception," by T. Hill, P. Lewicki, M. Czyzewska, and A. Boss, *Journal of Personality and Social Psychology*, 1989, *57*, 373–387. Copyright 1989 by the American Psychological Association. Reprinted by permission. **p. 97,** Figure 4.5 from "A Continuum of Impression Formation, from Category-Based to Individuating Processes: Influences of Information and Motivation on Attention and Interpretation," by S. T. Fiske, S. L. Neuberg, *Advances in Experimental Social Psychology*, 1990 *23*, 1–74. Copyright © 1990 by Academic Press. Reprinted by permission. **Chapter 5: p. 116,** Figure 5.1 adapted from *The Mathematical Theory of Communication*, by C. Shannon and W. Weaver. Copyright 1949 by the University of Illinois Press. Reprinted by permission. **p. 124,** Figure 5.5 from "Sociality of Solitary Smiling: Potentiation by an Implicit Audience," by A. J. Fridlund, *Journal of Personality and Social Psychology*,

1991, *60*, 229–240. Copyright © 1991 by the American Psychological Association. Reprinted by permission. **p. 131,** Figure 5.7 adapted from "An Arousal Model of Interpersonal Intimacy," by M. L. Patterson, *Psychological Review*, 1976, *83*, 235–245. Copyright 1976 by the American Psychological Association. Reprinted by permission. **Chapter 6: p. 152,** Figure 6.4 from "Cognitive Style and Political Belief Systems in the British House of Commons," by P. E. Tetlock, *Journal of Personality and Social Psychology*, 1984, *46*, 365–375. Copyright 1984 by the American Psychological Association. Reprinted by permission. **Chapter 7: p. 164,** Table 7.1 from "Anatomy of a Persuasion Schema: Targets, Goals, and Strategies," by B. G. Rule, G. Bisanz, and M. Kohn, *Journal of Personality and Social Psychology*, 1985, *48*, 1127–1140. Copyright 1981 by the American Psychological Association. Reprinted by permission. **p. 166,** Figure 7.1 from "Width of the Latitude of Acceptance as a Determinant of Attitude Change," by A. Eagly and K. Telaak, *Journal of Personality and Social Psychology*, 1972, *23*, 388–397. Copyright 1972 by the American Psychological Association. Reprinted by permission. **p. 168,** Figure 7.2 from "The Concepts of Balance, Congruity, and Dissonance," by R. B. Zajonc, *Public Opinion Quarterly*, 1960, *24*, 280–296. Copyright 1960 by Columbia University Press. **p. 178,** Figure 7.6 adapted from "The Elaboration Likelihood Model of Persuasion," by R. E. Petty and J. T. Cacioppo, *Advances in Experimental Social Psychology*, 1986, *19*, 123–205. Copyright © 1986 by Academic Press, Inc. Reprinted by permission. **p. 179,** Figure 7.7 from "Communicator Attributes and Persuasion Recipients' Access to Attitude-Relevant Information in Memory," by W. Wood and C. A. Kallgren, *Personality and Social Psychology Bulletin*, 1988, *14*, 172–182. Copyright © 1988 by Sage Publications, Inc. Reprinted by permission. **p. 184,** Figure 7.9 from "The Need for Cognition," by J. T. Cacioppo and R. E. Petty, *Journal of Personality and Social Psychology*, 1982, *42*, 116–131. Copyright 1982 by the American Psychological Association. Reprinted by permission. **p. 186,** Figure 7.10 adapted from "Attitude Change as a Function of Attitude Type and Argument Type," by M. G. Millar and K. U. Millar, *Journal of Personality and Social Psychology*, 1990, *59*, 217–228. Copyright 1990 by the American Psychological Association. Reprinted by permission. **p. 188,** Figure 7.11 adapted from "Inducing Resistance to Persuasion," by W. J. McGuire. In L. Berkowitz (Ed.), *Advances in Experimental Social Psychology*, Vol. 1, pp. 191–229. Copyright 1964 by Academic Press. Adapted by permission. **Chapter 8: p. 213,** Table 8.3 from "Generalized Expectancies for Internal versus External Control of Reinforcement," by J. B. Rotter, *Psychological Monographs*, 1966, 80, (1), Whole No. 609. Reprinted by permission of the author. **Chapter 9: p. 237,** Figure 9.3 adapted from "Gender Differences in the Initiation and Attribution of Tactile Intimacy," by V. J. Derlega, R. J. Lewis, S. Harrison, B. A. Winstead, and R. Constanza, *Journal of Nonverbal Behavior*, 1989, *13*, 83–96. Copyright © 1989 by Human Sciences Press, Inc. Reprinted by permission. **p. 238,** Figure 9.4 adapted from "Measurement of Romantic Love," by Z. Rubin, *Journal of Personality and Social Psychology*, 1970, *16*, 265–273. Copyright 1970 by the American Psychological Association. Reprinted by permission. **p. 239,** Table 9.3 from "A Theory and Method of Love," by C. Hendrick and S. Hendrick, *Journal of Personality and Social Psychology*, 1986, *50*, 392–402. Copyright 1986 by the American Psychological Association. Reprinted by permission. **p. 240,** Figure 9.5 based on "Changing Ingredients," September 10, 1985. Copyright © 1985 by The New York Times Company. Reprinted by permission. **p. 246,** Table 9.6 adapted from "Breakups Before Marriage: The End of 103 Affairs," by C. T. Hill, L. Rubin, and L. A. Peplau, *Journal of Social*

Chapter Opening Photographs

TO THE OWNER OF THIS BOOK:

We hope that you have found *Social Psychology for the 90's, Sixth Edition*, useful. So that this book can be improved in a future edition, would you take the time to complete this sheet and return it? Thank you.

Instructor's name: _____

Department: _____

School and address: _____

Year in school: _____ Major: _____

1. The name of the course in which I used this book is: _____

_____

2. What I like *most* about this book is: _____

_____

_____

3. What I like *least* about this book is: _____

_____

_____

4. What I would have liked *more of* in this book is: _____

_____

_____

5. What I would have liked *less of* in this book is: _____

_____

_____

6. Were all of the chapters of the book assigned for you to read?   Yes   No

   If not, which ones weren't? _____

7. On a separate sheet, please tell us anything else you would like us to know about the book. Thank you.

Optional:

Your name: _____   Date: _____

May Brooks/Cole quote you, either in promotion for *Social Psychology in the '90s, Sixth Edition*, or in future publishing ventures?

Yes: _____   No: _____

Sincerely,
Kay Deaux
Francis C. Dane
Lawrence S. Wrightsman

- -
FOLD HERE

BUSINESS REPLY MAIL
FIRST CLASS   PERMIT NO. 358   PACIFIC GROVE, CA

POSTAGE WILL BE PAID BY ADDRESSEE

ATT: *Deaux/Dane/Wrightsman* _____

Brooks/Cole Publishing Company
511 Forest Lodge Road
Pacific Grove, California 93950-9968

NO POSTAGE
NECESSARY
IF MAILED
IN THE
UNITED STATES

- -
FOLD HERE

2